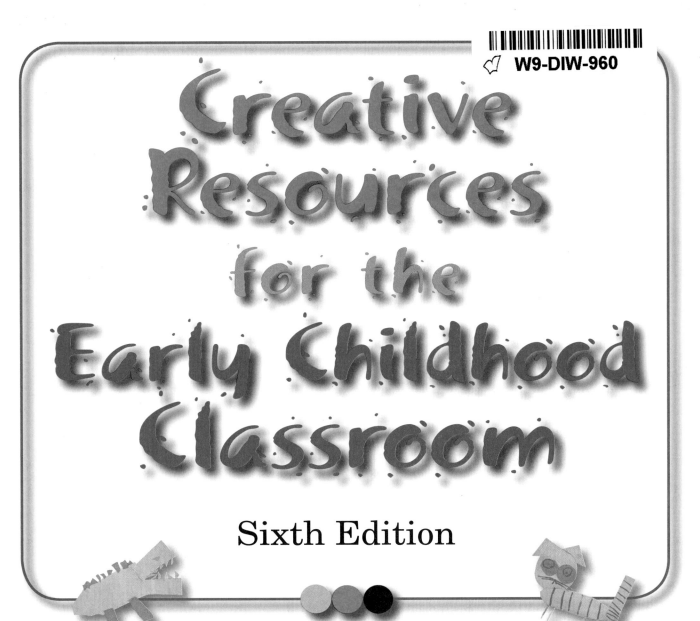

Creative Resources for the Early Childhood Classroom

Sixth Edition

Judy Herr,
University of Wisconsin–Stout

WADSWORTH
CENGAGE Learning

Australia • Brazil • Japan • Korea • Mexico • Singapore • Spain • United Kingdom • United States

Creative Resources for the Early Childhood Classroom, Sixth Edition
Judy Herr

Senior Publisher: Linda Schreiber-Ganster

Executive Editor: Mark David Kerr

Development Editor: Beth Kaufman

Assistant Editor: Genevieve Allen

Editorial Assistant: Greta Lindquist

Associate Media Editor: Elizabeth Momb

Marketing Manager: Kara Kindstrom

Senior Marketing Communications Manager: Heather L. Baxley

Content Project Management: PreMediaGlobal

Senior Art Director: Jennifer Wahi

Production Service: PreMediaGlobal

Manufacturing Planner: Rebecca Cross

Rights Acquisitions Specialist (Image, Text): Don Schlotman

Cover Designer: Bartay Studio

Cover Image: Children's artwork provided by the students of the Brookline Early Education Program (BEEP), Brookline, Massachusetts. Used with permission

Compositor: PreMediaGlobal

For product information and technology assistance, contact us at
Cengage Learning Customer & Sales Support, 1-800-354-9706

For permission to use material from this text or product, submit all requests online at **www.cengage.com/permissions**.
Further permissions questions can be emailed to **permissionrequest@cengage.com**.

Library of Congress Control Number: 2011936152

ISBN-13: 978-1-111-83102-8

ISBN-10: 1-111-83102-5

Wadsworth
20 Davis Drive
Belmont, CA 94002-3098
USA

Cengage Learning is a leading provider of customized learning solutions with office locations around the globe, including Singapore, the United Kingdom, Australia, Mexico, Brazil, and Japan. Locate your local office at **www.cengage.com/global**.

Cengage Learning products are represented in Canada by Nelson Education, Ltd.

For your course and learning solutions, visit **www.cengage.com**.

Purchase any of our products at your local college store or at our preferred online store **www.cengagebrain.com**

Printed in the United States of America
1 2 3 4 5 6 7 15 14 13 12 11

Brief Table of Contents

Table of Contents organized by Subject

FIELD TRIPS AND RESOURCE PEOPLE

Field Trips

Resource People

FINGERPLAYS AND CHANTS

GROUP TIME

LARGE-MUSCLE ACTIVITIES

MATH

MISCELLANEOUS

MUSIC

SENSORY ACTIVITIES

SOCIAL STUDIES

FEATURE BOXES

Preface

Why I Wrote This Book

Many years ago, while reviewing early childhood curriculum resources, it became apparent that few books were available that used a thematic approach for teaching young children. Moreover, an expanded resource that contained all of the curriculum areas for teaching preschool or kindergarten was nonexistent

As a result, my university students, colleagues, and alumni convinced me of the importance of such a book. Likewise, they convinced me of the significant contribution the book could make to early childhood teachers and, subsequently, the lives of young children. Teachers want to work smarter, not harder, by having one comprehensive book at their fingertips.

Before preparing the first manuscript, hundreds of early care and education, preschool, and kindergarten teachers were surveyed to ascertain their curriculum needs. In response, this reference book was designed, written, and tailored to their teaching needs using a thematic approach for use with two- through six-year-old children. Each theme contains a flowchart, theme goals, concepts for the children to learn, theme-related vocabulary words, music, fingerplays, science, social studies, dramatic play, creative art experiences, sensory, large-muscle activities, science, music, mathematics, cooking experiences, technology and multimedia, books, songs, field trips, and resource people. In addition, creative ideas for designing child-involvement bulletin boards and family letters have been included. Some of these resources were identified by the teachers included in the survey as being critical components that have been lacking in other curriculum guides. As the second, third, fourth, fifth, and sixth editions were developed, input was continuously sought from colleagues, teachers in training, and other individuals using the book.

How to Use This Book

In addition to the themes included in this book, other themes can and should be developed for teaching young children by integrating the activities in this book. It is the teacher's responsibility to thoughtfully select, plan, and introduce developmentally appropriate themes and culturally responsive learning experiences to promote positive outcomes for all children. Specifically, the teacher must tailor the curriculum to reflect the children's needs, interests, abilities, disabilities, experiences, and background. Consequently, all teachers need to be encouraged to carefully select, adapt, or change any of the activities in this book to meet the needs, abilities, interests, cultural background, and experiences of individuals as well as the group of children to ensure developmental appropriateness. The inside covers of this book should be used as handy references for checking developmental milestones, sometimes referred to as *emerging competencies*.

As you use this curriculum guide, you will note that some themes readily lend themselves to particular curriculum areas. As a result, the number of activities listed under each curriculum area will vary from theme to theme.

The detailed "Introduction" that follows is designed to help teachers use the book most effectively. It includes:

1. A discussion on how to develop the curriculum using a thematic approach
2. A list of possible themes
3. Suggestions for writing family letters
4. Methods for constructing and evaluating creative interactive bulletin boards
5. Criteria for selecting children's books
6. The importance of documentation boards

What's New in This Edition?

1. Brand-new activities and resources. Over 2500 new activities, books, and songs enrich this sixth edition. These activities are spread throughout the book, complement the existing themes, and are included in the new themes. Each theme begins with a curriculum web. This webbing helps teachers in recording possible ideas in an organized way. Webbing is a helpful tool designed to inform teachers of the major subconcepts that can be included under each theme. It is the teacher's responsibility to tailor the curriculum to make it developmentally appropriate, and linguistically and culturally engaging and challenging.

2. **New multicultural themes.** Five new multicultural themes have been added to this new edition: Chinese New Year, Cinco de Mayo, Diwali, Kwanzaa, and Ramadan. The themes for Hanukkah, Christmas, and Thanksgiving have also been refined and updated.

3. **New "going green" theme.** "Caring for Our Earth" has been added as a brand-new theme in this edition. It complements the existing themes of "Flowers," "Gardens," "Rain," and "Water."

4. **Brand-new color insert on using the digital camera in the early childhood classroom.** The brand-new colored insert in the middle of the book contains a wide variety of teacher-made materials and artifacts that illustrate how teachers can utilize the digital camera. Each artifact is aligned with the National Association for the Education of Young Children's (NAEYC) Teaching Standards. naeyc

5. **Expanded multicultural materials appendix.** This special appendix (Appendix B) has been expanded to include new books and other important multicultural resources.

6. **New and expanded reference and resource materials in each theme.** The sections on children's books that appear at the end of each theme have been carefully researched and updated to reflect the new publications related to each theme. All award-winning books related to the themes have been added. Likewise, many books that are no longer in print have been deleted.

7. **Introduction of additional recordings and songs for the themes.** A recording and song section containing music with related concepts has been revised and expanded for each theme where available.

8. **New technology and multimedia resources.** The former multimedia section for each theme has been updated. This section now contains computer software for young children and stories on DVDs.

Brand New Companion Website to Accompany the Text!

A new website accompanies this sixth edition of *Creative Resources for the Early Childhood Classroom*—accessible via www.cengagebrain.com. On the website, you will find invaluable materials on child assessment, curriculum planning, and other teacher resources that will assist you in providing a quality early childhood curriculum. Included under the section on assessment, there are forms for assessing young children's growth and development. The charts for emerging competencies can be used for assessment as well as for family conferences. In addition, examples of documentation boards are available that you can emulate for your classroom These colorful boards will show you many ways of documenting children's learning and development. Documentation should play an important role in the assessment process. Hung throughout the classroom, these boards can also add beauty. Families and other visitors will enjoy observing class activities recorded through photographs and the printed word.

The following is a list of the specific resources and documents that you will find on the Herr 6/e companion website—accessible through www.cengagebrain.com.

Assessing Young Children's Growth and Development Website Resources

- Activity Preferences: Self-Selected Play
- Anecdotal Record
- Documentation Boards/Panels
- Evaluating Documentation Boards/Panels
- Emerging Competencies: Two-Year-Olds–Six-Year-Olds
- Emerging Competencies: Two-Year-Olds
- Emerging Competencies: Three-Year-Olds
- Emerging Competencies: Four-Year-Olds
- Emerging Competencies: Five-Year-Olds
- Emerging Competencies: Six-Year-Olds
- Evaluation of an Activity
- Evaluating Documentation Boards/Panels
- Individual Child Profile
- Play Patterns Assessment Form

Curriculum-Planning Website Resources

- Block Plan Form
- Bulletin Board Letters: Lowercase
- Bulletin Board Letters: Uppercase
- Bulletin Board Numbers
- Curriculum Area Planning Web
- Evaluation of an activity
- Lesson Plan

Teacher Resources Website Resources

- Parent Letter
- Rainy Day Activities
- Teacher-Made Materials

Acknowledgments

During the years between the first and sixth editions of this book, there were many individuals whose creative ideas, support, and encouragement helped me. My sincere thanks to all of them:

- My colleagues in early childhood education who have worked with me at the University of Wisconsin–Stout, nationally and internationally.
- All students who have majored in early childhood education at the University of Wisconsin–Stout, the children who have participated in programs at the Child and Family Study Center, their families, and all children who have enjoyed the themes and activities presented in this book.
- And, finally, to my grandchildren Carson, Jeffrey, Eva, Madelyn, Marena, Vivian, and Evan, as well as all of the children throughout the world who have made my efforts worthwhile.
- My special thanks to individuals at Cengage Learning whose assistance and hard work made this book possible: Mark Kerr, Kara Kindstrom, Beth Kaufman, Jennifer Sacon, Genevieve Allen, Greta Lindquist, Elizabeth Momb, and Dewanshu Ranjan.
- Special thanks to Amy Schoenblum, an educator and multicultural consultant who assisted with the compilation of the new multicultural themes.
- Special thanks to Vicki Milstein, Min-Jen Wu Taylor, and the students of the Brookline Massachusetts Early Childhood Education Program for the beautiful original artwork that graces the sixth edition cover!
- I also want to extend my special thanks and dedicate this book to the three talented individuals who teach in the Child and Family Study Center at the University of Wisconsin–Stout whose support and contributions made this book possible: Jamie Lynch, Kathy Preusse, and Maggie Olson.

Reviewers

I am also grateful to my colleagues nationwide who served as reviewers during the development process:

Laurel Anderson, *Palomar College*

Laurel Bongiorno, *Champlain College*

Fredalene Bowers, *Indiana University of Pennsylvania*

Susan Christian, *Patrick Henry Community College*

Bessie Davis Cooke, *South Carolina State University*

Leanna Manna, *Villa Maria College;*

Vicki Milstein, *Principal, Brookline Massachusetts Early Education Program*

Jennifer Volkers, *Baker College*

and

Min-Jen Wu Taylor, *Early Childhood Educator, Brookline Massachusetts Early Education Program.*

Introduction

Why Use Thematic Curriculum Planning with Young Children?

The purpose of this introduction is to explain the process involved in curriculum planning for preschool and kindergarten children using the thematic, or unit, approach. Why use themes? Children's learning does not occur in naturally defined subject areas, so learning and development are integrated. Activities that stimulate one area of development and learning affect other areas as well. By organizing the curriculum around a theme, teachers can plan a meaningful child-centered curriculum that focuses on children's real life experiences and emerging interests, which makes the curriculum more meaningful. The theme represents a concept for children to investigate and provides a central focus that lends itself to the integration of curriculum areas. It also helps keep the curriculum interesting. With each new theme, the environment changes. New activities, props, books, music, songs, and other activities are introduced to stimulate the child's curiosity, imagination, and involvement.

A child's brain, like an adult's, is challenged by novelty, challenge, and feedback. Listening and speaking are the primary ways that preschool and kindergarten children learn new concepts and express their feelings and thoughts. Themes provide a language-rich environment through a variety of engaging, "hands-on," "minds-on," and "feelings-on" activities. When children are exposed to new themes, they gain new words and concepts more readily than when working individually or in small groups. Themes also provide concept development through a variety of engaging "hands-on," "minds-on," and "feelings-on" activities. The curriculum is more interesting when children encounter something they already know and care about. Themes also help children integrate skills and knowledge in meaningful ways. Moreover, themes also encourage parents to contribute to the curriculum. To support each theme, planning and construction ideas are included for bulletin boards, documentation boards, teacher-made materials, family letters, and a wide variety of classroom learning experiences.

Curriculum Planning

As you use this resource, remember that children learn best when they can self-select activities and interact with their environment using materials that are relevant to their lives. Therefore, many opportunities should be available for active learning—seeing, hearing, touching, tasting, self-expression, inquiry, discovery, and problem solving. Children need an inviting, enriched environment with an abundance of hands-on, minds-on, and feelings-on learning experiences. They also need many artifacts, materials, equipment, and choices to stimulate their curiosity and promote their creativity. To construct knowledge, they need to actively investigate and manipulate their environment. To provide these opportunities, the teacher's primary role is first to assess the children's needs, interests, abilities, experiences, learning styles, family values, and backgrounds. Using this assessment data, the teacher's next step is to create a stimulating, engaging environment where children can explore materials and discover relationships. To be meaningful, these experiences should be responsive and consistent with the child's development and culture.

Children learn by doing, and play is their work. Development proceeds when children have appropriate tools to develop new skills. For this, they need large blocks of time and flexible schedules. As a result, it is the author's intention that this book be used as a resource to help you design and carry out a child-centered curriculum. Specifically, the ideas in this book should help you to enrich, organize, and structure the children's environment, providing them an opportunity to make choices among a wide variety of activities that stimulate their natural curiosity.

Knowledge of child development and curriculum must be interwoven. To illustrate, play in the classroom should be child-centered and self-initiated. To provide an environment that promotes these types of play, it is the teacher's role to provide unstructured time, space, materials, and support. Using a theme-based approach to plan curriculum is one way to ensure that a wide variety of classroom experiences is provided. Successful early childhood programs have interesting, challenging, and engaging environments that are developmentally appropriate. Children need to learn to think, question, reason, and become active decision makers. They also need to reflect on and document what they are learning.

It is important that all curricula be adapted to match the developmental needs of children at a particular age or stage of development. An activity that is appropriate for one group of children may be inappropriate for another. To develop an appropriate curriculum, knowledge of the typical development of children is needed. For this reason, the inside covers of this book contain such information and may be helpful in making predictions about a child's developmental stage. Review these developmental milestones, or *emerging competencies* as they are often called, before selecting a theme or specific activities. The inside and back covers of this book contain forms that should be helpful in assessing the children's needs, interest, and abilities.

Theme Planning

A developmentally appropriate curriculum focuses on the emerging interests of the children. It integrates the children's needs, interests, abilities, and experiences and focuses on the whole child. Cognitive, social, emotional, and physical development are all included. Before planning aq curriculum, use the forms on the website to assess the children's development and interests. Record your observations. At the same time, note the children's interests and listen carefully. Children's informal conversations provide clues; this information is vital in selecting a theme that follows the direction of the children's interests and is personally meaningful to the children. After this, review your observations by discussing them with other staff members. A developmentally appropriate curriculum for young children cannot be planned without understanding their development. The curriculum must be relevant to their lives and emerge from their interests.

There are many methods for planning a curriculum other than using themes. In fact, you may prefer not to use a theme during parts of the year. If this is your choice, you might want to use the book as a source of ideas, integrating activities and experiences from a variety of the themes outlined in the book.

Planning an emergent child-centered curriculum using a theme approach involves several steps. Based upon assessment, the first step involves selecting a theme that is appropriate for the developmental level and emerging interests of your group of children. Themes based on the children's conversations and interests provide intrinsic motivation for exploration and learning. Meaningful experiences are more easily comprehended and remembered, and lead to new understandings. Moreover, curiosity, enjoyment of participation, and self-direction are heightened.

After selecting a theme, the next step is developing a flowchart which is often referred to as *webbing*. From the flowchart, goals, conceptual understandings, and vocabulary words can easily be extracted. The final step in curriculum planning is selecting hands-on activities based on the children's stages of development, interests, and available resources. While doing this, the covers of this book should be used as a reference to review emerging milestones for children of different ages. Depending upon the children's interests and the available teaching resources, themes may vary in length. A theme may be a day, three weeks, a week, a month, or even longer.

To help you understand the theme approach to curriculum development, each step of the process will be discussed. Included are assessing the children to identify themes related to the children's interests, needs, abilities, and experiences. After selecting a theme, the next step is developing a flowchart, theme goals, concepts, vocabulary, and activities. In addition, suggestions are given for writing family letters, designing bulletin boards, creating teacher-made materials, and selecting children's books.

Assessment

Assessment is important for planning curriculum, identifying children with special needs, and communicating a child's progress to families. Assessment provides a child's development status at a given time. It also provides information on a child or group of children's progress over time. Authentic assessment needs to be a continuous process of evaluating children's growth through their daily play activities. It involves a process of observing children during activities and engaging in thoughtful dialogue. Assessment is a process of observing children, recording their behaviors, and documenting their work. It involves showing what the children can do and have learned.

Assessment also involves records and descriptions of what you observe, see, and hear while the behavior is occurring. Logs and journals can be developed. The emerging developmental milestones on the inside covers of this text can be used as a checklist of behavior. For your convenience, samples of these forms can be downloaded from the website. This will help you create a profile of each child's individualized progress in developing skills. Your observations should tell what the child likes, doesn't like, has discovered, knows, and wants to learn.

Samples of the children's work should be maintained in an individual portfolio collection. A portfolio is a purposeful collection that documents the children's progress, achievements, and efforts. Included should be samples of the children's paintings, drawings, storytelling experiences, and oral and written language. Thus, the portfolio will include products and evidence of the children's accomplishments. The portfolio can also be used to communicate with parents and to demonstrate teacher accountability. The website contains documentation boards that can be used to showcase the children's or child's thinking and work.

Selecting a Theme

By reviewing the assessment materials, you can identify the children's emerging milestones and interests. This information will be important in selecting a theme that interests the children and in selecting developmentally appropriate learning experiences. A theme can be any topic of interest to young children.

When selecting a theme, remember that celebrating holidays can be controversial. You need to respect the diversity of the children and their families in your program and community. Therefore, it is important to seek input from families regarding holiday themes. Ask families how they feel. If some families object, respect those objections. In some cases, you can talk about a holiday rather than celebrate it. Then, too, the intent of a holiday can be encompassed in another theme. For example, Valentine's Day could be included in a theme on friendship. Remember, if used, a holiday theme should not be the focus of the curriculum for an extended period.

Three-year-old children primarily view holiday celebrations in terms of their own families. They need to learn about holiday activities that are concrete with simple information that is connected to their own familial experiences. Like three-year-old children, four-year-olds view holidays from the experiences they have had in their own families. Often, children these ages can remember a celebration from the previous year. Five- and six-year-olds enjoy learning about holidays and understand the reasons they are celebrated. They particularly enjoy preparing decorations, foods, and even invitations.

Flowcharts and Webbings

Once you have identified a theme that emerges out of the children's interests and you have available resources to use as support materials, the next step is to develop a flowchart. The flowchart is a simple way to record all possible subconcepts that relate to the major concept or theme. It includes a graphic picture of what may be included in the theme. To illustrate, plan a theme on apples. Begin this process by printing a copy of the Curriculum Area Planning Web form provided on the website. In the center on this form, print the word "apple." Then, using an encyclopedia as a resource, record the subconcepts that are related. Include origin, parts, colors, tastes, sizes, textures, food preparation, and nutrition. The following apples flowchart (from Theme #2, "Apples," within the text) includes these concepts. In addition, under each subconcept, list factual content that could be included. For example, apples may be colored green, yellow, or red. By using a thematic approach, we teach children the way that environments and humans interconnect. This process helps children make sense out of the human experience.

Apples

Tastes	Forms	Parts	Sizes	Origin
sweet	raw	seed	large	orchard
sour	cooked	core	small	seeds
	dried	meat		soil, sunshine
	baked	skin		water
		stem		trees
				blossoms
				fruit

Preparation

juice	jellies
pie	butter
cake	muffins
tarts	bread
sauce	pudding
cider	

Colors

red
yellow
green

Theme Goals

Once you have prepared a flowchart webbing, abstracting the theme goals is a simple process. Begin by reviewing the chart. Notice the subheadings listed. For the unit on apples, the subheadings include preparation, tastes, parts, sizes, forms, origin, texture, and colors. Writing each of these subheadings as a goal is the next step of the process.

Because there are eight subheadings, each of these can be included as a goal. In some cases, subheadings may be combined. For example, note the fourth goal listed. It combines several subheadings.

Through participation in the experiences provided by using apples as a curriculum theme, the children may learn:

1. Parts of an apple
2. Preparation of apples for eating
3. Forms of apples
4. The colors of apples
5. The origin of an apple
6. The tastes of apples
7. The sizes of apples
8. The texture of apples

Concepts

The concepts must be related to the goal; however, they are more specific. To write the concepts, study the goals. Then prepare sentences that are written in a simple form that children can understand. Examples of concepts for a unit on apples may include the following:

1. Apples grow on trees.
2. Seeds are planted in the soil to grow an apple tree.
3. A group of apple trees is called an *orchard*.
4. Water and sunshine are needed to make apple trees grow.
5. The flower on the apple tree is called a *blossom*.
6. An apple is a fruit.
7. An apple has five parts: seed, core, meat, skin, and stem.

8. Apples can be colored green, yellow, or red.
9. Apples can be large or small.
10. Bread, pies, puddings, and applesauce can be prepared from apples.
11. Cake, sauce, muffins, tarts, and juice may also be prepared from apples.

Vocabulary

The vocabulary should include new words that you want to informally introduce to the children. Vocabulary words need to be tailored to meet the specific needs of your group of children. The number of vocabulary words will vary, depending on the theme and the developmental level of the children. For example, it might be assumed that the children know the word *sweet,* but not *tart.* So, the definition of the word *tart* is included. Collectively, the following words could be introduced in this unit: apple, apple blossom, apple butter, core, and texture. Definitions for these words could include the following:

1. Apple—a fruit that is grown on a tree.
2. Apple blossom—a flower on the apple tree.
3. Apple butter—a spread for bread made from apples.
4. Core—the part of the apple that contains the seeds.
5. Texture—how something feels.

Activities

Now that you have learned how to develop goals related to a theme using a flowchart, you will need to learn how to select developmentally appropriate, engaging, hands-on activities. You will discover that many theme goals can be accomplished by additions to the environment, bulletin boards, field trips, music, science, social studies, stories, and resource people or family members at large-group time. Your major role as an adult, or teacher, is that of a facilitator, planning and preparing the environment to stimulate the child's natural curiosity.

To begin this process, review each goal and determine how it can be introduced in the classroom. For example, review the goals if you were going to develop a theme on apples. A bulletin board or game could introduce the three colors of apples. The children could also learn these colors through cooking experiences. Other vehicles for teaching the colors of apples would be placing the three colors of apples on a science table, eating apples at lunch time, sorting colored apple cards, and listening to apple-related stories.

The five parts of an apple could also be introduced through participation in a tasting or cooking experience, on a bulletin board, or even in a discussion on a field trip or at the snack table. Always remember that children need to observe and manipulate the concrete object while engaged in child-initiated or child-directed play that is teacher supported. For that reason, fresh apples could be cut horizontally and placed on the science table with a magnifying glass. Likewise, simultaneously, apple seeds and paper could be available on the art table to construct a collage. Always remember that the best activities for young children are hands-on, open-ended, and exploratory. That is, focus on the process, rather than the product. Children need to learn to think, reason, and become problem solvers. As a teacher, you should take the ideas in this book and use and adapt them for planning and preparing the environment. Always remember that successful early childhood programs provide interesting, challenging, and engaging environments that stimulate the child's curiosity and minds.

Family Letters

Communication between the child's home and school is important. It builds mutual understanding, cooperation, and partnerships with families. With the efficiency of modern technology, family letters are a form of written communication that can be shared on a weekly basis. These letters should always convey that parents and families are always welcome. Families can be invited to provide support and critical resources to the theme. Many have ideas, materials, stories, and expertise to share. By sharing, they can expose us to their culture and teach us about diversity. Chances are that they also have community connections for resource people, field trips, and materials.

Samples of family letters that you can adapt for each theme have been included in this book. The most interesting family letters are written in the active voice. It states the subject did something. To illustrate, "Mark's favorite activities today were playing with blocks and listening to stories on a DVD player."

When writing the family letter, consider the family's educational level and home language. Then write the letter in a clear, friendly, concise style. To do this, eliminate all words that are not needed. Limit the length of the letter to a page or two. To assist you with the process, an example of a family letter is included for each theme.

Family letters can be divided into three sections. Included should be a general introduction, school activities, and home activities. One way to begin the letter is by introducing new children or staff, or sharing something that happened the previous week. After this, introduce the theme for the coming week by explaining why it was chosen.

The second section of the family letter could include some of the goals and special activities for the theme. Share with the families all of the interesting things you will be doing at school throughout the week. By having this information, families can initiate verbal interaction with their child.

The third section of the family letter should be related to home activities. Suggest developmentally appropriate activities that the families can provide in the home. These activities may or may not relate to the theme. You may also want to include the words of new songs, fingerplays, and chants. This section can also be used to provide parenting information such as the developmental value of specific activities for young children. A format for writing family letters is introduced on the website. Also review the family letter that has been enhanced with a digital photograph in the center colored insert.

Bulletin Boards

Bulletin boards add color, decoration, and interest to the classroom. They also communicate what is happening in the classroom to families and other visitors. The most effective bulletin boards are interactive, involve the children, and are placed at their eye level. That is, the child will manipulate some pieces of the board. As a result, they are called *interactive* or *involvement bulletin boards*. Through the concrete experience of interacting with the bulletin board materials, children learn a variety of concepts and skills. Included may be size, shape, color, visual discrimination, hand-eye coordination, problem-solving skills, and so on.

Carefully study the bulletin boards included for each theme in this book. They are simple, containing a replica of objects from the child's immediate environment. Each bulletin board has a purpose. It teaches a skill or concept.

As you prepare the bulletin boards provided in this book, you will become more creative. Gradually, you will combine ideas from several bulletin boards as you develop new themes for curriculum. Rather than making bulletin boards, some teachers have reported that they use the ideas to make charts.

Some craft stores sell small projectors that enlarge images. This projector can be a useful tool for individuals who feel uncomfortable with their drawing skills. Using the projector, you can enlarge images from storybooks, coloring books, greeting cards, wrapping paper, and so on. Follow the directions for enlarging objects that accompany the projector, Using a pencil, color marker, or crayon, trace the outline of the image onto the paper or tagboard.

A digital camera is another useful tool for preparing bulletin boards. Photographs of young children support cognitive, social-emotional development and language development. Children love to have pictures taken during a field trip, or on special occasions, that can be posted on a bulletin board or tagboard. Parents also enjoy looking at the pictures. However, digital pictures do not need to be limited to taking the children's pictures for bulletin boards. They can be effectively used to make books, sequencing materials, charts, matching games, labeling lockers in the classroom, and so on. Pictures you take to make bulletin boards and teacher-made materials may be more meaningful than purchasing commercially prepared materials. The colored section of this book provides you with other ways that you can use a digital camera.

To make your bulletin board pieces more durable, laminate them. If your center does not have a laminating machine, use clear contact paper. This process works just as well, but it can be more expensive. Otherwise, some school specialty and office supply stores provide this service.

Titles for bulletin boards can be made from stencils, with plastic lettering, or by using a word processor. Using a word processor, you can use Microsoft software to prepare titles or labels. To do this, click on boldface first. Then, select a lettering size that would be in proportion to the size of the bulletin board and figures. After this, select a font. The font "Placard Condensed" is recommended because it represents a manuscript style that young children see in books. Uppercase and lowercase manuscript letters and numbers have been included on the website that can be used for bulletin board titles. Prepare lettering for bulletin boards by using these letters and placing colored construction paper in the printer.

In addition to providing these letters and numbers on the website, the simple art objects that are shown in the suggested bulletin boards in each theme are also included. You should be able to recreate these bulletin boards with very little effort or artistic skills.

Finally, the materials you choose to use on a bulletin board should be safe and durable. Careful attention should be given when selecting attachments. For two-, three-, and four-year-old children, adhesive Velcro and staples are preferred attachments. Caution: Pushpins may be used with older children under *careful supervision.*

Selecting Books

Books for young children need to be selected with care. Before selecting books, once again, refer to the covers and review the typical development for your group of young children. This information can provide a framework for selecting appropriate books.

There are some general guidelines for selecting books. First, children enjoy books that relate to their experiences. They also enjoy action. The words written in the book should be simple, descriptive, and within the child's understanding. The pictures should be large, be colorful, and closely represent the actions.

A book that is good for one group of children may be inappropriate for another. You must know the child or group of children for whom the story is being selected. Consider their interests, attention span, and developmental level.

Developmental considerations are important. Two-year-olds enjoy stories about familiar things they do, know, and enjoy. Commonplace adventure is a preference for three-year-olds. They like to listen to things that could happen to them, including stories about community helpers. Four-year-old children are not as self-centered. These children do not have to be part of every situation that they hear about. Many are ready for short and simple fantasy stories. Five-year-olds like stories that add to their knowledge—that is, books that contain new information and take them beyond the here and now. They also enjoy books with humor and exaggeration.

Documentation Boards and Panels

Documentation boards can illustrate the process and progress of learning. They can articulate the philosophy of the classroom and provide tangible evidence that the children are actively engaged in learning. Visual evidence such as photographs, work samples, and teacher's reflections can all be used. Documentation boards can communicate the theme, child development, celebration, skill acquisition, special events, and curricular milestones. To view some sample documentation boards, visit the Herr 6/e companion website at www.cengagebrain.com.

Curriculum-Planning Guide

We hope you find this book to be a valuable guide in planning curriculum for preschool and kindergarten children. The ideas should help you build a curriculum based on the children's natural interests. The book should also give you ideas so that your program will provide a wide variety of choices for children.

In planning a developmentally valid curriculum, consult the "Table of Contents by Subject." It has been prepared to allow you easy selection from all the themes. So pick and choose and make it your own! The various subjects included are shown in the following table:

Caution: Check for children's allergies when any food products will be used. As a safety precaution, none of the recipes in this book contain nuts or nut flavorings.

Table of Contents by Subject

 Arts and Crafts

 Cooking

 Dramatic Play

 Field Trips and Resource People

 Fingerplays and Chants

 Group Time
(Games, Language)

 Large Muscle

 Miscellaneous

 Math

 Music

 Science

 Sensory

 Social Studies

 Books

Technology/ Multimedia

Other Sources

Early childhood educators should refer to other Wadsworth/ Cengage Learning publications at www.cengage.com when developing appropriate curricula, including the following:

1. Charlesworth, Rosalind. *Experiences in Math for Young Children* (6th ed.).
2. Charlesworth, Rosalind, and Karen Lind. *Math and Science for Young Children*.

3. Charlesworth, Rosalind. *Understanding Child Development* (8th ed.).

4. Dolinar, Kathleen, Candace Boser, and Eleanor Holm. *Learning through Play: Curriculum and Activities for the Inclusive Classroom.*

5. Essa, Eva L. *A Practical Guide to Solving Preschool Behavior Problems* (5th ed.).

6. Essa, Eva L. *Introduction to Early Childhood Education* (5th ed.).

7. Gargiulo, R., and Jennifer Kilgo. *An Introduction to Young Children with Special Needs: Birth through Eight* (3rd ed.).

8. Gestwicki, Carol. *Home, School, and Community Relations: A Guide to Working with Parents* (6th ed.).

9. Jackman, Hilda. *Early Childhood Curriculum: A Child's Connection to the World* (4th ed.).

10. Herr, Judy. *Creative Learning Activities for Young Children.*

11. Herr, Judy, and Terri Swim. *Creative Resources for Infants and Toddlers.*

12. Kaster, Jean Bouza. *Growing Artists: Teaching the Arts to Young Children.*

13. Mayesky, M. *Creative Activities for Young Children.*

14. Machado, Jeanne M. (2010*). Early Childhood Experiences in Language Arts: Early Literacy* (9th ed.).

15. Nelson, Barbara A. (2011). *Week by Week: Plan for Documenting Children's Development* (5th ed.).

16. Ramirez, Gonzalo, Jr., and Jan Lee Ramirez. *Multiethnic Children's Literature: A Comprehensive Resource Guide.*

17. Schirrmacher, Robert. (2009). *Art and Creative Development for Young Children.*

Theme 1
ANTS

Colors
black
brown
rust
gray
red

Foods
insects
fruit
plants

Growth Stages
egg
larva
pupa
adult

Kinds
carpenter
weaver
leaf cutter
fire
cornfield
thief
army

Roles
queen
worker

Homes
underground
earthen mounds
inside trees
inside hollow
plants

Body Parts
head
antennae
eyes
mouth parts
trunk
six legs
wings (males and
young queens)

Importance
eat a large number
of insects
food source for birds,
frogs, and other animals

Theme Goals

Through participating in the experiences provided by this theme, the children may learn:

1. Kinds of ants
2. Ant body parts
3. Colors of ants
4. Roles of ants
5. Ant growth stages
6. Foods ants eat
7. Ant homes
8. Importance of ants

Concepts for the Children to Learn

1. An ant is a small insect with six legs.
2. There are many kinds of ants: carpenter, weaver, leaf cutter, fire, cornfield, thief, and army.
3. Ants can be black, brown, rust, gray, or red colored.
4. An ant's body has three main parts: head, trunk, and legs.
5. Ants have mouth parts, antennae, eyes, and mouth parts on their head.
6. Ants use their mouth parts to grasp food, carry their young, and fight enemies.
7. Ants use their antennae to smell, touch, taste, and hear.
8. Ants build homes inside trees, underground, and in hollow plants.
9. Ants eat other insects, plants, and fruits.
10. The queen ant lays the eggs.
11. Worker ants can carry things larger than their bodies.
12. Ants are a food source for birds, frogs, and other animals.

Vocabulary

1. **ant**—a type of small insect.
2. **antennae**—feelers on the head of an insect.
3. **colony**—a community or group of ants.
4. **mandibles**—pair of jaws that move from side to side.
5. **queen**—female ant that lays eggs.
6. **soldiers**—largest worker ants.
7. **workers**—female ants that build the nest, search for food, care for the young, and fight enemies.

Bulletin Board

The purpose of this bulletin board is to promote mathematical skills. To create the bulletin board, sketch anthills on heavy construction paper or tagboard. As illustrated, on each anthill make a dot to represent each ant. Using a felt-tip magic marker, print a numeral on each hill that represents a number of dots. If desired for durability, laminate each anthill or cover with transparent contact paper. If desired, small rubber or plastic ants may be purchased commercially; otherwise, they can be constructed out of black construction paper.

InBox

Dear Families,

Another week has quickly come and gone. Before we know it, summer will be here again! Have you noticed the grass getting greener and the birds in the trees? Nature is full of small wonders. This week in school, we will be learning about a group of "small wonders"—ants! We will learn many things about ants, those small picnic-joining insects! The children will learn about ant body parts, types of ants, the foods that ants eat, and the places where ants make homes, just to name a few!

At School

Learning experiences planned for this week include:

- Finding ants to create an ant farm for the classroom

- Going on a pretend picnic in the dramatic play area—ants included!

- Using small plastic ants as game pieces for classroom games

At Home

Try some of these ant activities at home this week.

- Create egg-carton ants! Cut a cardboard egg carton into three-cup sections. Paint as desired. Use chenille stems or yarn pieces to represent six legs and antennae. Add small pompons, pebbles, or seeds for the eyes, or use purchased craft eyes. Fun!

- Check out books about ants from the library. Some titles to look for are *Ant Cities* by Arthur Dorros and *Two Bad Ants* by Chris Van Allsburg.

- Take a slow walk around your home or neighborhood with your child and look for ants. Are they all the same size? Color? Can you figure out where their homes are? What do you think they eat?

Have a f-*ant*-astic week!

Arts and Crafts

1. Ant Prints

Set out several washable black and red ink pads and white paper. To create an ant, have each child press his or her index finger on the ink pad, and then make three prints in a row on the paper. Repeat process to make more ants. Provide black and red pens so children can add six legs and antennae.

2. Egg-Carton Ants

Cut cardboard egg cartons into three-section pieces. Children can paint their section as desired with "ant color" paints—black, brown, red, or gray. When dry, chenille stems or yarn pieces can be added to represent six legs and antennae. Eyes can be made by attaching small pompons, pebbles, seeds, or purchased small craft eyes.

3. Clay Ants

Provide clay or play dough as a medium for the children to create ants. Three small balls or circle shapes can be pushed together to create an ant body. Chenille stem pieces can be used for legs and antennae.

Cooking

Anthill Slaw

3 carrots, coarsely grated
3/4 cup raisins
1/2–3/4 cup mayonnaise
Juice from 1/2 lemon
Dash of salt and pepper

In a mixing bowl, combine carrots, raisins, and mayonnaise. Add more mayonnaise if needed. Add lemon juice, salt, and pepper. Mix again. Chill in the refrigerator for an hour.

Dramatic Play

Picnic (With Ants, of Course!)

Provide picnic props such as child-sized picnic table, backpack, tablecloth, picnic basket, cooler, thermos, plastic plates, and silverware. Plastic food items can be added. Have children assist in the preparation of paper ants that can be placed in the picnic area.

Field Trips and Resource People

Insect Specialist

Contact your local Department of Natural Resources or county 4-H agent to find out if there are any insect specialists in your area who could talk about ants or show examples of types of ants.

Fingerplays and Chants

Little Ants

One little ant, two little ants,
   (point to a finger for each number)
Three little ants I see.
Four little ants, five little ants,
Lively as can be.
Six little ants, seven little ants,
Eight in a bowl of glass.
Nine little ants, ten little ants,
Entertain our class.

Anthill

Once I saw an anthill,
   (make fist with one hand)
With no ants about.
So I said, "Dear little ants,
Won't you please come out?"
Then as if the little ants
Had heard my call,

One, two, three, four, five came out.
   (extend fingers one at a time)
And that was all.

Caught an Ant

One, two, three, four, five,
   (extend a finger for each number)
I caught an ant alive.
Six, seven, eight, nine, ten,
   (extend fingers of other hand)
I let it go again.
Why did I let it go?
   (shrug shoulders)
It bit my finger so.
Which one did it bite?
   (shrug shoulders)
The little one on the right.
   (hold up right pinkie finger)

Group Time

(Games, Language)

Ant Partners

Draw and cut out small matching ants from
different colors of construction paper. Place
the ants in a paper bag and have each child
take one. Play music and let the children
crawl around the room to find their "ant
partners" by matching up their ants. Then
have them hold hands with their partners
and sit to the side of the group until all
have found a partner. Collect the ants and
start the game again.

Large Muscle

Anthill Walk

Cut at least one large anthill shape out
of brown construction paper for each
child. Also cut several circles out of white
construction paper. Mix up the shapes and
tape them to the floor in a circle or trail.
Play music and let the children walk, skip,
or hop around the shape circle or trail.
Stop the music and have each child find an
anthill to stand on. Continue the game as
long as there is interest.

Math

1. **Ant Sort**
   Draw and cut out various-sized ants from
   different colors of paper. Laminate pieces to
   make them durable. Children can use the ant
   pieces for counting activities, as well as for
   sorting by attributes such as color and size.

2. **Anthill Math**
   Create several anthills from cardboard.
   Place a numeral on each anthill. Have the
   children place a corresponding number of
   ants on each hill. The numerals you place
   on each anthill can vary depending on the
   developmental abilities of the children in
   your classroom.

Music

1. **"The Ants Go Marching"**
   *(Sing to the tune of "When Johnny Comes
   Marching Home")*

   The ants go marching one by one.
   Hurrah, hurrah.
   The ants go marching one by one.
   Hurrah, hurrah.
   The ants go marching one by one.
   The little one stopped to wiggle its thumb.
   They all go marching,
   Marching to escape the rain.

   Continue with:

   The ants go marching two by two.
   The little one stopped to tie its shoe.

   The ants go marching three by three.
   The little one stopped to disagree.

   The ants go marching four by four.
   The little one stopped to shut the door.

   The ants go marching five by five.
   The little one stopped to learn to dive.

   The ants go marching six by six.
   The little one stopped to do some tricks.

   The ants go marching seven by seven.
   The little one stopped to wait for Devon.

The ants go marching eight by eight.
The little one stopped to shut the gate.

The ants go marching nine by nine.
The little one stopped to walk a line.

The ants go marching ten by ten.
The little one stopped to shout, "The End!"

2. "Six Little Ants"
(Sing to the tune of "Six Little Ducks")

Six little ants that I once knew,
Black ants, brown ants, gray ants, too.
But the busiest ants are the workers of the
     bunch.
They feed the babies with a munch, munch,
     munch.
Munch, munch, munch. Munch, munch,
     munch.
They feed the babies with a munch, munch,
     munch.

3. "Ants"
(Sing to the tune of "Mary Had a Little Lamb")

There's an ant trail underground,
Underground, underground.
There's an ant trail underground.
An ant colony lives down there.

The job of the queen is to lay the eggs,
Lay the eggs, lay the eggs.
The job of the queen is to lay the eggs.
That's all she has to do.

The worker ants have many jobs,
Many jobs, many jobs.
The worker ants have many jobs,
They do all the work.

4. "Little Black Ant"
(Sing to the tune of "I'm a Little Teapot")

I'm a little black ant on the ground.
I'm so tiny I can hardly be found.
Look very closely, then you'll see.
I'm scurrying around—just look at me!

Science

1. Ant Farm
If you and the children would like to watch ants close up, try making an ant farm. Begin by sifting soil or sand into a clean, clear container that has a lid or cover with holes punched in it. Next, search for some ants. Select ants from the same area so they will likely be from the same colony. Scoop the ants into a separate collecting jar and transfer them to the viewing container. Place a small piece of damp sponge into the container so the ants will have something to drink. Every three days or so, use an eyedropper to add a teaspoon of water to the sponge. Put a little food into the jar. Try to see what the ants are eating. Some ants like sweets, some like other insects, and some like seeds. Keep the ant farm in a dark place or cover it with a cloth when the ants are not being viewed. Ants will tend to dig deep tunnels, away from the light. You could also purchase an ant farm for classroom use.

2. Ant Watch
Place a cut piece of fruit or candy outside as ant bait. Check on the food piece periodically with the children to observe if ants have found it. Similarly, cracker or bread crumbs could be placed outside. Children may then be able to watch ants attempt to carry pieces to their nest.

Sensory

Additions to the Sensory Table

- Sand and small plastic ants with plastic jars and spoons
- Play dough, rolling pins, and circle cookie cutters (to create ants and anthills)

Social Studies

Ant Jobs
Ants work together to keep the ant colony alive. Each ant has work to do. Talk about the various roles or jobs that ants have in the colony.

Queen: The queen ant lays thousands and thousands of eggs. There is usually only one queen in a colony.

Workers: Workers are all females. They do the work in the ant city. They find food, store food, and take care of the ant eggs. They will also fight to protect the nest.

New Queens: New queens have wings. They use them to fly away to start new ant colonies. Their wings drop off, and then the queens lay eggs.

Books

The following books can be used to complement this theme:

Becker, Bonny. (2003). *An Ant's Day Off.* Illustrated by Nina Laden. New York: Simon and Schuster Books for Young Readers.

Brenner, Barbara. (1997). *Thinking about Ants.* Illustrated by Carol Schwartz. Greenvale, NY: Mondo.

Fowler, Allan. (1998). *Inside an Ant Colony.* Chicago: Children's Press.

Hall, Margaret. (2005). *Ants.* Mankato, MN: Capstone Press.

Hall, Margaret. (2007). *Hormigas/Ants.* Mankato, MN: Capstone Press.

Hartley, Karen, and Chris Marco. (2001). *Ant.* Des Plaines, IL: Heinemann Library.

Hodge, Deborah. (2004). *Ants.* Illustrated by Julian Mulock. Toronto: Kids Can Press.

Hoose, Hannah, and Phillip M. Hoose (1998). *Hey Little Ant.* Illustrated by Debbie Tilley. Berkeley, CA: Tricycle Press.

Kenney, Karen Latchana. (2010). *March the Ants.* Illustrated by Lisa Hedicker. Minneapolis, MN: Magic Wagon.

Kline, Suzy. (2009). *Horrible Harry and the Ant Invasion.* Illustrated by Frank Remkiewicz. New York: Penguin Group.

Lockwood, Sophie. (2008). *Ants.* Mankato, MN: Child's World.

Loewen, Nancy. (2004). *Tiny Workers: Ants in Your Backyard.* Illustrated by Brandon Reibeling. Minneapolis, MN: Picture Window Books.

McDonald, Megan. (2005). *Ant and Honey Bee, What a Pair!* Illustrated by G. Brian Karas. Cambridge, MA: Candlewick Press.

Nelson, Kristin L. (2004). *Busy Ants.* Minneapolis, MN: Lerner Publications.

Nickle, John. (1999). *The Ant Bully.* New York: Scholastic.

Owen, Ann. (2003). *The Ants Go Marching.* Illus. by Sandra D'Antonio. Minneapolis, MN: Picture Window Books.

Poole, Amy Lowry. (2000). *The Ant and the Grasshopper.* Aesop fable retold and illus. by Amy Lowry Poole. New York: Holiday House.

Prince, Joshya. (2007). *I Saw an Ant in a Parking Lot.* Illustrated by Macky Pamintuan. New York: Sterling.

Sayre, April Pulley. (2002). *Army Ant Parade.* Illustrated by Rick Chrustowski. New York: Henry Holt.

Sayre, April Pulley. (2005). *Ant, Ant, Ant! (An Insect Chant).* Illustrated by Trip Park. Minnetonka, MN: Northword Press

Tagliaferro, Linda. (2004). *Ants and Their Nests.* Mankato, MN: Capstone Press.

Vantrease, Norma. (2004). *Ants in My Pants.* Illustrated by Steve Cox. New York: Children's Press.

Young, Ed. (1995). *Night Visitors.* New York: Philomel Books.

Technology and Multimedia

The following technology and multimedia products can be used to complement this theme:

"The Ants Go Marching" [CD]. (2002). In *Ants Go Marching.* Wallingford, CT: Madacy Kids.

"Ants in My Pants" [CD]. (2001). In *Ants in My Pants.* Wallingford, CT: Madacy Kids.

"Ants Wear Underpants" [CD]. (2001). In *Ants Wear Underpants.* New York: BizzyBum.

The Ant Who Thought He Could Fly [audio book]. (2008). Scottsvalley, CA: CreateSpace.

"Farmer Brown Had Ten Green Apples" [CD]. (2002). In *Growing Up with Ella Jenkins.* Washington, DC: Smithsonian Folkways.

"Little Ants" [CD]. (2006). In *Start Smart Songs for 1's, 2's & 3's*. Long Branch, NJ: Kimbo Educational.

"Little Ant's Hill" [CD]. (2004). In *Laugh N Learn Silly Songs*. Long Branch, NJ: Kimbo.

NOVA: Ants—Little Creatures Who Run the World [DVD]. (2007). Boston: WGBH Boston.

"Rocks and Flowers" [CD]. (2009). In *More Please*. Olympia, WA: Aurora Elephant Music.

 Additional teaching resources to accompany this Theme can be found on the book's companion website. Go to www.cengagebrain.com to access the site for a variety of useful resources.

Theme 2
APPLES

Tastes
sweet
sour

Forms
raw
cooked
dried
baked

Parts
seed
core
meat
skin
stem

Sizes
large
small

Origin
orchard
seeds
soil, sunshine
water
trees
blossoms
fruit

Preparation
juice   jellies
pie   butter
cake   muffins
tarts   bread
sauce   pudding
cider

Colors
red
yellow
green

Theme Goals

Through participating in the experiences provided by this theme, the children may learn:

1. Parts of an apple
2. Preparation of apples for eating
3. Apple tastes
4. Colors of apples
5. Sizes of apples
6. The origin of apples

Concepts for the Children to Learn

1. An apple is a fruit.
2. An apple has five parts: seed, core, meat, skin, and stem.
3. Apples grow on trees; a group of apple trees is an orchard.
4. Trees need sunshine and water to blossom and grow fruit.
5. Apples can be eaten raw, cooked, dried, or baked.
6. Bread, butter, cakes, pies, pudding, applesauce, dumplings, butter, tarts, cider, bread, juice, muffins, and jelly can be prepared from apples.
7. Some apples taste sweet; others apples taste sour.
8. Apples can be green, yellow, or red.
9. Apples can be large or small.

Vocabulary

1. **apple**—a fruit that is grown on a tree. Apples can be colored red, green, or yellow.
2. **apple blossom**—a flower on the apple tree.
3. **apple butter**—a spread for bread made from apples.
4. **core**—the part of the apple that contains seeds.
5. **texture**—how something feels.

Bulletin Board

The purpose of this bulletin board is to develop the mathematical concept of sets, as well as to visually identify written numerals. Construct apples from red, green, and yellow tagboard. The number will depend on the developmental level of the children. Laminate the apples. Collect containers for baskets, such as large cottage cheese or pint berry containers. Cover the containers with paper if necessary. Affix numerals on baskets, beginning with 1. Staple the baskets to the bulletin board. The object is for the children to place the appropriate number of apples in each basket.

Family Letter

InBox

Dear Families,

Is it true that "an apple a day keeps the doctor away"? There are studies to support the nutritional value of apples and, therefore, the importance of including them in our diet. Next week a unit on apples will be introduced to the children. They will make many discoveries. Through active exploration and interaction, they will learn about the origin of apples, different flavors of apples, parts of apples, colors of apples, and ways apples can be prepared and eaten.

At School

Some classroom activities for this unit include:

- Preparing applesauce for Thursday's snack

- Drying apples in the sun

- Creating apple-shaped sponge prints in the art area

- Visiting the apple orchard! Arrangements have been made for a tour of the apple orchard on Wednesday morning. We will be leaving the center at 10:00 a.m. We would love to have families join us on this activity.

At Home

Apples are a tasty and nutritious food—and most children enjoy eating them. Try a variety of apple recipes for meals or snacks. Many people particularly like caramel apples.

Participating in cooking activities is a great way for children to learn.

Enjoy an apple with your child today!

Arts and Crafts

1. Apple Printing

Cut apple shapes from sponges. Have available individual shallow pans of red, yellow, and green tempera paint. Provide paper. The apple can be used as a painting tool. To illustrate, the children can place an apple half in the paint. After removing the excess paint, the apple can be placed on paper to create a print.

2. Seed Pictures

Collect: Apple seeds along with other seeds
Colored paper
Glue

Each child who chooses to participate should be provided with a small number of seeds. As they are distributed, discuss the seeds' similarities and differences. Provide uninterrupted time for the children to glue seeds onto paper and create pictures.

3. Shakers

Collect: Apple seeds
Paper plates (two per child)
Glue or stapler
Color crayons or felt-tip markers

The children can decorate the paper plates with color crayons or felt-tip markers. After this, the seeds can be placed between the two plates. To create the shakers, staple or glue the two plates together by securing the outer edges of the plates. The children can use the shakers as a means of self-expression during music or self-directed play.

Cooking

1. Caramel Apple Slices

Prepare the following recipe, which should serve 12 to 14 children.

1 pound caramels
2 tablespoons water
Dash of salt
6 crisp apples

Melt caramels with water in the microwave oven or double boiler, stirring frequently until melted. Stir in the salt. Pour the melted caramel over the sliced apples and cool before serving.

2. Applesauce

30 large apples
2 1/2 cups water
1 1/2 cups sugar
1 tablespoon Red Hots

1. Clean apples by peeling, coring, and cutting into small pieces.
2. Place the apples in a large kettle containing water.
3. Simmer the apples on low heat, stirring occasionally until soft.
4. Add the remaining ingredients.
5. Stir and simmer a few minutes.
6. Cool before eating.

3. Persian Apple Dessert
3 medium apples, cut up
2 to 3 tablespoons sugar
2 tablespoons lemon juice
Dash of salt

Place half the apples and the remaining ingredients in a blender. Cover and blend until coarsely chopped, about 20 to 30 seconds. Add remaining apples and repeat. Makes 3 servings.

4. Charoseths
6 medium apples, peeled or unpeeled
1/2 cup raisins
1/2 teaspoon cinnamon
1/2 cup chopped nuts (optional)
1/4 cup white grape juice

Chop the apples. Add the remaining ingredients. Mix well and serve.

5. Fruit Leather
2 cups applesauce
Vegetable shortening or oil

Preheat oven to 400 degrees. Pour applesauce onto greased, shallow pan. Spread to 1/8 inch in thickness. Place pan in oven and lower temperature to 180 degrees. Cook for approximately 3 hours until the leather can be peeled from the pan. Cut with scissors to serve.

6. Dried Apples
5 or 6 apples
2 tablespoons salt
Water

Peel, core, and cut apples into slices or rings 1/8 inch thick. Place apple slices in saltwater solution (2 tablespoons per 1 gallon water) for several minutes. Remove from the water. Place in 180-degree oven for 3 to 4 hours until dry. Turn apples occasionally.

Dramatic Play

Set Up an Apple Stand
Prepare an apple stand by providing the children with bags, plastic apples, a cash register, money, a stand, and bushel baskets. Encourage buying, selling, and packaging.

Field Trips

1. **Visit an Apple Orchard**
Observe the workers picking, sorting, and selling the apples. Call attention to the colors and types of apples.

2. **Visit a Grocery Store**
Observe all the forms of apples sold in a grocery store. Also, in the produce department, observe the different colors and sizes of apples. To show children differences in weight, take a large apple and place it on a scale. Note the weight. Then take a small apple and repeat the process.

Fingerplays and Chants

Apple Tree
Way up high in the apple tree
    (stretch arm up high)
Two little apples smiled at me.
    (hold up two fingers)
I shook that tree as hard as I could
    (make shaking motion)
Down came the apples.
    (make downward motions)
Mmmm—they were good.
    (smile and rub stomach)

Picking Apples
Here's a little apple tree.
    (left arm up, fingers spread)
I look up and I can see
    (look at fingers)
Big red apples, ripe and sweet,
    (cup hands to hold apple)

Big red apples, good to eat!
  (raise hands to mouth)
Shake the little apple tree.
  (shake tree with hands)
See the apples fall on me.
  (raise cupped hands and let fall)
Here's a basket, big and round.
  (make circle with arms)
Pick the apples from the ground.
  (pick and put in basket)
Here's an apple I can see.
  (look up to the tree)
I'll reach up. It's ripe and sweet.
  (reach up to upper hand)
That's the apple I will eat!
  (hands to mouth)

An Apple

An apple is what I'd like to be.
My shape would be round.
  (fingers in circular shape)
My color would be green.
  (point to something green)
Children could eat me each and every day.
I'm good in tarts and pies and cakes.
  (make these food shapes)
An apple is good to eat or to bake.
  (make stirring motion)

Apple Chant

Apples, apples, good to eat.
Apples, apples, juicy and sweet.
Pick them off the tree.
Buy them at the store.
Apples, apples,
We want more.

The Apple

Within its polished universe
The apple holds a star.
  (draw design of star with index finger)
A secret constellation
To scatter near and far.
  (point near and far)
Let a knife discover
Where the five points hide.
Split the shiny ruby
And find the star inside.
(After introducing the fingerplay, the
  teacher can cut an apple crosswise to
  find a star.)

Apple Tree

This is the tree
With leaves so green.
  (make leaves with fingers outstretched)
Here are the apples
That hang in between.
  (make fist)
When the wind blows
  (blow)
The apples will fall.
  (falling motion with hand)
Here is the basket to gather them all.
  (use arms to form basket)

Group Time
(Games, Language)

1. **What Is It?**
   Collect a variety of fruits such as apples,
   bananas, and oranges. Begin by placing one
   fruit in a bag. Choose a child to touch the
   fruit, describe it, and name it. Repeat with
   each fruit, discussing the characteristics.
   During the activity, each child should have
   an opportunity to participate.

2. **Transition Activity**
   The children should stand in a circle. As a
   record is played, the children pass an apple.
   When the record stops, the child holding
   the apple can get up to get a snack, put
   on outdoor clothes, clean up, and so on.
   Continue until all children have a turn. For
   older children, more than one apple may be
   successfully passed at a time.

3. **Picking Apples**
   Draw or paste a tree on a piece of tagboard
   or large piece of cardboard. Cut out apples
   from tagboard and place an alphabet letter
   on each apple. Laminate and attach Velcro
   to the backside of the apple. Place apples
   (letter-side down) on the tree with Velcro.
   Invite children to pick an apple and then
   try to identify the letter name.

   Sing the following song while the child picks
   the apple:

   Pick an apple from the apple tree,
   Say the letter (number, shape, color) name
     for me.

   Note: Shapes, colors, or numbers can be
   substituted for the alphabet letters on the
   apples.

Math

1. Cut apple shapes of various sizes from construction paper. Let the children sequence the shapes from smallest to largest.
2. Place a scale and various-sized apples on the math table. The children can experiment by weighing the apples.

Music

1. **"Little Apples"**
   (Sing to the tune of "Ten Little Indians")

   One little, two little, three little apples,
   Four little, five little, six little apples,
   Seven little, eight little, nine little apples,
   All fell to the ground.

   A variation for older children would be to give each child a number card (with a numeral from 1 through 9). When that number is sung, that child stands up. At the end of the fingerplay, all the children fall down.

2. **"Apples off My Tree"**
   (Sing to the tune of "Skip to My Lou")

   Pick some apples off my tree,
   Pick some apples off my tree,
   Pick some apples off my tree,
   Pick them all for you and me.

3. **"My Apple Tree"**
   (Sing to the tune of "The Muffin Man")

   Did you see my apple tree,
   Did you see my apple tree,
   Did you see my apple tree,
   Full of red apples?

Science

1. **Dried Apples**
   Using plastic knives, peel, core, and cut apples into slices or rings about 1/8 inch thick. Prepare a saltwater solution by mixing a tablespoon of salt in a gallon of water. Place the apples in this solution for several minutes. Remove from the solution. Place the apples in an 180-degree oven for 3 to 4 hours or until dry. Turn the apples occasionally.

2. **Oxidation of an Apple**
   Cut and core an apple into sections. Dip half the apple into lemon juice and place it on a plate. Place the remaining sections of apple on another plate. What happens to each plate of apples? Discuss the effects of the lemon juice coating, which keeps oxygen from the apples. As a result, they do not discolor as rapidly.

3. **Explore an Apple**
   Discuss the color, size, and shape of an apple. Then discuss the parts of an apple. Include the skin, stem, core, meat, and so on. Feel the apple. Then cut the apple in half. Observe the core and seeds. An apple is a fruit because it contains seeds.

Sensory

1. Cut different varieties of apples for a tasting party. This activity can easily be extended. On another day, provide the children applesauce, apple pie, apple juice, or apple cider to taste during snack or lunch.
2. Place several different kinds of seeds on the sensory table. In addition, to create interest, provide scoops, bowls, and bottles to fill.

Books

The following books can be used to complement this theme:

Aliki. (1991). *The Story of Johnny Appleseed.* New York: Simon & Schuster.

Berry, Lynne. (2010). *Ducking for Apples.* Illustrated by Hiroe Nakata. New York: Henry Holt.

Esbaum, Jill. (2009). *Apples for Everyone.* Washington, DC: National Geographic.

Farmer, Jacqueline. (2007). *Apples.* Illustrated by Phyllis Limbacher Tildes. Watertown, MA: Charlesbridge.

Fleming, Maria. (2005). *Five Shiny Apples.* Illustrated by Brenda Sexton. New York: Scholastic.

Gibbons, Gail. (2000). *Apples.* New York: Holiday House.

Hall, Zoe. (1996). *The Apple Pie Tree.* Illustrated by Shari Halpern. New York: Scholastic.

Harris, Calvin. (2008). *Apple Harvest.* Mankato, MN: Capstone Press.

Herman, Emmi S. (2003). *We All Fall for Apples.* New York: Scholastic.

Hodges, Margaret. (1997). *The True Tale of Johnny Appleseed.* New York: Holiday House.

Holub, Joan. (2003). *Apples and Honey.* Illustrated by Cary Pillo-Lassen. New York: Puffin Books.

Hubbell, Will. (2002). *Apples Here!* Morton Grove, IL: Albert Whitman and Company.

Hutchins, Pat. (2000). *Ten Red Apples.* New York: Greenwillow.

LeSieg, Theo. (1961). *Ten Apples Up on Top!* Illustrated by Roy Mc Kie. New York: Beginner Books.

Lipson, Eden Ross. (2009). *Applesauce Season.* Illustrated by Mordicai Gerstein. New York: Roaring Brook Press.

Marzollo, Jean. (1997). *I Am an Apple.* Illustrated by Judith Moffatt. St. Paul, MN: Cartwheel Books.

McNamara, Margaret. (2009). *Picking Apples.* Illustrated by Mike Gordon. New York: Aladdin Paperbacks.

Miller, Virginia. (2002). *Ten Red Apples.* Cambridge, MA: Candlewick Press.

Murphy, Patricia J. (2005). *A Visit to the Apple Orchard.* Mankato, MN: Capstone Press.

Naslund, Gorel Kristina. (2005). *Our Apple Tree.* Illustrated by Kristina Digman. New Milford, CT: Roaring Brook Press.

Patent, Dorothy Hinshaw. (1998). *Apple Trees.* Photos by William Munoz. Minneapolis, MN: Lerner Publications.

Rickert, Janet Elizabeth. (1999). *Russ and the Apple Tree Surprise.* Photos by Pete McGahan. Bethesda, MD: Woodbine House.

Robbins, Ken. (2002). *Apples.* New York: Atheneum Books for Young Readers.

Slade, Suzanne. (2009). *From Seed to Apple Tree: Following the Life Cycle.* Illus. by Suzanne Slade. Minneapolis, MN: Picture Window Books.

Snyder, Inez. (2005). *Apples to Applesauce.* Illustrated by Inez Snyder. New York: Children's Press.

Tagliaferro, Linda. (2007). *The Life Cycle of an Apple Tree.* Mankato, MN: Capstone Press.

VanHecke, Susan. (2009). *An Apple Pie for Dinner.* Illustrated by Carol Baicker-McKee. Tarrytown, NY: Marshall Cavendish.

Wallace, Nancy Elizabeth. (2000). *Apples, Apples, Apples.* Delray Beach, FL: Winslow Press.

Wellington, Monica. (2001). *Apple Farmer Annie.* New York: Dutton Books.

Technology and Multimedia

The following technology and multimedia products can be used to complement this theme:

"Aa Apple Song" [CD]. (2003). In *Fingerplays and Fun!* Buena Park, CA: Barbara Milne.

"Apples and Bananas" [CD]. (1996). In *One Light, One Song.* Cambridge, MA: Rounder/UMGD.

"Five Green Apples" [CD]. (2008). In *School Days.* Toronto: Casablanca Kids.

"I Love Apples" [CD]. (2002). In *Cousins Jamboree.* Richmond, VA: Holcomb Rock Road.

"Way Up High in the Apple Tree" [CD]. (2004). In *Toddler Twosome.* Redway, CA: Music for Little People.

Additional teaching resources to accompany this Theme can be found on the book's companion website. Go to www.cengagebrain.com to access the site for a variety of useful resources.

Theme 3
ART

Occupations
artist
weaver
designer
potter
painter
glassblower

Tools
paintbrushes   felt-tip markers
paper   needles
crayons   scissors
pencils   sewing machine
paint   pottery wheel
chalk
watercolors

Places
art studios
museums
parks
stores
homes
schools
craft shops

Uses
expressions of feelings
and thoughts
beauty
decoration
communication
enjoyment

Kinds
folk art
impressionist
modern
romantic
child created
crafts

Surfaces
paper
canvas
wood
metal
fabric
yarn
glass
ceramic
plastic
cement

Theme Goals

Through participating in the experiences provided by this theme, the children may learn:

1. The uses of art
2. Places where works of art can be found
3. Tools used for creating art
4. Surfaces used for art
5. Occupations associated with art
6. Kinds of art

Concepts for the Children to Learn

1. Art is an expression of feelings and thoughts.
2. Art can be used for decoration and beauty.
3. An artist uses art tools to make designs, pictures, or sculptures.
4. Brushes, scissors, paints, pencils, felt-tip markers, crayons, watercolors, chalk, needles, and paper are all tools for creating art.
5. Artists work in parks, stores, homes, schools, craft shops, and studios and at historical sites.
6. There are many kinds of art: folk, impressionistic, modern, crafts, romantic, and child created.
7. There are many surfaces that can be used for creating art.
8. Paper, canvas, wood, metal, fabric, yarn, glass, ceramic, plastic, and cement can all be used for art surfaces.
9. Artwork can be used for decorating our homes.

Vocabulary

1. **art**—a form of beauty. Paintings, drawings, and statues are kinds of art.
2. **artist**—a person who creates art.
3. **chalk**—a soft stone used as a tool for writing or drawing.
4. **crayon**—an art tool made of wax that comes in many colors.
5. **gallery**—a place that displays works of art.
6. **paint**—a colored liquid used for coloring and decorating objects.
7. **paintbrush**—a special type of brush that is a tool for applying paint.

Bulletin Board

The purpose of this bulletin board is to reinforce color-matching skills and develop visual perceptual skills. Construct a crayon-match bulletin board by drawing 16 crayons on white tagboard. Divide the crayons into pairs. Color each pair of crayons a different color. Include the colors pink, red, blue, yellow, purple, orange, brown, and green. Hang one from each pair on the top of the bulletin board and attach a corresponding colored string from the crayons. Hang the second set of crayons on the lower end of the bulletin board. A pushpin can be added to the bottom set of crayons, and the children can match the top crayons to their corresponding match on the bottom of the bulletin board.

Adjust the bulletin board to match the developmental needs and level of the children. For younger children, use fewer color choices. Let the children use the bulletin board during self-directed and self-initiated play periods. Repetition of this activity, providing it is initiated by the child, is important for assimilation.

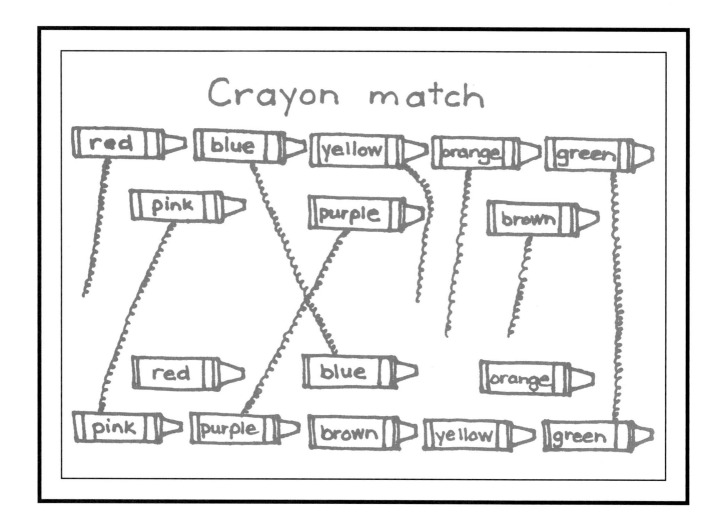

Family Letter

Dear Families,

Art is an expressive and aesthetic activity that can be enjoyed throughout life. It is also a curriculum theme that children always enjoy. During our focus on art this month, the children will be exploring many different types of art tools and surfaces. They will also be learning places where works of art can be found. Moreover, the artwork that they create will be displayed in an outdoor art gallery. You are invited to browse the gallery when you pick up your child from the center.

At School

Some of the artistic experiences planned include:

- Creating chalk murals on the sidewalk
- Staging an art gallery in the dramatic play area, and an outdoor art gallery
- Visiting on Tuesday with Bob Jones, a tour guide at the city museum. Mr. Jones will be sharing several art objects with us in our classroom.
- Exploring art tools
- Participating in a wide variety of art activities and exploring different types of painting surfaces

At Home

You can introduce the concepts of this theme into your home by collecting art tools and supplies and exploring them with your child. A fun art activity is applying tempera paint on paper using kitchen tools as applicators. Forks, potato mashers, and slotted spoons all work well. By participating in this activity, your child will be discovering interesting and creative ways for using kitchen tools as paint applicators. Art activities also provide opportunities for experimenting with color.

Have fun exploring art with your child!

 Arts and Crafts

1. Frames

During the course of this unit, with your assistance the children can frame their works of art by mounting them on sheets of colored tagboard. Using washable felt-tip markers, they can create a frame-like border. Older children may be able to do this unassisted. Display the works of art in the lobby or classroom—or outdoors, if weather permits.

2. Experimenting

In a unit on art, many kinds of art media need to be explored. Include the following art experiences:

- Felt-tip washable markers (both jumbo and skinny)
- Chalk (both wet and dry)
- Charcoal
- Pencils (both colored and lead)
- Crayons (jumbo, regular sized, and shavings)
- Paint (watercolors, tempera, and fingerpaint)
- Paper (colored construction, white, typing, tissue, newsprint, and tagboard)
- Other (tin foil, cotton, glitter, glue and paste, lace, scraps, crêpe paper, bags, waxed paper, yarn, and string)
- Tools for painting (marbles, string, fingers, brushes of all sizes, straws, and sponges)
- Play dough and clay
- Printing tools (stamps and ink pads, kitchen tools, sponges, potatoes, apples, and carrot ends)
- Seeds

3. Soap Painting

Pour two cups of soap flakes in a bowl. Then add two cups of water and beat until the mixture appears frothy. Let the children participate and point out how the mixture changes in appearance as it is beaten. Provide the children with large pieces of black or dark construction paper and painting brushes to use as tools to apply the paint.

4. Salt Painting

Premeasure 4 cups of salt and 1 cup of liquid starch. Let the children mix these two ingredients and add liquid food coloring. The mixture can be used to paint on an easel, paper, paper bags, newsprint, paper plates, or even large cardboard boxes outside on the play yard.

5. Squeeze-Bottle Painting

Pour liquid tempera paint into ketchup dispensers. Provide the children paper, and let them squeeze paint on paper.

6. Salt Dough Collage

Premeasure 1 cup salt, 4 cups flour, 3 T cooking oil, and 2 cups of cold water into a large, unbreakable bowl. The children take turns mixing the ingredients. If desired, add food coloring to the mixture. Then sprinkle a small amount of flour on a flat, washable surface. Demonstrate how to knead the dough, and let the children assist in the process. The dough can be molded into different shapes. When finished, the shapes need to dry.

7. Crayon Bundles

Using thick rubber bands, wrap three crayons together. Some bundles can contain the same color. Other bundles can contain three different colors. Provide paper and invite the children to color using the bundles.

8. Chunk Crayons

Save ends of old crayons. Remove the paper covers and place in muffin tins. Turn the oven on and set at 300 degrees. Place the tin in the oven, carefully monitoring the melting process. Remove the warm, melted crayons from the oven. Cool until set and remove from the tins. Provide the children the chunks of crayons and paper.

9. Silly Clay

Add 2 cups of white glue to 1 cup of liquid starch. Mix all of the ingredients in a bowl. Knead until smooth. If desired, food coloring can be added. After use, store in an airtight container.

 ## Cooking

1. **Graham Cracker Treat**
   Give each child a graham cracker, honey, and a brush to spread the honey. Top with grated cheese, raisins, or coconut.

2. **Cookie Decorating**
   Sugar cookies can be purchased commercially or baked and decorated. Recipes for the cookies and frosting follow.

3. **Drop Sugar Cookies**
   2 eggs
   2/3 cup vegetable oil
   2 teaspoons vanilla
   3/4 cup sugar
   2 cups flour
   2 teaspoons baking powder
   1/2 teaspoon salt

   Beat eggs with fork. Stir in oil and vanilla. Blend in sugar until mixture thickens. Add flour, baking powder, and salt. Mix well. Drop dough by teaspoons about 2 inches apart on an ungreased baking sheet. Flatten with the bottom of a plastic glass dipped in sugar. Bake at 400 degrees for 8 to 10 minutes or until delicate brown. Remove from baking sheet immediately. Makes about 4 dozen cookies that are 2 1/2 inches in diameter.

4. **Favorite Icing**
   1 cup sifted confectioners' sugar
   1/4 teaspoon salt
   1/2 teaspoon vanilla
   1 tablespoon water
   Food coloring

   Blend salt, sugar, and vanilla. Add enough water to make frosting easy to spread. Tint with food coloring. Allow children to spread on cookie with spatula or paintbrush.

5. **Colored Yogurt**
   Provide each child with a carton of vanilla yogurt. Then let them each select a bottle of their favorite color of food coloring. After adding a drop or two into their yogurt, they can stir it.

6. **Fruit-Flavored Yogurt**
   Provide each child with a carton of plain yogurt and a small cereal bowl. Encourage them to empty the yogurt into the small bowl. Then provide them blueberries, bananas, or raspberries to add to the yogurt.

 ## Dramatic Play

1. **Artist**
   Smocks, easels, and paint tables can be placed in the dramatic play area. The children can use the materials to pretend they are artists.

2. **Art Gallery**
   Mount pictures from magazines on sheets of tagboard. Let the children hang the pictures around the classroom. A cash register and play money for buying and selling the paintings can extend the play.

 ## Field Trips and Resource People

1. **Museum**
   Take a field trip to a museum, if one is available. Observe art objects. Point out and discuss color and form.

2. **Art Store**
   Take a walk to a nearby art store. Observe the many kinds of pencils, markers, crayons, paints, and other art supplies that are available.

3. Resource People
Invite the following people to show the children their artwork.

- Painter
- Potter
- Weaver
- Glassblower
- Sculptor

Fingerplays and Chants

Clay
> I stretch it.
>   (pulling motion)
> I pound it.
>   (pounding motion)
> I make it firm.
>   (pushing motion)
> I roll it.
>   (rolling motion)
> I pinch it.
>   (pinching motion)
> I make a worm.
>   (wiggling motion)

Painting
> Hands are blue.
>   (look at outstretched hands)
> Hands are green.
> Fingers are red,
> In between.
>   (wiggle fingers)
> Paint on my face.
>   (touch face)
> Paint on my smock.
>   (touch smock)
> Paint on my shoes.
>   (touch shoes)
> Paint on my socks.
>   (touch socks)

Group Time
(Games, Language)

Toward the end of the unit, collect all art projects and display them in an art gallery at your center. The children can help hang their own projects and decide where to have the gallery. If weather permits, the art gallery can be set up on the playground using low clotheslines and easels to display the art. If weather does not permit, a gallery can be set up in the classroom or center lobby, using walls and tables to display the art.

Large Muscle

1. Sidewalk Chalk
Washable colored chalk can be provided for the children to use outside on the sidewalk. After the activity, the designs can be removed with a hose. The children may even enjoy using scrub brushes to remove the designs.

2. Painting
Provide large paintbrushes or rollers and buckets of water for the children to paint the sidewalks, walls, and fences surrounding your center or school.

3. Foot Art
Prepare a thick tempera paint and pour a small amount in a shallow pan. Roll out long sheets of paper. The children can take off their shoes and socks, step into the tempera paint, and walk or dance across the sheets of paper. Provide buckets with soapy water and towels at the end of the paper for the children to wash their feet. Dry the foot paintings, and send them home with the children.

 **Math**

1. Counting Cans

Counting cans for this unit can be made from empty soup cans with filed edges. On each can, write a numeral. The number prepared will depend on the developmental needs of the children. Then provide an equal number of the following objects: pencils, pens, felt-tip markers, paintbrushes, crayons, chalk sticks, and sponges. The object is for the children to relate the number of objects to numerals on the can.

2. Measuring Art Tools

Art tools come in all different lengths. Provide a variety of art tools and rulers, or a tape measure that has been taped to the table. The children can measure the objects to find which one is the longest. Make a chart showing the longest tool and continuing to the shortest.

3. Sorting Art Supplies

A large ice cream pail can be used to hold pencils, pens, markers, crayons, glue bottles, and other supplies that can be sorted into shoeboxes.

 **Music**

"Let's Pretend"

(Sing to the tune of "Here We Are Together")

Let's pretend that we are artists,
are artists, are artists.
Let's pretend that we are artists
How happy we'll be.
We'll paint with our brushes,
and draw with our crayons.
Let's pretend that we are artists
How happy we'll be.

 **Science**

1. Art Tools

A variety of art tools can be placed on the science table. Included may be brushes, pencils, felt-tip markers, crayons, and chalk. The children can observe, smell, and feel the difference in the tools.

2. Charcoal

Place charcoal pieces and magnifying glasses on the science table.

3. Rock Writing

Provide the children with a variety of soft rocks. The children can experiment drawing on the sidewalks with them.

 **Sensory**

Additions to the Sensory Table

1. Goop

Mix together food coloring, 1 cup cornstarch, and 1 cup water in the sensory table. If a larger quantity is desired, double or triple the recipe.

2. Silly Putty

Mix food coloring, 1 cup liquid starch, and 2 cups of glue together. Stir constantly until the ingredients are well mixed. Add more starch as needed.

3. Wet Sand and Sand Mold Containers

Add sand to the sensory table. Then dampen the sand with water and add the sand molds and containers.

Social Studies

The Feel of Color

This activity can be introduced at large-group time. Begin by collecting colored construction paper. Individually hold up each color and ask the children how that particular color makes them feel. Adjectives that may be used include hot, cold, cheerful, warm, sad, tired, happy, and clean.

Books

The following books can be used to complement this theme:

Anholt, Laurence. (1994). *Camille and the Sunflowers: A Story about Vincent Van Gogh.* Hauppauge, NY: Barron's Educational Series.

Arnold, Katya. (2005). *Elephants Can Paint Too!* New York: Atheneum Books for Young Readers.

Auch, Mary Jane. (1996). *Eggs Mark the Spot.* New York: Holiday House.

Beaumont, Karen. (2005). *I Ain't Gonna Paint No More!* Illustrated by David Catrow. Orlando, FL: Harcourt.

DeRolf, Shane. (1997). *The Crayon Box That Talked.* Illustrated by Michael Letzig. New York: Random House.

Dodd, Emma. (2001). *Dog's Colorful Day: A Messy Story about Colors and Counting.* New York: Dutton Children's Books.

Eckler, Rebecca. (2010). *The Mischievous Mom at the Art Gallery.* Illustrated by Carrie Hartman. Toronto: Key Porter Kids.

Edwards, Pamela Duncan. (2001). *Warthogs Paint: A Messy Color Book.* Illustrated by Henry Cole. New York: Hyperion Books for Children.

Ehlert, Lois. (1997). *Hands.* San Diego, CA: Harcourt Brace.

Ericsson, Jennifer. (2007). *A Piece of Chalk.* Illustrated by Michelle Shapiro. New Milford, CT: Roaring Brook Press.

Gutman, Anne, and Georg Hallensleben. (2001). *Gaspard & Lisa at the Museum.* New York: Knopf.

Heide, Iris Van Der. (2006). *The Red Chalk.* Illustrated by Marije Tolman. Asheville, NC: Front Street.

Hubbard, Patricia. (1996). *My Crayons Talk.* Illustrated by G. Brain Karas. New York: Henry Holt.

Lynn, Sara. (1993). *Play with Paint.* Minneapolis, MN: Carolrhoda Books.

McArthur, Meher. (2010). *An ABC of What Art Can Be.* Los Angeles: J. Paul Getty Museum.

McDonnell, Patrick. (2006). *Art.* New York: Little, Brown.

Micklethwait, Lucy. (2004). *I Spy Shapes in Art.* New York: Greenwillow Books.

Mills, Claudia. (2005). *Ziggy's Blue-Ribbon Day.* Illustrated by R. W. Alley. New York: Farrar, Straus and Giroux.

Munoz, Isabel. (2005). *Es Mio / It's Mine.* Illustrated by Gustavo Mazali. New York: Scholastic.

Nikola, Lisa W. (2004). *Setting the Turkeys Free.* Illustrated by Ken Wilson-Max. New York: Hyperion Books for Children.

Rex, Michael. (2002). *Where Can Bunny Paint?* New York: Scholastic.

Reynolds, Peter. (2005). *The Dot.* Denton, TX: BrailleInk.

Rusch, Elizabeth. (2007). *A Day with No Crayons.* Illustrated by Chad Cameron. Flagstaff, AZ: Rising Moon.

Scieszka, Jon. (2005). *Seen Art?* Illustrated by Lane Smith. New York: Viking.

Snyder, Inez. (2003). *Wax to Crayons.* New York: Children's Press.

Thomson, Bill. (2010). *Chalk.* New York: Marshall Cavendish Children.

Watson, A., and the Staff of the Abby Aldrich Rockefeller Folk Art Center. (1992). *Folk Art Counting Book.* New York: Abrams.

Watt, Melanie. (2007). *Chester.* Toronto: Kids Can Press.

Watt, Melanie. (2010). *Chester's Masterpiece.* Toronto: Kids Can Press.

Whatley, Bruce. (2001). *Wait! No Paint!* New York: HarperCollins.

Wiesner, David. (2010). *Art and Max.* Boston: Clarion Books.

Wing, Natasha. (2007). *Go to Bed, Monster!* Illustrated by Sylvie Kantorovitz. Orlando, FL: Harcourt.

Winter, Jeanette. (1996). *Josefina.* Orlando: Harcourt Brace.

Ziefert, Harriet. (2003). *Lunchtime for a Purple Snake.* Paintings by Todd McKie. Boston: Houghton Mifflin.

Technology and Multimedia

The following technology and multimedia products can be used to complement this theme:

Art House, Vol. 1: Basic Shapes and Animals [DVD]. (2009). Marina del Rey, CA:: Clamorhouse Kids.

Harold and the Purple Crayon and More Harold Stories [DVD]. (2009). New York: Scholastic.

"Paint the Day Away" [CD]. (2009). In *For Those about to Hop.* Burbank, CA: Walt Disney Records.

Additional teaching resources to accompany this Theme can be found on the book's companion website. Go to www.cengagebrain.com to access the site for a variety of useful resources.

Painting Surfaces

There are many types of interesting surfaces that children can successfully use for painting. The list of possibilities is limited only by one's imagination. Included are:

- Construction paper
- Newsprint (plain or printed)
- Tissue paper
- Tracing paper
- Tin foil
- Clear or colored acetate
- Wood
- Cardboard (sheets or boxes)
- Paper tablecloths
- Paper place mats
- Waxed paper
- Boxes
- Leather scraps
- Sandpaper
- Paper towels
- Mirror
- Plexiglass
- Paper bags
- Cookie sheets
- Meat trays (plastic or styrofoam)
- Table surfaces
- Shopping bags
- Wrapping paper
- Shelf paper

Fingerpaint Recipes

Liquid Starch Method

Liquid starch
  (put in squeeze bottles)
Dry tempera paint in shakers

Put about 1 tablespoon of liquid starch on the surface to be painted. Let the child shake the paint onto the starch. Mix and blend the paint. *Note:* If this paint becomes too thick, simply sprinkle a few drops of water onto the painting.

Soap Flake Method

Soap flakes
A small amount of water

Mix soap and water in a small bowl. Beat until stiff with an eggbeater. Use white soap on dark paper, or add colored tempera paint to the soap and use it on light-colored paper. This gives a slight three-dimensional effect.

Wheat Flour Paste

3 parts water
1 part wheat flour
Coloring

Stir flour into water. Add coloring.

Uncooked Laundry Starch

A mixture of 1 cup laundry or liquid starch, 1 cup cold water, and 3 cups soap flakes will provide a quick fingerpaint.

Flour and Salt I

1 cup flour
1 1/2 cups salt
3/4 cup water
Coloring

Combine flour and salt. Add water. This has a grainy quality, unlike the other fingerpaints, providing a different sensory experience. Some children enjoy the different touch sensation when 1 1/2 cups of salt are added to the other recipes.

Flour and Salt II

2 cups flour
2 teaspoons salt
3 cups cold water
2 cups hot water
Coloring

Add salt to flour, then pour in cold water gradually and beat mixture with egg beater until it is smooth. Add hot water and boil until it becomes clear. Beat until smooth, then mix in coloring. Use 1/4 cup food coloring to 8 to 9 ounces of paint for strong colors.

Instantized Flour: Uncooked Method

1 pint water (2 cups)
1 1/2 cups instantized flour
  (the kind used to thicken
  gravy; regular flour may
  be lumpy)
Put the water in the bowl, and stir the flour into the water. Add color.

Cooked Starch Method

1 cup laundry starch
  dissolved in a small
  amount of cold water
5 cups boiling water added
  slowly to dissolve starch
1 tablespoon glycerin
  (optional)

Cook the mixture until it is thick and glossy. Add 1 cup mild soap flakes. Add color in separate containers. Cool before using.

Cornstarch Method

Gradually add 2 quarts water to 1 cup cornstarch. Cook until clear and add 1/2 cup soap flakes (like Ivory Snow). A few drops of glycerin or oil of wintergreen may be added.

Flour Method

Mix 1 cup flour and 1 cup cold water. Add 3 cups boiling water and bring all to a boil, stirring constantly. Add 1 tablespoon alum and coloring. Paintings from this recipe dry flat and do not need to be ironed.

Tips

1. Be sure you have running water and towels nearby or provide a large basin of water where children can rinse off.
2. Fingerpaint on smooth table, oilcloth, or cafeteria tray. Some children prefer

Fingerpaint Recipes (Continued)

to start fingerpainting with shaving cream on a sheet of oilcloth.

3. Food coloring or powdered paint may be added to the mixture before using, or allow each child to choose the colors he or she wants sprinkled on top of the paint.

4. Sometimes reluctant children are more easily attracted to the paint table if the fingerpaints are already colored. the colors he or she wants sprinkled on top of the paint.

4. Sometimes reluctant children are more easily attracted to the paint table if the fingerpaints are already colored.

Theme 4
BIRDS

Origin
eggs

Body
feathers
wings
tails
beaks
legs
eyes

Colors
blue
brown
black
red
gray
orange
green
pink

Types
turkeys
ducks
chickens
wild
pets

Foods
seeds
insects
crumbs
berries
worms
fish
small animals

Sizes
small
medium
large

Help
eat insects
create beauty

Homes
nests
trees
houses
cages

Theme Goals

Through participating in the experiences provided by this theme, the children may learn:

1. The bird's body parts
2. Types of birds
3. Bird homes
4. Foods that birds eat
5. Ways birds help
6. Sizes of birds
7. Colors of birds
8. Origins of birds

Concepts for the Children to Learn

1. There are many types of birds.
2. Turkeys, ducks, and chickens are birds.
3. Birds hatch from eggs.
4. Birds have feathers, wings, tails, legs, eyes, and beaks.
5. Birds live in nests, trees, houses, and cages.
6. Birds eat seeds, insects, crumbs, berries, and worms.
7. Some birds eat fish and small animals.
8. Some birds help us by eating insects.
9. Birds come in many sizes and colors.

Vocabulary

1. **bird**—an animal that has wings, feathers, and a beak.
2. **beak**—the part around a bird's mouth.
3. **bird feeder**—a container for bird food.
4. **birdwatching**—watching birds.
5. **feathers**—cover the skin of a bird.
6. **hatch**—to come from an egg.
7. **nest**—bed or home prepared by a bird. Birds make nests from leaves, small twigs, straw, and other things.
8. **perch**—a pole for a bird to stand on.
9. **wing**—movable body part that helps most birds fly.

Bulletin Board

The purpose of this bulletin board is to develop skills in eye-hand coordination, problem solving, and matching. To construct the board, cut 10 bird nests out of brown-colored tagboard. Draw a set of dots, beginning with 1, on each bird nest. Tack the nest on the bulletin board. Next, construct the same number of birds out of tagboard. Write a numeral on each bird beginning with 1. By matching the numeral on each bird to the number of dots on the nests, the children can help each bird find a home. The number of birds and nests on this bulletin board should match the children's developmental abilities.

InBox

Dear Families,

The children will be discussing our "feathered friends"—birds—during our next unit. They will be introduced to birds kept as pets and birds in the wild. In addition, they will discover the unique body parts of birds and the homes in which they live. By participating in class activities, the children will learn that birds are more similar than they are dissimilar.

At School

Some of the activities planned for the unit on birds include:

- Observing different types of bird nests with a magnifying glass at the science table
- Visiting with Jodi's pet canary on Wednesday
- Creating collages using birdseed and glue in the art area
- Making bird feeders to hang outdoors in our play yard
- Building birdhouses

At Home

Whether you live in the city or country, chances are there are birds nearby. If you have birds in your yard, the following game may be fun to play with your child. Set an egg or kitchen timer for 3 to 5 minutes. Then look out the window and see how many birds you can see. For each bird, drop a button in a jar. When the timer goes off, count how many buttons are in the jar. This game will strengthen your child's observation skills and increase his or her understanding of number concepts. Variations of this game would be to observe for cars, squirrels, or any other object that can be counted.

Happy birdwatching!

Arts and Crafts

1. Feather Painting

On the art table, place feathers, thin paper, and paint. Let the children experiment with different paint consistencies and types of feathers. *Suggestion:* Inexpensive feather dusters from discount stores are a good source of feathers. Individual feathers can be cut off as needed.

2. Birdseed Collages

Birdseed, paper, and white glue are needed for this activity. Apply glue to paper and sprinkle birdseed over the glue. For a variation, use additional types of seeds such as corn and sunflower seeds.

3. Eggshell Collage

Save eggshells and dye them. Crush the dyed shells into small pieces. Using glue, apply the eggshells to paper.

4. Robin Eggs

Cut easel paper into the shape of an egg. Provide light blue paint with sand for speckles.

5. Dyeing Eggs

Boil an egg for each child. Then let the children paint the eggs with nontoxic paint and easel brushes. The eggs can be eaten at snack time or taken home.

Cooking

1. Egg Salad Sandwiches

Eggs
Bread
Mayonnaise
Dry mustard (just a pinch)
Salt
Pepper

Boil, shell, and mash the eggs, adding enough mayonnaise to provide a consistent texture. Add salt, pepper, and dry mustard to flavor. Spread on the bread.

2. French Bread Recipe

1/2 cup water
2 packages fast-rising yeast
1 tablespoon salt
2 cups lukewarm water
7 to 7 1/2 cups all-purpose flour

Soften the yeast in 1/2 cup lukewarm water. Be careful that the water isn't too warm or the activity of the yeast will be destroyed. Add salt to 2 cups of lukewarm water in a large bowl. Gradually, add 2 cups of flour and beat well. Add the softened yeast and gradually add the remaining flour, beating well after each addition. Turn the soft dough out on a lightly floured surface and knead until elastic. Lightly grease a bowl and place the dough into it, turning once to grease surface. Let rise until double. Divide into 2 portions. Bake in a 375-degree oven until light brown, about 35 minutes. Serve at lunch or snack time. If any bread is left, place on a bird feeder.

3. Bird's Nest Salad

1 grated carrot
1/2 cup canned Chinese noodles
Mayonnaise to moisten
Peas or grapes

Have the children grate a carrot. Next, have them mix the carrot with 1/2 cup canned Chinese noodles and mayonnaise to moisten. Put a mound of this salad on a plate and push in the middle with a spoon to form a nest. Peas or grapes can be added to the nest to represent bird eggs. The nest could also be set on top of a lettuce leaf. Makes 2 salads.

Note: From *Super Snacks,* by J. Warren, 1982, Alderwood Manor, WA: Warren. Reprinted with permission.

4. Egg Foo Young

12 eggs
1/2 cup finely chopped onion
1/3 cup chopped green pepper
3/4 teaspoon salt
Dash of pepper
2 16-ounce cans bean sprouts, drained
Sauce:
2 tablespoons cornstarch
2 teaspoons sugar

2 cubes or 2 teaspoons chicken bouillon
Dash of ginger
2 cups water
3 tablespoons soy sauce

Heat oven to 300 degrees. Beat eggs in a large bowl. Add remaining ingredients, except sauce ingredients; mix well. Heat 2 tablespoons of oil in a large skillet. Drop egg mixture by tablespoons into skillet and fry until golden. Turn and brown other side. Drain on a paper towel. Continue to cook the remaining egg mixture, adding oil to skillet if necessary. Keep warm in a 300-degree oven while preparing sauce. Combine the first four sauce ingredients in a saucepan. Add water and soy sauce. Cook until mixture boils and thickens, stirring constantly.

5. Bird Nest Treat
1/4 cup butter or margarine (1/2 stick)
6–10 oz. regular marshmallows (about 40)
    or 4 cups miniature marshmallows

6 cups Rice Krispies

Melt butter in 3-quart saucepan. Add marshmallows and cook over low heat, stirring constantly, until marshmallows are melted and mixture is syrupy. Remove from heat.

Add Rice Krispies and stir until well coated.

Before cooling, shape into a bird's nest.

Dramatic Play

1. Birdhouse
Construct a large birdhouse out of cardboard. Place in the dramatic play area, allowing the children to imitate birds. Unless adequate room is available, this may be more appropriate for an outdoor activity. Bird accessories such as teacher-made beaks and wings may be supplied to stimulate interest.

2. Bird Nest
Place several bales of hay in the corner of a play yard, confining the materials to one area. Let the child rearrange the straw to simulate a bird nest.

3. Hatching
Here is a general idea of what you can say to create the hatching experience with young children. Say, "Close your eyes. Curl up very small, as small as you can. Lie on your side. Think of how dark it is inside your egg. Yes, you're in an egg! You're tiny and curled up and quiet. It's very dark. Very warm. But now, try to wiggle a little—just a little! Remember, your eggshell is all around you. You can wiggle your wingtips a little, and maybe your toes. You can shake your head just a little. Hey! Your beak is touching something. I think your beak is touching the eggshell. Tap the shell gently with your beak. Hear that? Yes, that's you making that noise. Keep tapping. A little harder. Something is happening. The shell has cracked—oh, close your eyes. It's bright out there. Now you can wiggle a little more. The shell is falling away. You can stretch out, stretch to be as long as you can make yourself. Stretch your feet. Stretch your wings. Doesn't that feel good, after being in that little egg? Stretch! You're brand new—can you stand up slowly? Can you see other new baby birds?"

Field Trips and Resource People

1. Pet Store
Take a field trip to a pet store. Arrange to have the manager show the children birds and birdcages. Ask the manager how to care for birds.

2. Bird Sanctuary
Take a field trip to a bird sanctuary, nature area, pond, or park. Observe where birds live.

3. Museum
Arrange to visit a nature museum or taxidermy studio to look at stuffed birds. Extend the activity by providing magnifying glasses.

4. Zoo
Visit the birdhouse. Observe the colors and sizes of birds.

5. Resource People

Invite resource people to visit the classroom. Suggestions include

- Wildlife management people
- Ornithologists
- Veterinarians
- Bird owners
- Birdwatchers
- Pet store owners

Fingerplays and Chants

Houses

Here is a nest for a robin.
  (cup both hands)
Here is a hive for a bee.
  (fists together)
Here is a hole for the bunny.
  (finger and thumb make circle)
And here is a house for me!
  (fingertips together to make roof)

Two Little Blackbirds

Two little blackbirds sitting on a hill,
  (close fists, extend index fingers)
One named Jack. One named Jill.
  (talk to one finger; talk to other finger)
Fly away, Jack. Fly away, Jill.
  (toss index fingers over shoulder
  separately)
Come back, Jack. Come back, Jill.
  (bring back hands separately with index
  fingers extended)

Bird Feeder

Here is the bird feeder. Here are seeds and
  crumbs.
  (left hand out flat, right hand cupped)
Sprinkle them on and see what comes.
  (sprinkling motion with right hand over
  left hand)
One cardinal, one chickadee, one junco,
  one jay,
  (join fingers of right hand and peck at
  the bird feeder once for each bird)
Four of my bird friends are eating today.
  (hold up four fingers of left hand)

If I Were a Bird

If I were a bird, I'd sing a song
And fly about the whole day long.
  (twine thumbs together and move hands
  like wings)
And when the night comes, go to rest,
  (tilt head and close eyes)
Up in my cozy little nest.
  (cup hands together to form nest)

Tap Tap Tap

Tap, tap, tap goes the woodpecker
  (tap with right pointer finger on inside
  of left wrist)
As he pecks a hole in a tree.
  (make hole with pointer finger and
  thumb)
He is making a house with a window
To peep at you and me.
  (hold circle made with finger and thumb
  in front of eye)

Stretch, Stretch

Stretch, stretch way up high:
On your tiptoes, reach the sky.
See the bluebirds flying high.
  (wave hands)
Now bend down and touch your toes.
Now sway as the North Wind blows.
Waddle as the gander goes!

Group Time
(Games, Language)

1. Little Birds

This is a movement game that allows for activity. To add interest, the teacher may use a tambourine for rhythm. One child can be the mother bird, and the remainder of the children can act out the story.

All the little birds are asleep in their nest.
All the little birds are taking a rest.
They do not even twitter, they do not even
  tweet.
Everything is quiet up and down the street.
Then came the mother bird and tapped
  them on the head.
They opened up one little eye and this is
  what was said,
"Come little birdies, it's time to learn to fly,
Come little birdies, fly way up in the sky."

Fly fly, oh fly away, fly, fly, fly
Fly fly, oh fly away, fly away so high.
Fly fly, oh, fly away, birds can fly the best.
Fly fly, oh, fly away, now fly back to your
    nest.

2. Who Is Inside?

The purpose of this game is to encourage the child to develop listening skills. To prepare for the activity, find a piece of large-muscle equipment such as a jungle gym to serve as the birdhouse. Cover it with a large blanket. To play the game, one child looks away from the group or covers his or her eyes. A second child should go into the birdhouse. The first child says, "Who is inside?" The second child replies, "I am inside the birdhouse." Then the first child tries to guess who is in the birdhouse by recognizing the voice. Other clues may be asked for, if voice alone does not work.

3. Little Red Hen

Tell the story of the Little Red Hen. After they have heard the story, let the children help make bread.

Large Muscle

1. Bird Nest Search

Hide strips of brown fabric around the room. Invite the children to search for "twigs" for a bird nest. When strips are found, glue onto a small plastic pool and place the "nest" in the dramatic play area.

2. Penguin Waddle

Explain to children how a penguin waddles. Place a small rubber ball between the knees of the children, so they can imitate the waddle of a penguin.

3. Egg Drop

Have the children walk while balancing a plastic egg on a large wooden spoon.

4. Egg Hunt

Hide plastic eggs on the outdoor playground or in the classroom. Ask children to search for eggs.

Math

1. Feather Sorting

During the self-directed activity period, place a variety of feathers on a table. Encourage the children to sort them according to attributes such as color, size, and texture. This activity can be followed with other sorting activities, including egg shapes and pictures of birds.

2. Cracked Eggs

Cut tagboard egg shapes. Using scissors, cut the eggs in half, making a jagged line. Record a numeral on one side of the egg and corresponding dots on the other side. The number of eggs prepared should reflect the children's developmental level.

3. Clothesline Birds

Create a clothesline stand by placing two wooden dowels into opposite ends of a board. Drill holes through each dowel near the top. Tie a rope from one dowel to another. Make birds in a variety of sizes. Have the children clip the birds onto the clothesline with clothespins, in order from smallest to largest or largest to smallest.

Music

1. "Birds"

(Sing to the tune of "Here We Go 'round the Mulberry Bush")

(The first verse remains the same, with the children walking around in a circle holding hands.)

This is the way we scratch for worms,
    scratch for worms, scratch for worms.
This is the way we scratch for worms so
    early in the morning.
      (children move foot in a scratching
      motion like a chicken)
This is the way we peck our food . . .
      (children peck)
This is the way we sit on our eggs . . .
      (children squat down)
This is the way we flap our wings . . .
      (bend arms at elbows and put thumbs
      under armpits, then flap)

This is the way we fly away . . .
> (children can "fly" anywhere they want,
> but return to the circle at the end of the
> verse)

2. "Pretty Birds"
(Sing to the tune of "Ten Little Indians")

One pretty, two pretty
Three pretty birdies.
Four pretty, five pretty,
Six pretty birdies.
Seven pretty, eight pretty,
Nine pretty birdies,
All sitting in a tree.

Science

1. Bird Feeders
Make bird feeders. Suet can be purchased from a butcher shop or the meat department of a supermarket. For each feeder, purchase 1/2 pound of suet, a 12-inch × 12-inch piece of netting, and birdseed. Begin by rolling the suet in birdseed. Place the seeded suet in the netting. Tie the four corners of the netting together, and hang in a tree or set outside on a window ledge for children to observe.

2. Grapefruit Cup Feeders
Place seeds in an empty grapefruit half. If possible, place the feeder in an observable location for the children. Some children may wish to take their feeders home.

3. Science Table
On the science table, provide magnifying glasses and the following items:
- Feathers
- Eggs
- Nests

4. Observing a Bird
Arrange for a caged parakeet to visit the classroom. A parent may volunteer, or a pet store may lend a bird for a week. Encourage the children to note the structure of the cage, the beauty of the bird, the food eaten, and the behavior of the bird.

5. Feed the Hummingbirds
Hang a hummingbird feeder near a classroom window. Encourage the children to help you mix the liquid to fill the hummingbird feeder. The recipe is as follows:

Hummingbird Food
2 cups water
1 cup sugar

Stir until dissolved. Pour liquid into feeder and encourage the children to watch for hummingbirds. Be sure to clean the feeder between refills.

6. Birds I Have Seen
Prepare a chart with all of the children's names and birds that can be identified in the local area. Title the chart "Bird Watch." Place a pair of binoculars and the chart on the science shelf. Encourage children to look outside for birds. If they see a bird, they can mark "yes" or place their picture on the corresponding bird chart behind their name.

Sensory

Additions to the Sensory Table
- Feathers and sand
- Eggshells
- Sticks and twigs for nests
- Worms and soil
- Water, rubber ducks, and other water toys
- Birdseed and measuring tools

Social Studies

1. Caring for Birds
Arrange for a pet canary to visit the classroom. The children can take turns feeding and caring for the bird. Responsibilities include cleaning the cage and providing water and birdseed. Also, a cuttlebone should be inserted in the bars of the cage within reach of the bird's bill. This bone will help keep the bird's bill sharp and clean, providing the bird uses it.

2. Bird Feeders

Purchase birdseed and small paper cups. The children can fill a cup with a small amount of seed. After this, the teacher can attach a small string to the cup for use as a handle. The bird feeders can then be hung in bushes outdoors. If bushes are not available, they can be placed on windowsills.

 **Books**

The following books can be used to complement this theme:

Aardema, Verna. (1995). *How the Ostrich Got Its Long Neck: A Tale from the Akamba of Kenya.* Illustrated by Marcia Brown. New York: Scholastic.

Appelt, Kathi, and Jane Dyer. (2000). *Oh My Baby, Little One.* San Diego, CA: Harcourt Brace.

Arnold, Caroline. (2010). *A Bald Eagle's World.* Minneapolis, MN: Picture Window Books.

Asch, Frank. (1999). *Baby Bird's First Nest.* San Diego, CA: Harcourt Brace.

Bates, Ivan. (2006). *Five Little Ducks.* Illustrated by Ivan Bates. New York: Scholastic.

Brenner, Barbara, and Julia Takaya. (1996). *Chibi: A True Story from Japan.* Illustrated by June Otani. New York: Clarion Books.

Carle, Eric. (2005). *10 Little Rubber Ducks.* New York: HarperCollins.

Earlry, Chris G. (2009). *Birds A to Z.* Richmond Hill, Ontario: Firefly Books.

Edwards, Richard. (1996). *Fly with the Birds.* Illustrated by Satoshi Kitamura. New York: Orchard Books.

Ehlert, Louis. (1997). *Cuckoo: A Mexican Folktale.* Orlando, FL: Harcourt Brace.

Ezra, Mark. (1997). *The Frightened Little Owl.* Illustrated by Gavin Rowe. New York: Crocodile Books.

Gibbons, Gail. (1998). *Soaring with the Wind: The Bald Eagle.* New York: William Morrow.

Giganti, Paul. (2005). *How Many Blue Birds Flew Away? A Counting Book with a Difference.* Illustrated by Donald Crews. New York: Greenwillow Books.

Grobler, Piet. (2005). *Little Bird's ABC.* Asheville, NC: Front Street.

Henkes, Kevin. (2009). *Birds.* Illustrated by Laura Dronzek. New York: Greenwillow Books.

Horacek, Petr. (2005). *Bird, Fly High.* Cambridge, MA: Candlewick Press.

Inches, Alison, and Cheryl Mendenhal. (2001). *Dizzy's Bird Watch.* New York: Simon Spotlight.

Jarkins, Sheila. (2008). *Marco Flamingo / Marco Flemenco.* McHenry, IL: Raven Tree.

Jarkins, Sheila. (2009). *The Adventures of Marco Flamingo under the Sea.* McHenry, IL: Raven Tree.

Johnson, Angela. (1994). *Mama Bird, Baby Birds.* Illustrated by Rhonda Mitchell. New York: Orchard Books.

Lopez, Blanca. (1995). *The Harvest Birds.* Illustrated by Enrique Flores. Emeryville, CA: Children's Book Press.

Maslowski, Steve. (2002). *Birds in the Fall.* North Mankato, MN: Smart Apple Media.

Maslowski, Steve. (2002). *Birds in the Spring.* North Mankato, MN: Smart Apple Media.

Maslowski, Steve. (2002). *Birds in the Summer.* North Mankato, MN: Smart Apple Media.

Maslowski, Steve. (2002). *Birds in the Winter.* North Mankato, MN: Smart Apple Media.

Massie, Diane Redfield, and Steven Kellogg. (2000). *The Baby BeeBee Bird.* Illustrated by Steven Kellogg. New York: HarperCollins.

McMillan, Bruce. (1995). *Nights of the Pufflings.* Boston: Houghton Mifflin.

Meddaugh, Susan. (1990). *Tree of Birds.* Boston: Houghton.

Morrison, Gordon. (1998). *Bald Eagle.* Boston: Houghton Mifflin.

Murphy, Mary. (2002). *I Like It When.* San Diego, CA: Red Wagon Books.

Owens, Mary Beth. (1993). *Counting Cranes.* Boston: Little, Brown.

Polacco, Patricia. (2001). *Mr. Lincoln's Way.* New York: Philomel Books.

Rau, Dana Meachen. (1995). *Robin at Hickory Street.* Illustrated by Joel Snyder. Norwalk, CT: Soundprints/Smithsonian Institution.

Rawson, Katherine. (2006). *If You Were a Parrot*. Illustrated by Sherry Rogers. Mt. Pleasant, SC: Sylvan Dell Publishing.

Reed, Lynn Rowe. (2010). *Basil's Birds*. New York: Marshal Cavendish.

Ritz, Karen. (2010). *Windows with Birds*. Honesdale, PA: Boyds Mills Press.

Runton, Andy. (2005). *Just a Little Blue*. Marietta, GA: Top Shelf.

Ryder, Joanne. (2003). *Wild Birds*. Illustrated by Susan Estelle Kwas. New York: HarperCollins Publishers.

Tagliaferro, Linda. (2004). *Birds and Their Nests*. Mankato, MN: Capstone Press.

Witte, Anna. (2004). *The Parrot Tico Tango*. Cambridge, MA: Barefoot Books.

Technology and Multimedia

The following technology and multimedia products can be used to complement this theme:

"Baby Chickie" [CD]. (1994). In *So Big*. Sherman Oaks, CA: Hap-Pal Music.

"Bold Little Bird" [CD]. (2009). In *More Please*. Olympia, WA: Aurora Elephant Music.

"The Little House" [CD]. (1996). In *Everything Grows*. Cambridge, MA: Rounder/UMGD.

"Little Parrot" [CD]. (2010). In *Funnier Little Fellas*. Portland, OR: Matt Clark.

"Robin in the Rain" [CD]. (1996). In *Singable Songs for the Very Young*. Cambridge, MA: Rounder/UMGD.

"Robin on a Wire" [CD]. (2009). In *More Please*. Olympia, WA: Aurora Elephant Music.

 Additional teaching resources to accompany this Theme can be found on the book's companion website. Go to www.cengagebrain.com to access the site for a variety of useful resources.

Theme 5
BLUE

Flowers
iris
lupine
Texas bluebonnets
crocus
colored carnations
lobelia

Objects
cars
bikes
sky
paint
blocks
toy trucks
magic markers
crayons

Color Mixing
blue + yellow = green
blue + red = purple

Food
blueberries
grapes

Symbolic
cold
sad

Theme Goals

Through participating in the experiences provided by this theme, the children may learn:

1. Blue is the color of many objects.
2. Some foods are a blue color.
3. Some flowers are colored blue.
4. Blue can be mixed with other colors.
5. The color blue can be symbolic.

Concepts for the Children to Learn

1. Blue is the name of a color.
2. Mixing blue with yellow makes green.
3. Mixing blue and red makes purple.
4. Many objects are colored blue.
5. Cars, bikes, blocks, and toy trucks can be colored blue.
6. Magic markers, paint, and crayons can be colored blue.
7. On sunny, clear days, the sky is a blue color.
8. Blueberries and grapes are examples of blue-colored foods.
9. Flowers can be colored blue.
10. Irises, Texas bluebonnets, lupines, crocuses, colored carnations, and lobelias are flowers that can be colored blue.
11. Blue is symbolic for being cold or sad.

Vocabulary

1. **blue**—a primary color.
2. **primary colors**—red, yellow, and blue.

Bulletin Board

The purpose of this bulletin board is to develop hand-eye coordination, visual discrimination, and problem-solving skills. A blue bulletin board can be constructed by focusing on familiar objects. Draw pictures of many familiar objects on tagboard. Color them various shades of blue. Cut out the objects and laminate. Next, trace the pictures, allowing 1/4-inch borders, on black construction paper. Cut out shadow pieces and hang on the bulletin board. Add a magnet piece to each shadow and picture. The children can match each picture to its corresponding shadow.

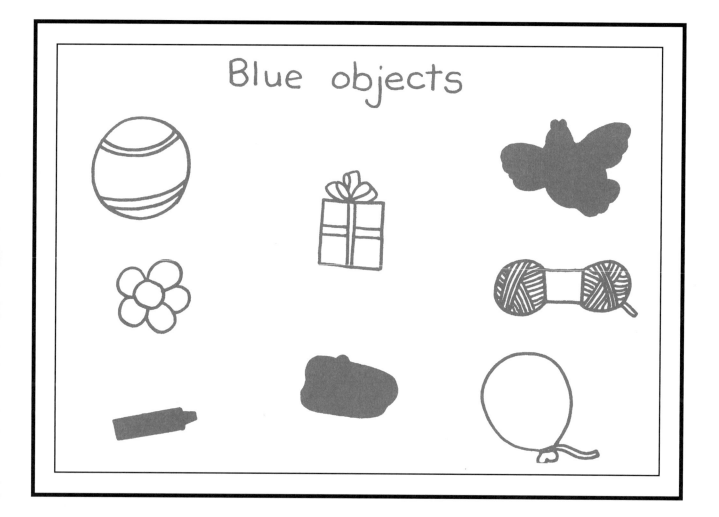

Family Letter

Dear Families,

Colors! Colors! Colors! Colors are all around us. In our curriculum, we will be focusing our activities on the color blue. The children will learn that blue can be mixed with red to make purple. When the color yellow is mixed with blue, green is created. The children will also become aware that many familiar objects are blue in color. Moreover, they will learn that the color blue has many associations, including sadness, cold, and music.

At School

Some of the learning experiences planned for this unit include:

- Singing a song called "Two Little Bluejays"

- Looking out our blue windows in the classroom

- Playing a paint store in the dramatic play area

- Fingerpainting with blue paint

- Eating blueberries for a snack

At Home

You can make almost any meal entertaining by occasionally adding a small amount of food coloring to one of your food items. Children often find this amusing. The food coloring adds interest to your food, and mealtimes become fun! Try adding a drop or two to milk, vanilla pudding, mashed potatoes, scrambled eggs, or cottage cheese. Does the color of a food affect its taste? (Try drinking green milk!) You be the judge! To further develop an awareness of color, identify foods that are red, blue, yellow, and so on. This improves memory, classification, and receptive and expressive language skills.

Have a great time helping your child discover the color blue!

Arts and Crafts

1. Arm Dancing

Provide each child with two blue crayons and a large sheet of paper. Play music, encouraging the children to color using both arms. Because of the structure of this activity, it should be limited to older children.

2. Sponge Painting

Collect sponge pieces, thick blue tempera paint, and sheets of light blue paper. If desired, clothespins can be clipped on the sponges and used as handles. To use as a tool, dip the sponge into blue paint and print on light blue paper.

3. Easel Ideas

- Feature different shades of blue paint at the easel.
- Use blue paint on aluminum foil.
- Add whipped soap flakes to blue paint.
- Add a container of yellow paint to the easel. Allow the children to mix the yellow and blue paints at the easel. This activity can be extended by providing red and blue tempera paint.

4. Fingerpainting

Blue fingerpaint and large sheets of paper should be placed in the art area.

5. Melted Crayon Design

Grate broken blue crayons. Place the shreddings on one square of waxed paper 6 inches × 6 inches. On top of the shreddings, place another 6-inch × 6-inch piece of waxed paper. Cover with a dish towel or old cloth. Apply heat with a warm iron for about 30 seconds. Let the sheets cool, and the child can trim them with scissors. These melted crayon designs can be used as nice sun catchers on the windows. *Caution:* This activity needs to be supervised closely. Only the teacher should handle the hot iron.

Cooking

1. Blueberries

Wash and prepare fresh or frozen blueberries for snack. Blueberry muffins are also appropriate for this theme.

2. Blueberry Muffins

2 tablespoons sugar
1 3/4 cups flour
2 1/2 teaspoons baking powder
3/4 teaspoon salt
1 egg
1/2 cup milk
1/3 cup vegetable oil

Spray a muffin tin with a nonstick spray or line it with paper liners. Mix all of the ingredients together. Add 2 tablespoons of sugar to 1 cup frozen or fresh blueberries. Mix slightly and gently add to the batter. Bake at 400 degrees for approximately 25 minutes.

3. Cream Cheese and Crackers

Tint cream cheese blue with food coloring and spread on crackers.

4. Cupcakes

Add blue food coloring to a white cake mix. Fill paper cupcake holders with the batter and bake as directed.

Dramatic Play

Paint Store

Provide paintbrushes, buckets, and paint sample books. The addition of a cash register, play money, and pads of paper will extend the children's play.

Field Trips

1. **"Blue" Watching**
Walk around your center's neighborhood and observe blue items. Things to look for include cars, bikes, birds, houses, and flowers. When you return, have the children dictate a list. Record their responses.

2. **Paint Store**
Visit a local paint store. Observe all the different shades of blue paint. Look carefully to see if they look similar. Ask the store manager for discarded sample cards. These cards can be added to the materials to use in the art area.

Group Time
(Games, Language)

1. **Bluebird, Bluebird**
The children should join hands and stand in a circle. Construct one bluebird necklace out of yarn and construction paper. Choose one child to be the first bluebird. This bluebird weaves in and out of the children's arms while the remainder of the children chant the song:

Bluebird, bluebird through my window
Bluebird, bluebird through my window
Bluebird, bluebird through my window
Who will be the next bluebird?

At this time, the child takes off the necklace and hands it to a child he or she would like to be the next bluebird.

2. **I Spy**
The teacher says, "I spy something blue that is sitting on the piano bench," or other such statements. The children will look around and try to figure out what the teacher has spied. Older children may enjoy taking turns repeating, "I spy something on the _____."

Large Muscle

1. **Painting**
Provide a bucket of blue-colored water and large paintbrushes. Encourage the children to paint the sidewalks, building, fence, sandbox, and so on.

2. **Blue Ribbon Dance**
Make blue streamer ribbons by attaching blue crêpe paper to unsharpened pencils. Play lively music and encourage the children to move to the music.

Math

1. **Muffin Math**
Make muffin cutouts on white or brown construction paper. Print a numeral on the top of each muffin. Use blue fingerpaint to place the corresponding number of "blueberries" on each muffin.

2. **Cube Tower**
Place blue Unifix cubes on a table. Roll a die and stack the corresponding number of cubes. Continue rolling and stacking until the tower falls over.

3. **Colored Craft Sticks**
Purchase a pack of colored craft sticks (or color your own). Have children sort the sticks into a matching colored cup.

Music

1. **"Two Little Bluejays"**
(Sing to the tune of "Two Little Blackbirds")
(To add interest, you can substitute names after the song has been sung several times. The children will enjoy hearing their names.)

Two little bluejays
sitting on a hill
One named Sue
One named Bill.

Fly away, Sue
Fly away, Bill.
Come back, Sue
Come back, Bill.

Two little bluejays
sitting on a hill
One named Sue
One named Bill.

2. **"Finding Colors"**
   (Sing to the tune of "The Muffin Man")

   Oh, can you find the color blue,
   The color blue, the color blue?
   Oh, can you find the color blue,
   Somewhere in this room?

Science

1. **Just One Drop**
   Each child will need a smock for this activity. Provide a glass of water and blue food coloring. Encourage the children to add a drop of blue food coloring to the water. Watch as the water becomes a light blue. Add a few more drops of food coloring, observing as the blue water turns a darker shade.

2. **Blue Color Paddles**
   Construct blue color paddles out of stiff tagboard and blue overhead transparency sheets. Make a form for the paddle out of tagboard, leaving the inside empty. Put the sheet of blue transparency paper on the back, glue, and trim. The children can hold the paddle up to their eyes and see how the colors have changed.

3. **Blue Windows**
   Place blue-colored cellophane or acetate sheets over some of the windows in the classroom. It is fun to look out the windows and see the blue world.

4. **Dyeing Carnations**
   On the science table, place the stem of a white carnation in a bottle of water with blue food coloring added. Observe the change of the petal colors.

Sensory

Additions to the Sensory Table

1. **Water with Blue Food Coloring**
   Add a few drops of blue food coloring to water.

2. **Blue Goop**
   Mix together blue food coloring, 1 cup cornstarch, and 1 cup of water.

Social Studies

Eye Color
Prepare an eye color chart with the children. Colors on the chart should include blue, brown, and green. Under each category, record the names of children who have that particular eye color. Extend the activity by adding the number of children with each color.

 Books

The following books can be used to complement this theme:

Anderson, Derek. (2006). *Blue Burt and Wiggles.* New York: Simon & Schuster Books for Young Readers.

Averbeck, Jim. (2008). *In A Blue Room.* Illustrated by Tricia Tusa. Orlando, FL: Harcourt.

Banks, Kate. (2005). *The Great Blue House.* Illustrated by George Hallensleben. New York: Farrar, Straus and Giroux.

Barnett, Mac. (2009). *Billy Twitters and His Big Blue Whale Problem.* Illustrated by Adam Rex. New York: Disney Hyperion Books.

Bogacki, Tomek, and Tomasz Bogacki. (1998). *Story of a Blue Bird.* New York: Farrar, Straus and Giroux.

Braun, Sebastien. (2010). *Meeow and the Blue Table.* London: Boxer.

Childress, Mark. (1996). *Joshua and the Big Bad Blue Crabs.* Illustrated by Mary B. Brown. Boston: Little, Brown.

Chrustowski, Rick. (2004). *Blue Sky Bluebird.* New York: Henry Holt.

Davies, Nicola. (1997). *Big Blue Whale.* Illustrated by Nick Maland. Cambridge, MA: Candlewick Press.

Dunbar, Polly. (2004). *Dog Blue.* Cambridge, MA: Candlewick Press.

Fine, Edith Hope, and Judith Pinkerton Josephson. (2007). *Armando and the Blue Tarp School.* Illustrated by Hernan Sosa. New York: Lee & Low Books.

Hausman, Gerald. (1998). *The Story of Blue Elk.* Illustrated by Kristina Rodanas. Boston: Houghton Mifflin.

Inkpen, Mick. (1996). *The Blue Balloon* (Vol. 1). Boston: Little, Brown.

Jones, Christianne C. (2007). *Splish, Splash, and Blue.* Illustrated by Christianne C. Jones. Minneapolis, MN: Picture Window Books.

Lionni, Leo. (1995). *Little Blue and Little Yellow.* New York: Mulberry Books.

Martin, Bill, Jr. (1992). *Brown Bear, Brown Bear, What Do You See?* Illustrated by Eric Carle. New York: Henry Holt.

Mills, Claudia. (2005). *Ziggy's Blue-Ribbon Day.* Illustrated by R. W. Alley. New York: Farrar, Straus and Giroux.

Onyefulu, Ifeoma. (1997). Chidi Only Likes Blue: An African Book of Colors. New York: Cobblehill.

Ostheeren, Ingrid, et al. (1996). *The Blue Monster.* New York: North South Books.

Ransom, Candice F. (2009). *The Old Blue Pickup Truck.* Illustrated by Jenny Mattheson. New York: Walker Book & Company.

Runton, Andy. (2005). *Just A Little Blue.* Marietta, GA: Top Shelf.

Salzmann, Mary Elizabeth. (2000). *Blue (Sandcastle I: What Color Is It?).* Minneapolis, MN: Abdo Publishing.

Schertle, Alice. (2008). *Little Blue Truck.* Illustrated by Jill McElmurry. Orlando, FL: Harcourt.

Schertle, Alice. (2009). *Little Blue Truck Leads the Way.* Illustrated by Jill McElmurry. Boston: Harcourt Children's Books.

Smallman, Steve. (2009). *The Monkey with a Bright Blue Bottom.* Illustrated by Steve Smallman. Intercourse, PA: Good Books.

Smee, Nicola. (2010). *What's the Matter, Bunny Blue?* London: Boxer.

Smith, Molly. (2007). *Blue Whale: The World's Biggest Mammal.* New York: Bearport Publishing.

Stephans, Helen. (2001). *Blue Horse.* New York: Scholastic.

Stewart, Joel. (2007). *Dexter Bexley and the Big Blue Beastie.* New York: Holiday House.

Stewart, Melissa. (2009). *Why Are Animals Blue?* Berkeley Heights, NJ: Enslow Elementary.

Stockland, Patricia M. (2009). *Blue.* Illustrated by Julia Woolf. Edina, MN: Magic Wagon.

Tafuri, Nancy. (2008). *Blue Goose.* New York: Simon & Schuster for Young Readers.

Winne, Joanne. (2000). *Blue in My World.* New York: Children's Press.

Wood, Audrey. (2005). *The Deep Blue Sea: A Book of Colors.* New York: Blue Sky Press.

Technology and Multimedia

The following technology and multimedia products can be used to complement this theme:

"Little Boy Blue" [CD]. (2010). In *No Fret Alphabet.* Buena Park, CA: Barbara Milne.

"Playing Blues" [CD]. (2002). In *Dancin' in the Kitchen.* New York: BizzyBum.

The Blue Elephant [DVD]. (2008). NY: The Weinstein Company.

Additional teaching resources to accompany this Theme can be found on the book's companion website. Go to www.cengagebrain.com to access the site for a variety of useful resources.

Transitions: Dismissal of Children

Smooth transitions are important when moving children from one activity to another. They help prevent disruptions and potential behavioral problems. By having the children move in groups assists in this process. The following strategies help support smooth transistions:

- Colors of clothing, types of clothing, and patterns of fabrics (stripes, polka dots, and plaid)
- Shoes (boots, shoes with buckles, shoes with ties, shoes with Velcro, slip-on shoes, and jelly shoes); also, number of eyelets on shoes, and number of buckles
- Ages in years
- Number of brothers or sisters
- Hair and eye color
- Birthdays in certain months
- Name cards
- First letter of names
- Last names
- Rhyming names
- Picking an animal or word that starts with the same sound as your name (Tiger-Tom)
- Giving each child a turn at something while putting rugs away (blowing a bubble, strumming a guitar, or hugging a puppet)
- Playing "I Spy" by saying, "I spy someone wearing blue pants and a Dora sweatshirt"
- Playing a quick game of "Simon Says" and then having Simon tell where the children are to go next
- Singing "Two Little Blackbirds":

Two little blackbirds sitting on a hill
One named Jack, one named Jill.
Fly away Jack, fly away Jill.
Come back Jack, come back Jill.
Two little blackbirds sitting on a hill,
One named Jack, one named Jill.

- Singing "I Have a Very Special Friend" (*Sing to the Tune of "Bingo"*):

I have a very special friend,
Can you guess his name-o?
J-A-R-E-D, J-A-R-E-D, J-A-R-E-D,
And Jared is his name-o.

- Singing "I'm Looking for Someone":

I'm looking for someone named Kristen,
I'm looking for someone named Kristen,
If there is someone named Kristen here now,
Stand up and take a bow. (Or "Stand up and go to lunch.")

- Singing "Where, oh, Where Is My Friend?":

Where, oh, where is my friend Travis?
Where, oh, where is my friend Travis?
Where, oh, where is my friend Travis?
Please come to the door.

- Singing "How Did You Come to School Today?":

How did you come to school today,
How did you come on Monday? (Child responds)
He came in a blue car,
Came in a blue car on Monday.

- Singing "One Elephant Went out to Play":

One elephant went out to play
Upon a spider's web one day.
He had such enormous fun
That he called for another elephant to come.

- Singing Goodbye Song (Sing to the tune of "Yankee Doodle"):

Now it's time to say goodbye,
We've had a lot of fun.
Goodbye (child's name) goodbye (child's name) and goodbye (child's name).
We had a lot of fun!

Transitions: Dismissal of Children (Continued)

Goodbye (child's name)
  goodbye (child's name) and
  goodbye (child's name).
Our time at school is done.

Group Dismissal

Opposed to having children move in groups, the entire group can be move from one activity to another. The following strategies are effective for moving the entire group of children at one time:

- Hop like a bunny.
- Walk as quiet as a mouse.
- Tiptoe.
- Walk backward.
- Count steps as you walk.
- Have footsteps for the group to walk on or a winding trail to follow.
- Sing "This Train" (*Sing to the tune of "This Train Is Bound for Glory"*):

(*You can change "lunchroom" to other words to fit the situation.*)
This train is bound for the
  lunchroom,
This train is bound for the
  lunchroom,
This train is bound for the
  lunchroom,
Katie, get on board.

Matthew, get on board.
Zachary, get on board.
Afton, get on board.

Fillers

- "One Potato"

One potato, two potato, three
  potato, four
Five potato, six potato, seven
  potato, more.

- "And One and Two"

And one and two and three
  and four,
And five and six and seven
  and eight.
(Repeat faster)

- "Colors Here and There"

Colors here and there,
Colors everywhere.
What's the name of this color
  here?

- "This Is What I Can Do"

This is what I can do,
Everybody do it, too.
This is what I can do,
Now I pass it on to you.

- "A Peanut Sat on a Railroad Track"

A peanut sat on a railroad
  track,
Its heart was all a-flutter.
Engine Nine came down the
  track,

Toot! Toot! Peanut butter!

The words peanut and peanut butter in the song can be substituted. Examples of other words include the following:.

- apple—applesauce
- banana—banana split
- orange—orange juice
- "Lickety Lick"

(*You can change "carrot" to any kind of cake.*)
Lickety lick, lickety lick,
The batter is getting all
  thickety thick.
What shall we bake?
What shall we bake?
A great, big beautiful carrot
  cake.

- "I Clap My Hands"

I clap my hands. (Echo)
I stamp my feet. (Echo)
I turn around. (Echo)
And it's really neat. (Echo)
I touch my shoulders.
  (Echo)
I touch my nose. (Echo)
I touch my knees. (Echo)
And that's how it goes.
  (Echo)

Theme 6
BREADS

Purpose
foods—meals and snacks
good health

Places Prepared
homes
restaurants
bakeries
supermarkets

Flatbreads
taco shells
pita bread
tortilla
lefse

Sizes
many

Shapes
round
twisted
oblong

Basic Ingredients
flour
water
milk
yeast
shortening

Yeast Breads
Danish pastries
croissants
rolls
breads
bagels
sweet rolls

Quick Breads
cornbread
biscuits
coffee cakes
muffins
popovers
scones
pancakes
waffles

Theme Goals

Through participating in the experiences provided by this theme, the children may learn:

1. The purpose of bread
2. The basic ingredients of bread
3. Places where bread is prepared
4. Types of yeast bread
5. Types of flatbread
6. Types of quick bread
7. Shapes of bread
8. Sizes of bread

Concepts for the Children to Learn

1. Bread is a healthy food.
2. The basic ingredients used in preparing bread are flour, water or milk, yeast, and shortening.
3. Bread can be prepared in homes, bakeries, supermarkets, and restaurants.
4. Breads come in many sizes.
5. Taco shells, pita bread, tortillas, and lefse are flatbreads.
6. Cornbread, biscuits, coffee cakes, muffins, popovers, scones, pancakes, and waffles are called quick breads.
7. Croissants, rolls, bagels, breads, Danish pastries, and sweet rolls are called yeast breads.
8. Breads can be shaped into different forms: round, twisted, and oblong.
9. Breads can be part of a meal or snack.

Vocabulary

1. **bread**—a food prepared by mixing flour or grain meal, water or milk, and shortening.
2. **crust**—the outside part of the bread.
3. **flour**—wheat that has been ground to a soft powder.
4. **yeast**—a food that makes the bread dough rise.

Bulletin Board

The purpose of this bulletin board is to promote hand-eye coordination, visual discrimination, and problem-solving skills, and call attention to various types of baked goods. Create this bulletin board by drawing baked goods on a piece of tagboard as illustrated. Pictures from magazines or computer-generated clip art could also be used. If drawn, color and add detail to the bakery items with felt-tip markers, cut out, and laminate. Trace these pieces onto black construction paper. Count out the pieces and attach to the bulletin board. Use map tacks or adhesive magnet pieces for children to match the corresponding baked good to its shadow.

Family Letter

Dear Families,

Did you know that bread is one of the most widely eaten foods? It is often called the "staff of life," and it provides a large share of people's energy and a small amount of plant protein. Special breads are also used in different cultural ceremonies. Our curriculum next week will focus on a theme related to breads. Activities will help your child learn the different types of bread and the ingredients of bread, including the purpose of yeast. Your child will also participate in making bread.

At School

Some of the curriculum activities related to the theme will include:

- Tasting many different kinds of breads
- Taking a field trip to the bakery
- Baking bread on Thursday and observing the action of yeast
- Making and selling baked goods in the bakery shop located in the dramatic play area

Family Involvement

If you prepare any special ethnic breads, we invite you to share them with our class. Please contact me so a time can be arranged. The children will enjoy having you in our class and learning about other types of breads.

At Home

We encourage you to participate in our celebration of bread. The next time you and your child are in the grocery store, find the bakery or bread department. Point out the different types and sizes of breads. Ask questions to help your child recognize similarities and differences.

Enjoy eating and discussing different types of bread with your child!

Arts and

Handwritten note: *making play dough*

1. Bread Collage

Provide magazine[...] and cut out pictur[...] breads. These pict[...] pasted to a piece [...] paper plate, creat[...] a bread coll[...]

2. Play Dough

The children can [...] assist in preparing play dough. If the mixture is left uncolored, it will resemble bread dough and have a similar consistency. Place three cups of flour and one cup of salt in a mixing bowl. Add 3/4 cup of water and stir. Keep adding small amounts of water and mix until the dough is workable but not sticky.

3. Muffin Tin Paint Trays

Fill muffin tins with various colors of paint in the art area for the children to use. Pastry brushes could be used as paint applicators.

4. Biscuit Cutter Prints

Place biscuit cutters and a shallow pan of paint out at the art table. The children can dip the biscuit cutter into the paint. After this, the biscuit cutter can be placed on a piece of construction paper. The children can repeat the process as desired.

5. Bread Sponge Painting

Cut sponges into different shapes and types of bread. Place the sponges and shallow trays of tempera paint on the art table. The children can dip a sponge into the paint and then press it onto a piece of paper to create a bread-shaped print.

Cooking

1. Bag Bread

3 cups of bread flour
2 packages of fast-rising yeast
1/4 cup sugar
1 1/2 teaspoon salt
1 1/2 cup warm water (125 to 130 degrees)
4 teaspoons vegetable oil

[...]n-size, heavy plastic, zipper-seal [...]g, place 1 1/2 cups flour, dry yeast, [...] Close. Let the children mix the [...]ts by shaking and working the bag [...] their fingers.

[...] oil and warm water to the [...]ts in the bag. Reseal the bag, and [...]rate to the children how to mix the [...]ts. Gradually add the remaining flour [...]il the mixture forms a stiff ball.

[...] your hands with a solid vegetable oil. Remove the dough from the bag and place on a lightly floured surface. Knead about 5 minutes. Small air pockets that appear as bubbles will form under the surface of the dough when it has been sufficiently kneaded. When they appear, let the children observe them.

Let the dough rest for 5–10 minutes. Grease two bread pans. Divide the dough in half. Shape into two loaves. Place each loaf in a greased bread pan. Cover with a kitchen towel. Let rise for an hour. Bake at 375 degrees for 25–30 minutes.

2. Pretzels

1 teaspoon salt
2 1/2 teaspoons sugar
1 package of fast-rising yeast
1 cup warm water (125 to 130 degrees)
1 tablespoon vegetable oil
1 egg yolk, beaten with 1 tablespoon water
3–3 1/2 cups flour

Combine 1 1/2 cups of flour, the dry yeast, sugar, and salt in a large bowl. Add the warm water and vegetable oil, and mix at low speed with an electric mixer for 3 minutes. Add an additional 1/2 cup flour and beat at high speed for 2–3 minutes. Stir in the remaining flour to form a soft dough. *Caution:* Use of the electric mixer needs to be carefully supervised.

Lightly flour a surface. Place the soft dough on the floured surface and knead for approximately 10 minutes. Grease a bowl with vegetable oil and place the dough in it to rise. Cover with a dish towel for 30–45 minutes.

Punch the air out of the dough and divide into 20 equal pieces. Demonstrate to the children how to roll a piece into a rope 12–14 inches long. Form the rope into a pretzel. Place on a greased baking sheet.

Cover again and let rise in a warm place for about 25 minutes.

Brush each of the pretzels with the egg yolk mixture. Preheat the oven to 375 degrees. Bake for 15 minutes and remove from pan. Place on a wire rack to cool.

3. Chapatis (pronounced "cha-PAH-tees")

This recipe, which comes from India, serves six; consequently, it will need to be adjusted to accommodate the number of children who need to be served.

1 1/2 cups of whole wheat flour
1/2 teaspoon salt
2/3 cup warm water
A small amount of cooking oil

Mix the flour and salt together in a bowl. Stir in water a small amount at a time until the mixture forms a ball.

On a floured surface, knead dough for 5–10 minutes until it is a smooth, sticky ball. Let rise in a covered bowl for 30 minutes.

Cut the dough into six pieces. Roll each piece out into a circle that is about 8 inches in diameter.

Lightly oil a frying pan and heat until it smokes. *Caution:* This portion of the activity needs to be carefully supervised to promote a safe environment.

Cook each circle of dough until it is brown and puffy on both sides. The chapatis are more flavorful when eaten warm.

4. Cheesy Puff Bread

3 3/4 cups bread flour
1 package fast-rising dry yeast
1 teaspoon salt
1/2 cup milk
2 tablespoons margarine
2 eggs
1 cup grated cheddar cheese
1/2 cup warm water
3 tablespoons sugar

Combine the dry yeast, sugar, salt, and 1 1/2 cups of the flour in a large mixing bowl. Heat the milk, water, and margarine on the stove or in the microwave oven until warm to the touch. Add the dry ingredients. Then beat at low speed with an electric mixer. Add 1/2 cup of the flour and the eggs. Beat at high speed for 2–3 minutes. Stir in the cheese and enough flour to make a soft dough.

On a lightly floured surface, knead the dough until it is elastic and smooth. Typically this will take 6–10 minutes. Place the dough in a greased bowl and let rise for 15–30 minutes.

Grease the entire inner surface of two 1 lb. coffee cans. Divide the dough into two equal pieces. Place each piece in a can. Cover the top of the can with a piece of aluminum foil. Let the dough rise for 35 minutes.

Bake for 30 minutes in a 375-degree oven. Remove from cans and cool on a wire rack.

5. Alphabet Toast

Pour milk into a small container and color with food coloring. (Make as many colors as desired.) Give each child a piece of bread and alphabet cookie cutters.

Encourage them to find the letter that their name begins with. Press the cutter lightly into the bread. Use a cotton swab to spread the colored milk on the letter. Place in toaster. The toast will come out brightly colored.

6. Toasted Tortilla Triangles

Cut corn tortillas into eight triangles. Place the wedges on cookie sheets. Sprinkle with grated Parmesan cheese. Bake at 350 degrees for 12–15 minutes until lightly browned and crisp.

 **Dramatic Play**

1. Bakery

Prepare the housekeeping area to resemble a bakery where the children can pretend to make breads and baked goods to sell to their classmates as customers. Provide the following items: aprons, baker's hats, bowls, mixing spoons, pans, rolling pins, muffin tins, measuring cups, egg cartons, empty bread and roll mix boxes, oven mitts or hot pads, a cash register, and posters or pictures depicting baked goods.

2. **Restaurant**

Prepare the housekeeping area as a restaurant. Provide props such as a tablecloth, dishes, cooking utensils, and a cash register with play money. Create menus by cutting pictures from magazines and gluing them onto construction paper. Include pictures of different baked goods.

Field Trips

1. **Bakery**

Arrange a visit to a local bakery. Observe the process of bread and baked goods production. Discuss a baker's job and uniform.

2. **Farm**

Take a trip to a farm where grains are grown. Notice the equipment and machinery used to plant and harvest the crops.

3. **Grocery Store**

Tour a grocery store and find the bakery department. The children can look at the many types of breads and ways they are packaged.

Fingerplays and Chants

Five Little Donuts

Down around the corner, at the bakery shop
There were five little donuts with sugar on top.
  (hold up five fingers)
Along came _____ (child's name), all alone.
And she (he) took the biggest one home.

(Continue the verses until all the donuts are gone.)

Group Time
(Games, Language)

1. **Bread-Tassting Party**

Bake or purchase various types and flavors of breads. Cut the bread into small pieces, and place these samples on paper plates for the children to taste. Discuss the types of breads, textures, flavors, and scents.

2. **Yeast Experiment**

To demonstrate the effects of yeast, try this experiment. Pour 1 package of dry yeast, ½ cup of sugar, and 1 cup of warm water into an empty soda bottle. Cover the bottle opening with a balloon and watch it expand.

3. ***The Little Red Hen***

Read the story of *The Little Red Hen* by Paul Galdone. After reading the story several times so that the children are familiar with the content, it can be acted out. Simple props can be provided to assist the children in creative dramatics and re-creating the story.

4. **Bread Basket Upset**

This game is played in a circle formation on chairs or carpet squares. One child is asked to sit in the middle of the circle as the baker. Hand a picture of a different type of bread—a bagel, a roll, a muffin, and others—to each of the other children. To play the game, the baker calls out the name of a bread. The children holding that particular bread exchange places. The game continues. When the baker calls out, "Bread Basket Upset," all of the children must exchange places, including the baker. The child who is unable to find a place is the new baker.

Large Muscle

1. **Tricycles**

During outdoor play, encourage children to use the tricycles for making bakery deliveries.

2. **Bread Trail**

Set up a bread trail in the classroom. Tape pictures of the bread on the floor, creating a trail. Have the children follow the trail by walking or hopping.

Math

1. **Favorite Bread Graph**

   After tasting various types of breads, the children can assist in making a class graph of their favorite types of breads. Across the top of a piece of tagboard, print the caption "Our Favorite Breads." Draw or paste pictures of different types or flavors of breads along the left-hand side of the tagboard.

   On the chart, place each child's name or picture next to the picture of his or her favorite bread. The results of the graph can be shared with the children using math vocabulary words such as most, more, fewer, least, and so on. Display the graph for future reference.

2. **Muffin Tin Math**

   Muffin tins can be used for counting and sorting activities based on the children's developmental level. For example, numerals can be printed in each cup, and the children can place the corresponding set of corn or toy pieces in each cup. Likewise, colored circles can be cut out of construction paper and glued to the bottom of the muffin cups. The children then can place objects of matching colors in the corresponding muffin cups.

3. **Pretzel Sort and Count**

   Provide each child with a cup containing various sizes and shapes of pretzels. Encourage the children to empty the cup onto a clean napkin or plate and sort the pretzels by size or shape. If appropriate, the children can count how many pretzels they have of each shape. Upon completion of the activity, the pretzels can be eaten by the children.

4. **Breadstick Seriation**

   Provide breadsticks or pictures of breadsticks of varying lengths. The children can place the breadsticks in order from shortest to longest.

Music

1. **"If I Had a Bagel"**

   (Sing to the tune "If I Had a Hammer")

   If I had a bagel.
   I'd eat it in the morning,
   I'd eat it in the evening,
   All over this land.
   I'd eat it for breakfast,
   I'd eat it for supper,
   I'd eat it with all my friends and sisters and brothers,
   All, all over this land.

2. **"Ten Little Donuts"**

   (Sing to the tune of "Ten Little Indians")

   One little, two little, three little donuts
   Four little, five little, six little donuts
   Seven little, eight little, nine little donuts
   Ten donuts in the bakery shop.

3. **"Let's Pretend"**

   (Sing to the tune of "Here We Are Together")

   Let's pretend that we are bakers,
   Are bakers, are bakers
   Let's pretend that we are bakers,
   As busy as can be.
   We'll knead all the dough out
   And bake loaves of bread.
   Let's pretend that we are bakers
   As busy as can be.

4. **"Down at the Bakery"**

   Down at the bakery what did I see?
   Five little cookies smiling at me.
   Along came (child's name) with a nickel one day.
   He bought the (color) one and took it away.
   (Continue singing until all cookies are gone.)

   Note: Make five different-colored cookies from construction paper. Laminate them, and attach Velcro or magnets to the back. Place on either a magnet board or a flannel board. Give five children a nickel each. As you call their name, invite them to take the corresponding color of cookie off the flannel or magnet board.

Science

1. **Bread Grains**
   On the science table, set out containers of grains used to make bread for the children to examine. Examples include wheat, corn, oats, and rye. Provide magnifying glasses for children to explore the grains.

2. **Weighing Bread Grains**
   The property of mass can be explored by providing a balance scale and bread grains at the science table. Scoops and spoons could be available to assist the children. The children can compare the grains. Encourage the use of vocabulary words such as heavier, lighter, more than, and less than.

3. **Baking Bread**
   The process of bread baking is definitely a science activity. The children can observe changes in substances and make predictions about the final outcome. Choose a bread recipe listed under the cooking section of this theme. Prepare a recipe chart for classroom use. Stress cooking safety with the children.

Sensory

1. Different types of grains can be placed in the sensory table. Examples include corn, rice, wheat, barley, and oats. Provide pails, scoops, measuring cups, flour sifters, and spoons to encourage active exploration.
2. Place play dough in the sensory table with rolling pins, measuring cups, muffin tins, and plastic knives.
3. Cooking utensils used for preparing baked goods can be placed in the sensory table with soapy water and dishcloths. The children can "wash" the items.

Social Studies

1. **Baker**
   The occupation of baker can be examined through books and discussion.

2. **Sharing Breads**
   Bake breads or muffins to give to a home for the elderly, the homeless, or some other organization. If possible, take a walk and have the children deliver them.

3. **Visitor**
   Invite people from various cultural backgrounds to bake or share breads originating from their native countries. As a follow-up activity, assist the children in writing thank-you notes.

Books

The following books can be used to complement this theme:

Anderson, Catherine. (2005). *Bread Bakery*. Chicago: Heinemann Library.

Asch, Frank. (2004). *Monsieur Saguette and His Baguette*. Toronto: Kids Can Press.

Brett, Jan. (1999). *Gingerbread Baby*. New York: G. P. Putnam.

Carle, Eric. (1995). *Walter the Baker*. New York: Simon & Schuster.

Czernecky, Stefan, et al. (1992). *The Sleeping Bread*. New York: Hyperion.

De Las Casas, Diane. (2009). *The Cajun Cornbread Boy: A Well-Loved Tale Spiced Up*. Illustrated by Marita Gentry. Gretna, LA: Pelican Publishing.

De Paola, Tomie. (1989). *Tony's Bread: An Italian Folktale*. New York: Putnam.

De Paola, Tomie. (1997). *Antonio the Bread Boy*. New York: G. P. Putnam.

Dooley, Norah. (1995). *Everybody Bakes Bread*. Illustrated by Peter J. Thornton. Minneapolis, MN: Carolrhoda Books.

Edelman, Julie, and Omar H. Davis. (2000). *Once upon a Recipe: Favorite Tales, Food and FUNtivities*. Illustrated by Omar H. Davis. Maplewood, NJ: Once Upon A Recipe Press.

Flanagan, Romie, and Alice K. (1998). *Mr. Santizo's Tasty Treats*. Chicago: Children's Press.

Gershator, David, et al. (1995). *Bread Is for Eating*. New York: Holt.

Granowsky, Alvin. (1996). *Help Yourself, Little Red Hen! (Another Side to the Story)*. Illustrated by Wendy Edelson and Jane K. Manning. Austin, TX: Raintree/Steck Vaughn.

Greeley, Valerie. (1990). *Where's My Share?* New York: Macmillan.

Head, Honor. (2010). *Bread*. Mankato, MN: Smart Apple Media.

Kleven, Elisa. (2001). *Sun Bread*. New York: Dutton Children's Books.

Levenson, George. (2004). *Bread Comes to Life: A Garden of Wheat and a Loaf to Eat*. Photography by Shmuel Thaler. Berkeley, CA: Tricycle Press.

Lindman, Maj. (1995). *Snipp, Snapp, Snurr and the Buttered Bread*. Morton Grove, IL: A. Whitman.

Linn, Dennis, Sheila Faabricant, and Francisco Miranda. (2006). *Making Heart-Bread*. Mahwah, NJ: Paulist Press.

Millen, C. M. (2004). *Blue Bowl Down*. Illustrated by Holly Meade. Cambridge, MA: Candlewick Press.

Morris, Ann. (1993). *Bread, Bread, Bread*. Illustrated by Ken Heyman. New York: Scholastic.

Rosenthal, Betsy R. (2006). *It's Not Worth Making a Tzimmes Over!* Illustrated by Ruth Rivers. Morton Grove, IL: Albert Whitman.

Snyder, Inez. (2005). *Grains to Bread*. New York: Children's Press.

Teevin, Toni. (2006). *What to Do?* New York: Clarion Books.

Technology and Multimedia

The following technology and multimedia products can be used to complement this theme:

"The Donut Song" (2004). In *Laugh N Learn Silly Songs*. Long Branch, NJ: Kimbo.

"Five Brown Buns" [CD]. (2008). In *Great Big Hits*. Toronto: Casablanca Kids.

Greg and Steve. (2007). "Muffin Man" [CD]. In *We All Live Together* (Vol. 2). Acton, CA: Youngheart Records.

"Hot Cross Buns" [CD]. (2004). In *Toddler Twosome*. Redway, CA: Music Little People.

"I Got a Job" [CD]. (2002). In *Growing Up with Ella Jenkins*. Washington, DC: Smithsonian Folkways.

"I'm a Pretzel" [CD]. (1994). In *So Big*. Sherman Oaks, CA: Hap-Pal Music.

"The Muffin Man" [CD]. (1995). In *Toddler Tunes: 26 Classic Songs for Toddlers*. Franklin, TN: Cedarmont Music, distributed by Benson Music Group.

"The Pretzel Store" [CD]. (2002). In *Buzz Buzz*. New York: Razor and Tie Music.

Shortnin' Bread" [CD]. (2002). In *Under a Shady Tree*. New York: Two Tomatoes.

Additional teaching resources to accompany this Theme can be found on the book's companion website. Go to www.cengagebrain.com to access the site for a variety of useful resources.

Theme 7
BRUSHES

Parts
handle
bristles

Users
all people
hairstylists
janitors and maids
dentists
artists
painters
animal groomers
manicurists

Kinds
paintbrush
scrub brush
toothbrush
hairbrush
clothes brush
vegetable brush
pastry brush
pet brush
eyebrow brush
nailbrush
makeup brush

Uses
cleaning
grooming and hygiene
painting
cooking

Materials
plastic
wood
nylon
hair

Theme Goals

Through participating in the experiences provided by this theme, the children may learn:

1. Parts of a brush
2. Kinds of brushes
3. Uses of brushes
4. Materials used to make brushes
5. Community helpers who use brushes for their work

Concepts for the Children to Learn

1. A brush is a tool.
2. A brush has two parts: handles and bristles
3. Brushes can be made from plastic, wood, nylon, and hair.
4. Everyone uses brushes.
5. Janitors, maids, and painters use brushes.
6. Hairstylists, manicurists, and animal groomers use brushes.
7. Brushes can be used for cleaning, grooming, painting, and cooking.
8. Scrub brushes are used for cleaning in our homes.
9. Toothbrushes help clean our teeth.
10. Hairbrushes, eyebrow brushes, and makeup brushes are used for grooming.
11. Vegetable brushes are used to clean vegetables.
12. Pastry brushes are used for baking and cooking.
13. Some people use brushes while working.
14. Animal groomers use pet brushes to groom dogs and horses.
15. Janitors and maids use scrub brushes.
16. Dentists use toothbrushes.
17. Hairstylists use hairbrushes.
18. Manicurists use nailbrushes.
19. Makeup brushes are used to apply powder and coloring to the face.
20. Painting brushes are tools to apply paint to surfaces.

Vocabulary

1. **bristle**—a short, stiff hair or threadlike object.
2. **brush**—a tool made of bristles or wires attached to a handle.
3. **dog brush**—a brush used to clean a dog's hair.
4. **groom**—to clean.
5. **handle**—the part of a brush that is held.
6. **powder brush**—a brush that is used to apply facial powder.
7. **toothbrush**—a small brush used to clean teeth.
8. **vegetable brush**—a stiff brush used to clean vegetables.

Bulletin Board

The purpose of this bulletin board is to promote the development of color identification and color-matching skills. Construct paint palettes and brushes out of tagboard. Use a different colored marker to draw paint spots on each palette and to "paint" the bristles of each brush. Laminate all the pieces. Attach the palettes to the bulletin board. Map tacks, putty, or Velcro may be used to place the brushes next to the corresponding color of paint palette.

Family Letter

Dear Families,

Did you ever stop to think about the number and types of brushes we use in a day? Brushes will be the next subject that we will explore. Each one has a different function and helps us do a different job. Through the activities related to the theme, the children will become aware of the many types and uses of brushes. In addition, they will be exposed to materials used in constructing brushes.

At School

Some of the learning experiences this week will include:

- Setting up a hairstylist shop in the dramatic play area (and discussing different hairstyles and colors)

- "Painting" outside with buckets of water and brushes

- Observing teeth being cleaned with electric and handheld brushes as we visit Dr. Smith's dental office on Thursday morning

- Painting with a variety of brushes at the easel each day

At Home

With your child, go through your home and locate brushes. Examples include toothbrushes, hairbrushes, paintbrushes, fingernail polish brushes, pastry brushes, and makeup brushes. Compare and sort the various brushes. This will help your child discriminate among weights, colors, sizes, textures, and shapes. The brushes can also be counted to determine which room contains the most and which contains the least number of brushes, which will promote the understanding of number concepts.

Paint a picture with your child today!

Arts and Crafts

1. Brush Painting
Place various brushes such as hairbrushes, makeup brushes, toothbrushes, and clothes brushes on a table in the art area. In addition, thin tempera paint and paper should be provided. Let the children explore the painting process with a variety of brushes.

2. Easel Ideas
Each day, change the type of brushes the children can use while painting at the easel. Variations may include sponge brushes, discarded toothbrushes, nail polish brushes, vegetable brushes, and makeup brushes.

3. Box House Painting
Place a large cardboard box outside. To decorate it, provide smocks, house-painting brushes, and tempera paint for the children.

Cooking

1. Cleaning Vegetables
Place several washtubs filled with water in the cooking area. Then provide children with fresh carrots and brushes. Encourage the children to clean the carrots using a vegetable brush. The carrots can be used to make carrot cake or muffins, or they can be added to soup.

2. Zucchini Bread
1 1/2 cups flour
3/4 cup sugar
1 teaspoon ground cinnamon
1/2 teaspoon of salt
1/4 teaspoon baking powder
1/2 teaspoon baking soda
1/4 teaspoon ground nutmeg
1 large egg, beaten
1 1/4 cups unpeeled zucchini, finely shredded
4 tablespoons corn oil
1/4 teaspoon lemon peel shredded
Heat oven to 350 degrees and grease an
8 × 4 × 2 loaf pan.

Mix the flour, cinnamon, baking soda, sugar, baking soda, nutmeg and salt in a large bowl. In another bowl, combine the shredded zucchini, lemon peel, egg, and cooking oil. Add to the flour mixture and stir until just moistened. The batter should be lumpy. Pour into the loaf pan and bake at 350 degrees for 55 to 60 minutes. Let cool for 8–10 minutes and removed from the pan. Zucchini bread is best wrapped and stored overnight before slicing as it will be easier for the children to handle while eating.

Dramatic Play

1. Hairstylist
Collect hair spray bottles, brushes, empty shampoo bottles, chairs, mirrors, hair dryers, and curling irons, and place in the dramatic play area. *Caution:* Cut the cords off the electrical appliances.

2. Water Painting
In an outdoor area, provide children with buckets of water and house paintbrushes. They can pretend to "paint" the building, sidewalks, equipment, and fence.

3. Shining Shoes
In the dramatic play area, place clear shoe polish, shoes, brushes, and shining cloths for the children to use to polish shoes. *Caution:* This activity needs to be carefully supervised.

Field Trips and Resource People

1. The Street Sweeper
Contact the city maintenance department. Invite them to clean the street in front of the center or school for the children to observe.

2. Artist's Studio
Visit a local artist's studio. Observe the various brushes used.

3. **Dentist's Office**
   Visit a dentist's office. Ask the dentist to demonstrate and explain the use of various brushes.

4. **Animal Groomer**
   Invite an animal groomer to school. Ask the groomer to show his or her equipment, emphasizing the importance of brushes.

Fingerplays and Chants

Brushes in My Home

These brushes in my home
Are simply everywhere.
I use them for my teeth each day,
   (brushing teeth motion)
And also for my hair.
   (hair-brushing motion)

We use them in the kitchen sink
   (scrubbing motion)
And in the toilet bowls,
   (scrubbing motion)
For putting polish on my shoes
   (touch shoes and rub)
And to waterproof the soles.

Brushes are used to polish the floors
   (polishing motions)
And also paint the wall,
   (painting motion)
To clean the charcoal barbecue,
   (brushing motion)
It's hard to name them all.

My Toothbrushes

I have a little toothbrush.
   (use pointer for toothbrush)
I hold it very tightly.
   (make tight fist)
I brush my teeth each morning
   (pretend to brush teeth)
And then again at night.

Shiny Shoes

First I loosen mud and dirt,
My shoes I then rub clean.
For shoes in such a dreadful sight,
Never should be seen.

I spread the polish on the shoes.
And then I let it dry.
I brush the shoes until they shine.
And sparkle in my eye.

Group Time
(Games, Language)

1. **Brush Hunt**
   Hide several brushes in the classroom. Have one child search for the brushes. When she or he gets close to them, clap loudly. When she or he is farther away, clap quietly.

2. **Brush of the Day**
   At group time each day, introduce a new brush. Discuss the shape, color, materials, and uses. Then allow the children to use the brush in the classroom during self-selected play period.

Large Muscle

Sidewalk Brushing
   Place buckets of water and paintbrushes for use outdoors on sidewalks, fences, and buildings.

Math

1. **Sequencing**
   Collect various-sized paintbrushes. Encourage the children to sequence them by height and width.

2. **Weighing Brushes**
   Place a balance scale and several brushes in the math area. Encourage the children to weigh and balance the brushes.

3. **Toothbrush Counting**
   Collect toothbrushes and cans. Label each can with a numeral. The children can place the corresponding number of brushes into each labeled can. If desired, the toothbrushes can be constructed out of tagboard.

Music

"Using Brushes"

(Sing to the tune of "Mulberry Bush")
This is the way we brush our teeth,
brush our teeth, brush our teeth.
This is the way we brush our teeth
So early in the morning.

(Variations:

- This is the way we brush our hair . . .
- This is the way we polish our nails . . .
- This is the way we paint the house . . .

Act out each verse, and allow the children to make up more verses.)

Science

1. Identifying Brushes

Inside the feely box, place various small brushes. The children can reach into the box, feel each object, and try to identify it by name.

2. Exploring Bristles

Add to the science table a variety of brushes and magnifying glasses. Allow the children to observe the bristles up close, noting similarities and differences.

Sensory

Place play plastic fruits and vegetables in the sensory table. Provide scrub brushes for the children to "clean and scrub" the fruits and vegetables.

Social Studies

1. Brushes Chart

Design a "Brushes in Our Classroom" chart. Encourage the children to find all that are used in the classroom.

2. Helper Chart

Design a helper chart. Include tasks such as sweeping floors, cleaning paintbrushes, and putting away brushes and brooms. This chart can encourage the children to use brushes every day in the classroom.

Books

The following books can be used to complement this theme:

Arnold, Katya. (2005). *Elephants Can Paint Too!* New York: Atheneum Books for Young Readers.

Beaumont, Karen. (2005). *I Ain't Gonna Paint No More!* Illustrated by David Catrow. Orlando, FL: Harcourt Children's Books.

Brown, Margaret. (2001). *The Dirty Little Boy.* Illustrated by Steven Salerno. Delray Beach, FL: Winslow Press.

DeGezelle, Terri. (2006). *Taking Care of My Hair.* Mankato, MN: Capstone Press.

Demi. (2000). *Liang and the Magic Paintbrush / Liang Hab Tug Cwg Mem Pleev Kws muaj Yeeg Siv.* Saint Paul, MN: Minnesota Humanities Commission, Motheread/Fatheread.

De Paola, Tomie. (1988). *The Legend of the Indian Paintbrush.* New York: G. P. Putnam.

De Paola, Tomie. (1998). *Bill and Pete to the Rescue.* New York: Putnam's.

Edwards, Pamela Duncan. (2001). *Warthogs Paint: A Messy Color Book.* Illustrated by Henry Cole. New York: Hyperion Books for Children.

Ehrlich, Fred. (2002). *Does a Lion Brush?* Illustrated by Emily Bolam. Brooklyn, NY: Blue Apple Books.

Fox, Lee. (2010). *Ella Kazoo Will Not Brush Her Hair.* Illustrated by Jennifer Plecas. New York:

Langreuter, Jutta, and Vera Sobat. (1997). *Little Bear Brushes His Teeth.* Illustrated by Vera Sobat. Brookfield, CT: Millbrook Press Trade.

Manning, Nick. (2001). *Wash, Scrub, Brush!* Illustrated by Mick Manning. Morton Grove, IL: Albert Whitman & Co.

Rex, Michael. (2002). *Where Can Bunny Paint?* New York: Scholastic.

Whatley, Bruce. (2001). *Wait! No Paint!* New York: HarperCollins.

Additional teaching resources to accompany this Theme can be found on the book's companion website. Go to www.cengagebrain.com to access the site for a variety of useful resources.

Technology and Multimedia

The following technology and multimedia products can be used to complement this theme:

"Brush Your Teeth" [CD]. (1996). In *Singable Songs for the Very Young.* Cambridge, MA: Rounder/UMGD.

Paint Applicators

Brushes are one of the primary ways to apply paint to a surface. Provide the children with a wide variety of brushes to use during this theme. Since there are many ways to apply paint. The size and shape of the following applicators produce unique results. Although some are recyclable, others are disposable.

Recyclable Examples

Paintbrushes, varying sizes and widths
Whisk brooms
Fingers and hands
Tongue depressors or craft sticks
Potato mashers
Forks and spoons
Toothbrushes
Aerosol can lids
Cookie cutters
Spray bottles

String or yarn
Roll-on deodorant bottles
Squeeze bottles (such as plastic ketchup containers)
Marbles and beads
Styrofoam shapes
Sponges
Feet
Spools
Rollers
Rags
Gauze

Disposable Applicators to Use with Paint

Twigs and sticks
String or yarn
Feathers
Pinecones
Rocks
Cloth
Cardboard tubes
Straws
Leaves
Cotton balls
Cotton swabs

BUBBLES

Coloring
food coloring

Purpose
bathing
cleaning
playing

Places Found
foods
bath
water and drinks

Tools for Making
straws
bubble rings
strings
funnels
coat hangers
pipes
berry baskets
six-pack rings

Sizes
large
medium
small

Ingredients
soap
water

Theme Goals

Through participating in the experiences provided by this theme, the children may learn:

1. Purposes of bubbles
2. Bubble ingredients
3. Tools for making bubbles
4. Colors of bubbles
5. Sizes of bubbles
6. Places bubbles are found

Concepts for the Children to Learn

1. Bubbles are formed from soap and water.
2. Bubbles have a skin that holds air inside.
3. Bubbles are in foods, baths, water, and drinks.
4. Food coloring can be used to add color to bubbles.
5. Bubbles can be made with straws, bubble rings, strings, and funnels.
6. Coat hangers, pipes, berry baskets, and six-pack rings can also be used to make bubbles.
7. Bubbles can be many sizes—large, medium, and small.
8. Bubbles can be used for bathing, cleaning, and playing.

Vocabulary

1. **bubble**—a circle that has a skin and contains air.
2. **bubble skin**—the outside of the bubble that holds the air.
3. **bubble solution**—a mixture of water and liquid soap.
4. **bubble wand**—a tool used to make bubbles.

Bulletin Board

The purpose of this bulletin board is to promote the active exploration of household items that can be used to make bubbles. Collect items such as chenille stems (chenille stems are made of a fine wire that is flexible and easy to bend. They can be purchased at craft stores or from early childhood catalogs that sell art and craft supplies), funnels, spools, six-pack rings, berry baskets, and scissors. Construct and label boxes or pockets to hold items on the bulletin board. Containers of bubble solution should be placed near the bulletin board for the children to experiment with to make bubbles with household items. Provide towels in the area to encourage the children to assist in wiping up spills.

 **Family Letter**

Dear Families,

What do you get when you mix water and soap? Bubbles! The children will make many fascinating discoveries as we focus on a bubbles theme. Through the experiences provided, the children will learn the ingredients used in making bubbles, the sizes of bubbles, and tools for making bubbles.

At School

Some of the learning experiences planned to highlight bubble concepts include:

- Washing dolls and dishes in the sensory table

- Testing many bubble solution recipes

- Making bubbles with common household items such as plastic berry baskets, funnels, straws, chenille stems, spools, and scissors

- Creating prints of bubbles in the art area

At Home

Try the following activities with your child to reinforce bubble concepts at home.

- Allow your child to assist in washing dishes after a meal. This experience will give your child a sense of responsibility and promote self-esteem, as well as heighten his or her awareness of the purpose of bubbles for cleaning.

- Prepare the following bubble solution with your child, then blow some bubbles with straws, bubble wands, and funnels! You need 1 cup of water, 2 tablespoons of liquid dish soap, and 1 tablespoon of glycerin (optional). Enjoy!

Have a good time with your child!

Arts and Crafts

Bubble Prints

For each bubble-print color desired, mix one part liquid tempera paint with two parts liquid dish soap in a small container. Place a straw in the solution and blow until the bubbles rise above the rim of the container. Remove the straw and place a piece of paper over the bubbles. As the bubbles break, they will leave a print on the paper. (Each child will need a straw for this activity. A pin may be used to poke holes near the top of the straws to prevent the children from accidentally sucking in the paint mixture.) *Variation:* Small bubble wands can be dipped into the paint bubble solution and blown so the bubbles will land on a piece of paper, either at the easel or on the ground outdoors.

Cooking

1. **Bubbly Beverage**

   6 oz. can frozen orange juice
   6 oz. can frozen lemonade
   6 oz. can frozen limeade
   6 oz. can frozen pineapple juice (optional)
   1 liter lemon-lime soda, chilled
   1 liter club soda, chilled

   Combine ingredients in a punch bowl or other large bowl. Stir to blend the ingredients. Serve over ice, if desired.

2. **Root Beer**

   5 gallons cold water
   5 lb. white sugar
   3 oz. bottle root beer extract
   5 lb. dry ice

   In a large stone crock or plastic container (do not use metal), mix sugar with 1 gallon of water. Add the remainder of the water and the root beer extract. Stir. Carefully add the dry ice. After the ice melts, the root beer can be transferred into other containers to store for 2–3 days.

Dramatic Play

1. **Housekeeping**

   Fill the sink in the dramatic play area with soapy water. Provide dishes, sponges, dish towels, and a dish rack for the children to wash the dishes.

2. **Hairstylist**

   Set up a hairstylist studio in the dramatic play area. Include props such as a cash register, empty shampoo and hair spray containers, mirrors, brushes, combs, barrettes, curlers, discarded hair dryers and curling irons, towels, and smocks. Display pictures of hairstyles and hair products. *Caution:* Cut the electric cords off the hair dryers and curling irons to prevent possible injuries.

Field Trips and Resource People

1. **Hairstylist**

   Visit a hairstylist to watch a customer receive a shampoo.

2. **Pet Groomer**

   Invite a pet groomer to demonstrate giving a dog a bath.

Fingerplays and Chants

Here Is a Bubble

Here is a bubble
   (make a circle with thumb and index finger)
And here is a bubble
   (make a bigger circle with two thumbs and index finger)
And here is a great big bubble I see.
   (make a large circle with arms)
Let's count the bubbles we've made.
One, two, three.
   (repeat prior actions)

Draw a Bubble

Draw a bubble, draw a bubble.
Make it very round.
   (make a shape in the air with index
   finger)
Draw a bubble, draw a bubble.
No corners can be found.
   (repeat actions)

Group Time
(Games, Language)

1. **What's Missing? (Game)**
Place several items used to prepare bubbles on a tray. At group time, show and discuss the items. To play the game, cover the tray with a towel and carefully remove one item. Have children then identify the missing item. The game can be made more challenging by adding more items to the tray, or by removing more than one item at a time.

2. **Bubbles (Creative Dramatics)**
Guide the children through a creative dramatics activity as they pretend to be bubbles. They can act out being:

   - A tiny bubble
   - A giant bubble
   - A bubble floating on a windy day
   - A bubble landing on the grass
   - A bubble floating high in the air
   - A bubble in a sink
   - A bubble in a piece of bread

3. **Favorite Bubble Gum Chart**
At the top of a piece of tagboard, print the caption "Our Favorite Bubble Gum." Along the left-hand side, glue bubble gum wrappers representing different brands or flavors. Present the chart at group time, and ask each child to choose one as his or her favorite. Record the children's names or place their pictures next to the response. If appropriate, count the number of "votes" each brand or flavor received and print them on the chart. Display the chart in the classroom and refer to it throughout the unit.

Math

1. **Bubble Count**
If appropriate, encourage the children to blow a set of bubbles that you specify. For example, if you say the number "three," the children would try to blow three bubbles.

2. **Bubble Wand Sort**
Collect small commercially manufactured bubble wands and place them in a small basket. These wands can be sorted by size or color. They could also be counted or placed in order by size.

3. **Geometric Bubble Shapes**
Attach the ends of two straws together with duct tape or paper clips, creating the desired shapes. Six straws will be needed to make a pyramid, and 12 to make a cube. The frames can be dipped into bubble solutions and observed.

Music

1. **"Pop! Goes the Bubble"**
(Sing to the tune of "Pop! Goes the Weasel")

   Soap and water can be mixed.
   To make a bubble solution.
   Carefully blow,
   Now, watch it go!
   Pop! Goes the bubble!

2. **"Can You Blow a Big Bubble?"**
(Sing to the tune of "The Muffin Man")

   Can you blow a big bubble?
   A big bubble, a big bubble?
   Can you blow a big bubble,
   With your bubble gum?

3. **"I'm a Little Bubble"**
(Sing to the tune of "I'm a Little Teapot")

   I'm a little bubble, shiny and round.
   I gently float down to the ground.
   The wind lifts me up and then I drop.
   Down to the dry ground where I pop.

4. "Ten Little Bubbles"
(Sing to the tune of "Ten Little Indians")

One little, two little, three little bubbles.
Four little, five little, six little bubbles.
Seven little, eight little, nine little bubbles.
Ten bubbles floating to the ground.

5. "Here's a Bubble"
(Sing to the tune of "Frère Jacques")

Here's a bubble, here's a bubble.
Big and round; big and round.
See it floating gently,
See it floating gently,
To the ground; to the ground.

Science

1. Bubble Solutions
Encourage the children to assist in preparing the following bubble solutions. *Note:* The use of glycerin in preparing the bubble solution is optional. It helps to provide a stronger skin on the bubble, but the solutions can be prepared without this ingredient.

Recipe #1
1/4 cup liquid dish soap
1/2 cup water
1 teaspoon sugar

Recipe #2 (for Outdoor Use)
3 cups water
2 cups liquid dish soap (such as Joy detergent)
1/2 cup light corn syrup

Recipe #3
2/3 liquid dish soap
1 gallon of water
1 tablespoon glycerin

2. Bubble Gadgets
Prepare a bubble solution and make some bubbles! Use the following to make great bubbles.

- Plastic berry baskets
- Chenille stems or thin electrical wire shaped into wands
- Six-pack holders
- Egg poacher trays
- Funnels
- Children's scissors—hold the blades and dip the finger holders into the bubble solution.
- Tin cans—open at both ends.
- Paper cups—poke a hole in the bottom of a paper cup. Dip the rim into a bubble solution and blow through the hole.
- Plastic straws—use a single straw or tape several together in a bundle.
- Straws and string—thread 3 feet of thin thread through two plastic straws. Tie the string together. Hold the straws and pull them to form a rectangle with the string. Dip into a bubble solution and pull upward. As you move the frame, a bubble will form. Bring the two straws together to close off the bubble. This technique requires practice.
- Hula hoop—fill a small wading pool with 2 inches of bubble solution. The hula hoop can be used as a giant wand by dipping the hoop in the solution and lifting it up carefully.

3. Wet and Dry
While blowing bubbles with the children, try touching a bubble with a dry finger. Repeat using a wet finger. What happens? You will observe that bubbles break when they touch an object that is dry.

4. Bubble Jar
Fill a small plastic bottle half-full of water. Add a few drops of food coloring, if desired. Add baby oil or mineral oil to completely fill the jar. Secure the bottle tightly. Then slowly tilt the bottle from side to side. When this occurs, the liquid in the jar resembles waves. Bubbles can be created by shaking the bottle. Encourage the children to observe these reactions.

5. Air Bubbles in Food
Examine the air bubbles in pieces of bread, Swiss cheese, and carbonated drinks.

6. Bubbling Raisins
Place two or three raisins in a small bottle of sparkling mineral water. Secure the cap and watch the bubbles form as the raisins sink and float.

 Sensory

1. **Wash Dolls**
   Fill the sensory table with warm water and add a few tablespoons of dish soap. Provide plastic dolls, washcloths, and towels.

2. **Dishwashing**
   Place plastic dishes and dishcloths in a sensory table filled with warm soapy water. A dish-drying rack could be set up nearby, or towels could be provided to dry the dishes.

3. **Bubble Bath**
   Purchase or make bubble bath soap to put at the sensory table along with scoops, measuring cups, and pails.

4. **Bubble Solution**
   The sensory table can be used to hold a bubble solution and bubble-making tools.

5. **Pumps and Water**
   Fill the sensory table with water. Add water pumps, turkey basters, and siphons to create air bubbles in the water.

 Books

The following books can be used to complement this theme:

Arnold, Tedd. (1995). *No More Water in the Tub.* New York: Dial Books.

Bergen, Stuart. (1996). *Fozzie's Bubble Bath.* Illustrated by Rick Brown. New York: Grosset & Dunlap.

Bourgeois, Paulette. (2006). *Franklin and the Bubble Gum.* Toronto: Kids Can Press.

Bradbury, Judy. (1997). *Double Bubble Trouble!* Illustrated by Cathy Trachok. Hightstown, NJ: McGraw-Hill.

Bradley, Kimberly Brubaker, and Margaret Miller. (2001). *Pop: A Book about Bubbles.* Illustrated by Margaret Miller. New York: HarperCollins.

Brown, Monica. (2010). *Chavela and the Magic Bubble.* Illustrated by Magaly Morales. Boston: Clarion Books.

De Paola, Tomie. (1996). *The Bubble Factory.* New York: Grosset & Dunlap.

De Paola, Tomie. (2000). *Strega Nona Takes a Vacation.* Edited by Margaret Frith and illustrated by Tomie De Paola. New York: Putnam.

Esbaum, Jill. (2006). *Estelle Takes a Bath.* Illustrated by Mary Newell DePalma. New York: Henry Holt.

Gerver, Jane E. (2004). *Bath Time.* Illustrated by Laura Ovresat. New York: Children's Press.

Goodman, Joan Elizabeth. (1996). *Bernard's Bath.* Illustrated by Dominic Catalano. Honesdale, PA: Boyds Mills Press.

Hitchcock, Coleen A. (2001). *Bubbly Bubble.* Illustrated by Jason Yoh. Aurora, OH: Greenleaf Book Group.

Hobbs, Leigh. (2004). *Fiona the Pig.* Philadelphia: Running Press Kids.

Hulme, Joy N. (1999). *Bubble Trouble.* Illustrated by Mike Cressy. New York: Children's Press.

Krensky, Stephan. (2004). *Bubble Trouble.* Illustrated by Jimmy Pickering. New York: Aladdin Paperbacks.

Krosoczka, Jarret J. (2003). *Bubble Bath Pirates.* New York: Viking.

Mahy, Margaret. (2009). *Bubble Trouble.* Illustrated by Polly Dunbar. New York: Clarion Books.

Mayer, Mercer. (1973). *Bubble, Bubble.* New York: Parents' Magazine Press.

Mayer, Mercer. (1997). *Just a Bubble Bath.* Utica, NY: Good Times Publishing.

Mooney, E. S., and Brothers Thompson. (2001). *Bubbles' Best Adventure Ever.* Illustrated by Brothers Thompson. New York: Scholastic.

O'Connor, Jane. (1997). *Benny's Big Bubble.* Illustrated by Tomie De Paola. New York: Price Stern Sloan.

Packard, Mary. (1995). *Bubble Trouble.* Illustrated by Elena Kuckarik. New York: Scholastic.

Wells, Rosemary. (2002). *Bubble-Gum Radar.* Illustrated by Jody Wheeler. New York: Hyperion Books for Children.

Wheeler, Lisa. (2004). *Bubble Gum, Bubble Gum.* Illustrated by Laura Huliska-Beith and Harriet Kasak Portfolio. New York: Little, Brown.

Woodruff, Elvira. (1990). *Tubtime.* New York: Holiday.

Technology and Multimedia

The following technology and multimedia products can be used to complement this theme:

"Bubbles" [CD]. (2000). In *Parachute Express.* Glendale, CA: Trio Lane.

"I'm Forever Blowing Bubbles" [CD]. (2009). In *Kids: Traditional Sing-Alongs!* Minneapolis, MN: C&B Productions.

"Tiny Tim" [CD]. (1998). In *Silly Songs.* Redway, CA: Music Little People.

The Tots and the Lovely Bubbly Surprise [video]. (1997). Troy, MI: Ragdoll Productions, distributed by Anchor Bay Entertainment.

 Additional teaching resources to accompany this Theme can be found on the book's companion website. Go to www.cengagebrain.com to access the site for a variety of useful resources.

Theme 9
BUILDINGS

Materials	Purpose	Types	Parts	Construction Workers
brick	shelter	homes	basement	carpenters
wood	storage	schools	rooms	electricians
cement		offices	windows	architects
steel		stores	doors	masons
glass		malls	roof	plumbers
		hospital or	walls	
		clinic	chimney	
		police station	ceilings	
		fire station	floors	
		library	frame	
		church		
		bank		
		restaurant		

Theme Goals

Through participating in the experiences provided by this theme, the children may learn:

1. Types of buildings
2. Purposes of buildings
3. Materials used to make buildings
4. Parts of a building
5. Workers who construct buildings

Concepts for the Children to Learn

1. A building has walls and a roof.
2. There are many types of buildings: homes, offices, stores, hospitals, malls, and clinics.
3. Police stations, fire stations, libraries, churches, banks, and restaurants are also buildings.
4. Buildings can be made of brick, wood, cement, steel, and glass.
5. Many workers help construct buildings: architects, carpenters, electricians, plumbers, and masons.
6. Buildings can be used for shelter and storage.
7. Most buildings have a frame, roof, walls, ceilings, windows, doors, and a floor.
8. Some buildings have a basement and chimney.

Vocabulary

1. **architect**—a person who designs a building.
2. **building**—a structure with walls and a window.
3. **carpenter**—a person who builds.
4. **ceiling**—the top "wall" of a room.
5. **electrician**—a person who wires a building for light, heat, and cooking.
6. **mall**—a building containing many stores.
7. **mason**—a person who lays cement, blocks, and bricks.
8. **plumber**—a person who installs water pipes, toilets, and sinks.
9. **roof**—the top covering of a building.
10. **room**—a part of a building set off by walls.
11. **skyscraper**—a very tall building.

Bulletin Board

The purpose of this bulletin board is to develop awareness of size as well as visual discrimination skills and hand-eye coordination. Construct house shapes out of tagboard ranging in size from small to large. Color the shapes and laminate. Punch a hole in the top of each house. Trace each house shape on black construction paper and cut out. Hang the shadow pieces on the bulletin board with a pushpin inserted in the top of each. During self-directed and self-initiated play, the children can match each colored house to the corresponding shadow piece by hanging it on the pushpin.

Family Letter

Dear Families,

Your home, the library, our school . . . these are all buildings with which your child is familiar. Buildings will be our next theme. Discoveries will be made regarding different kinds and parts of buildings, materials used to construct buildings, and construction workers who erect buildings.

At School

A sampling of the learning experiences includes:

- Building with various materials—such as cardboard boxes and milk cartons
- Working at the woodworking bench to practice supervised hammering, drilling, and sawing
- Weighing and balancing bricks
- Taking a walk to a construction site and observing the building process
- Identifying different types of buildings

At Home

You can reinforce building concepts on your way to and from the center by pointing out any buildings of interest, such as the fire station, police station, hospital, library, shopping mall, and restaurants. Children are naturally curious about why and how things happen. If you pass any construction sites, point out the materials and equipment used, as well as the jobs of the workers. This will help your child develop receptive and expressive language skills as well as stimulate his or her interest. Concepts of time can also be fostered if you are able to visit the construction site over an extended period of time. You and your child will be able to keep track of progress in the development of the building.

Enjoy your child as you reinforce concepts related to buildings.

Arts and Crafts

1. Our Home
Provide paper, crayons, and markers for each child to draw his or her home. Collect all of the drawings and place them in mural fashion on a large piece of paper to create a town. To extend this activity, have the children also draw buildings in the town to extend the mural. (This activity may be limited to kindergarten children or children who have reached the representational stage of art development.)

2. Blueprints
Blueprint paper, pencils, and markers should be placed in the art area. The children will enjoy marking on it. Older children may also enjoy using rulers and straight edges.

3. Building Shapes
Cut out building shapes from easel paper. Place at the easel, allowing children to paint their buildings.

4. Creating Structures
Save half-pint milk cartons. Rinse well and allow the children to paint, color, and decorate the cartons to look like buildings.

Cooking

Sugar Cookies
1 1/2 cups powdered sugar
1 cup margarine or butter
1 egg
1 teaspoon vanilla
2 1/2 cups all-purpose flour
1 teaspoon baking soda
1 teaspoon cream of tartar
Granulated sugar

Mix the powdered sugar, margarine, egg, and vanilla together. Stir in the flour, baking soda, and cream of tartar. Chill to prevent sticking while rolling out the dough. Heat the oven to 375 degrees. Roll out the dough. Cut into squares, triangles, diamonds, rectangles, and circles. Sprinkle with sugar. Place on a lightly greased cookie sheet. Bake until lightly browned, about 7 to 8 minutes. Give each child 3 to 5 cookies. Allow them to make buildings with their shapes before eating.

Dramatic Play

1. Library
Rearrange the dramatic play area to resemble a library. Include books, library cards, book markers, tables, and chairs for the children's use.

2. Buildings
Collect large cardboard boxes from an appliance dealer. The children can construct their own buildings and paint them with tempera paint.

3. Construction Site
Place cardboard boxes, blocks, plastic pipes, wheelbarrows, hard hats, paper, and pencils in the dramatic play area to represent a construction site.

Field Trips and Resource People

1. Building Site
Visit a local building site if available. Observe and discuss the people who are working, note how buildings look, and talk about safety. Take pictures. When the pictures are developed, post them in the classroom.

2. Neighborhood Walk
Take a walk around the neighborhood. Observe the various kinds of buildings. Talk about the different sizes and colors of the buildings.

3. Library
Visit a library. Observe how books are stored. Read the children a story while there. If possible, allow the children to check out books.

4. **Browsing at the Mall**
   Visit the shopping mall. Talk about the mall being a large building that houses a variety of stores. Visit a few of the stores that may be of special interest to the children. Included may be a toy store, a pet store, and a sporting goods store.

5. **Resource People**
   Invite people to visit the classroom, such as a

   • Construction worker
   • Carpenter
   • Electrician
   • Architect
   • Decorator or designer
   • Plumber

Fingerplays and Chants

The Carpenter's Tools
> The carpenter's hammer goes rap, rap, rap
> > (make hammering motion with fist)
> And his saw goes see, saw, see.
> > (make sawing motion with arm and hand)
> He planes and hammers and saws
> > (make motions for each)
> While he builds a building for me.
> > (point to yourself)

Carpenter
> This is the way he saws the wood
> > (make sawing motion)
> Sawing, sawing, sawing.
>
> This is the way she nails a nail
> > (make hammering motion)
> Nailing, nailing, nailing.
>
> This is the way he paints a building
> > (make brushing motion)
> Painting, painting, painting.

My House
> I'm going to build a little house.
> > (draw house with fingers by outlining in the air)
> With windows big and bright,
> > (spread out arms)

> With chimney tall and curling smoke
> > (show tall chimney with hands)
> Drifting out of sight.
> > (shade eyes with hands to look)
> In winter when the snowflakes fall
> > (use fingers to make the motion of snow falling downward)
> Or when I hear a storm,
> > (place hand to ear)
> I'll go sit in my little house
> > (draw house again)
> Where I'll be snug and warm.
> > (hug self)

Group Time
(Games, Language)

1. **Identifying Buildings**
   Collect several pictures of buildings that are easily identified such as a school, fire station, hospital, and home. Talk about each picture. Ask, "How do you know this is a school?" Discuss the function of each building. To help the children, pictures of buildings in their community can be used.

2. **Exploring Our Center**
   Explore your center. Walk around the outside and observe walls, windows, the roof, and so on. Explore the inside also. Check out the rooms, floor, walls, ceiling, and stairs. Colors, materials, and size are some things you can discuss. Allow the children to help make an "Our Center Has …" chart.

Large Muscle

Workbench
Call attention during group time to the woodworking bench, and explain the activities that can occur there. Try to encourage the children to practice pounding nails, sawing, drilling, and so forth during self-initiated play. ***Caution:*** This activity needs constant supervision.

 ## Math

1. **Weighing Bricks**
   Set out a heavy-duty balance scale and small bricks. The children can weigh and balance the bricks.

2. **Wipe-Off Windows**
   Cut out and laminate a variety of buildings with varying numbers of windows. Provide children with grease markers or watercolor markers. Encourage the children to count the number of windows of each building and print the corresponding numeral on the building. The numerals can be wiped off with a damp cloth. (This activity would be most appropriate for kindergarten children.)

3. **Blocks**
   Set out blocks of various shapes, including triangles, rectangles, and squares, for the children to build with.

 ## Music

"Go In and Out the Window"

Form a circle with the children and hold hands. While holding hands, have the children raise their arms up to form windows. Let each child have a turn weaving in and out the windows. Use the following chant as you play, and fill in a child's name in the blank space.

_____ goes in and out the windows,
In and out the windows,
In and out the windows.
_____ goes in and out the windows,
As we did before.

 ## Science

1. **Building Materials**
   Collect materials such as wood, brick, cement, metal, and magnifying glasses, and place on the science table. Encourage the children to observe the various materials up close.

2. **Mixing Cement**
   Make cement using a small amount of cement and water. Mix materials together in a large plastic ice cream bucket. Allow the children to help. The children can also observe and feel the wet cement. Caution: If a quick-dry-cement is used, the children shouldn't touch it because it can be harmful for their skin.

3. **Building Tools**
   Collect and place various tools such as a hammer, level, wedge, and screwdriver on the science table for the children to examine. Discuss each tool and demonstrate how it is used. Then place the tools in the woodworking area. Provide wood and styrofoam so that the children are encouraged to use the tools as a self-selected activity with close adult supervision.

 ## Sensory

1. **Wet Sand**
   Fill the sensory table with sand and add water. Provide cups, square plastic containers, bowls, and so forth for children to create molds with the sand.

2. **Wood Shavings**
   Place wood shavings in the sensory table.

3. **Scented Play Dough**
   Prepare scented play dough and place in the sensory table.

 ## Social Studies

1. **Buildings in Our Town**
   Make a chart with the children's names listed vertically on the right-hand side. Across the top of the chart, draw buildings or glue pictures of buildings that the

children have visited. Suggestions include a theater, supermarket, clinic, museum, post office, fire station, and so on. At group time, ask the children what buildings they have visited. Mark the sites for each child.

2. **Unusual Buildings**

Show pictures of unusual buildings cut from various magazines, travel guides, and so on. Allow the children to use their creative thinking by asking them the use of each building. All answers and possibilities should be acknowledged.

3. **Occupation Match**

Cut out pictures of buildings and the people who work in them. Examples would include a hospital and a nurse, or a fire station and a firefighter. Glue these pictures to a tagboard and laminate. The children should be encouraged to match each worker to the appropriate building.

 Books

The following books can be used to complement this theme:

Ackerman, Karen. (1995). *The Sleeping Porch.* Illustrated by Elizabeth Sayles. New York: William Morrow.

Adamson, Heather. (2008). *Homes in Many Cultures.* Mankato, MN: Capstone Press.

Attebury, Nancy Garhan. (2006). *Out and about at the Hospital.* Illustrated by Zachary Trover. Minneapolis, MN: Picture Window Books.

Barasch, Lynne. (2004). *A County Schoolhouse.* New York: Farrar, Straus and Giroux.

Barton, Byron. (1997). *Machines at Work.* New York: HarperCollins.

Cooper, Elisha. (1999). *Building.* New York: Greenwillow Books.

Dahl, Michael. (2004). *One Big Building: A Counting Book about Construction.* Illustrated by Todd Ouren. Minneapolis, MN: Picture Window Books.

Gordon, Sharon. (2007). *What's inside a Hospital? / Que Hay Dentro De Un Hospital?* Tarrytown, NY: Marshall Cavendish Benchmark.

Hautzig, David. (1994). *At the Supermarket.* New York: Orchard Books.

Hennessy, B. G. (2003). *Corduroy Goes to the Fire Station.* Illustrated by Lisa McCue. New York: Viking.

Hoban, Tana. (1997). *A Construction Zone.* New York: Greenwillow Books.

Keats, Ezra Jack. (1999). *Apt. 3.* New York: Viking.

Kemper, Bitsy. (2007). *Out and about at the Dentist.* Illustrated by Zachary Trover. Minneapolis, MN: Picture Window Books.

Kemper, Bitsy. (2007). *Out and about at the Greenhouse.* Illustrated by Zachary Trover. Minneapolis, MN: Picture Window Books.

Korman, Justine, Jan Gerardi, Justine Dorman-Fontes, and Jeffrey Scott. (2000). *Emmy's Dream House. Jellybean Books Just for Preschoolers.* Illustrated by Jan Gerardi. New York: CTW Books/ Random House.

Macken, JoAnn Early. (2008). *Building a Skyscraper.* Mankato, MN: Capstone Press.

Mayer, Mercer. (2005). *My Trip to the Hospital.* New York: HarperFestival.

Miller, Marilyn. (1996). *Behind the Scenes at the Shopping Mall.* Illustrated by Ingo Fast. Austin, TX: Raintree/Steck Vaughn.

Rey, Margret, and Alan J. Shalleck. (1985). *Curious George at the Fire Station.* Boston: Houghton Mifflin.

Rounds, Glen. (1995). *Sod Houses on the Great Plains.* New York: Holiday House.

Shelby, Anne. (1996). *The Someday House.* Illustrated by Rosanne Litzinger. New York: Orchard Books.

Smith, Alex T. (2009). *Once There Was a House, a House That Was a Home.* Wilton, CT: Tiger Tales.

Tarsky, Sue. (1998). *The Busy Building Book.* Illustrated by Alex Ayliffe. New York: G. P. Putnam's.

Teague, Mark. (2010). *Firehouse!* New York: Orchard Books.

Tolman, Marije, and Ronald Tolman. *The Tree House.* Honesdale, PA: Lemniscaat.

Yeoman, John. (1995). *The Do-It-Yourself House That Jack Built.* Illustrated by Quentin Blake. Colchester, CT: Atheneum.

Technology and Multimedia

The following technology and multimedia products can be used to complement this theme:

"The Corner Grocery Store" [CD]. (1996). In *The Corner Grocery Store.* Cambridge, MA: Rounder/UMGD.

The Man Who Walked between the Towers [DVD]. (2006). New York: Scholastic.

"There's No Place Like Home" [CD]. (2009). In *Kids: Traditional Sing-Alongs!* Minneapolis, MN: C&B Productions.

Additional teaching resources to accompany this Theme can be found on the book's companion website. Go to www.cengagebrain.com to access the site for a variety of useful resources.

Theme 10
CAMPING

Places
woods
campgrounds
parks
lakes
backyards

Equipment
tent
camper
lantern or flashlight
sleeping bag

Transportation
camper
car, pickup truck
motorcycle
van, canoe
bicycle, horse

Activities
boating
waterskiing
hiking
cooking outdoors
horseback riding
telling stories
fishing
birdwatching
observing wild animals

Foods
hot dogs
marshmallows
beans
fish
hamburgers

Theme Goals

Through participating in the experiences provided by this theme, the children may learn:

1. Places where people camp
2. Equipment used for camping
3. Camping transportation
4. Camping activities
5. Foods we eat while camping

Concepts for the Children to Learn

1. Camping is living outdoors in a tent or trailer.
2. A tent is used as a shelter when camping.
3. We can camp in the woods or at a campground.
4. We can also camp in a park, at a lake, or in our backyard.
5. Hot dogs, fish, hamburgers, marshmallows, and beans are all foods people eat while camping.
6. Foods often are cooked outdoors while camping.
7. Some people sleep in a camper instead of a tent.
8. A camper can be driven or attached to the back of a car or pickup truck.
9. Lanterns and flashlights are light sources used for camping.
10. A sleeping bag is a blanket used for camping.
11. Some people camp by a lake to waterski and go boating and fishing.
12. Some people take their bicycles and canoes on camping trips.
13. Birdwatching, hiking, and observing wild animals can be camping activities.
14. Some people enjoy storytelling while camping.

Vocabulary

1. **backpack**—a zippered bag worn on one's back to carry objects.
2. **campfire**—a fire that is made and carefully watched at a campground.
3. **camping**—living outdoors in sleeping bags, tents, cabins, or campers.
4. **campsite**—a place for tents and campers to park.
5. **hiking**—taking a long walk.
6. **lantern**—a covered light used for camping.
7. **recreational vehicle**—a living and sleeping area on wheels.
8. **sleeping bag**—a zippered blanket used for camping.
9. **tent**—a movable shelter made out of material.
10. **woods**—an area with many trees.

Bulletin Board

The purpose of this bulletin board is to develop color recognition skills and learn color words. In addition, visual discrimination, hand-eye coordination, and problem-solving skills are promoted. Construct several tents out of tagboard as illustrated. Make an identical set out of white tagboard. Color the first set of tents using the primary colors. Print the color names using corresponding colored markers onto the second set of tents. Laminate the materials. Staple the tents with color names to the bulletin board. Punch holes in the colored tents. Children can attach the tent to a pushpin on the corresponding color word tent.

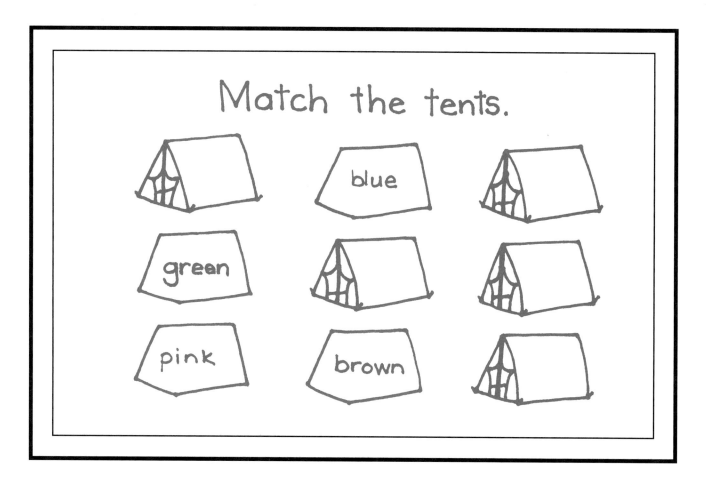

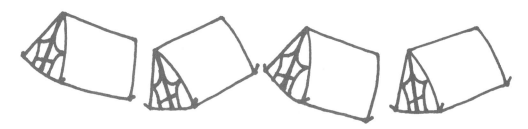

Family Letter

Dear Families,

With summer approaching, we will begin focusing on a fun family activity—camping! The children will become aware of camping activities. They will also learn about items and equipment that are commonly used while camping. From listening to the children's conversations, it sounds as if many have already been camping with their families. It should be fun to hear the camping stories they share!

At School

Some of the learning experiences planned include:

- Setting up the dramatic play area with a tent, sleeping bags, and other camping items
- Singing songs around a pretend campfire
- Going on a "bear hunt" (a rhythmic chant)
- Preparing foods that are eaten while camping
- Cleaning up after camping

At Home

Help your child create a tent by draping a sheet over a table. Provide a flashlight and a blanket or sleeping bag, and your child will be prepared for hours of indoor camping fun! Through dramatic play experiences, children relive and clarify situations and roles. They act out how they see the world and how they view relationships among people.

If you have any photographs or slides of family camping trips, we would be delighted if you would share them with us. Contact me and we can work out a time that would be convenient for you. Thanks!

Plan a camping trip with your child today!

Arts and Crafts

1. Easel Ideas

- Paint with leaves, sticks, flowers, and rocks.
- Paint with colors seen in the forest such as brown, green, yellow, and orange.
- Cut easel paper into the following shapes: tent, rabbits, chipmunks, and fish.

2. Camping Collage

Collect leaves, pebbles, twigs, pine cones, and so on. Provide glue and sturdy tagboard. Encourage the children to create a collage on the tagboard using the materials found while camping.

3. Tackle Box

Make two holes approximately 3 inches apart in the center of the lid of an egg carton. To form the handle, thread a cord through the holes and tie. Paint the box. In the box, place paper clips for hooks and S-shaped styrofoam pieces for worms.

Cooking

1. S'Mores

Place a large marshmallow on a square graham cracker. Next place a square of sweet chocolate on top of the marshmallow. After this, place the graham cracker on a baking sheet, and put into a 250-degree oven for about 5 minutes or until the chocolate starts to melt. Remove the s'more and press a second graham cracker square on top of the chocolate. Let cool for a few minutes, and serve while still slightly warm.

2. Venezuela Breakfast Cocoa

1/4 cup water
3 tablespoons cocoa
2 tablespoons sugar
2 cups milk
1 teaspoon vanilla

1. Bring the water to a boil in a saucepan.
2. Stir in the cocoa and sugar until they are blended. Turn the heat very low.
3. Slowly pour the milk into the saucepan with the cocoa mixture. Stir steadily to keep the mixture from burning. Continue cooking the mixture over low heat for about 2 minutes. Do not let it boil or skin will form on the top.
4. When the cocoa is hot, remove it from the stove and stir in the vanilla.
5. Carefully pour the cocoa into the cups. Serve warm.

Note: From *Many Hands Cooking,* by Terry Touff and Marilyn Ratner, 1974, New York: Thomas Y. Crowell. Reprinted with permission.

Dramatic Play

1. Camping

Collect various types of clothing and camping equipment, and place them in the dramatic play area or outdoors. Include items such as hiking boots, sweatshirts, raincoats, sleeping bags, backpacks, cooking tools, and a tent.

2. Puppets

Develop a puppet corner in the dramatic play area, including various animal puppets that would be seen while camping.

3. Going Fishing

Set up a rocking boat or a large box in the classroom or outdoors. Prepare paper fish with paper clips attached to them. Include a fishing pole made from a wooden dowel and a long string with a magnet attached to the end.

4. Going to the Beach

In the dramatic play area, set up lawn chairs, beach towels, buckets, shovels, sunglasses, and so on. Weather permitting, these items could also be placed outdoors.

Field Trips

1. **Department Store**
   Visit a department store or a sporting goods store where camping tents and other equipment are displayed.

2. **Picnic**
   Pack a picnic lunch or snack, and take it to an area campground.

3. **Camper Salesperson**
   Visit a recreational vehicle dealer, and tour a large mobile home.

Fingerplays and Chants

Five Little Bear Cubs

Five little bear cubs
Eating an apple core.
One had a sore tummy
And then there were four.

Four little bear cubs
Climbing in a tree.
One fell out
And then there were three.

Three little bear cubs
Playing peek-a-boo.
One was afraid
And then there were two.

Two little bear cubs
Sitting in the sun.
One ran away
And then there was one.

One little bear cub
Sitting all alone.
He saw his mommy
And then he ran home.

Group Time
(Games, Language)

1. **What's Missing**
   Have different pieces of camping equipment available to show the children. Include a canteen, portable stove, sleeping bag, cooking tools, lantern, and the like. Discuss each item, and then have the children close their eyes. Take one of the objects away and then have the children guess which object is missing.

2. **Camping Safety**
   Discuss camping safety. Include these points:
   - Always put out fires before going to sleep.
   - Swim in safe areas and with a partner.
   - When walking, or hiking away from your campsite, always have an adult with you.
   - Always wear a life jacket in the boat.

3. **Pack the Backpack**
   Bring a large backpack into the classroom. Also have many camping items available such as sweatshirts, flashlights, lanterns, food, raincoats, and so on. The teacher gives the children instructions that they are going to pretend to go on a hike to the beach. What is one thing they will need to bring along? Why? Continue until all of the children have had a chance to contribute.

4. **Campfire Story**
   Build a "campfire" by gluing empty toilet paper tubes or paper towel tubes together. (These will represent the logs.) Glue red, orange, and yellow tissue paper to the tops of the "logs" to represent the fire. Spread out a large blanket and place the "fire" in the middle. Turn off the lights and use a flashlight to read a camping story.

 Large Muscle

Caves

Using large packing boxes or barrels placed horizontally on the playground, allow the children to pretend to be wild animals in caves.

 Math

1. **Camping Scavenger Hunt**

   Before the children go outdoors, instruct them to find things on your playground that you would see while camping. Sort them and count them when they bring them into the classroom (five twigs, three rocks, etc.).

2. **Campers**

   Draw or paste tents onto the outside of a milk carton. Place a numeral on each tent. The children will place the corresponding number of campers into the tent. Use small people figurines for the campers. (If none are available, make people from construction paper.)

 Music

1. **"A Camping We Will Go"**

   (Sing to the tune of "The Farmer and the Dell")
   (The names in the song can be changed to different children's names.)

   A camping we will go.
   A camping we will go.
   Hi ho, we're off to the woods.
   A camping we will go.

   Saba will bring the tent.
   Oh, Saba will bring the tent.
   Hi ho, we're off to the woods.
   A camping we will go.

   Juan will bring the food.
   Oh, Juan will bring the food.
   Hi ho, we're off to the woods.
   A camping we will go.

2. **"Two Little Black Bears"**

   (Sing to the tune of "Two Little Blackbirds")

   Two little black bears sitting on a hill,
   One named Jack, one named Jill.
   Run away, Jack,
   Run away, Jill.
   Come back, Jack,
   Come back, Jill.
   Two little black bears sitting on a hill,
   One named Jack, one named Jill.

3. **Campfire Songs**

   Pretend that you are sitting around a campfire. Explain to the children that often people sing their favorite songs around a campfire. Encourage the children to name their favorite songs, and then sing some of them.

 Science

1. **Scavenger Hunt**

   While outside, have the children find plants growing, insects crawling, insects flying, a plant growing on a tree, a vine, a flower, bird feathers, a root, a seed, and so on.

2. **Sink or Float**

   Collect various pieces of camping equipment. Fill the water table with water, and let the children test which objects sink or float. If desired, make a chart.

3. **Magnifying Glasses**

   Provide magnifying glasses for looking at objects seen on a camping trip.

4. **Binoculars**

   Make binoculars by gluing or stapling toilet paper tubes together. If desired, children can decorate their binoculars with paint. Encourage children to find specific camping items by looking outside with their binoculars.

5. **Flashlight Fun**

   Give children flashlights to experiment with during naptime or when the lights have been dimmed. Encourage them to try to create shadows by holding their hands or other objects in front of the light.

Sensory

Sensory Table Additions

- Leaves
- Rocks
- Pebbles
- Mud and sand
- Twigs
- Evergreen needles and branches
- Water

Social Studies

1. **Pictures**

   Collect pictures of different campsites. Share them by displaying them in the classroom at the children's eye level.

2. **Camping Experiences**

   At group time, ask if any of the children have been camping. Let them tell the rest of the children what they did while they were camping. Ask where they slept, what they ate, where the bathroom was, and so on.

Books

The following books can be used to complement this theme:

Bauer, Marion Dane. (1995). *When I Go Camping with Grandma.* Illustrated by Allen Garns. Morago, CA: Bridgewater Books.

Birdseye, Tom. (2003). *Oh Yeah!* Illustrated by Ethan Long. New York: Holiday House.

Brillhart, Julie. (1997). *When Daddy Took Us Camping.* Niles, IL: Albert Whitman.

Brooks, Walter R. (2001). *Freddy Goes Camping.* Illustrated by Kurt Wiese. Woodstock, NY: Overlook Press.

Brown, M. K. (1995). *Let's Go Camping with Mr. Sillypants.* New York: Crown.

Christelow, Eileen. (1998). *Jerome Camps Out.* New York: Clarion.

Denton, P. J. (2007). *Camping Out.* Illustrated by Julia Denos. New York: Aladdin Paperbacks.

Duffey, Betsy. (1996). *Camp Knock Knock.* Illustrated by Fiona Dunbar. New York: Delacorte Press.

Eastman, Peter. (2005). *Fred and Ted Go Camping.* New York: Beginner Books.

Gifaldi, David. (2001). *Ben, King of the River.* Morton Grove, IL: Albert Whitman & Company.

Giff, Patricia Reilly. (1995). *Ronald Morgan Goes to Camp.* New York: Viking.

Hanson, Dave. (2006). *We're Going Camping.* Mankato, MN: Sea-to-Sea.

Henkes, Kevin. (1997). *Bailey Goes Camping.* New York: Mulberry Books.

Hermes, Patricia. (2009). *Emma Dilemma and the Camping Nanny.* Illustrated by Abby Carter. New York: Marshall Cavendish.

Huneck, Stephen. (2001). *Sally Goes to the Mountains.* New York: Harry N. Abrams.

James, Helen Foster. (2007). *S Is for S'Mores: A Camping Alphabet.* Illustrated by Lita Judge. Chelsea, MI: Sleeping Bear Press.

Jones, Christianne. (2007). *Camping in Green.* Illustrated by Todd Ouren. Minneapolis, MN: Picture Window Books.

Lakin, Patricia. (2009). *Camping Day.* Illustrated by Scott Nash. New York: Dial Books for Young Readers.

London, Jonathan. (2008). *Froggy Goes to Camp.* Illustrated by Frank Remkiewicz. New York. Viking Children's Books.

Lyon, Tammie. (2010). *Katie Goes Camping.* Mankato, MN: Picture Window Books.

Meyer, Susan. (2008). *Matthew and Tall Rabbit Go Camping.* Illustrated by Amy Huntington. Camden, ME: Down East Books.

Parish, Peggy. (1985). *Amelia Bedelia Goes Camping.* Illustrated by Lynn Sweat. New York: Greenwillow Books.

Parr, Todd. (2004). *Otto Goes to Camp.* New York: Little, Brown.

Polacco, Patricia. (2005). *The Graves Family Goes Camping.* New York: Philomel Books.

Rand, Gloria. (1996). *Willie Takes a Hike.* Illustrated by Ted Rand. Orlando, FL: Harcourt Brace.

Rey, H. A., & Margret Rey. (2007). *Curious George Goes Camping.* Boston: Houghton Mifflin.

Rosen, Michael. (1989). *We're Going on a Bear Hunt.* Illustrated by Helen Oxenbury. New York: Margaret K. McElderry Books.

Shaw, Nancy E. (1994). *Sheep Take a Hike.* Illustrated by Margot Apple. Boston: Houghton Mifflin.

Spohn, Kate. (2000). *Turtle and Snake Go Camping.* New York: Viking/Puffin.

Van Dusen, Chris. (2003). *A Camping Spree with Mr. Magee.* San Francisco: Chronicle Books.

Wolff, Ashley. (1999). *Stella and Roy Go Camping.* New York: Dutton Children's Books.

Technology and Multimedia

The following technology and multimedia products can be used to complement this theme:

"I Love Camping" [CD]. (2009). In *We Are the Not-Its!* Seattle, WA: Little Loopy Records.

Mercer Mayer's Just Me and My Dad [CD-ROM]. (1996). New York: GT Interactive Software.

"Sleeping Bag" [CD]. (2009). In *For Those about to Hop.* Burbank, CA: Walt Disney Records.

 Additional teaching resources to accompany this Theme can be found on the book's companion website. Go to www.cengagebrain.com to access the site for a variety of useful resources.

Theme 11
CARING FOR OUR EARTH

Picking Up Litter
aluminum cans
paper cups
plastic bags
paper

Recycling
cans
plastic
newspaper
computer paper
wrapping paper,
paper bags
cardboard
books
catalogs

Reuse
paper bags
cardboard books
catalogs
books
toys

Reducing Garbage
plant a garden
reuse paper and
plastic bags, reuse
cardboard boxes,
use both sides of
paper,
use washable
dishes

Making Compost
apple cores
bruised bananas
coffee grounds
(used)
fruit pulp
vegetable peelings
grass clippings

leaves
kitchen scraps
laundry lint
paper shreds
wiggly worms

Save Energy
turn off water
turn off lights
turn off electronics,
close refrigerator
door,
walk
ride bike
carpool

Being Kind
sharing books
planting a tree

Theme Goals

Through participating in the experiences provided by this theme, the children may learn:

1. Picking up litter
2. Recycling items
3. Reducing garbage
4. Making compost
5. Saving energy
6. Being kind

Concepts for the Children to Learn

1. Earth is our home, so we must care for it.
2. Reuse paper and plastic bags.
3. Use both sides of a piece of paper.
4. Use washable containers to reduce the amount of trash.
5. Plant a garden to reduce garbage.
6. Recycle cans, plastic bags, paper, magazines, wrapping paper, paper bags, computer paper, cardboard boxes, magazines, and catalogs.
7. Reuse paper, plastic, and cardboard boxes.
8. Compost can be made of apple cores, bruised bananas, coffee grounds, fruit pulp, vegetable peelings, and grass clippings.
9. Kitchen scraps, laundry lint, leaves, paper shreds, and wiggly worms can also be used to make compost.
10. You help the earth stay healthy when you save water.
11. Save water by turning the water off while you brush your teeth and by taking short showers.
12. Fill the bathtub only half full of water when taking a bath.
13. Turn off the lights if no one is in the room.
14. Turn off the television if no one is watching it.
15. Keep the refrigerator door closed.
16. Walk, ride your bike, or carpool to help keep air clean.
17. Pick up litter—aluminum cans, paper cups, plastic bags, and paper.

Vocabulary

1. **garbage**—food or items thrown away if they are not needed.
2. **compost**—vegetables, fruits, coffee grounds, and rotten leaves that are used to make the soil rich.
3. **pollute**—to make our earth unclean and unsafe.
4. **reuse**—to use items again so they are not put in the garbage. Paper bags can be reused.
5. **waste**—to throw away or make poor use of
6. **water**—a colorless liquid that people, plants, and animals need to live. We need water to drink, cook, and bathe.
7. **recycle**—to make new items from old items. Newspapers can be recycled to make paper plates, paper cups, cereal boxes, bags, and wrapping paper.

Bulletin Board

The purpose of this bulletin board is to promote an awareness of recycling as well as to promote visual discrimination and hand-eye coordination skills. At the bottom of the bulletin board, place four different felt bins labeled Glass, Aluminum, Plastic, and Paper. Above the bins, include pictures of a variety of recyclable items. Encourage the children to place the items into the appropriate bins.

Family Letter

InBox

Dear Families,

With the beautiful weather outside, we could not have asked for a better time to introduce our new theme, Taking Care of Our Earth. By participating in the activities related to this theme, the children will learn about the "3 R's," which are reduce, reuse, and recycle. One interesting activity will be making "compost stew." The children will become "environmental chefs" and learn how to make a compost stew. They will learn what materials can be included in compost and which ones won't break down and need to be recycled.

At School

Learning experiences for this week include:

- Sorting different recyclables
- Going on a "litter hunt" on our playground
- Making drums from reused yogurt containers
- Creating compost stew

At Home

Reducing and reusing are important. Every ton of recycled paper saves more than 3.3 cubic yards of landfill space. This is about the same amount of space as a small refrigerator. If you are not already recycling, begin now. Set aside a place to store your recyclable paper, plastic, and glass. Encourage your child to help gather and deposit these items in the right containers. Also, try incorporating some of the following ways of keeping our earth healthy into your home.

- Turn off lights and electronics that are not being used.
- Save water by turning off the faucet while brushing teeth.
- Replace regular light bulbs with energy-efficient ones.
- Fill the bathtub only one-half full.
- Reduce, Reuse, and Recycle!

Have a "green" week!

Arts and Crafts

Plastic Bottle Prints

Collect clean plastic bottles in different sizes and shapes. Provide the children with different colors of paint in shallow paint trays. The children can dip one end of the plastic bottle into the paint and then onto paper.

Scrap Paper Collage

Begin a collection of scrap paper in your classroom. Encourage the children to use the scrap paper to make a collage. Children can cut or tear paper into smaller pieces, and then glue it onto a larger piece of paper.

Bug Rocks

Take children out for a walk and have them choose a large rock. Provide children with paint and paintbrushes, and allow them to paint their rock to look like the bug of their choice.

Recyclable 3D Art

Collect different types of recyclables, glue, and tape for the children to use to turn into 3D art.

Leaf Rubbings

Collect leaves, paper, and crayons, and show the children how to place several leaves under a sheet of paper. Using the flat edge of crayon color, rub over paper. The image of leaves will appear.

Cooking

Fruit Kabobs

Gather different kinds of fruits such as bananas, strawberries, or peaches. Encourage the children to cut up the fruit using plastic knives. Then have them put the fruit onto kabob sticks. Challenge the children by asking them to make a pattern using the fruit.

Dramatic Play

Recycling Center

Gather different bins and label them with different pictures that represent plastic, aluminum, glass, and paper. Collect clean items that fit under each category (plastic bottles, soup cans, and newspaper). For the safety of the children, use pictures of glass items. Provide the children with a variety of clothing and gloves.

Greenhouse

Provide aprons, gardening gloves, artificial flowers, flower pots, shovels, and watering cans to create a greenhouse in dramatic play.

Field Trip and Resource People

Litter Pickup

Give children gloves to wear and take them for a walk to pick up litter on their playground or around the neighborhood.

Farmer's Market

Take children to a local farmer's market so they can see locally grown produce.

Botanist or Florist

Invite a botanist or florist to class to discuss the different parts of plants.

Recycling Center

Visit a recycling center and bring items from school that can be recycled.

Fingerplays and Chants

Flowers, Seeds, Leaves, and Roots
(Sing to the tune of "Head, Shoulders, Knees, and Toes")

Flowers, seeds, leaves, and roots.
    (Make circle above head, wiggle fingers
    down low, extend arms out from body,
    and touch toes.)
Leaves and roots.
Flowers, seeds, leaves, and roots.
Leaves and roots.
The parts of a plant are growing everyday.
    (Get down low and gradually grow
    taller.)
Flowers, seeds, leaves, and roots.
Leaves and roots.

Group Time

Going on a Nature Hike
In a large-group setting, talk about the
many things you would need to go on a
nature hike such as hiking boots, a hat, bug
spray, food, water, or a walking stick. Then
sing the following song:

Going on a nature hike, leaving right away.
If it doesn't rain, we'll stay all day!
Did you bring the _____?
    (Have child fill in something they would
    bring on a nature hike.)
Yes, I brought _____!
    (Repeat what the child said.)
Repeat until each child gets a turn to say
    something he or she would bring.

Large Muscle

Bug Hunt
Give the children nets and containers to
catch and store bugs in. Encourage them
to use the nets to chase and catch different
bugs to put into the containers. Allow them
to use magnifying glasses to look closely at
the bugs they catch.

Outdoor Scavenger Hunt
Take pictures of items from nature within
the school playground. Add the pictures to
a checklist of what the children have to find
on their scavenger hunt. Take the children
outside, and have them cross out each
picture as they find it.

Raking Leaves
Provide child-sized rakes for the children.
They can rake leaves into different
piles or make a maze to make their way
through.

Math

Sorting Caps
Collect different colored caps from plastic
bottles. Encourage the children to sort the
caps by colors and sizes. They can also make
patterns using the caps.

Leaf Sorting
Collect different types of leaves varying in
sizes and colors. Encourage the children to
sort the leaves by colors, sizes, and number
of points.

Counting Nature
Collect 10 different containers, and label
each container with a number from 1 to 10.
Gather items from nature such as rocks,
shells, flowers, leaves, or twigs. Encourage
children to look at the number on the
container and then count out that number
of items from nature.

Pick-Up Sticks
Make cards for the children with different
numbers. Collect twigs, similar in size, for
the children to pick up, and count according
to which number card they draw.

Music

Pick Up Litter
(Sing to the tune of "If You're Happy and You Know It")

If you see a piece of litter, pick it up!
If you see a piece of litter, pick it up!
You will make the world look better,
if you pick up all the litter.
If you see a piece of litter, pick it up!

Recycle for Our Earth
(Sing to the tune of "Mary Had a Little Lamb")

Hear the cans go crunch, crunch, crunch.
Crunch, crunch, crunch. Crunch, crunch,
   crunch.
Hear the cans go crunch, crunch, crunch.
Recycle for our earth.
Hear the paper go crinkle, crinkle, crinkle.
Crinkle, crinkle, crinkle. Crinkle, crinkle,
   crinkle.
Hear the paper go crinkle, crinkle, crinkle.
Recycle for our earth.
(Add verses for glass or plastic.)

Cleaning Up All the Litter
(Sing to the tune of "Hokey Pokey")

Put your litter bag in. Take your litter bag out.
Put your litter bag in and then you shake it
   all about.
You clean up all the litter and you turn
   yourself around.
That's what it is all about!

Science

Compost Stew
Encourage the children to help you start a
compost pile. Designate a covered bucket as
a place for children to throw scraps of their
food. Add worms to the compost bucket
and encourage children to check in on the
compost to see how it changes. After some
compost has been made, add it to soil and
plant a flower.

Decomposition Predictions
Explain the concept of decomposing.
Introduce the children to three to five
different items, and have them predict
which of them will decompose the fastest.
Graph the children's predictions on a chart.

Grow a Bean
Wrap a bean in a wet paper towel. Place
the paper towel inside a plastic bag. Place
the bag in a sunny window. Have children
make predictions on how many days it
will take for their bean to sprout. Children
can draw pictures on how their bean plant
changes.

Terrarium
Collect two liter bottles with caps to make
into individual terrariums. Remove the
label from the bottle. Cut the bottles about
two inches from the bottom of the bottle.
Fill the bottom of the bottle with soil, plant
a seed, and add a bit of water. Put the top
back on top of the base of the bottle. Place
the terrarium in a sunny spot so the seeds
can sprout.

A Tree's Age
Collect different cross sections of trees
in which the middle of the tree is visible.
Give the children magnifying glasses so
they can count how many rings are in the
middle of the tree to determine its age. Tell
the children each ring signifies one year of
growth in the tree.

Take-Apart Table
Collect old clocks, phones, cameras, and so
on, and place them on the table for fixing
and taking apart.

Eggshell Plants
Wash empty eggshells and fill with soil.
Then add a seed. When the plant grows,
the entire shell and plant can be planted
outdoors.

Recycling Bins
Create three recycling bins from sturdy
cardboard boxes. Label each box with
a picture and the word paper, metal, or
plastic. Then collect paper, metal, and

plastic items and place in a bushel basket. Encourage the children to sort the items into the appropriate bin. (In the parent letter, you could ask parents to contribute items for your recycling activity.)

Sensory

Outdoor Collage

Take the children outside. Draw a square or rectangle on a sidewalk, and tell them that is their "paper." You could also use a rope to outline a square or rectangle. Encourage the children to find things from nature to add to a collage.

Social Studies

Pollution

Collect either snow or rainwater. Run through a coffee filter. Then have the children observe what is left in the filter using both the naked eye and a magnifying glass. Explain in developmentally appropriate terms the impact of vehicle exhaust.

Books

The following books can be used to complement this theme:

Asch, Frank. (2004). *The Earth and I*. San Diego, CA: Harcourt Brace & Company.

Bass, Jules. (2008). *Herb, The Vegetarian Dragon*. Illustrated by Debbie Harter. Cambridge, MA: Barefoot Books.

Bergen, Lara. (2009). *Don't Throw That Away!* Illustrated by Betsy Snyder. New York. Little Simon.

Bethel, Ellie. (2008). *Michael Recycle*. Illustrated by Alexandra Colombo. San Diego, CA: Jonas Publishing/Worthwhile Books.

Bethel, Ellie. (2009). *Michael Recycle Meets Litterbug Doug*. Illustrated by Alexandra Colombo. San Diego, CA: Jonas Publishing/ Worthwhile Books.

Cherry, Lynne. (1990). *The Great Kapok Tree*. Orlando, FL: Harcourt Books.

Glaser, Linda. (2010). *Garbage Helps Our Garden Grow: A Compost Story*. Minneapolis, MN: Millbrook Press.

Green, Jen. (2005). *Why Should I Recycle?* Illustrated by Mike Gordon. Hauppauge, NY: Barron's Educational Series.

Green, Jen. (2005). *Why Should I Save Water?* Illustrated by Mike Gordon. Hauppauge, NY: Barron's Educational Series.

Hodgkins, Fran. (2005). *If You Were My Baby: A Wildlife Lullaby*. Illustrated by Laura J. Bryant. Nevada City, CA: Dawn Publications.

Inches, Alison. (2008). *I Can Save the Earth! One Little Monster Learns to Reduce, Reuse, and Recycle*. Illustrated by Viviana Garofoli. New York: Little Simon.

Koontz, Robin. (2002). *Composting: Nature's Recyclers*. Illustrated by Matthew Harrad. Minneapolis, MN: Picture Window Books.

Kowalski, Gary. (2009). *Earth Day: An Alphabet Book*. Illustrated by Rocco Baviera. Boston: Skinner House Books.

Kroll, Steven. (2009). *Stuff! Reduce, Reuse, Recycle*. New York: Marshall Cavendish.

Martin, Bill, Jr., and Michael R. Sampson. (2006). *I Love Our Earth*. Photographs by Dan Lipow. Watertown, MA: Charlesbridge.

Mayer, Mercer. (2008). *It's Earth Day!* New York: HarperFestival.

Mockford, Caroline. (2007). *What's This? A Seed's Story*. Cambridge, MA: Barefoot Books.

Murphy, Stuart J. (2004). *Earth Day: Hooray!* Illustrated by Renee Andriani. New York: HarperCollins.

Parr, Todd. (2010). *The Earth Book*. New York: Hachette Book Group.

Pfeffer, Wendy. (2003). *Wiggling Worms at Work*. Illustrated by Steve Jenkins. New York: HarperCollins.

Roca, Nurica. (2007). *The Three R's: Reuse, Reduce, Recycle*. Illustrated by Rosa M. Curto. Hauppauge, NY: Barron's Educational Series.

Scanlon, Liz Garton. (2009). *All the World.* Illustrated by Marla Frazee. La Jolla, CA: Simon & Schuster.

Siddals, Mary McKenna. (2010). *Compost Stew.* Illustrated by Ashley Wolf. New York: Tricycle Press.

Spinelli, Eileen. (2009). *Miss Fox's Class Goes Green.* Illustrated by Anne Kennedy. Morton Grove, IL: Albert Whitman & Company.

Wallace, Nancy Elizabeth. (2003). *Recycle Every Day.* New York: Marshall Cavendish.

Technology and Multimedia

The following technology and multimedia resources can be used to complement this theme:

Around the World with Earth Mama [CD]. (1997). Kennewick, WA: Rouse House.

Corr, Christopher, and Fred Penner. (2007). *Whole World* [CD and book]. Cambridge, MA: Barefoot Books.

Every Day Is Earth Day [CD]. (2004). Portland, OR: Crispy Records.

Little Green CD: 31 Exciting Earth Songs to Sing and Do! [CD]. (2008). London: TMa.

Reduce, Reuse, Recycle [CD]. (2010). London: CYP Limited.

Additional teaching resources to accompany this Theme can be found on the book's companion website. Go to www.cengagebrain.com to access the site for a variety of useful resources.

Theme 12
CARS, TRUCKS, AND BUSES

Inside Parts
horn
steering wheel
seats
blinkers
seat belts
radio
mirrors
clock
motor

Outside Parts
wheels
hood
headlights
trunk
mirrors
windshield
wipers
antenna

Safety
speed
seat belts
noise
activities
air bags
gasoline
handicapped accessible,
number of people,
sit until stopped

Kinds
Trucks
dump
fire
pickup
tank
semi
Cars
compact
van
station wagon
convertible
police

taxi
ambulance
Buses
school
city
tour

Colors
white
black
blue
green
yellow
silver, red

Uses
move objects
move people

Sizes
small
medium
large

Care
wash
wax
vacuum
repair

Theme Goals

Through participating in the experiences provided by this theme, the children may learn:

1. Kinds of cars, trucks, and buses
2. Care of vehicles
3. Uses of vehicles
4. Inside and outside parts of vehicles
5. Colors and sizes of vehicles
6. Safety factors

Concepts for the Children to Learn

1. Cars, trucks, and buses are used to move people.
2. There are many kinds of cars, trucks, and buses.
3. Trucks and buses are usually bigger than cars.
4. Trucks can be used to haul objects.
5. There are dump, fire, pickup, tank, and semi trucks.
6. Compact vans, station wagons, and convertibles are kinds of cars.
7. Special cars include police cars, taxis, and ambulances.
8. There are several kinds of buses, such as a city bus.
9. Cars, trucks, and buses come in many colors and sizes.
10. Cars, trucks, and buses can be white, black, green, blue, yellow, silver, and red.
11. Cars, trucks, and buses have inside and outside parts.
12. The horn, steering wheel, seats, blinkers, seat belts, mirror, clock, and motor are inside parts.
13. The wheels, hood, headlights, trunk door, mirrors, and windshield wipers are outside parts.
14. Seat belts help keep people safe; so does remaining seated until the vehicle stops.
15. Vehicles need care.
16. Vehicles need to be vacuumed, washed, waxed, and repaired.

Vocabulary

1. **bus**—a big machine that carries many people. Buses move people from place to place.
2. **car**—a machine used for moving people. Most cars have a motor and four wheels. Automobile is another word for cars.
3. **driver**—the person who drives a bus, car, or truck
4. **fuel**—gas used in the machine to produce power
5. **gas**—a liquid put in machines to make them move
6. **motor**—a machine that makes buses, cars, and trucks move
7. **passenger**—people who ride in buses, cars, and trucks
8. **truck**—a wheeled machine used to move people and big objects

Bulletin Board

The purpose of the bulletin board is to reinforce color-recognition and -matching skills, as well as to develop one-to-one correspondence concepts. In addition, visual discrimination, problem solving, and hand-eye coordination are promoted. Construct garage shapes out of tagboard. Color each garage a different color and hang on the bulletin board. Hang a pushpin or attach a Velcro piece in the center of each garage. Next, construct the same number of cars as garages from tagboard. Color each car a different color to correspond with the colors of the garages. Use a paper punch to make a hole in each car. The children can park each car in its corresponding colored garage. *Note:* Carefully supervise the use of pushpins.

Family Letter

Dear Families,

Cars, trucks, and buses—these are all transportation vehicles that your child sees daily. Because of the children's interest, we are beginning a unit on cars, trucks, and buses. Through participating in the planned activities, the children will learn that there are many colors, sizes, and kinds of cars, trucks, and buses. They will also learn the care of the inside and outside parts of a car.

At School

Some of the activities planned for this unit include:

- Painting with small cars at the art table

- Looking at and listening to many books and stories about trucks, buses, and cars

- Setting up a gas station in the dramatic play area

- Visiting with Officer Lewis from the police department, who will show the children his squad car at 10:30 a.m. on Thursday

At Home

You can foster the concepts of this unit at home by taking your child with you the next time you need to buy gas for your vehicle. There are many different types of trucks and cars to observe at the filling station. Also, provide soapy water and a sponge, and let your child help you wash the family vehicle. Children enjoy taking part in grown-up activities, and this helps build a sense of responsibility and self-esteem.

Enjoy your child as you explore concepts related to cars, trucks, and buses.

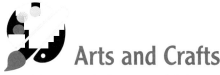

Arts and Crafts

1. **License Plate Rubbings**
   Place paper on top of a license plate. Using the side of a large crayon, rub across the top of the license plate.

2. **Car Track Painting**
   Provide several small plastic cars and trucks and large sheets of white paper. Also, have available low, flat pans of thin tempera paint. Encourage the children to take the cars and trucks and roll the wheels in the paint. They can then transfer the car to their own paper and make car or truck tracks on the paper.

3. **Designing Cars**
   Provide the children with large, appliance-sized cardboard boxes. To protect the floor surface, place a large sheet of plastic underneath. Provide the children with paint, markers, and collage materials to decorate the boxes as cars. When the cars dry, they can be moved into the block building, dramatic play area, or outdoor area.

Cooking

1. **Cracker Wheels**
   For this recipe, each child will need:

   4 round crackers
   1/2 hot dog
   1/2 a slice of 4-inch × 4-inch cheese

   Slice hot dogs and place on a cracker. Place cheese over the top. Place in oven at 350 degrees for 3 to 5 minutes, or microwave for 30 seconds. Let cool and eat.
   Note: Due to choking concerns, young children require careful supervision when eating hot dogs.

2. **Greek Honey Twists**
   3 eggs, beaten
   2 tablespoons vegetable oil
   1/2 teaspoon baking powder
   1/4 teaspoon salt
   1 3/4 to 2 cups all-purpose flour
   Vegetable oil
   1/4 cup honey

1 tablespoon water
Ground cinnamon to taste

Mix eggs, 2 tablespoons oil, baking powder, and salt in a large bowl. Gradually stir in enough flour to make a very stiff dough. Knead 5 minutes. Roll half the dough at a time as thin as possible on well-floured surface with a stockinet-covered rolling pin. Cut into wheel shapes. Twist into the shape of the numeral eight. Cover with a damp towel to prevent drying.

Heat 2 to 3 inches of oil to 375 degrees. Fry three to five twists at a time until golden brown, turning once, about 45 seconds on each side. Drain on paper towels. Heat honey and water to boiling; boil 1 minute. Cool slightly. Drizzle over twists; sprinkle with cinnamon. Makes 32 twists.

Note: From *Betty Crocker's International Cookbook,* 1980, New York: Random House. Reprinted with permission.

Dramatic Play

1. **Filling Station**
   Provide cardboard boxes for cars and hoses for the gas pumps. Also, make available play money and steering wheels.

2. **Bus**
   Set up a bus situation by lining up chairs in one or two long rows. Provide a steering wheel for the driver. A money bucket and play money can also be provided. If a steering wheel is unavailable, heavy round pizza cardboards can be used to improvise.

3. **Taxi**
   Set up two rows of chairs side by side to represent a taxi. Use a pizza cardboard, or other round object, as the steering wheel. Provide a telephone, dress-up clothes for the passengers, and a hat for the driver. A TAXI sign can also be placed by the chairs to invite play.

4. **Fire Truck**
   Contact the local fire chief and ask to use old hoses, fire hats, and firefighter clothing.

Field Trips and Resource People

1. **City Bus**
Take the children for a ride around town on a city bus. When boarding, allow each child to place his or her own money in the meter. Observe the length of the bus. While inside, watch how the bus driver operates the bus. Also, have a school bus driver visit and tell about the job and the importance of safety on a bus.

2. **Taxi Driver**
Invite a taxi driver to visit and show the features of the taxi.

3. **Patrol Car**
Invite a police officer to bring a squad car to the center. The radio, siren, and flashing lights can be demonstrated. Let the children sit in the car.

4. **Fire Truck**
Invite a local firefighter to bring a fire truck to the center. Let the children climb in the truck and observe the parts.

5. **Semi Truck Driver**
Invite a semi truck driver to bring the truck to school. Observe the size, number of wheels, and parts of the cab. Let the children sit in the cab.

6. **Ambulance**
Invite an ambulance driver to bring the vehicle to school. Let the children inspect the contents.

Fingerplays and Chants

Windshield Wiper
I'm a windshield wiper
(bend arm at elbow with fingers pointing up)
This is how I go
(move arm to left and right, pivoting at elbow)

Back and forth, back and forth
(continue back and forth motion)
In the rain and snow.
(continue back and forth motion)

Here Is a Car
Here is a car, shiny and bright.
(cup one hand and place on other palm)
This is the windshield that lets in the light.
(hands open, fingertips touching)
Here are wheels that go round and round.
(two fists)
I sit in the back seat and make not a sound.
(sit quietly with hands in lap)

The Car Ride
(The left arm, held out with a bent elbow and open palm, is the road; the right fist is a car.)

"Vroom!" says the engine
(place car on left shoulder)
As the driver starts the car.
(shake car)

"Mmmm," say the windows
As the driver takes it far.
(travel over upper arm)

"Errr," say the tires
As it rounds the final bend,
(turn at elbow, proceed over forearm)

"Ahhh," says the driver
As the trip comes to an end.
(stop car on left flattened palm)

School Bus
I go to the bus stop each day
(walk one hand across table)
Where the bus comes to take us away.
(stop, have other hand wait also)
We stand single file
(one behind the other)
And walk down the aisle
(step up imaginary steps onto bus)
When the bus driver talks, we obey.

Group Time
(Games, Language)

1. **Thank-You Note**
Write a thank-you note to a resource person. Allow the children to dictate and sign it.

2. Red Light, Green Light

Select one child to pretend to be a traffic light. The traffic light places his or her back to children lined up at the other end of the room. When the traffic light says, "Green light," or holds up green paper, the other children attempt to creep up on the traffic light. At any time the traffic light can say, "Red light," or hold up a red paper, and quickly turn around. Creeping children must freeze. Any child caught moving is sent back to the starting line. Play continues until one child reaches the traffic light. This child becomes the new traffic light.

Large Muscle

1. "Fill 'Er Up"

Tricycles, wagons, and scooters can be used outside on the playground. A gas pump can be constructed out of an old cardboard box with an attached hose.

2. Car, Car, Truck

Play this simple variation of "Duck, Duck, Goose" by substituting the words "Car, Car, Truck."

3. Wash a Car

If possible, wash a compact-size car. Provide a hose, sponges, brushes, a bucket, and soapy water. If an actual car is not available, children can wash tricycles, bicycles, scooters, and wagons.

4. Road Map Shower Curtain

Use permanent markers to color roads, trees, train tracks, buildings, and other landmarks on a shower curtain. Place the curtain on the floor, and encourage children to drive cars, trucks, or buses on the roads.

Math

1. Cars and Garages

Car garages can be constructed out of empty half-pint milk cartons. Collect and carefully wash the milk cartons. Cut out one side and write a numeral, starting with 1, on each carton. Next, collect a corresponding number of small miniature cars. Attach a strip of paper with a numeral from 1 to the appropriate number on each car's top. The children can drive each car into the garage with the corresponding numeral.

2. License Plate Match

Construct two sets of identical license plates. Print a pattern of letters or numerals on each set. Mix them up. Children can try to match the pairs.

3. Car, Truck, or Bus Sequencing

Cut out various-sized cars, trucks, or buses and laminate. Children can sequence them from largest to smallest and vice versa.

4. Sorting

Construct cars, trucks, and buses of different colors and laminate. Children can sort according to color.

5. Car Ramp

Roll a bus, car, and truck toy down a wooden ramp. Encourage children to determine which vehicle went the farthest or shortest distance.

Science

1. License Plates

Collect license plates from different states and different vehicles, and place them on a table for the children to explore.

2. Feely Box

Put transportation toys in a feely box. Include cars, trucks, and buses. Individually, let the children feel inside the box and identify the type of toy.

3. Road Materials

Place pieces of dirt, blacktop, and concrete in containers, and place them on a table for the children to explore.

Sensory

Sensory Table Additions

- Cars and trucks with wet sand

Social Studies

Discussion on Safety

Have a group discussion on safety when riding in a car. Allow children to come up with suggestions. Write them down on a chart, and display the chart in the classroom during the unit. The addition of pictures or drawings would be helpful for younger children.

Books

The following books can be used to complement this theme:

Barton, Byron. (2001). *My Car*. New York: Greenwillow.

Bingham, Caroline. (1996). *Race Car*. Mighty Machine series. New York: Dorling Kindersley.

Bingham, Caroline. (1998). *Monster Machines*. Mighty Machine series. New York: Dorling Kindersley.

Bloom, Suzanne. (2001). *The Bus for Us*. Honesdale, PA: Boyds Mills Press.

Bowman, Crystal. (2010). *The Boy on the Yellow Bus*. Cincinnati, OH: Standard Publishing.

Cuyler, Margery. (2009). *The Little Dump Truck*. Illustrated by Bob Kolar. New York: Henry Holt.

Dale, Penny. (2007). *The Boy on the Bus*. Cambridge, MA: Candlewick Press.

DeGezelle, Terri. (2006). *Garbage Trucks*. Mankato, MN: Capstone Press.

Haldane, Elizabeth. (2005). *Truck*. New York: DK Publishing.

Hamilton, Kersten R. (2008). *Red Truck*. Illustrated by Valeria Petrone. New York: Viking Children's Books.

Hort, Lenny. (2000). *The Seals on the Bus*. Illustrated by G. Brian Karas. New York: Henry Holt.

Hubbell, Patricia. (2006). *Cars: Rushing! Honking! Zooming!* Illustrated by Sean Addy and Megan Halsey. New York: Marshall Cavendish.

Hurd, Thacher. (1998). *Zoom City*. New York: HarperCollins Publishers.

Katz, Bobbi. (1997). *Truck Talk: Rhymes on Wheels*. St. Paul, MN: Cartwheel Books.

Kirk, David. (1999). *Miss Spider's New Car*. New York: Scholastic.

Lindeen, Carol K. (2005). *Fire Trucks*. Mankato, MN: Capstone Press.

Lindeen, Carol K. (2005). *Police Cars*. Mankato, MN: Capstone Press.

London, Jonathan. (2010). *I'm a Truck Driver*. Illustrated by David Parkins. New York: Henry Holt.

Maccarone, Grace. (1995). *Cars! Cars! Cars!* Illustrated by David A. Carter. New York: Scholastic.

McCarthy, Meghan. (2005). *The Adventures of Patty and the Big Red Bus*. New York: Alfred A. Knopf.

McMullan, Kate. (2002). *I Stink!* Illustrated by Jim McMullan. New York: Joanne Cotler Books.

Mills, J. Elizabeth. (2010). *The Spooky Wheels on the Bus*. New York: Scholastic/Cartwheel Books.

Mitton, Tony, and Ant Parker. (2005). *Cool Cars*. Boston: Kingfisher.

Oxlade, Chris. (1997). *Car (Take It Apart)*. Morristown, NJ: Silver Burdett.

Potts, Professor. (2009). *The Smash! Smash! Truck*. New York: David Fickling Books.

Radford, Derek. (1997). *Harry at the Garage*. Cambridge, MA: Candlewick Press.

Ransom, Candice F. (2009). *The Old Blue Pickup Truck*. Illustrated by Jenny Matheson. New York: Walker Book & Company.

Rex, Michael. (2004). *Truck Duck*. New York: G.P. Putnam.

Rooney, Ronnie. (2009). *The Wheels on the Bus*. Mankato, MN: Child's World.

Scarry, Richard. (1997). *Richard Scarry's Cars and Trucks and Things That Go*. New York: Golden Book.

Schertle, Alice. (2009). *Little Blue Truck Leads the Way*. Illustrated by Jill McElmurry. Boston: Harcourt Children's Books.

Schuh, Mari. (2009). *Fireboats in Action*. Mankato, MN: Capstone Press.

Schuh, Mari. (2009). *Fire Trucks in Action*. Mankato, MN: Capstone Press.

Singer, Marilyn. (2009). *I'm Your Bus*. New York: Scholastic Press.

Skultety, Nancy. (2005). *From Here to There*. Illustrated by Tammie Lyon. Honesdale, PA.: Boyds Mills Press.

Spangler, Brie. (2009). *The Grumpy Dump Truck*. New York: Alfred A. Knopf.

Stoeke, Janet Morgan. (2007). *The Bus Stop*. New York: Dutton Children's Books.

Strickland, Paul. (2000). *Truck Jam: A Pop-Up Book*. Brooklyn, NY: Ragged Bear.

Thompson, Kate. (2009). *Ten Little Racing Cars*. Illustrated by Charles Reasoner. Columbus, OH: School Specialty Publishing.

Walton, Rick. (2002). *Cars at Play*. Illustrated by James Lee Croft. New York: G.P. Putnam's Sons.

Williams, Linda D. (2005). *Dump Trucks*. Mankato, MN: Capstone Press.

Technology and Multimedia

The following technology and multimedia products can be used to complement this theme:

"Car, Car Song" [CD]. (1999). In *Five Little Monkeys*. Long Branch, NJ: Kimbo Educational.

Cars, Trucks, and Trains [CD]. (1997). Long Branch, NJ: Kimbo Educational.

"Drive My Car" [CD]. (2002). In *Under a Shady Tree*. New York: Two Tomatoes.

"Driving in My Car" [CD]. (2003). In *Fingerplays and Fun!* Buena Park, CA: Barbara Milne.

"Hooray for Farm Machines" [CD]. (1999). In *On the Farm with RONNO*. Long Branch, NJ: Kimbo Educational.

"Motoring" [CD]. (1996). In *People in Our Neighborhood*. Long Branch, NJ: Kimbo Educational.

Murphy, Jane Lawliss. (1997). *Cars, Trucks and Trains* [CD]. Long Branch, NJ: Kimbo Educational.

"Racecars" [CD]. (2009). In *People, Place and Things*. Coconut Grove, FL: In the Nick of Time.

"Seatbelt Buckled" [CD]. (2002). In *Cousins Jamboree*. Richmond, VA: Holcomb Rock Road.

Silly Car Songs [CD]. (2006). Columbus, OH: Tree House Entertainment.

"Truck Driver's Song" [CD]. (1999). In *We're on Our Way*. Sherman Oaks, CA: Hap-Pal Music.

"Wheels on the Bus" [CD]. (2002). In *Early Childhood Classics*. Sherman Oaks, CA: Hap-Pal Music.

"The Wheels on the Bus" [CD]. (2006). In *The Big Silly with Mr. Eric*. Atlanta, GA: Mr. Eric.

Additional teaching resources to accompany this Theme can be found on the book's companion website. Go to www.cengagebrain.com to access the site for a variety of useful resources.

Theme 13
CATS

Food
water
cat food

Body Parts
fur
legs
paws and claws
tail
whiskers
eyes
ears
nose
mouth

Care
food
water
grooming
exercise
shelter
medical care
gentle handling

Colors
black
brown
white
gray
yellow
calico

Places Cats Live
homes
barns
outdoors

Types
long haired
short haired
different colors
calico

Communication
purring
meowing

Theme Goals

Through participating in the experiences provided by this theme, the children may learn:

1. Types of cats
2. Body parts of a cat
3. Special care for cats
4. Foods that cats need
5. Places where cats live
6. Colors of cats
7. How cats communicate

Concepts for the Children to Learn

1. A cat is an animal with soft fur.
2. There are many different colors of cats.
3. Cats can be black, brown, white, gray, yellow, or calico.
4. Cats have legs, eyes, ears, a mouth, a nose, whiskers, paws, and claws.
5. Cats have fur on their skin.
6. Cats can have long or short fur.
7. Cats need to be cared for.
8. Cats need food, water, and exercise every day.
9. Cats also need shelter.
10. Cats can live in homes, barns, or outdoors.
11. Cats need to be handled gently.

Vocabulary

1. **cat**—an animal with soft fur that often is kept as a pet.
2. **calico**—a cat that has fur of many colors.
3. **coat**—hair or fur covering the skin.
4. **collar**—a band worn around the cat's neck.
5. **kitten**—a baby cat.
6. **leash**—a rope, chain, or cord that attaches to a collar.
7. **paw**—the cat's foot.
8. **pet**—an animal kept for pleasure.
9. **veterinarian**—an animal doctor.
10. **whiskers**—stiff hair growing around the cat's nose, mouth, and eyes.

Bulletin Board

The purpose of this bulletin board is to promote visual discrimination, pattern-matching, problem-solving, and hand-eye coordination skills. Construct cats' bodies and heads out of tagboard, coloring each a different color and fur pattern. Laminate all pieces. Attach cats' bodies to the bulletin board. Children then match the heads to the corresponding body.

Family Letter

Dear Families,

We have many exciting activities planned at school as we begin our study on cats. We will be learning about a cat's body structure, how to care and feed our cats, and different types of cats.

At School

Some of the learning experiences planned include:

- Taking field trips to the veterinarian's office and pet store

- Making a chart of different types of cats

- Setting up a cat-grooming area in dramatic play

- Listening to stories about cats

- Looking at pictures of cats

At Home

We will be learning the fingerplay "Two Little Kittens." You may want to try it with your child at home:

Two little kittens found a ball of yarn
   (hold up two fingers … cup hands together to form a ball)
As they were playing near a barn.
   (bring hands together, pointed upward for barn)
One little kitten jumped in the hay,
   (hold up one finger … make jumping, then wiggling, motions)
The other little kitten ran away.
   (make running motion with other hand)

Fingerplays and rhymes help children develop language vocabulary and sequencing skills.
The actions that often accompany fingerplays develop fine motor development.

Have fun with your child!

Arts and Crafts

1. **Pompon Painting**
   Set out several different colors of tempera paint. Using pompon balls, let children create their own designs on construction paper.

2. **Cat Mask**
   Using paper plates or paper bags along with paper scraps, yarn, crayons, scissors, and paint, let the children design cat masks.

3. **Paw Prints**
   Encourage the children to pretend they are cats, using their hands and paint to make prints.

Cooking

1. **Cheese Cat**
   English muffins
   Cheese slices

   Encourage the children to cut out a cat face on their own slice of cheese. Heat an oven or toaster oven to 300 degrees. Put the cheese on top of the English muffin, and bake long enough to melt the cheese.

2. **Cat Face**
   1/2 peach (head)
   Dried prunes (ears)
   Red Hots (eyes)
   Raisin (nose)
   Stick pretzels (whiskers)

   Create a cat face using the ideas above or a variety of other items.

Dramatic Play

1. **Cat Grooming**
   Provide the children with empty shampoo and conditioner bottles, brushes, combs, ribbons, collars, plastic bathtub, towels, and stuffed animal cats.

2. **Veterinarian's Office**
   Provide various medical supplies such as a stethoscope, bandages, and thermometers along with stuffed cats.

3. **Cats!**
   Let children pretend they are cats by using cat masks or costumes. Also, you may want to try using yarn balls, boxes to curl up in, and empty cat food boxes. Allow the children to act out the story "The Three Little Kittens" or other cat stories.

4. **Circus or Zoo**
   Lions, cheetahs, panthers, leopards, and tigers are also cats. Use large boxes for cages.

Field Trips and Resource People

1. **Pet Store**
   Take a field trip to a pet store. Ask the manager how to care for cats. Observe the different types of cats, cages, collars, leashes, and food.

2. **Veterinarian's Office**
   Take a field trip to a veterinarian's office or animal hospital. Compare the similarities to and differences from a doctor's office.

3. **Pet Supply Store**
   Visit a pet supply store and observe pet accessories.

4. **Resource People**
   Invite resource people. Suggestions include:
   - Cat groomer
   - Humane Society representative
   - Pet store owner
   - Veterinarian
   - Parents to bring in pet cats

Fingerplays and Chants

Mrs. Kitty's Dinner

Mrs. Kitty, sleek and fat,
    (put thumb up with fingers folded on
    right hand)
With her kittens four.
    (hold up four fingers on right hand)
Went to sleep upon the mat
    (make a fist)
By the kitchen door.

Mrs. Kitty heard a noise.
Up she jumped in glee.
    (thumb up on right hand)
"Kittens, maybe that's a mouse?
    (all five fingers on right hand up)
Let's go and see!"

Creeping, creeping, creeping on.
    (slowly sneaking with five fingers on
    floor)
Silently they stole.
But the little mouse had gone
    (mouse is thumb on left hand)
Back into his hole.

Three Cats

One little cat and two little cats
went out for a romp one day.
    (hold up one finger and then two fingers
    with other hand)

One little cat and two little cats
make how many cats at play?
    (ask how many that makes)
Three little cats had lots of fun
till growing tired away ran _____?
    (take one finger away and ask how many
    ran away)
I really think that he was most unkind
to the _____ little cats that were left
   behind.
    (ask how many are left)

Kitten Is Hiding

A kitten is hiding under a chair,
    (hide one thumb in other hand)
I looked and looked for her everywhere.
    (peer about with hand on forehead)

Under the table and under the bed,
    (pretend to look)
I looked in the corner and then I said,
"Come Kitty, come Kitty, I have milk for
   you."
    (cup hands to make dish and extend)
Kitty came running and calling, "Mew,
   mew."
    (run fingers up arm)

Two Little Kittens

Two little kittens found a ball of yarn
    (hold up two fingers … cup hands
    together to form a ball)
As they were playing near a barn.
    (bring hands together, pointed upward for
    barn)
One little kitten jumped in the hay,
    (hold up one finger … make jumping,
    then wiggling, motions)
The other little kitten ran away.
    (make running motion with other hand)

I Love Little Kitty

I love little kitty,
Her coat is so warm.
And if I don't hurt her,
She'll do me no harm.
So I'll not pull her tail,
Nor drive her away.
But kitty and I,
Very gently will play.

Group Time
(Games, Language)

1. **Copycats**

Have one child be the cat, and clap a
rhythm for the group. The other children
listen and then act as copycats. They clap
the same rhythm as the cat did. Another
child now becomes the cat and creates a
rhythm for the copycats to imitate.

2. **Nice Kitty**

One child is chosen to be the kitty. The
rest of the children sit in a circle. As the
kitty goes to each child in the circle, he or
she pets the kitty and says, "Nice kitty,"
but the kitty makes no reply. Finally, the

kitty meows in response to one child. That child must run around the outside of the circle as the kitty chases him or her. If the child returns to his or her original place before the kitty can catch him or her, the child becomes the new kitty. This activity is appropriate for four-, five-, and six-year-old children.

3. Listen Carefully

The children should sit in a circle. One child is selected to be the mother cat. After mother cat has left the room, choose several other children to be kittens. All of the other children cover their mouths with both hands, and the kittens start saying, "Meow, meow, meow." When the mother cat returns, she should listen carefully to find all of her kittens. When she has found them all, another child should be chosen to be mother cat, and the game can continue.

4. Farmer in the Dell

The children stand in a circle. And one child is chosen to be the farmer who is told to move in the middle of the circle. The farmer then selects a wife and brings her into the circle. This same pattern of selection continues throughout the song.

The farmer takes a wife,
The farmer takes a wife,
Heigh-ho, the derry-o,
The farmer takes a wife.
The wife takes a child,
The wife takes a child,
Heigh-ho, the derry-o,
The wife takes a child.
The child takes a nurse,
The child takes a nurse,
Heigh-ho, the dry-o,
The child takes a nurse.
The nurse takes a dog,
The nurse takes a dog,
Heigh-ho, a derry-o,
The nurse takes a dog.
The dog takes a cat,
The dog takes a cat,
Heigh-ho, a derry-o,
The dog takes a cat.
The cat takes a rat,
The cat takes a rat,
Heigh-ho, the derry-o,
The cat takes a rat.

The rat takes the cheese,
The rat takes the cheese,
Heigh-ho, the derry-o,
Heigh-ho, the derry-o,
The rat takes the cheese.
The cheese stands alone,
The cheese stands alone,
Heigh-ho, the derry-o,
The cheese stands alone.

The children can play "Farmer in the Dell."

Large Muscle

1. Bean Bag Toss

Make a cat shape on plywood with holes of different sizes cut out. The children can try from varying distances to throw bean bags through the holes.

2. Yarn Balls

Set up baskets at varying distances from a masking tape line on the floor. Toss yarn balls into the baskets.

3. Cat Pounce

Children pretend to be cats and pounce from one tape line to another.

4. Climbing Cats

Bring a wooden climber into the classroom or set it up outside. The children can pretend to be cats and climb on the climber.

5. Cat Movements

Write down all the words that describe how cats move. Allow the children to demonstrate the movements. Also, use music in the background.

6. Kitty, Kitty, Cat

Play a variation of "Duck, Duck, Goose" by saying "Kitty, Kitty, Cat."

Math

1. Matching Game

Have the children match the number of cats on a card to the correct numeral. (Cat stickers work well.)

2. How Many Paper Clips?

Make several different sizes of cats out of tagboard. Children measure each cat with the paper clips.

3. Whisker Count

Make several cat faces with one numeral on each face. Children attach the correct number of whiskers (chenille stems, felt, paper strips, etc.) according to the numeral on the cat.

Music

1. "Two Little Kittens"

(Sing to the tune of "Two Little Blackbirds")

Two little kittens sitting on a hill
One named Jack, one named Jill
Run away, Jack, run away, Jill
Come back, Jack, come back, Jill
Two little kittens sitting on a hill
One named Jack, one named Jill.

2. "Kitty"

(Sing to the tune of "Bingo")

I have a cat. She's very shy.
But she comes when I call Kitty.
K-I-T-T-Y
K-I-T-T-Y
K-I-T-T-Y
And Kitty is her name-o.

Variation: Let children think of other names.

3. "Three Little Kittens"

Three little kittens lost their mittens;
And they began to cry,
"Oh, mother dear, we very much fear
Our mittens we have lost."
"What! Lost your mittens! You naughty
      kittens!
Then you shall have no pie."
"Mee-ow, mee-ow, mee-ow, mee-ow."
"No, you shall have no pie."
The three little kittens they found their
      mittens;
And they began to cry,
"Oh, Mother dear, see here, see here!
Our mittens we have found."
"What! Found your mittens! You good little
      kittens!

Now you shall have some pie."
"Purr, purr, purr, purr,
Purr, purr, purr."

Science

1. Provide a scale and different cat items (such as cat toys, a collar, a food dish, etc.) to weigh.
2. During the social studies activity "Share Your Cat," arrange for a cat and a kitten to be in the classroom at the same time. With the help of parents, weigh the cats or kittens and discuss the differences with the children.
3. Set out a magnifying glass to observe different kinds of dry cat food.
4. Talk about a cat that has claws and one that is declawed. Ask various questions such as "Why do cats have claws?" "Why are cats declawed?" and "Where do cats go to be declawed?"
5. Discuss the various parts of a cat's body and how they can protect the cat (for example, fur and whiskers).
6. Discuss what a cat's body does when the cat senses danger.

Social Studies

1. Chart

With the children, make a chart of different types of cats.

2. Displays

Display different pictures of cats around the room.

3. Share Your Cat

Invite the children and the parents to bring in a pet cat on specified days. (Have your camera ready! Take pictures and display them on a bulletin board.) Encourage the children to talk about their cat's colors, likes, body, and so on.

4. Cat Safety

Discuss cat safety with the class. Items that may be discussed include why cats use their claws, what to do if you find a stray cat, and the uses of collars and leashes.

 **Books**

The following books can be used to complement this theme:

Bottner, Barbara. (2002). *The Scaredy Cats.* Illustrated by Victoria Chess. New York: Simon & Schuster for Young Readers.

Brown, Margaret Wise, Alice Provensen, and Martin Provensen. (2000). *The Color Kittens.* Illustrated by Alice Provensen and Martin Provensen. New York: Golden Books.

Carle, Eric. (1991). *Have You Seen My Cat?* Saxonville, MA: Picture Book Studio.

Dodd, Emma. (2010). *I Don't Want a Cool Cat.* New York: Little, Brown.

Doering, Amanda. (2005). *Cats ABC: An Alphabet Book.* Mankato, MN: Capstone Press.

Gag, Wanda. (1996). *Millions of Cats.* New York: Putnam.

Gallup, Tracy. (2006). *King Cat.* Traverse City, MI: Mackinac Island Press.

Gorbachev, Valeri. (2010). *The Best Cat.* Somerville, MA: Candlewick Press.

Hogrogian, Nonny. (2009). *Cool Cat.* New York: Roaring Brook Press.

Huseby, Victoria. (2009). *Cat.* Mankato, MN: Black Rabbit Books.

Ipcizade, Catherine. (2008). *Lions.* Mankato, MN: Capstone Press.

Kwon, Yoon-duck. (2007). *My Cat Copies Me.* La Jolla, CA: Kane/Miller.

Lakin, Patricia. (2007). *Clarence the Copy Cat.* Illustrated by John Manders. New York: Dragonfly Books.

Lewis, J. Patrick. (2009). *The Kindergarten Cat.* Illustrated by Ailie Busby. New York: Schwartz & Wade Books.

Litwin, Eric. (2010). *Pete the Cat: I Love My White Shoes.* Illustrated by James Dean. New York: Harper.

Martin, Bill, and Michael Sampson. (2008). *Kitty Cat, Kitty Cat, Are You Waking Up?* Illustrated by Laura J. Bryant. New York: Marshall Cavendish.

Nishizuka, Koko. (2009). *The Beckoning Cat: Based on a Japanese Folktale.* Illustrated by Rosanne Litzinger. New York: Holiday House.

Nodset, Joan L. (2008). *Come Back, Cat.* Illustrated by Steven Kellogg. New York: Harper Collins Children's Books.

Numeroff, Laura Joffe. (2009). *If You Give a Cat a Cupcake.* Illustrated by Felicia Bond. New York: Laura Geringer Books.

Picayo, Mario. (2008). *A Very Smart Cat / Una Gata Muy Inteligente.* Illustrated by Yolanda V. Fundora. New York: Editorial Campanita Books.

Rylant, Cynthia. (2006). *Mr. Putter and Tabby Spin the Yarn.* Illustrated by Arthur Howard. Orlando, FL: Harcourt.

Scotton, Rob. (2008). *Splat the Cat.* New York: HarperCollins.

Scotton, Rob. (2010). *Scaredy-Cat, Splat!* New York: Harper.

Simon, Seymour. (1991). *Big Cats.* New York: HarperCollins.

Smith, Linda. (2006). *Mrs. Crump's Cat.* Illustrated by David Roberts. New York: HarperCollins.

Spinelli, Eileen. (2007). *Callie Cat, Ice Skater.* Illustrated by Anne Kennedy. Morton Grove, IL: Albert Whitman.

Spinelli, Eileen, and Anne Mortimer. (2001). *Kittycat Lullaby.* Illustrated by Anne Mortimer. New York: Hyperion Press.

Tan, Amy, and Gretchen Shields. (2001). *SAGWA, the Chinese Siamese Cat.* Illustrated by Gretchen Shields. New York: Aladdin Paperbacks.

Teckentrup, Britta. (2008). *Grumpy Cat.* London: Boxer.

Thomson, Ruth. (2008). *The Life Cycle of a Cat.* New York: Powerkids Press.

Varon, Sara. (2006). *Chicken and Cat.* New York: Scholastic.

Walton, Rick. (2006). *The Remarkable Friendship of Mr. Cat and Mr. Rat.* Illustrated by Lisa McCue. New York: Putnam.

Weaver, Tess. (2007). *Cat Jumped In!*
    Illustrated by Emily Arnold McCully.
    New York: Clarion Books.

Technology and Multimedia

The following technology and multimedia products can be used to complement this theme:

"Itty Bitty Kitty in NYC" [CD]. (2001). In *Ants Wear Underpants*. New York: BizzyBum.

"Pete the Cat and His White Shoes" [CD]. (2006). In *The Big Silly with Mr. Eric*. Atlanta, GA: Mr. Eric.

"Three Little Kittens" [CD]. (1999). In *Sounds Like Fun*. Buena Park, CA: Barbara Milne.

"Three Little Kittens" [CD]. (2007). In *Nursery Rhymes and Good Ol' Times*. Oklahoma City, OK: Melody House.

Additional teaching resources to accompany this Theme can be found on the book's companion website. Go to www.cengagebrain.com to access the site for a variety of useful resources.

Theme 14
CHINESE NEW YEAR

Foods
puffed rice cakes (sweet
new year)
steamed buns (good luck)
shrimp (wealth and plenty)
beef (strength)
fried rice (harmony)
long noodles (long life)
duck (happiness)
pan-fried fish (luck)
cakes and candies (peace
and togetherness)

Preparation
cleans the house
shops for new clothes and
shoes,
decorates with red banner
brings flowers and candy
to extended family,
cooks for the feast

Color
red

Sounds
drums
cymbals
firecrackers and fireworks

Animals in Zodiac
rat
ox
tiger
rabbit
dragon
ram (sheep)
horse
monkey
rooster
dog
pig, snake

Symbols
oranges (wealth)
tangerines with leaves
(good luck),
flowers (rebirth)
dragon (strength)
twelve animals of the
Chinese zodiac,
red envelopes called
"lai see"

Celebration
celebrate for two weeks
welcomes spring,
greets bright moon
watches dragon parade
fireworks,
plays drums and cymbals,
receive presents and money
brings gifts to family and
friends,
wear bright clothing
say, "may you prosper",
eats, sings, talks, and
laughs

Theme Goals

Through participating in the experiences provided by this theme, the children may learn:

1. Chinese New Year celebrations
2. Preparation for Chinese New Year
3. Special foods prepared for Chinese New Year
4. Chinese New Year sounds
5. Red is the color that symbolizes Chinese New Year
6. Other symbols of Chinese New Year

Concepts for the Children to Learn

1. Chinese New Year is a holiday celebrated the first two weeks in January or February by Chinese people all over the world.
2. There are many symbols that are used for Chinese New Year.
3. Oranges are a symbol of wealth and flowers are symbols of rebirth.
4. Tangerines and leaves are symbols of good luck.
5. A dragon is a symbol of strength.
6. Chinese New Year is a time to welcome the beginning of spring.
7. Families prepare by cleaning, shopping and cooking.
8. Puffed rice, steamed buns, shrimp, beef, fried rice, long noodles, duck, pan-fried fish, cakes, and candies are eaten.
9. Special foods are eaten to bring luck, health, harmony, strength, happiness, peace, togetherness, and wealth in the new year.
10. Everyone gets new clothing or shoes and a haircut.
11. On New Year's Eve, there is a big dancing dragon parade and people wear bright clothing.
12. Doors and windows are opened to let the old year out and the new year in.
13. Children play drums and cymbals.
14. Firecrackers and fireworks are set off.
15. Some people dance together in a dragon costume at the parade.
16. Lanterns are used to greet the bright moon.
17. People eat, sing, talk, and laugh.
18. Children are given money in red envelopes.
19. Candy, flower, melon seeds, and cakes are given to family and friends.
20. Every person is born in a year of a particular animal—the rat, ox, tiger, rabbit, dragon, snake, horse, sheep, monkey, rooster, dog, or pig.

Vocabulary

1. **celebrate**—to observe a holiday and have a good time.
2. **cymbals**—two pieces of metal you can bang together to make music.
3. **feast**—a big, delicious meal.
4. **festival**—a party or celebration that usually happens every year.
5. **fireworks**—bright lights and loud noises.
6. **lai see**—red envelopes given to children during Chinese New Year.
7. **lantern**—a light usually used outside.
8. **parade**—people walking all together to celebrate.
9. **symbol**—something that stands for something else. For example, a heart can be a symbol of Valentine's Day.

Bulletin Board

The purpose of this bulletin board is to develop hand-eye coordination, visual-matching, and counting skills. Create this bulletin board by making and hanging five red envelopes numbered from 1 to 5. Cut out 15 gold circles for coins. Let your children take turns filling the envelopes with coins to match the numbers on the outside of each envelope.

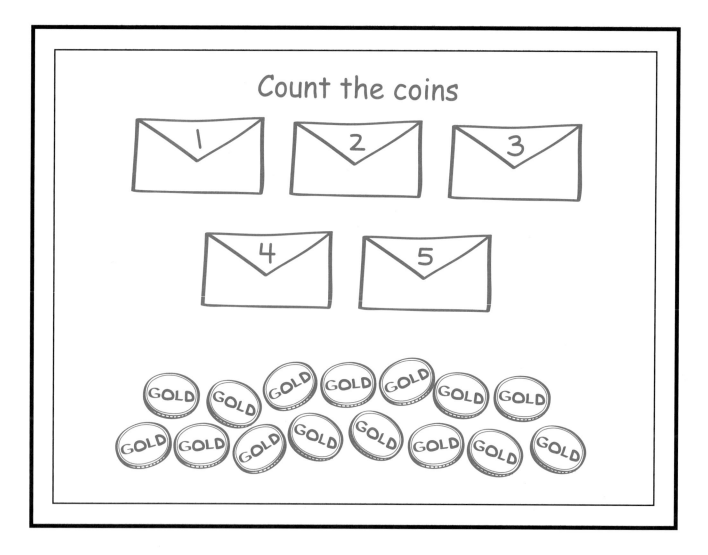

Family Letter

InBox

Dear Families,

Our next theme will focus on the exciting and colorful holiday of Chinese New Year. Many learning experiences have been planned to promote an awareness of the colors, sounds, and symbols of Chinese New Year. We are aware that many families do not celebrate this holiday, but we feel it is important for children to learn about and respect a diversity of customs.

The Chinese New Year is celebrated for two weeks to prepare for the arrival of spring. Everyone cleans out their homes and workplaces. Families go shopping for new clothing and shoes. Oranges are given as a symbol of money or wealth, along with tangerines, flowers, and sweets. Red banners with sayings and poems are hung on doorways and given to friends and family. A big parade on the last night features bright lanterns, firecrackers, drums, cymbals, and a huge dragon dance. There is always a big feast featuring symbolic foods to welcome the new year.

The Chinese calendar is based around the moon and divides the years into groups of 12. Each year is named for an animal in the zodiac. Every person is born in the year of a particular animal—the rat, ox, tiger, rabbit, dragon, snake, horse, sheep, monkey, rooster, dog, or pig. The belief is that people born in the year of a particular animal have traits or characteristics of that animal. You can find your animal and your child's animal on the chart on the back of this letter!

At School

Some of the Chinese New Year activities planned include:

- Making red envelopes and stuffing them with money made from tin foil

- Preparing traditional Chinese foods for snack

- A parade with cymbals, drums, and noisemakers

Gung hay fat choy—may you prosper!

The Chinese Zodiac

	Tiger: 1938, 1950, 1962, 1974, 1986, 1998, 2010 Tiger people are brave, powerful, loyal, and proud. Tigers make great friends.
	Rabbit: 1939, 1951, 1963, 1975, 1987, 1999, 2011 Rabbit people are lucky, happy, independent, affectionate, and gentle.
	Dragon: 1940, 1952, 1964, 1976, 1988, 2000, 2012 Dragon people are bold, successful, full of energy, and incredibly lucky.
	Snake: 1941, 1953, 1965, 1977, 1989, 2001, 2013 Snake people are wise and focused, and they trust their own judgment.
	Horse: 1942, 1954, 1966, 1978, 1990, 2002, 2014 Horse people are popular, cheerful, clever, and shy.
	Ram (Black or Gray Sheep): 1943, 1955, 1967, 1979, 1991, 2003, 2015 Sheep people are elegant, wise, sincere, and artistic.
	Monkey: 1944, 1956, 1968, 1980, 1992, 2004, 2016 Monkey people are quick, funny, original, clever, witty, and successful.
	Rooster: 1945, 1957, 1969, 1981, 1993, 2005, 2017 Rooster people are early risers, proud, alert, deep thinkers, and adventurous.
	Dog: 1946, 1958, 1970, 1982, 1994, 2006, 2018 Dog people are loyal friends, quick learners, and eager to please.
	Pig: 1947, 1959, 1971, 1983, 1995, 2007, 2019 People born in the Year of the Pig are intelligent, trustworthy, brave, and kind.
	Rat: 1948, 1960, 1972, 1984, 1996, 2008, 2020 People born in the Year of the Rat are loving, cheerful, charming, and hard-working.
	Ox: 1949, 1961, 1973, 1985, 1997, 2009, 2021 Ox people are easygoing, slow to anger, and self-assured.

Arts and Crafts

1. **Red Play Dough**
Make play dough and use red food coloring to make it red—the color of happiness. Animal-shaped cookie cutters (such as the animals in the Chinese zodiac) and rolling pins can extend this activity.

2. **Chinese Red and Yellow Paper Chains**
In advance, cut strips of red and yellow paper 2 inches wide (thinner if you want a daintier bracelet) and approximately 5 inches long. Teach the children to make a chain alternating red and yellow strips. First take a yellow strip, shape it into a ring, and tape the ends together. Then put a red strip through the yellow ring and tape the ends of the red strip together to form another ring. Continue this process until you have a chain. Hang the chains around the room or connect them all together to form one long chain.

3. **Red Door Hangers**
In advance, cut out red construction paper lengthwise (each strip will be 4.25 × 11 inches). Also prepare smaller white paper with New Year's wishes or sayings typed on them, such as these:

You are amazing
Good luck!
Happy New Year!
Health and happiness

Have the children glue a saying on their red door hanger. Punch a hole near the top center of the hanger. Put some red yarn through the hole, and tie it in a knot. Make the yarn loop big enough to hang on a doorknob.

4. **Red Envelopes**
At Chinese New Year, it is traditional for parents and elders to give gifts of "lucky money" to children. The money, which can vary from a small, new coin to a substantial sum, is always presented in a red envelope. Have the children make money out of foil and paper to put in the envelopes. Give them squares of red paper. Have them fold in the corners to meet in the middle and seal it with a gold sticker. If they wish, they can decorate the envelope to make it more special. The envelopes could be given to friends or family members.

5. **Painting Fireworks**
Explain fireworks to the children and show pictures if you have them. Hand out pieces of black paper. Have the children put small drops of paint on their picture and then blow these drops with a straw. Before the paint is dry, have them sprinkle glitter on the pictures. Have the children see if they can think of other ways to paint fireworks.

6. **Lanterns**
Provide a piece of 9-inch × 12-inch construction paper already folded in half in either direction. Using a pair of scissors, help them cut slits from the fold to within 1 inch of the opposite edge all along the fold (approximately 1 inch apart). Be sure to stop 1 inch before the edge. You may need to draw cutting lines before they begin. Then bend the paper into a cylinder and tape flaps together at the top and bottom. Punch two holes at the top of the lantern, and tie short strings to hang the lantern. The lanterns can be strung across your room on a string, or attached to a pole for holding a lantern parade.

7. **Chinese New Year Gift Bags**
Provide the children with paper bags and red washable magic markers. Encourage them to use the markers to create gift bags.

Cooking

1. Chinese Moon Cakes
1/4 cup sugar
2 egg yolks
1/2 cup salted butter
1 cup all-purpose flour
1 cup strawberry jam (or use a traditional can of red bean paste)

Preheat the oven to 375 degrees. Combine the butter, sugar, and 1 egg yolk and stir. Mix in the flour. Form the dough into one large ball and wrap it in plastic wrap. Refrigerate dough for half an hour. Unwrap the chilled dough and form small balls in the palms of your hand. Make a hole with your thumb in the center of each moon cake and fill with about half a teaspoon of jam. Brush each cake with the other beaten egg yolk (optional) and place on a cookie sheet. Bake for about 20 minutes or just until the outside edges are slightly brown. Makes 24.

2. Egg Fried Rice
1 1/2 cups uncooked instant rice
1 tablespoon sesame oil
Soy sauce to taste
2 eggs, beaten
1 teaspoon finely chopped fresh ginger root
1/4 cup finely chopped green onions
1 cup frozen peas and carrots (optional)

Bring water to a boil in a medium saucepan. Stir in rice and cover. Remove from heat and let stand 5 minutes. Fluff with a fork and drain any excess water. Heat oil in a large skillet over medium heat. Stir in rice, peas and carrots (optional), and soy sauce; heat for 5 minutes, then transfer rice to a bowl. Scramble the eggs in the same skillet, then stir in rice. Stir in ginger and green onions; heat through and serve for lunch or snack.

3. Long Life Noodles
8 cups lightly salted water
1/2 pound dried thin egg noodles or spaghetti
3 cups chicken broth or stock
1 tablespoon soy sauce, or to taste 1 teaspoon sesame oil
2 teaspoons cornstarch mixed with 4 teaspoons water
2 eggs, lightly beaten
3 green onions (spring onions), finely chopped
1/2–2/3 cup chopped cooked ham or chicken (optional).

Bring the salted water to a boil and parboil the noodles, using chopsticks to separate them. Rinse the noodles repeatedly in cold water and drain thoroughly. Divide the noodles equally among soup bowls. Bring the broth or stock to a boil over medium heat. Stir in the soy sauce, sesame oil, and pepper. Give the cornstarch and water a quick restir, and stir it in with the broth or stock. Remove the saucepan from the heat. Add the beaten egg, pouring it slowly through the tines of a fork and stirring rapidly in one direction for about 1 minute. Pour the hot broth over the noodles. Garnish with the chopped ham or chicken and green onion. Cool and serve for snack or lunch.

Dramatic Play

1. Shopping
Set up a grocery store in the dramatic play area. If possible, include oranges, tangerines, cakes, and candies—foods that are eaten during the holiday. To stimulate play, provide a cash register, shopping bags, and empty containers such as boxes, packages, and plastic bottles. Invite everyone to "go shopping" for the New Year's feast.

2. Cleaning House
Put on some music and provide cleaning supplies such as short brooms, dustpans, mops, plastic toy vacuums, and dust rags. Invite everyone to dust, wipe, and sweep to get the classroom ready for New Year.

3. Parade, Parade
Give children drums, shakers, cymbals, and animal masks. Invite them to march together and make a parade.

4. Dragon Dance

Paint a large dragon's head on a grocery bag. Attach a long piece of butcher paper for the body. Decorate it with glitter, sequins, and feathers to make it fancy. Have the children make up dances and take turns being the head and the body.

Field Trips and Resource People

Invite someone of Chinese descent, or someone who has visited China or been involved in a Chinese New Year celebration. Have them share with the children the things they heard, saw, and did during a Chinese New Year celebration. Encourage the visitor to bring any artifacts and pictures to share.

Fingerplays and Chants

Chinese New Year Story

Five strong dragons marching out the door,
   (hold up five fingers)
One ran away and then there were four.
   (running motion with hand)
Four strong dragons waving to you and me,
   (four fingers)
One climbed a tree, and then there were three.
   (climbing motion with fingers)
Three strong dragons breathing fire on your shoe,
   (three fingers)
One joined the lion dance and there were two.
   (say "roar")
Two strong dragons starting to run,
   (two fingers)
One got lost and then there was one.
   (one finger)
One strong dragon laughing having fun,
He fell asleep and then there were none!
   (make motions as if to fall asleep, and then put hands in lap)

Group Time
(Games, Language)

1. Drum and Flower Game

You will need a drum (traditional) or CD player, and a flower (real or paper). Have players sit in a circle. The person with the drum sits just outside the circle. As the drum beats, players pass the flower to the next person. When the drum stops, whoever is holding the flower must get up, go to the center of the circle, and do a crazy dance or bow. When the performer is finished, the game starts over, only this time the person who just performed gets to be the drummer!

2. Hot Orange Potato

Play hot potato with an orange (an important symbol in Chinese New Year).

3. Red Envelope Hunt

Remind children that red envelopes with money are given as gifts for the Chinese New Year. Hide a red envelope in the classroom and play a hide-and-seek game. For younger children, hide the envelope in an obvious place.

4. Year of the _____

Provide the children with verbal and visual clues to act like the animal of the current year, according to the Chinese zodiac. For example, 2011 = rabbit, 2012 = dragon, 2013 = snake, 2014 = horse, 2015 = snake, 2016 = monkey, 2017 = rooster, 2018 = dog, and so on. For example, for the year of the monkey (2016), you might try these:

- Happy monkey
- Sneaky monkey
- Hungry monkey
- Silly monkey
- Sad monkey
- Tired monkey
- Excited monkey

5. Red Color Games

Since red is seen everywhere at Chinese New Year's time, use the celebration to review the color with your children. Here are a few things to try.

- Select items of red clothing to wear, and encourage your children to do the same.

- Play an "I Spy" game with your children looking for red objects.
- Go for a "red walk" to find things that are red.

Math

1. Chinese New Year Puzzle
Mount pictures of oranges and flowers on tagboard. Cut into pieces. Laminate. The number of pieces will depend on the children's developmental age.

2. Lion Dance
Write the numbers 1 through 5 on pieces of paper, and hang them around the room where children can see them. Have the children hop, dance, or jump from 1 to 2 to 3 and so on all the way to 5 as they count and sing aloud:

(Sing to the tune of "If You're Happy and You Know It")

If you're in the lion dance, sing a 1
If you're in the lion dance, sing a 1
If you're in the lion dance, and you really
    want to dance, if you're in the lion
    dance, sing a 1
If you're in the lion dance, sing a 2
If you're in the lion dance, sing a 2
If you're in the lion dance, and you really
    want to dance, if you're in the lion
    dance, sing a 2
If you're in the lion dance, sing a 3
If you're in the lion dance, sing a 3
If you're in the lion dance, and you really
    want to dance, if you're in the lion
    dance, sing a 3
If you're in the lion dance, sing a 4
If you're in the lion dance, sing a 4
If you're in the lion dance, and you really
    want to dance, if you're in the lion
    dance, sing a 4
If you're in the lion dance, sing a 5
If you're in the lion dance, sing a 5
If you're in the lion dance, and you really
    want to dance, if you're in the lion
    dance, sing a 5

Music

1. "For Chinese New Year"
(Sing to the tune of "Skip to My Lou")

Sweep, sweep, sweep the floor.
Sweep, sweep, sweep the floor.
Sweep, sweep, sweep the floor.
Sweep the floor for New Year's.

Snip, snip, get a haircut.
Snip, snip, get a haircut.
Snip, snip, get a haircut.
Get a haircut for New Year's.

Shop, shop, shop for new clothes.
Shop, shop, shop for new clothes.
Shop, shop, shop for new clothes.
Shop for new clothes on New Year's.

Light, light, light the lanterns.
Light, light, light the lanterns.
Light, light, light the lanterns.
Light the lanterns for New Year's.

Beat, beat, beat the drums.
Beat, beat, beat the drums.
Beat, beat, beat the drums.
Beat the drums for New Year's!

2. "Gung Hay Fat Choy—Chinese New Year Song"
(This song wishes you good fortune and happiness. Sing as a fingerplay with the simple hand motions, or pass out rhythm instruments and have children play on the chorus. Keep a rhythm by patting hands together with one hand up, then the other.)

Chorus: Gung Hay Fat Choy, Gung Hay Fat Choy Sing Happy New Year, Gung Hay Fat Choy

1. The new moon tells us, exactly when (hold up one hand in C shape for crescent moon) To celebrate with family and friends (clap hands in rhythm) *(Sing chorus.)*
2. Clean up the house and get out the broom (pretend to sweep) Sweep out the old year, bring in the new *(Sing chorus.)*
3. Bring out the apples, the oranges too (hold out one fist, then the other) Their colors bring us joy and good luck too *(Sing chorus.)*

4. The dragon dances, the lanterns light
(place hands together, and snake around)
The firecrackers light up the night
(alternate right and left fist out with
fingers opening quickly to mimic shooting
fireworks) *(Sing chorus.)*

Source: From http://www.nancymusic.com.

3. "Dragon, Dragon"
(Sing to the tune of "Twinkle, Twinkle Little Star")

Dragon, dragon, dance around.
Dragon, dragon, touch the ground.
Dragon, dragon, shake your head.
Dragon, dragon, tongue so red.
Dragon, dragon, stamp your feet.
Dragon, dragon, coming down the street!

Source: Heather McPhail.

Science

1. Planting Seeds
Put small amounts of soil in small paper
cups. Distribute seeds for flowers that
are easy to grow, such as marigolds or
sunflowers. Place the cups in the sun, water
regularly, and watch the seeds grow.

2. Lantern Light
Light a lantern. Show the children how a
lantern works. Talk about other sources
of light (such as the sun, a lamp, a candle,
traffic lights, and so on).

Sensory

1. Preparing Food
Place play plastic fruits and vegetables in
the sensory table. Provide scrub brushes for
the children to clean and prepare the fruits
and vegetables for a Chinese New Year
feast.

2. Dusting
Place small, soft rags in the sensory table.
Invite children to use them to dust the area

(to clean up) to get ready for Chinese New
Year.

3. Clay Chinese Zodiac Animals
Make red clay. Place it in the sensory table
with animal cookie cutters that match the
animals of the Chinese New Year zodiac—
such as the monkey, snake, rabbit, horse,
rooster, and dog. Encourage the children
to use these during self-directed or self-
initiated play.

Social Studies

1. Chinese New Year Photographs
Display various pictures of the Chinese
New Year traditions at the children's eye
level. Examples would include pictures
of the dragon dance, the parade, the red
envelopes, the lanterns lit up at night, or a
family gathered around the feast table or an
altar of oranges and red envelopes.

2. Map It
Show a globe or world map and point to
where you are. Then show the children
where China is so they can understand that
many Chinese people live in China, and this
is where the holiday originates. Also explain
that there are Chinese people now living all
over the world—including right in the area
where you live.

3. Zodiac Signs
Prepare a piece of tagboard with zodiac
signs and pieces with each child's name
and birth date. Talk about the signs. Then
encourage each child to place his or her
picture under the correct sign.

Books

Ada, Alma F., and F. Isabel Campoy. (2006).
*Celebrate Chinese New Year with the Fong
Family (Stories to Celebrate).* Madrid:
Alfaguara Infantil.

Bouchard, David. (1999). *The Dragon New
Year: A Chinese Legend (Chinese Legends*

Trilogy). Illustrated by Zhong-Yang Huang. Atlanta, GA: Peachtree Publishers.

Chinn, Karen. (1997). *Sam and the Lucky Money.* Illustrated by Cornelius Van Wright and Ying-Hwa Hu. Logan, IA: Perfection Learning.

Compestine, Ying Chang. (2011). *The Runaway Wok: A Chinese New Year Tale.* New York: Dutton Juvenile.

Demi. (1999). *Happy New Year / Kung-his fa-ts'ai!* New York: Dragonfly Books.

Demi. (2003). *Happy, Happy Chinese New Year.* New York: Crown Books for Young Readers.

Dougherty, Terri. (2006). *Chinese New Year: Festival of New Beginnings.* Mankato, MN: Capstone Press.

Drew, Rosa, and Heather Phillips. (1999). *Celebrating Chinese New Year: Nick's New Year.* Illustrated by Cheryl Kirk Noll. Huntington Beach, CA: Creative Teaching Press.

Flannagan, Alice K. (2004). *Chinese New Year.* Illustrated by Svetlana Zhurkina. Minneapolis, MN: Compass Point Books.

Gleason, Carrie. (2008). *Chinese New Year (Celebrations in My World).* New York: Crabtree Publishing Company.

Holub, Joan, and Benrei Huang. (2003). *Dragon Dance: A Chinese New Year Lift-the-Flap Book.* New York: Puffin.

Hoyt-Goldsmith, Diane. (1999). *Celebrating Chinese New Year.* Illustrated by Lawrence Migdale. New York: Holiday House.

Jango-Cohen, Judith. (2004). *Chinese New Year.* On My Own: Holidays. Minneapolis, MN: Carolrhoda Books.

Katz, Karen. (2004). *My First Chinese New Year.* New York: Henry Holt.

Lin, Grace. (2003). *Dim Sum for Everyone.* New York: Dragonfly Books.

Lin, Grace (2004). *Kite Flying.* New York: Dragonfly Books.

Lin, Grace. (2008). *Bringing in the New Year.* New York: Knopf Books for Young Readers.

Marx, David E. (2002). *Chinese New Year.* Rookie Read-Aloud Holidays. Danbury, CT: Children's Press

Morrissey, Tricia. (2006). *Hiss! Pop! Boom! Celebrating Chinese New Year.* St. Paul, MN: Things Asian Press.

Otto, Carolyn. (2009). *Celebrate Chinese New Year with Fireworks, Dragons, and Lanterns.* National Geographic Holidays Around the World series. Washington, DC: National Geographic.

Roberts, Cindy. (2002). *Chinese New Years for Kids.* New York: Chinasprout.

Simonds, Nina, and Leslie Swartz. (2002). *Moonbeams, Dumplings and Dragon Boats: A Treasury of Chinese Holiday Tales, Activities and Recipes.* Illustrated by Meilo So. Boston: Harcourt Children's Books.

Thong, Roseanne. (2008). *Red Is a Dragon.* Illustrated by Grace Lin. San Francisco: Chronicle Books.

Vaughan, Marcia K. (1996). *The Dancing Dragon.* Illustrated by Stanley Wong Hoo Foon. New York: Mondo Publishing.

Waters, Kate. (1991). *Lion Dancer: Ernie Wan's Chinese New Year.* Reading Rainbow Books. New York: Scholastic Press.

Wong, Janet S. (2000). *This Next New Year.* Illustrated by Yangsook Choi. New York: Frances Foster Books/Farrar, Straus and Giroux.

Zucker, Jonny. (2003). *Lanterns and Firecrackers: A Chinese New Year Story (Festival Time).* Illustrated by Jan Barger Cohen. Hauppauge, NY: Barron's Educational Series.

Technology and Multimedia

The following technology and multimedia resources can be used to complement this theme:

Cooking with Kids: Celebrating Chinese New Year [video]. (2009). San Francisco: Ni Hao Productions.

Hanukkah and Chinese New Year [CD]. (2002). Long Branch, NJ: Kimbo.

Heart of the Dragon Ensemble. (2007). *Chinese New Years Music* [CD with book]. London: Arc Music.

Holiday Times: Songs, Stories, Rhymes and Chants for Christmas, Kwanza, Hanukkah, Chinese New Year and St. Patrick's Day

[CD]. (2000). Washington, DC: Smithsonian Folkways.

 Additional teaching resources to accompany this Theme can be found on the book's companion website. Go to www.cengagebrain.com to access the site for a variety of useful resources.

Theme 15
CHRISTMAS

Sounds
songs (carols)
bells

Colors
red
green
white

Foods
cookies
eggnog
candy canes

Symbols
ornaments
lights, gifts
stockings
Christmas cards
Santa Claus
star, garland
piñata, elves
wreaths, reindeer

Activities
decorating tree
hanging wreath
shopping
wrapping
giving gifts
sending cards
visiting families and
friends

Plants
trees
poinsettias
mistletoe
holly

Theme Goals

Through participating in the experiences provided by this theme, the children may learn:

1. Christmas colors
2. Christmas foods
3. Christmas plants
4. Christmas symbols
5. Christmas sounds
6. Christmas activities

Concepts for the Children to Learn

1. Christmas is a special time of the year for many people.
2. Red, green, and white are Christmas colors.
3. People make special foods during Christmas.
4. Cookies, eggnog, candy, and candy canes are Christmas foods.
5. Santa Claus, reindeer, stockings, and Christmas trees are symbols of Christmas.
6. Decorating Christmas trees and hanging a wreath are Christmas activities.
7. Christmas ornaments, lights, and garlands are hung on Christmas trees.
8. There are special Christmas songs.
9. A star is an ornament that can be placed on the top of the tree.
10. Bells and Christmas carols are sounds heard at Christmas.
11. Poinsettias, evergreen trees, holly, and mistletoe are Christmas plants.
12. Many people spend Christmas visiting their families and friends.
13. Some people hang special stockings that get filled with candy and small gifts.
14. Christmas is a time for giving and receiving gifts for some people.
15. Christians believe that Jesus was born on Christmas day.
16. People shop for gifts and wrap them in bright, pretty papers.
17. People send Christmas cards to their family and friends.

Vocabulary

1. **Christmas**—a special time of the year for some families.
2. **carol**—a Christmas song.
3. **evergreen tree**—a tree decorated for the Christmas holidays.
4. **ornament**—a decoration for the home or tree.
5. **piñata**—a brightly colored papier-mâché figure that is filled with candy and gifts.
6. **present**—a gift.
7. **reindeer**—animals used to pull Santa's sleigh.
8. **Santa Claus**—a jolly man who wears a red suit and symbolizes Christmas.
9. **star**—a treetop decoration.
10. **stocking**—a large Christmas sock.
11. **wreath**—a decoration made from evergreen branches.

Bulletin Board

The purpose of this bulletin board is to foster a positive self-concept, as well as name-recognition skills. Construct a stocking out of tagboard for each child in your class. Print the name across the top, and punch a hole in the top with a paper punch. Hang a Christmas poster or teacher-made poster in the center of the bulletin board. Next, attach pushpins to the bulletin board, allowing enough room for each stocking to hang on a pin. The children can hang their own stockings on the bulletin board as they arrive each day.

Family Letter

Dear Families,

The holiday season is approaching. As we drive through our neighborhoods, we are beginning to see decorations. Holiday songs are heard, and Santa is in the thoughts and sentences of many children. At school we will be participating in many Christmas activities. The children will learn the colors, plants, and symbols that are associated with the Christmas season. Perhaps not all children and families in our program celebrate this holiday, but we feel it is very important for children to learn about and respect others' beliefs. A general understanding and acceptance of other cultures can be interesting and fun.

At School

A few of the Christmas learning experiences planned include:

- Creating ornaments to decorate the classroom Christmas tree
- Painting with pine boughs at the easel
- Making Christmas cookies
- Designing Christmas cards in the art area
- Practicing songs for our holiday program.

At Home

Music and singing are wonderful ways to communicate our feelings, and we often have many feelings this time of year!

Reminder

Our last day of school will be December 23. School will open again on January 3 of the new year.

Enjoy singing Christmas carols with your child!

Arts and Crafts

1. **Christmas Chains**
   Cut sheets of red, green, and white construction paper into strips. Demonstrate how to form the links. The links can be pasted, taped, or stapled, depending on the developmental level of the children.

2. **Cookie Cutter Painting**
   Provide Christmas cookie cutters, paper, and shallow pans containing red and green paint. The children can apply the paint to the paper using the cookie cutters as printing tools.

3. **Rudolph**
   Begin the activity by encouraging the children to trace their shoe. This will be used for Rudolph's face. Then the children should trace both of their hands, which will be used as the reindeer's antlers. Finally, cut out a red circle to be used as the reindeer's nose. Have the children paste all the pieces together on a sheet of paper and add facial features.

4. **Designing Wrapping Paper**
   The children can design their own wrapping paper using newsprint, ink stampers, felt-tip colored markers, tempera paint, and so on. Glitter can also be glued onto the paper.

5. **Pine Bough Painting**
   Collect short pine boughs to use as painting tools. The tools can be placed at the easel or used with a shallow pan of tempera paint at tables.

6. **Candy Cane Marble Painting**
   Cut red construction paper into candy cane shapes. Marble paint with white tempera paint.

7. **Glittery Pinecones**
   Paint pinecones with tempera paint, sprinkle with glitter, and allow the paint to dry. The glittery pinecones can be used for classroom decorations, given as presents, or taken home.

8. **Paper Wreaths**
   Purchase green muffin tin liners. To make the paper wreaths, cut out a large ring from light tagboard or construction paper for each child in the class. The children can glue the green muffin tin liners to the ring, adding small pieces of red yarn, crayons, or felt-tip marker symbols to represent berries if desired.

9. **Play Dough Cookies**
   Using red, green, and white play dough and Christmas cookie cutters, the children can make play dough cookies.

10. **Favorite Play Dough**
    2 cups water
    1/2 cup salt
    Food coloring or tempera
    2 tablespoons salad oil
    2 tablespoons alum
    2 cups flour

    Combine and boil the water, salt, and food coloring until dissolved. Mix in the salad oil, alum, and flour while very hot. Knead approximately 5 minutes until smooth. Store in an airtight covered container.

11. **Gingerbread Play Dough**
    1 1/4 cup flour
    1/2 cup salt
    3 teaspoons cream of tartar
    1 cup water
    1 1/2 teaspoon vegetable oil
    2 tablespoons ground cinnamon
    1 teaspoon ground ginger

    Mix all ingredients and cook in a saucepan over medium heat while stirring frequently. When mixture begins to pull away from the sides of the pan, remove from heat and knead until smooth. Store in an airtight container.

 ## Cooking

1. **Candy Canes**
   Prepare the basic sugar dough recipe for cookie cutters (below). Divide the recipe in half. Add red food coloring to one-half of the dough. Show the children how to roll a piece

of red dough in a strip about 3 inches long by 1/2 inch wide. Repeat this process using the white dough. Then twist the two strips together, shaping into a candy cane. Bake the cookies in a 350-degree oven for 7 to 10 minutes.

2. **Basic Sugar Dough for Cookie Cutters**

   1/2 cup butter
   1 cup sugar
   1 egg
   1/2 teaspoon salt
   2 teaspoons baking powder
   2 cups flour
   1/2 teaspoon vanilla

   Cut into desired shapes. Place on lightly greased baking sheets. Bake 8 minutes at 400 degrees. This recipe makes approximately three to four dozen cookies.

3. **Eggnog**

   4 eggs (pasteurized)
   2 teaspoons vanilla
   4 tablespoons honey
   4 cups milk

   Beat all of the ingredients together until light and foamy. Pour into glasses or cups, and shake a little nutmeg on the top of the eggnog. This adds color and flavor. The recipe makes one quart. Eggnog should always be served immediately or refrigerated until snack or lunch. It should not be served to children who are allergic to eggs.

Dramatic Play

1. **Gift Wrapping**
   Collect and place in the dramatic play area empty boxes, scraps of wrapping paper, comic paper, wallpaper books, and scraps. Scissors, tape, bows, and ribbon should also be provided.

2. **North Pole**
   Create a sleigh out of cardboard or wood. Make reindeer headbands for the children to wear and pretend to pull the sleigh. Cover the floor with white felt or a white sheet.

Field Trips

1. **Christmas Tree Farm**
   Plan a trip to a Christmas tree farm so the children can cut down a Christmas tree. Check your state's licensing requirements regarding the use of fresh Christmas trees and decorations in the center or classroom.

2. **Caroling**
   Plan to go Christmas caroling at a local nursing home or even for another group of children. After caroling, Christmas cookies could be shared.

Fingerplays and Chants

Santa's Workshop
> Here is Santa's workshop.
>   (form peak with both hands)
> Here is Santa Claus.
>   (hold up thumb)
> Here are Santa's little elves
>   (wiggle fingers)
> Putting toys upon the shelves.

Here Is the Chimney
> Here is the chimney.
>   (make fist and tuck in thumb)
> Here is the top.
>   (cover with hand)
> Open it up quick
>   (lift hand up)
> And out Santa will pop.
>   (pop out thumb)

Five Little Christmas Cookies
(Hold up five fingers, take one away as directed by poem)

> Five little Christmas cookies on a plate by the door,
> One was eaten and then there were four.
>
> Four little Christmas cookies, gazing up at me,
> One was eaten and then there were three.

Three little Christmas cookies, enough for me and you,
One was eaten and then there were two.

Two little Christmas cookies sitting in the sun,
One was eaten and then there was one.

One little Christmas cookie, better grab it fast,
As you can see, the others surely didn't last.

Presents

See all the presents by the Christmas tree?
    (hand shades eyes)
Some for you,
    (point)
And some for me—
    (point)
Long ones,
    (extend arms)
Tall ones,
    (measure hand up from floor)
Short ones, too.
    (hand to floor—low)
And here is a round one
    (circle with arms)
Wrapped in blue.
Isn't it fun to look and see
    (hand shades eyes)
All of the presents by the Christmas tree?
    (arms open wide)

Group Time
(Games, Language)

1. Find the Christmas Bell
For this activity the children should be standing in a circle. One child is given a bell. Then the child should hide, while the remainder of the children cover their eyes. After the child has hidden, he or she begins to ring the bell, signaling the remainder of the children to listen for the sound and identify where the bell is hidden. Turns should be taken, allowing each child an opportunity to hide and ring the bell.

2. "Guess What's Inside?"
Place a familiar object inside a box. Let the children shake, feel, and try to identify the object. After this, open the box and show the children the object. This activity works well in small groups as well as large groups.

 Math

1. Christmas Card Sort
Place a variety of Christmas cards on a table in the math area. During self-selected or self-initiated periods, the children can sort by color, pictures, size, and so on.

2. Christmas Card Puzzles
Collect two sets of identical Christmas cards. Cut the covers off the cards. Cut one of each of the identical sets of cards into puzzle pieces. The matching card can be used as a form for the children to match the pieces.

Music

1. "Rudolph the Red-Nosed Reindeer"
(traditional)

2. "Jingle Bells"
(traditional)

3. "The Twelve Days of Christmas"
(traditional)

4. "We Wish You a Merry Christmas"
(traditional)

5. "Peppermint Stick Song"
Oh I took a lick of my peppermint stick
And I thought it tasted yummy.
Oh it used to hang on my Christmas tree,
But I like it better in my tummy.

6. "S-A-N-T-A"
(Sing to the tune of "B-I-N-G-O")

There was a man on Christmas Day
And Santa was his name-o.
S-A-N-T-A
S-A-N-T-A
S-A-N-T-A
And Santa was his name-o.

7. "Up on the House Top"
(traditional)

8. "Santa Claus Is Coming to Town"
(traditional)

9. "Circle Christmas Verse"

Two, four, six, eight.
Santa Claus don't be late;
Here's my stocking, I can't wait!
Two, four, six, eight.

10. "Christmas Chant"

With a "hey" and a "hi" and a "ho-ho-ho,"
Somebody tickled old Santa Claus's toe.
Get up ol' Santa, there's work to be done,
The children must have their holiday fun.
With a "hey" and a "hi" and a "ho-ho-ho,"
Santa Claus, Santa Claus,
GO-GO-GO!

11. "Santa's in His Shop"

(Sing to the tune of "The Farmer in the Dell")
(Pictures could be constructed for use singing about each toy.)

Santa's in his shop
Santa's in his shop
What a scene for Christmas
Santa's in his shop.
Other verses:
Santa takes a drum
The drum takes a doll
The doll takes a train
The train takes a ball
The ball takes a top
They're all in the shop
The top stays in the shop

Science

1. Making Candles

Candles can be made for Christmas gifts. This experience provides an opportunity for the children to see how a substance can change from solid to liquid and back to a solid form. The children can place pieces of paraffin in a tin can that is bent at the top, forming a spout. A red or green crayon piece can be used to add color.

The bottom of the tin cans should be placed in a pan of water and heated on the stove until the paraffin is melted. Meanwhile, the children can prepare small paper cups.

In the bottom of each paper cup mold, place a wick. Wicks can be made by tying a piece of string to a paper clip and a pencil. Then lay the pencil horizontally across the cup, allowing the string to hang vertically into the cup. When the wax is melted, the teacher should carefully pour the wax into the cup. After the wax hardens, the candles can be used as decorations or presents.

Caution: This activity should be restricted to four- and five-year-old children. Constant supervision of this activity is required for safety.

2. Add to the Science Area

- Pine needles and branches with magnifying glasses
- Pinecones with a balance scale
- Red, green, and white materials representing different textures

3. Bells

Collect bells of various shapes and sizes. Listen for differences in sounds in relation to the sizes of the bells.

4. Feely Box

A feely box containing Christmas items such as bows, cookie cutters, wrapping paper, nonbreakable ornaments, stockings, bells, candles, and so forth can be placed on the science table.

Sensory

1. Add to the Sensory Table

- Pine branches, needles, and cones
- Scented red and green play dough
- Icicles or snow (if possible) with thermometers
- Water for a sink-and-float activity, adding different Christmas objects such as bells, plastic stars, and cookie cutters
- Scents such as peppermint and ginger added to water

2. Holiday Cubes

Prepare ice cube trays using water that is colored with red or green food coloring. Freeze. Place in the sensory table.

 **Books**

The following books can be used to complement this theme:

Allen, Jonathan. (2008). *"I'm Not Santa!"* New York: Hyperion Books for Children.

Ammon, Richard. (1996). *An Amish Christmas.* Illustrated by Pamela Patrick. New York: Atheneum.

Balfe, Kevin, Glenn Beck, and Jason F. Wright. (2010). *The Christmas Sweater.* New York: Aladdin.

Banks, Kate. (2009). *What's Coming for Christmas?* Illustrated by Georg Hallensleben. New York: Farrar, Straus and Giroux.

Brett, Jan. (1990). *Christmas Reindeer.* New York: G. P. Putnam.

Brett, Jan. (2001). *Jan Brett's Christmas Treasury.* New York: G. P. Putnam.

Bright, Paul. (2009). *Grumpy Badger's Christmas.* Illustrated by Jane Chapman. Intercourse, PA: Good Books.

Brown, Margaret Wise. (1996). *On Christmas Eve.* Newly illustrated by Nancy Edwards Calder. New York: HarperCollins.

Carle, Eric. (2000). *Dream Snow.* New York: Philomel Books.

Ciavonne, Jean. (1995). *Carlos, Light the Farolito.* Illustrated by Donna Clair. New York: Clarion Books.

Cummings, E. E., and Chris Raschka. (2001). *Little Tree.* Illustrated by Chris Raschka. New York: Hyperion Press.

Davis, Rebecca. (1995). *The 12 Days of Christmas.* Illustrated by Linnea Asplind Riley. New York: Simon & Schuster.

Frazee, Marla. (2005). *Santa Claus: The World's Number One Toy Expert.* Orlando, FL: Harcourt.

Hobbie, Nathaniel. (2008). *Priscilla and the Great Santa Search.* Illustrated by Jocelyn Hobbie. New York: Little, Brown.

Hoffman, Mary. (1997). *An Angel Just like Me.* Illustrated by Cornelius Van Wright. New York: Dial Books.

Horacek, Petr. (2009). *Suzy Goose and the Christmas Star.* Somerville, MA: Candlewick Press.

Huckabee, Mike. (2010). *Can't Wait Till Christmas.* Illustrated by Jed Henry. New York: G.P. Putnam's Sons.

Lewis, Anne Margaret. (2008). *Santa Goes Green.* Illustrated by Elisa Chavarri. Traverse City, MI: Mackinac Island Press.

Martin, David. (2009). *Christmas Tree.* Illustrated by Melissa Sweet. Somerville, MA: Candlewick Press.

McGinley, Phyllis. (2010). *The Year without a Santa Claus.* Illustrated by John Manders. New York: Marshall Cavendish.

Milgrim, David. (2008). *Santa Duck.* New York: G.P. Putnam's Sons.

Moore, Clement Clarke. (2009). *The Night before Christmas.* Illustrated by Mary Engelbreit. New York: G.P. Putnam's Sons.

Obed, Ellen Bryan. (2009). *Who Would Like a Christmas Tree?* Illustrated by Anne Hunter. Boston: Houghton Mifflin Books for Children.

Pulver, Robin. (2010). *Christmas Kitten, Home at Last.* Illustrated by Layne Johnson. Chicago: Albert Whitman.

Radar, Laura. (2008). *When Santa Lost His Ho! Ho! Ho!* New York: HarperCollins Publishers.

Rawlinson, Julia. (2010). *Fletcher and the Snowflake Christmas.* Illustrated by Tiphanie Beeke. New York: Greenwillow Books.

Rustad, Martha E. H. (2009). *Christmas.* Mankato, MN: Capstone Press.

Rustad, Martha E. H. (2009). *Christmas in Many Cultures.* Mankato, MN: Capstone Press.

Rylant, Cynthia. (1997). *Silver Packages: An Appalachian Christmas Story.* Illustrated by Chris K. Soentpiet. New York: Orchard Books.

Scotton, Rob. (2009). *Merry Christmas, Splat.* New York: HarperCollins.

Shannon, David. (2010). *It's Christmas, David!* New York: Blue Sky Press.

Smith, Maggie. (2010). *Christmas with the Mousekins.* New York: Alfred A. Knopf.

Spirin, Gennady. (2009). *The Twelve Days of Christmas*. New York: Marshall Cavendish.

Stevens, Kathryn. (2010). *Christmas Trees*. Mankato, MN: Child's World.

Stevenson, James. (1996). *The Oldest Elf*. New York: William Morrow.

Tillman, Nancy. (2009). *The Spirit of Christmas*. New York: Feiwel and Friends.

True, Kelley. (2008). *The Dog Who Saved Santa*. New York: Holiday House.

Van Allsburg, Chris. (1985). *The Polar Express*. Boston: Houghton Mifflin.

Waldron, Jan L. (1997). *Angel Pig and the Hidden Christmas*. Illustrated by David M. McPhail. New York: Dutton.

Technology and Multimedia

The following technology and multimedia products can be used to complement this theme:

Arthur's Perfect Christmas [DVD]. (2000). Los Angeles: Sony Wonder.

The Berenstain Bears: Christmas Tree [DVD]. (2008). Los Angeles: Sony Wonder.

A Children's Christmas [CD]. (2000). The Learning Station. Long Branch, NJ: Kimbo Educational.

Children's Christmas Favorites [CD]. (1996). Hollywood, CA: Warner Bros.

Holiday Magic [CD]. (1996). Sherman Oaks, CA: Hap-Pal Music.

"Must Be Santa" [CD]. (1996). In *Singable Songs for the Very Young*. Cambridge, MA: Rounder/UMGD.

The Night before Christmas and More Christmas Stories [DVD]. (2002). New York: Scholastic.

Raffi's Christmas Album [CD]. (2002). Cambridge, MA: Rounder/UMGD.

Sing 'n' Sign Holiday Time [CD]. (2007). Long Branch, NJ: Kimbo Educational.

60 Christmas Carols for Kids [CD]. (2005). Wallingford, CT: Madacy Kids.

 Additional teaching resources to accompany this Theme can be found on the book's companion website. Go to www.cengagebrain.com to access the site for a variety of useful resources.

Gifts for Families and Friends

Wax Paper Placemats

Wax paper that is heavily
    waxed
Crayon shavings
Paper designs
Dish towel
Scissors

Use at least one of the
following:
Yarn   Lace
Fabric   Dried leaves

Cut the wax paper into 12-inch ×
20-inch sheets (two per mat).
Place crayon shavings between
the wax paper. Then decorate
with other items. Place towel
on wax paper and press with
warm iron until crayon melts.
Fringe the edges.

Craft Stick Picture Frames

Craft sticks (10 per frame)
Glue
Picture

Make a background of sticks
and glue the picture in place.
Add additional sticks around
the edges, front, and back for
the frame and for support. For
a freestanding frame, add more
craft sticks to both the front
and the back at the bottom.

Refrigerator Magnets

Small magnets
Glue
Any type of decoration (paper
    cutouts, plaster of Paris
    molds, yarn, styrofoam
    pieces, buttons, etc.)

Glue the decorations to the
magnet.

Service Certificate

Paper   Lace
Crayons   Ribbon
Pencils

Have the children write and
decorate a certificate that states
some service they will do for
their parents (for example, "This
certificate is good for washing
the dishes [or sweeping the floor,
picking up my toys, etc.]").

Ornaments

Plaster of Paris   Yarn
Any mold   Straw
Glitter

Pour the plaster of Paris into
the mold. Decorate with glitter
and let dry. If so desired, place
a straw into the mold and
string with yarn or thread.

Refrigerator Clothespin

Clothespins
Glue
Sequins, glitter, and beads
Small magnet

Let the children put glue on
one side of the clothespin.
Sprinkle this area with glitter,
sequins, or beads. Then assist
the child in gluing the magnet
to the other side.

Patchwork Flower Pot

Precut fabric squares
Glue
Tins (for glue)
Flower pots

Let the children soak the
fabric squares one at a time in
the glue. Press onto the pot in

a patchwork design. Let dry
overnight.

Snapshot Magnet

Snapshot
Plastic lid
Scissors (preferably pinking
    shears)
Glue
Magnet

Trace the outline of the lid
onto the back of the picture.
Cut out the picture, and glue it
onto the lid. Glue the magnet
to the underside of the lid.

Holiday Pin

Outline of a heart, wreath,
    and so forth, cut out of
    tagboard
Glue
Sequins, beads, buttons, and
yarn
Purchased backing for a pin

Let the children decorate the
cardboard figure with glue
and other decorating items.
Glue onto purchased backing
for a pin.

Flowers with Vase

Styrofoam egg carton
Chenille stem
Scissors
Glass jar or bottle
Liquid starch
Colored tissue paper (cut into
    squares)
Glue
Yarn
Paintbrush

Cut individual sections from
the egg carton, and punch

a hole in the bottom of each. Insert a chenille stem through the hole as a stem. Use the scissors to cut the petals.

For the vase: Using the paintbrush, cover a portion of the jar with liquid starch. Apply the tissue paper squares until the jar is covered. Add another coat of liquid starch. Dip the yarn into the glue, and wrap it around the jar. Insert the flower for a decoration.

Pinecone Ornament

Pinecones	Glue
Paint	Glitter
Paintbrush	Yarn

Paint the pinecones. Then roll the pinecones in the glue, and then into a dish filled with glitter. Tie a loop of yarn for hanging.

Paperweights

Glass furniture glides
Crêpe paper
Crayons
Glue
Plaster of Paris
Felt piece
Scissors

Children decorate a picture and then cut it to fit the glide. Place the picture face down into the recessed part of the glide. Pour plaster of Paris over the top of the picture and let it dry. Glue a felt piece over the plaster.

Rock Paperweight

Large rocks
Paint

Let the children paint a design on a rock they have chosen and give it to their parents as a present.

Soap Balls

1 cup Ivory Snow detergent
1/8 cup water
Food coloring
Colored nylon netting
Ribbon

Add the food coloring to the water, and then add the Ivory Snow detergent. Shape the mixture into balls or any shape. Wrap in colored netting and tie with a ribbon.

Closet Clove Scenter

Orange
Cloves
Netting
Ribbon

Have the children push the pointed ends of the cloves into an orange. Cover the orange completely. Wrap netting around the orange and tie it with the ribbon. These make good closet or dresser-drawer scenters.

Handprint Wreath

Colored construction paper
Scissors
Glue
Pencil
Cardboard or tagboard circle approximately 12 inches wide.

Let the children trace their hand and cut it out. Glue the palm of the hand to the cardboard circle. Using a pencil, roll the fingertips of the hand until curly.

Bird's Nest

1 can sweetened condensed milk
2 teaspoons vanilla
3 to 4 cups powdered milk
1 cup confectioners' sugar
Yellow food coloring

Mix all the ingredients together and add food coloring to tint the mixture to a yellow-brown color. Give each child a portion, and let him or her mold a bird's nest. Chill for 2 hours. If so desired, green-tinted coconut may be added for grass and put in the nest. Add small jellybeans for bird's eggs.

Flower Pots

Plaster of Paris
1/2-pint milk containers
Straws (three to four for each container)
Scissors
Construction paper
Paint
Paintbrush
Stapler

Cut the cartons in half and use the bottom half. Pour 1 to 3 inches of plaster into the containers. Stick three or four straws into the plaster and let harden. After plaster has hardened, remove the plaster very carefully from the milk carton. Let the children paint the plaster pot, make flowers from construction paper, and staple the flowers to the straws.

Cookie Jar

Coffee can with lid or oatmeal box
Construction paper
Crayons or felt-tip markers
Glue
Scissors

Gifts for Families and Friends (*continued*)

Cover the can with construction paper, and glue to seal. Let the children decorate their cans with crayons or felt-tip markers. For an added gift, make cookies in the classroom to send home in the jars.

Felt Printing
Felt
Glue
Wood block
Tempera paint
Scissors

Let the children cut the felt pieces into any shape. Glue the shape onto the wood block. Dip into a shallow pan of tempera paint. Print on newspaper to test.

Napkin Holder
Paper plates
Scissors
Yarn
Paper hole punch
Crayons
Clear shellac

Cut one paper plate in half. Place the inside together and punch holes through the lower half only. Use yarn to lace the plates together. Punch a small hole at the top for hanging. Decorate with crayons or felt-tip markers. Coat with shellac. May be used as a potholder, napkin, or card holder. *Caution:* This needs to be carefully supervised.

Clay Figures
4 cups flour
1 1/2 cup water

1 cup salt paint
Paintbrush

Combine flour, water, and salt. Knead for 5 to 10 minutes. Roll and cut dough into figures. (Cookie cutters work well.) Make a hole at the top of the figure. Bake in a 250-degree oven for 2 hours or until hard. When cool, paint to decorate.

Key Holder
8 craft sticks
Construction paper or a cutout from a greeting card
Self-adhesive picture hanger
Yarn

Glue five sticks together edge to edge. Cut one 3/4-inch piece of stick and glue it across the five sticks. Glue two sticks across the top parallel to the five sticks. Turn the sticks over. Cut paper or a greeting card to fit between the crossed sticks. Place on the self-adhesive hanger and tie yarn to the top for hanging.

Planter Trivets
7 craft sticks
Glue

Glue four craft sticks into a square, the top two overlapping the bottom ones. Fill in the open space with the remaining three, and glue into place.

Pencil Holder
Empty soup cans
Construction paper or contact paper

Crayons or felt-tip markers
Glue
Scissors

Cover the can with construction or contact paper. Decorate with crayons or markers, and use as a pencil holder.

Plaster Handprints
Plaster of Paris
1-inch-deep square container
Paint
Paintbrush

Pour plaster of Paris into the container. Have the child place his or her hand in the plaster to make a mold. Let the mold dry, and remove it from the container. Let the child paint the mold and give it as a gift with the following poem:

My Hands
Sometimes you get discouraged
Because I am so small
And always have my fingerprints
On furniture and walls.
But every day I'm growing up
And soon I'll be so tall
That all those little handprints
Will be hard for you to recall.
So here's a little handprint
Just for you to see
Exactly how my fingers looked
When I was little me.

CINCO DE MAYO

Foods

tacos
fajitas
guacamole
salsa
Mexican
meatball soup,
enchiladas

caramel
custard flan,
Mexican sugar
cookies,
quesadillas
Mexican
wedding cakes

Sounds

mariachi music
popular
Spanish music,
parade noises
maracas
Spanish
language

Symbols

flag of Mexico

Colors

Colors of the
Mexican flag:
red
green
white

Clothes

sombrero
poncho
colorful dresses
serape

Celebration

parades
fiestas (festivals)
food
music

dancing
language

Theme Goals

Through participating in the experiences provided by this theme, the children may learn:

1. Activities for celebrating Cinco de Mayo
2. Colors of Cinco de Mayo
3. Symbols of Cinco de Mayo
4. Foods eaten during Cinco de Mayo
5. Cinco de Mayo sounds
6. Clothing that may be worn during Cinco de Mayo

Concepts for the Children to Learn

1. Tacos, enchiladas, meatball soup, guacamole, salsa, fajitas, sugar cookies, Mexican wedding cakes, quesadillas, and caramel custard flan are enjoyed.
2. Parades are used to celebrate Cinco de Mayo.
3. Fiestas are celebrations that are fun and colorful, with live music, dancing, performances, and tasty foods.
4. Spanish music and mariachi music are played during Cinco de Mayo.
5. Some people play maracas (shakers) to celebrate.
6. Spanish is the dominant language spoken at Cinco de Mayo celebrations.
7. There are a lot of bright colors at Cinco de Mayo celebrations.
8. The colors red, green, and white are the colors of the Mexican flag.
9. People can be seen wearing sombreros, ponchos, and colorful clothing.

Vocabulary

1. **cape**—a piece of material that hangs loosely over the shoulders.
2. **Cinco de Mayo**—a holiday celebrating Mexican history.
3. **Mexico**—a country just south of the United States.
4. **fiesta**—a party linked to a holiday. Fiestas are used to celebrate Cinco de Mayo.
5. **piñata**—an empty papier-mâché object in the shape of an animal or person. It is filled with small toys or candy.
6. **serape**—a large, colorful blanket-like cape worn over a shirt.
7. **sombrero**—a hat that comes from Mexico with a large brim. Sombrero is the Spanish word for "hat."
8. **taco**—a corn shell filled with meat, lettuce, cheese, and salsa.
9. **guacamole**—a dip made out of a mashed avocado with tomato, onion, and garlic.
10. **mariachi**—a small Mexican band with guitars and singers.
11. **maracas**—instruments made from a hollow gourd and filled with small pebbles. Maracas are usually shaken in pairs to make music.
12. **quesadilla**—a toasted tortilla with melted cheese inside.
13. **poncho**—a piece of colorful fabric with a center opening for the head.
14. **tortilla**—a simple piece of flatbread made with corn and flour. In Spanish, tortilla means "little cake."

Bulletin Board

The purpose of this bulletin board is to promote visual discrimination, problem solving, and hand-eye coordination skills. To prepare the bulletin board, construct two of each item out of construction paper: guitars (any color), sombreros (tan), Mexican flags (green, white, and red), chili peppers (red or green), and maracas (any color). Hang one item of each pair on the left side of the bulletin board, and attach a red, green, or white piece of yarn to each shape. On the right side of the bulletin board, hang the matching picture shape. See illustration. Attach a pushpin to each of these picture shapes. The child can match the pictures by winding the correct string around the correct pushpin.

Family Letter

Dear Families,

It is May and spring is in the air! At school we are about to celebrate a new theme—the holiday of Cinco de Mayo. Spanish for the "fifth of May," Cinco de Mayo is a festive holiday celebrating Mexican pride and patriotism. The origin of the holiday is that on May 5, 1862, an outnumbered army of Mexican soldiers defeated an army of French and Mexican rebel soldiers in Mexico. The Mexican soldiers demonstrated great courage, unity, and patriotism—a deep love for their families, home, and country.

Today, Cinco de Mayo is celebrated in Mexico and by Mexican Americans in the United States. Big multiday festivals or "fiestas" are held with music, dancing, parades, and Mexican food. Whenever and however it is celebrated, the holiday is a celebration of Mexican culture.

Your children may not understand the history of the celebration, but they can help celebrate the day. At school, we will be immersed in activities related to Cinco de Mayo—everything from the foods, to the music, games, art projects, and, of course, a parade!

At School
A few of the learning experiences planned include:

- Listening to stories about Cinco de Mayo
- Cooking and tasting Mexican foods, such as tacos and guacamole
- Making Mexican flags, maracas, and piñatas
- Playing jumping bean games

At Home
If you'd like to integrate this curriculum unit into your home, consider making or eating Mexican foods such as tacos, enchiladas, quesadillas, Mexican hot chocolate (hot chocolate with cinnamon), and Mexican wedding cakes.

Ask your child about Cinco de Mayo!

Arts and Crafts

1. Maracas

Set out two small paper cups for each child to decorate with marking pens, or supply glue, glitter, and confetti to decorate with. Have children place 10–15 small dry beans into one of their cups. Help children place the empty cup on top of the bean cup and tape around the middle of the two cups. Small tissue paper streamers can also be taped to the two ends.

Have the children fingerpaint using red, white, and green paints—the colors of the Mexican flag.

2. Dancing Wands

You will need an empty paper towel tube for each child, plus green, white, and red tissue paper. Cut the tissue paper into 1" strips. Set out the tubes and some glue. Have children cover their tube with glue, then wrap a green, white, and red strip around the outside of their tube. When dry, have children tape or glue multiple strips of tissue paper coming out of one end of their tube. These can be used for a dance or parade.

3. Construction Paper Tacos

Cut out circle-shaped "tortillas" from a manila folder (approximately 6 inches in diameter). Cut out paper shapes like tomato pieces, shredded cheese, lettuce, and brown for meat. Let children glue them onto the "tortilla." Children can leave it flat like a soft taco (pizza style) or fold it over like a crispy taco.

4. Ponchos

Collect large paper grocery bags. Cut a whole in the top of each bag large enough for the child to put his or her head through. Provide the children with washable, colorful markers for decorating.

Cooking

1. Easy Guacamole

2 ripe avocados
1 small onion
1 clove garlic
1 small tomato
1 1/2 tbsp. lime juice (or juice of 1 fresh lime)
Salt and pepper to taste

Peel avocados and remove the pit. Peel and mince the onion and the garlic. Chop the tomato. Mash the avocado in a bowl (fun for the kids) and then stir in the remaining ingredients. Serve cold with tortillas or tortilla chips.

Tacos

Taco shells (hard or soft)
1 lb ground beef
1 package taco seasoning
Lettuce
Tomato
Grated cheese
Sour cream
Guacamole
Salsa

Prepare ground beef according to the taco seasoning package directions. Shred lettuce. Chop tomato. Put everything into separate bowls and let the children put together their own tacos. Demonstrate first by making your own taco in a taco shell.

3. Mexican Hot Chocolate

2 ounces unsweetened chocolate (two 1-ounce squares)
1/2 tsp. vanilla
1 tsp. ground cinnamon
4 tbsp. heavy cream
2 cups milk
2 egg yolks
2 tbsp. sugar
Optional: cinnamon sticks to stir

In a saucepan, stir together chocolate, vanilla, cinnamon, and cream. Cook over low heat! Heat, stirring constantly, until chocolate melts. Slowly add the two cups of milk, while stirring. Mix well. Let warm over low heat—DON'T LET IT BOIL! Beat egg yolks and sugar until foamy. Slowly pour about 1/4 of the chocolate mixture into the egg mixture, stirring constantly (we do this so the eggs heat slowly and you don't end up with scrambled eggs in your hot chocolate). Pour the egg-chocolate mixture back into the saucepan. Beat until mixture is frothy. Serve immediately with cinnamon sticks or spoons to stir with.

4. Polvorones (Mexican Sugar Cookies)

2 cups flour
3/4 cups sugar
1/2 tsp. cinnamon
1 cup butter or margarine

Preheat oven to 300 degrees. In a bowl, stir together flour, sugar, and cinnamon. Cream butter with a beater. Add flour mixture 1/2 cup at a time to the butter while still beating until it's mixed together. Spoon 1 tsp. dough and shape into a cookie. Repeat to make 2 dozen cookies. Place on ungreased cookie sheets and bake 25 minutes. (Optional: Sprinkle warm cookies with sugar and cinnamon.)

5. Mexican Wedding Cakes

1 cup butter
1/2 cup powdered sugar
2 cups all-purpose flour
1/4 tsp. salt
1/2 cup powdered sugar
1 tsp. vanilla

Preheat the oven to 400 degrees. Cream the butter and sugar until smooth. Add the salt, flour, and vanilla, which will make the mixture stiff. Show the children how to pinch off small pieces of dough and roll into a ball. Place on an ungreased cookie sheet. Bake for 12 minutes. When the cakes are removed from the oven and slightly cool, have the children roll them in powdered sugar.

6. Quesadillas

Large flour tortillas
Grated cheese (Monterey Jack or sharp or mild cheddar)

Heat a large frying pan to a medium-high heat. Add about 1/2 teaspoon of olive oil or

butter. Place one large flour tortilla in the pan and sprinkle cheese over it. Encourage the children to observe the tortillas as they are cooking.

Dramatic Play

Mexican Clothing
Place sombreros, ponchos, and serapes in the dramatic play area.

Field Trips and Resource People

1. Mexican American Cultural Center

If you live in an area with a large Mexican American population, arrange a visit to a Mexican American cultural center. Visit during a puppet show, performance, or other event that might be appropriate for your children.

2. Hispanic Volunteer

Invite a parent, a grandparent, or another person with a Hispanic background to share his or her clothing or instruments, read a story, or help prepare Cinco de Mayo foods.

Large Muscle

1. Avion (Hopscotch)

Using a piece of chalk, draw a hopscotch grid on an outdoor sidewalk. Each player takes a turn. They are not to step on a line while playing.

2. Canicas (Marbles)

Using a piece of chalk, draw a large circle on the sidewalk. This game may be played by two or more children. The players put several marbles inside the circle. The object of the game is to try to roll a marble from outside into the circle and hit other player's marbles. If they are successful, they take the marble. Taking turns, the winner is the person who takes the most marbles.

3. Cinco de Mayo Parade

Let your children help you plan a holiday parade to share with others. Put Mexican flags on sticks to carry. Let children shake their maracas. Let some children pretend to play guitars as they march. Make and wear ponchos by cutting head holes in large squares of material (or paper bags). Play or sing Mexican music as you march.

4. Jumping Bean Freeze!

Play Spanish music and have the children jump around like jumping beans. Then stop the music suddenly and have them "freeze" in place. Start the music and the fun begins again. Repeat until your group of jumping beans is tired out.

5. Mexican Hat Dance

Place a Mexican hat (sombrero) on the floor. Have your children stand in a circle around the hat. Choose one child to be "it." Have this child put on the hat and do a special dance movement. The rest of the children try to imitate the dancer in the middle. Variation: Children take turns dancing around the hat while others watch.

6. Mexican Jumping Beans

Explain to your children that Mexican jumping beans are beans that have a small caterpillar pupa inside. When the caterpillar gets warm, it twitches or jumps and makes the bean move. Have children roll up into small beans. Have them pretend they are getting hotter and hotter. Finally, have them start twitching, and then when they are really hot, have them start jumping around. Variation: Play some Mexican music for your children to twitch and jump to. When the music stops, have them roll back up into quiet beans.

7. Break the Piñata

Purchase or make a piñata filled with candies or small toys. One at a time, blindfold a child and turn her or him around a couple of times. Then encourage the child to hit the piñata with a large stick. **Caution:** Make sure that the other children are standing back and out of the way of the child with the stick.

Group Time
(Games and Language)

1. Bean Toss

Set out a large Mexican hat (sombrero) with the opening face down. Let children take turns tossing a small bean bag at the hat. See how many beanbags they can get to land on the brim or top of the hat. Alternatively, place the hat face up and toss the bean bags into the hat.

2. Pass the Hot Pepper

Explain to the children that sometimes Mexican food is made with hot, spicy peppers. Use a plastic pepper from your kitchen play area, or buy one in a craft store. Have the children sit on the floor in a circle. One player goes somewhere else in the room (or just outside the door) to hide his or her eyes. Pass the pepper quickly (it's hot!) around the circle until you say stop. The child holding the pepper hides it in his or her hands, lap, or under a leg. The other child comes back and tries to guess who has the pepper.

3. Pin the Tail on the Donkey

Pin up a large illustration of a donkey. Prepare a tail and add sticky tack to the back. Using a bandana, blindfold the children one at a time and have them try to pin the tail on the donkey. Write the child's name on the tail to see who wins.

4. La Lotería

Prepare two sets of identical cards using different pictures, stickers, or hand drawings (two beans, two chili peppers, two flowers, two tacos, etc.). You will need to have as many sets of cards as children in the group. Deal out the cards, one to each child. The child can look at his or her card. Shuffle your cards and turn them upside down. Choose a card. Then try to have the children guess who has the same card.

5. Benito Juarez Says

"Benito Juarez Says" is played the same way as "Simon Says." The child who is the leader says "Benito Juarez says hop on one foot." Until the leader says "Benito Juarez says stop" the children are to continue the action.

 Math

1. Counting in Spanish

Teach the children to count in Spanish. Play games using the Spanish numbers, or use your fingers to play counting games with numbers 1–5 or 1–10.

1. uno (oo-no)
2. dos (doss)
3. tres (trace)
4. cuatro (kwah-tro)
5. cinco (seen-ko)
6. seis (say-ees)
7. siete (see-ay-tay)
8. ocho (oh-cho)
9. nueve (nuay-vay)
10. diez (dee-ace)

 Music

1. "Come Join the Fun"

(Sing to the tune of "Frère Jacques")

Cinco de Mayo, Cinco de Mayo,
Is lots of fun, for everyone.
Many celebrations,
Loved ones get together.
Come join the fun, with everyone.

2. "Time to Celebrate"

(Sing to the tune of "Three Blind Mice")

Cinco de Mayo,
Cinco de Mayo.
Don't be late
To celebrate!
Time to dance around the square.
Time for flowers in your hair.
Time for lanterns everywhere.
Cinco de Mayo.
Cinco de Mayo.

3. Mexican Hat Dance

Encourage the children to stand around a sombrero. Play Mexican music and dance around the sombrero, clapping as you go. (If you do not have a sombrero, make one out of construction paper or cardboard.)

 Sensory

1. Colored Water

Change the color of the water in the sensory table each day, alternating between the colors red, white, and green. Provide the children with sponges, basters, unbreakable measuring cups, and measuring spoons.

2. Tissue Paper Coloring

Add strips of red or green tissue paper to the water in the sensory table. Encourage the children to observe what happens to the water. Then add water table toys.

 Social Studies

1. Spanish Language

Make a list of Spanish words your children already know on a large chart. Each day, add a new word or two with pictures if possible. Use the number and color words listed in the activities above and below.

2. Color Words

Teach your children how to say the names of colors in Spanish:

red = rojo (ROE-ho)
orange = naranja (nah-RAHN-hah)
yellow = amarillo (ah-maw-REE-yo)
green = verde (VAIR-day)
blue = azul (ah-SOOL)
purple = morado (morr-AH-doe)
white = blanca (BLAHN-kah)
black = negro (NAY-grow)

3. Buenos Amigos (Good Friends)

For this activity, you will need a timer, paper, and pen. Set the timer and encourage the children to say as many things they can think about their peers. Comments can be related to how they look, act, play, think, and so on. Record the comments for each child, and let him or her take them home.

Books

Ada, Alma Flor Ada, and F. Isabel Campoy. (2006). *Celebrate Cinco de Mayo with the Mexican Hat Dance.* Stories to Celebrate. Buenos Aires, Argentina: Alfaguara Infantil.

Cox, Judy. (2010). *Cinco de Mouse-o!* Illustrated by Jeffrey Ebbeler. New York: Holiday House.

Doering, Amanda. (2006). *Cinco de Mayo: Day of Mexican Pride.* First Facts, Holidays and Culture. Mankato, MN: Capstone Press.

Hall, M. C. (2010). *Cinco de Mayo.* Little World Holidays and Celebrations. Vero Beach, FL: Rourke Publishing.

Hill, Sandi. (1999). *Celebrating Cinco de Mayo: Fiesta Time!* Learn to Read: Read to Learn Holiday Series. Illustrated by Claude Martinot. Huntington Beach, CA: Creative Teaching Press.

Hoyt-Goldsmith, Diane. (2008). *Cinco de Mayo: Celebrating the Traditions of Mexico.* Photography by Lawrence Migdale. New York: Holiday House.

Levy, Janice. (2007). *Celebrate! It's Cinco de Mayo! ¡Celebramos! ¡Es el Cinco de Mayo!* (English and Spanish edition). Illustrated by Lorreta Lopez and translated by Miguel Arisa. Park Ridge, IL: Albert Whitman & Company.

Lowery, Linda, and Barbara Knutson. (2005). *Cinco de Mayo.* On My Own Holidays. Minneapolis, MN: First Avenue Editions.

Lowery, Linda, Barbara Knutson, and Julia Cisneros Fitzpatrick. (2005). *El Cinco de Mayo* (Spanish edition). On My Own Holidays. Minneapolis, MN: Ediciones Lerner.

McKissack, Fredrick, and Lisa Beringer McKissack. (2009). *Cinco de Mayo, Count and Celebrate!* Holidays—Count and Celebrate! Berkeley Heights, NJ: Enslow Elementary Publishers.

Otto, Caroline. (2008). *Holidays around the World: Celebrate Cinco de Mayo: with Fiestas, Music, and Dance.* Washington, DC: National Geographic Children's Books.

Riehecky, Janet, and Krystyna Stasiak. (2004). *Cinco de Mayo.* Circle the Year with Holidays. Danbury, CT: Children's Press.

Rissman, Rebecca. (2010). *Cinco de Mayo.* Holidays and Festivals. Portsmouth, NH: Heinemann Educational Books.

Schaefer, Lola M. (2000). *Cinco de Mayo.* Holidays and Celebrations. Mankato, MN: Capstone Press.

Wade, Mary Dodson, and Nanci R. Vargus. (2003). *Cinco de Mayo.* Rookie Read-About Holidays. Danbury, CT: Children's Press.

Worsham, Adria F. (2008). *Max Celebrates Cinco de Mayo.* Read It! Readers. Illustrated by Mernie Gallagher-Cole. Mankato, MN: Picture Window Books.

Technology and Multimedia

DJ's Choice: Cinco de Mayo Party Music [CD]. 2002. Edison, NJ: Turn up the Music.

Maya & Miguel: Cinco de Maya [DVD]. 2006. Los Angeles: Lion's Gate.

Various artists [CD]. 2002. *Cinco de Mayo.* Los Angeles: RCA International.

Additional teaching resources to accompany this Theme can be found on the book's companion website. Go to www.cengagebrain.com to access the site for a variety of useful resources.

Theme 17
CIRCUS

Foods
popcorn
peanuts
snow cones
cotton candy

Places
tents
wagons
parks
parades

Acts
trapeze
high wire
animal shows
clown
tumbling
bicycle
juggling

People
ringmaster
trapeze artist
tumblers
animal trainer
clowns
high-wire walker
makeup artist
costume designer

Animals
lions
horses
elephants
tigers
dogs
seals
bears

Theme Goals

Through participating in the experiences provided by this theme, the children may learn:

1. Different circus acts
2. People who work for a circus
3. Animals that perform in a circus
4. Places to watch a circus
5. Foods eaten at a circus

Concepts for the Children to Learn

1. The circus is a traveling show with people and animals.
2. The circus is fun.
3. Many adults and children enjoy the circus.
4. The circus can be performed under a big tent.
5. Often there are circus parades.
6. An animal trainer teaches animals tricks.
7. There are many circus animals.
8. Lions, horses, elephants, tigers, dogs, seals, and bears are all circus animals.
9. Circus wagons, people, and animals are in the parade.
10. Circus shows have colorful clowns.
11. Clowns wear makeup.
12. Clowns often do tumbling, juggling, and bicycle acts.
13. Music is played at the circus.
14. People and animals do special tricks in the circus.
15. Many people work at the circus.
16. The circus has a ringmaster, trapeze artist, animal trainers, high-wire walkers, makeup artists, and costume designers.
17. Popcorn, peanuts, snow cones, and cotton candy are foods that can be eaten at a circus.

Vocabulary

1. **circus**—traveling show with people and animals.
2. **circus parade**—a march of people and animals at the beginning of the performance.
3. **clowns**—people who wear makeup, act silly, and dress in silly clothes.
4. **makeup**—colored face paint.
5. **ringmaster**—person in charge of the circus performance.
6. **stilts**—long sticks that a performer stands on to be taller.
7. **trapeze**—short bar used for swinging.

Bulletin Board

The purpose of this bulletin board is to develop color recognition and matching skills. Construct eight clown faces with collars out of tagboard. Color each collar a different color using felt-tip markers. Hang these pieces on the bulletin board. Next, construct eight hat pieces out of tagboard. Color each one a different color, to correspond with the colors of the clowns' collars. Punch holes in the hats, and use pushpins to hold the hats above the appropriate clown. The children can match the colored hats to the clown wearing the same-colored collar.

Family Letter

Dear Families,

We are starting a unit that will be fun and exciting for everyone—the circus! Developing an awareness of special people and animals enhances an appreciation of others. It also stimulates children's curiosity to learn more about other people and people's jobs. The children will be learning about the many acts and performances of circus people and animals.

At School

Some of the many fun and exciting things we will be doing include:

- Listening to the story *Harriet Goes to the Circus* by Betsy and Giulio Maestro
- Dressing up in clown suits and applying makeup in the dramatic play area
- Acting out a small circus of our own
- Making clown face puppets
- Imitating circus clowns
- Looking at books containing circus animals
- Viewing the video *Circus*

We will have a very special visitor come to our room on Friday—a clown! He will show us how he applies his makeup and will perform for us. You are invited to join us for the fun at 3:00 p.m. to share in this activity.

At Home

It has been said that the circus is perhaps the world's oldest form of entertainment. Pictures of circus acts drawn over 3000 years ago have been discovered on walls of caves. Most children enjoy clowns and dressing up as clowns. Prepare clown makeup with your child by adding a few drops of food coloring to cold cream. Have your child use his or her fingers or a clean paintbrush to paint his or her face. This activity will help develop an awareness of colors, as well as help him or her realize that appearances can change but the person remains the same!

Enjoy your child!

Arts and Crafts

1. **Easel Ideas**
   - Clown face–shaped paper
   - Circus tent–shaped paper

2. **Circus Wagons**
   Collect old cardboard boxes and square food containers. The children can make circus wagons by decorating the boxes. When each child is through making his or her wagon, all of the boxes can be placed together for a circus train.

3. **Clown Face Masks**
   Provide paper plates and felt-tip markers to make paper plate clown masks. Glue the plate to a tongue depressor. The children can use the masks as puppets.

4. **Play Dough Animals**
   Prepare play dough by combining the following ingredients:

   2 cups flour
   1 cup salt
   1 cup hot water
   2 tablespoons oil
   4 teaspoons cream of tartar
   Food coloring

   Mix the ingredients. Then knead the mixture until smooth. This dough may be kept in a plastic bag or covered container. If the dough becomes sticky, add additional flour.

Cooking

Clown Snack
   Place a pear in the middle of a plate. Sprinkle grated cheese on the pear for hair. Add raisin eyes, a cherry nose, and a raisin mouth. Finally, make a ruffle collar from a lettuce leaf.

Dramatic Play

1. **Clown Makeup**
   Prepare clown makeup by mixing 1 part cold cream with 1 drop food coloring. Place clown makeup by a large mirror in the dramatic play area. The children apply makeup to their faces. Clown suits can also be provided if available. (Some programs may require parental permission slips for activities such as this.)

2. **Circus**
   Set up a circus in your classroom. Make a circle out of masking tape on the floor. The children can take turns performing in the ring. The addition of hula hoops, animal and clown costumes, tickets, and chairs would extend the children's play in this area.

3. **Animal Trainers**
   Each child can bring in his or her favorite stuffed animals on an assigned day. The children can pretend to be animal trainers for the circus. They may choose to act out different animal performances.

Field Trips and Resource People

1. **Clown Makeup**
   Invite a clown to demonstrate putting on makeup. Then have the clown put on a small skit and talk about the circus.

2. **The Circus**
   If possible, go to a circus or circus parade in your area.

Fingerplays and Chants

Going to the Circus

Going to the circus to have a lot of fun.
　(hold closed fist, and raise fingers to
　indicate number)
The animals parading one by one.
Now they are walking two by two,
A great big lion and a caribou.
Now they are walking three by three,
The elephants and the chimpanzee.
Now they are walking four by four,
A striped tiger and a big old bear.
Now they are walking five by five,
It makes us laugh when they arrive.

Elephants

Elephants walk like this and like that.
　(sway body back and forth)
They're terribly big; they're terribly fat.
　(spread arms wide in a circular motion)
They have no hands, they have no toes,
And goodness gracious, what a NOSE!
　(put arms together and sway for
　elephant nose)

Five Little Clowns

Five little clowns running through the door.
　(hold up one hand, put down one finger
　at each verse)
One fell down and then there were four.
Four little clowns in an apple tree.
One fell out and then there were three.
Three little clowns stirring up some stew.
One fell in and then there were two.
Two little clowns having lots of fun.
One ran away and then there was one.
One little clown left sitting in the sun.
He went home and then there were none!

Circus Clown

I'd like to be a circus clown
And make a funny face,
　(make a funny face)
And have all the people laugh at me
As I jump around the place.
　(act silly and jump around)

Group Time
(Games and Language)

1. **Circus Pictures**
Place pictures of clowns and circus things around the room at the children's eye level. Introduce the pictures at group time and discuss each picture.

2. **Who Took My Nose?**
Prepare red circles from construction paper. Seat the children in a circle. Give each child a red circle to tape on his or her nose. Then have everyone close their eyes. Tap one child. This child should get up and go to another child and take his or her nose. When the child returns to his or her place, the teacher claps her or his hands, and all the children open their eyes. The children then try to identify the child who took the nose.

3. **Clown Lotto**
Adhere clown face stickers, or draw simple clown faces, on several 2-inch × 2-inch pieces of tagboard. Also, prepare lotto boards using the same stickers or drawings. To play, turn all cards face down. Children take turns choosing a card from the table and seeing if it matches a picture on their game boards.

Large Muscle

1. **Tightrope Walker**
Provide a balance beam and a stick for the children to hold perpendicular to their bodies.

2. **Dancing Elephants**
Provide each child with a scarf and play music. The children can pretend to be dancing elephants.

3. **Bean Bag Toss**
Make a large clown or other circus person or animal bean bag toss out of thick cardboard. Cut the eyes, nose, and mouth holes all large enough for the bean bags to go through. For older children, assign each hole a certain number of points and maintain a score chart or card.

4. Can Stilts

Provide large tin cans with pre-bored holes on sides and thick string or twine for the children to make can stilts. Once completed, the children stand on the cans and walk around the room. Caution: Children need to be able to balance on the can tops for this to be a safe activity; therefore, this game is more appropriate for older children—four-, five-, six-, and seven-year-old children.

5. Tightrope Transition

As a transition, place a 10-foot line of masking tape on the floor. The children can pretend to tightrope walk over to the next activity.

6. Monkey, Monkey, Clown

Play "Duck, Duck, Goose," but change the words to "Monkey, Monkey, Clown."

 ## Math

1. Clown Hat Match

Make sets of matching colored hats. On one set, print a numeral. On the matching hats, print an identical number of dots. The children match the dots to the numbers.

2. Circus Sorting

Find several pictures of symbols that represent a circus. Also include other pictures. Place all pictures in a pile. The children can sort pictures into two piles. One pile will represent circus objects.

3. Growing Chart

Make a growing chart in the shape of a giraffe. If desired, another animal can be substituted. Record each child's height on the chart at various times during the year.

4. Unicycle Riders

Make unicycle cutouts, and write numerals on them. Have children stack the corresponding number of cutout clowns on each unicycle with Velcro.

 ## Music

1. "Circus"
(Sing to the tune of "Did You Ever See a Lassie?")

Let's pretend that we are clowns, are clowns, are clowns.
Let's pretend that we are clowns.
We'll have so much fun.
We'll put on our makeup and make people laugh hard.
Let's pretend that we are clowns.
We'll have so much fun.

Let's pretend that we are elephants, are elephants, are elephants.
Let's pretend that we are elephants.
We'll have so much fun.
We'll sway back and forth and stand on just two legs.
Let's pretend that we are elephants.
We'll have so much fun.
Let's pretend that we are on a trapeze, a trapeze, a trapeze.
Let's pretend that we are on a trapeze.
We'll have so much fun.
We'll swing high and swoop low and make people shout, "Oh!"
Let's pretend that we are on a trapeze.
We'll have so much fun!

2. "The Ringmaster"
(Sing to the tune of "The Farmer and the Dell")

The ringmaster has a circus.
The ringmaster has a circus.
Hi-ho the clowns are here.
The ringmaster has a circus.

The ringmaster takes a clown.
The ringmaster takes a clown.
Hi-ho the clowns are here.
The ringmaster takes a clown.

The clown takes an elephant ...

(Use clowns, elephants, lions, tigers, tight-rope walker, trapeze artist, acrobat, etc.)

Science

1. **Circus Balloons**
   Cut several pieces of tagboard into circles. If desired, cover the balloons with transparent contact or lamination paper. On each table, have three cups of colored water—red, yellow, and blue—with a brush in each cup. The children can mix all or any two colors and see which colors they can create for their circus balloons.

2. **Seal and Ball Color-Word Match**
   Cut several seals out of different-colored tagboard. Out of the same colors, cut several balls. Write the correct color on each ball. The children match each ball with the word on it to the correct seal.

3. **Sizzle Fun**
   Pour 1 inch of vinegar in a soda or catsup bottle. Put 2 teaspoons of baking soda inside a balloon. Quickly slip the open end of the balloon over the soda bottle. Watch the balloon fill with gas created by the interaction of the vinegar with the baking soda.

4. **Texture Clown**
   Construct a large clown from tagboard. Use different textured materials to create the clown's features. Make two sets. Place the extra set in a box or a bag. The children may pick a piece of textured material from the bag and match it to the identical textured piece used as a clown feature.

5. **High-Wire Balancers**
   Cut out the outline of a person, resembling an "X" shape with legs and arms apart, on tagboard or light cardboard. Tape a penny to the back of each foot. This will help the "high-wire walker" balance almost anywhere.

Sensory

1. Provide rubber or plastic animal figurines for the children to play with in the water table.

2. Make face paint to have the children practice painting on their cheeks or a friend's cheek. (Be sure to get parental permission first!) Encourage them to paint shapes or letters.

   Face Paint Recipe
   2 tsp. shortening
   1 tsp. flour
   Food coloring
   5 tsp. cornstarch
   3–4 drops glycerin
   Fragrance-free cream or lotion

Social Studies

1. **Circus Life**
   Read *You Think It's Fun to Be a Clown!* by David A. Adler. When finished, discuss the lives of circus people.

2. **Body Parts**
   Make a large clown out of tagboard. Make corresponding matching body parts such as arms, legs, ears, shoes, hands, and fingers. The children can match the parts.

Books

The following books can be used to complement this theme:

Argent, Kerry. (2005). *India the Showstopper.* Crows Nest, NSW Australia: Allen & Unwin.

Bardhan-Quallen, Sudipta. (2006). *Tightrope Poppy the High-Wire Pig.* Illustrated by Sarah Dillard. New York: Sterling Pub.

Bond, Michael. (1992). *Paddington at the Circus.* Illustrated by John Lobban. New York: HarperCollins.

Bronson, Linda. (2001). *The Circus Alphabet.* New York: Henry Holt.

Chwast, Seymour. (1993). *The Twelve Circus Rings.* Orlando, FL: Harcourt Brace.

Dahl, Michael, and Lucie Papineau. (2006). *Gilda the Giraffe and Marvin the Marmoset.* Illustrated by Marisol Sarrazin. Minneapolis, MN: Picture Window Books.

Damjan, Mischa. (2002). *The Clown Said No.* Illustrated by Gian Casty. New York: North-South Books.

Dodds, Dayle Ann. (2003). *Where's Pup?* Illustrated by Pierre Pratt. New York: Dial Books for Young Readers.

Downs, Mike. (2005). *You See a Circus: I See.* Illustrated by Anik McGrory. Watertown, MA: Charlesbridge.

Duncan, Lois. (2002). *Song of the Circus.* Illustrated by Meg Cundiff. New York: Philomel Books.

Ehlert, Lois. (1992). *Circus.* New York: HarperCollins.

Flaconer, Ian. (2001). *Olivia Saves the Circus.* New York: Atheneum.

Fleischman, Paul, and Kevin Hawkes. (2004). *Sidewalk Circus.* Illustrated by Kevin Hawkes. Cambridge, MA: Candlewick Press.

Gordon, Lynn. (2010). *Circus Fantastico: A Magnifying Mystery.* Illustrated by Molly Idle. Denver, CO: Accord Publishing.

Gottfried, Maya. (2003). *Last Night I Dreamed a Circus.* Illustrated by Robert Rahway Zakanitch. New York: Alfred Knopf.

Hartland, Jessie. (2005). *Clementine in the City.* New York: Viking.

Klise, Kate. (2010). *Little Rabbit and the Meanest Mother on Earth.* Illustrated by M. Sarah Klise. Boston: Harcourt Children's Books.

Langen, Annette, Constanza Droop, and Laura Lindgren. (2000). *Felix Joins the Circus.* Illustrated by Constanza Droop. New York: Abbeville Press.

McFarlane, Sheryl. (2006). *What's That Sound? At the Circus.* Illustrated by Kim LaFave. Ontario: Fitzhenry & Whiteside.

Millman, Issac. (2003). *Moses Goes to the Circus.* New York: Frances Foster Books.

Munro, Roxie. (2006). *Circus.* San Francisco: Chronicle Books.

Paxton, Tom. (1997). *Engelbert Joins the Circus.* Illustrated by Roberta Wilson. New York: William Morrow.

Rex, Adam. (2006). *Tree-Ring Circus.* Orlando, FL: Harcourt.

Romanelli, Serena. (2005). *Little Bobo's Circus Adventure.* Illustrated by Hans de Beer. New York: North-South Books.

Schumaker, Ward. (1997). *Sing a Song of Circus.* Orlando, FL: Harcourt Brace.

Slate, Joseph. (2002). *Miss Bindergarten Plans a Circus with Kindergarten.* Illustrated by Ashley Wolff. New York: Dutton Children's Books.

Van Dusen, Chris. (2009). *The Circus Ship.* Somerville, MA: Candlewick Press.

Villeneuve, Anne. (2010). *The Red Scarf.* Toronto: Tundra Books.

Whitford Paul, Ann. (2003). *Little Monkey Says Good Night.* Illustrated by Ann Whitford Paul. New York: Melanie Kroupa Books.

Wright, Johanna. (2009). *The Secret Circus.* New York: Roaring Brook Press.

Ziefert, Harriet. (2005). *Circus Parade.* Illustrated by Tanya Roitman. Maplewood, NJ: Blue Apple Books.

Technology and Multimedia

The following technology and multimedia products can be used to complement this theme:

Alphabet Circus [DVD]. (2004). Conroe, TX: Rock 'N Learn.

Bridwell, Norman. 2010. *Clifford at the Circus* [audio book]. New York: Scholastic.

Circus Calyope [CD]. (2006). Sikeston, MO: Carlisle Music.

"Clown Song" [CD]. (1997). In *Turn on the Music.* Sherman Oaks, CA: Hap-Pal Music.

"Three Ring Circus" [CD]. (2009). In *People, Place and Things.* Coconut Grove, FL: In the Nick of Time.

Additional teaching resources to accompany this Theme can be found on the book's companion website. Go to www.cengagebrain.com to access the site for a variety of useful resources.

Theme 18
CLOTHING

Colors and Sizes
many

Workers
tailor
seamstress
salesperson
laundromat assistant
shoe repair person

Uses
ceremonial
protection
decoration
identification
costumes

Kinds
pants, uniforms
dresses, sweaters
skirts, shirts
shoes, boots
socks, hats
gloves, coats
pajamas, scarves
kilts, ponchos
turbans, kaftans
kimonos

Care
wash
dry
mend
press
steam
polish
brush

Equipment
sewing machine
washing machine
dryer
iron
ironing board
brushes
steamer
needle
clothespins
hangers

Theme Goals

Through participating in the experiences provided by this theme, the children may learn:

1. Kinds of clothing
2. Clothing workers
3. Uses of clothing
4. Care of clothing
5. Clothing equipment
6. Colors and sizes of clothing

Concepts for the Children to Learn

1. Clothing is a covering for our body.
2. Pants, dresses, shirts, skirts, coats, pajamas, uniforms, kilts, ponchos, kimonos, kaftans, and sweaters are some of the clothing we wear on our bodies.
3. Shoes, socks, and boots are clothing for our feet.
4. Gloves and mittens are coverings for our hands.
5. Hats, turbans, and scarves are coverings for our head.
6. Protection, decoration, and identification are uses for clothing.
7. Clothes identify workers.
8. Policemen and firefighters wear uniforms.
9. There are many colors and sizes of clothing.
10. Clothing needs to be taken care of.
11. Clothing can be washed, dried, steamed, pressed, and mended.
12. Clothing needs to be cleaned.
13. Tailors and seamstresses help make and mend clothing.
14. Sewing machines are used to make clothing.
15. People wear clothing for ceremonies.
16. Brides may wear a bridal gown for a wedding ceremony.
17. Costumes, such as those worn for Halloween, are also clothing.
18. A shoe repair person mends shoes.
19. Clothespins and hangers are used to hang clothes.
20. Needles and thread, brushes, and irons are needed to care for clothing.

Vocabulary

1. **clothespin**—a clip used to hang clothes on a clothesline or a hanger.
2. **clothing**—a covering for the body.
3. **coat or jacket**—a piece of clothing that is often used for warmth and is worn over other clothing.
4. **dryer**—an appliance that dries clothes.
5. **hat**—clothing that covers our head.
6. **laundromat**—a place to clean clothes.
7. **shirt**—clothing that covers the chest and sometimes the arms.
8. **shoes**—clothing for our feet.
9. **skirt**—clothing that hangs from the waist.
10. **washing machine**—an appliance used to clean clothes.

Bulletin Board

The purpose of this bulletin board is to develop visual perception and discrimination skills. A "Sort the Clothes" bulletin board can be an addition to the clothing unit. Construct shorts and shirt pieces out of tagboard. The number used will depend on the size of the bulletin board and the developmental appropriateness for the children. Draw a pattern on a pair of shorts and the same pattern on one of the shirts. Continue by drawing a different pattern for each shorts and shirt set. Hang the shorts on the bulletin board, and hang a pushpin on top of the shorts, so the children can hang the corresponding patterned shirt on top of the shorts.

Family Letter

InBox

Dear Families,

We will be beginning a unit on clothing. Through participation in this unit, the children will learn about many different kinds of clothing. They will also become aware of the uses, purposes, and care of clothing.

At School

Some of the learning experiences planned for this unit include:

- Sorting clothes hangers by color
- Going to a laundromat in the dramatic play area
- Making newspaper skirts at the art table
- Washing doll clothes in the sensory table

We will also be taking a walk to the Corner Laundromat on Tuesday afternoon. We will be looking at the big laundry carts, washers and dryers, and folding tables. If you would like to join us, please contact me. We will be leaving the center at 3:00 p.m.

Parent Involvement

If you have any special clothes worn for celebrations or ceremonies, we invite you to share them with our class. Please contact me so a time can be arranged for your visit. The children will enjoy having you in the class and learning about the significance of the apparel.

At Home

You can foster the concepts introduced in this unit by encouraging your child to select what he or she will wear to school each day. To promote independence, begin by placing your child's clothes in a low drawer, allowing easy access to the clothing. To make mornings more enjoyable, encourage your child to select clothes at night that can be worn the next day. Find a location to place the clothes. Also, if your child has doll clothes, fill the kitchen sink or a tub with soapy water, and let your child wash the doll clothes. This will help your child learn how to care for clothing.

Have fun exploring clothing concepts with your child!

Arts and Crafts

1. Dress the Paper Doll

Prepare clothing out of construction paper scraps to fit paper dolls. For younger children, the dolls can be precut. Older children may be able to cut their own dolls if the lines are traced on paper and a simple pattern is provided.

2. Newspaper Skirts

Depending on the developmental level of the children, newspaper skirts can be constructed in the classroom. Begin by stapling about 10 sheets of newspaper across at the top. Draw a bold line about 2 inches from the staples. Then instruct the children to vertically cut from the bottom edge of the paper, all the way up to the bold line, creating strips. String pieces can be attached by stapling to the top of both sides to enable the skirt to be tied in the back.

3. Easel Ideas

- Feature clothes-shaped easel paper.
- Paint using tools created by attaching small sponges to a clothespin.

Cooking

1. Graham Crackers

Wear chef uniforms, and make your own graham crackers for a snack.

1/2 cup margarine
2/3 cup brown sugar
1/2 cup water
2 3/4 cups graham flour
1/2 teaspoon salt
1/2 teaspoon baking powder
1/8 teaspoon cinnamon

Beat margarine and sugar till smooth and creamy. Add the remainder of the ingredients and mix well. Let the mixture sit for 30 to 45 minutes. Sprinkle flour on a board or tabletop. Roll out dough to 1/8 inch thick. Cut the dough into squares, logs, or other shapes. Place on an oiled cookie sheet. Bake at 350 degrees for 20 minutes until lightly browned. This recipe should produce a sufficient quantity for eight children.

2. Irish Gingerbread

1 or 2 teaspoons butter
2 cups flour
1 1/2 teaspoon baking soda
1 teaspoon cinnamon
1 teaspoon ground ginger
3/4 teaspoon salt
1 egg
2 egg yolks
1 cup molasses
1/2 cup soft butter
1/2 cup sugar
1/2 cup quick-cooking oatmeal
1 cup hot water

Preheat the oven to 350 degrees. Grease the bottom of the baking pan with 1 or 2 teaspoons of butter. Measure the flour, baking soda, cinnamon, ginger, and salt; sift them together onto a piece of waxed paper. In a mixing bowl, combine the butter with the sugar by stirring them with the mixing spoon until they are blended. Add the egg and egg yolks. With the mixing spoon, beat the mixture until it is fluffy. Stir in the molasses.

Add the sifted dry ingredients, the oatmeal, and the hot water one-fourth at a time to the egg and molasses mixture, stirring after each addition. Pour the mixture into the greased pan. Bake 50 to 55 minutes. Test with a toothpick. Make gingerbread people with cookie cutters. Decorate: Make clothes for the gingerbread people using coconut, nuts, raisins, and other tasty items.

Note: From *Many Hands Cooking,* by Terry Touff and Marilyn Ratner, 1974, New York: Thomas Y. Crowell. Reprinted with permission.

3. Pita or Pocket Bread

1 package of yeast
1/4 cup lukewarm water
3 cups flour (white, whole wheat, or any combination)
2 teaspoons salt

Dissolve the yeast in the water, and add the flour and salt. Stir into a rough sticky ball. Knead on a floured board or table until smooth, adding more flour if necessary. Divide the dough into six balls, and knead each ball until smooth and round. Flatten each ball with a rolling pin until 1/4 inch thick and about 4 to 5 inches in diameter.

Cover the dough with a clean towel, and let it rise for 45 minutes. Arrange the rounds upside down on baking sheets. Bake in a 500-degree oven for 10 to 15 minutes or until brown and puffed in the center. The breads will be hard when they are removed from the oven but will soften and flatten as they cool. When cooled, split or cut the bread carefully and fill with any combination of sandwich filling.

Dramatic Play

1. Clothing Store
Place dress-up clothing on hangers and a rack. A cash register, play money, bags, and small shopping carts can also be provided to extend the play.

2. Party Clothes
Provide dressy clothes, jewelry, shoes, hats, and purses.

3. Uniforms
Collect occupational clothing and hats, such as police officer shirts and hats, a firefighter's hat, nurse and doctor lab coats, and artist smocks. High school athletic uniforms can also be provided. After use, store this box so the uniforms are available upon request for other units.

4. Hanging Clothes
String a low clothesline in the classroom or outdoors. Provide clothespins and doll clothes for the children to hang up.

5. Laundromat
Collect two large, appliance-sized boxes. Cut a hole in the top of one to represent a washing machine, and cut a front door in the other to represent a dryer. A laundry basket, empty soap box, and play clothing may be welcome additions to extend the play.

Field Trips and Resource People

1. Clothing Store
Visit a children's clothing store. Look at the different colors, sizes, and types of clothing.

2. Tailor or Seamstress
Invite a tailor or seamstress to visit your classroom to show the children how he or she makes, mends, and repairs clothing. The seamstress can demonstrate tools and share some of the clothing articles he or she has made.

3. Laundromat
Take a walk to a local laundromat. Observe the facility. Point out the sizes of the different kinds of washing machines and dryers. Explain the use of the laundry carts and folding tables.

Fingerplays and Chants

Three Buttons
Here's a button
   (make circle shape with thumb and
   index finger)
And here's a button
   (make circle shape with other thumb
   and index finger)
A great big button, I see.
   (make circle shape with arms above head)
Shall we count them?
Are you ready?
One, two, three!
   (make all three circles in succession)

One, Two, Buckle My Shoe
One, two, buckle my shoe.
Three, four, shut the door.
Five, six, pick up sticks.
Seven, eight, lay them straight.
Nine, ten, a big fat hen.
Nine, ten, say it again.

Group Time
(Games and Language)

Look Closely

While the children are sitting on the floor in a circle, call out the clothes items that one child is wearing. For example, say, "I see someone who is wearing a red shirt and pants." The children can look around the circle and say the name of the child who is wearing those items.

Large Muscle

1. **Clothespin Drop**

Collect clothespins and a series of jars with mouth openings of varying widths. The children can stand near the jar and drop the clothespins into it. To ensure success, the younger children should be guided to try the jar with the largest opening.

2. **Bean Bag Toss**

Bean bags can be tossed into empty laundry baskets.

3. **Clothes Race**

Fill bags with large-sized clothing items. Give a bag to each child. Signal the children to begin dressing up with the clothing. The object is to see how quickly they can put on all of the clothes items in the bag over their own clothing. This activity is more appropriate for five-, six-, and seven-year-olds, who have better large motor coordination and development.

Math

1. **Clothes Seriation**

Provide a basketful of clothes for the children to line up from largest to smallest. Include hats, sweatshirts, shoes, and pants. Use clothing items whose sizes are easily distinguishable.

2. **Line 'Em Up**

Print numerals on clothespins. The children can attach the clothespins on a low clothesline and sequence them in numerical order.

3. **Hanger Sort**

Colored hangers can be sorted into laundry baskets or on a clothesline by color.

4. **Sock Match**

Collect many different pairs of socks. Combine in a laundry basket. The children can find the matching pairs and fold them.

Science

1. **Fabric Sink and Float**

Provide various kinds of clothing and fabric on the science table along with a large tub of water. The children can test the different types of clothing to see which will sink and which will float. Some clothing articles will sink, whereas other clothing articles float until they become saturated with water. After a test has been made, the clothes can be hung to dry.

2. **Cleaning Fabric**

Give each child a piece of fabric. Set a bowl of mud, paint, ketchup, and markers on the table. Ask them to get their fabric dirty. After the children have gotten their fabric dirty, give them a brush and water and ask them to try to clean it. After a few minutes of trying with water, ask them to report their progress and ask what they think might help clean it. Provide laundry soap for the children to rub into the fabric. Discuss the difference in cleaning the fabric. What changes do they see? Why?

Note: This activity will require the table to be covered and should be completed near the sink and on noncarpeted floors.

Sensory

1. Washing Clothes
Fill the sensory table with soapy water and let the children wash doll clothing. After being washed, the clothes can be hung on a low clothesline.

2. Add to the Sensory Table
Place a variety of clothespins in the sensory table. Encourage the children to clip the pins together to create various forms.

Social Studies

1. Weather Clothing
Bring in examples of clothing worn in each of the four seasons. Provide four laundry baskets. Label each basket with a picture representing a hot sunny day, a rainy day, a cold day, and a fall or spring day. Then encourage the children to sort the clothing according to the weather label on the basket.

2. Who Wears It?
At group time, hold up clothing items and ask the children who would wear it. Include baby clothes, sports uniforms, occupational clothing, ladies clothes, men's clothes, and others.

Books

The following books can be used to complement this theme:

Adamson, Heather. (2008). *Clothes in Many Cultures.* Mankato, MN: Capstone Press.

Ahlberg, Allan. (2001). *The Man Who Wore All His Clothes.* Illustrated by Katharine McEwan. Cambridge, MA: Candlewick Press.

Bae, Hyun-Joo. (2007). *New Clothes for New Year's Day.* La Jolla, CA: Kane/Miller. – Korean.

Beaton, Claire. (1996). *Clothes / La Ropa.* Hauppauge, NY: Barron's.

Bechtold, Lisze. (2008). *Sally and the Purple Socks.* New York: Philomel Books.

Blankenship, Lee Ann. (2005). *Mr. Tuggle's Troubles.* Illustrated by Karen Dugan. Honesdale, PA: Boyds Mills Press.

Blessing, Charlotte. (2009). *New Old Shoes.* Illustrated by Gary R. Philips. Raynham Center, MA: Pleasant St. Press.

Cullen, Catherine Ann. (2001). *The Magical, Mystical, Marvelous Coat.* Illustrated by David Christiana. Boston: Little, Brown.

Davidson, Susannah. (2006). *The Emperor's New Clothes.* Illustrated by Mike Gordon. Tulsa, OK: EDC Publishing.

Dodd, Dayle Ann. (2002). *The Kettles Get New Clothes.* Illustrated by Jill McElmurry. Cambridge, MA: Candlewick Press.

Ehrlich, Fred. (2005). *Does a Chimp Wear Clothes?* Illustrated by Emily Bolam. Maplewood, NJ: Blue Apple Books.

Emberley, Rebecca. (2002). *My Clothes / Mi Ropa.* Boston: Little, Brown.

Emery, Joanna. (2005). *Stinky Clothes.* Illustrated by Richard Rossi. New York: Children's Press.

Goode, Diane. (1999). *The Dinosaur's New Clothes.* New York: Blue Sky Press.

Keller, Holly. (1995). *Rosata.* New York: Greenwillow.

Lacome, Julie. (2000). *Ruthie's Big Old Coat.* Cambridge, MA: Candlewick Press.

Lasky, Kathryn. (1999). *The Emperor's Old Clothes.* Illustrated by David Catrow. San Diego, CA: Harcourt Brace.

Lewis, J. Patrick, and Chris Sheban. (2000). *The Shoe Tree of Chagrin: A Christmas Story.* Illustrated by Chris Sheban. Mankato, MN: Creative Editions.

Lucas, David. (2004). *Halibut Jackson.* New York: Knopf, distributed by Random House.

Murphy, Stuart. (1996). *A Pair of Socks.* Illustrated by Lois Ehlert. New York: HarperCollins.

Nelson, Robin. (2003). *From Cotton to T-Shirt.* Minneapolis, MN: Lerner.

Parnell, Robyn. (2005). *My Closet Threw a Party.* Illustrated by Jimmy Pickering. New York: Sterling Pub.

Reidy, Hannah. (2005). *All Sorts of Clothes.* Illustrated by Emma Dodd. Minneapolis, MN: Picture Window Books.

Rosenthal, Betsy R. (2010). *Which Shoes Would You Choose?* Illustrated by Nancy Cote. New York: G.P. Putnam's Sons.

Salas, Laura Purdie. (2006). *Whose Coat Is This?* Illustrated by Amy Bailey Muehlenhardt. Minneapolis, MN: Picture Window Books.

Shea, Bob. (2007). *New Socks.* New York: Little, Brown.

Slegers, Liesbet. (2009). *Clothes.* New York: Clavis Pub.

Small, David. (1996). *Fenwick's Suit.* New York: Farrar, Straus and Giroux.

Spinelli, Eileen. (2001). *In My New Yellow Shirt.* Illustrated by Hideko Takahashi. New York: Henry Holt.

Szekeres, Cyndy. (2000). *Toby's Rainbow Clothes.* New York: Little Simon.

Thiesing, Lisa. (2006). *The Scarecrow's New Clothes: A Silly Thriller with Peggy the Pig.* New York: Dutton Children's Books.

Wollman, Jessica. (2002). *Andrew's Bright Blue T-Shirt.* Illustrated by Ana Lopez Escriva. New York: Doubleday Book for Young Readers.

Woods, Samuel G. (2001). *Kid's Clothes: From Start to Finish.* Woodbridge, CT: Blackbirch Press.

Technology and Multimedia

The following technology and multimedia products can be used to complement this theme:

"Blue Suede Shoes" [CD] (2000). In *Bean Bag Rock & Roll.* Long Branch, NJ: Kimbo Educational.

"Boots" [CD]. (2010). In *Best of Laurie Berkner Band.* New York: Two Tomatoes.

"Bring Your Clothes" [CD]. (2001). In *Whaddaya Think of That?* New York: Two Tomatoes.

The Day Jimmy's Boa Ate the Wash and More Back to School Stories [DVD]. (2005). New York: Scholastic.

"Dressin' Up" [CD]. (2009). In *We Are the Not-Its!* Seattle, WA: Little Loopy Records.

"Mary Wore Her Red Dress" [CD]. (1996). In *Everything Grows.* Cambridge, MA: Rounder/UMGD.

"Running Shoes" [CD]. (2010). In *Lots of Fun.* Atlanta, GA: Mr Greg's Musical Madness.

"Shoes" (2004). In *Circle Time Activities.* Long Branch, NJ: Kimbo Educational.

"Sneakers" [CD]. (2009). In *People, Place and Things.* Coconut Grove, FL: In the Nick of Time.

"This Hat" [CD]. (2002). In *Under a Shady Tree.* New York: Two Tomatoes.

"Tina Took Her Tap Shoes" [CD]. (1999). In *We're on Our Way.* Sherman Oaks, CA: Hap-Pal Music.

 Additional teaching resources to accompany this Theme can be found on the book's companion website. Go to www.cengagebrain.com to access the site for a variety of useful resources.

Dramatic Play Clothes

The following list contains names of male and female clothing articles to save for use in the dramatic play area:

aprons	scarves	slippers	suspenders
boots	leotards	robes	billfolds
pajamas	swimsuits	slacks	ties
shirts	socks	sweaters	belts
dresses	purses	ponchos	tutus
skirts	jewelry:	coats	turbans
kaftans	rings	earmuffs	bridal veils
kilts	bracelets	raincoats	capes
kimonos	necklaces	snow pants	
hats	clip-on earrings	shorts	
gloves and mittens	shoes	sweatsuits	

Theme 19
COMMUNICATION

Written
books
newspapers
magazines
letters
greeting cards
printed words

Verbal
talking
singing
sounds

Alarm
flashing lights
car horns
fire alarms
sirens

Equipment
telephone
television
telegraph
fax machine
radio, CDs
video recorder
DVDs, computer
e-mail
compact disc player
cell phone

Nonverbal
listening
body movements
sign language
dancing
pantomime
drawings

Visual
letters
numbers
greeting cards
signs
pictures
art
artifacts

Theme Goals

Through participating in the experiences provided by this theme, the children may learn:

1. Visual communication skills
2. Nonverbal communication skills
3. Verbal communication skills
4. Communication equipment
5. Types of written communication
6. Ways of communicating alarm

Concepts for the Children to Learn

1. Talking, singing, and making sounds are forms of communication.
2. Listening is a way to hear.
3. Our hands and face can communicate our feelings.
4. Sign language is a way of communication.
5. Body movements, dancing, drawing, and pantomiming are forms of nonverbal communication.
6. There are many types of equipment used for communicating.
7. Telephones, cell phones, televisions, faxes, radios, video recorders, computer disks, and computers are equipment used for communicating.
8. Letters and greeting cards are ways of communicating.
9. Machines can transmit messages.
10. Using letters, numbers, and signs are ways of communicating.
11. Books, magazines, letters, greeting cards, and printed words are forms of written communication.
12. Pictures, artifacts, and art are forms of visual communication.
13. Flashing lights, car horns, fire alarms, and sirens communicate alarm.

Vocabulary

1. **alphabet**—letter symbols that are used to write a language.
2. **card**—a piece of folded paper with a design. Cards are sent to people on special occasions: birthdays, holidays, celebrations, or when they are ill.
3. **communication**—sharing information. There are many ways to share information. The telephone, computer, a book, or a letter can all be used to share information.
4. **computer**—a machine that stores and gets information.
5. **fax machine**—a machine that copies a message and sends it to another person or place.
6. **letter**—a paper with a written or typed message.
7. **newspaper**—words printed on paper.
8. **sign language**—making symbols with our hands to communicate.
9. **signs**—symbols.
10. **cell and telephones**—devices used to talk to someone in another place.

Bulletin Board

The purpose of this bulletin board is to help children learn their home telephone number. Construct two telephone handsets for each child. See the illustration. Affix each child's telephone number to the handset. Laminate this cards. The children can practice dialing their home phone numbers by "pressing" the appropriate pad on the handset.

Family Letter

InBox

Dear Families,

We will begin talking about communication next week and emphasizing how we share our feelings and ideas with others. Through this unit, the children will become aware of the different ways we communicate: through our voices, letters, using hand signals, and body language. They will also become familiar with machines that are used to help us communicate, such as the television, radio, computer, cell phone, and telephone.

At School

Some of the learning experiences planned for this unit include:

- A sign language demonstration
- A phone booth in the dramatic play area
- A computer in the writing center
- Songs and books about communication
- A wireless telephone on the science table

At Home

It is important for children to learn their telephone number for safety purposes. Help your children learn your home telephone number. (This is also something we will be practicing at school.) To make practicing more fun, construct a toy telephone with your child. Two paper cups or empty tin cans and a long piece of rope, string, or yarn are needed to make a telephone. Thread the string through the two cups and tie knots on the ends. Have two people hold the cups and pull the string taut. Take turns talking and listening. The sound vibrations travel through the string—and you won't hear a busy signal!

Enjoy your children as you share concepts and experiences related to communication.

Arts and Crafts

1. Easel Idea
Cut easel paper in the shape of a book, CD, radio, or other piece of communication equipment.

2. Stationery
Provide the children with various stencils or stamps to make their own stationery. It can be used as a gift for a parent or a special person. Children could then dictate a letter to a relative or friend.

Dramatic Play

1. Post Office
In the dramatic play area, place a mailbox, envelopes, old cards, paper, pens, old stampers, ink pads, hats, and mailbags. During self-selected or self-initiated play periods, the children can play post office.

2. Television
Obtain an older discarded television console (from before the digital era) to use for puppetry or storytelling experiences. Remove the back and set, leaving just the wooden frame. If desired, make curtains.

3. Radio Station
Place an old microphone, or one made from a styrofoam ball and cardboard, with CDs in the dramatic play area.

4. Puppet Show
Place a puppet stand and a variety of puppets in the dramatic play area for the children to use during the self-selected or self-directed play period.

Field Trips and Resource People

1. Post Office
Visit a local post office. Encourage the children to observe how the mail is sorted.

2. Radio Station
Visit a local disc jockey at the radio station.

3. Television Station
If available, visit a local television station. Observe the cameras, microphones, and other communication devices.

4. Sign Language Demonstration
Invite someone to demonstrate sign language.

Fingerplays and Chants

Body Talk
When I smile, I tell you I'm happy.
(point at the corner of mouth)
When I frown I tell you that I'm sad.
(pull down corners of mouth)
When I raise my shoulders and tilt my head
I tell you "I don't know."
(raise shoulders, tilt head, raise hands, and shake head)

Helpful Friends
Mail carriers carry a full pack
Of cards and letters on their backs.
(hold both hands over one shoulder)
Step, step, step! Now ring, ring, ring!
(step in place and pretend to ring bell)
What glad surprises do they bring?

My Hands
My hands can talk
In a special way.
These are some things
They help me to say:
"Hello"
(wave)
"Come Here"
(beckon toward self)
"It's A-OK"
(form circle with thumb and pointer)
"Now Stop"
(hand out, palm up)
"Look"
(hands shading eyes)

"Listen"
   (cup hand behind ear)
Or "It's far, far away"
   (point out into the distance)
And "Glad to meet you, how are you today?"
   (shake neighbor's hand)

Group Time
(Games and Language)

1. **Telephone**
Play the "telephone" game by having the children sit in a circle. Begin by whispering a short phrase into a child's ear. Then that child whispers your message to the next child. Continue until the message gets to the last child. The last child repeats the message out loud. It is fun to see how much it has changed. (This game is most successful with older children.)

2. **What's Missing?**
Place items that are related to communication on a tray. Include a stamp, a telephone, a CD, a portable radio, and other items. The children can examine the objects for a few minutes. After this, they should close their eyes while you remove an object. Then let the children look at the tray and identify which object is missing.

3. **Household Objects Sound Like . . .**
Make a tape of different sounds around the house. Include a radio, television, alarm clock, telephone, vacuum cleaner, flushing toilet, door bells, egg timer, and other sounds. Play the tape for the children, letting them identify the individual sounds.

Large Muscle

Charades

Invite children one at a time to come to the front of the group. Then whisper something in the child's ear, such as "You're very happy." The child then uses his or her hands, face, feet, arms, and so forth to communicate this feeling to the other children. The group of children then identifies the demonstrated feeling.

Math

1. **Phone Numbers**
Make a list of the children's names and telephone numbers. Place the list by a toy telephone.

2. **Stamp Sort**
Paste a variety of samples of different shapes and colors onto construction paper. Laminate and cut out. Encourage the children to sort the stamps by size and color.

Music

1. **"Call a Friend"**
(Sing to the tune of "Row, Row, Row Your Boat")

Call, call, call a friend.
Friend, I'm calling you.
Hi, hello, how are you?
Very good, thank you!

2. **"Twinkle, Twinkle Traffic Light"**
(Sing to the tune of "Twinkle, Twinkle Little Star")

Twinkle, twinkle traffic light
Standing on the corner bright.
Green means go, we all know
Yellow means wait, even if you're late.
Red means STOP!
   (pause)
Twinkle, twinkle traffic light
Standing on the corner bright.

3. **"I'm a Little Mail Carrier"**
(Sing to the tune of "I'm a Little Teapot")

I'm a little mail carrier, short and stout.
Here is my hat, and here is my pouch.
   (point to head, point to side)

I walk around from house to house,
Delivering mail from my pouch.
  (pretend to take things out of a bag)

Science

1. **Telephones**
   Place telephones, real or toy, in the classroom to encourage the children to talk to each other. Also, make your own telephones by using two large empty orange juice concentrate cans. After washing the cans, connect with a long string. The children can pull the string taut. Then they can take turns talking and listening to each other.

2. **Sound Shakers**
   Using identical small orange juice cans, pudding cups, or empty film containers, fill pairs of the containers with different objects. Included may be sand, coins, rocks, rice, salt, and the like. Replace the lids. Make sure to secure the lids with glue or heavy tape to avoid spilling. To make the containers self-correcting, place numbers or like colors on the bottoms of the matching containers.

3. **Feely Box**
   Prepare a feely box that includes such things as a CD, a pen, a pencil, block letters, an envelope, and anything else that is related to communication. The children can place their hand in the box and identify objects using their sense of touch.

4. **Vibrations**
   Encourage the children to gently place their hand on the side of a piano, guitar, CD player, radio, television, and so forth in order to feel the vibrations. Then have the children feel their own throats vibrate as they speak. A tuning fork can also be a teaching aid when talking about vibrations.

6. **Telephone Parts**
   Dismantle an old telephone, and put it on the science table for the children to discover and explore the parts.

Social Studies

1. **Thank You**
   Let the children dictate a group thank-you letter to one of your resource visitors or field trip representatives. Before mailing the letter, provide writing tools for children to sign their names.

2. **Sign Language**
   Learn some simple sign language to teach the children in your classroom. Some ideas include thank you (touch hand to chin and pull down), please (rub chest), and friend (cross pointer fingers).

Books

The following books can be used to complement this theme:

Aliki. (1996). *Hello! Good-Bye.* New York: Greenwillow.

Austin, Margot, and David McPhail. (1999). *A Friend for Growl Bear.* Illustrated by David McPhail. New York: HarperCollins.

Bakur-Weiner, Marcella, and Jill Neimark. (2010). *I Want Your Moo.* Illustrated by Jairo Barragan. Washington, DC: Magination Press.

Banks, Kate. (2006). *Max's Words.* Illustrated by Boris Kulikov. New York: Farrar, Straus and Giroux.

Borlenghi, Patricia. (1992). *From Albatross to Zoo: An Alphabet Book in Five Languages.* Illustrated by Piors Harper. New York: Scholastic.

Brown, Marc Tolon. (1997). *Arthur's TV Trouble.* Boston: Little, Brown.

Buck, Nola. (1996). *Sid and Sam.* Illustrated by G. Brian Karas. New York: HarperCollins.

Button, Lana. (2010). *Willow's Whispers.* Illustrated by Tania Howells. Toronto: Kids Can Press.

Cheng, Andrea. (2000). *Grandfather Counts.* Illustrated by Ange Zhang. New York: Lee and Low Books.

Cronin, Doreen. (2000). *Click, Clack, Moo: Cows That Type.* Illustrated by Betsy Lewin. New York: Simon & Schuster for Young Readers.

Dodds, Dayle Ann. (1992). *Do Bunnies Talk?* Illustrated by Arlene Dubanevich. New York: HarperCollins.

Donaldson, Julia. (2010). *What the Ladybug Heard.* Illustrated by Lydia Monks. New York: Henry Holt.

Evans, Lezlie. (1999). *Can You Count Ten Toes?* Illustrated by Denis Roche. Boston: Houghton Mifflin.

Finn, Carrie. (2007). *Manners on the Telephone.* Illustrated by Chris Lensch. Minneapolis, MN: Picture Window Books.

Gibbons, Gail. (1993). *Puff—Flash—Bang: A Book about Signals.* New York: William Morrow.

Hubbard, Patricia. (1996). *My Crayons Talk.* Illustrated by G. Brian Karas. New York: Henry Holt.

Isadora, Rachel. (2010). *Say Hello!* New York: G.P. Putnam's Sons.

King, Mary Ellen. (1997). *A Good Day for Listening.* Harrisburg, PA: Morehouse Publishing.

Law, Diane. (2006). *Count around the World in 5 Languages.* New York: North-South.

Lester, Helen. (1995). *Listen, Buddy.* Illustrated by Lynn Munsinger. Boston: Houghton Mifflin.

Ljungkvist, Laura. (2001). *Toni's Topsy-Turvy Telephone Day.* New York: Harry N. Abrams.

Peterson, Jeanne Whitehouse. (1994). *My Mama Sings.* Illustrated by Sandra Speidel. New York: HarperCollins.

Pleau-Murissi, Marilyn. (2003). *The Phone Call.* Montreal: Chouette.

Prezler, June. (2007). *Why Do Birds Sing? A Book about Animal Communication.* Mankato, MN: Capstone Press.

Schotter, Roni. (2006). *The Boy Who Loved Words.* Illustrated by Giselle Potter. New York: Schwartz & Wade Books

Shapiro, Arnold. (1997). *Mice Squeak, We Speak.* Illustrated by Tomie de Paola. New York: G. P. Putnam.

Showers, Paul. (1991). *Listening Walk* (revised edition). New York: HarperCollins.

Weinstein, Ellen. (2008). *Everywhere the Cow Says "Moo!"* Illustrated by Kenneth Anderson. Honesdale, PA: Boyds Mills Press.

Wheeler, Cindy. (1998). *More Simple Signs.* New York: Viking.

Ziefert, Harriet. (1999). *Talk, Baby!* Illustrated by Emily Bolam. New York: Henry Holt.

Technology and Multimedia

The following technology and multimedia products can be used to complement this theme:

"Bananaphone" [CD]. (1996). In *Bananaphone.* Cambridge, MA: Rounder/UMGD.

Click Clack Moo: Cows That Type and More Fun on the Farm [DVD]. (2009). New York: Scholastic.

"Run Baby Run" [CD]. (2009). In *More Please.* Olympia, WA: Aurora Elephant Music.

"Telephone" [CD]. (2002). In *Buzz Buzz.* New York: Razor and Tie Music.

Tossing, Gaia. (1995). *Sing 'n Sign for Fun!* [CD]. Glenview, IL: Heartsong.

Additional teaching resources to accompany this Theme can be found on the book's companion website. Go to www.cengagebrain.com to access the site for a variety of useful resources.

CONSTRUCTION TOOLS

Safety
storage
use
care
electrical
childproof
goggles
handle with care

Types
electric
hand-powered

Names
drill
wrench
screwdriver
saw, hammer
pliers, clamp
level, wedge
nails, screws
ruler, plane
pencil, chalk
tweezers
plane, scissors

Uses
clamping
drilling holes
measuring
cutting
pounding
building

Theme Goals

Through participating in the experiences provided by this theme, the children may learn:

1. Types of tools
2. Names of common tools
3. Uses of tools
4. Tool safety

Concepts for the Children to Learn

1. A tool is something that helps you do work.
2. Tools can be electric or hand-powered.
3. Tools are helpful when building.
4. Pliers, tweezers, and clamps hold things.
5. Tools can be used for measuring, cutting, pounding, and building.
6. Tools can also be used for drilling holes and clamping.
7. Drills, nails, and screws make holes.
8. Planes, saws, and scissors cut materials.
9. Hammers and screwdrivers are used to put in and remove nails and screws.
10. A level and plane are tools to help make wood straight.
11. A wrench is used to open or tighten things.
12. A wedge is used to split materials.
13. Rulers are used for measuring.
14. To be safe, tools need to be handled with care.
15. Goggles should be worn to protect our eyes when using tools.
16. Pencils and chalk are marking tools.
17. After use, tools need to be put away and stored.

Vocabulary

1. **tool**—a device for doing work. Hammers and screwdrivers are tools.
2. **clamp**—a tool used to join or hold things.
3. **drill**—a tool that cuts holes.
4. **hammer**—a tool used to insert or remove objects such as nails.
5. **plane**—a tool used for shaving wood.
6. **pliers**—a tool used for holding objects.
7. **ruler**—a measuring tool.
8. **saw**—a cutting tool with sharp edges.
9. **screwdriver**—a tool used to turn screws.
10. **wedge**—a tool used for splitting.
11. **wrench**—a tool that opens and tightens things.

Bulletin Board

The purpose of this bulletin board is to develop awareness of tool types, as well as to foster visual discrimination skills. A shadow tool match bulletin board can be constructed by drawing six or seven tool pieces on tagboard. See the illustration. These pieces can be colored and then cut out. Next, trace the tools on black construction paper to make shadows of each piece. These shadow pieces can be attached to the bulletin board. Magnet pieces can be applied to both the shadows and the colored tool pieces. Otherwise, a pushpin can be placed above the shadow and a hole can be punched in the colored tool piece. The children can match the colored tool piece to its corresponding-shaped shadow.

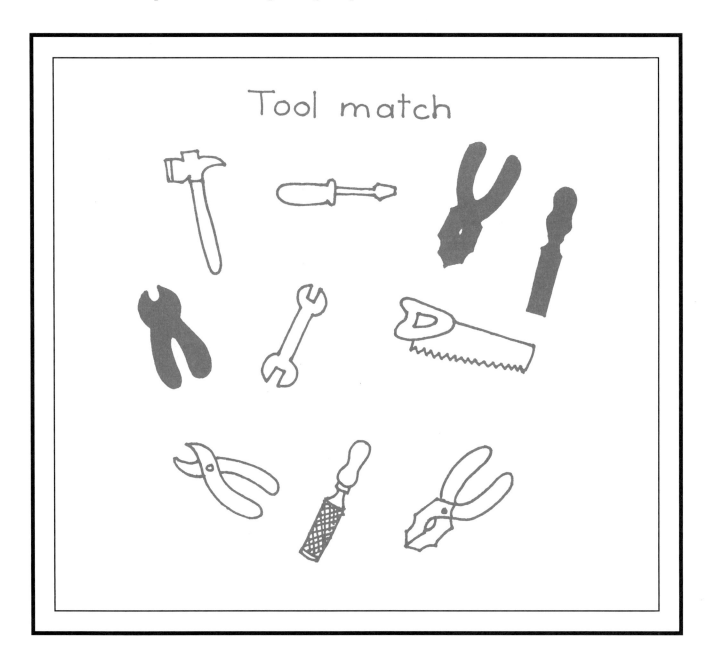

Family Letter

InBox

Dear Families,

Construction tools will be the focus of our next curriculum unit. This unit will help your child become more aware of many kinds of tools, their purposes, and tool safety. While exploring the classroom activities, the children will have opportunities to use many hand tools at the woodworking bench.

At School

Some of the activities the children will participate in include:

- Painting with screwdrivers and wrenches

- Exploring wood shavings in the sensory table

- Setting up a mechanic's shop where the children can pretend to fix cars

- Visiting with Mr. Smith, a local shoe repairman, on Wednesday. Mr. Smith will show us the tools and techniques he uses to repair shoes.

- Exploring woodworking tools with Bob the builder, who will show us how to use woodworking tools

At Home

To promote the development of language skills, recall with your child the tools you use in your home—from cooking and cleaning tools to gardening tools. Count the number of tools that are in each room of your house. Which room contains the most tools? This activity can promote the mathematical concepts of rational counting and the vocabulary concepts of most and least.

Have fun with your child!

Arts and Crafts

1. Rulers
Set rulers and paper on the table. The children can then experiment with creating lines and geometric shapes.

2. Tool Print
Pour a small amount of thick, colored tempera paint in a flat pan. Also, provide the children with miniature tools such as wrenches, screwdrivers, and paper. The children then can place the tools in the paint pan, remove them, and make prints with them on paper.

Cooking

3 cups brown sugar
3 cups margarine or butter
6 cups oatmeal
1 tablespoon baking soda
3 cups flour

Place all of the ingredients in a bowl. Let the children use clean, child-size wooden hammers to mash and knead. Form into small balls and place on an ungreased cookie sheet. Butter the bottom of a glass. Dip the bottom of the glass into a saucer with sugar. Use the glass to flatten the balls. Bake in an oven preheated to 350 degrees for 10 to 12 minutes. Makes 15 dozen.

Dramatic Play

1. The Carpenter
Place a carpentry box with scissors, rulers, and masking tape in the woodworking area. Also, provide large cardboard boxes and paint, if desired.

2. Shoemaker Store
Set up a shoemaker's store. Provide the children with shoes, toy hammers, smocks, cash registers, and play money. The children can act out mending, buying, and selling shoes.

Field Trips and Resource People

1. Shoe Repair Store
Visit a shoe repair store. Observe a shoe being repaired.

2. Woodworker
Invite into the classroom a parent or other person who enjoys woodworking as a hobby.

Fingerplays and Chants

Carpenter's Hammer
The carpenter's hammer goes rap, rap, tap
   (make hammer motion)
And his saw goes see, saw, see.
   (make saw motions)
He planes and measures and
   hammers and saws
   (act out each one)
While he builds a house for me.
   (draw house with index fingers)

Johnny's Hammer
(Say the same words, adding one hammer each time. Children are to pretend to hammer using various body parts:

Verse 1: one hand hitting leg.
Verse 2: two hands hitting legs.
Verse 3: use motions for verses 1 and 2, plus tap one foot.
Verse 4: verses 1, 2, and 3, plus tap other foot.
Verse 5: verses 1 to 4, plus nod head. At the end of verse 5, say, "Then he goes to sleep," and place both hands by the side of your head.

You can also change the name used in the fingerplay to include names of children in your classroom.)

Johnny works with one hammer,
   one hammer, one hammer.
Johnny works with one hammer, then he
   works with two.

The Cobbler
Cobbler, cobbler, mend my shoe.
   (point to shoe)
Get it done by half past two.
   (hold up two fingers)
Half past two is much too late.
Get it done by half past eight.
   (hold up eight fingers)

Group Time
(Games, Language)

1. Tool of the Day
Each day of this unit, introduce a "tool of the day." Explain how each tool is used and who uses it. If possible, leave the tool out for children to use on the woodworking bench. *Caution:* The use of tools needs to be closely supervised.

2. Thank-You Letter
Using a pencil as a tool, let the children dictate a thank-you note to any resource person or field trip site coordinator who has contributed to the program.

Large Muscle

The Workbench
In the woodworking area, place various tools, wood, and goggles for the children to use. It is very important to discuss the safety and limits used when at the workbench before this activity. An extra adult is helpful to supervise this area.

Math

1. Use of Rulers
Discuss how rulers are used. Provide children with rulers so that they may measure various objects in the classroom. Allow them to compare the lengths. Also, measure each child and construct a chart including each child's height.

2. Weighing Tools
Place scales and a variety of tools on the math table. Let the children explore weighing the tools.

Music

1. "This Is the Way"
(Sing to the tune of "Mulberry Bush")

This is the way we saw our wood, saw our
   wood, saw our wood.
This is the way we saw our wood, so early in
   the morning.

(Other verses: Pound our nails
                  Drill a hole
                  Use a screwdriver)

2. "Johnny Works with One Hammer"
Johnny works with one hammer,
One hammer, one hammer.
   (make hammering motion with right
   hand)
Johnny works with one hammer
Then he works with two.
Johnny works with two hammers …
   (motion with left and right hands)
Johnny works with three hammers …
   (motion with both hands and right foot)
Johnny work with four hammers …
   (motion with both hands and both feet)
Johnny works with five hammers …
   (motion with both hands and feet and
   with head)
Then he goes to bed.

Science

1. Exploring Levels
Place levels and wood scraps on a table for the children to explore while being closely supervised.

2. Hammers

Collect a variety of hammers, various-sized nails, and wood scraps or styrofoam. Allow the children to practice pounding using the different tools and materials while closely supervising them.

3. The Wide World of Rulers

Set up a display with different types and sizes of rulers. Paper and pencils can also be added to create interest.

 Sensory

1. Scented Play Dough

Prepare play dough and add a few drops of extract such as peppermint, anise, or vanilla. Also, collect a variety of scissors, and place in the art area with the play dough.

Caution: The use of scissors needs to be closely supervised.

2. Wood Shavings

Place wood shavings in the sensory table along with scoops and pails.

 Social Studies

1. Tool Safety

Discuss the safe use of tools. Allow the children to help decide what classroom rules are necessary for using tools. Make a chart containing these rules to display in the woodworking area.

2. Helper Chart

Design a helper chart for the children to assist with the cleanup and care of the classroom tools. Each day select new children to assist, assuring that everyone gets a turn. To participate, the children can be responsible for cleaning the dirty tools and putting them away.

 Books

The following books can be used to complement this theme:

Adamson, Heather. (2004). *A Day in the Life of a Construction Worker*. Mankato, MN: Capstone Press.

Araki, Mie. (2003). *The Magic Toolbox*. San Francisco: Chronicle Books.

Barton, Byron. (1995). *Tools*. New York: HarperCollins.

Boekhoff, Patti Marlene. (2006). *What Does a Construction Worker Do?* Berkeley Heights, NJ: Enslow Elementary.

Boelts, Maribeth. (1997). *Little Bunny's Cool Tool Set*. Illustrated by Kathy Parkinson. Morton Grove, IL: A. Whitman.

Brady, Peter. (1996). *Bulldozers. Mankato*, MN: Bridgestone Books.

Fleming, Denise. (2002). *Alphabet under Construction*. New York: Henry Holt.

Hoban, Tana. (1997). *Construction Zone*. New York: Greenwillow.

Kilby, Don. (2003). *At a Construction Site*. Tonawanda, NY: Kids Can Press.

Klinting, Lars. (1996). *Bruno the Carpenter*. New York: Holt.

Macken, JoAnn Early. (2008). *Construction Crew*. Mankato, MN: Capstone Press.

Macken, JoAnn Early. (2008). *Construction Tools*. Mankato, MN: Capstone Press.

Macken, JoAnn Early. (2009). *Building a House*. Mankato, MN: Capstone Press.

Miura, Taro. (2006). *Tools*. San Francisco: Chronicle Books

Neitzel, Shirley. (1997). *The House I'll Build for the Wren*. Illustrated by Nancy Winslow Parker. New York: Greenwillow.

Olson, K. C. (2004). *Construction Countdown*. Illustrated by David Gordon. New York: Henry Holt.

Pallotta, Jerry. (2006). *The Construction Alphabet Book*. Illustrated by Rob Bolster. Watertown, MA: Charlesbridge.

Parish, Herman. (2006). *Amelia Bedelia under Construction*. Illustrated by Lynn Sweat. New York: Greenwillow Books.

Schaefer, Lola. (2006). *Toolbox Twins*. Illustrated by Melissa Iwai. New York: Henry Holt.

Schomp, Virginia. (1998). *If You Were a Construction Worker*. New York: Benchmark Books.

Shulman, Lisa. (2002). *Old McDonald Had a Woodshop*. Illustrated by Ashley Wolff. New York: G.P. Putnam.

Singer, Marilyn. (2006). *Let's Build a Clubhouse*. Illustrated by Timothy Bush. New York: Clarion Books.

Sobel, June. (2006). *B Is for Bulldozer: A Construction ABC*. Illustrated by Melissa Iwai. Orlando, FL. Harcourt.

Sturges, Philemon. (2006). *I Love Tools!* Illustrated by Shari Halpern. New York: HarperCollins.

Wallace, John. (1997). *Building a House with Mr. Bumble*. Cambridge, MA: Candlewick Press.

Williams, Linda D. (2005). *Dump Trucks*. Mankato, MN: Capstone Press.

Winne, Joanne. (2001). *A Day with a Carpenter*. New York: Children's Press.

Technology and Multimedia

The following technology and multimedia products can be used to complement this theme:

"A Bulldozer Operator I Will Be" [CD]. (2007). In *50 Learning Songs*. Stow, OH: Twin Sisters Productions.

"Cement Mixer" and "Ding Dong Digger (The Power Shovel)" [CD] (1997). In *Cars, Trucks and Trains*. Long Branch, NJ: Kimbo Educational.

"The Community Helper Hop" [CD] (1996). In *People in Our Neighborhood*. Long Branch, NJ: Kimbo Educational. (This song discusses construction workers—builders, carpenters, bricklayers, plasterers, painters, plumbers, and electricians.)

"Fix it Up" [CD]. (2009). In *For Those about to Hop*. Burbank, CA: Walt Disney Records.

"If I Had a Hammer" [CD]. (2006). In *Train Songs and Other Tracks*. Mission Viejo, CA: Stargazer Productions.

 Additional teaching resources to accompany this Theme can be found on the book's companion website. Go to www.cengagebrain.com to access the site for a variety of useful resources.

Science Materials and Equipment

Teachers need to continuously provide science materials for the classroom. Materials that can be collected include:

acorns and other nuts
aluminum foil
ball bearings
balloons
binoculars
bird nests
bones
bowls and cups
clock
cocoons
corks
dishpans
drinking straws
drums
egg cartons
eggbeaters
eyedroppers and basters
fabric scraps
filter paper
flashlights
flowers
gears
insect nests
insects
jacks
kaleidoscopes

locks and keys
magnets (varying strengths and sizes)
magnifying glasses with good lenses
marbles
measuring cups and spoons
microscopes
milk cartons
mirrors (all sizes)
moths
musical instruments
newspapers
nails, screws, and bolts
paper bags
paper of various types
paper rolls and spools
plants
plastic bags
plastic containers with lids (many sizes)
plastic tubing
pots, pans, trays, and muffin tins
prisms
pulleys

rocks
rubber tubing
rulers
safety goggles (child size)
sandpaper
scales
scissors (assorted sizes)
screen wire
sieves, sifters, and funnels
seeds
spatulas
sponges
stones
string
styrofoam
tape
thermometers
tongs and tweezers
tools such as hammer and pliers
tuning forks
waxed paper
weeds
wheels
wood and other building materials

Theme 21
CONTAINERS

Uses	Types	Materials
packaging liquids and solids	boxes	glass
carrying items	jars	aluminum
	cans	steel
	bags	cardboard
	bottles	paper
	baskets	plastic
	bowls	fabric
		wood

Theme Goals

Through participating in the experiences provided by this theme, the children may learn:

1. Types of containers
2. Materials used to make containers
3. Container uses

Concepts for the Children to Learn

1. There are many kinds of containers.
2. Boxes, jars, cans, bags, and bottles are containers.
3. Bowls, baskets, and pockets are containers.
4. Containers are used to hold and carry things.
5. Containers can be made from many materials.
6. Boxes are usually made from cardboard and paper.
7. Cans are made from aluminum or steel.
8. Fruit juice, soup, and paint are stored in cans.
9. Jars are usually made from glass or plastic.
10. Bags can be paper, plastic, or fabric.
11. Bottles are made from glass or plastic.
12. Bottles usually have caps on them.
13. Baskets can be made from wood or plastic.
14. Many items are sold in containers.

Vocabulary

1. **bag**—a container made of paper, cloth, or plastic that can be closed at the top. Bags are used to carry objects and food.
2. **basket**—a container used to hold objects and foods. Baskets come in many sizes.
3. **bottle**—a container made of glass or plastic for holding liquids such as milk and juice. Most bottles have caps.
4. **bowl**—a deep dish. Bowls can hold soup, cereals, and other food.
5. **can**—a container that can hold food or paint.
6. **container**—a box, jar, or can that is used to hold food or objects.

Bulletin Board

The purpose of this bulletin board is to promote the development of visual discrimination, hand-eye coordination, problem-solving, and memory skills. Create the containers by sketching them onto heavy tagboard. Use felt-tip markers to add color and details. Laminate and cut out the containers. Trace the cutout container pieces onto black construction paper. Cut out these pieces and attach to the bulletin board. A magnet strip should be attached to the containers and the shadow pieces. The children can match each container shape to its shadow on the bulletin board.

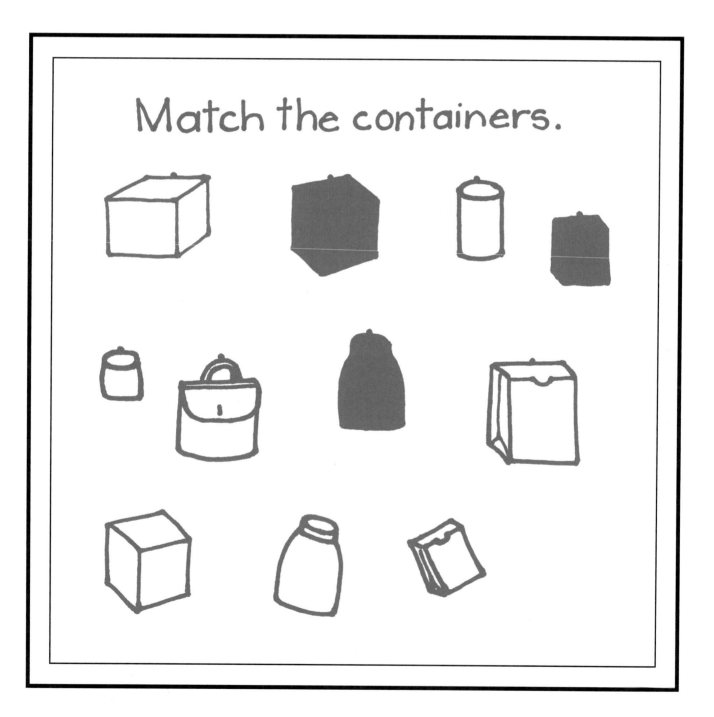

Family Letter

Dear Families,

Try to imagine a world without boxes, jars, bags, baskets, or bowls. It's hard to do! There are so many kinds of containers—we use them every day and probably never realize it. This week at school, we will focus on the subject of containers. The children will learn about types of containers, typical materials used to make containers, and items that come in containers.

At School

As we learn about containers this week at school, the children will be:

- Making prints with plastic berry baskets and paint in the art area.

- Playing in our classroom grocery store set up in the dramatic play area. We could use your help. Please save and send empty, clean food containers to school. We will use the boxes, bottles, and jars as grocery items in the dramatic play area. Thank you.

- Sorting various containers by type and materials.

Parent Involvement

If you have special containers reflecting your culture or heritage, we invite you to share them with our class. Please contact me so a time can be arranged for your visit. The children will enjoy having you share with us!

At Home

You can help your child make discoveries about containers. A few things to try include the following:

- Look in your refrigerator or kitchen and find containers. How many are boxes, cans, bottles, and so on?

- Make a milk carton bird feeder. Cut a large rectangle in the side of a clean half-gallon milk carton. Fill the bottom of the carton with birdseed. Hang the bird feeder outside where it can be observed.

Have a good week!

Arts and Crafts

1. Basket Prints
Collect plastic berry baskets, construction paper, and paints. Pour paint(s) into shallow trays. Have the children dip the bottom of the plastic berry baskets in paint, and then press them on construction paper.

2. Jar Prints
Save and clean baby food jars. Provide the jars, construction paper, and paint(s). Pour the paint(s) into individual trays, just covering the bottoms. Children can turn the jars over and dip the tops of the baby food jars in the paint, then press them on their paper to create prints.

3. Zipper-Seal Plastic Bag Painting
Materials needed include tempera paints and small zipper-seal plastic bags—one per child. Ask each child which two colors of paint he or she would like. Put a small amount of the two colors of paint into a zipper-seal plastic bag. Carefully seal the bags. Apply cellophane or masking tape for added safety. The children can then squeeze their bags to mix the colors. The bag can be placed on a table, and fingers can be used to fingerpaint without getting messy.

4. Colored Salt Jars
Create several colors of salt (or sand) by adding teaspoons of tempera paint powder to bowls of salt. Stir well. Collect baby food jars and lids. To create a colored salt jar, the children spoon different colors of salt into the jar, creating layers of beautiful colors. Fill jars to the top and secure lids tightly. If desired, squeeze glue around the jar rim before placing the lid on.

Cooking

1. Container Cookies
1/2 cup butter or margarine
1/2 cup shortening
1 cup sugar
1 egg
2 tablespoons milk
1/2 teaspoon vanilla
2 1/4 cups flour
1/2 teaspoon baking soda
1/2 teaspoon salt
Filling choices:
Pie filling—any flavor
Jam or jelly
Chocolate chips
Raisins
Toasted coconut
Sugar

Beat butter (or shortening) in a large mixing bowl with an electric mixer on medium speed, about 30 seconds. Add sugar and beat until fluffy. Add egg, milk, and vanilla. Beat well. In a medium mixing bowl, combine flour, baking soda, and salt. With the electric mixer on low, gradually add the flour mixture to the butter mixture, beating well. Cover and chill dough in the freezer about 20 minutes or until firm to handle. Divide dough in half. Shape each half into a roll 3 inches thick and 3 inches long. Wrap in plastic wrap. Freeze at least 6 hours or up to 6 months.

When ready to bake the cookies, preheat oven to 375 degrees. Unwrap one roll of dough. Slice the roll crosswise to make 16 slices about 1/8-inch thick. Repeat with the other roll. Place half of the slices 2 inches apart on ungreased cookie sheets. In the center of the circles, place 2 teaspoons of desired filling(s). Top each with a plain slice of dough. Press a floured fork around the edges to seal well. Sprinkle with a little sugar.

Bake for 12 to 15 minutes or until edges are golden brown. Place cookies on rack to cool.

2. Butter in a Jar
Pour 1/3 cup of whipping cream in a clean small jar. Secure lid tightly. Allow children to take turns shaking the jar until a lump of butter forms. This will take several minutes. Pour off liquid, add a dash of salt, and stir. Spread butter on crackers to enjoy.

3. Pita Pocket Sandwiches
Use pita bread to create yummy pocket sandwiches. Cut rounds of pita bread in half, creating pocket-shaped pieces. Fill with favorite sandwich ingredients. Try sloppy joes, tuna salad, or ham and cheese.

Dramatic Play

Grocery Store

To create a grocery store in the dramatic play area, provide props such as a cash register, posters of various foods, smocks or shirts, paper and plastic grocery bags, and empty, clean food containers. A note can be sent home requesting help with this project. Set food containers on shelves or in baskets to resemble a grocery store.

Fingerplays and Chants

There Was a Little Turtle

by Vachel Lindsay

There was a little turtle,
    (make small circle with hands)
He lived in a box.
    (make box with both hands)

He swam in a puddle,
    (wiggle hands)
He climbed on the rocks.
    (climb fingers of one hand up over the other)

He snapped at a mosquito,
    (clap hands)
He snapped at a flea,
    (repeat)
He snapped at a minnow,
    (repeat)
He snapped at me!
    (point to self)
He caught the mosquito,
    (catching motion with hands and arms)
He caught the flea,
    (repeat)
He caught the minnow,
    (repeat)
But he didn't catch me!
    (shake head from side to side)

Group Time
(Games, Language)

1. Mystery Box

Collect a box with a lid. Color or decorate as desired. Secretly place an object inside the box. At group time, begin by saying, "There is something in my box. What do you think it might be?" Give identifying clues until the children guess what the object is.

2. Cookie Jar

Have the children sit on the floor, with their legs crossed, in a circle formation. The children should repeat this rhythmic chant with the teacher while clapping their hands together and then clapping their hands on their thighs:

Someone took a cookie from the cookie jar.
Who took a cookie from the cookie jar?
Mara took a cookie from the cookie jar.
(Mara): Who me?
(All): Yes, you!
(Mara): Couldn't be!
(All): Then who?
(Mara, naming another child): ——— took a cookie from the cookie jar.
Use each child's name.

3. Hiding Game

Collect three small boxes. Set out the boxes in a row, and place a bean or button under one of the boxes. While the children watch, move the order of the cups several times. Ask the children to guess which cup the bean is under. The bean or button can be hidden again, and the game repeated.

Large Muscle

1. Box Obstacle Course

Collect large cardboard boxes. Open the tops and bottoms, and lay boxes on their sides to create tunnels. Place the boxes in a maze-type course and let children discover ways to complete the course. They could run, walk, crawl, or hop from beginning to end.

2. Inside a Barrel

Say, "You are *outside* a big barrel. Now get in it. You are *inside* the barrel—now get out of it. You are *underneath* the barrel—now get out from under it. You are on *top* of the barrel—now get down from it."

3. Unwrapping a Present

Say, "It is your birthday, and you are going to get a present. Show me the shape of the box. How big is the box? Feel the box. Hold the box. Shake the box. Unwrap the box. Take the present out. Put the present back into the box. Rewrap the box."

4. Movin' Through

Providing there is sufficient space, this activity can be successfully introduced indoors or outdoors. Ask the children to show you with their body how they would move to get through:

- Sand
- Mud
- Ice cream
- The ocean
- Peanut butter
- Paste
- Tempera paint
- Mashed potatoes
- Pudding
- Chocolate chip cookies
- Apple sauce

Math

1. Container Sort

Collect various containers and place in a laundry basket. Encourage children to find ways to sort the containers. Containers could be sorted by type, size, or construction material.

2. Pocket Count

During a group time, have the children individually stand up and take note of the pockets on their clothes. Assist in counting the number of pockets each child has. If appropriate, the information could be recorded and put on a graph to be displayed. Repeat the activity on a different day and compare the results.

3. How Many?

Place a number of small objects (such as paper clips, dice, marbles, and buttons) in a clear plastic bag or a jar. Let children guess how many of the objects are in the bag. Count the objects together. Repeat with a different number of objects.

4. Container Stack

Roll a die. The number that is rolled is the number of containers to be stacked. Continue rolling and stacking. See how many containers can be stacked before the containers fall.

Music

1. "I Have Something in My Pocket"
(Traditional)

I have something in my pocket that belongs across my face.
I keep it very close at hand in a most convenient place.
I'm sure you couldn't guess it if you'd take a long, long while.
So, I'll take it out and put it on,
It's a great, big, happy smile.

2. "Tony Has Three Pockets"
(Sing to the tune of "Mary Wore a Red Dress")
(Insert individual children's names and substitute articles of clothing that could have pockets, such as a dress, pants, a jacket, etc.)

Tony has three pockets,
Three pockets, three pockets.
Tony has three pockets,
On his shirt today.

3. "A Tisket, a Tasket"
(Traditional)

A tisket, a tasket, a green and yellow basket.
I wrote a letter to my love
And on the way I dropped it.
I dropped it, I dropped it
And on the way I dropped it.
I wrote a letter to my love
And on the way I dropped it.

Science

1. **Insect Keeper**

   Collect milk cartons or similar-sized cardboard boxes. For each insect keeper, cut a rectangle out of each side of a clean carton or box. Glue or tape the top closed. Decorate if desired. After an insect or two are found, put the insects, along with a twig and grass, in the carton. Quickly insert box in the leg portion of an old nylon stocking (or cover with netting), and use a twist tie or rubber band to fasten the top.

2. **Rubber Band Guitar**

   Each child will need a small box or carton, such as an individual cereal box, check box, or half-pint milk carton. For each "guitar," cut a rectangle in one side of a box or carton. Decorate as desired. Wrap each container with four or five rubber bands. The children can pluck or strum the rubber bands to create sounds.

3. **Wave Jar**

   Fill a clear jar half full with water. Add a few drops of food coloring, if desired. Pour mineral oil to fill the jar. Secure the lid tightly. Watch what happens as the jar is gently tilted back and forth. Individual wave jars can be made using baby food jars.

4. **Sound Jars or Boxes**

   Collect 10 identical small boxes. Fill the containers, as pairs, with five different materials such as popcorn kernels, pennies, sand, nails, cotton balls, rubber bands, paper clips, and the like. Secure caps or lids, and place containers on a table. Encourage children to shake the containers to find the matching sound containers.

5. **Musical Jars**

   Fill five or six identical-sized jars with varying amounts of water. Add drops of food coloring to water if desired. Encourage children to gently tap the sides of the jars with a metal spoon to create sounds. The jars will produce low to high sounds. Some children may be able to arrange the jars from lowest to highest sounds.

6. **Fish in a Bottle**

   Save and clean a 2-liter plastic soda bottle. Fill the bottle one-quarter full with water. Add a few drops of blue food coloring to the water and swirl to mix. Barely blow up some small balloons and tie ends closed. Use a permanent marker to draw eyes, gills, and mouths on balloons to make them look like fish. Push the balloons into the bottle, and securely fasten the cap of the bottle. Hold the bottle on its side, and it will look like fish in the water. Gently rock the bottle back and forth to create waves.

Sensory

The following materials can be added to the sensory table:

- Plastic bottles, funnels, and colored water
- Plastic jars, animals, and sand
- Berry baskets, plastic zoo animals, and grains
- Zipper-seal plastic bags, scoops, and sand

Books

The following books can be used to complement this theme:

Battle-Lavert, Gwendolyn. (2000). *The Shaking Bag*. Illustrated by Aminah Brenda Lynn Robinson. Morton Grove, IL: A. Whitman.

Boyd, Lizi. (1991). *Willy and the Cardboard Boxes*. New York: Viking.

Braun, Sebastien. (2009). *Meeow and the Big Box*. London: Boxer Books.

Brimmer, Larry Dance. (2001). *The Big, Beautiful, Brown Box*. Illustrated by Christine Tripp. New York: Children's Press.

Burningham, John. (1996). *The Shopping Basket.* Cambridge, MA: Candlewick Press.

Cleminson, Katie. (2009). *Magic Box: A Magical Story.* New York: Hyperion Books.

Craig, Helen. (2003). *Susie and Alfred in the Night of the Paper Bag Monsters.* Cambridge, MA: Candlewick Press.

De Varennes, Monique. (2007). *The Jewel Box Ballerinas.* Illustrated by Ana Juan. New York: Schwartz & Wade Books.

Fitzgerald, Ella. (2003). *A-Tisket, A-Tasket.* Illustrated by Ora Eitan. New York: Philomel Books.

Jeffries, Alison. (2004). *Sam and the Bag.* Illustrated by Dan Andreasen. Orlando, FL: Harcourt.

McAllister, Angela. (2003). *Harry's Box.* Illustrated by Jenny Jones. New York: Bloomsbury Children's Book.

Miller, Sara Swan. (2001). *Cat in the Bag.* Illustrated by Ben Mahan. New York: Children's Press.

Neitzel, Shirley. (1995). *The Bag I'm Taking to Grandma's.* Illustrated by Nancy Winslow Parker. New York: Greenwillow Books.

Patricelli, Leslie. (2007). *The Birthday Box: Happy Birthday to Me!* Cambridge, MA: Candlewick Press.

Ruzzier, Sergio. (2010). *Hey, Rabbit!* New York: Roaring Brook Press.

Spiegelman, Art. (2008). *Jack and the Box.* New York: Raw Junior.

Tibo, Gilles. (1995). *Simon and His Boxes.* Plattsburgh, NY: Tundra Books.

Young, Ed. (2004). *I, Doko: The Tale of a Basket.* New York: Philomel Books.

Technology and Multimedia

The following technology and multimedia products can be used to complement this theme:

"A Tisket, A Tasket" [CD]. (2004). In *Toddler Twosome.* Redway, CA: Music Little People.

"Buckets and Cans" [CD]. (2009). In *For Those about to Hop.* Burbank, CA: Walt Disney Records.

"I'm a Little Teapot" [CD]. (2007). In *Nursery Rhymes and Good Ol' Times.* New Oklahoma City, OK: Melody House.

"Ten Green Bottles" [CD]. (2002). In *Growing Up with Ella Jenkins.* Washington, DC: Smithsonian Folkways.

"Who Stole the Cookies from the Cookie Jar?" [CD]. (1998). In *Silly Songs.* Redway, CA: Music Little People.

Additional teaching resources to accompany this Theme can be found on the book's companion website. Go to www.cengagebrain.com to access the site for a variety of useful resources.

Theme 22
CREATIVE MOVEMENT

Accessories
ballet shoes
tap shoes
costumes
makeup

Feelings
happy
sad
angry
surprised

Types of Dance
ballet
tap
jazz
social
folk
modern
street dancing
line dancing
hula

Sound Sources
CD player
digital music (MP3) player
DVD player
drums
guitar
rhythm sticks
band

Body Movements
twist
slide
wave arms
yoga
alone
with partner
in group
shapes
sports

Theme Goals

Through participating in the experiences provided by this theme, the children may learn:

1. Creative movement accessories
2. Creative movement sound sources
3. Body movements used in creative movement
4. Expression of feelings through creative movement
5. Types of dance

Concepts for the Children to Learn

1. People can dance to the sound of music.
2. The CD player, MP3 player, DVD player, and drums are all sound sources used for dance.
3. The guitar, rhythm sticks, and a band are also sound sources for creative movement.
4. Dancing and moving can be done alone, with a partner, or in a group.
5. Our bodies can move in many different ways to the sound of music
6. There are many types of dance.
7. Ballet, tap, jazz, and social are some types of dances.
8. Folk, modern, street, and line are other types of dances.
9. Happy, sad, angry, and surprised are feelings that can be expressed through dance.
10. There are many types of dancers.
11. Some dancers wear special costumes and makeup.
12. Ballet and tap dancers wear special shoes.
13. Our bodies can move to the sound of drums, guitars, and rhythm sticks.
14. We can twist, slide, and wave our arms during dance.

Vocabulary

1. **ballet**—movement that usually tells a story.
2. **dance**—a pattern of body movements to the sound of music.
3. **movement**—change in body position.
4. **music**—sounds made by instruments or voices.

Bulletin Board

The purpose of this bulletin board is to promote the development of one-to-one correspondence skills and to match a set to a written numeral. Construct tank tops, each of a different color, from a sheet of tagboard. See the illustration. Print a numeral that would be developmentally appropriate for the group of children on each tank top. Draw a corresponding number of black dots below each numeral. Construct a tutu ruffle from white tagboard for each top. Place colored dots on each ruffle. Trace ruffles onto black construction paper. Laminate all pieces. Staple tank tops and shadow ruffles to the bulletin board. The children can match the ruffles with dots to the corresponding tank top, using holes in the white ruffles and pushpins in the shadow ruffles.

Family Letter

Dear Families,

Children love to dance, and they are constantly on the move. We will begin a curriculum unit on creative movement. Throughout the classroom activities, the children will discover the different ways our bodies move, and also learn about various forms of dance. Some of the activities include:

- Singing songs and moving to music
- Dancing in the dance studio that will be set up in the dramatic play area
- Watching other people move
- Participating in an aerobics class

Parental Involvement

If you have any special ethnic dances you enjoy, we invite you to share them with our class. Please contact me so a time for your visit can be arranged. The children will enjoy having you visit our class and learning new types of dances.

Field Trip

On Thursday, at 2:30 p.m., we will be taking a bus to a dance studio. At the studio, we will observe dancers and learn a few steps from a dance instructor. To assist with the trip, we need several parents to accompany us. Please call the school if you are available.

At Home

As your child develops, you will observe increased control and interest in perfecting and improving motor skills. To foster the development of large muscle skills, balance, and body coordination, provide opportunities each day for vigorous play. Give suggestions such as "How fast can you hop?", "How far can you hop on one foot?", and so on. Also, ask your child to walk on a curved line, a straight line, or a balance beam.

Enjoy your child!

Arts and Crafts

1. **Stencils**

   The teacher can construct stencils from tagboard. Shapes such as shoes, ballerinas, circles, and so forth can be made and added to the art table for use during self-selected activity periods.

2. **Musical Painting**

   Provide a CD, DVD, or MP3 player with headphones and a CD, DVD, or playlist of children's music or classical music at the easel. The children can listen and move their brushes to the music if desired.

Cooking

1. **Orange Buttermilk Smoothie**

   1 quart buttermilk
   3 cups orange juice
   1/2 teaspoon cinnamon
   1/4 cup honey
   Enjoy!

   This recipe serves 14 children. Mix the ingredients for fifteen seconds. Then pour 1/2 cup into plastic cups or containers with lids. Let the children creatively shake their smoothie and drink at snack time.

2. **Indian Flatbread**

   2 cups all-purpose flour
   1/4 cup unflavored yogurt
   1 egg, slightly beaten
   1 1/2 teaspoons baking powder
   1 teaspoon sugar
   1/4 teaspoon salt
   1/4 teaspoon baking soda
   1/2 cup milk
   Vegetable oil
   Poppy seeds

   Mix all ingredients except milk, vegetable oil, and poppy seeds. Stir in enough milk to make a soft dough. Turn dough onto lightly floured surface. Demonstrate kneading the bread by folding the outside edge of the dough over onto itself and then pushing the dough away with the heels of your hands.

Lightly flour the children's hands and let them take turns creatively kneading the bread. Add just enough flour to keep the dough from sticking while kneading. When the dough is elastic, smooth and no longer sticky it has been kneaded enough. Then place in a container or large bowl that has a top. Grease the inside of the container. Cover and let rest in a warm place for 3 hours.

Divide the dough into 6 or 8 equal parts. Flatten each part on a lightly floured surface, rolling it into a 6-inch × 4-inch leaf shape about 1/4 inch thick. Brush with vegetable oil; sprinkle with poppy seeds.

Place 2 cookie sheets in oven; heat oven to 450 degrees. Remove hot cookie sheets from oven; place breads on cookie sheets. Bake until firm, 6 to 8 minutes. Makes 6 to 8 breads.

Note: From *Betty Crocker's International Cookbook*, 1980, New York: Random House. Reprinted with permission.

Dramatic Play

1. **Dance Studio**

   Add to the dramatic play area tap shoes, tutus, ballet shoes, tights, and leotards. Provide a CD player with CDs, a DVD player with music- or dance-related DVDs, or an MP3 player.

2. **Fitness Gym**

   Add to the dramatic play area a small mat, headbands, wristbands, sweatshirts, sweatpants, leotards, and music.

Field Trips and Resource People

1. **Field Trips**

   - Dance studio
   - Health club
   - Gymnasium

2. Resource People

Invite the following people to class to talk with the children:

- A dancer or dance instructor
- A gymnast
- An aerobics instructor

Fingerplays and Chants

Hands on Shoulders

(Follow actions described for each line)

Hands on shoulders
Hands on knees.
Hands in front of you, if you please.
Touch your shoulders,
Now your nose,
Now your head and now your toes.
Hands go up high in the air,
Now touch your ears,
Then touch your hair.
Hands way up high just like before.
Now clap your hands,
One, two, three, four!

Clap, Two, Three, Four!

Clap, two, three, four, five, six, seven.
(clap hands)
Shake, two, three, four, five, six, seven.
(shake fingers)
Slap, two, three, four, five, six, seven.
(slap knees)
Roll, two, three, four, five, six, seven.
(rotate hands over each)
Snap, two, three, four, five, six, seven.
(snap fingers)
Tap, two, three, four, five, six, seven.
(pound fists)
Push, two, three, four, five, six, seven.
(push hands forward)
Clap, two, three, four, five, six, seven.
(clap hands)

My Wiggles

I can reach high. (stretch up high)
I can reach low. (touch the ground)
I'll touch my head. (touch head)

And then my toes. (touch toes)
I'll wiggle my fingers. (move fingers)
And touch them, too. (touch fingers)
I'm having fun. (point to self)
And so are you! (point to another person)
We'll stretch up to the ceiling. (stretch up high)
And reach out to the wall. (reach arms to the side)
We'll bend to touch our knees and toes. (touch knees, then toes)
Then stand up straight and tall. (stand up straight)

Taller, Smaller

When I stretch up, I feel so tall. (stand up and reach hands up into the air)
When I bend down, I feel so small. (crouch down)
Taller, taller, taller, taller. (slowly stand and raise arms)
Smaller, smaller, smaller, smaller. (slowly crouch down)
Into a tiny ball. (tuck in arms and head)

Group Time
(Games and Language)

1. Balloon Bounce

Blow up balloons for the children to use at group time. Play music and have children bounce the balloons up in the air. Let the balloons float to the ground when the music ends. Supervision is required for this activity. Broken balloons should be immediately removed from the environment.

2. Toy Movements

Form a circle and move like different toys. Try to include as many actual toys as you can, so that the children can observe each toy moving, and then can more easily pretend to be that toy.

- Jack-in-the-box
- Wind-up dolls
- Roll like a ball
- Skates

3. **Rag Doll**
Repeat the following poem as the child creates a dance with a rag doll:
If I were a rag doll
And I belonged to you,
Whenever I would try to dance,
This is what I'd do.

Large Muscle

1. **Streamer and Music Activity**
In the music area provide streamers. Play a variety of music, allowing the children, if desired, to move to the different rhythms.

2. **Do As I Say**
Provide the children verbal cues for moving. For example, say, "Move like you are sad," "Show me that you are tired," "You just received a special present," and "Show me how you feel."

3. **Animal Movement**
Ask a child to act out the way a certain animal moves. Examples include frog, spider, caterpillar, butterfly, and so on.

4. **Balance**
Add a balance beam or balance strip to the indoor or outdoor environment.

5. **Roly-Poly**
The children can stretch their bodies out on the floor. When touched by a teacher, the child rolls into a tight ball.

6. **Dancing Cloud**
Using an inflated white balloon or ball, let the children stand in a circle and bounce or hit it to each other.

7. **Obstacle Course**
Set up an obstacle course indoors or outdoors depending on the weather. Let the children move their bodies in many different ways. They can run or crawl through the course. Older children may enjoy hopping or skipping.

Math

1. **Matching Leotards to Hangers**
Using plastic hangers, prepare a numeral on each of the hangers. Provide the children with a box of leotards. Have a printed numeral on each. Encourage the children to match the numbered leotard with the identically numbered hanger.

2. **Following Steps**
Using tagboard, cut out some left feet and right feet. Write the numerals from 1 to 10 on the feet and arrange them in numerical order. Place the footprints on the floor, securing them with masking tape. Encourage the children to begin the walk on the numeral 1 and continue in the correct sequence.

3. **Ballet Puzzle**
Purchase a large poster of a ballet dancer. Laminate the poster or cover it with clear contact paper. Cut the poster into several large shapes. Place the puzzle in the manipulative area. During self-selected play periods, the children can reconstruct the puzzle.

Science

1. **Magnet Dancers**
On a piece of tagboard, draw pictures of 3-inch dancers. Stickers or pictures from magazines can also be used. Cut out the dancers, and attach paper clips to the back side. Use a small box and a magnet to make these dancers move. Hold up the dancers on one side of the box, and move up the dancer by holding and moving a magnet on the other side of the box.

2. **Kaleidoscopes**
On the science table, put a number of kaleidoscopes. The tiny figures inside appear to be dancing.

3. Dancing Shoes

Place various types of dancing shoes at the science table. Let the children compare the shape, size, color, and texture of the shoes. The children may also enjoy trying on the shoes for size and dancing in them.

Social Studies

Social Dancing

Let each child choose a partner. Encourage the children to hold hands. Play music as a background, so the partners can move together.

Books

The following books can be used to complement this theme:

Applegate, Katherine. (2009). *Don't Tap Dance on Your Teacher.* Illustrated by Brian Briggs. New York: HarperTrophy.

Asher, Sandy, and Kathryn Brown. (2001). *Stella's Dancing Days.* Illustrated by Kathryn Brown. San Diego, CA: Harcourt Brace.

Barrows, Annie. (2009). *Ivy & Bean Doomed to Dance.* Illustrated by Sophie Blackall. San Francisco: Chronicle Books.

Boynton, Sandra. (2008). *Let Us Dance, Little Pookie.* New York: Robin Corey Books.

Capucilli, Alyssa Satin. (2010). *Katy Duck Goes to Dance Class.* Illustrated by Henry Cole. New York: Little Simon.

Clay, Kathryn. (2010). *Ballet Dancing.* Mankato, MN: Capstone Press.

Clay, Kathryn. (2010). *Jazz Dancing.* Mankato, MN: Capstone Press.

Clay, Kathryn. (2010). *Tap Dancing.* Mankato, MN: Capstone Press.

Cocca-Leffler, Maryann. (2009). *My Dance Recital.* New York: Robin Corey Books.

Craig, Lindsey. (2010). *Dancing Feet!* Illustrated by Marc Brown. New York: Alfred A. Knopf.

Durango, Julia. (2006). *Cha-Cha Chimps.* Illustrated by Eleanor Taylor. New York: Simon & Schuster Books for Young Readers.

Duvall, Jill D. (1997). *Meet Rory Hohenstein, a Professional Dancer.* Photography by Lili S. Duvall. Chicago: Children's Press.

Esbensen, Barbara Juster. (1995). *Dance with Me.* Illustrated by Megan Lloyd. New York: HarperCollins.

Evans, Nate, and Laura Joffe Numeroff. (2008). *The Jellybeans and the Big Dance.* Illustrated by Lynn Munsinger. New York: Abrams Books for Young Readers.

Felix, Monique, and Jan Wahl. (2008). *Bear Dance.* Mankato, MN: Creative Editions.

French, Jackie. (2007). *Josephine Wants to Dance.* Illustrated by Bruce Whatley. New York: Abrams Books for Young Readers.

Gray, Libba Moore. (1995). *My Mama Had a Dancing Heart.* Illustrated by Raul Colon. New York: Orchard Books.

Grimm, Jakob. (1996). *The Twelve Dancing Princesses.* Retold by Jane Ray. New York: Dutton.

Hakala, Marjorie. (2009). *Mermaid Dance.* Illustrated by Mark Jones. Maplewood, NJ: Blue Apple Books.

Holabird, Katharine, and Helen Craig. (2000). *Angelina and the Princess.* Illustrated by Helen Craig. Middleton, WI: Pleasant Company.

Howells, Tania, and Tera Johnson. (2008). *Berkeley's Barn Owl Dance.* Toronto: Kids Can Press.

Hudson, Cheryl Willis. (2010). *My Friend Maya Loves to Dance.* Illustrated by Eric Velasquez. New York: Abrams Books for Young Readers.

Hueston, M. P. (2010). *The All-American Jump and Jive Jig.* Illustrated by Amanda Haley. New York: Sterling.

Hutchins, Pat. (2007). *Barn Dance!* New York: Greenwillow Books.

Isadora, Rachel. (1997). *Lili Backstage.* New York: G.P. Putnam.

Kroll, Virginia L. (1996). *Can You Dance, Dalila?* Illustrated by Nancy Carpenter. New York: Simon & Schuster.

Loredo, Elizabeth. (1997). *Boogie Bones*. Illustrated by Kevin Hawkes. New York: G.P. Putnam.

Manning, Maurie J. (2008). *Kitchen Dance*. New York: Clarion Books.

Pinkwater, Daniel. (2006). *Dancing Larry*. Illustrated by Jill Pinkwater. New York: Marshall Cavendish.

Sauer, Tammi. (2009). *Chicken Dance*. Illustrated by Dan Santat. New York: Sterling.

Schomp, Virginia. (1997). *If You Were a … Ballet Dancer*. Tarrytown, NY: Marshall Cavendish.

Sis, Peter. (2001). *Ballerina!* New York: Greenwillow.

Stutson, Caroline. (2010). *Cats' Night Out*. Illustrated by J. Klassen. New York: Simon & Schuster Books for Young Readers.

Thomas, Peggy. (2008). *Snow Dance*. Illustrated by Paul Fracklam. Gretna, LA: Pelican.

Thomassie, Tynia. (1996). *Mimi's Tutu*. Illustrated by Jan Spivey Gilchrist. New York: Scholastic.

Troupe, Thomas Kingsley. (2010). *If I Were a Ballerina*. Illustrated by Heather Heyworth. Mankato, MN: Capstone Press.

Willems, Mo. (2009). *Elephants Cannot Dance!* New York: Hyperion Books for Children.

Technology and Multimedia

The following technology and multimedia products can be used to complement this theme:

"Alligator Stomp" [CD]. (2001). In *Jack in the Box*. Long Branch, NJ: Kimbo Educational.

Building Better Bodies and Brains: Creative Movements [CD]. (2010). Oklahoma City, OK: Melody House.

"Cho, Cho, Cho" [CD]. (2001). In *Jack in the Box*. Long Branch, NJ: Kimbo Educational.

Come Play Yoga [CD]. (2008). New York: Karma Kids Yoga.

"Dance & Sing" [CD]. (2010). In *Lots of Fun*. Atlanta, GA: Mr Greg's Musical Madness.

Dance Party Fun (2001). Long Branch, NJ: Kimbo Educational.

Dance with the Animals [DVD]. (2006). Conroe, TX: Rock 'N Learn.

"The Freeze Dance" [CD]. (2009). In *People, Places and Things*. Coconut Grove, FL: In the Nick of Time.

Gotta Dance [CD]. (1996). Long Branch, NJ: Kimbo Educational.

"The Hokey Pokey" [CD]. (2006). In *Josh Levine for Kids*. New York: Josh Levine.

Joining Hands in Other Lands [CD]. (1993). Long Branch, NJ: Kimbo Educational.

"Let Me See You Boogaloo" [CD]. (2007). In *Keep on Singing and Dancing*. Oklahoma City, OK: Melody House.

"Mexican Hat Dance" [CD]. (2001). In *Jack in the Box*. Long Branch, NJ: Kimbo Educational.

"Monkey Dance" [CD]. (2010). In *Lots of Fun*. Atlanta, GA: Mr Greg's Musical Madness.

Motown Dances [CD]. (1998). Long Branch, NJ: Kimbo Educational.

Moving with Mozart [CD]. (1997). Long Branch, NJ: Kimbo Educational.

Physical Ed [CD]. (2000). Melbourne, FL: The Learning Station.

"Shake, Rattle and Roll" [CD]. (2001). In *Dance Party Fun*. Long Branch, NJ: Kimbo Educational.

"Shake, Rattle and Roll," "Peppermint Twist," and "Whole Lotta Shakin'" [CD]. (2000). In *Bean Bag Rock & Roll*. Long Branch, NJ: Kimbo Educational.

"Stretch," "Stomp and Clap," "Side Slide," "Musical Hula Hoops," and "Can You Keep Your Balance?" [CD]. (2000). In *Physical Ed*. Long Branch, NJ: Kimbo Educational.

"When I'm Down I Get Up and Dance" [CD]. (1994). In *So Big*. Sherman Oaks, CA: Hap-Pal Music.

A World of Parachute Play [CD]. (1997). Long Branch, NJ: Kimbo Educational.

 Additional teaching resources to accompany this Theme can be found on the book's companion website. Go to www.cengagebrain.com to access the site for a variety of useful resources.

Movement Activities

Encourage the children to creatively explore and express themselves by moving to music of various tempos and sounds.

Listen to the Drum

(Accessory: drum)
Fast
Slow
Heavy
Soft
Big
Small

Choose a Partner

Make a big shape.
Go over.
Go under.
Go through.
Go around.

To Become Aware of Time

Run very fast.
Walk very slowly.
Jump all over the floor quickly.
Sit down on the floor slowly.
Slowly grow up as tall as you can.
Slowly curl up on the floor as small as possible.

To Become Aware of Space

Lift your leg up in front of you.
Lift it up backward or sideways.
Lift your leg and step forward, backward, sideways, and around and around.
Reach up to the ceiling.
Stretch to touch the walls.
Punch down to the floor.

To Become Aware of Weight

To feel the difference between heavy and light, the child should experiment with his or her own body force.

Punch down to the floor hard.
Lift up your arms slowly and gently.
Stomp on the floor.
Walk on tiptoe.
Kick out one leg as hard as you can.
Very smoothly and lightly, slide one foot along the floor.

Moving Shapes

1. Try to move like something huge and heavy: an elephant, tugboat, or bulldozer.
2. Try to move like something small and heavy: a fat frog, or a heavy top.
3. Try moving like something big and light: a beach ball, a parachute, or a cloud.
4. Try moving like something small and light: a feather, a snowflake, a flea, or a butterfly.

Put Yourself Inside Something

(Examples could include a bottle, box, or barrel.)

You're *outside* of something—now get into it.
You're *inside* of something—now get out of it.
You're *underneath* something.
You're *on top of* something.
You're *beside* or *next to* something.
You're *surrounded* by it.

Pantomime

1. You're going to get a present. What is the shape of the box? How big is the box? Feel it. Hold it. Unwrap it. Take it out. Put it back in.
2. Think about an occupation. How does the worker act?
3. Show me that it is cold (or hot).
4. You are two years old (or 16, 80, etc.).
5. Show me: It's very early in the morning (or late in the afternoon).
6. Show me: What is the weather like?
7. Pretend you are driving, typing, or raking leaves.
8. Take a partner. Pretend you're playing ball.

Theme 23
DAIRY PRODUCTS

Value
healthy food choice
builds strong bones

Forms
fresh
frozen
canned
processed

Sources
cows
goats
sheep
llamas

Containers for Storing
cartons
bottles
pails
bags
boxes

Types
butter
cream cheese
cottage cheese
cheddar cheese
mozzarella cheese
colby cheese
milk
ice cream
yogurt

Places to Purchase
supermarkets
minimarts
cheese factories
restaurants

Theme Goals

Through participating in the experiences provided by this theme, the children may learn:

1. Sources of dairy products
2. Types of dairy products
3. Forms of dairy products
4. Places to purchase dairy products
5. Containers used to store dairy products
6. Value of dairy products

Concepts for the Children to Learn

1. Cows, goats, sheep, and llamas provide milk.
2. Milk can be used to make butter, cheese, ice cream, and yogurt.
3. There are many kinds of cheese, such as cottage cheese, cream cheese, cheddar cheese, mozzarella, and colby.
4. Dairy products can be purchased fresh, frozen, canned, or processed.
5. We can buy dairy products at supermarkets, minimarts, cheese factories, and restaurants.
6. Cartons, bottles, pails, bags, and boxes are used to store dairy products.
7. Dairy products are good, healthy choices.
8. Dairy products help build strong bones and bodies.

Vocabulary

1. **can**—to prepare food for future use.
2. **carton**—a box or container to hold food or other objects.
3. **cheese factory**—a place where cheese is made or sold.
4. **cream**—the fatty part of milk. Cream is a yellowish-white color.
5. **dairy product**—a product made from milk.
6. **frozen**—food that is kept very cold. It is frozen so it can be eaten at a later time.
7. **minimart**—a very small store that sells food.
8. **yogurt**—a milk product that can be sweetened and flavored with fruit.

Bulletin Board

The purpose of this bulletin board is to help children identify ice cream as a dairy product, as well as recognize the printed word. This is designed as a check-in or attendance bulletin board. Each child is provided a bulletin board piece with his or her name on it. When the children arrive each day at school, they should be encouraged to place their names on the bulletin board.

To create the bulletin board, cut an ice cream cone out of tagboard or construction paper for each child in the class. Color or decorate each cone as desired. Print the child's name on the ice cream cone. Laminate the pieces, or cover with clear contact paper. Use pushpins or adhesive magnet pieces to attach the ice cream cones to the bulletin board.

Family Letter

Dear Families,

Did you know that the average person in the United States consumes about 550 pounds of dairy products each year? Dairy products provide us with one of our main sources of protein. We will be learning about dairy products in our classroom. The children will learn sources of dairy products, values of dairy products, types of dairy products, forms of dairy products, places dairy products can be purchased, and containers used to hold dairy products.

At School

Some of the learning activities the children will participate in include:

- Preparing milkshakes, homemade vanilla pudding, and strawberry yogurt in the cooking area
- Creating a dairy collage, yogurt print cups, and ice cream cone sponge paints in the art area
- Hearing stories related to the dairy theme
- Visiting the dairy department of a grocery store
- Looking at books featuring dairy products
- Identifying foods prepared with dairy products

At Home

At home, to reinforce the dairy product concepts, you can:

- Encourage your child to prepare instant pudding with you for a snack or a dessert.
- Have your child identify the foods being served at mealtimes that are dairy products.
- Browse through newspaper ads or magazines and have your child identify dairy products.
- Take your child grocery shopping and have him or her show you where the dairy section of the store is located.

Enjoy your child!

Arts and Crafts

1. **Buttermilk Chalk Pictures**
   Dip colored chalk into a small container of buttermilk, or brush construction paper with buttermilk. Use the chalk to create designs on construction paper.

2. **Dairy Product Paint Containers**
   Use empty dairy product containers to hold paint for use at the art table or easel. Examples include milk cartons, yogurt cups, and cottage cheese containers.

3. **Whipped Soap Painting**
   The following mixture can be made to represent ice cream or cottage cheese. Mix one cup of Ivory Snow flakes with 1/2 cup of warm water in a bowl. The children can beat the mixture with a hand eggbeater until it is fluffy. Add more water, if necessary. Apply mixture with paintbrushes or fingers to construction paper. For a variation, food coloring can be added to the paint mixture.

4. **Ice Cream Cone Sponge Painting**
   Cut sponges into shapes of ice cream cones and scoops of ice cream. Provide shallow trays of various colors of paints. Designs are created by dipping the sponge in the paint and then pressing it onto a piece of construction paper.

5. **Yogurt Cup Prints**
   Collect empty yogurt cups of various shapes and sizes. Wash them thoroughly. Prepare shallow trays of paint. Create designs by inverting a yogurt cup, dipping it into the paint, and then applying it to construction paper. Repeat the process as desired.

Cooking

1. **Milk Shake**
   For each shake, combine 1/2 cup of vanilla ice cream and 1 cup of milk in a blender. If desired, flavor the shake with one of the following: 1/2 cup fresh berries, 1/2 banana, or 2 tablespoons chocolate syrup.

2. **Grilled Cheese Sandwich**
   Assist the children in making cheese sandwiches. Provide plastic knives for the children to spread soft butter or margarine on the outside of sandwiches. Turn over and place a cheese slice between the two pieces of bread.

   Under adult supervision, place the sandwiches on a heated skillet or electric grill until golden brown, turning once.

3. **Homemade Vanilla Pudding**
   1/8 teaspoon salt
   2 cups milk
   3 tablespoons cornstarch
   1/2 cup white granulated sugar
   2 slightly beaten egg yolks
   1 tablespoon softened butter or margarine
   2 teaspoons vanilla

   Combine cornstarch, sugar, and salt in a medium saucepan. Stir in the milk. Over medium heat, cook and stir constantly until the mixture thickens and comes to a boil. Stir and boil 1 minute. In a small bowl, blend half of the hot mixture into the egg yolks. Pour the egg mixture back into the saucepan and cook until the mixture boils, stirring constantly. Remove the pan from the heat and add the butter and vanilla. Allow the pudding to cool slightly, and spoon into a serving bowl or individual dishes. Refrigerate. This recipe makes 4 servings.

4. **Strawberry Yogurt Surprise**
   3 oz. package strawberry-flavored gelatin
   1 cup boiling water
   1/2 cup cold water
   1 cup strawberry yogurt

   Dissolve gelatin in the boiling water. Stir in cold water. Chill until thickened but not set. Beat gelatin and fold in yogurt. Pour into serving dish. Refrigerate until firm. This recipe makes 4 servings.

Dramatic Play

1. **Ice Cream Shop**
Clothes and props for an ice cream shop can be placed in the dramatic play area. Include items such as empty, clean ice cream pails and cartons; ice cream scoops; plastic parfait glasses and bowls; plastic spoons; empty ice cream cone boxes; napkins; aprons; and a cash register with play money. Prepare and display posters in the area that portray various ice cream products and flavors.

2. **Dairy Farm**
Turn the dramatic play center into a dairy farm where the children can pretend to do chores. Display pictures of farms and cows and provide overalls, boots, hats, pails, hoses, and other appropriate props.

3. **Grocery Store: Dairy Department**
Set up the dramatic play area to resemble the dairy department of a grocery store. Include props such as milk cartons, cottage cheese containers, yogurt cups, sour cream containers, ice cream pails and cartons, butter boxes, cheese packages, and a cash register. Display pictures of dairy foods.

Field Trips

1. **The Grocery Store**
Visit a grocery store and locate the dairy section. Look at the types of dairy products available.

2. **Ice Cream Shop**
Take a trip to an ice cream shop. Count the flavors of ice cream available. Purchase a cone for each of the children.

3. **Dairy Farm**
Visit a dairy farm. Ask the farmer to show the housing, equipment, and food supplies needed to care for dairy cows.

Fingerplays and Chants

Ice Cream
I'm licking my ice cream.
I'm licking it fast.
It's dripping down my arm.
It's disappearing fast.

Little Miss Muffet
Little Miss Muffet
Sat on a tuffet
Eating her curds and whey.
Along came a spider
And sat down beside her
And frightened Miss Muffet away!

This Little Cow
This little cow eats grass.
  (hold up fingers of one hand, bend down one finger)
This little cow eats hay.
  (bend down another finger)
This little cow drinks water.
  (bend down another finger)
And this little cow does nothing
  (bend down another finger)
but lie and sleep all day.

Group Time
(Games and Language)

1. **Dairy Charts**
Print the caption "Foods Made from Milk" across the top of a piece of tagboard. During group time, present the chart and record the children's responses. Display the chart and refer to it throughout the theme.
   Additional language charts could be made about types of cheeses, ice cream, and yogurt.

2. **Cheese-Tasting Party**
Cut various types of cheese into small slices or pieces. Place the cheese pieces on paper plates for the children to taste. Discuss types of cheeses, textures, flavors, and colors.

 **Math**

1. **Dairy Sort**

   Collect different types of food-product containers, including dairy products. Place all of the containers in a basket. Encourage the children to sort out the containers representing dairy products from the other food-product containers.

2. **Dairy Lids**

   Collect lids and caps from milk jugs. They can be recycled and used for game pieces, creating patterns, and counting activities.

3. **Favorite Ice Cream Graph**

   The children can assist in making a graph of their favorite ice cream flavors. Begin by printing the caption "Our Favorite Ice Cream Flavors" across the top of a piece of tagboard. Draw or paste pictures of different flavors of ice cream along the left-hand side of the tagboard. Each child's name or picture is placed next to the picture of his or her favorite ice cream flavor. The results of the graph should be shared with the children using math vocabulary words: most, more, fewer, least, and so on. Display the graph for further reference.

   Additional graphs could be made depicting the children's favorite flavors of yogurt, cheese, or milk.

 Music

1. **"The Farmer in the Dell"**

   (Continue after the first verse with additional verses:

   The farmer takes the wife/husband.
   The wife/husband takes the nurse.
   The nurse takes the dog.
   The dog takes the cat.
   The cat takes the rat.
   The rat takes the cheese.

   The final verse is at the bottom.)

   The farmer in the dell,
   The farmer in the dell,
   Hi-ho, the dairy-o
   The farmer in the dell.

(Final verse)

The cheese stands alone.
The cheese stands alone.
Hi-ho, the dairy-o,
The cheese stands alone.

2. **"Old MacDonald Had a Farm"**
   (Traditional)

   Old MacDonald had a farm,
   Ee i ee i oh!
   And on his farm he had some chicks,
   Ee i ee i oh!
   With a cluck-cluck here,
   And a cluck-cluck there
   Here a cluck, there a cluck,
   Everywhere a cluck-cluck
   Old MacDonald had a farm
   Ee i ee i oh!

   Old MacDonald had a farm,
   Ee i ee i oh!
   And on his farm he had some cows,
   Ee i ee i oh!
   With a moo-moo here,
   And a moo-moo there
   Here a moo, there a moo,
   Everywhere a moo-moo

   Old MacDonald had a farm
   Ee i ee i oh!
   Old MacDonald had a farm,
   Ee i ee i oh!
   And on his farm he had some pigs,
   Ee i ee i oh!
   With an oink-oink here,
   And an oink-oink there
   Here an oink, there an oink,
   Everywhere an oink-oink,
   Old MacDonald had a farm
   Ee i ee i oh!

3. **"We Like Ice Cream"**
   (Sing to the tune of "Are You Sleeping?")

   We like ice cream, we like ice cream.
   Yes, we do! Yes, we do!
   Vanilla and strawberry,
   Chocolate and mint.
   Yum, yum, yum.
   Yum, yum, yum!

4. "Drink Your Milk"
(Sing to the tune of "My Darling Clementine")

Drink your milk.
Drink your milk.
Drink your milk every day.
It is good for your teeth and bones.
Drink your milk every day.

5. "Cows"
(Sing to the tune of "Mulberry Bush")

This is the way we feed the cows,
Feed the cows, feed the cows.
This is the way we feed the cows,
On the dairy farm each day.
This is the way we milk the cows,
Milk the cows, milk the cows.
This is the way we milk the cows,
On the dairy farm each day.

Science

1. Making Butter
Fill baby food jars half-full with whipping cream and replace lids. The children can take turns shaking the jars until the cream separates. (The mixture will first look like whipping cream, then like overwhipped cream, and finally it will be obvious that separation has occurred.) Pour off the remaining liquid. Rinse the butter in cold water several times and drain. Add salt to taste. Let the children spread the butter on crackers or bread.
Caution: Supervise this activity carefully because of the use of glass jars.

2. Making Ice Cream
Collect the following ingredients:
1 cup milk
1/2 cup sugar
1/4 teaspoon salt
3 beaten egg yolks
1 tablespoon vanilla
2 cups whipping cream

In a saucepan, combine milk, sugar, salt, and egg yolks. Stir constantly over medium heat until bubbles appear around the edge of the pan. Cool mixture at room temperature. Stir in vanilla and whipping cream. Pour into an ice cream maker, and follow the manufacturer's directions. Recipe makes 1 quart of ice cream.

3. Science Table Additions
Additions to the science table may include:
- Pictures of dairy cows
- Books about milking cows and dairy animals
- Containers of grain, corn, and hay along with magnifying glasses
- Pictures of goats, sheep, and llamas

Sensory

Additions to the Sensory Table
- Sand, scoops, and empty milk cartons
- Water and empty, clean yogurt and cottage cheese containers
- Cotton balls, spoons, ice cream scoops, bowls, and empty, clean ice cream pails

Social Studies

1. Sharing a Treat
Prepare a dairy food with the children and share it with another class, a senior citizens' group, or another community group.

2. Role of the Dairy Farmer
Invite a dairy farmer to the classroom to discuss his or her occupation. The equipment and tools used to farm could also be shown and discussed.

3. Dairy Allergies
Discuss dairy allergies. Provide dairy-free alternatives for the children to sample. Differences in taste and smell can be discussed. Some ideas include soymilk and rice milk.

 **Books**

The following books can be used to complement this theme:

Cazet, Denys. (2000). *Minnie and Moo and the Thanksgiving Tree.* New York: DK.

Clifford, Rowan. (2005). *Rodeo Ron and His Milkshake Cows.* New York: Alfred A. Knopf.

Daly, Kathleen N., and Tibor Gergeby. (2001). *The Good Humor Man.* Illustrated by Tibor Gergeby. New York: Golden Books.

Emberley, Ed. (2003). *Thanks, Mom!* Boston: Little, Brown.

Foskett-Cordsen, Carol. (2005). *The Milkman.* Illustrated by Douglas B. Jones. New York: Dutton Children's Books.

French, Vivian. (2001). *Oliver's Milk Shake.* Illustrated by Alison Bartlett. New York: Orchard Books.

Green, Emily K. (2007). *Milk, Yogurt, and Cheese.* Minneapolis, MN: Bellwether Media.

Godfrey, Neale S. (1995). *Here's the Scoop: Follow an Ice-Cream Cone around the World.* Illustrated by Randy Verougstraete. Morristown, NJ: Silver Burdett Press.

Head, Honor. (2010). *Milk, Cheese, and Eggs.* Mankato, MN: Smart Apple Media.

Howe, James. (2009). *Horace and Morris Say Cheese (Which Makes Delores Sneeze!).* Illustrated by Amy Walrod. New York: Atheneum Books for Young Readers.

Johnson, Christian, and Spencer Johnson. (2003). *Who Moved My Cheese?* Illustrated by Steve Pileggi. New York: G.P. Putnam's Sons.

Katz, Jill. (2003). *Dairy Products.* Mankato, MN: Smart Apple Media.

Mahy, Margaret. (1999). *Simply Delicious!* Illustrated by Jonathan Allen. New York: Orchard Books.

Malachy, Doyle. (2002). *Cow.* Illustrated by Angelo Rinaldi. New York: Margaret K. McElderry Books.

Murphy, Andy. (2003). *Out and about at the Dairy Farm.* Illustrated by Anne McMullen. Minneapolis, MN: Picture Window Books.

Nolan, Lucy. (2003). *A Fairy in a Dairy.* Illustrated by Laura J. Bryant. New York: Marshall Cavendish.

Parker, Victoria. (2010). *All about Dairy.* Mankato, MN: QEB Pub.

Pinkwater, Daniel. (1999). *Ice Cream Larry.* Illustrated by Jill Pinkwater. New York: Marshall Cavendish.

Rey, Margret, and Alan J. Shalleck. (1989). *Curious George Goes to an Ice Cream Shop.* Boston: Houghton Mifflin.

Santoro, Scott. (1999). *Isaac the Ice Cream Truck.* New York: Henry Holt.

Schuh, Mari C. (2006). *The Milk Group.* Mankato, MN: Capstone Press.

Shaw, Charles Green. (2000). *It Looked Like Spilt Milk.* New York: HarperCollins Publishers.

Simmons, Toni. (2003). *The Cheese Chase: Why Dogs Chase Cats: An African-American Folktale.* Edina, MN: Beaver's Pond Press.

Sokol, Edward. (2000). *Meet Stinky Magee.* New York: HarperCollins Publishers.

 Technology and Multimedia

The following technology and multimedia products can be used to complement this theme:

Alphabet Road: "F" Is for Farm: Do You Know Where Milk Comes From? [DVD]. (2006). Herndon, VA: Go Babies.

"Milkshake" [CD]. (2007). In *Bottle of Sunshine.* Baltimore: Milkshake Music.

"Milkshake Song" [CD]. (2010). In *Songs for Wiggleworms.* Chicago: Bloodshot Records.

 Additional teaching resources to accompany this Theme can be found on the book's companion website. Go to www.cengagebrain.com to access the site for a variety of useful resources.

Theme 24
DENTIST

Hygienist's Tools
dental floss
toothbrush
mirror
toothpaste
toothpick
fluoride rinse

Purpose
keeping teeth healthy
checks teeth
treats teeth
fills cavities
medical treatment
prevention training
braces
pulls teeth

Dentist's Tools
lights
X-ray machine
drills
picks
file

Helpers
hygienist
receptionist

Office Furnishings
chairs
desk
patient's chair
telephone
file cabinets
computer

Theme Goals

Through participating in the experiences provided by this theme, the children may learn:

1. The dentist's purpose
2. How the dentist helps us
3. The dentist's tools
4. The hygienist's tools
5. Dental office furnishings

Concepts for the Children to Learn

1. The dentist is a doctor who helps keep our teeth healthy.
2. Teeth are used to chew food.
3. Teeth should be brushed with toothpaste after each meal.
4. A hygienist helps the dentist.
5. The dentist checks teeth, treats teeth, fills cavities, and pulls teeth.
6. The dentist places braces on some people to straighten their teeth.
7. A dentist has helpers.
8. A receptionist makes a time for people to see the dentist.
9. A hygienist cleans and X-rays people's teeth.
10. A dentist removes decay from our teeth with a drill.
11. Pictures of our teeth are called X-rays.
12. Dental floss, toothpicks, and a fluoride rinse help clean between teeth.
13. The dentist's office has special machines and special chairs.
14. The dentist has an office with furniture.
15. Chairs, desks, a telephone, computer, and file cabinets are office furniture.

Vocabulary

1. **cavity**—decay on the tooth.
2. **dental floss**—a string used to clean between the teeth.
3. **dentist**—a person who helps to keep our teeth healthy.
4. **hygienist**—the dentist's assistant who cleans teeth.
5. **teeth**—small white structures in our mouth used to chew food.
6. **toothbrush**—a brush to clean our teeth.
7. **toothpaste**—a paste to clean our teeth.
8. **toothpick**—a stick-like tool used for removing food particles between our teeth.
9. **X-ray**—to take a picture.

Bulletin Board

The purpose of this bulletin board is to promote the development of a positive self-concept and assist in developing name recognition skills. Prepare an attendance bulletin board by constructing a toothbrush out of tagboard for each student and teacher. See the illustration. Color the toothbrushes with colored felt-tip markers, and print the children's and teachers' names on them. Laminate. Punch holes in each toothbrush. Check who has brushed their teeth by observing the toothbrush hung on the bulletin board.

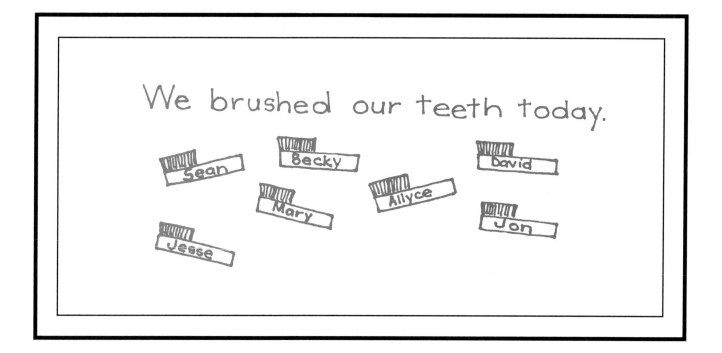

Family Letter

InBox

Dear Families,

We are continuing our study of community helpers with a unit on the dentist. The dentist is an important helper for us because our teeth are very important. Children are very aware of their teeth at this age. Many of the older five-year-olds will soon begin losing their baby teeth. Through the experiences provided in this curriculum unit, the children may learn that the dentist is a person who helps us keep our teeth healthy. They will also spend some time learning about the importance and techniques of proper tooth care.

At School

Some of the experiences planned for the unit include:

- Making toothpaste
- String painting with dental floss at the art table
- Painting with discarded toothbrushes at the easel
- Exploring tools that a dentist uses

Special Visitor

On Tuesday, we will meet Mrs. Jones, the dental hygienist at Dr. Milivitz's dental clinic. Mrs. Jones will discuss proper toothbrushing and will pass out toothbrush kits. You are invited to join our class at 10:00 a.m. for her visit.

At Home

Good habits start young! Dental cavities are one of the most prevalent diseases among children. It has been estimated that 98 percent of school-aged children have at least one cavity. You and your child can spend some time each day brushing your teeth together. Sometimes a child will brush more effectively if someone else is with him or her. It is important for children to realize that they are the primary caretakers of their teeth!

Have fun with your child!

Arts and Crafts

1. **Easel Ideas**
   - Paint with discarded toothbrushes.
   - Paint on tooth-shaped easel paper.

2. **Toothbrushes and Splatter Screen**
   Provide construction paper, splatter screens, and discarded toothbrushes. The children can splatter paint onto the paper using the toothbrush as a painting tool.

3. **Dental Floss Painting**
   Provide thin tempera paint, paper, and dental floss. The child can spoon a small amount of paint onto the paper and can hold on to one end of the dental floss while moving the free end through the paint to make a design.

Cooking

Happy Teeth Snacks

- Apple wedges
- Orange slices
- Asparagus
- Cheese chunks
- Milk
- Cucumber slices
- Cauliflower pieces

Dramatic Play

Dental Office
Provide white shirts, cotton balls, paper and pencils, a phone, clipboards, and chairs in the dramatic play area. Set up as a dental office with a front desk, waiting area, and examination office.
Note: Remind children to not put cotton balls or fingers in each other's mouths.

Field Trips and Resource People

1. **The Dentist**
   Visit the dentist's office. Observe the furnishings and equipment.

2. **The Hygienist**
   Invite a dental hygienist to visit the classroom. Ask the hygienist to discuss tooth care and demonstrate proper brushing techniques. After the discussion, provide each child with a disclosing tablet which contains a dye that highlights bacterial plaque on tooth surfaces. Let each child look into a mirror to see where more brushing and flossing are needed.

Fingerplays and Chants

My Toothbrush
> I have a little toothbrush.
> (use pointer finger)
> I hold it very tight.
> (make hand into fist)
> I brush my teeth each morning,
> and then again at night.
> (use pointer finger and pretend to brush)

Brushing Teeth
> I move the toothbrush back and forth.
> (pretend to brush teeth)
> I brush all of my teeth.
> I swish the water to rinse them and then,
> (puff out cheeks to swish)
> I look at myself and smile.
> (smile at one another)

My Friend the Toothbrush
> My toothbrush is a tool.
> I use it every day.
> I brush and brush and brush and brush
> to keep the cavities away.
> (pretend to brush teeth)

Group Time
(Games and Language)

Pass the Toothpaste

Play music and pass a tube of toothpaste around the circle. When the music stops, the person who is holding the toothpaste stands up and claps his or her hands three times (or some similar action). Repeat the game.

Large Muscle

1. **Drop the Toothbrush**
   Set a large, plastic, open-mouth bottle on the floor. Encourage the children to try to drop the toothbrushes into the mouth of the bottle.

2. **Sugar, Sugar, Toothbrush**
   Play like "Duck, Duck, Goose." The "toothbrush" tries to catch the "sugar" before it gets around the circle to where the "toothbrush" was sitting. Game can continue until interest diminishes.

Music

1. **"Brushing Teeth"**
   (Sing to the tune of "Mulberry Bush")
   This is the way we brush our teeth,
    brush our teeth, brush our teeth.
   This is the way we brush our teeth,
    so early in the morning.

2. **"Clean Teeth"**
   (Sing to the tune of "Row, Row, Row Your Boat")

Brush, brush, brush your teeth
Brush them every day.
We put some toothpaste on our brush
To help stop tooth decay.

Science

1. **Tools**
   Place some safe dental products on the sensory table. Include a mirror, dental floss, toothbrush, toothpaste, and so on. A dentist may even lend you a model of a set of teeth.

2. **Acid on Our Teeth**
   Show the children how acid weakens the enamel of your teeth. Place a hard-boiled egg in a bowl of vinegar for 24 hours. Observe how the eggshell becomes soft as it decalcifies. The same principle applies to our teeth if the acid is not removed by brushing. (This activity is most appropriate with older children.)

3. **Making Toothpaste**
   In individual plastic bags, place 4 teaspoons of baking soda, 1 teaspoon salt, and 1 teaspoon water. Add a drop of food-flavoring extract such as peppermint or orange. The children can mix their own toothpaste.

4. **Sugar on Our Teeth**
   Sugar found in sweet food can cause cavities on tooth enamel if it is not removed by rinsing or brushing. To demonstrate the effect of brushing, submerge white eggshells into a clear glass of cola for 24 hours. Observe the discoloration of the eggshell. Apply toothpaste to the toothbrush. Brush the eggshell, removing the stain. Ask the children, "What caused the stain?"

5. **Flossing Teeth**
   Use empty egg cartons to represent teeth. Cut pieces of yarn for the children to practice "flossing" teeth. Discuss the importance of flossing teeth daily.

Sensory

Additions to the Sensory Table

- Toothbrushes and water
- Peppermint extract added to water

Books

The following books can be used to complement this theme:

Adler, David A. (1997). *A Young Cam Jansen and the Lost Tooth.* Illustrated by Susanna Natti. New York: Viking.

Barber, Tom. (2004). *Open Wide.* Illustrated by Lynne Chapman. London: Chrysalis Children's.

DeGezelle, Terri. (2006). *Taking Care of My Teeth.* Mankato, MN: Capstone Press.

Finnegan, Evelyn M. (1995). *My Little Friend Goes to the Dentist.* Illustrated by Diane R. Houghton. Scituate, MA: Little Friend Press.

Frost, Helen. (1999). *Brushing Well.* Mankato, MN: Pebble Books.

Frost, Helen. (1999). *Going to the Dentist.* Mankato, MN: Pebble Books.

Gomi, Taro. (1994). *The Crocodile and the Dentist.* Brookfield, CT: Millbrook Press.

Hall, Kirsten. (1994). *The Tooth Fairy.* Illustrated by Nan Brooks. Chicago: Children's Press.

Hallinan, P. K. (2002). *My Dentist, My Friend.* Nashville, TN: Ideals Publishing.

Hoban, Lillian. (1987). *Arthur's Loose Tooth: Story and Pictures.* New York: Harper Collins.

Keller, Laurie. (2000). *Open Wide: Tooth School Inside.* New York: Holt.

Kemper, Bitsy. (2007). *Out and about at the Dentist.* Illustrated by Zachary Trover. Minneapolis, MN: Picture Window Books.

Klein, Adria F. (2006). *Max Goes to the Dentist.* Illustrated by Mernie Gallagher-Cole. Minneapolis, MN: Picture Window Books.

London, Jonathan. (2004). *Zack at the Dentist.* Illustrated by Jack Medoff. New York: Scholastic.

MacDonald, Amy. (1996). *Cousin Ruth's Tooth.* Illustrated by Marjorie Priceman. Boston: Houghton Mifflin.

Mayer, Mercer. (2003). *Just Going to the Dentist.* New York: Goler Books.

McGhee, Alison. (2004). *Mrs. Watson Wants Your Teeth.* Illustrated by Harry Bliss. Orlando, FL: Harcourt.

Mercier, Johanne. (2004). *Caillou at the Dentist.* Montreal: Chouette.

Moffat, Julia. (2005). *My Dentist Is Not a Monster.* Illustrated by Anni Axworthy. Worthington, OH: Brighter Child.

Murkoff, Heidi Eisenberg. (2002). *What to Expect When You Go to the Dentist.* Illustrated by Laura Rader. New York: HarperFestival.

Murphy, Patricia J. (2005). *A Visit to the Dentist's Office.* Mankato, MN: Capstone Press.

Ready, Dee. (1997). *Dentists.* Chicago: Children's Press.

Rosenberry, Vera. (2002). *Vera Goes to the Dentist.* New York: Henry Holt.

Sage, Angie. (2001). *Molly at the Dentist.* Atlanta, GA: Peachtree.

Schuh, Mari C. (2008). *At the Dentist.* Mankato, MN: Capstone Press.

Simms, Laura. (1998). *Rotten Teeth.* Illustrated by David Catrow. Boston: Houghton Mifflin.

Steig, William. (1997). *Doctor De Soto.* New York: Farrar, Straus and Giroux.

Stockham, Jess. (2011). *Dentist.* Auburn, ME: Child's Play International.

Swanson, Diane. (2002). *Dentist and You.* Toronto: Annick Press.

Thaler, Mike. (2000). *Fang the Dentist.* Illustrated by Jared Lee. Mahwah, NJ: Troll Press.

Thaler, Mike. (2005). *The Dentist from the Black Lagoon.* Illustrated by Jared Lee. New York: Scholastic.

Thomas, Pat. (2008). *Do I Have to Go to the Dentist? A First Look at Healthy Teeth.* Hauppauge, NY: Barron's Educational Series.

Tourville, Amanda Doering. (2009). *Brush, Floss, and Rinse: Caring for Your Teeth and Gums*. Illustrated by Ronnie Rooney. Minneapolis, MN: Picture Window Books.

Ziefert, Harriet. (2008). *ABC Dentist*. Maplewood, NJ: Blue Apple Books.

Technology and Multimedia

The following technology and multimedia products can be used to complement this theme:

"Brush Your Teeth." [CD]. (1996). In *Singable Songs for the Very Young*. Cambridge, MA: Rounder/UMGD.

"A Bulldozer Operator I Will Be" [CD]. (2007). In *50 Learning Songs*. Stow, OH: Twin Sisters Productions.

"Doctor, Doctor" [CD]. (1996). In *People in Our Neighborhood*. Long Branch, NJ: Kimbo Educational.

"I Got a Job" [CD]. (2002). In *Growing Up with Ella Jenkins*. Washington, DC: Smithsonian Folkways.

Open Wide, Tooth School Inside and 4 More Fantastic Children's Stories [DVD]. (2007). New York: Scholastic.

"Tiger with a Toothbrush" [CD]. (1999). In *We're On Our Way*. Sherman Oaks, CA: Hap-Pal Music.

Additional teaching resources to accompany this Theme can be found on the book's companion website. Go to www.cengagebrain.com to access the site for a variety of useful resources.

Theme 25
DIWALI
(pronounced "di-vahl-ee")

Foods
cakes
candies
lassi (yogurt shakes)
kheer (rice pudding)
vegetable curry

Sounds
fireworks and firecrackers

Symbols
tiny lights
clay lamps called "diya"
rangoli patterns
Hindu gods and goddesses

Celebration
five days long every autumn
candy and sweets
gifts
cards
new clothes
gold and jewelry
clean homes

decorate shrines in homes
rangoli patterns
oil lamps
feasts
card games
fireworks, firecrackers, and sparklers
Lakshmi

Theme Goals

Through participating in the experiences provided by this theme, the children may learn:

1. How Diwali is celebrated
2. Foods prepared and eaten during Diwali
3. Sounds of Diwali celebrations
4. Symbols of this important holiday

Concepts for the Children to Learn

1. Diwali is a holiday celebrated for five days in October and/or November.
2. People who follow the Hindu religion (and some other religions) in India and throughout the world celebrate Diwali.
3. The holiday shows respect to Hindu gods and goddesses.
4. Shrines are decorated in peoples' homes.
5. Families feast for lunch or dinner.
6. At home, everyone prepares by cleaning and decorating.
7. People wear new clothes and dress up for the holiday.
8. Some people wear gold jewelry.
9. Families send cards to each other.
10. People give sweets such as cakes, cookies, and candy for gifts.
11. Colorful patterns (rangoli) are painted on the ground outside.
12. People feast on vegetable curry dishes, yogurt shakes (lassi), and rice pudding (kheer).
13. Clay lamps (diya) and candles are lit up to make everything bright.
14. Fireworks and firecrackers are set off.
15. Children believe that when they are sleeping, they are visited by a goddess (Lakshmi) who brings them candy and presents.
16. Children play card games and other games together.

Vocabulary

1. **candle**—a wax shape with a string wick that is burned to give off light.
2. **celebrate**—to observe a holiday and have a good time.
3. **curry**—a spice from the curry leaf used in Indian foods.
4. **Diwali**—a five-day holiday celebrated by Hindus all over the world.
5. **diya lamp**—a small oil lamp made from baked clay.
6. **feast**—a big, delicious meal.
7. **festival**—a party or celebration that usually happens every year.
8. **fireworks**—bright lights and loud noises.
9. **Hindu**—a religion with origins in India.
10. **rangoli** pattern—decorative designs made using powdered stone and created during festivals.

Bulletin Board

The purpose of this bulletin board is to promote name recognition, visual discrimination, and hand-eye coordination skills. Trace and cut a candle for each child in the class from tagboard, and print each child's name on the flame section of the candle (all in plain tagboard). Cut out the candle pieces. Trace and cut out a flame for each child in the class in red construction paper. Then print each child's name on a flame. Laminate and cut out the flame pieces. Have the children match each red flame with name to the matching candle.

Family Letter

InBox

Dear Families,

Our next theme is the holiday of Diwali (pronounced "di-vahl-ee"). Depending upon the position of the moon each year in October or November, Diwali is celebrated by people who follow the Hindu religion, as well as people who are Sikh or Jain.

Officially, Diwali marks the time when Lord Rama and his wife Sita return to Ayodhya after 14 years of exile, having been sent away by his father, the king of Ayodhya. Today, the holiday is celebrated in India and around the world as the "Festival of Light." People light candles and clay lamps called "diya" to light the path for Rama and Sita and to show the power of good over evil.

Diwali celebrations—which last for five days—also include dazzling fireworks displays, sweets and other mouthwatering dishes, prayers to gods and goddesses, new clothing, and gift giving. Families clean their homes and decorate with lights and flowers. Brightly colored rangoli patterns (decorative designs) are drawn outside on floors and pavement as a sign of welcome, usually with rice flour and water.

For children, the magic of Diwali happens at night while they are sleeping. The belief is that a goddess named Lakshmi visits homes on Diwali and leaves presents and candies for the children to find in the morning. The more lamps they light, the more likely it is that Lakshmi will be tempted to visit.

At School

Some of the Diwali activities planned include:

- Preparing traditional Indian shakes and rice pudding
- Cleaning up and dressing up to get ready for Diwali
- Coloring rangoli patterns with colored chalk
- Making the sounds of firecrackers

At Home

If you or anyone you know celebrates Diwali at home, you might want to make and send Diwali cards, make a curry dish, eat in an Indian restaurant, or light candles and lamps to display in your windows.

Parent Involvement

If you have special knowledge or experience celebrating Diwali, we would love to have you share it with our class. Please contact me so a time can be arranged for your visit.

Enjoy learning about Diwali with your child!

Arts and Crafts

1. Happy Diwali Banner

Cut a large piece of butcher paper and paint the words "Happy Diwali!" on it. Once it is dry, invite the children to make handprints using fingerpaint. You might want to add the outline of a few candles so children can color these in too. Hang the banner for everyone to see and enjoy.

2. Colored Chalk Rangolis

Show a picture or two of rangoli patterns from a book about Diwali (or on the Internet). Draw some shape outlines or designs on the pavement outside. Invite the children to work together to color and decorate the designs using colored chalks. (Or, draw an 8–10-inch circle for each child to color his or her own rangoli on the pavement outside.) You can also provide some colored sand to decorate the rangoli. **Variation:** You can also sketch an easy-to-color rangoli design on an 8 1/2 × 11 piece of paper and photocopy for each child to color.

3. Candleholders (Diyas)

Give children some modeling clay or play dough in different colors. Show them how to make "Diwali lamps" or "diyas" by molding the clay into small bowl shapes. Add pieces of yarn for pretend wicks. Line up the lamps on a windowsill for a festive look.

Cooking

1. Rice Pudding (Kheer)

3 cups cooked white rice
3 cups 2% milk
1/2 cup granulated sugar
1/4 teaspoon salt (optional)
2 tablespoons butter or margarine
1 teaspoon vanilla extract

Combine rice, milk, sugar, salt, and butter in saucepan. Cook over medium heat until thickened, 25 to 30 minutes, stirring often. Add vanilla. Pour into serving dishes. Serve warm or cold.

2. Pineapple Basundi

2 1/2 cups low-fat warm milk
3/4 cup pineapple (grated)
5 teaspoons sugar
A few strands of saffron
1/4 teaspoon cardamom powder
1/4 cup pineapple (cubed)

Soak the saffron in a bowl with 2 tablespoons of warm milk. In a nonstick pan, boil the milk. Stir continuously until the milk reduces to half its original volume. Add the saffron and cardamom powder, and mix well. Refrigerate. In a nonstick pan, mix the pineapple and sugar. Cook for 6 minutes, stirring continuously. Set to cool. Add the pineapple mixture to the chilled milk and then mix. Garnish with pineapple cubes.

3. Indian Vegetable Rice

2 tablespoons vegetable oil
1 onion, thinly sliced
1/2 teaspoon ground cumin
1 cup basmati rice
2 cups water
3/4 tsp salt
3/4 cup frozen mixed vegetable

In a pan, heat oil and sauté onion and cumin. Stir-fry the onions until tender. Rinse the rice and add it to the pan, along with 2 cups of water. Add salt and frozen vegetables. Cover the pan and boil over high heat. Reduce the heat and cook for approximately 30 minutes, stirring after 10 minutes to mix the spices evenly.

4. Chocolate Cereal Diyas (Candleholders)

1 cup chocolate chips
2 tablespoons butter
2 cups rice crispy cereal
Mini-cupcake pan and liners or
    aluminum foil

Prepare diya molds by lining the mini-cupcake pan with liners or foil. Set aside. Fill a large pot or double boiler with water. Bring to boil. Add chocolate chips and butter to a small bowl and place over the boiling water, or add to top of double boiler. Melt, stirring gently. (*Note:* A microwave can also be used on low to melt the chocolate.) When smooth, add the cereal. Remove from heat and mix well. Cool slightly.

Pour a small amount of the mixture into the prepared diya molds. Press into shape with the back of a spoon. Allow to cool and harden in the refrigerator. When cool, gently remove from molds.

5. **Coconut Treats**
1 cup sweet (flavored) cream cheese
1/2 cup flaked coconut
Dried apricot halves

Mix sweetened cream cheese with flaked coconut and roll into small balls. Use fingers to soften dried apricot halves. Stuff the apricots with the coconut-cheese balls.

Dramatic Play

1. **Clean Up for Diwali**
Remind children that everyone cleans their house to get ready for the special holiday of Diwali. Have the children do a big "cleanup" in their preschool room.

2. **Jewelry Shop**
Remind children that everyone dresses up for the special holiday of Diwali. Set out materials your children can use to make jewelry, such as aluminum foil or sparkly pipe cleaners. You might also include paper shapes that can be decorated with glitter glue or sequins and then strung on yarn for a necklace.

3. **Wrapping Station**
Place tissue paper, wrapping paper scraps, tape, and ribbons on a table. Provide a variety of little objects such as blocks, pretend food, and small toys for children to wrap as pretend gifts for Diwali.

Fingerplays and Chants

1. **Diwali Candles One—Two—Three**
Diwali candles one—two—three.
(Hold up fingers on the count)

Diwali candles just for me!
(Point to self)
Candles to the left, candles to the right
(Hold up fingers on left hand and then hold up fingers on the right)
Diwali candles, burn all night!
(Hold up and wiggle 10 fingers like burning flames)

2. **One Little, Two Little, Three Little Candles**
One little, two little, three little candles
(Hold up 1, 2, then 3 fingers)
Four little, five little, six little candles
(Hold up 4, 5, then 6 fingers)
Seven little, eight little, nine little candles
(Hold up 7, 8, then 9 fingers)
Ten little candles burning!
(Hold up and wiggle all 10 fingers)

Field Trips and Resource People

1. **Host a Visitor**
Invite someone who celebrates Diwali to come visit. Have them share with the children the things they enjoy about celebrating Diwali. Encourage the visitor to bring any artifacts and pictures to share.

2. **Indian Shops**
If you live in an area where there is a strong Indian community, consider visiting some Indian shops during the time when people are preparing for Diwali. An Indian market would expose the children to the many different spices, colors, ingredients, and smells there are. A sari shop would give the children a colorful look at dressing up for the holiday. Teach them to greet others with "Happy Diwali."

Group Time
(Games and Language)

1. **Decorate for Diwali**
Clean and decorate your space together. Invite children to sweep, dust, put away

toys, and use wipes to clean surfaces. Then hang streamers, paper chains, flower garlands (string flower shapes cut from colored paper onto pieces of yarn), and other decorations together.

2. **Flashlight Jamboree**
Hand out small flashlights and have the children explore using the beams of light to find things, light up dark spaces (cubbies and closets), and make shadows or patterns on the walls or floor.

Large Muscle

1. **Boom Boom Firecrackers**
Roll out a few long strips of large bubble wrap (the largest bubble size available) and have the children run, jump, or dance down the strip, making firecracker sounds with their feet.

2. **Musical Chairs + 1**
This is a noncompetitive version of a popular game that you can play to celebrate Diwali. Place a group of chairs in a double row with the chairs back-to-back. The total number of chairs for preschoolers can be the same number as the number of children playing. Play a fun musical track, and have the children walk around the chairs in a single line. When you stop the music, the children have to rush to find the nearest seat and sit down. Repeat again and again. Continue the game in this way till all the players are tired out and giggling.

Math

1. **Count Off**
With chalk, draw a circle of 10-inch circles on the pavement outside with the same number of 10-inch circles as the number of children in your group. Have your children stand in the circle, each one on a 10-inch

circle. Start them singing the following song, and walking one step at a time to the right as they say each number (1, 2, 3, 4, etc.). Encourage the child whose name is called to pretend to eat! Then repeat the song and have the children continue walking with the count. If walking around a circle is challenging, have the children hold hands as they walk.
One, two, three, four
(child's name) at the kitchen door.
Five, six, seven, eight.
Eating (curry, kheer, or rice pudding) off her plate.
It's Diwali!
Variation: The same activity can be done inside or outside without circles.

2. **Candle Sort**
Sort various candles by size, shape, and color.

3. **Light Walk**
Take a walk with the children and record the number of lights (lamps, candles, and light fixtures) observed on the walk. If appropriate, the lights might be classified into categories such as "lamps" and "fixtures."

4. **Which is bigger?**
Collect a variety of stick (taper) candles in different sizes. Encourage the children to order from biggest to smallest.

Music

1. **The People at Diwali**
(Sing to the tune of "The Wheels on the Bus")
Oh, the people at Diwali light the lights
light the lights, light the lights
(Children wave fingers to show flickering light)
Oh, the people at Diwali light the lights,
All over town.
Oh, the sounds at Diwali, boom boom boom

boom boom boom, boom boom boom
   (Children close and open their fingers)
Oh the sounds at Diwali, boom boom boom,
All over town.
Oh, the sweets at Diwali, yum yum yum
Yum yum yum, yum yum yum
   (Children rub their belly)
Oh, the sweets at Diwali, yum yum yum
All over town.

2. Little Lamps

(Sing to the tune of "London Bridge")
Little lamps are burning bright,
Burning bright, burning bright.
Little lamps are burning bright,
Happy Diwali.
See them lighting up the night,
Up the night, up the night.
See them lighting up the night,
Happy Diwali.

Social Studies

1. Celebration Collage

Cut pictures of people getting together, smiling, and laughing. Include pictures of older people, middle-aged people, children, and babies. You might want to seek out pictures of people eating together. Provide glue sticks and 8 1/2-inch × 11-inch paper. Invite children to make collages of families and friends celebrating together.

2. Diwali around the World

Show pictures in a children's book of Diwali celebrations. Invite the children to tell you what they see.

3. Brothers and Sisters

On the last (fifth) day of Diwali, brothers and sisters get together to strengthen their bonds. Invite children to tell you about their brothers and sisters. Ask, "What do you like to play together?" "How do you take care of your brothers or sisters?" and "How do your brothers and sisters take care of you?"

Sensory

1. Bubble Wrap

Fill the sensory table with pieces of bubble wrap (or Styrofoam packing pieces) for the children to make the sounds of firecrackers.

Books

Das, Prodeepta. (2004). *I Is for India*. World Alphabets. London: Frances Lincoln Children's Books.

Dickmann, Nancy. (2011). *Diwali*. Fiestas. Portsmouth, NH: Heinemann Raintree.

Gardeski, Christina Mia. (2000). *Diwali*. Rookie Read-About Holidays. New Haven, CT: Children's Press.

Gilmore, Rachna. (2000). *Lights for Gita*. Illustrated by Alice Priestley. Gardiner, ME: Tilbury House Publishers.

Heiligman, Deborah. (2008). *Celebrate Diwali: With Sweets, Lights, and Fireworks*. Holidays around the World. Washington, DC: National Geographic Children's Books.

Jordan, Denise M. (2002). *Diwali*. Heinemann Read and Learn. Portsmouth, NH: Heinemann.

Kumar, Manisha, and Monica Kumar. (2006). *Diwali: A Festival of Lights and Fun / Diwali: Kushiyon Ka Tyohaar*. Illustrated by Sona and Jacob. San Jose, CA: MeeraMasi.

Makhijani, Pooja. (2007). *Mama's Saris*. Illustrated by Elena Gomez. New York: Little Brown & Company Books for Young Readers.

Preszler, June. (2006). *Diwali: Hindu Festival of Lights*. First Facts. Mankato, MN: Capstone Press.

Sandhu, Rupi K. (2008). *Twinkling Lights, Diwali Nights*. Bloomington, IN: Trafford Publishing.

Somaiah, Rosemarie, and Ranjan Somaiah. (2006). *Indian Children's Favourite Stories*. North Clarendon, VT: Tuttle Publishing.

Strain Trueit, Trudi. (2006). *Diwali.* Rookie Read-About Holidays. New Haven, CT: Children's Press.

Torpie, Kate, Chester Fisher, and Susan Labella. (2008). *Diwali.* Celebrations in My World. New York: Crabtree Publishing.

Zucker, Jonny. (2004). Illustrated by Jan Barger Cohen. *Lighting a Lamp: A Diwali Story.* Hauppauge, NY: Barron's Educational Series.

Technology and Multimedia

Global Wonders: India [DVD]. 2008. Hollywood, CA: Paramount Pictures.

Additional teaching resources to accompany this Theme can be found on the book's companion website. Go to www.cengagebrain.com to access the site for a variety of useful resources.

Theme 26
DOCTORS AND NURSES

Tools
rubber hammer
stethoscope
thermometer
scale
medicine

Kinds
eye
ear
feet
teeth
animal
baby

Clothing
white lab coat
gloves
masks

Purposes
community helpers
help people
help animals

Places of Work
hospitals
clinics
home care
schools

241

Theme Goals

Through participating in the experiences provided by this theme, the children may learn:

1. The purpose of doctors and nurses
2. Kinds of doctors and nurses
3. Places doctors and nurses work
4. Tools used by doctors and nurses
5. Clothing worn by doctors and nurses

Concepts for the Children to Learn

1. Doctors and nurses are community helpers.
2. Doctors and nurses help to keep people and animals healthy.
3. Doctors and nurses work in clinics, hospitals, schools, and homes.
4. Lab coats, gloves, and masks are clothing doctors and nurses may wear.
5. Special doctors and nurses care for our eyes, ears, feet, and teeth.
6. An animal doctor is called a veterinarian.
7. A pediatrician is a children's doctor.
8. Doctors and nurses use many tools.
9. A stethoscope is a tool used to check heartbeats and breathing.
10. Thermometers are used to check body temperature.
11. A scale is used to check people's weight.
12. A rubber hammer is used to check people's reflexes.
13. Sometimes doctors give people medicine to make them feel better.

Vocabulary

1. **doctor**—a man or woman who helps keep our bodies healthy.
2. **nurse**—a man or woman who usually assists the doctor.
3. **ophthalmologist**—an eye doctor.
4. **patient**—a person who goes to see a doctor.
5. **pediatrician**—a children's doctor.
6. **stethoscope**—a tool for checking heartbeat and breathing.
7. **thermometer**—a tool for checking our body temperature.
8. **veterinarian**—an animal doctor.

Bulletin Board

The purpose of this bulletin board is to develop skills in identifying written numerals and matching sets to numerals. Construct bandages out of manila tagboard as illustrated, or use purchased adhesive bandages. Laminate. Collect small boxes and cover with white paper if necessary. The number of boxes will be dependent on the developmental age of the children. Plastic bandage boxes or 16-count crayon boxes may be used. On each box, place a numeral. Affix the box to a bulletin board by stapling. The children can place the proper number of bandages in each box.

InBox

Dear Families,

I hope everyone in your family is happy and healthy! Speaking of healthy, we are starting a unit on doctors and nurses. The children will be learning about the different types of doctors and nurses and how they help people. They also will be introduced to some of the tools used by doctors and nurses.

At School

A few of the learning experiences planned include:

- Listening to the story *Tommy Goes to the Doctor*
- Taking our temperatures with forehead strips and recording them on a chart in the science area
- Dressing up as doctors and nurses in the dramatic play area
- Experimenting with syringes (no needles!) and water at the sensory table
- Listening to and looking at books related to doctors and nurses

At Home

There are many ways to integrate this curriculum unit into your home. To begin, discuss the role of your family doctor. Talk about your child's visit to a physician. This will help to alleviate anxiety and fears your child may have about the procedures and setting. Let your child help you prepare this nutritious snack at home. We will be making it for Wednesday's snack as well.

Fruit Smoothie

1 cup lowfat yogurt
2 cups fresh or frozen berries
2 tablespoons frozen orange juice concentrate

Combine all of the ingredients and blend. Process the mixture until smooth. If desired, thin by adding additional orange juice.

Model positive attitudes toward health for your child.

Arts and Crafts

1. Cotton Swab Painting
Place cotton swabs, cotton balls, and tempera paint on a table in the art area. The cotton swabs and balls can be used as painting tools.

2. Body Tracing
Trace the children's bodies by having them lie down on a large piece of paper. The body shape can be decorated at school by the child with crayons and felt-tip markers. The shapes could also be taken home and decorated with parental assistance.

3. Eyedropper Painting
Provide eyedroppers, thin tempera paint, and absorbent paper. Designs can be made by using the eyedropper as a painting tool. Another method is to prepare water colored with food coloring in muffin tins. Using heavy paper towels with construction paper underneath for protection, the children will enjoy creating designs with the colored water.

Cooking

1. Mighty Mixture
Mix any of the following:

A variety of dried fruit (apples, apricots, pineapple, and raisins)
A variety of seeds (pumpkin and sunflower)

2. Vegetable Juice
Prepare individual servings of vegetable juice in a blender by adding 1/2 cup of cut-up vegetables and 1/4 cup of water. Add salt to taste. Vegetables that can be used include celery, carrots, beets, tomatoes, cucumbers, and zucchini.

Dramatic Play

1. Doctors and Nurses
Make a prop box for a doctor and nurse. Include a white coat, rubber gloves, a forehead strip thermometer, gauze, tape, masks, eyedroppers, an eye chart, cots, blankets, pencils and paper, empty and washed medicine bottles, a stethoscope, a scale, and syringes without needles. A first-aid kit including gauze and tape, adhesive bandages, a sling, and Ace bandages can be placed in this box. Place the prop boxes in the dramatic play area.

2. Animal Clinic
Place stuffed animals with the doctor tools in the dramatic play area.

3. Eye Doctor Clinic
Ask a local eye doctor for discontinued eyeglass frames. Place the frames with a wall chart in the dramatic play area.

Field Trips and Resource People

1. Doctor's Office
Visit a doctor's office.

2. Resource Person
Invite a nurse or doctor to visit the classroom. Encourage him or her to talk briefly about his or her job. He or she can also share some of the tools with the children.

3. The Hospital
Visit a local hospital.

Fingerplays and Chants

Miss Polly's Dolly
Miss Polly had a dolly that was sick, sick, sick.
(cradle arms and look sad)
She called for the doctor to come quick, quick, quick.
(clap hands three times)
The doctor came with his coat and his hat.
(point to your shirt and head)
And rapped on the door with a rap, rap, rap.
(pretend to knock three times)

He looked at the dolly and he shook his head
    (shake head)
And he said, "Miss Polly, put her straight to
    bed."
    (shake finger)
Then he wrote on a paper for some pills,
    pills, pills.
    (hold left hand out flat, pretend to write
    with right hand)
I'll be back in the morning with my bill, bill,
    bill.
    (hold left hand out flat, wave it up and
    down as if waiting to be handed cash)

Note: The doctor may be male or female.
    Substitute pronouns.

Five Little Children

Five little children, playing in a tree. (hold
    up five fingers)
One fell out and broke his knee. (touch
    knee)
Mommy (Daddy) called the doctor, (hold
    fist to ear)
And the doctor said,
"No more children playing in a tree!" (shake
    pointed index finger)
Four little children . . . (repeat actions as
    above)
Three little children . . .
Two little children . . .
One little child . . .

Group Time
(Games and Language)

1. **Doctor, Doctor, Nurse**
Play "Duck, Duck, Goose" inserting the
words, "Doctor, Doctor, Nurse."

2. **What's Missing?**
Place a variety of doctors' and nurses' tools
on a large tray. Tell the children to close
their eyes. Remove one item from the tray.
Then have the children open their eyes
and guess which item has been removed.
Continue playing the game using all of the
items as well as providing an opportunity
for each child.

Math

1. **Weight and Height Chart**
Prepare a height and weight chart out of
tagboard. Record each child's height and
weight on this chart. Repeat periodically
throughout the year to note physical
changes.

2. **Tongue Depressor Dominoes**
Make a set of dominoes by writing on
tongue depressors. Divide each tongue
depressor in half with a felt-tip marker.
On each half place a different number of
dots. Consider the children's developmental
level in determining the number of dots
to be included. Demonstrate to interested
children how to play dominoes.

3. **Bandage Lotto**
Construct a bandage lotto game using
various sizes and shapes of bandages. Trace
each bandage onto a piece of tag board
using a permanent felt-tip marker. The
bandages can be matched to the shapes on
the tagboard.

Music

1. **"The Doctor in the Clinic"**
(*Sing to the tune of "Farmer in the Dell"*)

The doctor in the clinic.
The doctor in the clinic.
Hi-ho the derry-o,
The doctor in the clinic.

The doctor takes a nurse . . .
The nurse takes a patient . . .
The patient gets help . . .
The patient gets better . . .

2. **"To the Hospital"**
(*Sing to the tune of "Frére Jacques"*)

To the hospital, to the hospital,
We will go, we will go.
We will see the doctors,
And we'll see the nurses,
Dressed in scrubs, dressed in scrubs.

Science

1. **Thermometer**
   Place a variety of unbreakable thermometers on the science table. Include a candy, a meat, and an outdoor thermometer. Also include a strip thermometer that can be safely used on children's foreheads.

2. **Casts**
   Ask personnel at a local hospital to save clean, discarded casts. Place the casts on the science table, allowing the children to observe the materials, try them on for size, as well as feel their weight. The children may also enjoy decorating the casts.

3. **Stethoscope**
   Place a stethoscope on the science table for the children to experiment with. After each child uses it, wipe the ear plugs with alcohol to prevent the transmission of disease.

4. **Doctors' Tools**
   In a feely box, place several tools that a doctor uses. Include a thermometer, gauze, a stethoscope, a rubber hammer, and tongue depressors.

5. **Making Toothpaste**
   Mix 4 teaspoons baking soda, 1 teaspoon salt, and 1 teaspoon peppermint flavoring. Then add just enough water to form a thick paste.

Social Studies

Pictures
Display various health-related pictures in the room at the children's eye level. Include doctors and nurses. Pictures should depict males and females in both of these health-related fields.

Books

The following books can be used to complement this theme:

Beatty, Andrea, and Pascal Lemaitre. (2008). *Doctor Ted.* New York: Simon & Schuster.

Bennett, Howard J. (2006). *Lions Aren't Scared of Shots: A Story for Children about Visiting the Doctor.* Illustrated by M. S. Weber. Washington, DC: Magination Press.

Bond, Michael, Karen Jankel, and R. W. Alley. (2001). *Paddington Bear Goes to the Hospital.* Illustrated by R. W. Alley. New York: HarperCollins.

Brazelton, T. Berry. (1996). *Going to the Doctor.* Photos by Alfred Womack. Reading, MA: Addison Wesley.

Charlip, Remy, and Burton Supree. (2001). *Mother Mother I Feel Sick Send for the Doctor Quick Quick Quick.* Illustrated by Remy Charlip. Berkeley, CA: Tricycle Press.

Civardi, Anne. (2005). *Going to the Doctor.* Illustrated by Stephen Cartwright. Tulsa, OK: EDC Pub.

Cole, Joanna. (2005). *My Friend the Doctor.* Illustrated by Maxie Chambliss. New York: HarperCollins.

Cousins, Lucy. (2001). *Doctor Maisy.* Cambridge, MA: Candlewick Press.

Davison, Martine. (1992). *Robby Visits the Doctor.* Illustrated by Nancy Stevenson. New York: Random House.

Dooley, Virginia. (1996). *Tubes in My Ears: My Trip to the Hospital.* Illustrated by Miriam Katin. Greenvale, NY: Mondo Publications.

Ehrlich, H. M. (2005). *Dr. Duck and the New Babies.* Illustrated by Laura Rader. Maplewood, NJ: Blue Apple Books.

Fiedler, Sonja. (2006). *Say Ahh!* New York: North-South.

Gordon, Sharon. (2007). *What's inside a Hospital?/Que Hay Dentro De Un Hospital?* Tarrytown, NY: Marshall Cavendish Benchmark.

Hoena, B. A. (2004). *A Visit to the Doctor's Office.* Mankato, MN: Capstone Press.

Kottke, Jan. (2000). *A Day with a Doctor.* New York: Children's Press.

Liebman, Daniel. (2000). *I Want to Be a Doctor.* Toronto: Firefly Books.

Lloyd, Sam. (2007). *Doctor Meow's Big Emergency.* New York: Henry Holt.

London, Jonathan. (2002). *Froggy Goes to the Doctor.* Illustrated by Frank Remikiewicz. New York: Viking.

Marx, David F. (2000). *Hello, Doctor.* Illustrated by Mark A. Hicks. New York: Children's Press.

Marzollo, Jean. (2001). *Shanna's Doctor Show.* Illustrated by Shane Evans. New York: Jump at the Sun/Hyperion Books for Children.

Mayer, Mercer. (2005). *My Trip to the Hospital.* New York: HarperFestival.

McCue, Lisa. (2005). *Corduroy Goes to the Doctor.* New York: Viking.

Miller, Marilyn. (1996). *Behind the Scenes at the Hospital.* Illustrated by Ingo Fast. Austin, TX: Raintree/Steck Vaughn.

Moses, Amy. (1997). *Doctors Help People.* Mankato, MN: Child's World.

Murkoff, Heidi E. (2001). *What to Expect When You Go to the Doctor.* New York: HarperFestival.

Murphy, Liz. (2007). *ABC Doctor.* Maplewood, NJ: Blue Apple Books.

Sanschagrin, Joceline. (2008). *Caillou: The Doctor.* Illustrated by Pierre Brignaud. Montreal: Chouette Publishing.

Schomp, Virginia. (1998). *If You Were a Veterinarian.* Tarrytown, NY: Marshall Cavendish.

Seligmann, Jean H. (1975) *Tommy Visits the Doctor.* NY: Random House.

Thaler, Mike. (1995). *The School Nurse from the Black Lagoon.* Illustrated by Jared Lee. New York: Scholastic.

Wells, Rosemary. (2001). *Felix Feels Better.* Cambridge, MA: Candlewick Press.

Technology and Multimedia

The following technology and multimedia products can be used to complement this theme:

"Doctor Knickerbocker" [CD]. (2008). In *Name Games.* Toronto: Casablanca Kids.

"I Got a Job" [CD]. (2002). In *Growing Up with Ella Jenkins.* Washington, DC: Smithsonian Folkways.

Additional teaching resources to accompany this Theme can be found on the book's companion website. Go to www.cengagebrain.com to access the site for a variety of useful resources.

Theme 27
DOGS

Body Parts
fur
four legs
paws
tail
ears
eyes
nose
mouth

Food
water
dog food
dog treats

Safety
diseases
rabies

Communicate
growling
barking
wagging tail
pawing
licking

Supplies
collars
bones
leashes
brushes

Colors
yellow
brown
black
white
mixed

Care
exercise
food
water
sleep
grooming

Occupational Uses
police and
security dog
Seeing Eye dog
hunting
farming
ranching

Sizes
large
medium
small

Homes
doghouses
kennels
house

Theme Goals

Through participating in the experiences provided by this theme, the children may learn:

1. Dog's body parts
2. Sizes of dogs
3. Foods dogs eat
4. Supplies dogs need
5. Occupational uses of dogs
6. Dog homes
7. Dog safety
8. Colors of dogs
9. Special care of dogs
10. How dogs communicate

Concepts for the Children to Learn

1. A dog is an animal.
2. There are many different sizes of dogs.
3. Dogs have keen senses of smell and hearing.
4. Dogs growl, paw, lick, wag their tail, and bark to communicate.
5. Dogs may bark at strangers to protect their owners and their space.
6. Children should not pet strange dogs.
7. Dogs have four legs, eyes, ears, a mouth, a nose, paws, and a tail.
8. Dogs have fur on their skin.
9. Dogs need water and dog food.
10. Police dogs help police officers.
11. Seeing Eye dogs help people who are blind and cannot see.
12. Hunting dogs help hunters.
13. Some dogs, like herding dogs, help farmers or ranchers.
14. There are many different kinds of dogs.
15. Dogs need care.
16. Dogs need food, water, sleep, and exercise.
17. Dogs need to have their toenails clipped.
18. Some dogs need to be groomed.
19. Dogs can live in doghouses, in kennels, or in a house.
20. Dogs can be many different colors.

Vocabulary

1. **dog**—a domesticated animal that usually lives with humans.
2. **bone**—an object a dog chews on.
3. **coat**—hair or fur covering the skin.
4. **collar**—a band worn around the dog's neck.
5. **doghouse**—a place for dogs to sleep and keep warm.
6. **guide dog**—a dog trained to help people who are blind or need help.
7. **leash**—a rope, chain, or cord that attaches to a collar.
8. **obedience school**—a school where dogs are taught to obey.
9. **paw**—the dog's foot.
10. **pet**—an animal kept for pleasure.
11. **puppy**—a baby dog.
12. **veterinarian**—an animal doctor.
13. **whiskers**—stiff hair growing around the dog's nose, mouth, and eyes.

Bulletin Board

The purpose of this bulletin board is to develop visual discrimination, problem-solving, color recognition, and matching skills. Prepare the bulletin board by cutting dog shapes out of tagboard or construction paper. Add details using felt-tip markers. Use rubber cement to attach a different colored paper collar to each dog's neck. Also, cut out dog dishes from colored construction paper. Attach the pieces to the bulletin board as illustrated. Attach lengths of yarn or string for children to match the color of each dog's collar to the corresponding dog dish.

Family Letter

Dear Families,

We will begin a curriculum unit on a favorite subject of children of all ages—dogs! Through the classroom activities, we will be learning about a dog's basic physical features such as the coat and body parts. We will also learn about caring for a dog, the roles of dogs in people's lives, dog training, as well as factors families need to consider when choosing a dog. This curriculum unit is designed to encourage the children to develop an awareness of and respect for dogs as pets.

At School

Some of the learning experiences planned include:

- Creating paw prints at the art table (dipping paw-shaped sponges into paint and applying them to paper)
- Sorting various-sized dog biscuits
- Listening to the children's stories about their own dogs
- Setting up a "pet store" in the dramatic play area, complete with stuffed animals and many dog accessories
- Baking dog biscuits

At Home

To foster parent-child interaction and reinforce some of the concepts we are working on at school, try some of the following ideas:

- Look through magazines to find pictures of dogs and puppies. Help your child tear out some of the pictures. This activity is good for the development of fine motor and visual discrimination skills. An interesting collage can be made by gluing these pictures onto a piece of paper.
- If you don't have access to a dog, visit a pet shop to observe the puppies. At the same time, note all of the dog supplies available.

Enjoy your child!

 Arts and Crafts

1. **Dog Puppets**
   Provide socks, paper bags, or paper plates to make dog puppets.

2. **Dog Masks**
   Use fake fur ears and chenille stems for whiskers.

3. **Bone Printing**
   Provide different meat bones, a tray of tempera paint, and paper to make prints.

4. **Bone Painting**
   Cut easel paper in bone shapes.

 Cooking

1. **Hot "Dog" Kebabs on a Stick**
   1 package hot dogs, cut up
   2 green peppers, cut up
   Cherry tomatoes
   Paper plates and napkins
   Skewers

   Place two pieces of green pepper, two cherry tomatoes, and two hot dog pieces on each child's plate. Show the children how to thread the ingredients on skewers. Bake the kabobs in a preheated oven for 15 minutes at 350 degrees. Due to choking hazards, children should be watched carefully when eating hot dogs.

2. **Dog Biscuits—for Dogs!**
   2 1/2 cups whole wheat flour
   1/2 cup powdered dry milk
   1/2 teaspoon salt
   1/2 teaspoon garlic powder
   6 tablespoons margarine, shortening, or
        meat drippings
   1 egg
   1 teaspoon brown sugar
   1/2 cup ice water

   Combine flour, milk, salt, and garlic powder. Cut in the shortening. Mix in egg. Add enough water so that mixture forms a ball. Pat the dough to a half-inch thickness on a lightly oiled cookie sheet. Cut with cutters and remove scraps. Bake 25 to 30 minutes at 350 degrees. This recipe may be varied by adding pureed soup greens, protein powder, and so on.

3. **Healthy Dog Biscuits**
   1 3/4 cups beef or chicken broth
   1 package dry yeast
   2 cups whole wheat flour
   1/2 cup cornmeal
   1 teaspoon salt
   1/3 cup safflower oil
   1/3 cup finely chopped fresh mint
   1 egg, lightly beaten with 1 teaspoon of water

   To proof yeast:
   Heat broth in a small saucepan to 105 degrees. Sprinkle in yeast, stir to dissolve, and remove from heat. Let the mixture stand at room temperature for 5 minutes. ***Caution:*** If the broth is too hot, it will kill the yeast.

   To make biscuits:
   Pour the yeast mixture into the bowl of a standing mixer fitted with a paddle attachment. Add the whole wheat flour, cornmeal, salt, oil, and mint. Mix on medium speed until a soft dough is formed.
   Remove to a well-floured surface. Knead 10–12 times, or just until the texture is smooth. Cover the dough with a kitchen towel. Let stand for 20 minutes.

   To shape biscuits:
   Roll out into a 1/4-inch-thick rectangle. Using a bone-shaped cookie cutter, cut shapes starting from the edge of the dough and working toward the center so that fewer scraps remain. Gather up scraps. Knead together until smooth. Reroll to cut additional biscuits. Place 1/2 inch apart on parchment-linked baking sheets.

   To bake biscuits:
   Brush the tops with the egg mixture. Place on the center oven rack. Bake in a 400-degree oven for 45–50 minutes or until lightly browned, reversing the baking sheets halfway through the baking time. Turn off the oven. Keep the biscuits inside the oven for 30 minutes to crisp. Remove. Cool. Store in plastic bags.

When finished:
Dog biscuits can be sent home with children or donated to a local animal shelter.

Makes 30 six-inch biscuits.

4. Hush Puppies
Vegetable oil
2 1/4 cups yellow cornmeal
1 teaspoon salt
2 tablespoons finely chopped onion
3/4 teaspoon baking soda
1 1/2 cups buttermilk

Heat oil (about 1 inch deep) in a deep frying pan to 375 degrees. Mix cornmeal, salt, onion, and baking soda in a bowl. Add buttermilk. Drop the mixture by spoonfuls into hot oil. Fry until brown, about 2 minutes. ***Caution:*** This activity should be carefully supervised.

Dramatic Play

1. Pet Store
Simulate a pet store using stuffed animals. Include a counter complete with a cash register and money. Post a large "Pet Store" sign. Set out many stuffed dogs with collars and leashes. Children will enjoy pretending they have a new pet.

2. Veterinarian's Office
Use some medical equipment and stuffed dogs to create a veterinarian's office.

3. Pet Show
Encourage the children to bring a stuffed animal to school. Children can pretend that their stuffed animals can do tricks. Have ribbons available for them to look at and award to each other.

4. Doghouse
Construct a doghouse from a large cardboard box. Provide dog ears and tails for the children to wear as they imitate the pet.

Field Trips and Resource People

1. Pet Store
Take a field trip to a pet store. While there, ask the manager how to care for dogs. Observe the different types of cages, collars, leashes, food, and toys.

2. Veterinarian's Office
Take a field trip to a veterinarian's office or animal hospital. Compare its similarities and differences with a doctor's office.

3. Kennel
Visit a kennel and observe the different sizes of cages and dogs.

4. Variety Store
Visit a variety store and observe pet accessories.

5. Grocery Store
Take a field trip to the grocery store and purchase the ingredients needed to make dog biscuits.

6. Dog Trainer
Invite an obedience trainer to talk about teaching dogs.

7. Additional Resource People
- Veterinarian
- Pet store owner
- Parents (bring in family dogs)
- Humane Society representative
- Representative from a kennel
- Dog groomer
- Person with a Seeing Eye dog (guide dog)

Fingerplays and Chants

Frisky's Doghouse
This is Frisky's doghouse;
(pointer fingers touch to make a roof)
This is Frisky's bed;
(motion of smoothing)

Here is Frisky's pan of milk;
  (cup hands)
So that he can be fed.

Frisky has a collar
  (point to neck with fingers)
With his name upon it, too;
Take a stick and throw it,
  (motion of throwing)
He'll bring it back to you.
  (clap once)

Five Little Puppies Playing in the Sun

Five little puppies were playing in the sun.
  (hold up hands, fingers extended)
This one saw a rabbit, and he began to run.
  (bend down first finger)
This one saw a butterfly, and he began to race.
  (bend down second finger)
This one saw a cat, and he began to chase.
  (bend down third finger)
This one tried to catch his tail, and he went round and round.
  (bend down fourth finger)
This one was so quiet, he never made a sound.
  (bend down thumb)

Five Little Puppies Jumping on the Bed

Five little puppies jumping on the bed,
  (hold up five fingers)
One fell off and bumped his head,
  (hold up one finger—tap head)
Mama called the doctor and the doctor said,
"No more puppies jumping on the bed."
  (shake index finger)

Group Time
(Games and Language)

1. **The Dog Catcher**
   Hide stuffed dogs or those cut from construction paper around the classroom, and have children find them.

2. **Child-Created Stories**
   Bring in a picture of a dog or a stuffed dog. Encourage the children to tell you a story about the picture or the stuffed dog. While each child speaks, record the words. Place the story in the book corner.

3. **Dog Chart**
   Make a chart listing the color of each child's dog. A variation would be to have the children state their favorite color of dog. This activity can be repeated using size.

4. **Doggie, Doggie, Where's Your Bone?**
   Bring in a clean bone or a bone cut from construction paper. Sit the children in a circle. Choose one child to be the dog. Have the child pretending to be the dog sit in the middle. The doggie closes his or her eyes. A child from the circle sneaks up and takes the bone. Children call, "Doggie, doggie, where's your bone? Someone stole it from your home!" The "dog" gets three guesses to find out who has the bone.

5. **The Lost Dog**
   (This is a variation of the "Dog Catcher" game.) Using the children's stuffed animals from home, have the children trade dogs so that each is holding another's pet. One child begins by hiding the dog he or she is holding while the other children cover their eyes. He or she tells the owner, "Your dog is lost, but we can help you find it." As the dog owner looks, he or she can put the pet he or she is holding on his or her carpet square to free both hands. The group gives "hot" and "cold" clues to indicate whether the child is close to or far away from the pet. When the child finds his or her pet, he or she is the next one to hide a pet.

6. **Doggy, Doggy, Where is Your Bone?**
   Sit the children in a circle formation. Then place a chair in the center of the circle. Place a block under the chair. Select one child, the dog, to sit on the chair and close his or her eyes. Then point to another child. This child must try to get the dog's bone from under the chair without making a noise. After the child returns to his or her place in the circle, all of the children place their hands behind them. Then, in unison, the children say, "Doggy, Doggy, where's your bone?" During the game, each dog has three guesses about who has the bone.

Large Muscle

1. Pretending
Encourage the children to dramatize the following movements:

- A big dog
- A tiny dog
- A dog with heavy steps
- A dog with light steps
- A happy dog
- A sad dog
- A mad dog
- A loud dog
- A quiet dog
- A hungry dog
- A tired dog
- A curious dog
- A sick dog

2. Dog Hoops
Provide hoops for the children to jump through as they imitate dogs.

3. Scent Walk
Place prints of dog paws on the play yard leading to different activities. Encourage the child to crawl to each activity.

4. Tracks
If snow is available, make tracks with boots that have different treads. Encourage children to follow one track.

5. Bean Bag Bones
Provide round bean bags or make special bone-shaped bean bags. Encourage the children to throw them into a large dog food bowl.

Math

1. Dog Bones
Cut dog bone shapes of four different sizes from tagboard. Encourage the children to sequence them.

2. Classifying Dog Biscuits
Purchase three sizes of dog biscuits. Using dog dishes, have the children sort them according to size and type.

3. Weighing Biscuits
Using the scale, encourage the children to weigh different sizes and amounts of dog biscuits.

Music

1. "Bingo"
There was a farmer who had a dog
And Bingo was his name-o.
B-I-N-G-O
B-I-N-G-O
B-I-N-G-O
And Bingo was his name-o.

2. "Six Little Dogs"
(*Sing to the tune of "Six Little Ducks"*)

Six little dogs that I once knew,
fat ones, skinny ones, fair ones too.
But the one little dog with the brown curly fur,
He led the others with a grr, grr, grr.
Grr, grr, grr
Grr, grr, grr
He led the others with a grr, grr, GRR!

Science

1. Additions to the science table or area may include:

   - A magnifying glass with bones, dog hair, and dog food
   - Dog toys of different sizes, including some with squeakers
   - A balance scale and dry dog food

2. During a cooking activity, prepare dog biscuits. Biscuit recipes are listed under "Cooking."

Social Studies

1. Share Your Dog
Individually invite the parents to bring their child's pet to school.

2. Pictures of Dogs
Display pictures of different types of dogs.

3. Bulletin Board

Prepare a bulletin board with pictures of the children's dogs.

4. Digital Photographs

Take digital photographs of dog-related field trips and of resource people who helped teach the class about dogs. Share them at group time. (These digital photographs can be posted on the family bulletin board or inserted into family letters.)

5. Dog Biscuits

Prepare dog biscuits and donate them to the local animal shelter. (See the "Cooking" section of this theme.)

6. Chart

Make a chart, including each child's name and the type, size, and name of his or her pet. Count the number of dogs, cats, birds, and other pets. Discuss the most popular names.

7. Dogs

Using pictures or a real dog, talk about a dog's body. Some dogs have long noses so they can smell things very well; others have short hair to live in hot climates. Discuss why some dogs are good guard dogs. Discuss how dogs' tongues help them to cool off on hot days. Also talk about what else a dog's rough tongue is used for.

 Books

The following books can be used to complement this theme:

Baek, Matthew J. (2008). *Be Gentle with the Dog, Dear!* New York: Dial Books for Young Readers.

Bansch, Helga. (2009). *I Want a Dog!* New York: North-South.

Boland, Janice, and Brian G. Karas. (1998). *A Dog Named Sam.* New York: Puffin.

Braeuner, Shellie. (2009). *The Great Dog Wash.* Illustrated by Robert Neubecker. New York: Simon & Schuster.

Calmenson, Stephanie. (2007). *May I Pet Your Dog?* Illustrated by Jan Ormerod. New York: Clarion Books.

Dodd, Emma. (2008). *I Don't Want a Posh Dog.* New York: Little, Brown.

Gal, Susan. (2010). *Please Take Me for a Walk.* New York: Alfred A. Knopf.

Garcia, Cristina. (2008). *The Dog Who Loved the Moon.* Illustrated by Sebastia Serra. New York: Atheneum Books for Young Readers.

Gutman, Anne, and Georg Hallensleben. (2001). *Gaspard and Lisa at the Museum.* New York: Knopf.

Harper, Isabelle. (1996). *Our New Puppy.* Illustrated by Barry Moser. New York: Scholastic.

Herman, R. A. (2005). *Gomer and Little Gomer.* Illustrated by Steve Haskamp. New York: Dutton Children's Books.

Hest, Amy. (2008). *The Dog Who Belonged to No One.* Illustrated by Amy Bates. New York: Abrams Books for Young Readers.

Jarka, Jeff. (2009). *I Love That Puppy!* New York: Henry Holt.

Jenkins, Emily. (2008). *Skunkdog.* Illustrated by Pierre Pratt. New York: Farrar, Straus and Giroux.

Katz, Bobbi. (2010). *Nothing but a Dog.* Illustrated by Jane Manning. New York: Dutton Children's Books.

Kennedy, Marlane. (2009). *The Dog Days of Charlotte Hayes.* New York: Greenwillow Books.

King, Stephen Michael. (2005). *Mutt Dog!* Orlando, FL: Harcourt.

Koontz, Dean Ray. (2009). *I, Trixie Who Is Dog.* Illustrated by Janet Cleland. New York: Putnam's Sons.

LeFrak, Karen. (2008). *Jake the Ballet Dog.* Illustrated by Marcin Baranski. New York: Walker and Co.

Masurel, Claire. (1997). *No, No, Titus!* Illustrated by Shari Halpern. New York: North South Books.

McDonnell, Christine. (2009). *Dog Wants to Play.* Illustrated by Jeff Mack. New York: Viking.

Moore, Eva. (1996). *Buddy: The First Seeing Eye Dog.* Illustrated by Don Bolognese. New York: Scholastic.

Pinkwater, Daniel. (2010). *I Am the Dog.* Illustrated by Jack E. Davis. New York: Harper.

Ries, Lori. (2009). *Good Dog, Aggie!* Illustrated by Frank W. Dormer. Watertown, MA: Charlesbridge.

Rylant, Cynthia. (2006). *Mr. Putter and Tabby Spin the Yarn.* Illustrated by Arthur Howard. Orlando, FL: Harcourt.

Saenz, Benjamin Alire. (2009). *The Dog Who Loved Tortillas / La Perrita Que Le Encantaban Las Tortillas.* Illustrated by Geronimo Garcia. El Paso, TX: Cinco Puntos Press.

Slade, Suzanne. (2009). *From Puppy to Dog: Following the Life Cycle.* Illustrated by Jeff Yesh. Minneapolis, MN: Picture Window Books.

Stevens, Janet, and Susan Stevens-Crummel. (2009). *My Big Dog.* New York: Dragonfly Books.

Stuve-Bodeen, Stephanie. (2010). *A Small, Brown Dog with a Wet, Pink Nose.* Illustrated by Linzie Hunter. New York: Little, Brown.

Tagliaferro, Linda. (2004). *Dogs and Their Puppies.* Mankato, MN: Capstone Press.

Waber, Bernard. (2010). *Lyle Walks the Dogs: A Counting Book.* Illustrated by Paulis Waber. Boston: Houghton Mifflin.

Wahman, Wendy. (2009). *Don't Lick the Dog: Making Friends with Dogs.* New York: Henry Holt.

Wells, Rosemary, and Susan Jeffers. (2001). *McDuff Goes to School.* Illustrated by Susan Jeffers. New York: Hyperion Press.

Willems, Mo. (2010). *City Dog, Country Frog.* New York: Hyperion Books for Children.

Technology and Multimedia

The following technology and multimedia products can be used to complement this theme:

"Alice the Beagle" [CD]. (2005). In *Sing-a-Move-a-Dance.* Eau Claire, WI: North Side Music.

Bark, George [DVD]. (2009). New York: Scholastic.

"BINGO" [CD]. (2002). In *Early Childhood Classics.* Sherman Oaks, CA: Hap-Pal Music.

"Dog Gone Gone Dog Gone" [CD]. (2009). In *More Please.* Olympia, WA: Aurora Elephant Music.

Harry the Dirty Dog and More Terrific Tails [DVD]. (2003). New York: Scholastic.

"How Much Is That Doggie in the Window?" [CD]. (2008). In *Great Big Hits.* Toronto: Casablanca Kids.

"I've Got a Little Dog" [CD]. (2009). In *People, Place and Things.* Coconut Grove, FL: In the Nick of Time.

"I Want to Be a Dog" [CD]. (2000). In *10 Carrot Diamond.* Vancouver, BC: Hug Bug Records.

"My Dog Rags" (2004). In *Laugh N Learn Silly Songs.* Long Branch, NJ: Kimbo.

"Snuggle with Your Puppy" [CD]. (2000). In *Charlotte Diamond's World.* Vancouver, BC: Hug Bug Records.

"Where Has My Little Dog Gone?" [CD]. (1999). In *Sounds Like Fun.* Buena Park, CA: Barbara Milne.

"Who Let the Dogs Out?" (2001). In *Dance Party Fun.* Long Branch, NJ: Kimbo Educational.

 Additional teaching resources to accompany this Theme can be found on the book's companion website. Go to www.cengagebrain.com to access the site for a variety of useful resources.

Theme 28
EASTER

Symbols

baskets

rabbits

eggs

chicks and ducklings

bonnets

Special Foods

colored eggs

hot cross buns

candies

Celebrations

egg hunts

parades

Spring Holiday

new life

religious for some people*

* Some center personnel may elect to include an Easter theme with an emphasis on the spring holiday as opposed to the traditional religious emphasis.

Theme Goals

Through participating in the experiences provided by this theme, the children may learn:

1. Easter celebrations
2. Easter symbols
3. Special foods served at Easter
4. Easter as a spring holiday

Concepts for the Children to Learn

1. Easter is a holiday celebrated on a Sunday.
2. Many families celebrate Easter.
3. At Easter time, eggs are colored and decorated.
4. There are many symbols of Easter, including baby animals, baskets, rabbits, and eggs.
5. Colored eggs and plastic eggs filled with candy may be hidden.
6. Baby animals born in the spring are a sign of new life.
7. Bonnets (hats) may be worn at Easter time.
8. Easter is often celebrated with egg hunts and parades.

Vocabulary

1. **basket**—a woven container.
2. **bonnet**—a kind of hat that ties under the chin and is worn by a girl or woman.
3. **bunny**—a baby rabbit.
4. **chick**—a baby chicken.
5. **duckling**—a baby duck.
6. **dye**—to change the color of something.
7. **Easter**—a holiday in spring that always is on a Sunday.
8. **hatch**—to break out of a shell.
9. **holiday**—a day of celebration.
10. **spring**—the season of the year when plants begin to grow.

Bulletin Board

The purpose of this bulletin board is to promote the correspondence of sets to written numerals. Construct baskets out of stiff tagboard. Write a numeral beginning with the number 1 on each basket as illustrated. Carefully attach these to the bulletin board by stapling all the way around the bottom of the baskets. Construct many small Easter eggs. Encourage the children to deposit the corresponding number of Easter eggs in the numbered baskets. Care needs to be taken when removing the eggs. The number of baskets provided should reflect the developmental level of the children. If available, you might want to try using lightweight Easter baskets. They are harder to hang up but may prove to be more sturdy.

InBox

Dear Families,

"Here comes Peter Cottontail, hopping down the bunny trail. . . ." Easter is on its way and is the next curriculum theme we will explore. This is an exciting holiday for children. Through the planned learning experiences, the children will learn ways that families celebrate Easter and the symbols representing Easter. Included will be customs such as the Easter bunny, Easter baskets, and foods that are usually associated with Easter. Perhaps not all children and families celebrate this holiday, but we feel it is very important for children to learn about and respect others' beliefs.

At School

Learning experiences planned to reinforce concepts of Easter include:

- A special visitor for the week—a rabbit! The children will assist in taking care of the rabbit.
- A hat shop in the dramatic play area with materials to create Easter bonnets
- Easter grass and plastic eggs in the sensory table
- An egg hunt! On Friday, we will search our play yard for hidden eggs and place them in our baskets.
- Listening to Easter stories

At Home

Be adventurous and try some dyes from natural materials. Natural dyeing is not new; natural dyes were the original Easter egg colors the world over. To make purple eggs, purchase a box of frozen blackberries. Thaw and place in a saucepan. Add eggs and cover with water plus 1 tablespoon of vinegar. Bring the water to a boil and simmer for 20 minutes. Afterward, take the pan off the heat source and let stand for approximately 20 minutes.

Enjoy the holiday with your children!

 Arts and Crafts

1. **Easter Collages**
   Collect eggshells, straw, Easter grass, or plant seeds for making collages. Place on the art table with sheets of paper and glue.

2. **Colorful Collages**
   Use pastel-colored sand and glue to make collages.

3. **Wet Chalk Eggs**
   Use wet chalk to decorate paper cut in the shape of eggs in pastel colors. Show the children the difference between wetting the chalk in vinegar and in water. The vinegar color will be brighter.

4. **Easel Ideas**
   Cut egg-shaped easel paper or basket-shaped paper. Clip to the easel. Provide pastel paints at the easel. To make the paint more interesting, add glitter.

5. **Milk Carton Easter Baskets**
   Cut off the bottom 4 inches from milk cartons. Provide precut construction paper or wallpaper and yarn to cover the baskets. Include small bits of paper or bright cloth to glue on the cartons. Make a handle using a thin strip of paper that is stapled to the carton. Use the baskets for the children's snack.

6. **Plastic Easter Baskets**
   Easter baskets can be made by using the green plastic baskets that strawberries and blueberries come in from the grocery store. Cut thin strips of paper that children can practice weaving through the holes. This activity is most successful with older children.

7. **Color Mixing**
   Provide red-, yellow-, and blue-dyed water in shallow pans. Provide the children with medicine droppers and absorbent paper cut in the shape of eggs. Also, the children can use medicine droppers to apply color to the paper. Observe what happens when the colors blend together.

8. **Rabbit Ears**
   Construct rabbit ears out of heavy paper. Attach them to a band that can be worn around the head, fitting it for size. These ears may stimulate creative movement as well as dramatic play.

 Cooking

1. **Decorating Cupcakes**
   Let the children use green frosting, dyed coconut, and jellybeans to decorate cupcakes that they can put into their Easter baskets. Cake mixes can be used to make the cupcakes. Follow the directions on the box. Place paper liners in a muffin pan to ensure easy removability.

2. **Bunny Food**
   Carrot sticks, celery, and lettuce can be available for snack.

3. **Egg Sandwiches**
   Use the boiled eggs the children have decorated to make egg salad or deviled eggs for snack time.

4. **Carrot and Raisin Salad**
   4 cups grated carrots
   1 cup raisins
   1/2 cup mayonnaise or whipped salad
       dressing
   Place ingredients in a bowl and mix
       thoroughly.

5. **Bunny Salad**
   For each serving, place one lettuce leaf on a plate. Put one canned pear half with the cut side down on top of the lettuce leaf. Add sections of an orange to represent the ears. Decorate the bunny face by adding grated carrots, raisins, or maraschino cherries to make eyes, a nose, and a mouth.

Dramatic Play

1. **Flower Shop**
   Plan a flower shop for the dramatic play area. Include spring plants, baskets, and Easter lilies.

2. **Egg Center**
   Create a colored egg center to be used during self-directed play. Some children put stickers on plastic eggs, some sell the eggs, and others buy them.

3. **Costume Shop**
   Place costumes for bunny use, Easter baskets, and Easter eggs in the dramatic play area. The children can take turns hiding the eggs and going on hunts.

4. **A Bird Nest**
   Place a nest with eggs in the dramatic play area. Also provide bird masks, a perch, and other bird items in the area for use during self-initiated play.

5. **Easter Clothes**
   Bring in Easter clothes for the children to dress up in. Suits, dresses, hats, purses, gloves, and dress-up shoes should be included.

6. **Hat Shop**
   Make a hat shop. Place hats, ribbons, flowers, netting, and other decorations in the dramatic play area. The children can decorate the hats. If appropriate, plan an Easter parade.

Field Trips

1. **The Farm**
   Take a trip to a farm to see baby animals.

2. **The Hatchery**
   Visit a hatchery on a day that they are selling chicks.

3. **Neighborhood Walk**
   Take a walk around the neighborhood and look for signs of new life.

4. **Rabbit Visit**
   Bring some rabbits to school for the children to observe.

Fingerplays and Chants

The Duck

I waddle when I walk.
    (hold arms elbow high and twist trunk side to side, or squat down)
I quack when I talk.
    (place palms together and open and close)
And I have webbed toes on my feet.
    (spread fingers wide)
Rain coming down
Makes me smile, not frown
    (smile)
And I dive for something to eat.
    (put hands together and make diving motion)

My Rabbit

My rabbit has two big ears
    (hold up index and middle fingers for ears)
And a funny little nose.
    (join other three fingers for nose)
He likes to nibble carrots
    (move thumb away from other two fingers)
And he hops wherever he goes.
    (move whole hand jerkily)

Group Time
(Games and Language)

1. **The Last Bunny**
   This is a game for 10 or more players. It is more fun with a large number. An Easter rabbit is chosen by counting out or drawing straws. All the other players stand in a circle. The Easter rabbit walks around the circle and taps one player on the back, asking, "Have you seen my bunny helper?"
   "What does it look like?" asks the player.

The Easter rabbit describes the bunny helper. He or she may say, "She is wearing a watch and blue shoes." The player tries to guess who it is. When he or she names the right person, the Easter rabbit says, "That's my helper!" and the other player chases the bunny helper outside and around the circle. If the chaser catches the bunny helper before he or she can return to his or her place, the chaser becomes the Easter rabbit. If the bunny helper gets there first, then the first Easter rabbit must try again. The Easter rabbit takes the place in the circle of whoever is the new Easter rabbit.

Note: From *Games and How to Play Them,* by Anne Rockwell, 1973, New York: Thomas Y. Crowell.

2. Outdoor Egg Hunt

Plan an egg hunt outdoors, if possible. Hide the boiled eggs that the children have decorated, candy eggs in wrappers, or small Easter candies in clear plastic bags. The children can use the baskets they have made to collect their eggs, then, weather permitting, eat the boiled eggs for a snack outdoors.

Large Muscle

1. Bunny Trail

Set up a bunny trail in the classroom. Place tape on the floor, and have children hop over the trail. To make it more challenging, add a balance beam to resemble a bridge.

2. Eggs in the Basket

The children can practice throwing egg-shaped or regular beanbags into a large basket or bucket.

3. Rabbit Tag

Make egg-shaped beanbags to play rabbit tag. To play the game, the children stand in a circle, with one child being the rabbit. The rabbit walks around the circle with a beanbag balanced on his or her head and drops a second beanbag behind the back of another child. The second child must put the beanbag on his or her head and follow the rabbit around the circle once. Each child must keep the beanbag balanced—if it drops, it must be picked up and replaced on the head. If the rabbit is tagged, he or she chooses the next rabbit. If the rabbit returns to the empty spot in the circle, the second child becomes the rabbit. This is an unusual game in that the action is fairly slow but it's still very exciting.

4. Egg Rolling

Place mats on the floor and have children roll across with their arms at their sides. For older children, you can place the mat on a slightly inclined plane and have children roll down, and then have them try to roll back up, which is more challenging.

Math

1. Egg Numerals

Collect five small boxes. Put numerals from 1 to 5 (or 1 to 10, for older children) on the eggs. Let the children place the correct number of cotton balls or markers into each egg.

2. Easter Seriation

Cut different-sized tagboard eggs, chicks, ducklings, and rabbits. The children can place the items in a row from the smallest to the largest.

Music

1. "Did You Ever See a Rabbit?"

(*Sing to the tune of "Did You Ever See a Lassie?"*)

Did you ever see a rabbit, a rabbit, a rabbit?
Did you ever see a rabbit, a rabbit, on Easter morn?
He hops around so quietly
And hides all the eggs.
Did you ever see a rabbit, on Easter morn?

2. "Easter Bunny" Chant

Where, oh, where is the Easter Bunny,
Where, oh, where is the Easter Bunny,
Where, oh, where is the Easter Bunny,
Early Easter morning?
Find all the eggs and put them in a basket,
Find all the eggs and put them in a basket,
Find all the eggs and put them in a basket,
Early Easter morning.

3. "Easter Eggs"

(*Sing to the chorus of "Jingle Bells"*)

Easter eggs, Easter eggs,
Hidden all around.
Come my children look about
And see where they are found.

Easter eggs, Easter eggs,
They're a sight to see.
One for Tom and one for Ann
And a special one for me!

Insert names of children in your classroom.

4. "Easter Eggs" Chant

Easter eggs here and there,
Easter eggs everywhere.
What's the color of the
Easter egg here?

Science

1. Incubate and Hatch Eggs

Check the yellow pages of your telephone book to see if any hatcheries are located in your area.

2. Dyeing Eggs

Use natural products to make egg dye. Beets make deep red dye, cranberries make light red dye, spinach leaves make green dye, and blackberries make blue dye. To make dyed eggs, pick two or three colors from the list. Make the dye by boiling the fruit or vegetable in small amounts of water. Let the children put a cool hard-boiled egg in a nylon stocking and dip it into the dye. Keep the egg in the dye for several minutes. Pull out the nylon and check the color. If it is dark enough, place the egg on a paper towel to dry. If children want to color the eggs with crayons before dyeing, you can show how the wax keeps liquid from getting on the egg.

3. Science Table Additions

- Bird nests
- Empty bird eggs
- Different kinds of baskets
- An incubator
- Newly planted seeds
- Flowers still in bud (place the stems in water, and children can watch them open)
- Pussy willows

4. Basket Guessing

Do reach-and-feel using a covered basket. Place an egg, a chick, a rabbit, a doll's hat, some Easter grass, and so on in a large Easter basket. Let the children place their hands into the basket individually and describe the objects they are feeling.

Sensory

1. Sensory Table Activities

Add to the sensory table:

- Cotton balls with scoops and measuring cups
- Birdseed or beans
- Straw or hay and plastic eggs
- Plastic chicks and ducklings with water
- Easter grass, eggs, and small straw mats
- Dirt with plastic flowers and leaves
- Dyed, scented water, and water toys
- Sand, shovels, and scoops

2. Clay Cutters

Make scented clay. Place on the art table with rabbit, duck, egg, and flower cookie cutters for the children to use during self-directed or self-initiated play.

Social Studies

1. Family Easter Traditions

During large-group discussion, ask the children what special activities their families do to celebrate Easter. Their families may go to church, eat together, have egg hunts, or do other things that are special on this day.

2. **Sharing Baskets**

Decorate eggs or baskets to give to a home for the elderly. If possible, take a walk and let the children deliver them.

 **Books**

The following books can be used to complement this theme:

Adams, Adrienne. (1991). *Easter Egg Artists.* Madison, WI: Demco Media.

Anderson, R. P. (2009). *Happy Easter Curious George.* Boston: Houghton Mifflin Harcourt.

Auch, Mary Jane. (1996). *Eggs Mark the Spot.* New York: Holiday House.

Berenstain, Jan. (2008). *The Berenstain Bears' Baby Easter Bunny.* Illustrated by Jan Berenstain. New York: HarperFestival.

Brett, Jan. (2010). *The Easter Egg.* New York: G. P. Putnam's Sons.

Bryant, Megan. (2010). *A Surprise for the Easter Bunny.* Illustrated by Ivanka and Lola. New York: Price Stern Sloan.

Chaconas, Dori. (2008). *Looking for Easter.* Illustrated by Margie Moore. Morton Grove, IL: Albert Whitman & Co.

Church, Caroline. (2010). *Here Comes Easter.* London: Scholastic.

Dunrea, Olivier. (2009). *Ollie's Easter Eggs.* Boston: Houghton Mifflin Books for Children.

Elschner, Geraldine. (2004). *The Easter Chick.* Illustrated by Alexandra Junge. New York: North-South Books.

Engelbreit, Mary. (2006). *Queen of Easter.* New York: HarperCollins.

Fisher, Aileen Lucia. (1997). *The Story of Easter.* Illustrated by Stefano Vitale. New York: HarperCollins.

Garfield, Valarie, and Julie Durrell. (2001). *Sergeant Sniff's Easter Egg Mystery.* Illustrated by Julie Durrell. New York: HarperFestival.

Garland, Michael. (2005). *The Great Easter Egg Hunt.* New York: Dutton Children's Books.

Haley, Amanda. (2008). *Easter Has Eggs.* New York: Sterling Pub.

Haugen, Brenda. (2004). *Easter.* Illustrated by Sheree Boyd. Minneapolis, MN: Picture Window Books.

Hulme, Joy N. (2010). *Easter Babies: A Springtime Counting Book.* Illustrated by Dan Andreasen. New York: Sterling Pub.

Katz, Karen. (2008). *Where Are Baby's Easter Eggs?* New York: Little Simon.

Kroll, Steven. (2008). *The Biggest Easter Basket Ever.* New York: Scholastic.

Maccarone, Grace. (2006). *Peter Rabbit's Happy Easter.* Illustrated by David McPhail. New York: Scholastic.

Mercer, Mayer. (2007). *It's Easter, Little Critter!* New York: HarperFestival.

Merrick, Patrick. (2010). *Easter Bunnies.* Mankato, MN: The Child's World.

Milich, Melissa. (1997). *Miz Fannie Mae's Fine New Easter Hat.* Illustrated by Yong Chen. Boston: Little, Brown.

Mortimer, Anne. (2010). *Bunny's Easter Egg.* New York: Katherine Tegen Books.

Numeroff, Laura Joffe. (2010). *Happy Easter, Mouse!* New York: HarperCollins.

Potter, Beatrix. (2009). *Peter Rabbit Easter Egg Hunt.* London: Frederick Warne.

Stalder, Paivi. (2009). *Ernest's First Easter.* Illustrated by Frauke Weldin. New York: North-South Books.

Tegen, Katherine Brown. (2005). *The Story of the Easter Bunny.* Illustrated by Sally Anne Lambert. New York: HarperCollins.

Tudor, Tasha. (2001). *A Tale for Easter.* New York: Simon & Schuster.

Walburg, Lori, and James Bernadin. (1999). *The Legend of the Easter Egg.* Illustrated by James Bernadin. Grand Rapids, MI: Zondervan.

Wilhelm, Hans. (2004). *Quacky Ducky's Easter Egg.* New York: HarperCollins Publishers.

Zolotow, Charlotte. (1998). *The Bunny Who Found Easter.* Boston: Houghton Mifflin.

Technology and Multimedia

The following technology and multimedia products can be used to complement this theme:

A Bunnyland Easter [CD]. (2002). Wallingford, CT: Madacy Kids.

The Easter Bunny Is Coming to Town [DVD]. (2008). Los Angeles: Warner Bros.

The Easter Egg Adventure [DVD]. (2005). Century City, CA: First Look Pictures.

"The Easter Rabbit" [CD]. (2003). In *Teddy and Friends*. LaCrosse, WI: Platinum Disc.

"Easter Time Is Here Again" [CD]. (1997). In *Holiday Songs and Rhythms*. Freeport, NY: Activity Records and Educational Activities.

"So Early Easter Morning," "Bunny-Pokey," and "Like a Bunny Would" [CD]. (1993). In *Holiday Piggyback Songs*. Long Branch, NJ: Kimbo Educational.

 Additional teaching resources to accompany this Theme can be found on the book's companion website. Go to www.cengagebrain.com to access the site for a variety of useful resources.

Easter Eggs

Where did the custom of coloring Easter eggs come from? No one knows for sure. In any case, the Easter holiday centers around eggs for young children. Here are some projects you might like to try.

- To hard-cook eggs: Place eggs in a saucepan and add enough cold water to cover at least 1 inch above the eggs. Heat rapidly to boiling and remove from heat. Cover the pan and allow to stand for 22 to 24 minutes. Immediately cool the eggs in cold water.

- Make a vegetable dye solution by adding a teaspoon of vinegar to 1/2 cup of boiling water. Drop in food coloring and stir. The longer the egg is kept in the dye, the deeper the color will be.

- Add a teaspoonful of salad oil to a dye mixture and mix in the oil well. This results in a dye that produces swirls of color. Immerse the egg in the dye for a few minutes.

- Draw a design on an egg with a crayon before dyeing it. The dye will not stay on the areas with the crayon marks, and the design will show through.

- Wrap rubber bands, string, yarn, or narrow strips of masking tape around an egg to create stripes and other designs. Dip the egg in dye and allow to dry before removing the wrapping.

- Draw a design on the egg using a piece of wax. Place the egg in dye. Repeat the process again, if desired, dipping the egg in another color of dye. *Caution:* The lighted candle is to be used by an adult only.

- Felt-tip markers can be used to decorate dyed or undyed eggs.

- Small stickers can be used on eggs.

- Craft items such as sequins, glitter, ribbons, and small pompons can be used with glue to decorate eggs.

- Apply lengths of yarns, string, or thread to the eggs with glue, creating designs, and allow these to dry.

- Egg creatures can be created by using markers, construction paper, feathers, ribbon, lace, cotton balls, fabric, and buttons. To make an egg holder, make small cardboard or construction paper cylinders. A toilet paper or paper towel tube can be cut to make stands as well.

- Save the shells from the eggs to use for eggshell collages. Crumble the shells and sprinkle over a glue design that has been made on paper or cardboard.

Theme 29
EGGS

Sizes
small (insect)
large (ostrich)

Shapes
round (toad, frog, and fish)
oval (bird)
spherical (tortoise)

Colors
clear, white
tan, black
blue, speckled

Uses
food for humans
(bird eggs)
food for animals
preparation of vaccines
(bird eggs)
cosmetics (bird eggs)

Kinds
bird, insect
spider, toad
frog, fish
reptiles (snakes, lizards,
turtles, alligators, and
crocodiles)

Locations
nests, trees
grass, rock ledges
sand, lakes
ponds, oceans
grocery stores

Theme Goals

Through participating in the experiences provided by this theme, the children may learn:

1. Animals that produce eggs
2. Colors of eggs
3. Sizes of eggs
4. Shapes of eggs
5. Places to find eggs
6. Uses of eggs

Concepts for the Children to Learn

1. There are many kinds of eggs.
2. Birds, insects, spiders, toads, frogs, fish, and reptiles (including snakes, lizards, turtles, and alligators) lay eggs.
3. Eggs can be found in many locations.
4. Eggs can be found in nests, trees, grass, and rock ledges.
5. Eggs can also be found in the sand, in lakes, in ponds, in oceans, and in grocery stores.
6. An egg is the first stage in the development of an animal.
7. Eggs are made by the female.
8. Birds are the only animals that sit on their eggs to keep them warm.
9. Eggs can be different colors, including white, tan, black, blue, speckled, and clear.
10. Eggs range in size from tiny eggs, such as insects' eggs, to very large eggs, like those of an ostrich.
11. Birds lay only a few eggs at a time. Other animals may lay thousands of small eggs.
12. Bird eggs are generally oval in shape. Other animals have eggs that are different shapes.
13. Some people eat chicken eggs.
14. Chicken eggs can be prepared to be eaten in many ways (such as boiled, scrambled, fried, or poached).
15. Chicken eggs are sold in grocery stores by the dozen.
16. Chicken eggs are also used to prepare vaccines, animal feeds, fertilizers, and some cosmetics.
17. Eggs have many uses.
18. Bird eggs can be food for humans or other animals.

Vocabulary

1. **egg**—a roundish object covered with a shell or membrane that is laid by the female of birds, reptiles, fish, and amphibians.
2. **hatch**—to come out of an egg.
3. **incubate**—to sit on eggs in order to hatch them.
4. **incubator**—a machine-type box for keeping bird eggs at a certain temperature so that they will hatch.
5. **shell**—the outer covering of most eggs.

Bulletin Board

The purpose of this bulletin board is to promote correspondence skills. To prepare the bulletin board pieces, trace and cut the nests from yellow tagboard. Then trace and cut the eggs from white tagboard. Attach dots and print numerals on each nest as illustrated. The number of nests prepared and numerals utilized should be developmentally appropriate for the group of children.

Family Letter

InBox

Dear Families,

We will be having an "egg-stra" special week as we make discoveries about eggs. We usually think of chicken eggs when we hear the word "egg"—but there are so many different kinds of animals that lay eggs. Your child will learn about many animals that lay eggs, places eggs can be found, and uses of eggs during our week focusing on the theme of eggs.

At School

A few of the week's highlights include:

- Going on an egg walk! Weather permitting, we plan on walking through the park to look for various types of eggs, looking underneath logs and leaves. Care to join us?

- Creating mosaic designs with eggshells. You can help us by saving and cleaning eggshells. Please bring them to school by Friday morning.

- Observing chicken eggs in an incubator. Mr. Johnson (Matt's dad) will be bringing an incubator and five fertilized eggs for us to watch. Chicken eggs hatch in about 21 days. We'll keep you posted!

At Home

There are many ways to bring our egg unit into your home. Some ideas to try include:

- Preparing a meal or snack with your child that uses eggs as an ingredient

- Comparing the sizes of small, medium, large, and extra-large eggs while at a grocery store with your child

- Going to the library and checking out children's books about eggs. Some titles to look for include the following:

    Scrambled Eggs by Dr. Seuss

    Hedgie's Surprise by Jan Brett

    Egg: A Photographic Story of Hatching by Robert Burton

Have an "egg-cellent" week!

Arts and Crafts

1. **Eggshell Mosaic**
   Save and clean eggshells. Children can color eggshells with markers or paint. Then, have children spread glue on a piece of cardboard, tagboard, or construction paper. Eggshells can be broken into smaller pieces and placed in the glue to create a design.

2. **Egg Carton Caterpillar**
   Collect cardboard egg cartons, chenille stems, crayons, black felt-tip washable markers, green tempera paint and brushes. Cut egg cartons in half lengthwise. Help children fold a chenille stem in half and poke it into the top of the first section of the egg carton to represent the antennas. Children can then use the other materials as desired to to draw the eyes and mouth and decorate their caterpillar.

3. **Painting with Feathers**
   Provide construction paper, feathers (available at craft stores), and paint. Children can use the feathers to apply the paint to the paper.

4. **Clay Eggs**
   Children can use clay or play dough to create various sizes and colors of eggs. Allow to dry if desired.

Cooking

1. **Noodle Nests**
   12 ounces butterscotch chips
   3 cups chow mein noodles, cooked
   Optional: jellybeans

   Melt butterscotch chips in microwave or saucepan over low heat. Stir in noodles. Drop by teaspoonfuls onto waxed paper. Immediately top with jellybeans if desired. Let stand until firm. Makes about 36 pieces.

2. **Egg Foo Young**
   6 eggs
   1/4 cup instant minced onion
   2 tablespoons chopped green pepper
   1/2 teaspoon salt
   Dash of pepper
   16 ounces of bean sprouts (if canned, be sure to drain)

   Sauce:
   1 tablespoon cornstarch
   2 teaspoons sugar
   1 cube chicken bouillon
   Dash of ginger
   1 cup water
   2 tablespoons soy sauce

   Heat oven to 300 degrees. In a large bowl, beat eggs well. Add the remaining ingredients, except sauce ingredients. Mix well. Heat 2 tablespoons oil in a large skillet. Drop the egg mixture by tablespoonfuls into the skillet. Fry until golden. Turn and brown the other side. Drain on a paper towel. If necessary, add additional oil to the skillet and cook the remaining egg mixture. Keep warm in a 300-degree oven while preparing the sauce. Combine the first four ingredients in a small saucepan. Add water and soy sauce. Cook until the mixture boils and thickens, stirring constantly.

3. **Southwestern Eggs**
   1 pound bulk chorizo or pork sausage
   1/2 cup chopped onion
   1 1/4 cups mild salsa
   4 eggs
   3/4 cup shredded mozzarella cheese

   Cook the sausage and onion in a 10-inch skillet until the sausage is brown; drain. Stir in the salsa and heat. Spread the mixture evenly in a skillet. Make four indentations in the mixture with the back of a spoon. Break one egg into each indentation. Cover and cook over low heat about 12 minutes or until whites are set and yolks have thickened. Sprinkle with cheese. Serve with sour cream if desired.

4. **Painted Egg Cookies**
   Cookies:
   1/3 cup butter or margarine
   1/4 cup sugar
   1 egg
   2/3 cup honey
   3/4 teaspoon vanilla
   2 3/4 cups flour

1 teaspoon baking soda
1/2 teaspoon salt

"Paint":
1 egg yolk
1/4 teaspoon water
Food coloring

In a large mixing bowl, beat the butter and sugar until fluffy. Add the egg, honey, and vanilla. Beat well. Combine the flour, baking soda, and salt. Gradually add the flour mixture to the butter mixture. Beat well. Cover and chill for 1 hour.

Set oven to 350 degrees. Grease the cookie sheets if necessary. Divide the dough in half, keeping one-half chilled. Roll the dough on a lightly floured surface to a 1/4-inch thickness. Cut with an egg-shaped (oval) cookie cutter. Place 1 inch apart on cookie sheets. Repeat with the remaining dough.

Beat the egg yolk and water in a small mixing bowl. Divide the yolk mixture between three or four small bowls. Add two to three drops of different food colors to each bowl and mix well. With a clean small paintbrush, pastry brush, or cotton swab, paint cookies as desired. Bake 6 to 8 minutes or until golden.

Dramatic Play

1. **Grocery Store**
   Ask parents to save empty, clean food containers (boxes, jars, plastic bottles, etc.) to be used as props and supplies for a grocery store. Include empty, clean egg cartons of various-sized eggs.

2. **House**
   Provide empty, clean egg cartons; egg beaters; wire whisks; bowls; small frying pans; and turners as additional props to the housekeeping area.

3. **Bird Store**
   Create a bird store in the dramatic play area. Display posters and pictures of birds. Provide clean bird cages, stuffed toy and craft birds, and plastic bird eggs. Check out

bird books from the library, and include them in the area.

Field Trips and Resource People

1. **Farm**
   Plan a field trip to a farm where children can observe young chickens, turkeys, or ducks.

2. **Zoo**
   Eggs of many reptiles, amphibians, and birds may be observed at some zoos.

3. **4-H Agent**
   Contact your local 4-H agent for information regarding area people involved in hatcheries. Invite one to talk to the children about eggs and incubators.

4. **Grocery Store**
   While at the grocery store, observe the egg section.

Fingerplays and Chants

Eggs in a Nest
Here's an egg in a nest up in a tree.
(make fist with right hand and place in palm of cupped left hand)
What's inside? What can it be?
(shrug shoulders)
Peck, peck, peck,
Peep, peep, peep.
Out hatches a little bird,
(wiggle fingers or fisted hand)
Cute as can be!

Humpty Dumpty
Humpty Dumpty sat on a wall,
Humpty Dumpty had a great fall,
All the king's horses and all the king's men,
Couldn't put Humpty Dumpty together again.

My Turtle

This is my turtle,
(make fist and extend thumb)
He lives in a shell.
(hide thumb in fist)
He likes his home very well.
He pokes his head out when he wants to eat
(extend thumb)
And pulls it back in when he wants to sleep.
(hide thumb in fist)

Hatching Chickens

Five eggs and five eggs
(hold up one hand and then the other)
Are underneath a hen.
Five eggs and five eggs
(hold up all fingers)
And that makes 10.
The hen keeps the eggs warm for three long
weeks
(hold up three fingers)
Snap go the shells with tiny little beaks.
(snap fingers)
Crack, crack, the shells go.
(clap four times)
The chickens, every one,
Fluff out their feathers
In the warm spring sun.
(make circle of arms)

Group Time
(Games and Language)

1. **Egg Habitats**
Ask the children, "If you could go looking for
an egg right now, where would you look?"
Have children name places eggs can be
found—nests, grass, water, sand, ponds, sea,
or trees. Record the children's responses on
a large sheet of paper or tagboard. Display
the sheet in the classroom.

2. **Game: "Egg, Egg, Who's Got the Egg?"**
For this game, a plastic, paper, or hard-
boiled egg can be used. The children sit in
a circle formation. One child is chosen to be
the chicken or bird and sits in the center of
the circle with the egg in front of him or her.
The "chicken" closes his or her eyes. A child
from the circle is silently chosen to sneak
up and take the egg. All children then put

their hands behind their backs and call,
"Egg, egg, who's got the egg?" The "chicken"
then has three chances to guess who is
holding the egg.

Large Muscle

1. **Egg Maze**
Create a maze on the floor using classroom
blocks. Older children may be able to help!
Then, encourage children to roll and push
a hard-boiled or plastic egg through the
maze as quickly as possible. Tools such as
brushes, small brooms, or spoons could be
used to roll the egg.

2. **Egg Relay**
In this activity, a spoon is used to transport
a hard-boiled egg from one location
to another. The game can be played
individually or children can be in teams, if
appropriate.

Math

1. **Balancing Eggs**
Provide a balance scale and a hard-boiled
egg. If appropriate, children can estimate
how many of a specific object (crayons,
cubes, or blocks) they think will equal the
egg in weight. Then the children can count
(and possibly record) the actual number it
takes to balance the egg. The activity can be
repeated with various objects. Results can
be compared.

2. **Egg Sort**
Create and cut various egg shapes out of
construction paper or tagboard. Decorate
pieces as desired. Laminate pieces for
durability. Encourage children to sort the
eggs by various attributes such as size,
color, and patterns.

3. **Egg Carton Math**
Using a permanent marker, randomly
number the egg cups in an egg carton from

1 to 12 (or use fewer numerals or sets of dots, if appropriate). Put a button or bread tag in the carton and close the lid. Children shake the carton, open the lid, and identify the number the piece landed on.

Music

1. **"Here's a Little Birdie"**
(*Sing to the tune of "I Know a Little Kitty"*)

Here's a little birdie
Hatching from its shell.
First comes its beak,
Then comes its head.
He's working very, very hard,
His wings he gives a flap.
Then he lies down to rest and dry off,
Now what do you think of that?!
Peck, peck, peck, peck, peck, peck, peck,
   peck,
Peep!

2. **"Egg Choices"**
(*Sing to the tune of "If You're Happy and You Know It"*)

If you like your eggs scrambled,
Clap your hands.
   (clap, clap)
If you like your eggs scrambled,
Clap your hands.
   (clap, clap)
If you like your eggs scrambled,
And it's your favorite way to make 'em,
If you like your eggs scrambled,
Clap your hands.
   (clap, clap)
Additional verses:

If you like your eggs fried,
Touch your toes . . .

If you like your eggs hard-boiled,
Snap your fingers . . .

3. **"Red Hen, Red Hen"**
(*Sing to the tune of "Baa, Baa, Black Sheep"*)

Red hen, red hen, have you eggs for me?
Yes, sir. Yes, sir. A lot as you can see.
One to hard-boil.

Another one to fry.
One to scramble.
And Easter eggs to dye.
Red hen, red hen, have you eggs for me?
Yes, sir. Yes, sir. A lot as you can see.

Science

1. **Eggshell Garden**
Save and clean eggshell halves. Provide potting soil and seeds (such as radish or marigold). Have children fill each shell with soil and a few seeds. Add a spoonful of water to each shell. Place eggshell halves in the cups of an empty egg carton. Once the plants have grown, they can be transplanted into the ground or a larger container after crushing the eggshells.

2. **Will an Egg Float?**
All fresh, raw chicken eggs sink in water. However, salt mixed or dissolved in water can make an egg float. Place a raw egg in a clear glass filled with water. If appropriate, older students can count and record how many individual teaspoons of salt are mixed in the water to make the egg float.

3. **Vinegar and Eggs**
Gently place a raw egg in a clear glass or jar filled with vinegar. Observe what happens to the egg over a period of three to four days. (After two days, the shell will soften and begin to disappear. After three days, most of the calcium will have dissolved, leaving only a bladder.)

4. **Egg to Frog (or Toad)**
Hatching frog or toad eggs is a great way to observe eggs. In the spring, search local ponds for jelly-like masses of eggs. They are usually found underwater among weeds or grasses near shore. Prepare a tank or glass jar for the eggs and tadpoles. Changes occur fast, and children will be able to observe them. (If ponds are not locally accessible, check a biological supply house or ask a high school biology teacher.)

FALL

Changes
leaves turn color and fall
temperature cooler
darker earlier
days are shorter

Clothing
sweaters
coats
scarves
long-sleeved shirts
long pants

Holidays
Columbus Day
Halloween
Thanksgiving

Activities
football
raking leaves
walks
bike rides
harvesting foods
camping
soccer

Theme Goals

Through participating in the experiences provided by this theme, the children may learn:

1. Changes in fall
2. Fall holidays
3. Fall clothing
4. Fall activities

Concepts for the Children to Learn

1. Fall is one of the four seasons; it comes after summer and before winter.
2. There are many changes in the fall.
3. Leaves turn color in the fall.
4. It gets dark outside earlier in the day.
5. In some places, the weather becomes cooler in the fall.
6. The days become shorter in the fall.
7. Leaves fall from some trees in the fall.
8. Columbus Day, Halloween, and Thanksgiving are some fall holidays.
9. Scarves and sweaters may need to be worn in the fall to keep warm.
10. Long-sleeved shirts, long pants, and coats may also need to be worn in the fall.
11. Pumpkins and apples can be harvested in the fall.
12. Football and soccer are fall sports.
13. People take walks, ride bikes, and camp in the fall.
14. Leaves may also be raked in the fall.

Vocabulary

1. **fall**—the season between summer and winter.
2. **Halloween**—the holiday when people wear costumes and go trick-or-treating.
3. **Columbus Day**—a holiday to honor explorer Christopher Columbus's arrival in America.
4. **season**—a time of the year.
5. **Thanksgiving**—a holiday to express thanks.

Bulletin Board

The purpose of this bulletin board is to foster a positive self-concept as well as **develop name recognition skills**. Construct an acorn for each child. Print the children's names on the acorns. See illustration. Laminate and punch holes in the acorns. Children can hang their acorns on pushpins on the bulletin board when they arrive.

InBox

Dear Families,

Where we live, the days are getting shorter, the temperature is getting colder, and the leaves are changing color. It's the perfect time to introduce our next unit—fall. By participating in the experiences provided throughout this unit, children will become more aware of changes that take place in the fall. They will also learn about fall holidays, clothing, and activities.

At School

A few of this week's learning experiences include:

- Recording the temperature and the changing colors of the leaves
- Making leaf rubbings in the art area
- Raking leaves on our playground during outdoor time

We will also be taking a fall walk around the neighborhood to observe the trees in their peak changes. We will be leaving Thursday at 10:00 a.m. Please feel free to join us. It will be a scenic tour.

At Home

To develop classification skills, help your child sort leaves by their color, type, or size.

Fingerplays promote language and vocabulary skills. This fingerplay is one we will be learning this week. Enjoy it with your child at home!

Autumn

Autumn winds begin to blow.
   (blow)
Colored leaves fall fast and slow.
   (make fast and slow motions with hands)
Twirling, whirling all around,
   (turn around)
'Til at last, they touch the ground.
   (fall to the ground)

Enjoy your child as you explore experiences related to the unit on fall.

Arts and Crafts

1. Fall Collage

After taking a walk to collect objects such as grass, twigs, leaves, nuts, and weeds, collages can be made in the art area.

2. Leaf Rubbings

Collect leaves, paper, and crayons, and show the children how to place several leaves under a sheet of paper. Using the flat edge of the crayon, rub over paper. The image of the leaves will appear.

3. Pumpkin Seed Collage

Wash and dry pumpkin seeds, and place them in the art area with glue and paper. The children can make pumpkin seed collages.

4. Leaf Screen Painting

Use a lid from a box that is approximately 9 inches × 12 inches × 12 inches. Cut a rectangle from the lid top, leaving a 1 1/2-inch border. Invert the lid and place a wire screen over the opening. Tape the screen to the border. Arrange the leaves on a sheet of paper. Place the lid over the arrangement. Dip a toothbrush into thin tempera paint and brush across the screen. When the tempera paint dries, remove the leaves.

Cooking

1. Apple Banana Frosty

1 golden delicious apple, diced
1 peeled, sliced banana
1/4 cup milk
3 ice cubes

Blend all the ingredients in a blender. Serves four children.

2. Apple Salad

6 medium apples
1/2 cup raisins
1/2 teaspoon cinnamon
1/4 cup white grape juice

Peel and chop the apples. Mix well and add the remaining ingredients. Serves 10 children.

Dramatic Play

1. Fall Wear

Set out warm clothes such as sweaters, coats, hats, and blankets to indicate cold weather coming. The children can use the clothes for dressing up.

2. Football

Collect football gear, including balls, helmets, and jerseys, and play on the outdoor playground.

Field Trips

1. Neighborhood Walk

Take a walk around the neighborhood when the leaves are at their peak of changing colors. Discuss differences in color and size.

2. Apple Orchard

Visit an apple orchard. Observe the apples being picked and processed. If possible, let children pick their own apples from a tree.

3. Pumpkin Patch

Visit a pumpkin patch. Discuss and observe how pumpkins grow and their size, shape, and color. Let the children pick a pumpkin to bring back to the classroom.

Fingerplays and Chants

Autumn

Autumn winds begin to blow.
   (blow)
Colored leaves fall fast and slow.
   (make fast and slow falling motions with hands)

Twirling, whirling all around
    (turn around)
'Til at last, they touch the ground.
    (fall to the ground)

Leaves

Little leaves fall gently down
Red and yellow, orange and brown.
    (flutter hands like leaves falling)
Whirling, whirling around and around.
    (turn around)
Quietly without a sound.
    (put finger to lips)
Falling softly to the ground
    (begin to fall slowly)
Down and down and down and down.
    (lie on floor)

Little Leaves

The little leaves are falling down
    (use hands to make falling motion)
Round and round, round and round.
    (turn around)
The little leaves are falling down,
    (use hands to make falling motion)
Falling to the ground.
    (fall to ground)

Twirling Leaves

The autumn wind blows—Oooo Oooo Oooo.
    (make wind sounds)
The leaves shake and shake, then fly into
    the sky so blue.
    (children shake)
They whirl and whirl around them, twirl
    and twirl around.
    (turn around in circles)
But when the wind stops, the leaves sink
    slowly to the ground.
Lower, lower, lower, and land quietly
    without a sound.
    (sink very slowly and very quietly)

Large Muscle

Raking Leaves

Child-sized rakes can be provided. The children can be encouraged to rake leaves into piles.

Math

1. **Weighing Acorns and Pinecones**
A scale, acorns, and pinecones for the children to weigh can be added to the science table.

2. **Leaf Math**
Out of construction paper or tagboard, prepare pairs of various-shaped leaves. The children can match the identical leaves.

Music

1. **"Little Leaves"**
(*Sing to the tune of "Ten Little Indians"*)

One little, two little, three little leaves.
Four little, five little, six little leaves.
Seven little, eight little, nine little leaves.
Ten little leaves fall down.

2. **"Happy Children Tune"**
(*Sing to the tune of "Did You Ever See a Lassie?"*)
(*While singing the song, children can keep time by pretending to rake leaves, jump in the leaves, etc.*)

Happy children in the autumn,
In the autumn, in the autumn.
Happy children in the autumn
Do this way and that.

3. **"Pretty Leaves Are Falling Down"**
(*Sing to the tune of "London Bridge"*)

Pretty leaves are falling down, falling down,
    falling down.
Pretty leaves are falling down, all around
    the town.
    (wiggle fingers)
Let's rake them up in a pile, in a pile, in a
    pile.
Let's rake them up in a pile, all around the
    town.
    (make raking motions)
Let's all jump in and have some fun,

have some fun, have some fun.
Let's all jump in and have some fun, all
   around the town.
   (jump into circle)

Social Studies

Bulletin Board

Construct a bulletin board using bare
branches to represent a tree. Cut out leaves
from colored construction paper and print
one child's name on each. At the beginning
of the day, children can hang their name on
the tree when they arrive.

Science

1. **Leaf Observation**
   Collect leaves from a variety of trees. Place
   them and a magnifying glass on the science
   table for the children to explore.

2. **Temperature Watch**
   Place a thermometer outside. A large
   cardboard thermometer can also be
   constructed out of tagboard with movable
   elastic or ribbon for the mercury. The
   children can match the temperature on
   the cardboard thermometer with the
   outdoor one.

3. **Weather Calendar**
   Construct a calendar for the month.
   Record the changes of weather each day by
   attaching a symbol to the calendar. Symbols
   should include clouds, sun, snow, rain, and
   so on.

4. **Color Change Sequence**
   Laminate or cover with contact paper several
   leaves of different colors. The children can
   sort, count, and classify the leaves.

Books

The following books can be used to complement
this theme:

Arnosky, Jim. (1993). *Every Autumn Comes the
   Bear.* New York: G.P. Putnam.

Berger, Carin. (2008). *The Little Yellow Leaf.*
   New York: Greenwillow Books.

Bullard, Lisa. (2010). *Leaves Fall Down:
   Learning about Autumn Leaves.* Illustrated
   by Nadine Takvorian. Mankato, MN:
   Picture Window Books.

Bunting, Eve, and James Ransome. (2001).
   Peepers. Illustrated by James Ransome. San
   Diego, CA: Harcourt Brace.

Cocca-Leffler, Maryann. (2010). *Let It Fall.* New
   York: Cartwheel Books.

Curry, Don L. (2004). *Fall Leaves.* Illustrated
   by Don L. Curry. New York: Children's
   Press.

Ehlert, Lois. (1991). *Red Leaf, Yellow Leaf.*
   Orlando, FL: Harcourt Brace.

Ehlert, Lois. (2005). *Leaf Man.* Orlando, FL:
   Harcourt.

Emmett, Jonathan. (2009). *Leaf Trouble.* New
   York: Chicken House.

Fowler, Allan. (1992). *How Do You Know It's
   Fall?* Chicago: Children's Press.

Fowler, Allan. (1993). *It Could Still Be a Leaf.*
   Chicago: Children's Press.

George, Lindsay Barrett. (1995). *In the
   Woods: Who's Been Here?* New York:
   Greenwillow.

Sensory

1. **Leaves**
   Place a variety of leaves in the sensory
   table. Try to include moist and dry
   examples for the children to compare.

2. **Pumpkins**
   Place pumpkins, hammers, and golf tees in
   the sensory table. The children can practice
   pounding the golf tees into the pumpkins.
   Note: This activity must be carefully
   supervised.

Glaser, Linda. (2001). *It's Fall!* Illustrated by Susan Swan. Brookfield, CT: Millbrook Press.

Hall, Zoe, and Shari Halpern. (2000). *Fall Leaves Fall!* Illustrated by Shari Halpern. New York: Scholastic.

Harshman, Marc, Cheryl Ryan, and Wade Zahares. (2001). *Red Are the Apples.* Illustrated by Wade Zahares. San Diego, CA: Gulliver Books.

Hawk, Fran. (2009). *Count Down to Fall.* Illustrated by Sherry Neidigh. Mount Pleasant, SC: Sylvan Dell Publishing.

Hunter, Anne. (1996). *Possum's Harvest Moon.* Boston: Houghton Mifflin.

Hutchings, Amy. (1994). *Picking Apples and Pumpkins.* Illustrated by Richard Hutchings. St. Paul, MN: Cartwheel Books.

Kelley, Marty. (1998). *Fall Is Not Easy.* Madison, WI: Zino Press Children's Books.

Lee, Huy Voun. (2005). *In the Leaves.* New York: Holt.

Maass, Robert. (1990). *When Autumn Comes.* New York: Holt.

Maestro, Betsy C. (1994). *Why Do Leaves Change Color?* Illustrated by Loretta Krupinski. New York: HarperCollins.

Marzollo, Jean. (1998). *I Am a Leaf.* Illustrated by Judith Moffatt. New York: Scholastic.

O'Malley, Kevin. (2004). *Lucky Leaf.* New York: Walker & Co.

Raczka, Bob. (2007). *Who Loves the Fall?* Illustrated by Judy Stead. Morton Grove, IL: Albert Whitman.

Rawlinson, Julia. (2006). *Fletcher and the Falling Leaves.* Illustrated by Tiphanie Beeke. New York: Greenwillow Books.

Robbins, Ken. (1998). *Fall Leaves.* New York: Scholastic.

Roca, Nuria. (2004). *Fall.* Hauppauge, NY: Barron's Educational Series.

Rockwell, Anne F. (1989). *Apples and Pumpkins.* Illustrated by Lizzy Rockwell. New York: Simon & Schuster.

Russo, Marisabina. (1994). *I Don't Want to Go Back to School.* New York: Greenwillow.

Rustad, Martha E. H. (2008). *Animals in Fall.* Mankato, MN: Capstone Press.

Rustad, Martha E. H. (2008). *Leaves in Fall.* Mankato, MN: Capstone Press.

Rylant, Cynthia. (1999). *Poppleton in Fall.* Illustrated by Mark Teague. New York: Blue Sky Press.

Rylant, Cynthia, and Jill Kastner. (2000). *In November.* Illustrated by Jill Kastner. San Diego, CA: Harcourt Brace.

Saunders-Smith, Gail. (1997). *Autumn Leaves.* Mankato, MN: Pebble Books.

Schuette, Sarah L. (2007). *Let's Look at Fall.* Mankato, MN: Capstone Press.

Spafford, Suzy. (2003). *Fall Is for Friends.* New York: Scholastic.

Spetter, Jung-Hee. (1998). *Lily and Trooper's Fall.* Asheville, NC: Front Street, Lemniscaat.

Thompson, Lauren. (2006). *Mouse's First Fall.* Illustrated by Buket Erdogan. New York: Simon & Schuster Books for Young Readers.

Wallace, Nancy Elizabeth. (2003). *Leaves! Leaves! Leaves!* New York: Cavendish Children's Books.

Zagwyn, Deborah Turney. (1997). *The Pumpkin Blanket.* Berkeley, CA: Tricycle Press.

 # Technology and Multimedia

The following technology and multimedia products can be used to complement this theme:

"Autumn," "Season Song," and "Leaves" [CD]. (1995). In *Piggyback Songs.* Long Branch, NJ: Kimbo Educational.

"Five Little Pumpkins" [CD]. (1996). In *Singable Songs for the Very Young.* Cambridge, MA: Rounder/UMGD.

"It's Fall Again" [CD]. (2001). In *Seasonal Songs in Motion*. Melbourne, FL: The Learning Station.

Seasonal Songs in Motion [CD]. (2001). Melbourne, FL: The Learning Station.

"What Falls in the Fall" [CD]. (2001). In *Whaddaya Think of That?* New York: Two Tomatoes.

White, Linda. (1997). *Too Many Pumpkins* [video]. Somers, NY: Live Oak Productions.

Additional teaching resources to accompany this Theme can be found on the book's companion website. Go to www.cengagebrain.com to access the site for a variety of useful resources.

Fall Nature Recipes

Cattails

Use them in their natural color or tint by shaking metallic powder over them. Handle carefully. The cattail is dry and feels crumbly. It will fall apart easily.

Crystal Garden*

Place broken pieces of brick or terra-cotta clay in a glass bowl or jar. Pour the following solution over this:

4 teaspoons water
1 teaspoon ammonia
4 teaspoons bluing
1 teaspoon Mercurochrome
4 teaspoons salt

Add more of this solution each day until the crystal garden has grown to the desired size.

Note: Adult supervision is required.

* This activity should be carefully observed if in a classroom with preschool children.

Drying Plants for Winter Bouquets

Strip the leaves from the flowers immediately. Tie the flowers by their stems with string and hang them with the heads down in a cool, dry place away from the light. Darkness is essential for preserving their color. Thorough drying takes about two weeks.

Preserving Fall Leaves

Place alternate layers of powdered borax and leaves in a box. The leaves must be completely covered. Allow them to stand for four days. Shake off the borax, and wipe each leaf with liquid floor wax. Rub a warm iron over a cake of paraffin, then press the iron over the front and back of each leaf.

Preserving Magnolia Leaves

Mix two parts of water with one part of glycerin. Place stems of the magnolia leaves in the mixture and let them stand for several days. The leaves will turn brown and last several years. Their surface may be painted or sprayed with silver or gold paint.

Pressing Wildflowers

When gathering specimens, include the roots, leaves, flowers, and seed pods. Place between newspapers, laying two layers of blotters underneath the newspaper and two on top to absorb the moisture. Change the newspapers three times during the week. Place between two sheets of corrugated cardboard and press. It usually takes 7 to 10 days to press specimens. Cardboard covered with cotton batting is the mounting base. Lay the flower on the cotton and cover with cellophane or plastic wrap to preserve the color.

Treating Gourds

Soak gourds in water for two hours. Scrape them clean with a knife. Rub with fine sandpaper. While still damp, cut an opening to remove seeds.

Theme 31
FAMILIES

Activities	Purpose	Members
celebrations	care	mothers, fathers
eating	protect	stepparents, sisters
reading	love	brothers, grandmothers
playing	teach	grandfathers, aunts
working		uncles, nephews
reunions		nieces, cousins
vacationing		adopted members
camping		deceased members

Theme Goals

Through participating in the experiences provided by this theme, the children may learn:

1. The members in a family
2. Purpose of families
3. Family activities

Concepts for the Children to Learn

1. A family is a group of people who usually live together.
2. Mothers, fathers, sisters, and brothers are family members.
3. Grandmothers, grandfathers, aunts, uncles, cousins, nephews, nieces, and stepparents are family members.
4. Eating, working, reading, and playing are all family activities.
5. Families often vacation together.
6. Families may often have reunions.
7. Families teach us about our world.
8. Family members care for and protect us.
9. There are many different types of families: one-parent, two-parent, blended, and extended.

Vocabulary

1. **aunt**—sister of a parent.
2. **blended**—people from two or more families living together.
3. **brother**—a boy having the same parents as another person.
4. **children**—young people.
5. **cousin**—son or daughter of an uncle or aunt.
6. **extended**—includes aunts, uncles, grandparents, and cousins.
7. **family**—people living together.
8. **father**—male parent.
9. **grandfather**—father of a parent.
10. **grandmother**—mother of a parent.
11. **love**—feeling of warmth toward another.
12. **mother**—female parent.
13. **nephew**—son of a brother or sister.
14. **niece**—daughter of a brother or sister.
15. **one-parent family**—a child or children who lives with only one parent, a father or mother.
16. **sister**—a girl having the same parents as another person.
17. **uncle**—brother of a parent.

Bulletin Board

The purpose of this bulletin board is to foster an awareness of various family sizes, as well as to identify family members. Construct a name card for each child from tagboard. Print each child's name on one of the tagboard pieces. Then cut people figures as illustrated. Laminate the name cards and people. Staple the name cards to a bulletin board as illustrated. Individually, the children can affix the people in their family after their name using tape, sticky putty, or a stapler.

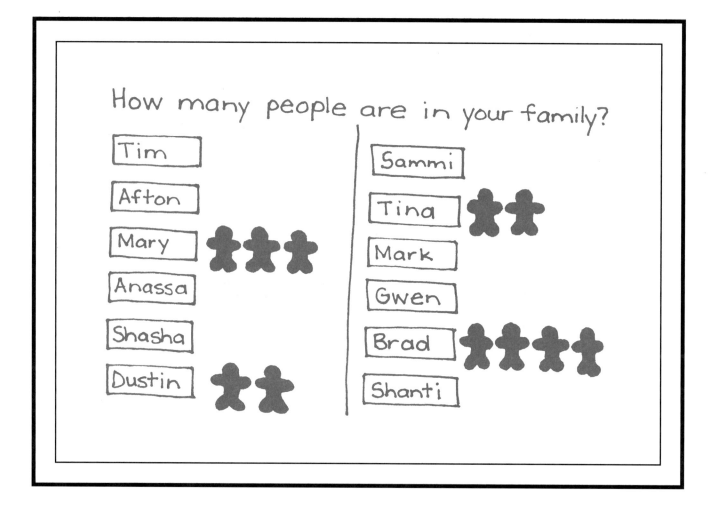

Family Letter

Dear Families,

Our next unit will focus on families. Through this unit, the children will develop an understanding of various types of families—nuclear, extended, blended, and step. They will also discover what family members do for each other, as well as activities that families can participate in together.

At School

A few of this unit's highlights include:

- Creating pictures of our families on a bulletin board
- Looking at photographs of classmates' families. To assist us with this unit, please send a picture of your family to school with your child. We will place the photograph in a special photo album to look at in the reading area.

At Home

There are several activities you can do at home to foster the concepts of this unit. Begin by looking through family photographs with your child. While doing this, discuss family traditions or customs. You can also encourage your child to dictate a letter to you to write to a grandparent or other relative. Plan and participate in a family activity. This could be as simple as taking a walk together or going on a picnic.

We invite you and your family to visit us. This includes moms, dads, brothers, sisters, grandparents, and other relatives! If you are interested in coming, please let me know!

Enjoy your family this week!

Arts and Crafts

1. Family Collage

The children can cut out pictures of people from magazines. The pictures can be pasted on a sheet of paper to make a collage.

2. My Body

Trace each child's body on a large piece of paper. The children can use crayons and felt-tip markers to color their own body picture. When finished, display the pictures around the room or in the center's entrance.

Cooking

1. Jelly

Cut whole-wheat bread into house shapes for a snack one day. Put raisins and jelly on the table with plastic knives. Let children choose their own topping.

2. Gingerbread Families

1 1/2 cups whole-wheat pastry flour
1 teaspoon baking soda
1/2 teaspoon salt
1/2 teaspoon ginger
1 teaspoon cinnamon
1/4 cup oil
1/4 cup maple syrup
1/4 cup honey
1 large egg

Preheat oven to 350 degrees. Measure all of the dry ingredients into a bowl and mix well. Measure all wet ingredients into a second bowl and mix well. Add the two mixtures together. Pour the combined mixture into an 8-inch-square pan and bake for 30 to 35 minutes. When cool, roll the gingerbread dough into thin slices and provide cookie cutters for children to cut out a gingerbread family. Decorate the figures with standard icing, candies, cookie decorations, or sprinkles or jimmies. Enjoy for snack time.

3. Raisin Bran Muffins

4 cups raisin bran cereal
2 1/2 cups all-purpose flour
1 cup sugar
2 1/2 teaspoons baking soda
1 teaspoon salt
2 eggs, beaten
2 cups buttermilk
1/2 cup cooking oil

Stir the cereal, flour, sugar, baking soda, and salt together in a large mixing bowl. In a separate bowl beat the eggs, buttermilk, and oil together. Add this mixture to the dry ingredients, and stir until moistened. The batter will be thick. Spoon the batter into greased or lined muffin cups, filling 3/4 full. Bake in a 375-degree oven for 20 to 25 minutes, and remove from pans.

4. Kabbat Hamudth

(This is a meatball soup served during Ramadan, a Muslim family celebration)

For the meatballs:

1 pound choice ground beef
14 oz. box cream of rice cereal
1/2 teaspoon salt

Combine ingredients and mix well. Add a little water if necessary. Puree in small batches. Divide mixture into 30 balls. Cover and chill.

For the stuffing:

1 medium onion, chopped
1/2 pound choice ground beef
1/2 cup drained chickpeas
1/4 cup chopped fresh parsley
1 scant teaspoon ground allspice

Brown onions and beef in a 10-inch skillet. Drain fat, and add remaining stuffing ingredients. Set aside.

To form meatballs, flatten each ball with your fingertips. Place 2–3 teaspoons of the stuffing in the center, and re-form beef into a ball around the stuffing. Cover and chill.

For the soup:

2–3 medium onions, quartered
1 pound turnips, chopped
2 tablespoons olive oil

16 cups beef broth
1 pound Swiss chard, coarsely chopped
1/2 cup drained canned chickpeas
1 teaspoon ground allspice (optional)
Salt and pepper to taste
3–4 tablespoons finely chopped fresh mint leaves, or 2 teaspoons dried mint leaves
1/2 cup lemon juice

Sauté onions and turnips in olive oil until onions are translucent. Bring broth to boil, lower heat, and add onions, turnips, Swiss chard, and chickpeas. Season with allspice, salt, and pepper. Simmer until turnips are soft. Add mint and lemon juice. About 20 minutes before serving, add meatballs.

Serve in bowls with two to three meatballs per serving. Caution must be taken regarding the temperature of the soup.

5. **Mexican Salad for a Family Gathering**
1 pound hamburger
I head of lettucre
1 8 ounce bag of taco chips
1 package of taco seasoning mix
3 large tomatoes
1 cup chopped onion
8 ounces of grated cheddar cheese
1 15-ounce can of rinsed and drained dark red kidney beans
1 bottle of Thousand Island dressing.

Brown the hamburger in a skillet. Add the taco seasoning to the hamburger, add the beans, and stir well. Then cut the tomatoes, chop the onion, and tear the lettuce into bite-sized pieces. Mix. Crumble the chips, and place on top of this mixture. Then add the browned hamburger. Pour the dressing on top, and mix. Sprinkle the grated cheese on top of the salad.

Dramatic Play

1. **Baby Clothing**
Arrange the dramatic play area for washing baby dolls. Include a tub with soapy water, washcloths, drying towels, play clothes, a brush, and a comb.

2. **Family Picnic**
Collect items to make a picnic basket. Include paper napkins, cups, plates, plastic eating utensils, and so on.

3. **Dollhouse**
Set up a large dollhouse for children to play with. These can be constructed from cardboard. Include dolls to represent several members of a family.

Fingerplays and Chants

1. **Grandma's and Grandpa's Glasses**
Here are Grandma's glasses.
   (make small circles with fingers over eyes)
Here is Grandma's hat.
   (fold hands over head)
This is the way she folds her hands
   (fold hands)
And lays them in her lap.
   (place hands in lap)
Here are Grandpa's glasses.
   (make bigger circles with fingers over eyes)
Here is Grandpa's cap.
   (pretend to put baseball cap on head)
This is the way he folds his arms
   (fold arms across chest)
Just like that!

2. **My Family**
This is the mother, kind and dear
   (begin with hands clasped, and then show thumbs)
This is father, sitting near
   (show forefingers)
This is the brother, strong and tall
   (show middle finger)
This is my sister who plays with her ball
   (show ring finger)
This is baby, the smallest of all
   (show little finger)
See my whole family, large and small
   (show all fingers)

3. Cookie Jar

(This is a rhythmic chant. You could introduce an alternating leg-hand clap to emphasize the rhythm.)

Someone ate the cookies in the cookie jar.
Who ate the cookies in the cookie jar?
(Sung Jee) ate the cookies in the cookie jar.
(Sung Jee) ate the cookies in the cookie jar?
Who, me?
Yes, you.
Couldn't be.
Then who ate the cookies in the cookie jar?

(Repeat using another child's name)

4. Children

"It's time for my children to go to bed,"
The nice and happy mother (father) said.
"Now I must count them up to see,
If all my children are home with me."
One child, two children, three children, dear,
   (hold up three fingers in succession)
Four children, five children, YES, they are
   all here.
   (hold up remaining fingers in succession)
They're the dearest little children alive,
One, two, three, four, five.
   (hold up each finger in succession)

5. Five Little Robins

Five little robins lived in a tree.
A father, mother, and babies three.
   (hold up fingers of one hand)
Father caught a worm,
   (point to thumb)
Mother caught a bug,
   (point to index finger)
This one got the bug,
   (point to middle finger)
This one got the worm,
   (point to ring finger)
And this one sat and waited his turn.
   (point to pinky finger)

6. Home Sweet Home

A nest is a home for a blue jay.
   (cup hands to form a nest)
A hive is a home for a bee.
   (turn cupped hands over)
A hole is a home for a rabbit.
   (make a hole shape with hands)
And a house is a home for me.
   (make roof shape with peaked hands)

Group Time
(Games and Language)

A Hundred Ways to Get There
During outdoor or group play, form a large circle. Begin the game by choosing a child to cross the circle by skipping, hopping, jumping, crawling, running, and so on. Once the circle has been crossed, the child takes the place of another person, who then goes across the circle in another manner. Each child can try to think of something new.

Large Muscle

Neighborhood Walk
Take a walk through a neighborhood and have children identify different homes. Observe the colors and sizes of the homes.

Math

1. Families: From Biggest to Smallest
Cut out pictures of several members of a family from magazines. The children can place the members from largest to smallest, and then from smallest to largest. They can also identify which family member is the biggest and which is the smallest.

2. Family Member Chart
Graph the number of family members for each child's family on a chart.

Music

"Family Helper"
(Sing to the tune of "Here We Are Together")

It's fun to be a helper, a helper, a helper.
It's fun to be a helper, just any time.
Oh, I can set the table, the table, the table.
Oh, I can set the table at dinner time.

Oh, I can dry the dishes, the dishes, the dishes.
Oh, I can dry the dishes, and make them
   shine.

Field Trips and Resource People

Family Day
Invite moms, dads, sisters, brothers,
grandfathers, grandmothers, and other
family members to a tea at your early
childhood center.

Science

1. **Sounds**
   Record different sounds from around the
   house that families hear daily, such as a
   crying baby, teeth being brushed, telephone
   ringing, toilet flushing, doorbell ringing,
   water running, electric shaver, alarm
   clock, and so on. Play the recording for the
   children to identify the correct sound.

2. **Feely Box**
   Place objects pertaining to a family into a
   box. Include items such as a baby rattle, a
   toothbrush, a comb, a baby bottle, and so
   on. The children feel the objects and try to
   identify them.

3. **Animal Families**
   Gerbils or hamsters with young babies in
   a cage can be placed on the science table.
   Observe daily to see how they raise their
   babies. Compare the animal behavior with
   that of the children's own families.

Sensory

1. Washing baby dolls in lukewarm, soapy
   water
2. Washing dishes in warm water
3. Washing doll clothes and hanging them
   up to dry

4. Cars and houses placed on top of several
   inches of sand

Social Studies

Family Pictures
1. Display posters of all types of families.
   At group time, discuss ways that
   families help and care for each other.
2. Ask each child to bring in a family
   picture. Label each child's picture and
   place on a special bulletin board with
   the caption "Our Families."
3. Discuss different family holidays
   and celebrations. One example is the
   Muslim celebration of Ramadan. Each
   year. Muslims around the world observe
   the religious period of Ramadan by
   refraining from food, water, television,
   and other activities from sunrise to
   sunset. The fasting lasts for 28 days.
   Fasting teaches patience, discipline,
   and humility. Families and friends
   gather before sunrise (*Suhour*) and
   after sunset for meals. Children learn
   that the Prophet Mohammed broke
   his fast on dates. Families then mostly
   have soup, because it is easy on the
   stomach and also helps rehydrate the
   thirsty.

Books

The following books can be used to complement
this theme:

Aubrey, Annette. (2007). *Flora's Family.*
   Illustrated by Patrice Barton. Laguna Hills,
   CA: QEB.

Bailey, Debbie. (1999). *Families.* Illustrated by
   Susan Huszar. Toronto: Annick Press.

Bee, William. (2005). *Whatever.* Cambridge, MA:
   Candlewick Press.

Berenstain, Stan. (2009). *The Berenstain
   Bears' Family Reunion.* Illustrated by
   Jan Berenstain. New York: HarperCollins
   Publishers.

Brown, Margaret Wise. (2005). *The Runaway Bunny*. Illustrated by Clement Hurd. New York: HarperCollins Publishers.

Bruchac, Joseph. (2010). *My Father Is Taller Than a Tree*. Illustrated by Wendy Haperin. New York: Dial Books for Young Readers.

Buckley, Helen E. (1994). *Grandmother and I*. Illustrated by Jan Ormerod. New York: Lothrop, Lee & Shepard.

Bullard, Lisa. (2003). *My Family: Love and Care, Give and Share*. Illustrated by Brandon Reibeling. Minneapolis, MN: Picture Window Books.

Buller, Jon, and Susan Schade. (2006). *I Love You, Good Night*. Illustrated by Bernadette Pons. New York: Little Simon.

Bunting, Eve. (2010), *Will It Be a Baby Brother?* Illustrated by Beth Spiegel. Honesdale, PA: Boyds Mills Press.

Carle, Eric. (2000). *Does a Kangaroo Have a Mother, Too?* New York: HarperCollins Publishers.

Carlson, Nancy. (2004). *My Family Is Forever*. New York: Viking.

Clements, Andrew. (2005). *Because Your Daddy Loves You*. Illustrated by Andrew Clements. New York: Clarion Books.

Cole, Joanna. (2010). *I'm a Big Brother*. Illustrated by Maxie Chambliss. New York: HarperCollins.

Cole, Joanna. (2010). *I'm a Big Sister*. Illustrated by Maxie Chambliss. New York: HarperCollins.

Combs, Bobbie, Desiree Keane, and Brian Rappa. (2001). *ABC: A Family Alphabet Book*. Illustrated by Desiree Keane and Brian Rappa. Ridley Park, PA: Two Lives.

Cox, Judy. (2003). *My Family Plays Music*. Illustrated by Elbrite Brown. New York: Holiday House.

De Paola, Tomie. (2010). *My Mother Is So Smart*. New York: G.P. Putnam's Sons.

Downey, Roma, and Justine Gasquet. (2001). *Love Is a Family*. Illustrated by Justine Gasquet. New York: HarperCollins.

Edmonds, Barbara Lynn. (2000). *When Grown-Ups Fall in Love*. Eugene, OR: Barby's House Books.

Garden, Nancy. (2004). *Molly's Family*. Illustrated by Sharon Wooding. New York: Farrar, Straus and Giroux.

Gutman, Anne, and Georg Hallensleben. (2005). *Daddy Cuddles*. San Francisco: Chronicle Books.

Gutman, Anne, and Georg Hallensleben. (2005). *Mommy Loves*. San Francisco: Chronicle Books.

Hest, Amy. (2001). *Kiss Good Night*. Illustrated by Anita Jeram. Cambridge, MA: Candlewick Press.

Homel, David. (2006). *Travels with My Family*. Illustrated by Marie-Louise Gay. Toronto: Groundwood Books.

Isadora, Rachel. (2006). *What a Family! A Fresh Look at Family Trees*. New York: G.P. Putnam's Sons.

Joosse, Barbara. (2005). *Nikolai, the Only Bear*. Illustrated by Renata Liwska. New York: Philomel Books.

King-Smith, Dick. (2008). *The Mouse Family Robinson*. Illustrated by Nick Bruel. New York: Roaring Brook Press.

Kingsbury, Karen. (2008). *Let's Go on a Mommy Date*. Illustrated by Dan Andreasen. Grand Rapids, MI: Zonderkidz.

Leedy, Loreen. (1995). *Who's Who in My Family*. New York: Holiday House.

Lish, Ted. (2002). *It's Not My Job*. Illustrated by Charles Jordan. Victorville, CA: Munchweiler Press.

Long, Sylvia. (2002). *Hush Little Baby*. San Francisco: Chronicle Books.

Mayer, Mercer. (2004). *Bye-Bye, Mom and Dad*. New York: HarperFestival.

Medearis, Angela. (2004). *Snug in Mama's Arms*. Illustrated by John Sandford. Columbus, OH: Gingham Dog Press.

Meyers, Susan. (2004). *Everywhere Babies*. Illustrated by Marla Frazee. San Diego, CA: Harcourt.

Morris, Ann. (1995). *The Daddy Book*. Photography by Ken Heyman. Parsippany, NJ: Silver Press.

Morris, Ann. (1995). *The Mommy Book*. Photography by Ken Heyman. Parsippany, NJ: Silver Press.

Murphy, Mary. (2003). *I Kissed the Baby!* Cambridge, MA: Candlewick Press.

Norac, Carl. (2005). *My Daddy Is a Giant.* Illustrated by Ingrid Godon. New York: Clarion Books.

Ohi, Ruth. (2005). *Me and My Sister.* Toronto: Annick Press.

Pellegrini, Nina. (1991). *Families Are Different.* New York: Holiday House.

Penn, Audrey. (2006). *The Kissing Hand.* Illustrated by Ruth Harper and Nancy Leak. Terre Haute, IN: Tanglewood Press.

Perl, Erica S. (2006). *Ninety-Three in My Family.* Illustrated by Mike Lester. New York: Abrams Books for Young Readers.

Polacco, Patricia. (2005). *The Graves Family Goes Camping.* New York: Philomel Books.

Porter-Gaylord, Laurel. (2004). *I Love My Daddy Because.* Illustrated by Ashley Wolf. New York: Dutton Children's Books.

Porter-Gaylord, Laurel. (2004). *I Love My Mommy Because.* Illustrated by Ashley Wolf. New York: Dutton Children's Books.

Rathmann, Peggy. (2003). *The Day the Babies Crawled Away.* New York: G.P. Putnam's Sons.

Rau, Dana Meachen. (2007). *Family Photo.* Illustrated by Mike Gordon. New York: Children's Press.

Schindel, John. (1995). *Dear Daddy.* Illustrated by Dorothy Dononue. Niles, IL: Albert Whitman.

Schuette, Sarah L. (2009). *Families.* Mankato, MN: Capstone Press.

Schwartz, Amy. (1994). *A Teeny Tiny Baby.* New York: Orchard Books.

Shapiro, Jody Fickes. (2007). *Family Lullaby.* Illustrated by Cathie Felstead. New York: Greenwillow Books.

Smith, Lane. (2003). *The Happy Hocky Family Moves to the Country.* New York: Viking.

Sullivan, Sarah. (2010). *Once upon a Baby Brother.* Illustrated by Tricia Tusa. New York: Farrar, Straus and Giroux.

Vigna, Judith. (1997). *I Live with Daddy.* Niles, IL: Albert Whitman.

Walker, Sally M. (2008). *The Vowel Family: A Tale of Lost Letters.* Illustrated by Kevin Luthardt. Minneapolis, MN: Carolrhoda Books.

Willis, Jeanne. (2008). *Mommy, Do You Love Me?* Illustrated by Jan Fearnley. Cambridge, MA: Candlewick Press.

Winthrop, Elizabeth. (2005). *Squashed in the Middle.* Illustrated by Pat Cummings. New York: Henry Holt.

Wolff, Ashley. (2004). *Me Baby, You Baby.* New York: Dutton Children's Books.

Zamorano, Ana. (1997). *Let's Eat!* Illustrated by Julie Vivas. New York: Scholastic.

Zemach, Margot. (2005). *Eating Up Gladys.* Illustrated by Kaethe Zemach. New York: Arthur A. Levine Books.

Technology and Multimedia

The following technology and multimedia products can be used to complement this theme:

"Cousins Jamboree" [CD]. (2002). In *Cousins Jamboree.* Richmond, VA: Holcomb Rock Road.

"Down on Grandpa's Farm" [CD]. (1996). In *One Light, One Song.* Cambridge, MA: Rounder/ UMGD.

"Helping Mommy in the Kitchen" [CD]. (1997). In *Turn on the Music.* Sherman Oaks, CA: Hap-Pal Music.

Is Your Mama a Llama? And More Stories about Growing Up [DVD]. (2009). New York: Scholastic.

"My Grandpa" [CD]. (2002). In *Dancin' in the Kitchen.* New York: BizzyBum.

"The Family" [CD]. (2003). In *Teddy and Friends.* LaCrosse, WI: Platinum Disc.

"Why Did I Have to Have a Sister?" [CD]. (2000). In *10 Carrot Diamond.* Vancouver, BC: Hug Bug Records.

 Additional teaching resources to accompany this Theme can be found on the book's companion website. Go to www.cengagebrain.com to access the site for a variety of useful resources.

Snack Ideas for Young Children

Milk

1. Dips (yogurt, cottage cheese, and cream cheese)
2. Cheese (balls, wedges, cutouts, squares, faces, etc.)
3. Yogurt and fruit
4. Milk punches made with fruits and juices
5. Conventional cocoa
6. Cottage cheese (add pineapple, peaches, etc.)
7. Cheese fondues (preheated—no open flames in classroom)
8. Shakes (mix fruit and milk in a blender)

Meats

1. Meat strips, chunks, and cubes (beef, pork, chicken, turkey, ham, and fish)
2. Meatballs and small kabobs
3. Meat roll-ups (cheese spread, mashed potatoes, spinach, lettuce leaves, or tortillas)
4. Meat salads (tuna, other fish, chicken, turkey, etc.) as spreads for crackers, as stuffing for celery, and rolled in spinach or lettuce
5. Sardines
6. Stuffing for potatoes, tomatoes, and squash

Eggs

1. Hard-boiled
2. Deviled (use different flavors)
3. Egg salad spread
4. Eggs any style that can be managed
5. Egg as a part of other recipes
6. Eggnog

Fruits

1. Use standard fruits, but be adventurous: pomegranates, cranberries, pears, peaches, apricots, plums, berries, pineapples, melons, grapes, grapefruit, and tangerines
2. Kabobs and salads
3. Juices and juice blends
4. In muffins, yogurt, and milk beverages
5. Fruit "sandwiches"
6. Stuffed dates, prunes, and so on
7. Dried fruits (raisins, currants, prunes, apples, peaches, apricots, dates, and figs)

Vegetables

1. Variety—sweet and white potatoes, cherry tomatoes, broccoli, cauliflower, radishes, peppers, mushrooms, zucchini, all squashes, rutabaga, avocados, eggplant, okra, pea pods, turnips, pumpkin, sprouts, and spinach
2. Almost any vegetable can be served raw with or without dip
3. Salads, kabobs, and cutouts
4. Juices and juice blends
5. Soup in a cup (hot or cold)
6. Stuffed—celery, cucumbers, zucchini, spinach, lettuce, cabbage, squash, potatoes, and tomatoes
7. Vegetable spreads
8. Sandwiches

Dried Peas and Beans

1. Kidney beans, garbanzos, limas, lentils, yellow and green peas, pintos, and black beans
2. Beans and peas mashed as dips or spreads
3. Bean, pea, or lentil soup in a cup
4. Roasted soybeans
5. Three-bean salad

Pastas

1. Different shapes and thicknesses
2. Pasta with butter and poppy seeds
3. Cold pasta salad
4. Lasagna noodles (cut for small sandwiches)
5. Chow mein noodles (wheat or rice)

Breads

1. Use a variety of grains— whole wheat, cracked wheat, rye, cornmeal, oatmeal, bran, grits, and so on
2. Use a variety of breads— tortillas, pocket breads, crêpes, pancakes, muffins, biscuits, bagels, popovers, and English muffins
3. Toast—plain, buttered, cinnamon, and with spreads
4. Homemade yeast and quick breads

5. Fill and roll-up crêpes, and pancakes
6. Waffle sandwiches

Cereals, Grains, and Seeds

1. Granola
2. Slices of rice loaf or rice cakes
3. Dry cereal mixes (not pre-sweetened)
4. Seed mixes (pumpkin, sunflower, sesame, poppy, caraway, etc.)
5. Roasted wheat berries, wheat germ, and bran as roll-ins, as toppings, or as finger mix
6. Popcorn with toppings of grated cheese or flavored butters
7. Stir into muffins or use as a topping

Theme 32
FARM ANIMALS

Shelters	Kinds	Sounds	Uses	Food
barns	horses	hee-haw	transportation	corn
stables	cows	moo	milk	hay
sheds	chickens	cluck	food	oats
	pigs	oink		silage
	goats	baa		water
	sheep			

Theme Goals

Through participating in the experiences provided by this theme, the children may learn:

1. Kinds of farm animals
2. Uses for farm animals
3. Farm animal shelters
4. Food for farm animals
5. Sounds of farm animals

Concepts for the Children to Learn

1. A farm animal lives on a farm.
2. Barns, stables, and sheds are homes for farm animals.
3. Horses are farm animals that can be used for transportation.
4. Cows, chickens, pigs, sheep, and goats are farm animals that can be used for food.
5. Some cows and goats give milk.
6. Some chickens give eggs.
7. Farm animals eat corn, hay, oats, and silage.
8. Farm animals can be recognized by the sounds they make.

Vocabulary

1. **barn**—building used to house farm animals and store grain.
2. **farmer**—person who cares for farm animals.
3. **herd**—a group of animals.
4. **stable**—building for horses and cattle.

Bulletin Board

The purpose of this bulletin board is to foster visual discrimination, problem-solving, perceptual, and numeral recognition skills. Out of tagboard, construct red barns as illustrated. The number of barns constructed will depend on the developmental level of your group of children. Place a numeral on each red barn. Construct the same number of black barns by tracing around the red barns onto black construction paper. After cutting out, place small white circles (dots from a paper punch) onto the black barns. Laminate all barns. Staple black barns to the board. Punch a hole in each red barn window. During self-selected activity periods, the children can hang red barns on pushpins of corresponding black barns.

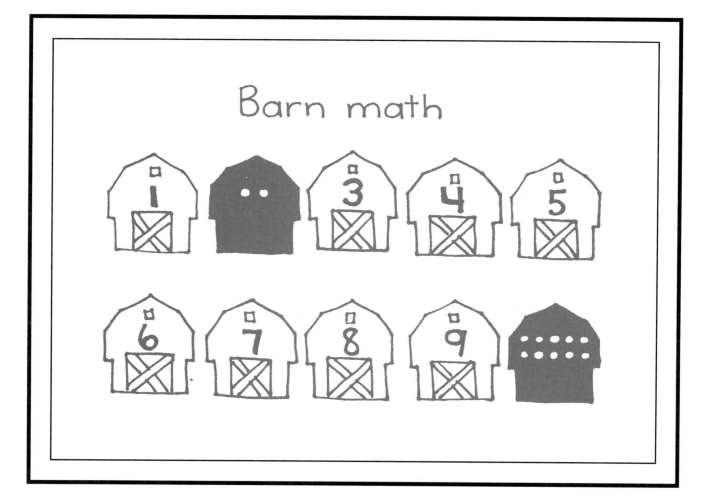

Family Letter

InBox

Dear Families,

Farm animals will be the focus of our next curriculum unit. The children will be learning the many different ways that farm animals help us. They will become aware of the difference between pets and farm animals. The children will also discover that farm animals need homes and food.

At School

Some of the learning activities scheduled for this week include:

- Making a barn out of a large cardboard box for the dramatic play area
- Tasting different kinds of eggs, milk, and cheese for breakfast one day
- At the science table, observing and comparing the many grains and seeds that farm animals eat
- Dressing up like farmers and farm animals
- Making buttermilk chalk pictures
- Listening to stories about farm animals
- Reciting fingerplays representing farm animals

At Home

There are many ways you can integrate this unit into your family life. To stimulate imagination and movement skills, ask your child to imitate different farm animals by walking and making that animal's noise. Also, your child will be learning this rhyme at school. You can also recite it at home to foster language skills.

If I Were a Horse
If I were a horse, I'd gallop all around.
(slap thighs and gallop in a circle)
I'd shake my head and say, "Neigh, neigh."
(shake head)
I'd prance and gallop all over town.

Enjoy your child as you explore experiences related to farm animals.

Arts and Crafts

1. **Yarn Collage**
   Provide the children with several types and lengths of yarn. Include clipped yarn, yarn fluffs, and frayed yarn in several different colors, along with paper.

2. **Texture Collage**
   On the art table, provide several colors, shapes, and types of fabric for creating a texture collage during the self-selected activity period for the children.

3. **Buttermilk Chalk Picture**
   Brush a piece of cardboard with 2 to 3 tablespoons of buttermilk, or dip chalk in buttermilk. Create designs using colored chalk as a tool.

4. **Eggshell Collages**
   Collect eggshells and crush into pieces. Place the eggshells in the art area for the children to glue on paper. Let dry. If desired, the shells can be painted. If preparation time is available, eggshells can be dyed with food coloring by the teacher before the activity.

5. **Sponge Prints**
   Cut farm animal shapes out of sponges. If a pattern is needed, cut out of a coloring book. Once cut, the sponge forms can be dipped into a pan of thick tempera paint and used as a tool to apply a design.

Cooking

1. **Make Butter**
   Fill baby food jars half-full with whipping cream. Allow the children to take turns shaking the jars until the cream separates. First it will appear like whipping cream, then like overwhipped cream, and, finally, an obvious separation will occur. Pour off the liquid and taste. Wash the butter in cold water in a bowl several times. Drain off milky liquid each time. Taste, and then wash again until nearly clear. Work the butter in the water with a wooden spoon as you wash. Add salt to taste. Let the children spread the butter on crackers or bread. *Note:* Carefully supervise the use of glass jars in this activity.

2. **Purple Cow Drink Mix**
   1/2 gallon milk
   1/2 gallon grape juice
   6 ice cubes
   Mix the ingredients in a blender for one minute. Drink. Enjoy! This recipe will serve approximately 20 children.

3. **Animal Crackers**
   Serve animal crackers for snack.

4. **Corn Bread**
   2 cups cornmeal
   1 teaspoon salt
   1/2 teaspoon baking soda
   1 1/2 teaspoons baking powder
   1 tablespoon sugar
   2 eggs
   1 1/2 cups buttermilk
   1/4 cup cooking oil

   Heat oven to 400 degrees. Sift cornmeal, salt, soda, baking powder, baking soda, and sugar into a bowl. Stir in unbeaten eggs, buttermilk, and cooking oil until all ingredients are mixed. Pour the batter into a greased 9-inch × 9-inch pan or cob-shaped pans. Bake for 30 minutes until lightly browned.

5. **Hungry Cheese Spread**
   8 ounces of goat cheese or soft cream cheese
   1/4 cup soft butter
   1 teaspoon salt
   1 tablespoon paprika
   1 teaspoon dry mustard
   1 1/2 tablespoons caraway seeds

   Blend the cheese and butter in the mixing bowl. Add the remaining ingredients. Mix them well. Put the blended cheese into a small serving bowl. Chill in the refrigerator for at least 30 minutes before serving.

   Note: From *Many Hands Cooking,* by Terry Touff Cooper and Marilyn Ratner, 1974, New York: Thomas Y. Crowell.

Dramatic Play

1. **Farmer**
   Clothes and props for a farmer can be placed in the dramatic play area. Include items such as hats, scarves, overalls, boots, and so on.

2. **Saddle**
   A horse saddle can be placed on a bench in the classroom. The children can take turns sitting on it, pretending they are riding a horse.

3. **Barn**
   A barn and plastic animals can be added to the classroom. The children can use blocks as accessories to make pens, cages, and the like.

4. **Veterinarian**
   Collect materials to make a veterinarian prop box. Stuffed animals can be used as patients.

5. **Transition Time Dramatic Play**
   During transition time, encourage the children to imitate different farm animals. They may gallop like a horse, hop like a bunny, waddle like a duck, move like a snake, and so on.

Field Trips and Resource People

1. **Farmer**
   Invite a farmer to talk to the children. If possible, have him or her bring a small farm animal for the children to touch and observe.

2. **The Farm**
   Visit a farm. Observe the animals and machinery.

3. **Milk Station**
   Visit a milk station if there is one in your area.

4. **Grocery Store**
   Visit the dairy section of a grocery store. Look for dairy products.

Group Time
(Games, Language)

1. **Duck, Duck, Goose**
   Ask the children to squat in a circle formation. Then ask one child to walk around the outside of the circle, lightly touching each child's head and saying, "Duck," for each one. When he or she touches another child and says, "Goose," that child chases him or her around the circle. If the child who was "it" returns to the "goose's" place without being tagged, the tapped child becomes "it." This game is appropriate for older four-, five- and six-year-old children.

2. **Thank You**
   Write a thank-you note as a follow-up activity after a field trip or a visit from a resource person.

Large Muscle

1. **Tricycles**
   During outdoor play, encourage children to use tricycles and wagons for hauling.

2. **Barn**
   Construct a large barn out of a large cardboard box. Let all the children help paint it outdoors. When dry, the children can play in it.

Math

1. **Puzzles**
   Laminate several pictures of farm animals; coloring books are a good source. Cut the pictures into puzzles for the children.

2. **Grouping and Sorting**
   Collect plastic farm animals. Place in a basket, and let the children sort them according to size, color, where they live, how they move, and so on.

3. Hen and Chick Match

Make 10 hen cutouts, and place a numeral from 1 to 10 and corresponding dots on each hen. Give each child one hen cutout. Make 10 chick cutouts that will fit inside a plastic Easter egg, and again place a numeral from 1 to 10 and corresponding dots on each chick. Place chicks inside eggs, and place eggs in a basket. The children will take turns picking an egg and determining if the chick matches the number on their hen. The children should continue taking turns picking eggs until they find a match.

Music

1. "Old MacDonald Had a Farm"
(Traditional)

2. "The Animals on the Farm"
(Sing to the tune of "The Wheels on the Bus")

The cows on the farm go moo, moo, moo.
Moo, moo, moo, moo, moo, moo.
The cows on the farm go moo, moo, moo all
    day long.

The horses on the farm go neigh, neigh,
    neigh.
Neigh, neigh, neigh, neigh, neigh, neigh.
The horses on the farm go neigh, neigh,
    neigh all day long.

(Additional verses: pigs—oink; chicken—cluck; sheep—baa; and turkeys—gobble)

3. "The Farmer in the Dell"
(Traditional)

The farmer in the dell,
The farmer in the dell,
Hi-ho the dairy-o
The farmer in the dell.

The farmer takes a wife (husband).
The farmer takes a wife (husband).
Hi-ho the dairy-o
The farmer in the dell.

(The other verses are as follows)
The wife (husband) takes the child
The child takes the nurse
The nurse takes the dog

The dog takes the cat
The cat takes the rat
The rat takes the cheese.

(The final verse:)
The cheese stands alone.
The cheese stands alone.
Hi-ho the dairy-o
The cheese stands alone.

4. "This Little Piggy"

This little piggy went to market,
    (wiggle big toe)
This little piggy stayed home,
    (wiggle second toe)
This little piggy had roast beef,
    (wiggle third toe)
This little piggy had none,
    (wiggle fourth toe)
And this little piggy cried, "Wee-wee-wee!"
    all the way home. (wiggle little toe)

Science

1. Sheep Wool

Place various types of wool on a table for the children to observe. Included may be wool clippings, lanolin, dyed yarn, yarn spun into thread, wool cloth, and wool articles such as mittens and socks.

2. Feathers

Examine various types of feathers. Use a magnifying glass. Discuss their purposes, such as keeping birds warm and helping ducks to float on water. Add the feathers to the water table to see if they float. Discuss why they float.

3. Tasting Dairy Products

Plan a milk-tasting party. To do this, taste and compare the following types of milk products: cow milk, goat milk, cream, skimmed milk, whole milk, cottage cheese, sour cream, butter, margarine, and buttermilk. ***Caution:*** Check for children's allergies before all food-related activities.

4. Eggs

Taste different kinds of eggs. Let children choose from scrambled, poached, deviled, hard-boiled, and fried eggs. This could also be integrated as part of the breakfast menu.

5. Cheese Types

Observe, taste, and compare different kinds of cheese. Examples include Swiss, cheddar, colby, cottage cheese, and cheese curds.

6. Egg Hatching

If possible, contact a hatchery to borrow an incubator. Watch the eggs hatch in the classroom.

7. Feels like the Farm

Construct a feely box containing farm items. Examples may include an ear of corn, hay, sheep wool, a turkey feather, a hard-boiled egg, and so on.

Sensory

1. Farm Animal Sound Bingo

Record a child making a farm animal sound or download the sound from the Internet. Find photographs or clipart of the animal, and glue them onto a cardboard bingo card. Play each sound, and ask the child to put a button over the corresponding animal.

2. Additions to the Sensory Table

- Different types of grain, such as oats, wheat, barley, and corn, and measuring devices
- Wool and feathers
- Sand and plastic farm animals
- Provide materials to make a barnyard. Include soil, hay, farm animals, barns, farm equipment toys, and so on

Social Studies

Farm Animal of the Day

Throughout the week, let children take care of and watch baby farm animals. Suggestions include a piglet, chicks, small ducks, a rabbit, or a lamb.

Books

The following books can be used to complement this theme:

Aliki. (1992). *Milk from Cow to Carton* (revised edition). New York: HarperCollins.

Baker, Keith. (1994). *Big Fat Hen.* San Diego, CA: Harcourt Brace.

Bates, Ivan. (2006). *Five Little Ducks.* Illustrated by Ivan Bates. New York: Scholastic.

Battaglia, Aurelius. (2005). *Animal Sounds.* Illustrated by Aurelius Battaglia. New York: Random House.

Beaumont, Karen. (2004). *Duck, Duck, Goose! A Coyote's on the Loose!* New York: HarperCollins.

Beshara, Crystal. (2009). *When I Visit the Farm.* Montreal: Lobster Press.

Blackstone, Stella. (2006). *There's a Cow in the Cabbage Patch.* Cambridge, MA: Barefoot Books.

Brown, Margaret Wise. (2002). *Big Red Barn.* New York: Rayo.

Bruss, Deborah, and Tiphanie Beeke. (2001). *Book! Book! Book!* Illustrated by Tiphanie Beeke. New York: Arthur A. Levine.

Bunting, Eve. (2007). *Hurry! Hurry!* Illustrated by Jeff Mack. Orlando, FL: Harcourt Children's Books.

Church, Caroline Jayne. (2008). *Ping Pong Pig.* New York: Holiday House.

Cooper, Elisha. (2010). *Farm.* New York: Orchard Books.

Cowley, Joy. (2003). *Mrs. Wishy-Washy Makes a Splash.* Illustrated by Elizabeth Fuller. New York: Philomel Books.

Cronin, Doreen, and Betsy Lewin. (2000). *Click, Clack, Moo: Cows That Type.* Illustrated by Betsy Lewin. New York: Simon & Schuster.

Crum, Shutta. (2009). *Thunder-Boomer!* Illustrated by Carol Thompson. New York: Clarion Books.

Davidson, Susanna. (2006). *The Little Red Hen.* Illustrated by Daniel Postgate. London: Usborne.

DeSeve, Randall. (2010). *Mathilda and the Orange Balloon.* Illustrated by Jen Corace. New York: Balzer & Bray.

Duffield, Katy. (2003). *Farmer McPeepers and His Missing Milk Cows.* Illustrated by Kathy Duffield. Flagstaff, AZ: Rising Moon.

Elliot, David. (2008). *On the Farm.* Illustrated by Holly Meade. Somerville, MA: Candlewick Press.

Henderson, Kathy. (1996). *Counting Farm.* Cambridge, MA: Shaw's Candlewick Press.

Himmelman, John. (2010). *Pigs to the Rescue.* New York: Henry Holt.

Hoena, B. A. (2004). *A Visit to the Farm.* Mankato, MN: Capstone Press.

Hutchins, Pat. (1994). *Little Pink Pig.* New York: Greenwillow.

Jackson, Ellen. (1995). *Brown Cow, Green Grass, Yellow Mellow Sun.* Illustrated by Victoria Raymond. New York: Hyperion.

Kasza, Keiko. (2003). *My Lucky Day.* New York: G.P. Putnam's Sons.

Landstrom, Lena. (2005). *Four Hens and a Rooster.* New York: Douglas & McIntyre.

Lesser, Carolyn. (1995). *What a Wonderful Day to Be a Cow.* Illustrated by Melissa Bay Mathis. New York: Knopf.

Martin, Bernard, Bill Martin Jr., and Michael Sampson. (2005). *Chicken Chuck.* Illustrated by Steven Salerno. New York: Marshall Cavendish.

Milord, Susan. (2005). *Three about Thurston.* Boston: Houghton Mifflin.

Minne, Brigitte. (2004). *The Best Bottom.* New York: Milk & Cookies Press.

Newton, Jill. (2010). *Crash Bang Donkey!* Chicago: Albert Whitman.

Palatini, Margie, and Richard Egielski. (2001). *The Web Files.* Illustrated by Richard Egielski. New York: Hyperion Press.

Perl, Erica S. (2004). *Chicken Bedtime Is Really Early.* Illustrated by George Bates. New York: Abrams.

Scarry, Richard. (2004). *The Rooster Struts.* New York: Golden Books.

Schubert, Leda. (2010). *Feeding the Sheep.* Illustrated by Andrea U'Ren. New York: Farrar, Straus and Giroux.

Smee, Nicola. (2006). *Clip-Clop.* London: Boxer Books.

Spinelli, Eileen. (2009). *Princess Pig.* Illustrated by Tim Bowers. New York: Alfred A. Knopf.

Stohner, Anu. (2005). *Brave Charlotte.* Illustrated by Henrike Wilson. New York: Bloomsbury Children's Books.

Sturghes, Philemon. (1999). *The Little Red Hen Makes a Pizza.* New York: Dutton Children's Books.

Sykes, Julie. (1997). *Dora's Eggs.* Illustrated by Jane Chapman. Wilton, CT: Tiger Tales.

Teague, Mark. (2009). *Funny Farm.* New York: Orchard Books.

Thomas, Jan. (2008). *A Birthday for Cow!* Orlando, FL: Harcourt.

Van Petter, Bruce. (2010). *Tucker Took It!* Honesdale, PA: Boyds Mills Press.

Waring, Richard. (2001). *Hungry Hen.* Illustrated by Caroline Jayne Church. New York: HarperCollins.

Weinstein, Ellen. (2008). *Everywhere the Cow Says "Moo!"* Illustrated by Kenneth Anderson. Honesdale, PA: Boyds Mills Press. (Different languages)

Wild, Margaret. (2009). *Piglet and Granny.* Illustrated by Stephen Michael King. New York: Abrams Books for Young Readers.

Wilson, Karma. (2010). *The Cow Loves Cookies.* Illustrated by Marcellus Hall. New York: Margaret K. McElderry Books.

Technology and Multimedia

The following technology and multimedia products can be used to complement this theme:

Alphabet Road: "F" Is for Farm—Do You Know Where Milk Comes From? [DVD]. (2006). New York: GoBabies.

"Baby Chickie" [CD]. (1994). In *So Big.* Sherman Oaks, CA: Hap-Pal Music.

"Barnyard Boogie" [CD]. (2005). In *Sing-a-Move-a-Dance.* Eau Claire, WI: North Side Music.

"BINGO" [CD]. (2002). In *Early Childhood Classics*. Sherman Oaks, CA: Hap-Pal Music.

"The Color Farm?" [CD]. (2007). In *Sing to Learn with Dr. Jean*. Oklahoma City, OK: Melody House.

Dance with the Animals. [DVD]. (2006). Conroe, TX: Rock 'N Learn Inc..

"Down on Grandpa's Farm" [CD]. (1996). In *One Light, One Song*. Cambridge, MA: Rounder/UMGD.

"Farmer in the Dell" [CD]. (2007). In *Nursery Rhymes and Good Ol' Times*. Oklahoma City, OK: Melody House.

"Giddyup Pony" [CD]. (2000). In *Charlotte Diamond's World*. Vancouver, BC: Hug Bug Records.

Giggle, Giggle, Quack and More Stories by Doreen Cronin [DVD]. (2009). New York: Scholastic.

"Here Comes the Cow" and "Hop Like a Bunny" [CD]. (1974). In *It's Fun to Clap*. Long Branch, NJ: Kimbo Educational.

"I Know a Chicken" [CD]. (2010). In *Best of Laurie Berkner Band*. New York: Two Tomatoes.

"Neat Nanny Goat," "Piggly, Wiggly, Pizza Pig," and "Skiing Sheep" [CD]. (1994). In *A to Z: The Animals and Me*. Long Branch, NJ: Kimbo Educational.

"Old MacDonald Had a Farm," "Six Little Ducks," "Little White Duck," and "B-I-N-G-O" [CD]. (1997). In *Six Little Ducks*. Long Branch, NJ: Kimbo Educational.

"Old McDonald" [CD]. (2002). In *Early Childhood Classics*. Sherman Oaks, CA: Hap-Pal Music.

"Old McDonald" [CD]. (2007). In *Nursery Rhymes and Good Ol' Times*. Oklahoma City, OK: Melody House.

On the Farm [CD]. (1999). Long Branch, NJ: Kimbo Educational.

 Additional teaching resources to accompany this Theme can be found on the book's companion website. Go to www.cengagebrain.com to access the site for a variety of useful resources.

Theme 33
FEELINGS

Verbal
yelling
crying
talking
singing
laughing
whispering

Nonverbal
smiling
frowning
jumping
hitting
petting
hugging
kissing

Types
happy, sad
lonely, tired
surprised, angry
excited, friendly
afraid, hungry
sorry, depressed
loved

Causes
people
situations
sickness

Theme Goals

Through participating in the experiences provided by this theme, the children may learn:

1. Types of feelings
2. Verbal expressions of feelings
3. Nonverbal expressions of feelings
4. Causes for our feelings

Concepts for the Children to Learn

1. Everyone has feelings.
2. Feelings show how we feel.
3. Feelings change.
4. Feelings are caused by people, situations, and sickness.
5. Loved, happy, sad, excited, sorry, and surprised are types of feelings.
6. Lonely, tired, angry, afraid, hungry, and depressed are feelings.
7. Friendliness and love are also feelings.
8. People can share their feelings verbally.
9. Yelling, crying, talking, singing, and laughing are ways to verbally express feelings.
10. People show their feelings nonverbally.
11. Kissing, hugging, and petting are examples of showing feelings nonverbally.
12. Frowning, jumping, and hitting are other ways people can show feelings nonverbally.

Vocabulary

1. **afraid**—the feeling of being unsure of or frightened about something.
2. **feelings**—the way you feel about something in your mind. Happiness and love are feelings.
3. **happy**—a feeling of being glad.
4. **sad**—the feeling of being hurt or unhappy.
5. **smile**—a facial expression of pleasure or happiness.
6. **surprise**—a feeling from something unexpected.

Bulletin Board

The purpose of this bulletin board is to help the children become aware of happy, sad, and mad feelings, as well as recognize their printed names. Prepare individual name cards for each child. Then prepare different expressive faces such as happy, sad, and angry. Staple faces to top of bulletin board. See the illustration for an example. If available, magnetic strips may be added to the bulletin board under faces and pieces affixed to name cards, or pushpins may be placed on the board and holes punched in name cards. The children may place their names under the face they decide they feel like when arriving at school. Later, during large-group time, the board can be reviewed to see if any of the children's feelings have changed.

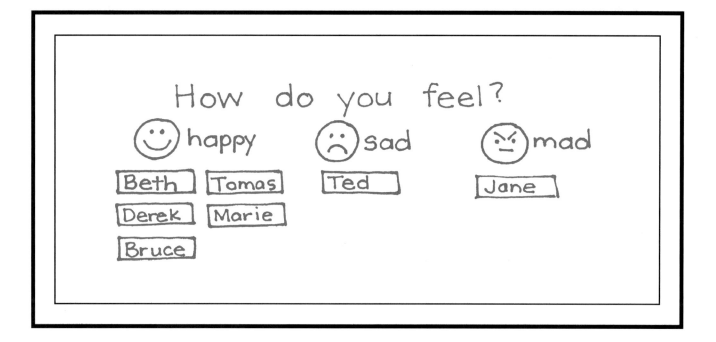

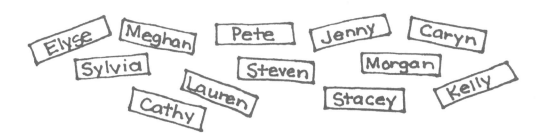

Family Letter

Dear Families,

Emotions and feelings will be the focus of our next curriculum unit. Throughout each day, the children experience many feelings, ranging from happiness to sadness. The purpose of this unit is to have the children develop an understanding of feelings. Feelings are something we all share, and feelings are acceptable. We will also be exploring ways of expressing different feelings.

At School

Some of the learning experiences planned for this unit include:

- Listening to and discussing the book *Alexander and the Terrible, Horrible, No Good, Very Bad Day* by Judith Viorst

- Singing songs about our feelings

- Drawing and painting to various types of music

- Expressing feelings through music

Our Special Visitor

"Clancy the Clown" will be visiting the children on Thursday at 3:00 p.m. The children are all looking forward to this special visitor. You are encouraged to join us and share their excitement.

At Home

To help your child identify situations that elicit feelings, have your child cut or tear pictures from discarded magazines that depict events or situations that make your child feel happy or sad. These pictures can then be glued or pasted on paper to create a feelings collage.

Talking with your child about your feelings will encourage parent-child communication. Tell your child what things make you feel various ways. Then ask your child to share some feelings.

Make your child happy today!

Arts and Crafts

1. **Drawing to Music**

   Play various types of music, including jazz, classical, and rock, and let the children draw during the self-selected activity period. Different tunes and melodies might make us feel a certain way.

2. **Play Dough**

   Using play dough is a wonderful way to vent feelings. Prepare several types and let the children feel the different textures. Color each type a different color. Add a scent to one, and to another add a textured material such as sawdust, rice, or sand. A list of play dough recipes can be found later in this theme.

3. **Footprints**

   Mix tempera paint. Pour the paint into a shallow jelly roll pan approximately 1/4-inch deep. The children can dip their feet into the pan. After this, they can step directly onto paper. Using their feet as an application tool, footsteps can be made. This activity could be used to create a mural to hang in the hall or lobby.

Cooking

1. **Happy Rolls**

   1 package fast-rising dry yeast
   1 cup warm water
   1/3 cup sugar
   1/3 cup cooking oil
   3 cups flour
   Dash of salt

   Measure the warm water and pour it into a bowl. Sprinkle the yeast on top of the water. Let the yeast settle into the water. Mix all of the ingredients in a large bowl. Place the dough on a floured board to knead it. Demonstrate how to knead, letting each of the children take turns kneading the bread. This is a wonderful activity to work through emotions. After kneading it for about 10 minutes, put the ball of dough into a greased bowl. If kneaded sufficiently, the top of the dough should have blisters on it. Cover the bowl and put in the sun or near heat. Let it rise for about an hour or until doubled. Take the dough out of the bowl. Punch it down, knead for several more minutes, and then divide the dough into 12 to 15 pieces. Roll each piece of dough into a ball. Place each ball on a greased cookie sheet. Let the dough rise again until doubled. Bake at 450 degrees for 10 to 12 minutes. A happy face can be drawn on the roll with frosting.

2. **Berry "Happy" Shake from Finland**

   10 fresh strawberries or 6 tablespoons frozen sliced strawberries in syrup, thawed
   2 cups cold milk
   1 1/2 tablespoons sugar or honey

   Wash the strawberries (if fresh) and cut out the stems. Cut the strawberries into small pieces. (If you are using frozen strawberries, drain the syrup into a small bowl or cup and save it.) Pour the milk into the mixing bowl. Add the strawberries. If you are using fresh strawberries, add the sugar or honey. If you are using frozen strawberries, add 3 tablespoons of the strawberry syrup instead of sugar. Beat with the egg beater for 1 minute. Pour the drink into glasses.
   Note: From *Many Hands Cooking,* by Terry Touff Cooper and Marilyn Ratner, 1974, New York: Thomas Y. Crowell.

3. **Danish Smile Berry Pudding**

   1 10-ounce package frozen raspberries, thawed
   1 10-ounce package frozen strawberries, thawed
   1/4 cup cornstarch
   2 tablespoons sugar
   1/2 cup cold water
   1 tablespoon lemon juice

   Puree berries in blender or press through sieve. Mix cornstarch and sugar in 1 1/2-quart saucepan. Gradually stir in water; add puree. Heat to boiling, stirring constantly. Boil and stir 1 minute. Remove from heat. Stir in lemon juice. Pour into dessert dishes or serving bowl. Cover and refrigerate at least 2 hours. Serve with half-and-half if desired. Makes 6 servings.

Note: From *Betty Crocker's International Cookbook,* 1980, New York: Random House.

Dramatic Play

1. **Flower Shop**
   Plastic flowers, vases, and wrapping paper can be placed in the dramatic play area. Make a sign that says "Flower Shop." The children may want to arrange, sell, deliver, and receive flowers.

2. **Post Office**
   Collect discarded greeting cards and envelopes. The children can stamp and deliver the cards to one another.

3. **Puppet Center**
   A puppet center can be added to the dramatic play area. Include a variety of puppets and a stage.

Fingerplays and Chants

I Looked inside My Looking Glass
   I looked inside my looking glass
      (pinch index finger and thumb together to form a circle)
   To see what I could see.
      (hold a circle over each eye)
   It looks like I'm happy today,
      (smile)
   Because that smiling face is me.
      (continue smiling and point to oneself)

Stand Up Tall
   Stand up tall
      (stand up straight)
   Hands in the air.
      (hold hands over head in the air)
   Now sit down
   In your chair.
      (sit on chair)

Clap your hands
   (clap hands)
And make a frown.
   (frown)
Smile and smile.
   (smile)
Hop like a clown.
   (stand up and hop)

Group Time
(Games and Language)

Happy Feeling
Discuss happiness. Ask each child to name one thing that makes him or her happy. Record each answer on a "Happiness Chart." Post the chart for the parents to observe as they pick up their children.

Large Muscle

1. **Mirrors**
   The children should sit as pairs facing each other. Select one child to make a "feeling face" at the partner. Let the other child guess what feeling it is. A variation of this activity would be to have partners face each other. When one child smiles, the partner is to imitate his or her feelings.

2. **Simon Says**
   Play "Simon Says" using emotions:
   "Simon Says walk in a circle feeling happy . . ."
   "Simon Says walk in a circle feeling sad . . ."

Math

Face Match
Collect two small shoe boxes. On one shoe box, draw a happy face. On the other box, draw a sad face. Cut faces of people from magazines. The children can sort the pictures accordingly.

Music

1. "Feelings"
(Sing to the tune of "Twinkle, Twinkle Little Star")

I have feelings.
You do, too.
Let's all sing about a few.

I am happy.
   (smile)
I am sad.
   (frown)
I get scared.
   (wrap arms around self)
I get mad.
   (make a fist and shake it)

I am proud of being me.
   (hands on hips)
That's a feeling, too, you see.
I have feelings.
   (point to self)
You do, too.
   (point to someone else)
We just sang about a few.

2. "If You're Happy and You Know It"
(Traditional)
(For additional verses, change the emotions and actions)

If you're happy and you know it
Clap your hands.
   (clap twice)
If you're happy and you know it
Clap your hands.
   (clap twice)
If you're happy and you know it
Then your face will surely show it.
If you're happy and you know it
Clap your hands.
   (clap twice)

3. "I Have Something in My Pocket"

I have something in my pocket.
It belongs across my face.
I keep it very close at hand.
In a most convenient place.
I bet you could guess it,
If you guessed a long, long while
So I'll take it out and put it on,
It's a great big happy SMILE!

4. "For He's a Jolly Good Fellow"

For he's a jolly good fellow,
For he's a jolly good fellow,
For he's a jolly good fellow,
Which nobody can deny.
Which nobody can deny,
Which nobody can deny,
For he's a jolly good fellow,
For he's a jolly good fellow,
For he's a jolly good fellow,
Which nobody can deny.

We won't go home until morning,
We won't go home until morning,
We won't go home until morning,
'Till daylight doth appear.
'Till daylight doth appear,
'Till daylight doth appear,
We won't go home until morning,
We won't go home until morning,
We won't go home until morning,
'Till daylight doth appear.

Resource People

1. A Clown
Invite a clown to the classroom. You may ask the clown to dress and apply makeup for the children. After the clown leaves, provide makeup for the children.

2. Musician
Invite a musician to play a variety of music for the children to express feelings.

3. Florist
Invite a florist to visit your classroom and show how flowers are arranged. Talk about why people send flowers. If convenient, the children could visit the florist, touring the greenhouses.

Science

1. **Sound Tape**
   Tape various noises that express emotions; suggestions include sounds such as laughter, cheering, growling, shrieking, crying, and so on. Play these sounds for the children, letting them identify the emotion. They may also want to act out the emotion.

2. **Communication without Words**
   Hang a large screen or sheet with a bright light behind it. The children can go behind the screen and act out various emotions. Other children guess how they are feeling.

3. **How Does It Feel?**
   Add various pieces of textured materials to the science table. Include materials such as soft fur, sandpaper, rocks, and cotton. Encourage the children to touch each object and explain how it feels.

Sensory

Texture Feelings
Various textures can create feelings. Let the children express their feelings by adding the following to the sensory table:

- Cotton
- Water (warm or with ice)
- Black water
- Blue water
- Sand
- Pebbles
- Dirt with scoops
- Plastic worms with water

Social Studies

Pictures
Share pictures of individuals engaged in different occupations such as doctors, firefighters, beauticians, florists, nurses, bakers, and so on. Discuss how these individuals help us and how they make us feel.

Books

The following books can be used to complement this theme:

Aboff, Marcie. (2010). *Everyone Feels Scared Sometimes*. Illustrated by Damian Ward. Mankato, MN: Capstone Press.

Brisson, Pat. (2010). *Sometimes We Were Brave*. Illustrated by France Brassard. Honesdale, PA: Boyds Mills Press.

Brown, Laurie Krasny. (1996). *When Dinosaurs Die: A Guide to Understanding Death*. Illustrated by Marc Tolon Brown. Boston: Little, Brown.

Cabrera, Jane. (2005). *If You're Happy and You Know It!* New York: Holiday House.

Carle, Eric. (1995). *The Very Lonely Firefly*. New York: Philomel Books.

Carlson, Nancy L. (1997). *ABC I Like Me*. New York: Viking.

Crary, Elizabeth. (1992). *I'm Frustrated*. Dealing with Feelings series. Illustrated by Jean Whitney. Seattle, WA: Parenting Press.

Crary, Elizabeth. (1992). *I'm Mad*. Dealing with Feelings series. Illustrated by Jean Whitney. Seattle, WA: Parenting Press.

Crary, Elizabeth. (1992). *I'm Proud*. Dealing with Feelings series. Illustrated by Jean Whitney. Seattle, WA: Parenting Press.

Crary, Elizabeth. (1996). *I'm Excited*. Dealing with Feelings series. Illustrated by Jean Whitney. Seattle, WA: Parenting Press.

Crary, Elizabeth. (1996). *I'm Furious*. Dealing with Feelings series. Illustrated by Jean Whitney. Seattle, WA: Parenting Press.

Crary, Elizabeth. (1996). *I'm Scared*. Dealing with Feelings series. Illustrated by Jean Whitney. Seattle, WA: Parenting Press.

Curtis, Munzee. (1997). *When the Big Dog Barks*. Illustrated by Susan Ayishai. New York: Greenwillow.

Cusimano, Maryann K., and Satomi Ichikawa. (2001). *You Are My I Love You.* New York: Philomel Books.

Danneberg, Julie, and Judith Dufour Love. (2000). *First Day Jitters.* Illustrated by Judith Dufour Love. Watertown, MA: Charlesbridge.

Dunbar, Polly. (2008). *Happy Hector.* Cambridge, MA: Candlewick Press.

Emberley, Ed. (1997). *Glad Monster, Sad Monster: A Book about Feelings.* Illustrated by Anne Miranda. Boston: Little, Brown.

Freymann, Saxton, and Joost Elffers. (1999). *How Are You Feeling?* New York: Arthur A. Levine.

Genechten, Guido Van. (2005). *The Cuddle Book.* New York: HarperCollins.

Grover, Lorie Ann. (2008). *Hug Hug!* Illustrated by Rebecca Malone. New York: Little Simon.

Harper, Charise Mericle. (2010). *Cupcake: A Journey to Special.* New York: Disney-Hyperion.

Heling, Kathryn. (2009). *I Wish I Had Freckles Like Abby.* McHenry, IL: Raven Tree Press.

Henkes, Kevin. (2000). *Wemberly Worried.* New York: Greenwillow.

Hills, Tad. (2009). *Duck and Goose, How Are You Feeling? How Are You Feeling?* New York: Schwartz & Wade Books.

Hodgkinson, Leigh. (2010). *Smile!* New York: Balzer & Bray.

Isadora, Rachel. (2009). *Happy Belly, Happy Smile.* Boston: Harcourt Children's Books.

Julian, Alison. (2001). *Brave as a Bunny Can Be.* Minneapolis, MN: Waldman House.

Klise, Kate. (2006). *Why Do You Cry? Not a Sob Story.* Illustrated by M. Sarah Klise. New York: H. Holt.

Lachner, Dorothea. (1995). *Andrew's Angry Words.* Illustrated by Tjong-Khing The. New York: North South Books.

Markes, Julie. (2001). *Good Thing You're Not an Octopus!* Illustrated by Maggie Smith. New York: HarperCollins.

McAllister, Angela. (2006). *Brave Bitsy and the Bear.* Illustrated by Tiphanie Beeke. New York: Clarion Books.

McGhee, Alison. (2006). *A Very Brave Witch.* Illustrated by Harry Bliss. New York: Simon & Schuster Books for Young Readers.

Murphy, Mary. (2000). *I Feel Happy, and Sad, and Angry, and Glad.* New York: Dorling Kindersley.

Raffi. (2005). *If You're Happy and You Know It.* Illustrated by Cyd Moore. New York: Alfred A. Knopf, distributed by Random House.

Seeger, Pete, and Paul DuBois Jacobs. (2005). *Some Friends to Feed: The Story of Stone Soup.* Illustrated by Michael Hays. New York: G.P. Putnam's Sons.

Seuss, Dr. (1996). *My Many Colored Days.* Edited by Lou Fancher and illustrated by Steve Johnson. New York: Knopf.

Smee, Nicola. (2006). *Funny Face.* New York: Bloomsbury Children's Books.

Spelman, Cornelia Maude. (2002). *When I Feel Sad.* Illustrated by Kathy Parkinson. Morton Grove, IL: A. Whitman.

Spelman, Cornelia. (2004). *When I Miss You.* Illustrated by Kathy Parkinson. Morton Grove, IL: Albert Whitman.

Spinelli, Eileen. (2006). *When You Are Happy.* Illustrated by Geraldo Valerio. New York: Simon & Schuster Books for Young Readers.

Stamp, Jorgen. (2009). *Flying High.* New York: Enchanted Lion Books.

Stanley, Mandy. (2006). *How Do You Feel?* New York: Little Simon.

Stohner, Anu. (2009). *Brave Charlotte and the Wolves.* Illustrated By Henrike Wilson. New York: Bloomsbury.

Tankard, Jeremy. (2007). *Grumpy Bird.* New York: Scholastic.

Thompson, Colin. (2008). *The Big Little Book of Happy Sadness.* La Jolla, CA: Kane/Miller.

Verdick, Elizabeth. (2010). *Calm-Down Time.* Illustrated by Marieka Heilen. Minneapolis, MN: Free Spirit.

Verroken, Sarah. (2009). *Feeling Sad.* Brooklyn, NY: Enchanted Lion Books.

Viorst, Judith (1972). *Alexander and the Terrible, Horrible, No Good, Very Bad Day.* Illustrated by Ray Cruz. New York: Simon and Schuster.

Wagenbach, Debbie. (2010). *The Grouchies.* Washington, DC: Magination Press.

Wilson, Karma. (2008). *Bear Feels Scared.* Illustrated by Jane Chapman. New York: Margaret K. McElderry Books.

Yolen, Jane. (2008). *Sad, Mad, Glad Hippos.* Illustrated by Steve Mack. Toronto: Key Porter Books.

Technology and Multimedia

The following technology and multimedia products can be used to complement this theme:

"A Friend in Need," "It's a Great Day," "It's All Right," and "Squabbles Hugs" [CD]. (1994). In *Get Up and Grow.* Long Branch, NJ: Kimbo Educational.

"A Little Bit Afraid" [CD]. (2002). In *Cousins Jamboree.* Richmond, VA: Holcomb Rock Road.

"Angry," "Sad," and "Scared." (1986). In *Singing, Moving and Fun.* Long Branch, NJ: Kimbo Educational.

"Celebrate Your Courage" [CD]. (2010). In *Lots of Fun.* Atlanta, GA: Mr Greg's Musical Madness.

"Everyone's Afraid of Something" [CD]. (2009). In *People, Place and Things.* Coconut Grove, FL: In the Nick of Time.

"Friends" [CD]. (1992). In *Nelson Gill / Friends.* Long Branch, NJ: Kimbo Educational.

"Hang on Friend" [CD]. (2002). In *Cousins Jamboree.* Richmond, VA: Holcomb Rock Road.

"Happy" [CD]. (2004). In *Circle Time Activities.* Long Branch, NJ: Kimbo Educational.

"Happy Days" [CD]. (2000). In *Bean Bag Rock and Roll.* Long Branch, NJ: Kimbo Educational.

"Happy Rappy" [CD]. (1994). In *Yes, I Can Songs (with RONNO).* Long Branch, NJ: Kimbo Educational.

"How Are You Today—Please?" [CD]. (1995). In *Piggyback Songs.* Long Branch, NJ: Kimbo Educational.

"I Can Do It" [CD]. (2002). In *Cousins Jamboree.* Richmond, VA: Holcomb Rock Road.

"If You're Happy and You Know It" [CD]. (2006). In *Josh Levine for Kids.* New York: Josh Levine.

"Out of Green Paint Blues" [CD]. (2009). In *People, Place and Things.* Coconut Grove, FL: In the Nick of Time.

"Smile" [CD]. (2002). In *Under a Shady Tree.* New York: Two Tomatoes.

"Talking Sharing Blues" [CD]. (2010). In *Funnier Little Fellas.* Portland, OR: Matt Clark.

"When I'm Down I Get Up and Dance" [CD]. (1994). In *So Big.* Sherman Oaks, CA: Hap-Pal Music.

 Additional teaching resources to accompany this Theme can be found on the book's companion website. Go to www.cengagebrain.com to access the site for a variety of useful resources.

Recipes for Doughs and Clays

Clay Dough
3 cups flour
3 cups salt
3 tablespoons alum

Combine ingredients and slowly add water, a little at a time. Mix well with spoon. As mixture thickens, continue mixing with your hands until it has the feel of clay. If it feels too dry, add more water. If it is too sticky, add equal parts of flour and salt.

Play Dough
2 cups flour
1 cup salt
1 cup hot water
2 tablespoons cooking oil
4 teaspoons cream of tartar
Food coloring

Mix well. Knead until smooth. This dough may be kept in a plastic bag or covered container and used again. If it gets sticky, more flour may be added.

Favorite Play Dough
2 cups water
1/2 cup salt
Food coloring or tempera paint
2 tablespoons cooking oil
2 tablespoons alum
2 cups flour

Combine and boil water, salt, and food coloring or paint until dissolved. While very hot, mix in oil, alum, and flour. Knead (approximately 5 minutes) until smooth. Store in covered, airtight containers.

Oatmeal Dough
2 cups oatmeal
1 cup flour

1/2 cup water

Combine ingredients. Knead well. This dough has a very different texture, is easily manipulated, and looks different. Finished projects can be painted when dry.

Baker's Clay #1
1 cup cornstarch
2 cups baking soda
1 1/2 cups cold water

Combine ingredients. Stir until smooth. Cook over medium heat, stirring constantly until mixture reaches the consistency of slightly dry mashed potatoes.

Turn out onto plate or bowl, covering with damp cloth. When cool enough to handle, knead thoroughly until smooth and pliable on cornstarch-covered surface.

Store in tightly closed plastic bag or covered container.

Baker's Clay #2
4 cups flour
1 1/2 cups water
1 cup salt

Combine ingredients. Mix well. Knead 5 to 10 minutes. Roll out to 1/4-inch thickness. Cut with decorative cookie cutters or with a knife. Make a hole at the top.

Bake at 250 degrees for 2 hours or until hard. When cool, paint with tempera paint and spray with clear varnish or paint with acrylic paint.

Cloud Dough
3 cups flour
1 cup oil
Scent (oil of peppermint, wintergreen, lemon, etc.)
Food coloring

Combine ingredients. Add water until easily manipulated (about 1/2 cup).

Sawdust Dough
2 cups sawdust
3 cups flour
1 cup salt

Combine ingredients. Add water as needed. This dough becomes very hard and is not easily broken. It is good to use for making objects and figures that one desires to keep.

Salt Dough
4 cups salt
1 cup cornstarch
Water

Combine salt and cornstarch with sufficient water to form a paste. Cook over medium heat, stirring constantly.

Cooked Clay Dough
1 cup flour
1/2 cup cornstarch
4 cups water
1 cup salt
3 or 4 pounds flour
Food coloring if desired

Stir slowly and be patient with this recipe. Blend the 1 cup flour and cornstarch with cold water. Add salt to the water, and boil. Pour the boiling salt and water solution into the flour and cornstarch paste, and cook over high heat until clear.

Add the additional flour and coloring to the cooked solution and knead. After the clay has been in use, if it is too moist, add flour; if dry, add water. Keep in covered container. Wrap dough with damp cloth or towel. This dough has a very nice texture and is very popular with all age groups. May be kept 2 or 3 weeks.

Play Dough
5 cups flour
2 cups salt
4 tablespoons cooking oil
Water

Mix ingredients, adding water to right consistency. Powdered tempera may be added in with flour, or food coloring may be added to finished dough. This dough may be kept in a plastic bag or covered container for approximately 2 to 4 weeks. It is better used as play dough rather than leaving objects to harden.

Used Coffee Grounds
2 cups used coffee grounds
1/2 cup salt
1 1/2 cups oatmeal

Combine ingredients and add enough water to moisten. Children like to roll, pack, and pat this mixture. It has a very different feel and look, but it's not good for finished products. It has a very nice texture.

Mud Dough
2 cups sterile potting soil
2 cups sand
1/2 cup salt
Water

Combine ingredients and add enough water to make pliable. Children like to work with this mixture. It has a nice texture and is easy to use. This cannot be picked up easily to save for finished products. It can be used for rolling and cutouts.

Soap Modeling
2 cups soap flakes
Water

Add enough water to moisten and whip until consistency is right for molding. Use soap such as Ivory Snow, Dreft, Lux, or the like. Mixture will have very slight flaky appearance when it can be molded. It is very enjoyable for all age groups and is easy to work. Also, the texture is very different from other materials ordinarily used for molding. It may be put up to dry, but articles are very slow to dry.

Soap and Sawdust
1 cup whipped soap
1 cup sawdust
Water

Mix ingredients well together. This gives a very different feel and appearance. It is quite easily molded into different shapes by all age groups. May be used for 2 to 3 days if stored in a tight plastic bag.

Bath Time Soap Flake Play Dough
4 cups soap flakes
1 cup water

Put the soap flakes into a large bowl. Gradually add the water, mixing constantly until the mixture is dough-like. Make a variety of figures. Save the figures on a plate for the next bath time.

Best Play Dough Ever
1 cup flour
1 cup water
2 teaspoons cream of tartar
1/2 cup salt
1 tablespoon oil
Food coloring (optional)

Stir all ingredients together, and cook over medium-high heat for 5 minutes or until the right consistency. Store in a plastic bag or airtight container.

Changes in Your Hands Play Dough
2 cups baking soda
1/2 cup water
1 cup cornstarch

Add soda and starch to water. Mix with fork until smooth. Boil mixture over medium heat for 1 minute or until it thickens. Spoon onto wax paper or plate until it cools. This dough will respond to the warmth of the hands and will change as the child works with it. If the play dough is still soft and a little sticky, it is too fresh. Provide time for it to cool slightly.

Easy Play Dough
3/4 cup water
1/4 cup salt
1 1/2 teaspoons oil
1 tablespoon alum
Food coloring
1 cup flour

Mix salt and water and bring to full rolling boil. Set on a cooling rack. Stir in oil, alum, and food coloring.

Recipes for Doughs and Clays (Continued)

Quickly mix in flour and knead.

Cookie Cutter Play Dough

2 cups flour
1/2 cup salt
1/2 plus 1/4 cup water

Mix flour and salt in a bowl. Add 1/2 cup water and stir for a few minutes. Slowly add 1/4 cup water while turning dough in a bowl. Form dough into a ball. Knead for 5 minutes. Shape dough into desired shapes, adding enough water to join pieces together, or use cookie cutters. Bake at 250 degrees for 15–30 minutes until hard. Let cool completely. Paint with acrylic paints.

Cornstarch Play Dough

1/2 cup salt
1/4 cup water
1 cup cornstarch
Food coloring

Mix ingredients thoroughly and cook over low heat, stirring constantly until it forms a lump. Add food coloring of desired color.

Creamy Play Dough

2 cups flour
Water
2 cups salt

Mix flour and salt. Add enough water to make a creamy consistency. Add powdered paint or other coloring.

Crêpe Paper Clay

1 cup crêpe paper clippings (one color)

1 cup warm water
1/2 to 2/3 cup non-self-rising wheat flour

Cut crêpe paper very finely. Place clippings in bowl and cover with water. Set aside for several hours until soft. Pour off excess water. Add 1/2 cup flour and stir thoroughly. Pour onto floured board and knead. Add flour until mixture is like a piecrust.

Fun Play Dough

2 cups water
1/2 cup salt
Food coloring or tempera paints
2 tablespoons oil
2 cups flour
2 tablespoons alum

Combine water, salt, and coloring, and boil until salt is dissolved. While very hot, mix in oil, alum, and flour. Knead until smooth. Store in airtight container.

Indefinitely Pliable Play Dough

1 cup salt
3/4 cup water
1/2 cup cornstarch

Mix cold ingredients on top of a double boiler, preferably with a wooden spoon. For colored play dough, add a few drops of food coloring. Heat over boiling water; keep stirring until balls form around the spoon. Cover with a damp cloth until cool enough to handle, then

work into a smooth ball. This hardens in the air but keeps pliable indefinitely in a plastic bag in the refrigerator. It can be formed into shapes and painted when hard.

Kool-Aid Play Dough #1

1 cup sifted flour
3 tablespoons oil
1/2 cup salt
1 package Kool-Aid (unsweetened)
1 cup boiling water

Mix flour, salt, oil, and Kool-Aid. Add boiling water. Stir together. Knead mixture until it forms into a soft dough.

Kool-Aid Play Dough #2

2 1/2 cups flour
2 packages unsweetened Kool-Aid
3 tablespoons vegetable oil
1/2 cup salt
1/2 teaspoon alum
2 cups boiling water

Mix flour, Kool-Aid, salt, oil, and alum. Stir in water. Knead.

Microwave Play Dough

2 cups flour
1 cup salt
1/2 cup cornstarch
1 tablespoon alum
2 cups water
Food coloring
1 tablespoon cooking oil

Add the oil, water, and food coloring and mix thoroughly. Microwave 4 1/2 to 5 minutes until thick, stirring every minute. Cool mixture. Knead on table, knead in color.

Salt Modeling Clay

1 cup non-self-rising wheat flour
1/2 cup salt
1 teaspoon powdered alum
1/3 to 1/2 cup water
Food coloring

Combine flour, salt, and alum in a bowl. Add water a little at a time, and stir into the flour mixture until it is like piecrust dough. Knead until dough is thoroughly mixed and has a smooth consistency. This clay is white.

Sand and Cornstarch Play Dough

1 cup sand
1/2 cup cornstarch
1 teaspoon powdered alum
3/4 cup hot water
Food coloring if desired

Mix sand, cornstarch, and alum. Add hot water, stirring vigorously. Add food coloring if desired. Cook over medium heat until thick, stirring constantly.

Stretch Play Dough

1 cup liquid starch
2 cups white glue
Food coloring

Mix ingredients in a bowl. Knead with hands until smooth. Food coloring may be added with starch. Store in covered container.

Goop

2 cups salt
1 cup cornstarch
1 cup water

Cook salt and 1/2 cup water for 4–5 minutes. Remove from heat. Add cornstarch and 1/2 cup water. Return to heat. Stir until mixture thickens. Store goop in plastic bag.

FEET

Purpose
walking
hopping
running
jumping
skipping
balance

Parts
toes
toenails
sole
heel
bones
ligaments
muscles

Care
keep feet clean and dry
cut toenails when needed
wear correctly fitting
footwear

Coverings

shoes　　socks　　boots　　slippers　　　　sports

sandals　　　　　　rain　　　　　roller skates, roller blades

slip-on shoes　　　snow　　　　　ice skates, golf shoes

Velcro® closure shoes　hiking　　water shoes, football shoes

tie shoes　　　　　cowboy　　　　baseball shoes

buckle shoes　　　ski　　　　　　tennis shoes

ballet shoes

Theme Goals

Through participating in the experiences provided by this theme, the children may learn:

1. Parts of the foot
2. Ways to take care of feet
3. Coverings worn on the feet
4. Purpose of feet

Concepts for the Children to Learn

1. Our feet help us balance while standing.
2. Our feet also help us to walk, hop, skip, run, jump, and dance.
3. There are six parts to our feet.
4. Toe, toenails, sole, heel, bones, ligaments, and muscles are all parts of our feet.
5. Feet need special care.
6. Our feet need to be kept clean and dry.
7. Toenails need to be cut.
8. Footwear should fit the feet.
9. There are many types of coverings for our feet.
10. Socks, slippers, shoes, boots, and sports shoes are all coverings for our feet.
11. There are many types of shoes.
12. Sandals, slip-on, Velcro closure, tie, and buckled are different types of shoes.
13. Cowboy, hiking, snow, and rain are types of boots.
14. Special footwear is worn for some sports and activities.
15. Roller skates and ice skates can also cover our feet.
16. Golf, water, football, tennis, and ballet shoes are also coverings for our feet.

Vocabulary

1. **cobbler**—a person who mends shoes.
2. **foot**—end part of the leg, on which a person stands.
3. **footwear**—covering for the feet. Shoes, slippers, boots, and sandals are footwear.
3. **podiatrist**—foot doctor.
4. **shoe**—a covering for the foot.
5. **sole**—bottom of the foot.
6. **toe**—a digit at the end of the foot.
7. **toenail**—a nail that grows on the end of each toe.

Bulletin Board

The purpose of this bulletin board is to develop beginning graphing skills. Create this bulletin board by drawing a buckle shoe, slip-on shoe, Velcro closure shoe, and tie shoe. Decorate each shoe as desired. Cut out tagboard squares and print a child's name on each one. Laminate all pieces. Staple each shoe to the left side of the bulletin board. Attach a row of pushpins to the right of each shoe. As each child arrives, he or she can hang a name card in the row that corresponds with the shoe type he or she is wearing that day. After all name cards have been placed on the bulletin board, count the number of shoes in each row. Which has more? Which has less?

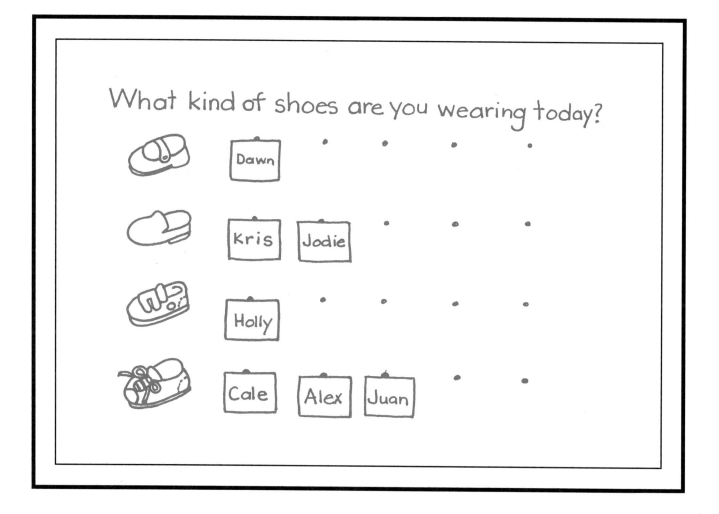

Family Letter

Dear Families,

Did you know that the human foot has 26 bones—14 of which are in the toes? No wonder your feet can ache at the end of a long day! This week we will learn the purpose and parts of our feet. We will also learn about foot care and coverings.

At School

During this busy week, we will:

- Make prints of our feet with paint!
- Find matching pairs of socks (sounds like doing laundry, doesn't it?)
- Experiment with various shoe fasteners—such as laces, buckles, and Velcro
- Look at footwear worn for different activities, including relaxing, sports, and cold weather

At Home

To reinforce the concepts of this unit at home, go on a "shoe hunt" with your child. Count the number of shoes each family member has. Count the total number of shoes and boots in your house. How many have laces? How many are slip-on shoes? Do any have Velcro® or buckles? How many are worn indoors? Which ones are worn outdoors? Also, have your child help with the laundry. He or she can help by finding matching pairs of socks and distributing them to the person who wears them!

Have a nice week!

Arts and Crafts

1. Foot Painting
Set out different colors of tempera paint in trays on the floor. The children can take turns dipping a bare foot (or feet) in the paint and then stepping on butcher or construction paper, creating footprints. Have buckets of warm soapy water and towels nearby to assist in the clean-up process.

2. Sock Puppets
Collect clean discarded socks, yarn, buttons, fabric scraps, pompons, and glue. Place materials on the art table. Children can use the supplies to design sock puppets.

3. Shoebox Art
Save shoeboxes of various sizes. Place the boxes on the art table with construction paper, markers, crayons, glue, and craft odds and ends. Children can use the materials to design creations of their choice.

4. Shoelace Painting
Provide containers of paint, paper, and shoelaces. The children can apply the paint to the paper using the shoelaces as painting tools.

5. Shoe Prints
On the art table, place a few discarded shoes, trays of paint, and construction paper. Children can dip the soles of the shoes in the paint and then press on paper, creating a print of the shoe.

Cooking

Foot French Toast
2 eggs, slightly beaten
1 tablespoon sugar
1/2 teaspoon salt
1/4 teaspoon cinnamon
1/2 cup milk
2 tablespoons margarine or butter
6 slices of bread

Cut slices of bread into sock or foot shapes. Heat griddle or frying pan to medium heat (340 degrees). Combine the first five ingredients in a shallow bowl. Melt margarine on griddle. Dip bread in egg mixture, coating both sides. Cook about 4 minutes on each side or until golden brown. Serve with maple syrup or powdered sugar.

Dramatic Play

Shoe Store
Collect a variety of shoes, shoeboxes, pictures of shoes, rulers, a cash register, and play money. Arrange materials and chairs in the dramatic play area to resemble a shoe store.

Field Trips and Resource People

1. Shoe Store
Plan a trip to a shoe store. Note the selection and variety of sizes. Which shoes are worn for special activities or sports?

2. Podiatrist
Make arrangements for the children to visit a podiatrist's office. What special equipment does the doctor have to take care of feet?

Fingerplays and Chants

I Clap My Hands
I clap my hands,
  (clap)
I touch my feet,
  (touch feet)
I jump up from the ground.
  (jump)
I clap my hands,
  (clap)
I touch my feet,
  (touch feet)
And turn myself around
  (turn around)

I clap my hands,
  (clap)
I touch my feet,
  (touch feet)
I sit myself right down,
  (sit on floor)
I clap my hands,
  (clap)
I touch my feet,
  (touch feet)
I do not make a sound.

I Am a Cobber

I am a cobbler,
  (point to self)
And this is what I do:
Rap-tap-a-tap
To mend my shoe.
  (pound fist into palm of other hand)

Night Time

Before I jump into my bed,
  (jump)
Before I dim the light,
  (pretend to turn light off)
I put my shoes together,
  (put hands together)
So they can talk at night.
I'm sure they would be lonesome,
If I tossed one here and there,
  (move one hand to right—one hand to left)
So I put them close together,
  (put hands together)
For they're a friendly pair.

Shiny Shoes

First I loosen mud and dirt,
  (pretend to brush off dirt)
My shoes I then rub clean.
  (rubbing motion)
For shoes in such a dreadful sight,
Never should be seen.
  (move hands behind back)
Next I spread the polish on,
  (slow, rubbing motion)
And then I let it dry.
I brush, and brush, and brush, and brush.
  (brushing motion)
How those shoes shine! Oh, my!
  (extend hand and smile)

Walking in the Snow

Let's go walking in the snow,
  (walking motion with legs)

Walking, walking, on tiptoe.
  (tiptoe)
Lift your one foot way up high,
  (lift one foot)
Then the other to keep it dry.
  (lift other foot)
All around the yard we skip,
  (skip)
Watch your step or you might slip.
  (pretend to slip)

Two Little

Two little feet go tap, tap, tap.
  (tap feet on floor)
Two little hands go clap, clap, clap.
  (clap)
A quiet leap up from a chair,
  (jump)
Two little arms reach high in the air.
  (raise hands above head)
Two little feet go jump, jump, jump.
  (hop)
Two little fists go thump, thump, thump.
  (pound fists)
One little body goes round, round, round.
  (turn around)
And one little child sits quietly down.
  (sit down)

This Little Piggy

This little piggy went to market.
  (touch big toe)
This little piggy stayed home.
  (touch second toe)
This little piggy had roast beef.
  (touch third toe)
This little piggy had none.
  (touch fourth toe)
And this little piggy cried, "Wee, wee, wee,"
All the way home.
  (touch little toe)

Group Time
(Games and Language)

1. **"One, Two, Buckle My Shoe"**
    (Using teacher-made materials or commercially available pictures, teach or review this nursery rhyme with the children. Upon mastery of the rhyme, encourage children to act it out.)

One, two, buckle my shoe.
Three, four, shut the door.
Five, six, pick up sticks.
Seven, eight, lay them straight.
Nine, ten, a big fat hen.

2. **"Cobbler, Cobbler, Mend My Shoe"**
(To play the game, have the children sit in a circle formation. Select one child to be the cobbler and sit in the center with his or her eyes closed. The children in the circle pass a shoe around as they chant the following nursery rhyme.)

Cobbler, cobbler, mend my shoe.
Have it done by half past two.
Stitch it up and stitch it down.
Now see with whom the shoe is found.

(When the chant is finished, the shoe is no longer passed. At this point, all children in the circle put their hands behind their backs. Then the "cobbler" opens his or her eyes and tries to guess who has the shoe.)

Large Muscle

1. **Feet Movement**
Have the children think of movements and activities that require their feet, such as walking, running, skipping, hopping (on one foot, two feet), and jumping. Practice these movements outdoors or in a large indoor area.

2. **Follow the Footprints**
Cut foot shapes out of construction paper. Place them on the floor, and have children follow the paper footprint trail.

Math

1. **Sock Sort**
Collect pairs of clean socks of a variety of sizes, materials, and colors. Place the socks in a laundry basket. Children can find matching pairs of socks.

2. **Shoe Seriation**
Collect shoes of various sizes. Encourage the children to put the shoes in order by size from smallest to largest.

3. **How Many Footsteps?**
Have the children count how many footsteps it takes to get from a designated beginning spot (such as a chair) to the window. How many footsteps does it take to reach the door? The sink? The calendar? If appropriate, record the information on a chart and compare results.

Music

1. **"Tie Your Shoes"**
(Sing to the tune of "Row Your Boat")

Tie, tie, tie your shoes.
Pull the laces tight.
Make two loops and twist them 'round.
Until you've got it right!

2. **"What Are You Wearing on Your Feet?"**
(Sing to the tune of "Mary Had a Little Lamb")
(Insert child's name and footwear as appropriate)

What are you wearing on your feet,
On your feet, on your feet?
What are you wearing on your feet,
On your feet today?
Tony is wearing tie shoes,
Tie shoes, tie shoes.
Tony is wearing tie shoes
On his feet today.
Suzanne is wearing buckle shoes …
Chandler is wearing hiking boots …

3. **"I Have Something Very Special"**
(Sing to the tune of "She'll Be Coming 'Round the Mountain")

I have something very special on my legs,
They are right at the very end of my legs.
They help me walk and run,
They help me jump and hop.
Have you guessed what's very special?
They're my feet!

Science

1. **Foot X-Rays**
   Contact the local hospital radiation department and ask to borrow X-rays of feet. In the classroom, hold the X-rays up to a light source and let the children observe the many bones of a foot.

2. **Animal Tracks**
   With the children, look for animal tracks in the soil, sand, or snow. Use reference books to try to identify the animal that created the prints.

Sensory

Sensory Walk
Collect several plastic washtubs. Fill each with a few inches of various materials such as water, dry oats, cornmeal, rocks, sand, birdseed, cotton balls, and so on. Have the children remove their shoes and socks and get in a line formation. Place the buckets on the floor, and have the children follow the "leader" as he or she walks carefully through the tubs of materials. How did each feel on their feet?

Social Studies

Footwear of Long Ago
Borrow old shoes and boots from a local museum, historical society, or theater group. Have the children make comparisons of footwear worn long ago and today's footwear. What materials were used to make the boots and shoes? What kinds of fasteners were used?

Books

The following books can be used to complement this theme:

Badt, Karin Luisa. (1994). *On Your Feet!* Chicago: Children's Press.

Binch, Caroline. (2001). *Silver Shoes.* New York: DK Publishing.

Blessing, Charlotte. (2009). *New Old Shoes.* Illustrated by Gary R. Phillips. Raynham Center, MA: Pleasant St. Press.

Brown, Jonathan A. (2007). *Animal Feet and Legs.* Milwaukee, WI: Weekly Reader Early Library.

Burgard, Anna Marlis. (2005). *Flying Feet: A Story of Irish Dance.* San Francisco: Chronicle Books.

Carle, Eric. (1997). *From Head to Toe.* New York: HarperCollins.

Cleary, Beverly. (1997). *The Growing-Up Feet.* New York: Mulberry Books.

Craig, Lindsey. (2010). *Dancing Feet!* Illustrated by Marc Brown. New York: Alfred A. Knopf.

Daniels, Teri, and Travic Foster. (1999). *The Feet in the Gym.* New York: Winslow Press.

Defelice, Cynthia C., and Robert Andrew Parker. (2000). *Cold Feet.* New York: DK Publishing.

DeGezelle, Terri. (2006). *Taking Care of My Hands and Feet.* Mankato, MN: Capstone Press.

Dolenz, Micky. (2006). *Gakky Two-Feet.* Illustrated by David Clark. New York: Putnam.

Ellis, Sarah. (2006). *The Queen's Feet.* Illustrated by Dusan Petricic. Calgary, AB: Red Deer Press.

Emerson, Scott, and Howard Post. (1999). *The Magic Boots.* Layton, UT: Gibbs Smith.

Hall, Peg. (2003). *Whose Feet Are These? A Look at Hooves, Paws, and Claws.* Illustrated by Ken Landmark. Minneapolis, MN: Picture Window Books.

Hayles, Marsha. (2009). *Bunion Burt.* Illustrated by Jack E. Davis. New York: Margaret K. McElderry.

Hess, Nina. (2004). *Whose Feet?* Illustrated by John Kanzler. New York: Random House.

Keeler, Patricia. (2006). *Drumbeat in Our Feet.* New York: Lee & Low Books.

Knowlton, Laurie Lazzaro. (1995). *Why Cowboys Sleep with Their Boots On.* Gretna, LA: Pelican.

Lynch, Wayne. (2003). *Whose Feet Are These?* Milwaukee, WI: Gareth Stevens.

May, Kara, and Jonathon Allen. (2000). *Joe Lion's Big Boots.* New York: Larousse Kingfisher Chambers.

Morris, Ann. (1998). *Shoes, Shoes, Shoes.* New York: Mulberry Books.

Murphy, Stuart. (1996). *A Pair of Socks.* Illustrated by Lois Ehlert. New York: HarperCollins.

O'Brien, Claire. (1997). *Sam's Sneaker Search.* Illustrated by Charles Fuge. New York: Simon & Schuster.

Pearson, Susan. (2005). *Hooray for Feet!* Illustrated by Roxanna Baer-Block. Maplewood, NJ: Blue Apple Books.

Pearson, Susan. (2008). *Feet Are Neat!* Maplewood, NJ: Begin Smart Books.

Perkins, Wendy. (2007). *Let's Look at Animal Feet.* Mankato, MN: Pebble Plus.

Posner, Pat. (2002). *Princess Fidgety Feet.* Bel Air, CA: Brighter Child.

Quinlan, Patricia, and Linda Hendry. (1996). *Baby's Feet.* Willowdale, ON: Annick Press.

Rayner, Catherine. (2008). *Harris Finds His Feet.* Intercourse, PA: Good Books.

Rosenthal, Betsy R. (2010). *Which Shoes Would You Choose?* Illustrated by Nancy Cote. New York: G.P. Putnam's Sons.

Salzmann, Mary Elizabeth. (2008). *What Has Webbed Feet?* Edina, MN: ABDO.

Sayre, April Pulley, and Jeff Sayre. (2003). *One Is a Snail, Ten Is a Crab: A Counting by Feet Book.* Illustrated by Randy Cecil. Cambridge, MA: Candlewick Press.

Seuss, Dr. (1996). *Foot Book.* New York: Random House.

Simmons, Jane. (2001). *Daisy: The Little Duck with Big Feet.* Boston: Little, Brown.

Souza, D. M. (2007). *Look What Feet Can Do.* Minneapolis, MN: Lerner Publications.

Stevenson, James. (2004). *Flying Feet: A Mud Flat Story.* New York: Greenwillow Books.

Stower, Adam. (2004). *Two Left Feet.* Illustrated by Graham Howells. New York: Bloomsbury Children's Books.

Vail, Rachel. (2007). *Righty and Lefty: A Tale of Two Feet.* Illustrated by Matthew Cordell. New York: Scholastic.

Verdick, Elizabeth. (2004). *Feet Are Not for Kicking.* Minneapolis, MN: Free Spirit.

Technology and Multimedia

The following multimedia products can be used to complement this theme:

"Boots" [CD]. (2010). In *Best of Laurie Berkner Band.* New York: Two Tomatoes.

"Meet De Feet" [CD]. (2001). In *Fittersitters.* Long Branch, NJ: Kimbo Educational.

"Running Shoes" [CD]. (2010). In *Lots of Fun.* Atlanta, GA: Mr Greg's Musical Madness.

"Shake a Toe" [CD]. (1996). In *Rise and Shine.* Cambridge, MA: Rounder/UMGD.

"Something in my Shoe" [CD]. (1996). In *Rise and Shine.* Cambridge, MA: Rounder/UMGD.

"Ten Fingers and Toes" [CD]. (2001). In *Ants Wear Underpants.* New York: BizzyBum.

"Tina Took Her Tap Shoes" [CD]. (1999). *We're on Our Way.* Sherman Oaks, CA: Hap-Pal Music.

"Walk, Walk, Walk" [CD]. (1996). In *Rise and Shine.* Cambridge, MA: Rounder/UMGD.

Additional teaching resources to accompany this Theme can be found on the book's companion website. Go to www.cengagebrain.com to access the site for a variety of useful resources.

Theme 35
FIREFIGHTERS

Clothing
hats
coats
mask
boots
gloves
uniform

Job
fight fires
inspect buildings
teach fire safety
provide medical treatment

Vehicles
fire trucks
water trucks
rescue vehicles

Safety
fire drills
smoke detectors

Fire Station
garage
workroom
kitchen
sleeping room
bathrooms

Equipment
fire hydrant
fire extinguisher
hoses
nozzles
axes
ladders
telephone
communication radio

Theme Goals

Through participating in the experiences provided by this theme, the children may learn:

1. The firefighter's job
2. Clothing worn by firefighters
3. Vehicles used by firefighters
4. Firefighting equipment
5. Areas inside a fire station
6. Fire safety

Concepts for the Children to Learn

1. Men and women who fight fires are called firefighters.
2. Firefighters help keep our community safe.
3. Firefighters fight fires, inspect buildings, teach fire safety, and provide medical treatment.
4. Firefighters wear special hats and clothing.
5. Firefighters wear hats, coats, boots, masks, gloves, and uniforms.
6. The fire station has a garage, kitchen, workroom, bathrooms, and sleeping rooms.
7. The fire station has a special telephone number.
8. Firefighters have special equipment.
9. Ladders, hoses, and water are needed to fight fires.
10. Nozzles control the water.
11. The hoses are connected to the fire hydrant.
12. Firefighters have special vehicles.
13. Rescue vehicles assist in accidents.
14. Fire and water trucks are driven to fires.
15. Firefighters check buildings to make sure they are safe.
16. Firefighters teach us fire safety and may provide medical safety.
17. Fire extinguishers can be used to put out small fires.
18. Fire drills teach us what to do in case of a fire.
19. Smoke detectors warn people about fires.
20. Call 911 to report a fire.

Vocabulary

1. **firefighter**—a person whose work is to put out fires.
2. **fire alarm**—a sound that warns people about fire.
3. **fire drill**—practice for teaching people what to do in case of a fire.
4. **fire engines**—trucks carrying tools and equipment needed to fight fires.
5. **fire extinguisher**—equipment that puts out fires.
6. **fire station**—a building that provides housing for firefighters and fire trucks.
7. **helmet**—a protective hat.
8. **hose**—a tube that water flows through.

Bulletin Board

The purpose of this bulletin board is to develop an awareness of clothing worn by firefighters and to reinforce color-matching skills. Likewise, this board promotes the development of hand-eye coordination, visual discrimination, and problem-solving skills. From tagboard, construct five firefighter hats. Color each hat a different color. Then construct five firefighter boots from tagboard. Color-coordinate boots to match the hats. Laminate all of the pieces. Staple hats in two rows across the top of the bulletin board as illustrated. Staple boots in a row across the bottom of the bulletin board. Affix matching yarn to each hat. Children can match each hat to its correspondingly colored boot by winding the string around a pushpin in the top of the boot.

Family Letter

Dear Families,

Because next week is Fire Prevention Week, we have decided that it would be fun and educational to focus on some very important community helpers—firefighters. The children will become more aware of the role of the firefighter, the clothing worn by firefighters, and the fire station. We will also learn how to use the telephone to call the emergency fire number.

At School

We have many activities planned for this unit! On Monday, we will paint a large box to create our own fire engine to use during the week in the dramatic play area. On Tuesday, a real fire engine will visit the parking lot so the children can see how many tools firefighters need to take along on the job. We'll also be making fire helmets and practicing our fire drill procedures.

At Home

To ensure your family's safety, talk with your child about what would happen in the event of a fire in your house. You can do this calmly, without frightening your child. Practice taking a fire escape route from the child's bedroom, the playroom, the kitchen, and other rooms of your house. Establish a meeting place so that family members can go to the same location in the event of a fire.

Enjoy your child as you share the importance of safety in the event of a fire.

Arts and Crafts

1. **Firefighters' Hats**
   Provide materials for the children to make fire hats. The hats can be decorated with foil, crayons, or paint. The emergency number 911 may be printed on the crown.

2. **Charcoal Drawings**
   Provide real charcoal at the easels to be used as an application tool.

3. **Crayon Melting**
   Place wax crayons and paper on the art table for the children to create a design during self-initiated or self-directed play. Place a clean sheet of paper over the picture. Apply a warm iron. Show the children the effect of heat. This activity needs to be carefully supervised. The caption "crayon melting" may be printed on a bulletin board. On the board, place the children's pictures, identifying each by name in the upper-left corner.

Cooking

Firehouse Baked Beans
   Purchase canned baked beans. To the beans, add cut-up hot dogs, cut lengthwise, and extra ketchup. Heat and serve for snack.

Dramatic Play

1. **Firefighters**
   Place firefighting clothes such as hats, boots, and coats for children to wear. Sometimes fire station personnel will allow schools to borrow some of their clothing and equipment. Also, provide a bell to use as an alarm. To extend play, a vacuum cleaner hose or a length of garden hose can be included to represent a water hose.

2. **Fire Truck**
   A fire truck can be cut from a cardboard refrigerator box. The children may want to paint the box yellow or red. A steering wheel and chairs may be added.

Field Trips and Resource People

1. **Fire Station**
   Take a trip to a fire station. Observe the clothing worn by firefighters, the building, the vehicles, and the tools.

2. **Firefighter**
   Invite a firefighter to bring a fire truck to your school. Ask the firefighter to point out the special features such as the hose, siren, ladders, light, and special clothing kept on the truck. If permissible and safe, let the children climb onto the truck.

Fingerplays and Chants

The Firefighter
   This brave firefighter is going to bed.
      (hold up right thumb)
   Down on the pillow he lays his head.
      (place right thumb on left palm)
   He wraps himself in a blanket tight
      (curl fingers around thumb)
   And wants to sleep this way all night.
      (close eyes)
   But the fire alarm rings! He opens his eyes!
      (open eyes wide)
   Quickly he's dressed and down the pole he slides.
      (right hand slides down left arm in a grip motion)
   Then he climbs on the truck, to the fire he goes. (hands grip imaginary steering wheel)
   Out goes the fire with water from a hose.
      (pretend to hold hose and spray)

Ten Little Firefighters
   Ten little firefighters
   Sleeping in a row:
      (extend both hands, showing fingers)
   Ding, dong, goes the fire bell,

(shake fire bell with one hand)
And down the pole they go.
　(make fists and place on top of each
　other to slide down the pole)
Turn the engine on, oh, oh, oh
　(pretend steering the fire truck)
Using the big hose, so, so, so.
　(pretend holding hosing and aiming
　at fire)
When the fire is out, home so slow.
　(pretending steering fire truck)
Back to bed, all in a row.
　(extend both hands, showing fingers
　again)

Group Time
(Games and Language)

Language Experience
Review safety rules. Write the rules on a large piece of paper. These rules can also be included in a family letter as well as posted in the classroom.

Large Muscle

1. **Firefighter's Workout**
Lead children in a firefighter's workout. Do exercises such as jumping jacks, knee bends, leg lifts, and running in place. Ask children why they think firefighters need to be in good physical condition for their job.

2. **Obstacle Course**
Make an obstacle course. Let children follow a string or piece of tape under chairs or tables, over steps, and across ladders. This activity can be planned for indoors or outdoors.

Math

1. **Sequencing**
Cut a piece of rubber tubing into various lengths. The children can sequence the pieces from shortest to longest.

2. **Emergency Number**
If developmentally appropriate, teach the children how to dial a local emergency number using play telephones. Above the phones, post a large chart containing the emergency number(s).

Music

"Down by the Station"
Down by the station early in the morning
See the great big fire trucks all in a row.
Hear the jangly fire bell sound a loud alarm
　now—
Chug chug, clang clang, off we go!

Science

"Fire" Paintings
Provide red and yellow paint. Invite children to experiment mixing the colors with their hands. What did they observe? The finished paintings can be "fires."

Sensory

1. Fill the sensory table with water. Provide cups and rubber tubing to resemble hoses and funnels.

2. Place sand in the sensory table. Add fire engines, firefighter dolls, craft sticks to make fences, and blocks to make buildings or houses.

Social Studies

1. **Safety Rules**
Discuss safety rules dealing with fire. Let children generate ideas about safety. Write their ideas on chart paper and display. Discuss why fire drills are a good idea. Practice "Stop, drop, and roll" procedures.

2. Fire Inspection Tour

Tour the classroom or building looking for fire extinguishers, emergency fire alarm boxes, and exits.

3. Fire Drill

Schedule a fire drill. Before the drill, talk to the children about fire drill procedures.

 **Books**

The following books can be used to complement this theme:

Armentrout, David, and Patricia Armentrout. (2009). *The Fire Department*. Vero Beach, FL: Rourke Publishing.

Bingham, Caroline. (2003). *Fire Truck*. New York: DK Publishing.

Boelts, Maribeth, and Terry Widener. (2004). *The Firefighters' Thanksgiving*. New York: Putnam's.

Bond, Felicia. (2003). *Poinsettia and the Firefighters*. New York: HarperCollins.

Clemesha, David, and Andrea Griffing Zimmerman. (2007). *Fire Engine Man*. New York: Henry Holt.

Clemson, David, and Wendy Clemson. (2007). *Firefighters to the Rescue*. Milwaukee, WI: Gareth Stevens.

Cuyler, Margery, and Arthur Howard. (2001). *Stop, Drop, and Roll (A Book about Fire Safety)*. Illustrated by Arthur Howard. New York: Simon & Schuster.

Demarest, Chris L. (2000). *Firefighters A to Z*. New York: Margaret K. McElderry Books.

Gergoli, Tibor. (2003). *The Great Big Fire Engine Book*. New York: Random/Golden.

Goodwin, Laura. (2009). *This Is the Firefighter*. New York: Disney Hyperion Books.

Graham, Thomas. (2008). *Five Little Firefighters*. New York: H. Holt.

Grambling, Lois G. (2007). *My Mom Is a Firefighter*. New York: HarperCollins.

Hamilton, K. R. (2005). *Firefighters to the Rescue!* Illustrated by Rich Davis. New York: Viking.

Harper, Jamie. (2009). *Miss Mingo and the Fire Drill*. Somerville, MA: Candlewick Press.

Hayward, Linda. (2001). *A Day in a Life of a Firefighter*. New York: Dorling Kindersley.

Hubbell, Patricia. (2007). *Firefighters! Speeding! Spraying! Saving!* Tarrytown, NY: Cavendish Children.

Jacobs, Paul DuBois, and Jennifer Swender. (2010). *Fire Drill*. Illustrated by Huy Voun Lee. New York: Henry Holt.

Johnson, Stephen. (2009). *My Little Red Fire Truck*. New York: Simon & Schuster Books for Young Readers.

Klein, Adria F. (2009). *Max Goes to the Fire Station*. Illustrated by Mernie Gallagher-Cole. Minneapolis, MN: Picture Window Books.

Kole MacLean, Christine. (2002), *Even Firefighters Hug Their Moms*. New York: Dutton Children's Books.

Kottke, Jan (2000). *A Day with Firefighters*. New York: Children's Press.

Liebman, Dan, (1999). *I Want to Be a Firefighter*. Buffalo, NY: Firefly Books.

Lindeen, Carol K. (2005). *Fire Trucks*. Mankato, MN: Capstone Press.

MacLean, Christine Cole. (2002). *Even Firefighters Hug Their Moms*. New York: Dutton Children's Books.

Meyer, Sandra E. (2005). *Buddy Goes to the Fire Station*. Illustrated by Deanne Hooker. Bloomington, IN: Trafford Publishing.

Murphy, Stuart J. (2003). *3 Little Firefighters*. Illustrated by Bernice Lum. New York: HarperCollins.

Owen, Ann. (2004). *Protecting Your Home: A Book about Firefighters*. Illustrated by Eric Thomas. Minneapolis, MN: Picture Window Books.

Rey H. A., and Margret Rey. (2004). *Curious George and the Firefighters*. Boston: Houghton Mifflin.

Schuh, Mari. (2009). *Fireboats in Action*. Mankato, MN: Capstone Press.

Schuh, Mari. (2009). *Fire Safety in Action*. Mankato, MN: Capstone Press.

Schuh, Mari. (2009). *Fire Stations in Action*. Mankato, MN: Capstone Press.

Schuh, Mari. (2009). *Fire Trucks in Action*. Mankato, MN: Capstone Press.

Slater, Dashka. (2006). *Firefighters in the Dark.* Illustrated by Nicoletta Ceccoli. Boston: Houghton Mifflin.

Spanyol, Jessica. (2008). *Clemence and His Noisy Little Fire Engine.* Cambridge, MA: Candlewick Press.

Tourville, Amanda Doerring. (2009). *Fire Trucks.* Edina, MN: Magic Wagon.

Wax, Wendy, and Naomi Wax. (2008). *Even Firefighters Go to the Potty.* Illustrated by Stephen Gilpin. New York: Simon & Schuster.

Whiting, Sue. (2008). *The Firefighters.* Illustrated by Donna Rawlins. Cambridge, MA: Candlewick Press.

Technology and Multimedia

The following multimedia products can be used to complement this theme:

"Drive the Fire Truck" [CD]. (2010). In *Songs for Wiggleworms.* Chicago: Bloodshot Records.

"Firefighter" [CD]. (2008). In *Songs for the Whole Day.* Nashville, TN: Lamon Records.

Fire Songs and Safety Tips [DVD]. (2008). Barrington, ILL: Marshall Publishing and Promotions.

Lights and Ladders [DVD]. (2007). Dallas, TX: NCircle Entertainment.

Spend a Day with Firefighters [DVD]. (2003). Century City, CA: First Look Home Entertainment.

"Stop, Drop and Roll" [CD]. (2006). In *The Big Silly with Mr. Eric.* Atlanta, GA: Mr. Eric.

What I Want to Be! [DVD]. (2002). Los Angeles, CA: Image Entertainment.

Additional teaching resources to accompany this Theme can be found on the book's companion website. Go to www.cengagebrain.com to access the site for a variety of useful resources.

FISH

Size
small
medium
large
very large

Habitat
lakes
oceans
ponds
rivers
fish farms
aquariums

Foods
insects
snails
worms
other fish
fish food
cornmeal

Colors
blue
brown
gray
black
orange
white
red
yellow
green

Kinds
northern pike
sea horse
salmon
trout
lobster
guppy
catfish
shark
eel

Parts
eyes
fins
gills
scales
mouth
tail

Importance
food
entertainment
sports
pets

Theme Goals

Through participating in the experiences provided by this theme, the children may learn:

1. Homes for fish
2. The importance of fish
3. Colors of fish
4. Foods for fish
5. Kinds of fish
6. Sizes of fish
7. Parts of fish

Concepts for the Children to Learn

1. A fish is an animal that lives in the water.
2. Most fish have two eyes, fins, gills, scales, a mouth, and a tail.
3. Fish vary in size.
4. There are small, medium-sized, large, and very large fish.
5. There are many colors of fish.
6. Blue, brown, gray, white, black, red, yellow, green, and orange are some of the colors of fish.
7. Fish may live in lakes, oceans, ponds, rivers, fish farms, and aquariums.
8. Fish need food and water to live.
9. Insects, snails, plants, worms, fish food, smaller fish, and cornmeal are foods fish eat.
10. There are many kinds of fish.
11. Some kinds include northern pike, sea horse, guppy, catfish, shark, salmon, trout, lobster, and eel.
12. Fish are important to people.
13. Fish provide food and entertainment.
14. Fishing can be a sport.

Vocabulary

1. **fish**—a fish is an animal that lives in the water.
2. **fin**—the part that moves to help fish swim.
3. **fish farm**—a place to raise fish for food.
4. **gills**—the part of the fish's body that helps it get air.
5. **scales**—skin covering of fish and other reptiles.
6. **school**—a group of fish.
7. **tail**—the end body part that helps fish move.

Bulletin Board

The purpose of this bulletin board is to promote identification of written numerals, as well as match a set to a written numeral. To prepare the bulletin board, begin by drawing and cutting fish shapes from construction paper. Decorate the fish as desired, and print a numeral on each fish. Make another set of identical fish shapes from black construction paper to create fish "shadows." Cut small circles out of white construction paper to represent the fishes' air bubbles. Staple the fish shadows to the bulletin board. Above each fish shadow, staple a set of air bubbles. Children can then match the numerals on the fish to the corresponding set of air bubbles. The fish can be attached to the bulletin board with pushpins or small adhesive magnet pieces.

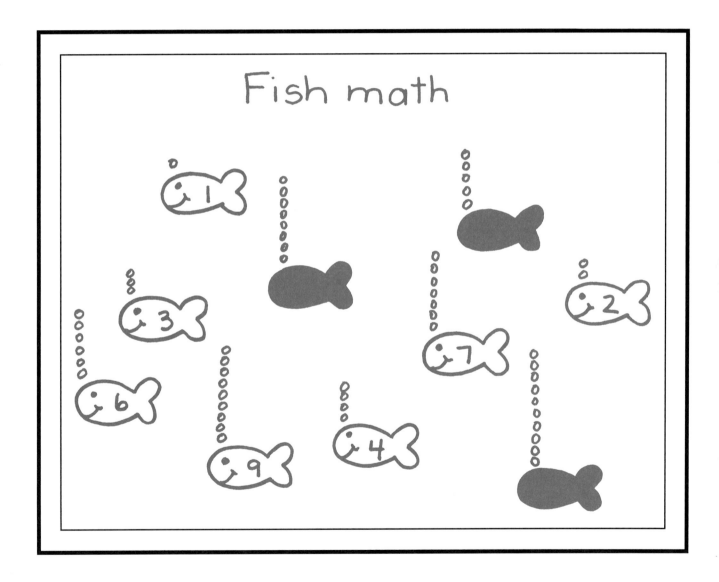

Family Letter

Dear Families,

Our next theme will focus on fish. Through participating in the experiences provided by this theme, the children will learn the color, size, kinds, and parts of a fish. They will also learn where fish live and the role fish play in our lives.

At School

Learning experiences that have been planned to complement this theme include:

- Visiting a pet store to observe different types and colors of fish. We will also purchase fish to bring back to our classroom.

- Listening to the story *Fish Eyes* by Lois Ehlert

- Sorting, counting, and eating various fish-shaped crackers

- Fishing in the dramatic play area

- Observing minnows at the sensory table

At Home

- Prepare a tuna salad using a favorite recipe with your child.

- Point out fishing gear in the sports section of a department store or in a catalog.

- Check out children's books about fish from the library. Look for:

    Fishes by Brian Wildsmith

    Fish Is Fish and *Swimmy* by Leo Lionni

    Gone Fishing by Earlene R. Long

    A Million Fish . . . More or Less by Patricia C. McKissack

Enjoy your child as you explore experiences related to fish!

Arts and Crafts

1. **Aquarium Crayon Resist**
   After observing fish or listening to stories about them, encourage the children to use crayons to draw fish on a piece of white construction paper. Then, the children can paint over their crayon drawing with a thin wash of blue tempera or water color. The wax will repel the water paints, leaving an interesting effect.

2. **Fish Sponge Painting**
   Cut sponges into fish shapes. Place the sponges on the art table with paper and several shallow trays of paint. Use thick tempera paint the color of fish. Also provide paper. The children can make prints by dipping the sponges into the paint and then pressing them onto paper.

3. **Fish Rubbings**
   Cut fish shapes out of tagboard, adding details as desired. Place the fish shapes on the art table along with paper and crayons. The children can create designs by placing a tagboard fish beneath a piece of paper and rubbing over the top of the paper with a crayon. Repeat as discussed.

4. **Tackle Box Paint Container**
   Use a discarded, clean tackle box as a container to hold paints at the art table. Paints can be placed in individual compartments, providing several choices for the children.

Cooking

1. **Swimming Fish Snack**
   8 ounces soft cream cheese
   Blue food coloring
   1 box rectangular-shaped crackers
   2 cups small fish-shaped crackers (any flavor)

   Add a few drops of blue food coloring to the cream cheese and stir. For each serving, spread cream cheese on a large, rectangular cracker. Place a few fish-shaped crackers on top of the cream cheese.

2. **Fish Mix Snack**
   2 cups toasted oat cereal
   2 cups pretzel sticks
   2 cups small fish-shaped crackers (any flavor)
   1/4 cup melted margarine
   2 teaspoons Worcestershire sauce

   Combine oat cereal, pretzels, and fish-shaped crackers in a bowl. In a small bowl, stir together melted margarine and Worcestershire sauce. Drizzle over cereal mixture and toss to coat evenly. Transfer into a 13" × 9" baking pan and bake in a 300-degree oven for 30 minutes, stirring occasionally. Remove from oven and cool. Makes approximately six cups.

3. **Tuna Salad**
   1 can of tuna (3 1/4 ounces), drained
   1/4 cup mayonnaise, salad dressing, or plain yogurt
   1/4 cup finely chopped apple
   3 tablespoons sunflower seeds
   4 slices of bread or 2 English muffins

   Combine the tuna, mayonnaise, apple, and sunflower seeds in a bowl. Chill if desired. Toast the bread or English muffins. Spread tuna mixture on toasted muffins. Makes four servings.

4. **Tartar Sauce for Fish Sticks**
   1/2 cup mayonnaise or salad dressing
   1 tablespoon finely chopped pickle or pickle relish
   1 teaspoon dried parsley
   1/2 teaspoon grated onion or onion flakes

   Combine all ingredients and chill. Bake frozen fish sticks as directed on the package, and serve with tartar sauce.

Dramatic Play

1. **Gone Fishing**
   Set up a fishing area in the dramatic play center. Provide props such as a wooden rocking boat, a small wading pool, life vests, hats, tackle boxes, nets, and fishing poles. Fishing poles can be made by attaching string to a short dowel or paper towel tube. Tie a small magnet to the end of the string. Attach paper clips to the construction paper fish. Then, go fishing!

2. **Bait and Tackle Shop**
   Provide props to simulate a bait and tackle shop in the dramatic play area. Items can include a cash register, play money, plastic or paper fish of varying sizes, nets, fishing lures (remove hooks), tackle boxes, coolers, fishing poles, and life vests. Display pictures of fish and people fishing.

Field Trips and Resource People

1. **Lake, Pond, or Stream**
   If possible, visit a small body of water to observe a fish habitat. Watch for people fishing. (For safety purposes, the body of water will have to be carefully chosen. Likewise, additional supervision may be required.)

2. **Pet Store**
   Visit a pet store to see many types of fish as well as aquariums and fish supplies. Purchase one or more goldfish to take back to your classroom.
   Note: Water needs to be dechlorinated before placing goldfish in it.

3. **Bait and Tackle Shop**
   Make arrangements to visit a bait and tackle shop. Observe the many types of fishing poles and lures as well as boat safety items.

4. **State or National Fish Hatchery**
   These make a wonderful field trip. They also have coloring books and other activities for the children.

5. **Fish Sportsman or Sportswoman**
   Invite a parent or another person who enjoys fishing to come talk with the children. Ask the person to bring fishing gear and pictures of fishing trips and fish caught.

Fingerplays and Chants

Fish Story
> One, two, three, four, five
>   (hold up fingers while counting)
> Once I caught a fish alive.
> Six, seven, eight, nine, ten
>   (hold up additional fingers)
> Then I let it go again.
> Why did I let it go?
> Because it bit my finger so.
> Which finger did it bite?
> The little finger on the right.
>   (hold up pinky on the right hand)

Group Time
(Games and Language)

1. **Fish Memory Game**
   Collect items associated with fish and place on a tray. At group time, show the tray containing the items and name them. To play the game, cover the tray with a towel. Then ask the children to recall the names of items on the tray. To vary the game, play again, this time removing an item from the tray while covered. The children then try to name the item missing from the tray. To ensure success, begin the activity with few objects. Additional objects can be added depending on the developmental maturity of the children.

2. Go Fish!

Cut fish shapes out of various colors of construction paper. Attach a paper clip to each fish. Make a fishing pole by tying a string to a short dowel. Attach a small magnet to the end of the string. At group time, present the fishing pole and fish. Place the fish on the floor and allow the children to take turns fishing. As a fish is caught, the child removes it from the magnet and names the color. Repeat until all of the children have had a turn. The game can be varied by drawing a basic shape and printing a numeral or a letter on each fish for the children to identify.

 Math

1. Sort the Fish
Purchase a variety of small plastic fish or construct some out of tagboard. Put them in a large pail. The children can sort the fish by size, color, and type.

2. Fish Seriation and Measurement
Trace and cut fish shapes out of construction paper. Encourage the children to place them in order from smallest to largest. If developmentally appropriate, provide rulers and yardsticks for the children to measure the fish.

3. Fishbowl Math
Print numerals or sets of dots on small plastic fish. Place the fish in a clean bowl or container. The children can use small nets to take turns scooping out a fish and stating the numeral or counting the dots.

4. Fish Cracker Sort
Purchase a variety of flavors of small, fish-shaped crackers. For each child, place a few of each kind of cracker in a paper cup. Before eating the crackers, encourage the children to sort the crackers. If appropriate, the children can count the number of each cracker flavor.

 Music

1. "I'm a Little Fish"
(Sing to the tune of "I'm a Little Teapot")

I'm a little fish in the lake so blue,
There are so many things that I can do.
I can swim around with my tail and fin.
The water's fine—just jump right in.

2. "Goldfish"
(Sing to the tune of "Have You Ever Seen a Lassie?")

Have you ever seen a goldfish, a goldfish, a
  goldfish?
Have you ever seen a goldfish, just
  swimming all around?
He swims this way and that way,
And this way and that way.
Have you ever seen a goldfish, just
  swimming all around?

3. "Six Little Fish"
(Sing to the tune of "Six Little Ducks")

Six little fish that I once knew,
Fat ones, skinny ones, fair ones, too.
But the one little fish who was the leader of
  the crowd.
He led the other fish around and around.

 Science

1. Aquarium
Set up an aquarium to place on the science table. Let the children take turns feeding the fish. Provide pictures and books about fish.

2. Balance Scale
On the science table, place a balance scale and clean aquarium rocks. The children can use spoons and measuring cups to transfer the rocks into the scale containers. After this, they can experiment with the balance.

3. Fish-Tasting Party

Plan a tasting party. Prepare fish using different methods, such as baked, broiled, fried, and prepared in a casserole. The results of the children's favorite fish preparation method can be discussed and charted.

4. Worm Farm

Fill a transparent plastic container with soil. Place 6–12 worms in the container. Then wrap black paper around the container. Sprinkle corn meal or grated carrots on top of the soil.

Sensory

1. Aquarium Rocks

Place a bag of clean aquarium rocks at the sensory table. Provide cups, bowls, and pails for the children's use. Add water, if desired.

2. Plastic Fish

Purchase small plastic fish and place at the sensory table with water, strainers, and pails.

3. Minnows

Purchase minnows from a bait store. Place the minnows in a sensory table filled with cold water. Stress the importance of being gentle with the fish and follow through with limits set for the activity. After participating in this activity, the children need to wash their hands.

4. Plastic Boats

Place small plastic boats in a sensory table filled with water. Also provide small plastic people to ride in and fish from the boats.

Books

The following books can be used to complement this theme:

Babin, Claire. (2008). *Gus Is a Fish*. Illustrated by Olivier Tallec. New York: Enchanted Lion Books.

Barner, Bob. (2000). *Fish Wish*. New York: Holiday House.

Bright, Paul. (2008). *Fidgety Fish and Friends*. Illustrated by Ruth Galloway. Wilton, CT: Tiger Tales.

Bunting, Eve. (2001). *Gleam and Glow*. Illustrated by Peter Sylvada. San Diego, CA: Harcourt.

Butterworth, Chris. (2006). *Sea Horse: The Shyest Fish in the Sea*. Illustrated by John Lawrence. Cambridge, MA: Candlewick Press.

Carle, Eric. (2004). *Mister Seahorse*. New York: Philomel Books.

Carney, Margaret, and Janet Wilson. (2001). *The Biggest Fish in the Lake*. Illustrated by Janet Wilson. Toronto: Kids Can Press.

Cole, Joanna. (1997). *Magic School Bus Goes Upstream: A Book about Salmon on Migration*. Illustrated by Bruce Degen. New York: Scholastic.

Cousins, Lucy. (2005). *Hooray for Fish!* Cambridge, MA: Candlewick Press.

Cronin, Doreen. (2006). *Click, Clack, Splish, Splash: A Counting Adventure*. Illustrated by Betsy Lewin. New York: Atheneum Books for Young Readers.

Diesen, Deborah. (2008). *The Pout-Pout Fish*. Illustrated by Dan Hanna. New York: Farrar, Straus and Giroux.

Donaldson, Julia. (2008). *The Fish Who Cried Wolf*. New York: Arthur A. Levine.

Donovan, Gail. (2001). *A Fishy Story*. New York: Night Sky Books.

Ehlert, Lois. (1990). *Fish Eyes: A Book You Can Count On*. New York: Harcourt Brace.

Frazier, Craig. (2006). *Stanley Goes Fishing*. San Francisco: Chronicle Books.

Gall, Chris. (2006). *Dear Fish*. New York: Little, Brown.

Geist, Ken. (2007). *The Three Little Fish and the Big Bad Shark*. New York: Cartwheel Books/Scholastic.

Grant, Joan. (2005). *Cat and Fish*. Illustrated by Neil Curtis. Vancouver, BC: Simply Read Books.

Knox, Barbara. (2003). *Under the Sea: Counting Ocean Life*. Mankato, MN: Capstone Press.

Using the Digital Camera in the Early Childhood Classroom

In today's early childhood classrooms, the digital camera can be used effectively to help teachers reach their instructional goals. In this special section, we have included some specific examples of how digital images can be used to support classroom organization and management, curriculum planning, and parent-teacher communication. We have also included some specific examples of teacher-made classroom activities and student artifacts. Try these out in your own classrooms!

CUBBY TAGS

Artifact Goal: Classroom Management

Directions: Cubby tags can be made by taking a child's photo and adding his or her name.

Then display the tag in the child's personal cubby space for ease of recognition.

Aligns with NAEYC Teaching Standard 9: Physical Environment

naeyc

Does anything look familiar?

LOST AND FOUND POSTER

Artifact Goal: Classroom Management

Directions: Lay out lost and found items on a table. Take a picture and add a caption. Enlarge if desired. Display the photo poster on the entrance door or parents' bulletin board. As items are claimed, mark the photo poster with an "X" or remove it.

Aligns with NAEYC Teaching Standard 7: Families

naeyc

STOREROOM ORGANIZATION POSTER

Artifact Goal: Classroom Management

Directions: To help keep teaching materials organized, take a photograph of the area such as this storage cabinet. Print and post the photo nearby on a door, shelf, or bin.

Aligns with NAEYC Teaching Standard 9: Physical Environment

naeyc

TEACHER IDENTIFICATION POSTER

Artifact Goal: Classroom Management

Directions: On a piece of tagboard, insert the titles and names of all classroom personnel. Attach colored photographs and display the poster in the entrance to the classroom. If desired, add the individual teacher's credentials to the chart.

Aligns with NAEYC Teaching Standard 10: Leadership and Management

naeyc

Imagine Room

Head Teachers

Assistants

Volunteers

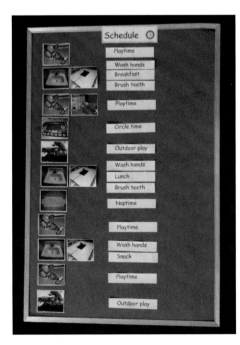

DAILY SCHEDULE CHART

Artifact Goal: Classroom Management

Directions: Using photographs that illustrate classroom routines, create your daily schedule. Add text to describe the photographs. Post at the children's eye level to provide a visual reminder of the daily classroom routine.

Aligns with NAEYC Teaching Standard 3: Teaching

naeyc

CLASSROOM RULES POSTER

Artifact Goal: Classroom Management

Directions: Take photographs to represent basic classroom rules. Mount the photographs on a piece of tagboard, and add text to provide visual clues for the children.

Aligns with NAEYC Teaching Standard 1: Relationships

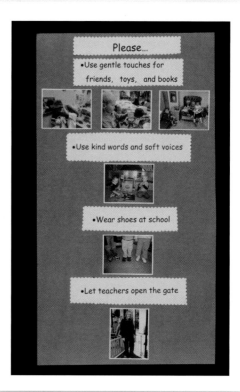

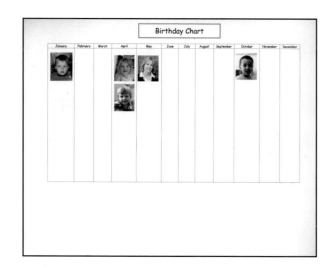

BIRTHDAY CHART

Artifact Goal: Classroom Communication

Directions: Create a chart showing the 12 months of the year. Insert photographs of the children and teachers into the month representing their birthday. Add the date of the individual's birthday on the lower right-hand side of the photograph.

Aligns with NAEYC Teaching Standard 1: Relationships

naeyc

FAMILY LETTER SAMPLE
Artifact Goal: Home-School Communication

Directions: Add interest to your family letters by inserting a variety of photographs that highlight the children's activities, introduce new classmates or teachers, and share weekly reminders.

Aligns with NAEYC Teaching Standard 7: Families

naeyc

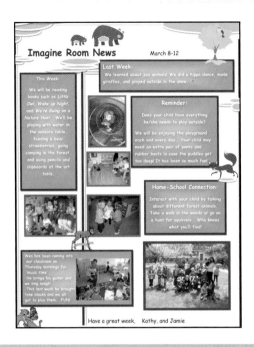

SAMPLE BULLETIN BOARDS
Artifact Goal: Classroom Display

Hats off to Children!
Directions: Display photographs of children wearing a variety of different hats. This bulletin board can be used to support a variety of themes in this book, including "Occupations," "Hats," and "Winter."

Aligns with NAEYC Teaching Standard 2: Curriculum

naeyc

Friends
Directions: Display photographs of children positively interacting with each other in various play situations. Captions could include "How do friendships develop?" or "What makes a good friend?"

Aligns with NAEYC Teaching Standard 1: Relationships

naeyc

STUDENT DIPLOMA

Artifact Goal: Classroom Memento

Directions: Using a diploma template, insert a child's picture, fill in the form, and print on cardstock paper. If desired, additional pictures can be added to highlight the child's school experiences.

Aligns with NAEYC Teaching Standard 7: Families

naeyc

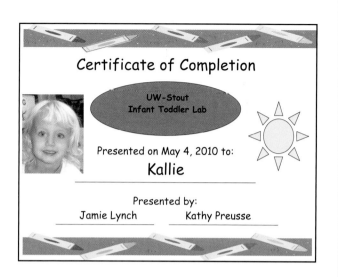

Certificate of Completion

UW-Stout
Infant Toddler Lab

Presented on May 4, 2010 to:

Kallie

Presented by:

Jamie Lynch   Kathy Preusse

PARENT OR CAREGIVER GIFTS

Artifact Goal: Classroom Memento

Directions: Photos can be used to personalize gifts throughout the year. If developmentally appropriate, allow individual children to glue on their photograph, print their name, and add the date.

Some other ideas for gifts that include photographs include:
- Winter handprint
- Spring flower
- Summer rainbow
- Fall leaf
- Valentine
- Pumpkin
- Puppet

Aligns with NAEYC Teaching Standard 7: Families

naeyc

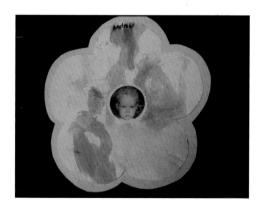

COLORFUL PUPPIES ACTIVITY

Artifact Goal: Classroom Activity

Description: Take photographs of puppies playing with different colored pieces of felt. Place each of the photographs in a transparent sheet protector. Arrange in a three-ring binder. Then insert felt pieces adjacent to the corresponding color.

Related Themes: "Colors" and "Animals"

Aligns with NAEYC Teaching Standard 3: Teaching

naeyc

ANIMAL LOTTO GAME

Artifact Goal: Classroom Activity

Directions: Photograph a variety of objects related to the current theme such as the zoo animals pictured. Print two copies of each person, animal, or object. Use one photograph to construct a game board, and the other photograph for the matching game piece. See the illustration. *Note:* There is only one row of pictures on the lotto board. Instead of covering the object when a match is found, the children are to place the matching photograph directly under it in the box provided. This strategy makes it easier for the children to identify when they have finished the game.

Aligns with NAEYC Teaching Standard 3: Teaching

naeyc

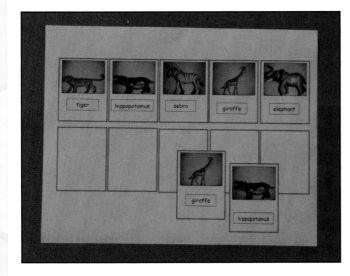

APPLE-TASTING CHART

Artifact Goal: Classroom Activity

Directions: Following an apple-tasting activity, allow the children to place their photograph in the graph column based upon their taste preference. When everyone has posted their photograph, follow up with a counting activity to identify preferences.

Related Themes: "Apples," "Birds," "Bread," "Cars," "Cats," "Dogs," "Flowers," "Fruits and Vegetables," and "Pets"

Aligns with NAEYC Teaching Standard 3: Teaching

naeyc

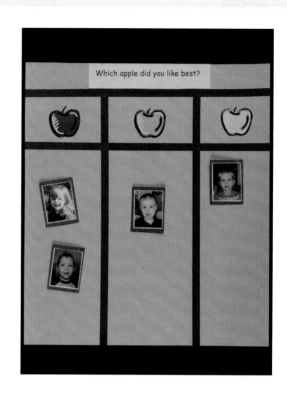

BLOCK SORT

Artifact Goal: Classroom Activity

Directions: Title a piece of tagboard "Sort the Legos." Encourage the children to play with the blocks by sorting them into groups. Take a photograph of each group of blocks, and ask the children how the blocks were sorted. Make the photograph into a card as illustrated. Post the cards on a bulletin board.

Related Themes: "Colors," "Shapes," and "Cars"

Aligns with NAEYC Teaching Standard 3: Teaching

naeyc

BUILDING BLOCKS
Artifact Goal: Classroom Activity

Directions: Take photographs of several local public buildings. Tape them to unit blocks, and add to the block area. Encourage the children to build using the blocks.

Related Themes: "Buildings," "Home," and "Occupations"

Aligns with NAEYC Teaching Standard 3: Teaching

naeyc

COOKIE JAR
Artifact Goal: Classroom Activity

Directions: Make a cookie jar from clip art, laminate it, and tape it to a metal cookie or pizza pan. Laminate cookies printed from clip art, and attach magnets to the backside. While singing, "Who took the cookies from the cookie jar?" add a child's photograph and finish the verse using his or her name

Related Themes: "Friends" and "Containers"

Aligns with NAEYC Teaching Standard 3: Teaching

naeyc

FIELD TRIP BOOKS
Artifact Goal: Classroom Activity

Directions: Take photographs during a field trip or when a resource person is invited to the classroom. Assemble the photographs into a book format (as illustrated) and add text. Using a felt-tip marker, highlight the concepts that were emphasized

Related Themes: This activity can be adapted to a variety of themes, including "Apples," "Occupations," "Buildings," "Firefighters," "Circus," "Families," "Farm," "Animals," "Gardens," "Health," "Homes," and so on.

Aligns with NAEYC Teaching Standard 3: Teaching

naeyc

FRIEND BLOCKS
Artifact Goal: Classroom Activity

Directions: Take full-body photographs of the children. Cut out the images and attach to wooden blocks as illustrated. Attach the back of a small piece of Velcro over the face on each photograph. Print out index-size faces of the children. Laminate these pieces, and attach the opposite side of the Velcro to the back. This process will allow the faces to be moved from block to block.

Related Themes: "Friends" and "Families"

Aligns with NAEYC Teaching Standards 3: Teaching

naeyc

FRIENDS LACING CARDS
Artifact Goal: Classroom Activity

Directions: Take photographs of the children playing. Make a 5- × 7-inch print or larger of each photograph. Mount on construction paper or tagboard. Laminate and punch holes around the entire photograph. Tie a shoelace in one corner.

Related Themes: Photographic lacing cards can be adapted to almost any theme.

Aligns with NAEYC Teaching Standard 3: Teaching

naeyc

LET'S GO WALKING
Artifact Goal: Classroom Activity

Directions: Take photographs of several locations along a familiar walking route. Make a map by sequencing the photographs on a heavy piece of paper. Print one map per child or small group. Take a walk, letting the children be the guides using the picture map.

Related Themes: This can be adapted to themes such as "Buildings," "Homes," and "Trees."

Aligns with NAEYC Teaching Standard 3: Teaching

naeyc

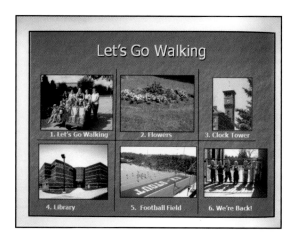

MEMORY MATCH GAME

Artifact Goal: Classroom Activity

Directions: Take photographs of several items associated with a day at school or the current theme. Print two copies of each photograph. Arrange one set of photographs on a large piece of tagboard, add a title, and laminate. The remaining photographs should be individually mounted on smaller tagboard pieces and laminated. They should be used as matching game pieces.

Aligns with NAEYC Teaching Standard 2: Curriculum

naeyc

MY NAME IS …

Artifact Goal: Classroom Activity

Directions: Construct a card using a child's photograph and name. Provide several sets of pinch-type wooden clothespins marked with alphabet letters. *Note:* One side of a clothespin should have the uppercase letter, and the other side should contain the lowercase letter. The child constructs his or her name by attaching the appropriate clothespins.

Related Themes: "Communications," "Friends," and "Mail Carrier"

Aligns with NAEYC Teaching Standard 3: Teaching

naeyc

OPEN THE BARN DOOR
Artifact Goal: Classroom Activity

Directions: Create a barn scene with a hinged door on a piece of tagboard. Attach a wheel to the back of the door that has a variety of farm animals. Give each child a turn to open the barn door, identify the animal, and demonstrate its sound. Turn the wheel after the child finishes to expose a new farm animal.

Related Themes: "Friends" and "Farm Animals"

Aligns with NAEYC Teaching Standard 3: Teaching

naeyc

PICTURE BALL GAME
Artifact Goal: Classroom Activity

Directions: Attach the back part of a Velcro piece on different parts of the ball. Use photographs of the children's faces, as illustrated, and attach to a variety of colors or shapes as game pieces. Move the ball by rolling, bouncing, or throwing from one child to another. The child catching the ball needs to identify the closest color, shape, and friend.

Related Themes: "Colors," "Shapes," "Friends," and "Valentine's Day"

Aligns with NAEYC Teaching Standard 3: Teaching

naeyc

PICTURE PUZZLES

Artifact Goal: Classroom Activity

Directions: Take photographs of several group activities. Print 8- × 10-inch photographs on cardstock. Cut the puzzles into pieces. The number of pieces will be dependent on the developmental level of the children.

Related Themes: This activity can be adapted to many themes, as well as field trips.

Aligns with NAEYC Teaching Standard 3: Teaching

naeyc

PUMPKIN PATCH

Artifact Goal: Classroom Activity

Directions: Decorate a box to represent a pumpkin patch. Add slits on the top to accommodate craft sticks. Attach laminated clip art pumpkins to the craft sticks. Adhere photographs of the children's faces to the pumpkins. Sing, "Who picked the pumpkin from the pumpkin patch?" Respond by inserting a child's name: "____ picked the pumpkin from the pumpkin patch." As a child's name is sung, he or she takes the pumpkin from the patch.

Related Themes: "Garden," "Fall," "Orange," and "Halloween"

Aligns with NAEYC Teaching Standard 3: Teaching

naeyc

RECIPE CHART
Artifact Goal: Classroom Activity

Directions: Create a recipe chart by taking photographs of the ingredients needed. Add text, as illustrated, to describe the process

Related Themes: "Apples," "Fruits and Vegetables," "Bread," "Eggs," "Fish," "Thanksgiving," and "Valentine's Day"

Aligns with NAEYC Teaching Standard 3: Teaching

naeyc

Let's Make Pudding

Pour | JELL-O INSTANT | into |
Add |
Shake |
Eat ! |

SENSORY TABLE SEARCH
Artifact Goal: Classroom Activity

Directions: Tape children's photographs to the bottom of a sensory table. Fill the table with cotton balls or other sensory material and scoops. However, avoid sand since it would scratch the photographs. Encourage the children to manipulate the materials to find pictures of their classmates and themselves.

Related Themes: "Friends," "Birds," "Farm Animals," "Cats," "Insects and Spiders," "Occupations," "Pets," and "Zoo Animals"

Aligns with NAEYC Teaching Standard 3: Teaching

naeyc

TEACHER-MADE BOOKS
Artifact Goal: Classroom Activity

Directions: Use photographs and related text to tell a story. Place each page in a plastic sleeve. Then arrange in a three-ring binder and place in the classroom library. This activity can be adapted to almost any theme. It can also be used as a follow-up to field trips.

Aligns with NAEYC Teaching Standard 3: Teaching

naeyc

TEN IN THE BED GAME
Artifact Goal: Classroom Activity

Directions: Using clip art, make a bed and quilt. Attach to a piece of tagboard or foam board to give body. Add small strips of the back side of Velcro to the top of the bed. Then cut the children's faces from photographs. Behind each face, add the top Velcro strip. Sing "Ten in the Bed," removing a child's picture after each verse.

Related Themes: "Numbers," "Health," and "Music"

Aligns with NAEYC Teaching Standard 3: Teaching

naeyc

WHOSE _____?
VISUALS

Artifact Goal: Classroom Activity

Directions:

Whose Nose?
Directions: Fold a piece of cardstock in half, cut slits to make a flap, add text, and paste a photograph inside. See illustration.

Whose Shoes?
Directions: Photograph children wearing a variety of types of shoes—laces, buckles, slip-on, straps, Velcro, and others. See illustration.

Whose Hat?
Fill an inexpensive photo album with photographs of children wearing different types of hats. Use text to describe the type of hat (e.g., sports or occupational).

Whose Name?
Take photographs of all of the children in the class. Print each classmate's name on an individual piece of tagboard and on the back of each picture. Encourage the children to match the names with the picture. By turning over the picture and matching the print, the child can see if the correct name was matched to the picture.

Aligns with NAEYC Teaching Standard 3: Teaching

naeyc

Kreloff, Elliot. (2007). *Harry Bear and Friends Count Fish.* Maplewood, NJ: Blue Apple Books.

McMissack, Patricia C. (1996). *A Million Fish More or Less.* (1996). New York: Random House Children's Books.

Lindeen, Carol K. (2005). *Clown Fish.* Mankato, MN: Capstone Press.

Lindeen, Carol K. (2004). *Life in a Ocean.* Mankato, MN: Capstone Press.

Lionni, Leo. (2005). *Fish Is Fish.* New York: A. A. Knopf.

Lionni, Leo. (1973). *Swimmy.* New York: A. A. Knopf.

London, Jonathan. (2002). *Where the Big Fish Are.* Cambridge, MA: Candlewick Press.

Long, Earlene R. (1987). *Gone Fishing.* Illustrated by Richard Brown. Boston, MA: Houghton Mifflin Harcourt.

MacDonald, Suse. (2007). *Fish, Swish! Splash, Dash!* New York: Little Simon.

Martin, David. (2005). *Piggy and Dad Go Fishing.* Illustrated by Frank Remkiewicz. Cambridge, MA: Candlewick Press.

Parker, Steve. (2005). *Fish.* New York: DK Children.

Pfister, Marcus. (1992). *The Rainbow Fish.* Translated by J. Alison James. New York: North South Books.

Pfister, Marcus. (1995). *Rainbow Fish to the Rescue.* Translated by J. Alison James. New York: North South Books.

Pfister, Marcus. (2000). *The Adventures of Rainbow Fish.* New York: North South Books.

Pully Sayer, Apri. (2004). *Trout, Trout, Trout! A Fish Chant.* Illustrated by Trip Park. Chanhassen, MN: Northword Press.

Rosen, M. J. (2005). *Fishing with Dad: Lessons of Love and Lure from Father to Son.* New York: Artisan.

Ryder, Joanne. (1997). *Shark in the Sea.* Illustrated by Michael Rothman. New York: William Morrow.

Rylant, Cynthia, and Arthur Howard. (2001). *Mr. Putter and Tabby Feed the Fish.* Illustrated by Arthur Howard. San Diego, CA: Harcourt Brace.

Scillian, Devin. (2010). *Memoirs of a Goldfish.* Illustrated by Tim Bowers. Ann Arbor, MI: Sleeping Bear Press.

Sill, Cathryn P. (2002). *About Fish: A Guide for Children.* Illustrated by John Sill. Atlanta, GA: Peachtree Publishers.

Stockdale, Susan. (2008). *Fabulous Fishes.* Atlanta, GA: Peach Tree Publishers

Sullivan, Jody. (2006). *Parrotfish.* Mankato, MN: Capstone Press.

Sullivan, Jody. (2007). *Puffer Fish.* Mankato, MN: Capstone Press.

Wildsmith, Brian. (1987). *Fishes.* London: Oxford University Press.

Wood, Audrey. (2004). *Ten Little Fish.* Illustrated by Bruce Wood. New York: Blue Sky Press.

Yoo, Taeeun. (2007). *The Little Red Fish.* New York: Dial Books for Young Readers.

Technology and Multimedia

The following multimedia products can be used to complement this theme:

"Baby Fish" [CD]. (2007). In *Dr. Jean's Silly Songs.* Oklahoma City, OK: Melody House.

Fish [DVD]. (2007). New York: DK Publishing.

"Five Little Fish" [CD]. (2007). In *Dr. Jean's Silly Songs.* Oklahoma City, OK: Melody House.

"The Goldfish" [CD]. (2010). In *Best of Laurie Berkner Band.* New York: Two Tomatoes.

"Have You Ever Been Fishing?" [CD]. (2007). In *Keep on Singing and Dancing.* Oklahoma City, OK: Melody House.

"Octopus' Garden" [CD]. (1999). In *Five Little Monkeys.* Long Branch, NJ: Kimbo Educational.

The Rainbow Fish: Dazzle the Dinosaur [DVD]. (1997). Los Angeles: Sony Wonder.

"Slippery Fish" [CD]. (1985). In *10 Carrot Diamond.* Vancouver, BC: Hug Bug Records.

"Splishin' and Splashin'" [CD]. (2000). In *Charlotte Diamond's World*. Vancouver, BC: Hug Bug Records.

Swimmy—and More Classic Leo Lionni Stories [DVD]. (2005). New York: Scholastic.

"Three Little Fishies" [CD]. (2009). In *A Frog Named Sam*. Milwaukee, WI: Bartlett Ave. Records.

What Makes a Fish a Fish? [DVD]. (2007). Annie Crawley. Seattle, WA: Dive Into Your Imagination.

What's in the Sea? (1990). Long Branch, NJ: Kimbo Educational.

Who Lives in the Sea? [DVD]. (2007). Annie Crawley. Seattle, WA: Dive Into Your Imagination.

 Additional teaching resources to accompany this Theme can be found on the book's companion website. Go to www.cengagebrain.com to access the site for a variety of useful resources.

FLOWERS

Containers

vases

pots

window boxes

planters

Uses

beauty

decoration

perfume

dye for clothing

gifts

ceremonial

food

Plant Parts

petals

stem

leaves

roots

buds

seeds

Names

violet, tulip

carnation

rose, lilac, lily

sunflower

orchid, magnolia

petunia, marigold

pansy

Places

wild

soil

water

greenhouses

gardens

homes

Care

water

soil

sunshine

air

pollination (bees)

Theme Goals

Through participating in the experiences provided by this theme, the children may learn:

1. Parts of the flower
2. Names of flowers
3. Places flowers grow
4. Uses of flowers
5. Containers that hold flowers
6. Care of flowers

Concepts for the Children to Learn

1. A flower is a plant.
2. Flowers add beauty to our world.
3. Flowers can be used for decoration.
4. Most flowers have a smell.
5. Vases, pots, window boxes, and planters are all flower containers.
6. Flowers need soil, water, sunshine, and air to grow.
7. Bees pollinate flowers.
8. Sometimes flowers are given to people for special reasons, such as holidays, birthdays, or if someone goes to the hospital.
9. Flowers are used at weddings.
10. Some flowers are used to make perfume.
11. Dye for clothing can be made from flowers.
12. There are many parts to flowers.
13. Seeds, roots, stem, leaves, buds, and petals are all parts of a flower.
14. Flowers need water to grow in the soil.
15. Flowers can be grown in the wild, in greenhouses, in gardens, and in homes.
16. Violets, tulips, carnations, roses, lilacs, lilies, sunflowers, orchids, magnolias, petunias, marigolds, and pansies are all names of flowers.

Vocabulary

1. **flower**—the colored part of a plant that blossoms.
2. **greenhouse**—a glass house for growing plants. Plants that need light, heat, and protection from the weather are grown in a greenhouse.
3. **leaves**—growth from the stem of a plant. Most leaves are green.
4. **petal**—colored part of a flower.
5. **root**—the part of the plant that usually grows under the ground.
6. **seed**—the part of the plant that produces a new plant.
7. **stem**—the stalk of the plant that bears buds and shoots.
8. **shoot**—a newly grown plant part.

Bulletin Board

The purpose of this bulletin board is to develop visual discretion, problem-solving, and color-matching skills, as well as to foster the correspondence of sets to written numerals. Cut large numerals out of tagboard. Color each number a different color. Next, create tulips out of tagboard. The number will depend on the maturity of the children. Color each tulip the same color as its corresponding numeral: for example, three blue tulips for a blue numeral 3. The children can hang the appropriate number of tulips on the bulletin board next to each numeral. Moreover, the children can match the colored tulips to the corresponding colored numeral to make this activity self-correcting.

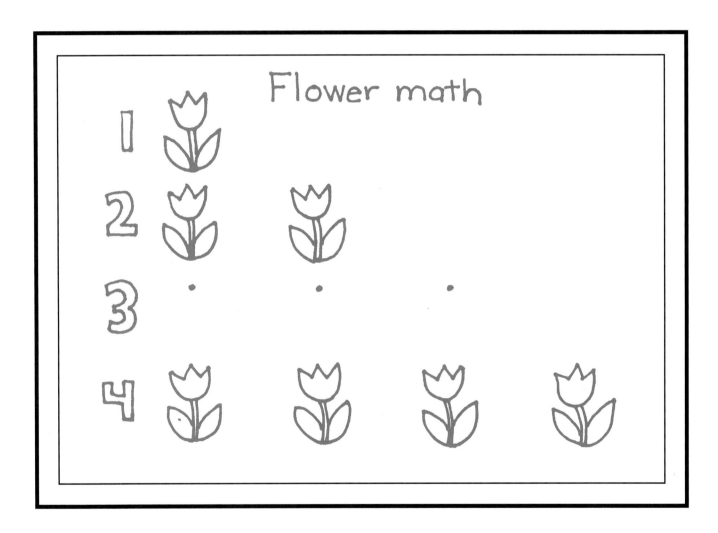

Family Letter

Dear Families,

Hello! As spring arrives and all the flowers begin to bloom, we will begin a unit on flowers. Through this unit the children will learn about the care, uses, and parts of a flowering plant. They will also learn about places where flowers are grown as well as the names of flowers and their containers.

At School

Some of the learning experiences planned to help the children make discoveries about flowers include:

- Listening to the story *Quiet in the Garden* by Aliki
- Planting seeds and observing and measuring the growth of various flowers
- Visiting a floral shop
- Reciting fingerplays

At Home

If you are planning to plant a garden in your yard this spring, let your child help you. Another activity would be to examine the plants and flowers you have growing in your house.

To develop language skills, we will be learning this fingerplay in school. Let your child teach it to you.

Daisies

One, two, three, four, five
   (pop up fingers, one at a time)
Yellow daisies all alive.
Here they are all in a row.
   (point to fingers standing)
The sun and the rain will help them grow.
      (make a circle with fingers, flutter
      fingers for rain)

Enjoy your child!

Arts and Crafts

1. **Muffin Cup Flowers**
    For younger children, prepare shapes of flowers and leaves. The older children may be able to do this themselves. Attach the stems and leaves to muffin tin liners. Add a small amount of perfume to the flower for interest.

2. **Easel**
    Cut easel paper into flower shapes.

3. **Seed Collages**
    Place a pan containing a variety of seeds in the middle of the art table. In addition, supply glue and paper for the children to form a collage.

4. **Egg Carton Flowers**
    Cut the sections of an egg container apart. Attach chenille stems for stems, and decorate with watercolor markers.

5. **Flower Mobile**
    Bring in a tree branch and hang from the classroom ceiling. Let the children make flowers and hang them on the branch for decoration.

6. **Paper Plate Flowers**
    Provide snack-sized paper plates, markers, crayons, and colored construction paper. The children may use these materials to create a flower.

Cooking

1. **Fruit Candy**
    Fruit grows on trees and plants. A flower blossom grows on the trees or plants. The flowers produce fruit.
    1 pound dried figs
    1 pound dried apricots
    1/2 pound dates
    2 cups oats
    1/2 cup raisins

Put fruit and 2 cups of oats through a food grinder. Press into a buttered 9-inch × 13-inch pan. Chill and enjoy!

2. **Pudding Fruit Salad**
    2 boxes sugar-free instant vanilla pudding
    3 bananas, sliced into 1/4-inch pieces
    2 oranges, peeled and sectioned
    1 30-ounce can fruit cocktail
    1 11-ounce can mandarin oranges

    Combine all of the ingredients and mix until the pudding is dissolved. As the pudding absorbs the juices from the canned fruit, it will thicken. Cool two hours before serving.

Dramatic Play

1. **Garden**
    Aprons, small garden tools, a tin of soil, seeds, watering cans, pots, and vases can all be provided. Pictures of flowers with names on them can be hung in the classroom.

2. **Gardener**
    Gather materials for a gardener prop box. Include gloves, seed packets, sun hat, handheld spade or hoe, stakes for marking, watering cans, and so on.

3. **Flower Shop**
    In the dramatic play area, set up a flower shop complete with plastic flowers, boxes, containers, watering cans, a misting bottle, and a cash register. Artificial corsages would also be a fun addition.

4. **Flower Arranging**
    Artificial flowers and containers can be placed in the dramatic play area. The children can make centerpieces for the lunch table. Also, a centerpiece can be made for the science table, the lobby, and the secretary, director, or principal.

Field Trips and Resource People

1. Florist
Arrange to visit a local floral shop. Observe the different kinds of flowers. Then watch the florist design a bouquet or corsage.

2. Walk
Walk around the neighborhood, observing different types and colors of flowers.

Fingerplays and Chants

My Garden
> This is my garden
>   (extend one hand forward, palm up)
> I'll rake it with care
>   (raking motion with fingers)
> And then some flower seeds
>   (planting motion)
> I'll plant in right there.
> The sun will shine
>   (make circle with hands)
> And the rain will fall
>   (let fingers flutter down to lap)
> And my garden will blossom
>   (cup hands together, extend upward
>   slowly)
> And grow straight and tall.

Daisies
> One, two, three, four, five
>   (pop up fingers, one at a time)
> Yellow daisies all alive.
> Here they are all in a row.
>   (point to fingers standing)
> The sun and the rain will help them grow.
>   (make a circle with fingers, flutter
>   fingers for rain)

Flower Play
> If I were a little flower
> Sleeping underneath the ground,
>   (curl up)

> I'd raise my head and grow and grow
>   (raise head and begin to grow)
> And stretch my arms and grow and grow
>   (stretch arms)
> And nod my head and say,
>   (nod head)
> "I'm glad to see you all today."

Group Time
(Games and Language)

Hide the Flower
Choose one child to look for the flower. Ask him or her to cover his or her eyes. Ask another child to hide a flower. After the flower is hidden and the child returns to the group, instruct the first child to uncover his or her eyes and find the flower. Clues can be provided. For example, if the child approaches the area where the flower is hidden, the remainder of the children can clap their hands.

Math

1. Flower Growth
Prepare sequence cards representing flowers at various stages of growth. Encourage the children to sequence them.

2. Flower Match
Cut pictures of flowers from magazines or seed catalogs. If desired, mount the pictures. The children can match them by kind, size, color, and shape.

3. Measuring Seed Growth
Plant several types of seeds. At determined intervals, measure the growth of various plants and flowers. Maintain a chart comparing the growth.

4. Flower Petal Math
Make a flower stem and place a circle on it. Place a number in the circle. The children should glue the corresponding number of petals onto the circle to create a flower.

Music

"Flowers"

(Sing to the tune of "Pop! Goes the Weasel")

All around the forest ground
There's flowers everywhere.
There's pink, yellow, and purple, too.
Here's one for you.

Science

1. **Flowers**

   Place a variety of flowers on the science table. Encourage the children to compare the color, shape, size, and smell of each flower.

2. **Planting Seeds**

   Plant flower seeds in a styrofoam cup. Save the seed packages and mount on a piece of tagboard. Place this directly behind the containers, on the science table. Encourage the children to compare their plants. When the plant starts growing, compare the seed packages to the plant growth.

3. **Carnation**

   Place a white carnation in a vase containing water with red food coloring added. Watch the tips of the carnation petals gradually change colors. Repeat the activity using other flowers and colors of water.

4. **Observing and Weighing Bulbs**

   Collect flower bulbs and place on the science table. Encourage the children to observe the similarities and differences. A balance scale can also be added.

5. **Microscopes**

   Place petals from a flower under a microscope for the children to observe.

Sensory

Additions to the Sensory Table

- Soil and plastic flowers
- Water and watering cans

Books

The following books can be used to complement this theme:

Aliki. (2009). *Quiet in the Garden.* New York: Greenwillow Books.

Ashman, Sarah, and Nancy Parent. (2004). *Holly Bloom's Garden.* Illustrated by Lori Mitchell. New York: Flashlight Press.

Barry, Frances. (2008). *Big Yellow Sunflower.* Cambridge, MA: Candlewick Press.

Bodach, Vijaya Khisty. (2007). *Flowers.* Mankato, MN: Capstone Press.

Bodach, Vijaya Khisty. (2007). *Leaves.* Mankato, MN: Capstone Press.

Bodach, Vijaya Khisty. (2007). *Roots.* Mankato, MN: Capstone Press.

Brenner, Barbara. (2004). *Good Morning, Garden.* Illustrated by Denise Ortakales. Chanhassen, MN: NorthWord Press.

Bruce, Lisa. (2000). *Fran's Flowers.* Illustrated by Rosalind Beardshaw. New York: HarperCollins.

Burrowes, Adjoa J. (2000). *Grandma's Purple Flowers.* New York: Lee & Low Books.

Cheng, Andrea. (2003). *Goldfish and Chrysanthemums.* Illustrated by Michelle Cheng. New York: Lee & Low Books.

Davis, Nancy. (2009). *A Garden of Opposites.* New York: Schwartz & Wade Books.

Ehlert, Lois. (2003). *Planting a Rainbow.* San Diego, CA: Harcourt.

Ehlert, Lois. (2001). *Waiting for Wings.* San Diego, CA: Harcourt.

Elschner, Geraldine. (2007). *Max's Magic Seeds.* Illustrated by Jean-Pierre Corderoch. New York: Penguin Young Readers Group.

Fausch, Karen, and Laura Jane Coats. (2001). *The Window Box Book.* Illustrated by Laura Jane Coats. New York: Little Bookroom.

Greenstein, Elaine. (2004). *One Little Seed.* New York: Viking.

Gunderson, Jessica. (2008). *Friends and Flowers.* Illustrated by Cori Doerrfeld. Minneapolis, MN: Picture Window Books.

Helbrough, Emma, and Maggie Silver. (2007). *How Flowers Grow.* Illustrated by Catherine-Anne MacKinnon. Eveleth, MN: Usborne Books.

Henkes, Kevin. (2010). *My Garden.* New York: Greenwillow Books.

Hickman, Pamela, and Heather Collins. (2000). *Plant Book (Starting with Nature).* Illustrated by Heather Collins. Toronto: Kids Can Press.

Howard, Fran. (2005). *Bumble Bees.* Mankato, MN: Capstone Press.

Lach, William. (2010). *My Friend the Flowers.* Illustrated by Doug Kennedy. New York: Abrams Books for Young Readers.

Lerner, Carol. (2002). *Butterflies in the Garden.* New York: HarperCollins.

Love, Pamela. (2004). *Lighthouse Seeds.* Illustrated by Linda Warner. Camden, ME: Down East Books.

Lucht, Irmgard. (1995). *The Red Poppy.* Illustrated by Frank Jacoby-Nelson. New York: Hyperion.

Marzollo, Jean. (1996). *I'm a Seed.* Madison, WI: Demco Media.

Milne, A. A. (2000). *The Magic Hill.* Illustrated by Isabel Bodar Brown. New York: Dutton Children's Books.

Murphy, Mary. (2002). *Koala and the Flower.* Brookfield, CT: Roaring Brook Press.

Noda, Takayo. (2006). *Song of the Flowers.* New York: Dial Books for Young Readers.

Park, Linda Sue. (2005). *What Does Bunny See? A Book of Colors and Flowers.* Illustrated by Maggie Smith. New York: Clarion Books.

Parker, Kim. (2005). *Counting in the Garden.* New York: Orchard Books.

Pomeroy, Diana. (1997). *Wildflower ABC: An Alphabet of Potato Prints.* Orlando, FL: Harcourt Brace.

Rawlinson, Julia. (2009). *Fletcher and the Springtime Blossoms.* Illustrated by Tiphanie Beeke. New York: Greenwillow Books.

Reynolds, Peter. (2009). *Rose's Garden.* Somerville, MA: Candlewick Press.

Rockwell, Anne F. (1999). *Bumblebee, Bumblebee, Do You Know Me? A Garden Guessing Game.* New York: HarperCollins.

Svatos, Ladislav. (1976). *Dandelion.* New York: Doubleday Co.

Schaefer, Lola M. (2003). *Pick, Pull, Snap.* Illustrated by Lindsay Barrett George. New York: Greenwillow Books.

Schaefer, Lola M. (2000). *This is the Sunflower.* Illustrated by Donald Crew. New York: Greenwillow Books.

Stanley, Mandy. (2006). *Lettice the Flower Girl.* New York: Simon & Schuster Books for Young Readers.

Stoker, Joann, and Gerald Stoker. (1999). *ABC Book of Flowers for Young Gardeners.* Columbia, SC: Summerhouse Press.

Sun, Chyng-Feng. (1996). *Cat and Cat-Face.* Illustrated by Lesley Liu. Boston: Houghton Mifflin.

Wade, Mary Dodson. (2009). *Flowers Bloom!* Berkeley Heights, NJ: Enslow Elementary.

Wade, Mary Dodson. (2009). *Seeds Sprout!* Berkeley Heights, NJ: Enslow Publishing.

Wellington, Monica. (2005). *Zinnia's Flower Garden.* New York: Dutton Children's Books.

Wojtowicz, Jennifer. (2005). *The Boy Who Grew Flowers.* Illustrated by Steve Adams. Cambridge, MA: Barefoot Books.

Technology and Multimedia

The following technology and multimedia products can be used to complement this theme:

Chrysanthemum and More Kevin Henkes Stories [DVD]. (2009). New York: Scholastic.

"Each of Us Is a Flower" [CD]. (2000). In *10 Carrot Diamond.* Vancouver, BC: Hug Bug Records.

"Flower Garden" [CD]. (1995). In *Piggyback Songs*. Long Branch, NJ: Kimbo Educational.

Flowers and Seeds [video]. (1994). Princeton, NJ: Films for the Humanities.

"Flowers in the Snow" [CD]. (2006). In *Train Songs and Other Tracks*. Mission Viejo, CA: Stargazer Productions.

Flowers, Plants and Trees [video]. (1987). Tell Me Why series. Marina del Rey, CA: Penguin Productions.

Flowers, Plants and Trees [DVD]. (2008). Dallas, TX: NCircle Entertainment.

"The Garden Song" [CD]. (2000). In *10 Carrot Diamond*. Vancouver, BC: Hug Bug Records.

"Gardener at Home" and "The Seed Song" [CD]. (1999). In *On the Farm with RONNO*. Long Branch, NJ: Kimbo Educational.

"In Grandma's Garden" [CD]. (1988). In *Rainbow of Songs*. Long Branch, NJ: Kimbo Educational.

Plant [DVD]. (2006). New York: DK Publishing .

Raffi. (1994). "Spring Flowers" [CD]. In *Bananaphone*. Cambridge, MA: Shoreline. Available from Kimbo Educational, Long Branch, NJ.

Reading Rainbow. *My Little Island* [DVD]. Lincoln, NE: GNP Educational Media.

 Additional teaching resources to accompany this Theme can be found on the book's companion website. Go to www.cengagebrain.com to access the site for a variety of useful resources.

Theme 38
FRIENDS

Who	Activities	Places	Why
self	play	school	to help
mothers	share	neighborhood	to enjoy
fathers	learn	home	
brothers	talk	park	
sisters	listen		
cousins	work		
grandmothers			
grandfathers			
aunts, uncles			
boys, girls			
neighbors, pets			

Theme Goals

Through participating in the experiences provided by this theme, the children may learn:

1. Who friends are
2. Why we have friends
3. Activities we can do with our friends
4. Places we can make friends

Concepts for the Children to Learn

1. A friend is someone who I like and who likes me.
2. My friends are special to me.
3. We can have friends at school, in our neighborhood, in our homes, and at the park.
4. Our brothers and sisters can be our friends.
5. Friends can help us with our work.
6. We enjoy playing with our friends.
7. We share and learn with friends.
8. Friends talk and listen to us.
9. A pet can be a friend.
10. Friends can be boys or girls.
11. Mothers, fathers, grandmothers, grandfathers, aunts, uncles, and cousins can be our friends.

Vocabulary

1. **cooperating**—working together to help someone.
2. **friend**—a person we enjoy.
3. **giving**—sharing something of your own with others.
4. **like**—feeling good about someone or something.
5. **pal or buddy**—other words for "friend."
6. **sharing**—giving and taking turns.
7. **togetherness**—being with one another and sharing a good feeling.

Bulletin Board

The purpose of this bulletin board is to call attention to print. It will help the children recognize their own and their friends' names. The bulletin board can also be used by the teacher as an attendance check. Prepare the board by constructing name cards for each child as illustrated. Then laminate and punch holes in each card. When the children arrive at school, they can attach their name cards to the bulletin board with pushpins.

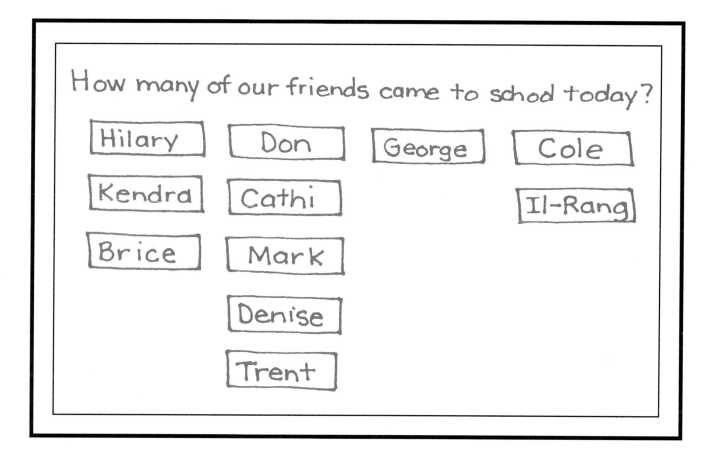

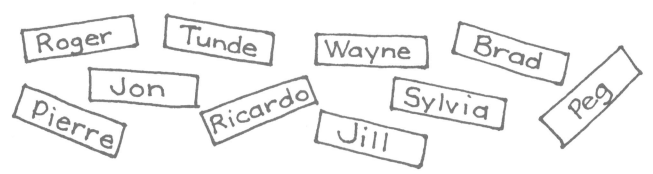

Family Letter

InBox

Dear Families,

We will be starting a curriculum unit on friends, which will include discovering people of all ages and even animal friends. The children have made many new friends at school, with whom they are learning to take turns, cooperate, work, and play. Through this unit, the children will become more aware of what a friend is and activities friends can do together. Moreover, they will learn the importance of prosocial behavior.

At School

Highlights of the learning experiences in this unit include:

- Making cookies for our friends
- Sending notes to pen pals
- Creating a friendship chain with strips of paper
- Looking at pictures of our friends at school in our classroom photo album
- Reciting fingerplays related to friendships
- Singing songs related to friendships

At Home

Your child may enjoy looking at photo albums of family and friends. Perhaps a friend could be invited to come and play with your child. We will be learning a poem about friends to promote an enjoyment of language and poetry.

Friends

I like my friends,
So when we are at play,
I try to be very kind,
and nice in every way.

Be your child's best friend!

Arts and Crafts

1. Friendship Chain

Provide strips of paper for the older children to print their names on. For those children who are not interested or unable, print their names for them. When all the names are on the strips of paper, the children can connect them to make a chain. The chain can symbolize that everyone in the class is a friend.

2. Friendship Exchange Art

Provide each child with a piece of construction paper with "To: _____" printed in the upper-left corner and "From: _____" printed on the bottom. The teacher assists the children in printing their names on the bottom of the paper and the name of the person to their right on the top of the paper. Using paper scraps, tissue paper squares, fabric scraps, and glue, each child will construct a picture for a friend. When finished, have each child pass the paper to the friend for whom it was made.

Cooking

1. Friendship Brownies

3/4 cup butter or margarine, softened
1 cup sugar
3 eggs
2 1-ounce squares unsweetened chocolate, melted and cooled
1 teaspoon vanilla
1 1/4 cups all-purpose flour
1/2 teaspoon baking powder
1/4 teaspoon salt

Cream butter and sugar; beat in eggs. Blend in chocolate and vanilla. Stir flour with baking powder and salt. Add to creamed mixture. Mix well. Spread in a greased 9- × 9- × 2-inch baking pan. Bake at 350 degrees for 25 to 30 minutes. Cool. If desired, sift powdered sugar over the top. Cut into bars. Yields 24 bars.

2. Cupcake Cones

Purchase a cake mix and ice cream cone. Follow the directions on the back of the cake mix box. Pour 1/4 cup of batter in an ice cream cone. Place the cones in muffin tins. Bake 15–18 minutes at 400 degrees. Cool and serve for dessert.

3. Italian Pizza Muffins

24 ounces of canned tomato sauce
1 1/2 teaspoons Italian seasoning
1 teaspoon garlic powder
12 whole-wheat English muffins
24 ounces of grated mozzarella cheese

Heat the over to 425 degrees. Mix the tomato sauce, Italian seasoning, and garlic powder, and heat. Spread the muffins on a baking sheet and toast. On each muffin half, spread 2 teaspoons of tomato sauce. Then sprinkle the mozzarella cheese on each muffin. Return to the oven, observing closely, until the cheese melts.

Dramatic Play

1. Puppet Show

Set up a puppet stage with various types of puppets. The children can share puppets and act out friendships using the puppets in various situations.

2. A Tea Party

Provide dress-up clothes, play dishes, and water in the dramatic play area.

Field Trips and Resource People

1. The Zoo

Take a trip to the zoo to observe animals.

2. The Nursing Home

Visit a nursing home, allowing the children to interact with elderly friends.

3. Resource People

Invite the following community helpers into the classroom because young children would consider them our friends:

- Police officer
- Trash collector
- Janitor or custodian
- Firefighter
- Doctor, nurse, or dentist
- Principal or director

Fingerplays and Chants

Friends

I like my friends.
So when we are at play,
I try to be very kind
and nice in every way.

Five Little Friends

(Hold up five fingers; subtract one with each action)

Five little friends playing on the floor,
One got tired and then there were four.
Four little friends climbing in a tree,
One jumped down and then there were three.
Three little friends skipping to the zoo,
One went for lunch and then there were two.
Two little friends swimming in the sun,
One went home and then there was one.
One little friend going for a run,
Decided to take a nap and then there were none.

Large Muscle

1. Double Balance Beam

Place two balance beams side by side, and encourage two children to hold hands and cross together.

2. Bowling Game

Set up pins or plastic bottles. With a ball, have the children take turns knocking down the pins.

3. Outdoor Obstacle Course

Design an obstacle course outdoors that is specifically designed for two children to go through at one time. Use balance beams, climbers, slides, and so on. Short and simple obstacle courses seem to work the best.

Math

1. Group Pictures

Take pictures of the children in groups of two, three, four, and so on. Make separate corresponding number cards. The children then can match the correct numeral to the picture card.

2. Friend Charts

Take individual pictures of the children and chart them according to hair color, eye color, and so on. Encourage the children to compare their looks to the characteristics of their friends.

Music

1. "Do You Know This Friend of Mine?"

(Sing to the tune of "The Muffin Man")

Do you know this friend of mine,
This friend of mine,
This friend of mine?
Do you know this friend of mine?
His name is _____.
Yes, we know this friend of yours,
This friend of yours,
This friend of yours.
Yes, we know this friend of yours.
His name is _____.

2. "The More We Are Together"

(Sing to the tune of "Have You Ever Seen a Lassie?")
(Insert names of children in your classroom)

The more we are together, together, together,
The more we are together, thc happier
    we'll be.
For your friends are my friends, and my
    friends are your friends.
The more we are together, the happier
    we'll be.
We're all in school together, together,
    together,
We're all in school together, and happy
    we'll be.
There's Ali and Keisha and Jenny and Ben,
There's ____ and ____ and ____ and ____.
We're all in school together and happy
    we'll be.

3. "Beth Met a Friend"

(Sing to the tune of "The Farmer in the Dell")
(Insert names of children in your classroom for each verse)

Beth met a friend,
Beth met a friend,
When she came to school today,
Beth met a friend.

4. The More We Get Together

The more we get together,
Together, together.
The more we get together,
The happier we'll be.
For your friends are my friends,
And my friends are your friends.
The more we get together,
The happier we'll be.

Science

1. Comparing Heartbeats

Provide stethoscopes for the children to listen to their friends' heartbeats.

2. Fingerprints

Ink pads and white paper can be provided for the children to make fingerprints. Also, a microscope can be provided to encourage the children to compare their fingerprints.

3. Friends' Voices

Tape the children's voices throughout the course of the day. The following day, leave the tape recorder at the science table. The children can listen to the tape and try to guess which classmate is talking.

4. Animal Friends

Prepare signs for the animal cages listing the animals' daily food intake and care.

Sensory

The sensory table is an area where two to four children can make new friends and share. Materials that can be added to the sensory table include:

- Shaving cream
- Play dough
- Sand with toys
- Water with boats
- Wood shavings
- Silly Putty
- Dry pasta with scoops and a balance scale
- Goop:

    Mix equal parts of white glue and liquid starch. Food coloring can be added for color. Store in an airtight container.
    Mix water and cornstarch. Add cornstarch to the water until you get the consistency that you want.
Caution: Carefully supervise children while playing with sensory materials.

Social Studies

Friends Bulletin Board

Ask the children to bring pictures of their friends into the classroom. Set up a bulletin board in the classroom where these pictures can be hung for all to see. Remind the children that friends can be family members and animals too.

 ## Books

The following books can be used to complement this theme:

Agee, Jon. (2005). *Terrific.* New York: Hyperion Books for Children.

AlAbdullah, Raina, and Kelly DiPucchio. (2010). *The Sandwich Swap.* Illustrated by Tricia Tusa. New York: Disney-Hyperion Books.

Aliki. (1995). *Best Friends Together Again.* New York: Greenwillow.

Anderson, Derek. (2006). *Blue Burt and Wiggles.* New York: Simon & Schuster Books for Young Readers.

Berger, Carin. (2010). *Forever Friends.* New York: Greenwillow Books.

Blabey, Aaron. (2008). *Pearly Barley and Charlie Parsley.* Asheville, NC: Front Street.

Brett, Jan. (2008). *Gingerbread Friends.* New York: G.P. Putnam's Sons.

Bruna, Dick. (2001). *Dick Bruna's 1st Picture Books: Miffy's Animal Friends.* New York: Kodansha International.

Chapman, Jane, and Claire Freedman. (2009). *When We're Together.* Intercourse, PA: Good Books.

Cohn, Aden, and Dan Sullivan. (1999). *Friends of a Feather.* Illustrated by Dan Sullivan. Denver, CO: Accord Publishing.

Cousins, Lucy. (2010). *I'm the Best.* Somerville, MA: Candlewick Press.

Davidson, Susanna. (2006). *The Little Red Hen.* Illustrated by Daniel Postgate. London: Usborne.

Fuchs, Diane Marcial. (1995). *A Bear for All Seasons.* Illustrated by Kathryn Brown. New York: Holt.

Fucile, Tony. (2009). *Let's Do Nothing.* Somerville, MA: Candlewick Press.

Gorbachev, Valeri. (2005). *That's What Friends Are For.* New York: Philomel Books.

Hatkoff, Craig, Isabella Hatkoff, and Paula Kahumba. (2006). *Owen and Mzee: The True Story of a Remarkable Friendship.* Illustrated by Peter Greste. New York: Scholastic.

Heide, Florence Parry, and Sylvia Van Clief. (2003). *That's What Friends Are For.* Illustrated by Holly Meade. Cambridge, MA: Candlewick Press.

Hutchins, Pat. (1996). *Titch and Daisy.* New York: Greenwillow.

Joosse, Barbara M. (2010). *Friends (Mostly).* Illustrated by Tomaso Milian. New York: Greenwillow Books.

Keller, Holly. (2007). *Help! A Story of Friendship.* New York: Greenwillow Books.

Klein, Tali, and Corey Rosen Schwartz. (2006). *Hop! Plop!* Illustrated by Olivier Dunrea. New York: Walker.

Kroll, Virginia. (2005). *Forgiving a Friend.* Illustrated by Paige Billin-Frye. Morton Grove, IL: Albert Whitman.

Kruusval, Catarina. (2008). *Franny's Friends.* Stockholm, NY: R&S Books.

Lionni, Leo. (1996). *It's Mine!* New York: Dragonfly Books.

Miller, J. Phillip, and Sheppard Greene. (2001). *We All Sing with the Same Voice.* Illustrated by Paul Meisel. New York: HarperCollins.

Monson, A. M. (1997). *Wanted: Best Friend.* Illustrated by Lynn Munsinger. New York: Dial Books.

Reiser, Lynn. (1997). *Best Friends Think Alike.* New York: Greenwillow.

Seeger, Laura Vaccaro. (2007). *Dog and Bear: Two Friends, Three Stories.* New Milford, CT: Roaring Brook Press.

Seeger, Pete, and Paul DuBois Jacobs. (2005). *Some Friends to Feed: The Story of Stone Soup.* Illustrated by Michael Hays. New York: G.P. Putnam's Sons.

Shaw, Hannah. (2008). *Sneaky Weasel.* New York: Alfred A. Knopf.

Spinelli, Eileen. (1994). *Lizzie Logan Wears Purple Sunglasses.* Illustrated by Melanie Hope Greenberg. New York: Simon & Schuster Books for Young Readers.

Teckentrup, Britta. (2008). *Grumpy Cat.* London: Boxer.

Valckx, Catharina. (2005). *Lizette's Green Sock.* New York: Clarion Books.

Willems, Mo. (2008). *I Will Surprise My Friend!* New York: Hyperion Books for Children.

Willems, Mo. (2010). *Let's Say Hi to Friends Who Fly!* New York: Balzer & Bray.

Yerrid, Gable. (2007). *Marley's Treasure.* Illustrated by Jennifer Fitzgerald. Scottsdale, AZ: Yorkville Press.

"Friends" [CD]. (1997). In *Turn on the Music.* Sherman Oaks, CA: Hap-Pal Music.

"Make New Friends" [CD]. (2004). In *Toddler Twosome.* Redway, CA: Music Little People.

"Mary and Her Friends" [CD]. (2009). In *More Please.* Olympia, WA: Aurora Elephant Music.

"The Sharing Song" [CD]. (1996). In *Singable Songs for the Very Young.* Cambridge, MA: Rounder/UMGD.

"We Go Together" (2000). In *Bean Bag Rock and Roll.* Long Branch, NJ: Kimbo Educational.

"Will You Be My Friend?" [CD]. (2001). In *Ants Wear Underpants.* New York: BizzyBum.

Technology and Multimedia

The following technology and multimedia products can be used to complement this theme:

Additional teaching resources to accompany this Theme can be found on the book's companion website. Go to www.cengagebrain.com to access the site for a variety of useful resources.

Transition Activities

Clean-Up Time

"Do You Know What Time It Is?"
(Sing to the tune of "The Muffin Man")

Oh, do you know what time it is,
What time it is, what time it is?
Oh, do you know what time it is?
It's almost clean-up time. (Or "It's time to clean up.")

"Clean-Up Time"
(Sing to the tune of "London Bridge")

Clean-up time is already here,
Already here, already here.
Clean-up time is already here,
Already here.

"This Is the Way"
(Sing to the tune of "Mulberry Bush")

This is the way we pick up our toys,
Pick up our toys, pick up our toys.
This is the way we pick up our toys,
At clean-up time each day.

"Oh, It's Clean-Up Time"
(Sing to the tune of "Oh, My Darling Clementine")

Oh, it's clean-up time,
Oh, it's clean-up time,
Oh, it's clean-up time right now.
It's time to put the toys away,
It is clean-up time right now.

"A Helper I Will Be"
(Sing to the tune of "The Farmer in the Dell")

A helper I will be.
A helper I will be.
I'll pick up the toys and put
    them away.
A helper I will be.

"We're Cleaning Up Our Room"
(Sing to the tune of "The Farmer in the Dell")

We're cleaning up our room.
We're cleaning up our room.
We're putting all the toys away.
We're cleaning up our room.

"It's Clean-Up Time"
(Sing to the chorus of "Looby Loo")

It's clean-up time at school.
It's time for boys and girls
To stop what they are doing
And put away their toys.

"Time to Clean Up"
(Sing to the tune of "Are You Sleeping?")
(Specific toys can be mentioned in place of "toys")

Time to clean up.
Time to clean up.
Everybody help.
Everybody help.
Put the toys away, put the
    toys away.
Then sit down. (Or, "Then
    come here.")

"Clean-Up Time"
(Sing to the tune of "Hot Cross Buns")

Clean-up time.
Clean-up time.
Put all of the toys away.
It's clean-up time.

Routines

"Passing Around"
(Sing to the tune of "Skip to My Loo")

(Fill in appropriate child's name and substitute the napkin for any object that needs to be passed at mealtime)

Brad, take a napkin and pass
    them to Sara.
Sara, take a napkin and pass
    them to Tina.
Tina, take a napkin and pass
    them to Eric,
Passing around the napkins.

"Put Your Coat On"
(Sing to the tune of "Oh, My Darling Clementine")
(You can change coat to any article of clothing)

Put your coat on.
Put your coat on.
Put your winter coat on now.
We are going to play outside.
Put your coat on right now.

"Time to Go Outside"
(Sing to the tune of "When Johnny Comes Marching Home")

When it's time for us to go
    outside
To play, to play,
We find a place to put our toys
Away, away.
We'll march so quietly to the
    door.
We know exactly what's in
    store
When we go outside to play
    for a little while.

"We're Going on a Walk"
(Sing to the tune of "The Farmer in the Dell")

We're going for a walk.
We're going for a walk.
Hi-ho, the dairy-o,
We're going for a walk.
Additional verses:

What will we wear? …
What will we see? …
How will we go? …
Who knows the way? …

"Find a Partner"
(Sing to the tune of "Oh, My Darling Clementine")

Find a partner, find a partner,
Find a partner right now.
We are going for a walk.
Find a partner right now.

"Walk Along"
(Sing to the tune of "Clap Your Hands")
(Change walk to any other types of movement—jump, hop, skip, crawl)

Walk, walk, walk along,
Walk along to the bathroom.
____ and ____ walk along,
Walk along to the bathroom.

"We're Going …"
(Sing to the tune of "Go in and out the Window")

We're going to the bathroom,
We're going to the bathroom,
We're going to the bathroom,
And then we'll wash our hands.

"It's Time to Change"
(Sing to the tune of "Hello, Everybody")

It's time to change, yes
    indeed,
Yes indeed, yes indeed.
It's time to change, yes indeed
Time to change groups. (Or,
    "Time to go outside.")

FROGS

Colors
green
brown

Foods
insects
earthworms
spiders
minnows

Life Stages
egg
tadpole
adult frog

Body Parts
eyes
mouth
tongue
skin
legs

Movement
swim
jump
walk
climb

Places
water
trees
ground

Theme Goals

Through participating in the experiences provided by this theme, the children may learn:

1. Life stages of frog development
2. Body parts of frog development
3. Ways frogs move
4. Places frogs live
5. Foods frogs eat
6. Colors of frogs

Concepts for the Children to Learn

1. A frog is an animal with two long back legs.
2. Frogs have eyes, a mouth, a tongue, legs, and skin covering their body.
3. Frogs may live in many places.
4. Frogs can live in water, in trees, and on the ground.
5. Frogs can swim, climb, walk, and jump.
6. Frogs eat insects, earthworms, spiders, and minnows.
7. Frogs are colored green and brown.
8. The three life stages of a frog are egg, tadpole, and adult frog.

Vocabulary

1. **frog**—a frog is an animal with two long back legs.
2. **amphibian**—an animal that begins its life in the water, and then grows to live on land.
3. **frog**—a small animal with bulging eyes and long back legs.
4. **metamorphosis**—change, such as when a tadpole changes into a frog.
5. **tadpole**—a tiny, fishlike baby frog.

Bulletin Board

The purpose of this bulletin board is to foster a positive self-concept as well as name recognition skills. Construct a frog and lily pad shape out of tagboard for each child in your class. Print a child's name on each frog. Laminate all pieces. Staple the lily pads to the board. Punch a hole in the top of each frog piece with a paper punch. Attach a pushpin several inches above each lily pad. The children can hang their own frogs on the bulletin board as they arrive each day.

Family Letter

Dear Families,

What is usually green, has four legs, and jumps? You've guessed it—a frog! As we head into spring, we will begin a unit to discover many fascinating things about frogs. As you know, a frog is an amphibian, which means it spends part of its life in water and part on land. Frogs are related to toads, but they are not the same animal. The children will learn the life stages, body parts, and movements of a frog.

At School

A few of the week's learning experiences include:

- Watching tadpoles! Mr. Larson (Scott's dad) has volunteered to bring in some tadpoles, which we will place in an unused aquarium for maximum viewing. We will be able to observe the tadpoles' growth and development into frogs. Stop in our classroom and take a look!

- Listening to books about frogs, including *Jump, Frog, Jump!* by Robert Kalan and *The Wide-Mouthed Frog* by Keith Faulkner

- Playing leapfrog—a jumping game

At Home

You can foster the concepts of this unit at home by going to the library with your child and checking out books about frogs. Also, when you are near a lake or pond with your child, look for frogs or frog habitats.

Have a hoppin' good week!

Arts and Crafts

1. **Lily Pads**
   Cut large lily pad shapes out of construction paper. Children can decorate the shapes with green crayons, markers, tempera paint, or watercolor paint. A small, white flower shape can be added, if desired.

2. **Frog Sponge Painting**
   Cut new sponges into simple frog and lily pad shapes. Children can use the sponges to dip in green paint and press on construction paper to create designs.

3. **Green Play Dough Frogs**
   Use a play dough recipe in this book to make green play dough. Encourage the children to make frog shapes. If desired, the frog shapes can be set out to dry, creating a permanent object.

4. **Egg Carton Frog**
   Collect cardboard egg cartons, construction paper, markers, small pompons, and paint. Cut egg carton cups apart. Children can then use the materials as desired to create a frog, using the pompons to represent eyes.

Cooking

1. **Frog Cookies**
   With the children, prepare a batch of sugar cookie dough. Demonstrate how to roll three balls (one large and two smaller) and place on a cookie sheet so that they will resemble a frog head with two large eyes when baked. The frog cookies can be decorated with green frosting, chocolate chips, and string licorice.

2. **Frog Floats**
   Lime sherbet
   Mini marshmallows
   Lemon-lime soda

   Place a scoop of sherbet in a clear cup or bowl. Pour a small amount of soda in a cup. Add two small marshmallows on top of the sherbet to resemble the eyes of a frog. Enjoy!

Dramatic Play

Frogs

Use green tagboard, markers, scissors, and 1-inch-wide elastic to create frog masks. Cut a large lily pad shape out of green tagboard, butcher paper, or fabric. Place items in the dramatic play area. The children can pretend to be frogs in a pond or act out favorite frog songs and fingerplays.

Field Trips

1. **Zoo**
   Visit the amphibian section of a zoo. Observe many kinds of colors of frogs. How are they the same? How are they different?

2. **Pond**
   If available, visit a pond area in the spring or summer. Look for tadpoles and frog habitat.

Fingerplays and Chants

Mr. Bullfrog

Here's Mr. Bullfrog,
   (left hand in fist position, thumb upright)
Sitting on a rock.
Along comes a little boy (or girl),
   (walking motion with fingers of right hand)
Mr. Bullfrog jumps, kerplop!

Little Frog

A little frog in a pond am I,
   (make fist with hand)
Hippity, hippity, hop.
   (move fist up and down)
And I can jump in the air so high,
   (raise fist into the air)
Hippity, hippity, hop.
   (move fist up and down)

Five Little Frogs

Five little frogs sitting on a log.
    (extend fingers on one hand)
This little frog is still a pollywog.
    (point to thumb)
This little frog wears a happy grin.
    (point to index finger)
This little frog is tall and thin.
    (point to middle finger)
This little frog can jump very high.
    (point to ring finger)
This little frog wants to fly.
    (point to little finger)
So he calls out, "Ribbit!" and a bird flies by,
And takes him for a ride way up to the sky!
    (make wings with both hands)

Little Green Frog

A little green frog once lived in a pool.
    (hold up fist)
The sun was hot and the water cool.
He sat in the pool the whole day long,
And sang a dear little, funny little song.
"Jaggery do, quaggery dee,
No one was ever as happy as me!"

Ten Little Froggies

Ten little froggies sitting on a lily pad.
    (all fingers up)
The first one said, "Let's catch a fly."
    (right pinkie down)
The second one said, "Let's go hide."
    (right ring finger down)
The third one said, "Let's go for a swim."
    (right middle finger down)
The fourth one said, "Look, I'm in!"
    (right pointer down)
The fifth one said, "Let's dive."
    (right thumb down)
The sixth one said, "There went five!"
    (left thumb down)
The seventh one said, "Where did they go?"
    (left pointer down)
The eighth one said, "Ho, ho."
    (left middle finger down)
The ninth one said, "I need a friend."
    (left ring finger down)
The tenth one said, "This is the end."
    (left pinkie down)

Tadpole, Tadpole

Tadpole, tadpole, swimming all around.
    (use hands to make swimming
    motion)
Swishing your tail without a sound.
    (continue using hands to make
    swimming motion)
Soon you will change into a little frog.
    (make one hand into a tight fist to
    represent frog)
Tadpole, tadpole, little polliwog.
    (maintain hand in the tight fist)

Group Time
(Games and Language)

Who Is the Frog?

The purpose of this game is to promote the development of listening skills. The children sit in a circle formation. Begin by choosing one child to sit in the middle with his or her eyes closed. Another child is silently chosen to be the "frog" and say the word "ribbit" three times. Afterward, the child in the middle tries to identify who the "frog" is. Continue playing the game until all children have had a turn to play or until the group begins to lose interest.

Large Muscle

Leapfrog

Have each child find a partner. Child number one squats down on his or her hands and knees, while child number two straddles and jumps over the first child. Then, the children switch roles and the action continues!

Math

1. **Sets of Frogs**

   Cut out frog shapes from green tagboard or felt. Children can use the frog shapes for counting activities or frog-counting songs.

2. Frogs: From Biggest to Smallest

Cut out frog shapes of various sizes from construction paper, tagboard, or felt. The children can place the pieces in order from largest to smallest and then from smallest to largest.

3. Frog Board Game

Cut out lily pads from green construction paper, and arrange in a row on a piece of tagboard. Decorate remaining tagboard to resemble a pond (cattails, grass, etc.). Have children roll a die and make the frog "hop" on the corresponding number of lily pads. The game is over when a frog reaches the last lily pad.

Music

1. "Ten Little Froggies"

(Sing to the tune of "Ten Little Indians")

One little, two little, three little froggies.
Four little, five little, six little froggies.
Seven little, eight little, nine little froggies.
Ten frogs in the pond.

2. "Five Green Speckled Frogs"

Five green speckled frogs
Sitting on a speckled log,
Eating the most delicious bugs. Yum! Yum!

One jumped into the pool,
Where it was nice and cool.
Now there are four green speckled frogs.
  (continue with additional verses,
  counting down to zero/none)

3. "Jumping Frogs"

(Sing to the tune of "Jingle Bells")

Jumping frogs, jumping frogs, jumping all
  around
Looking for worms and bugs to eat,
They make a croaking sound. Oh!
Jumping frogs, jumping frogs, in the pond
  they go,
Splishing, splashing, and swimming around,
Moving to and fro.

Science

1. Observing Tadpoles

In the spring, carefully collect tadpoles from a pond or lake area. Place tadpoles in a clean aquarium filled with water obtained from the pond or lake. The aquarium can be placed on the science table for the children to observe. Occasionally, add fresh pond or lake water. When the tadpoles begin to grow legs, place a piece of wood in the aquarium. (The young frogs will soon need a place to rest out of the water.) Eventually, return the frogs to their habitat.

2. Metamorphosis

Draw or collect pictures from children's science magazines that depict the life cycle of a frog. Pictures should include frog eggs, a tadpole, a tadpole with its tail shrinking and legs sprouting, and a frog. Discuss the word *metamorphosis*. Check the library for books that show frogs at various stages of development.

3. African Dwarf Frogs

Place African dwarf frogs in an aquarium that is filled with water. These frogs are swimmers and do not need time out of the water. Place magnifying glasses near the aquarium and encourage children to observe the characteristics of the frogs.

Sensory

1. Plastic Frogs

Place purchased plastic frogs in a water-filled sensory table. Add small strainers and nets.

2. Cork Frogs

Using permanent markers, color several corks green. Insert a green chenille stem in the center of each cork and bend it to resemble frog legs. Add details to frogs using markers. Place frogs in a sensory table that has been filled with water. If desired, attach a string to the cork frogs so they can be pulled around in the water.

 Books

The following books can be used to complement this theme:

Anderson, Judith. (2009). *Once There Was a Tadpole.* Illustrated by Mike Gordon. Hauppauge, NY: Barron's.

Arnosky, Jim. (2002). *All About Frogs.* New York: Scholastic.

Asher, Sandy. (2005). *Too Many Frogs!* Illustrated by Keith Graves. New York: Philomel Books.

Barkan, Joanne. (2007). *Frogs and Friends.* Illustrated by Claudine Gevry. Pleasantville, NY: Reader's Digest Children's Books.

Barry, Frances. (2008). *Little Green Frogs.* Cambridge, MA: Candlewick Press.

Bauer, Marion Dane. (2005). *If Frogs Made the Weather.* Illustrated by Dorothy Donohue. New York: Holiday House.

Behler, John L. (2005). *Frogs: A Chorus of Color.* New York: Sterling Publishing.

Bentley, Dawn, and Salina Yoon. (1999). *The Icky Sticky Frog.* Santa Monica, CA: Piggy Toes Press.

Bishops, Nic. (2008*). Nic Bishop Frogs.* New York: Scholastic.

Burris, Priscilla. (2002). *Five Green and Speckled Frogs.* New York: Scholastic.

Calmenseon, Stephanie, and Denise Brunkus. (2001). *The Frog Principal.* New York: Scholastic.

Carney, Elizabeth. (2009). *Frogs!* Washington, DC: National Geographic.

Florian, Douglas. (2001). *Lizards, Frogs, and Polliwogs.* San Diego, CA: Harcourt.

Franco, Betsy. (2009). *Pond Circle.* Illustrated by Stefano Vitale. New York: Margaret K. McElderry Books.

Faulkner, Keith. (1996). *The Wide Mouth Frog.* Illustrated by Jonathan Lambert. New York: Dail Publisher.

French, Vivian. (2000). *Growing Frogs.* Illustrated by Alison Bartlett. Cambridge, MA: Candlewick Press.

Fridell, Ron. (2001). *The Search for Poison-Dart Frogs.* New York: Franklin Watts.

Gibbons, Gail. (2002). *Tell Me, Tree: All about Trees for Kids.* Boston: Little, Brown.

James, Betsy. (1999). *Tadpoles.* New York: Dutton Children's Books.

Kalan, Robert. (2003). *Jump Frog Jump.* New York: Greenwillow Books.

Kelly, Martin. (2000). *Five Green and Speckled Frogs.* Brooklyn, NY: Handprint.

Lechner, John. (2005). *A Froggy Fable.* Cambridge, MA: Candlewick Press.

Lindeen, Carol K. (2004). *Life in a Pond.* Mankato, MN: Capstone Press.

Lionni, Leo. (1996). *It's Mine!* New York: Dragonfly Books.

Lionni, Leo. (2005). *Fish Is Fish.* New York: A. A. Knopf.

Lobel, Arnold. (2009). *The Frogs and Toads All Sang.* Color by Adrienne Lobel. New York: HarperCollins.

London, Jonathan. (2002). *Froggy Goes to the Doctor.* New York: Viking Children's Press.

London, Jonathan. (2006). *Froggy Rides a Bike.* New York: Viking Children's Press.

London, Jonathan. (2007). *Froggy Loves Books.* New York: Scholastic.

London, Jonathan. (2007). *Froggy Plays T-Ball.* New York: Viking Children's Press.

London, Jonathon, and Frank Remkiewicz. (2000). *Froggy Bakes a Cake.* New York: Grosset & Dunlap.

London, Jonathon, and Frank Remkiewicz. (2000). *Froggy Goes to Bed.* New York: Viking.

London, Jonathon, and Frank Remkiewicz. (2000). *Froggy's Best Christmas.* New York: Viking.

London, Jonathon, and Frank Remkiewicz. (2000). *Froggy's First Kiss.* New York: Puffin.

London, Jonathon, and Frank Remkiewicz. (2001). *Froggy Eats Out.* New York: Viking.

London, Jonathon, and Frank Remkiewicz. (2001). *Froggy Plays Soccer.* New York: Puffin.

London, Jonathon, and Frank Remkiewicz. (2001). *Froggy's Halloween.* New York: Puffin.

Lunis, Natalie. (2010). *Green Tree Frogs: Colorful Hiders.* New York: Bearport Publishing.

Markle, Sandra. (2006). *Slippery, Slimy Baby Frogs.* New York: Walker and Company.

Milbourne, Anna, and Patricia Donaera. (2007). *Tadpoles and Frogs.* Illustrated by Zoe Wray. Eveleth, MN: Usborne Books.

Moffett, Mark. (2008). *Face to Face with Frogs.* Washington, DC: National Geographic.

Netherton, John. (2001). *Red-Eyed Tree Frogs.* Minneapolis, MN: Lerner Publications.

Novak, Matt. (2008). *My Froggy Valentine.* New Milford, CT: Roaring Brook Press.

Parenteau, Shirley. (2007). *One Frog Sang.* Illustrated by Cynthia Jabar. Cambridge, MA: Candlewick Press.

Parker, Steve. (1999). *It's a Frog's Life.* Illustrated by Philip Bishop, Robin Carter, and Robert Morton. Pleasantville, NY: Reader's Digest Children's Books.

Prelutsky, Jack. (2002). *The Frogs Wore Red Suspenders.* New York: Greenwillow Books.

Riches, Sara. (2000). *Fat Frogs on a Skinny Log.* New York: Scholastic.

Simon, Francesca. (1999). *Hugo and the Bully Frogs.* Illustrated by Caroline Jayne Church. London: David & Charles Children's Books.

Sweeney, Alyse. (2010). *Frogs.* Mankato, MN: Capstone Press.

Talley, Linda, and Itoko Maeno. (2001). *Toad in Town.* Kansas City, MO: MarshMedia.

Willems, Mo. (2010). *City Dog, Country Frog.* Illustrated by Jon J. Murth. New York: Hyperion Books for Children.

Willis, Jeanne. (2003). *Tadpole's Promise.* Illustrated by Tony Ross. New York: Atheneum Books for Young Readers.

Wilson, Karma. (2007). *A Frog in the Bog.* Illustrated by Joan Rankin. New York: McElderry Books.

Winer, Yvonne. (2002). *Frogs Sing Songs.* Illustrated by Tony Oliver. Watertown, MA: Charlesbridge.

Yang, Belle. (2009). *Foo: The Flying Frog of Washtub Pond.* Cambridge, MA: Candlewick Press.

Technology and Multimedia

The following multimedia products can be used to complement this theme:

Amphibian [DVD]. (2008). New York: DK Publishing.

"Can You Leap Like a Frog?" [CD]. (2000). In *Kids in Action: Greg and Steve.* Acton, CA: Greg and Steve Productions.

"Five Little Frogs" [CD]. (1996). In *Singable Songs for the Very Young.* Cambridge, MA: Rounder/UMGD.

"The Foolish Frog" [CD]. (1998). In *Birds, Beasts, Bugs and Fishes Little and Big.* Washington, DC: Smithsonian Folkways.

"A Frog Named Sam" [CD]. (2009). In *A Frog Named Sam.* Milwaukee, WI: Bartlett Ave. Records.

The Frog Prince [DVD]. (2005). Burbank, CA: Walt Disney Home Entertainment.

"Frogs Eat Butterflys" [CD]. (2010). In *What Are the Odds?* New York: Monkey Monkey Music.

Frog Song [CD]. (2000). Toronto: Dan Gibson Solitudes.

"Frog Went a Courtin" [CD]. (2007). In *Nursery Rhymes and Good Ol' Times.* New Oklahoma City, OK: Melody House.

Miss Spider's Froggy Day in Sunny Patch [DVD]. (2007). Los Angeles: Lionsgate.

Really Wild Animals: Totally Tropical Forest [DVD]. (2005). Washington, DC: National Geographic.

Totally Tropical Rain Forest [DVD]. (2004). Washington, DC: National Geographic.

 Additional teaching resources to accompany this Theme can be found on the book's companion website. Go to www.cengagebrain.com to access the site for a variety of useful resources.

Theme 40
FRUITS AND VEGETABLES

Characteristics
- seeds
- fruits
- vegetables
- shapes
- size
- colors

Forms
- fresh
- frozen
- canned
- raw
- cooked
- peeled

Care Needs
- sunlight
- water
- plants
- seeds

Names of Fruits
- banana
- mango
- apricot
- cherry
- grape
- apple
- orange
- grapefruit

Places Grown
- yard
- garden
- trees
- vines
- underground

Names of Vegetables
- carrot
- radish
- potato
- bean
- corn

Preparation
- peeled
- raw
- cooked
- frozen
- canned
- dried

Theme Goals

Through participating in the experiences provided by this theme, the children may learn:

1. Names of common fruits and vegetables
2. Care needs of fruits and vegetables
3. Places fruits and vegetables are grown
4. Preparation of fruits and vegetables
5. Forms in which fruits and vegetables can be served
6. Fruit or vegetable seeds
7. Characteristics of fruits and vegetables

Concepts for the Children to Learn

1. A fruit is usually the sweet-tasting part of a plant.
2. A vegetable is a plant used for food to eat.
3. Fruits and vegetables are grown from seeds and plants.
4. Fruits and vegetables come in many shapes, sizes, and colors.
5. Fruits and vegetables need sunlight and water to grow.
6. Apples, apricots, oranges, grapefruits, cherries, and mangoes are fruits that are grown on trees.
7. Grapes are grown on vines and bananas are grown on trees.
8. Carrots, radishes, and potatoes are vegetables that are grown in the ground. Beans and corn are grown on plants.
9. Fruits and vegetables can be bought fresh, frozen, or canned.
10. Some people grow fruits and vegetables in home gardens.
11. Most fruits and vegetables can be eaten raw or cooked.
12. We eat some fruits and vegetables with their skin; some we need to peel first. Some fruits have seeds.

Vocabulary

1. **cook**—to prepare food by heating.
2. **frozen**—chilled or refrigerated to make solid.
3. **fruit**—usually a sweet-tasting part of a plant.
4. **garden**—ground used to grow plants.
5. **produce**—agriculture products such as fruits and vegetables.
6. **ripe**—ready to be picked and eaten.
7. **roots**—part of a plant that grows downward into the soil and is edible in some plants (potatoes, turnips, radishes, onions, and carrots).
8. **seeds**—part of a plant used for growing a new crop and edible in some plants (sunflower and pumpkin).
9. **soil**—portion of earth; dirt used for growing.
10. **sprout**—to begin to grow.
11. **stems**—part of a plant used for transporting food and water and edible in some plants (celery).
12. **vegetable**—part of a plant that can be eaten.
13. **vine**—plant with a long, slender stem.

Bulletin Board

The purpose of this bulletin board is to observe the growth of a lima bean seed. Prepare by placing a moist paper towel in a small plastic bag, along with a lima bean (seed). Sprouting will occur faster if the seeds have been presoaked overnight. Staple each bag to the bulletin board as illustrated and place a child's name beside each one. Additional watering may be needed throughout this unit.

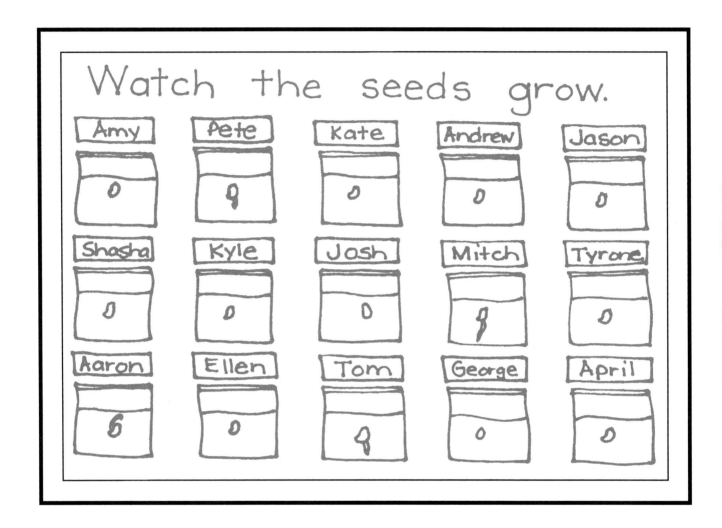

Family Letter

Dear Families,

Hello again! We hope that everyone in your family is healthy and happy. Speaking of health, we are starting a new curriculum unit on fruits and vegetables. Through the experiences planned for this unit, the children will learn the names of many fruits and vegetables, their forms, and places they are grown. Also, they will discover ways many different fruits and vegetables can be prepared and how they taste.

At School

Some of the many fun-filled learning activities scheduled for this unit include:

- Planting lima beans (seeds) to sprout. Take a look at our bulletin board this week.
- Playing the role of a gardener or farmer in the dramatic play area
- Matching pictures of vegetables to where they are grown (trees, vines, underground, etc.)
- Having a fruit- and vegetable-tasting party during a snack
- Visiting a produce section at the grocery store
- Listening to a story called *Strego Nona's Garden* by Tomie De Paola.

At Home

There are many ways you can integrate this unit's concepts into your family life. To help develop memory and language skills, ask your child which vegetables or fruits he or she tried during the week. Then let your child help you prepare them at home. Cooking often tempts a child to try new foods.

Enjoy your child!

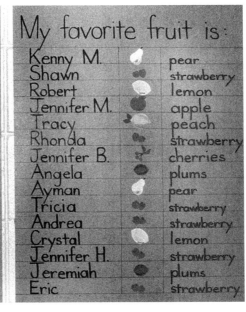

My favorite vegetable:

Name		Vegetable
Kenny M.		pumpkin
Shawn		corn
Robert		radishes
Jennifer M.		corn
Tracy		peas
Angela		potato
Ayman		carrots
Jennifer B.		peas
Tricia		carrots
Andrea		carrots
Rhonda		carrots
Crystal		cucumber
Jennifer H.		carrots
Jeremiah		pumpkin
Eric		corn

My favorite fruit is:

Kenny M.		pear
Shawn		strawberry
Robert		lemon
Jennifer M.		apple
Tracy		peach
Rhonda		strawberry
Jennifer B.		cherries
Angela		plums
Ayman		pear
Tricia		strawberry
Andrea		strawberry
Crystal		lemon
Jennifer H.		strawberry
Jeremiah		plums
Eric		strawberry

Arts and Crafts

1. Seeds

Save several seeds from fruits and vegetables for the children to make a seed collage. When seeds are securely glued, children can also paint them if desired. The collage can be secured to a bulletin board.

2. Cutting Vegetable and Fruit Shapes

Cut easel paper into a different shape of fruit or vegetable every day. Dry Kool-Aid mix can be added to the paint to give it a "fruity" smell.

3. Mold with Play Dough

The children can mold and create fruits and vegetables out of clay and play dough. Another option would be to color and scent the play dough. Examples might include orange-scented orange, lemon-scented yellow, and banana-scented yellow.

4. Potato Prints

Cut potatoes in half. The children can dip them in paints and stamp the potatoes on a large sheet of paper.

5. Paint with Celery Leaves

Mix some thin tempera paint. Use celery leaves as a painting tool.

6. Lemon Play Dough

2 cups water
3 teaspoons liquid food coloring
2 tablespoons cooking oil
2 1/2 cups flour
5 tablespoons cream of tartar
2 or 3 drops lemon oil

In a large pot, combine water, food coloring, and oil. Add flour, salt, and cream of tartar. Over medium heat, cook and stir for about 5 minutes, until a ball of dough forms. Cool the dough for 5 minutes, and then knead it with your hands until smooth. Add additional flour if necessary. Store in an airtight container in the refrigerator when not using.

Cooking

1. Vegetable Dip

1 cup plain yogurt
1 cup mayonnaise
1 tablespoon dill weed
1 teaspoon seasoned salt

Mix all the ingredients together and chill. Serve with fresh, raw vegetables.

2. Ants on a Log

Cut celery into pieces and spread with cream cheese. Top with raisins, coconut, or grated carrots.

Note: Celery is difficult for younger children to chew.

3. Applesauce

4 apples
1 tablespoon water
2 tablespoons brown sugar or honey

Wash the apples and cut into small pieces. Dip the pieces into water and roll in brown sugar or honey. Serves eight.

4. Banana Rounds

4 medium bananas
1/2 cup yogurt
3 tablespoons honey
1/8 teaspoon nutmeg
1/8 teaspoon cinnamon
1/4 cup wheat germ

The children can participate by peeling the bananas and slicing them into "rounds." Measure the spices, wheat germ, and honey. Blend this mixture with yogurt and bananas. Chill before serving. Serves eight.

5. Finnish Strawberry Shake

20 fresh strawberries
4 cups milk
3 tablespoons sugar

Wash strawberries and remove stems. Cut strawberries into small pieces. Combine milk, sugar, and strawberries in a large mixing bowl or blender. Beat with an eggbeater or blend for 2 minutes. Pour strawberry shakes into individual glasses. Makes four to eight servings.

Variation: Raspberries or other sweet fruit may be used instead.

6. Banana Sandwiches

1/2 or 1 banana per child
Honey

Peel the bananas and slice them in half lengthwise. Spread honey on one-half of the banana and top with the other half.

7. Healthy Popsicles

16 ounces unflavored yogurt
6 bananas
2 6-ounce cans of orange juice concentrate

Mix all of the ingredients in a blender, and freeze in popsicle or ice cube trays.

Dramatic Play

Grocery Store

Plan a grocery store containing many plastic fruits and vegetables, a cash register, grocery bags, and play money if available. The children can take turns being a produce clerk, cashier, and price tagger.

Field Trips

1. Grocery Store

Take a trip to the grocery store to visit the produce department. Ask the clerk to show the children how the food is delivered.

2. Visiting a Farm

Visit a farm. Ask the farmer to show the children the fruits and vegetables grown on the farm.

3. Visit a Farmers' Market

Visit a farmers' market. Purchase fruits and vegetables that can be used for snacks.

4. Visit an Orchard

Visit an apple or fruit orchard. Observe how the fruit is grown. If possible, pick some fruit to bring back to the classroom.

Fingerplays and Chants

My Garden

This is my garden
   (extend one hand forward, palm up)
I'll rake it with care
   (make raking motion on palm with three fingers of other hand)
And then some seeds
   (planting motion)

I'll plant in there.
The sun will shine
    (make circle with arms)
And the rain will fall
    (let fingers flutter down to lap)
And my garden will blossom
    (cup hand together, extend upward
    slowly)
And grow straight and tall.

Dig a Little Hole

Dig a little hole.
    (dig)
Plant a little seed.
    (drop seed)
Pour a little water.
    (pour)
Pull a little weed.
    (pull and throw)
Chase a little bug.
    (chasing motion with hands)
Heigh-ho, there he goes.
    (shade eyes)
Give a little sunshine
    (circle arms over head)
Grow a little bean!
    (hands grow upward)

Apple Tree

Way up high in the apple tree
    (hold arms up high)
Two little apples smiled at me.
    (look at two hands up high)
I shook that tree as hard as I could.
    (shake arms)
Down came the apples,
    (arms fall)
Mmm, were they good!
    (rub tummy)

Bananas

Bananas are my favorite fruit.
    (make fists as if holding banana)
I eat one every day.
    (hold up one finger)
I always take one with me
    (act as if putting one in pocket)
When I go out to play.
    (wave good-bye)
It gives me lots of energy
    (make a muscle)
To jump around and run.
    (move arms as if running)

Bananas are my favorite fruit.
    (rub tummy)
To me they're so much fun!
    (point to self and smile)

Vegetables and Fruits

The food we like to eat that grows
On vines and bushes and trees
Are vegetables and fruits, my friends,
Like cherries, grapes, and peas.
Apples and oranges and peaches are
    fruits
And so are tangerines,
Lettuce and carrots are vegetables,
Like squash and beans.

Group Time
(Games and Language)

1. **Carrot, Carrot, Corn**
   Play "Duck, Duck, Goose," but substitute "Carrot, Carrot, Corn."

2. **Hot Potato**
   The children sit in a circle, and the teacher gives one child a potato. Teacher then plays lively music and the children pass the potato around the circle. When the music suddenly stops, the child with the potato must stand up and say the name of a fruit or vegetable. Encourage children to think of a fruit or vegetable that hasn't been named yet.

3. **Fruit Basket Upset**
   Ask the children to sit in a circle formation on chairs or on carpet squares. Then ask one child to sit in the middle of the circle as the chef. Hand pictures of various fruits to the rest of the children. Continue the game by asking the chef to call out the name of a fruit. The child holding that particular fruit exchanges places. If the chef calls out, "Fruit basket upset," all of the children must exchange places, including the chef. The child who fails to find a place is the new chef. A variation of this game would be vegetable or bread basket upset. This game is appropriate for older children.

Large Muscle

Place child-sized plastic hoes, shovels, rakes, and watering cans around the outdoor sand area.

Math

1. **Fruit and Vegetable Match**
   Cut out various fruits and vegetables from a magazine. Trace their shapes onto tagboard. Have children match the fruit or vegetable to the correct shape on the tagboard.

2. **Seriation**
   Make five sizes of each vegetable or fruit you want to use. Have children place in order from smallest to largest, or from largest to smallest.

3. **Measuring**
   The children can measure their bean sprouts. Maintain a small chart of their measurements.

4. **Parts and Wholes**
   Cut apples in half at snack time to introduce the concepts of parts and wholes.

5. **Grouping Pictures**
   Cut pictures of fruits and vegetables for the children to sort according to color, size, and shape.

Music

1. **"The Vegetable Garden"**
   (Sing to the tune of "Mulberry Bush")

   Here we go 'round the vegetable garden,
   The vegetable garden, the vegetable garden,
   Here we go 'round the vegetable garden,
   So early in the morning.

Other verses:
This is the way we pull the weeds …
This is the way we water the plants …
This is the way we eat the vegetables …

2. **"Vegetables"**
   (Sing to the tune of "Mary Had a Little Lamb")

   I'm a tomato, red and round,
   Red and round, red and round.
   I'm a tomato, red and round,
   Seated on the ground.

   I'm a corn stalk, tall and straight,
   Tall and straight, tall and straight.
   I'm a corn stalk, tall and straight
   And I taste just great.

Science

1. **Cut and Draw**
   Cut out or draw many different fruits and vegetables from tagboard or construction paper scraps. Also make a tree, a vine, and some soil. Have children classify the fruit by where it's grown—on a tree, on a vine, or underground.

2. **Tasting Center**
   Cut small pieces of various fruits and set up a tasting center. Include apple slices, banana slices, melon balls, peach slices, and so on. Encourage the children to taste and compare different fruits and vegetables.

3. **Tasting Party**
   Plan a vegetable-tasting party. Cut small pieces of vegetables. Also, have children taste raw vegetables and compare them to the same vegetable cooked.

4. **Identify by Smelling**
   Place one each of several fruits and vegetables in small cups and cover with aluminum foil. Punch a small hole in the top of the aluminum foil. Then have the children smell the cups and try to identify each fruit or vegetable.

5. Carrot Tops in Water

Cut off the top of a carrot and place it in a shallow dish of water. Observe what happens day to day. Given time, the top of the carrot should sprout.

6. Colored Celery Stalks

Place celery stalks into water colored with food coloring. Observe what happens to the leaves of celery.

7. Fruit Dehydration

Provide plastic knives and a variety of fruit for the children to slice. Discuss with children how the fruit looks and feels. Place the sliced fruit in a dehydrator. Dry fruit overnight. The next day, invite the children to discuss the differences in how the fruit looks and feels. Introduce the concept of dehydration (taking the liquid out). Strawberries, bananas, pineapple, apples, and grapes usually have a significant change after dehydrating.

Sensory

1. Preparing Fruits and Vegetables

Wash vegetables and fruits to prepare for eating at snack time.

2. Fruit and Vegetable Scrub

Place play fruits and vegetables in the sensory table. Provide scrub brushes for the children to clean and scrub the fruits and vegetables.

Social Studies

1. Field Trip to a Garden

Plan a field trip to a large garden. Point out different fruits and vegetables. If possible, have the children pull radishes and carrots.

2. Hang Pictures

On a bulletin board in the classroom, hang pictures of fruits and vegetables.

3. Fruit and Vegetable Book

The children can make a fruit and vegetable book. Possible titles include "My Favorite Fruit Is . . . ," "My Favorite Vegetable Is . . . ," "I Would Like to Grow . . . ," and "I Would Most Like to Cook . . ." The children can paste pictures or adhere stickers to the individual pages.

Books

The following books can be used to complement this theme:

Alda, Arlene. (2006). *Did You Say Pears?* Toronto: Tundra Books.

Aston, Dianna Hutts. (2007). *A Seed Is Sleepy.* Illustrated by Sylvia Long. San Francisco: Chronicle Books.

Bodach, Vijaya Khisty. (2007). *Fruits.* Mankato, MN: Capstone Press.

Bosca, Francesca. (2001). *The Apple King.* Illustrated by Giuliano Ferri. New York: North-South Books.

Bunting, Eve. (2006). *One Green Apple.* Illustrated by Ted Lewin. New York: Clarion Books.

Chandler, Lynda E. (2001). *Fruits and Vegetables.* New York: Dover Publishers.

De Paola, Tomie. (2009). *Strega Nona's Garden.* New York: G.P. Putnam's Sons.

Ehlert, Lois. (1994). *Eating the Alphabet: Fruits and Vegetables from A to Z.* Orlando, FL: Harcourt Brace.

Fowler, Allan. (1996). *It's a Fruit, It's a Vegetable, It's a Pumpkin.* Illustrated by Robert L. Hillerich. Chicago: Children's Press.

Gaiman, Neil. (2009). *Blueberry Girl.* Illustrated by Charles Vess. New York: HarperCollins Publishers.

Gibbons, Gail. (2007). *The Vegetables We Eat.* New York: Holiday House.

Gordon, Elizabeth, and M. T. Ross. (2000). *Mother Earth's Children: The Frolics of the Fruits and Vegetables.* Illustrated by M. T. Ross. New York: Derrydale Books.

Gourley, Robin. (2009). *Bring Me Some Apples and I'll Make You a Pie: A Story about Edna Lewis.* New York: Clarion Books.

Hall, Zoe. (1996). *The Apple Pie Tree.* Illustrated by Shari Halpern. New York: Scholastic.

Lin, Grace. (2009). *The Ugly Vegetables.* Watertown, MA: Charlesbridge.

Mcky, Katie. (2006). *Pumpkin Town! Or, Nothing Is Better and Worse Than Pumpkins.* Illustrated by Pablo Bernasconi. Boston: Houghton Mifflin.

Miranda, Anne. (2001). *To Market, to Market.* Illustrated by Janet Stevens. San Diego, CA: Harcourt Brace.

Ray, Deborah Kogan. (2002). *Lily's Garden.* Brookfield, CT: Roaring Brook Press.

Ray, Jane. (2008). *The Apple-Pip Princess.* Cambridge, MA: Candlewick Press.

Rockwell, Anne. (2005). *Apples and Pumpkins.* Illustrated by Lizzy Rockwell. New York: Simon & Schuster.

Rosa-Mendoza, Gladys. (2002). *Fruits and Vegetables = Frutas y Vegetales.* Illustrated by Linda Holt Ayriss. Wheaton, IL: Me+mi Publishing.

Rubel, Nicole. (2002). *No More Vegetables.* New York: Farrar, Straus and Giroux.

Schaefer, Lola M. (2003) *Pick, Pull, Snap.* Illustrated by Lindsay Barrett George. New York: Greenwillow Books.

Schuette, Sarah. (2003). *An Alphabet Salad: Fruits and Vegetables from A to Z.* Mankato, MN: A+ Books.

Schuette, Sarah L. (2003). *The Alphabet Soup: Fruits and Vegetables from A to Z.* Mankato, MN: Capstone Press.

Schuette, Sarah L. (2003). *Eating Pairs: Counting Fruits and Vegetables by Twos.* Mankato, MN: Capstone Press.

Schuh, Mari C. (2006). *The Fruit Group.* Mankato, MN: Capstone Press.

Schuh, Mari C. (2006). *The Vegetable Group.* Mankato, MN: Capstone Press.

Sloat, Teri, and Betty Huffmon. (2004). *Berry Magic.* Anchorage: Alaska Northwest Books.

Tagliaferro, Linda. (2007). *The Life Cycle of an Apple Tree.* Mankato, MN: Capstone Press.

Technology and Multimedia

The following technology and multimedia products can be used to complement this theme:

"All Kinds of Farms," "Hello Harvest Moon," and "Gardener at Home" [CD]. (1999). In *On the Farm with RONNO.* Long Branch, NJ: Kimbo Educational.

"Apples and Bananas" [CD]. (1985). In *One Light, One Sun.* Cambridge, MA: Rounder/UMGD

"Apples and Bananas" and "Aikendrum" [CD]. (1999). In *Five Little Monkeys.* Long Branch, NJ: Kimbo Educational.

"Let's Sing about Food" [CD]. (1994). In *Get Up and Grow.* Long Branch, NJ: Kimbo Educational.

Reading Rainbow. (2007). *Gregory, the Terrible Eater* [DVD]. Lincoln, NE: GNP Educational Media.

"Rhubarb Pie" [CD]. (2010). In *Laurie Berkner: Under a Shady Tree.* New York: Two Tomatoes.

"Vegetable Soup Song" and "Vegetables" [CD]. (1995). In *Piggyback Songs.* Long Branch, NJ: Kimbo Educational.

"Veggie Power" [CD]. (1994). In *Fun 'n' Friendly (RONNO).* Long Branch, NJ: Kimbo Educational.

"Vixen Who Makes Vegetable Soup" [CD]. (1994). In *A to Z: The Animals and Me.* Long Branch, NJ: Kimbo Educational.

Where Food is Grown [DVD]. (2001). Wynnewood, PA: Schlessinger Media.

 Additional teaching resources to accompany this Theme can be found on the book's companion website. Go to www.cengagebrain.com to access the site for a variety of useful resources.

Cooking Vocabulary

The following vocabulary words can be introduced through cooking experiences:

bake	cube	grate	mince	scrub	stir
beat	cut	grease	mix	shake	strain
boil	dice	grill	pare	shred	stuff
broil	dip	grind	peel	sift	tear
brown	drain	heat	pit	simmer	toast
chop	freeze	knead	pour	slice	toss
cool	frost	mash	roast	spread	whip
core	fry	marinate	roll	sprinkle	
cream	garnish	measure	scrape	squeeze	

GARDENS

Type	Purpose	Place
rock	food	window box
vegetable	beauty	indoor
flower	hobby	community
terrarium		rooftop

Plants	Tools	Care
bulbs	hoe	sunshine
seeds	rake	water
plants	spade	fertilizer
roots	hose	warmth
	watering can	soil

Theme Goals

Through participating in the experiences provided by this theme, the children may learn:

1. Purposes of gardens
2. Places of gardens
3. Tools used for gardening
4. Care of gardens
5. Types of plants grown in a garden
6. Types of gardens

Concepts for the Children to Learn

1. Gardens produce vegetables, fruits, and beautiful flowers.
2. Gardens need care.
3. Plants need sunshine, water, soil, fertilizer, and warmth to grow.
4. Plants are living things.
5. Some people garden for a hobby.
6. We plant gardens by placing bulbs, seeds, plants, or roots in the ground.
7. Fruits, vegetables, and flowers can be planted in our gardens.
8. Many tools are needed for gardening.
9. A watering can or hose can be used for watering gardens.
10. A hoe, rake, and spade are gardening tools.
11. There are many places where gardens can be planted.
12. Gardens can be housed on rooftops, in window boxes, and in terrariums.
13. Rock, flower, vegetable, and terrarium are types of gardens.

Vocabulary

1. **bulb**—a type of seed.
2. **flower**—part of the plant that has colored petals.
3. **garden**—a place to grow plants.
4. **greenhouse**—building for growing plants and flowers.
5. **leaf**—flat, green part of a plant.
6. **rake**—a tool with teeth or prongs.
7. **root**—part of the plant that grows into the ground.
8. **seed**—part of the plant from which a new plant will grow.
9. **soil**—top of the ground.
10. **stem**—part of the plant that holds the leaves and flowers.
11. **vegetable**—a plant that can be eaten.
12. **weed**—a plant that is not needed.

Bulletin Board

The purpose of this bulletin board is to foster visual discrimination skills.
To prepare the bulletin board, construct five or six watering cans out of tagboard.
Color each one a different color with felt-tip markers and hang on the bulletin
board. Attach a string to each watering can. Next, construct the same number
of small rakes out of tagboard. Color each one using the same colors you used
for the watering cans. Attach a pushpin to the top of each rake. The children
can match each watering can to the corresponding colored rake by winding the
string around the correct pushpin.

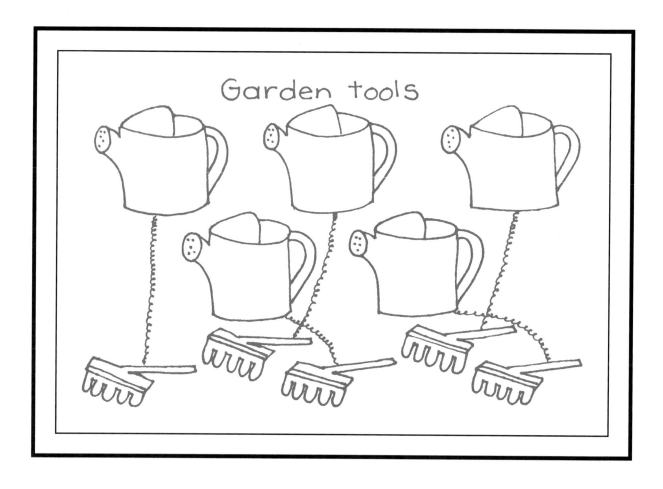

Family Letter

InBox

Dear Families,

"Mary, Mary, quite contrary, how does your garden grow?" That familiar nursery rhyme sums up our next curriculum unit—gardens! We will be exploring the purposes, types, and places for flower and vegetable gardens. We will also learn the names of garden tools and the care that gardens need.

At School

Some of the learning experiences planned to foster concepts related to gardens include:

- Enjoying a flower shop set up in the dramatic play area

- Dramatizing the story of *The Big Turnip*

- Preparing a section of our play yard for a garden. The children will help decide which seeds to plant.

- Playing with mud in the sensory table

At Home

If you have a garden, ask your child to help you water, weed, and care for it. If you don't have a garden, take a walk and observe how many plants you can find that are cared for by people. What are the plants? What colors are they? How are they cared for?

Help your child plant seeds such as corn, beans, and pumpkin that sprout quickly. Then help them develop a vocabulary for describing plant growth: plant, sprout, unfold, bloom, blossom, and flower.

Carrot tops make attractive plants. Cut the tops of carrots off 1/4 inch from the stem to make a carrot-top garden. Place carrot tops in a shallow pie tin and pour 1/4 inch of water in the tin. Soon roots will appear, the greens will grow, and your child will be able to observe the growth.

Enjoy your child!

Arts and Crafts

1. **Leaf Rubbings**

   Take the children on a leaf walk. The children choose a couple of large leaves to bring back to school. Place the leaves between two sheets of paper, and rub with flat, large crayons across the top sheet of paper.

2. **Stencils**

   Cut stencils out of tagboard of various-shaped leaves or vegetables (see patterns). Laminate the stencils. The children can use crayons, pencils, or marking pens to make the leaf or vegetable outlines. These stencils can be used as the front of the "Salad and Soup Party" invitations listed under the "Social Studies" activities.

3. **Decorating Vases**

   Collect tin cans or milk cartons for the children to use as vases. If cans are used, file the sharp edges or cover them with masking tape. The children can decorate the containers with colored paper, gift wrapping paper, or wallpaper. Greeting cards may also be useful for this activity.

4. **Root Painting**

   Dig up old plants (nontoxic), and save the roots and stems. Put paint in containers and take the children, roots, paper, and paint outside to create a painting. The children will use the roots as "paintbrushes."

 ## Cooking

1. **Vegetable Soup**

   Begin with a consommé or soup base. Add whatever vegetables, such as beans that children want to add and can help to prepare. Make the soup a day ahead so that all of the vegetables will be cooked thoroughly.

2. **Indian Cucumbers and Tomatoes with Yogurt**

   2 medium cucumbers
   2 green onions with tops, chopped
   1 teaspoon salt
   2 tomatoes, chopped
   1/2 clove garlic, finely chopped
   2 tablespoons snipped parsley
   1/2 teaspoon ground cumin
   1/8 teaspoon pepper
   1 cup unflavored yogurt

   Cut cucumbers lengthwise into halves. Scoop out seeds. Chop cucumbers. Mix cucumbers, green onions, and salt. Let stand 10 minutes. Add tomatoes. Mix remaining ingredients except yogurt. Toss with cucumber mixture. Cover and refrigerate at least 1 hour. Drain thoroughly. Just before serving, fold in yogurt. Makes 6 servings.

   Note: From *Betty Crocker's International Cookbook,* 1980, New York: Random House.

3. **Lettuce or Spinach Roll-Ups**

   On clean lettuce or spinach leaves, spread softened cream cheese or cottage cheese. If desired, sprinkle with grated carrots. Roll them up. Chill and serve.

4. **Carrot Cookies**

   1/2 cup honey
   1 egg
   1/2 cup margarine
   1 cup whole-wheat flour
   1 1/4 teaspoons baking powder
   1/4 teaspoon salt
   1/2 cup rolled oats
   1/2 cup wheat germ
   1/2 cup grated raw carrots
   1/2 cup raisins
   1 teaspoon vanilla

   Mix all ingredients in a bowl. Drop mixture by spoonfuls onto a lightly greased cookie sheet. Flatten each ball slightly. Bake in a 350-degree oven for approximately 12 minutes.

5. **Jungle Juice**

   Place one banana, 2 cups of orange juice, and a pinch of ginger into an electric blender. Then blend until smooth and serve.

6. Fruit Salad

In a large bowl combine 1 cup of small marshmallows, 1 cup of crushed pineapple, 1 cup of mandarin oranges, 1 cup of shredded coconut, and 1 cup of plain or vanilla yogurt. Serve immediately; otherwise, chill until served.

Dramatic Play

1. Flower Shop

Create a flower shop by gathering plastic flowers and plants. If desired, flowers can be made from tissue paper and chenille stems. Collect different kinds of vases and also styrofoam or sponge blocks so the children can make flower arrangements. A cash register, aprons, money, and sacks can also be provided to encourage play.

2. Gardening Center

Gather tools, gloves, hats, seeds, and plastic flowers or plants. The children can pretend to plant and grow seeds. Provide seed catalogs and order blanks for children to choose seeds to order.

3. Fruit Stand

Set up a fruit stand by using plastic fruits and vegetables. Aprons, a cash register, market baskets or bags, and play money can also be used to encourage play. The children can take turns being the owner and the shopper.

4. Sandbox

The children can experiment with gardening tools in the sandbox.

Field Trips/ Resource People

1. Field Trips

Take a field trip to the following places:

- A flower garden
- A vegetable garden
- A flower shop
- A farmers' market
- A greenhouse
- A conservatory
- A park
- The produce section of a grocery store
- A natural food store

2. Resource People

- Gardeners
- Florist to demonstrate flower arranging

Fingerplays and Chants

Seeds

Some little seeds have parachutes
To carry them around
    (cup hand downward)
The wind blows them swish, swish, swish.
    (flip fingers outward from parachute)
Then gently lays them on the ground.
    (let hand gently float down and rest on lap)

Relaxing Flowers

Five little flowers standing in the sun
    (hold up five fingers)
See their heads nodding, bowing one by one?
    (bend fingers several times)
Down, down, down comes the gentle rain
    (raise hands, wiggle fingers, and lower arms to simulate falling rain)
And the five little flowers lift their heads up again!
    (hold up five fingers)

How It Happens

A muddy hump,
    (make a fist using both hands)
A small green lump,
    (poke up thumbs together as one)
Two leaves and then
Two leaves again
    (raise forefinger of each hand from fist, then middle fingers)
And shooting up, a stem and cup.
    (put elbows, forearms, and hands together, fingers slightly curved)

One last shower,
> (rain movements with spread arms and fingers)

Then a flower.
> (elbows, forearms together with hands wide apart, palms up)

Little Flowers

The sun comes out and shines so bright
> (join hands over head in circle)

Then we have a shower.
> (wiggle fingers coming down)

The little bud pushes with all its might
> (one hand in fist, other hand clasped over; move hands up slowly)

And soon we have a flower.
> (join thumbs and spread fingers for flower)

Mr. Carrot

Nice Mr. Carrot
Makes curly hair.
> (hand on head)

His head grows underneath the ground,
> (bob head)

His feet up in the air.
> (raise feet)

And early in the morning
I find him in his bed
> (close eyes, lay head on hands)

And give his feet a great big pull
> (stretch legs out)

And out comes his head.

Flowers

Flowers tall,
> (hands held high)

Flowers small,
> (hands held low)

Growing by the garden, wall
Flowers red
> (cup both hands to form a flower)

Nod each head
> (move cupped hands in a forward motion)

Flowers gay
Seem to say,
> (cupped hands sway back and forth)

Come and join us in our play.

Group Time
(Games and Language)

Huckle Buckle Bean Stalk

A small object such as a plastic flower or acorn may be used for hiding. All the players cover their eyes, except the one who hides the object. After it is hidden, the players stand up and begin to look for it. When one locates it, he or she doesn't let others know the placement. Instead, he or she quietly takes a seat, saying, "Huckle buckle bean stalk." The game continues until all players have located the object. The first child to find the object usually hides it the next time. This game is appropriate for older children.

 Large Muscle

Leaf Jumping

This is an active skill game that can be played indoors or outdoors. Cut out large cardboard leaves, and arrange them in an irregular line, as they might appear on a stem. The closer they are together, the harder the game will be. Beginning at one end, each player tries to jump over the leaves without touching them. Older children may try to skip or hop over the leaves.

 Math

1. **Sorting Beans**

   Mix together several shapes and colors of large, dried beans. The children can sort the beans by size and color.

2. **Inchworm Measuring**

   A good introduction for this activity is the story *Inch by Inch* by Leo Lionni. Cut two or three dozen inchworms out of felt. Then cut out flowers of various heights—with long or short stems. Encourage the children to place worms along each stem from bottom to top of the flower. How many inchworms tall is each flower? After this, have the children count the inchworms.

Music

"A Little Seed"

(Sing to the tune of "I'm a Little Teapot")
Here's a little seed in the dark, dark ground.
Out comes the warm sun, yellow and round.
Down comes the rain, wet and slow.
Up comes the little seed, grow, grow, grow!

Science

1. **Growing Grass**

   Germinate grass seeds by placing a damp sponge in a pie tin of water and sprinkling seeds on the sponge. The children will notice tiny sprouts after a few days. Experiment by putting one sponge in the freezer, one near a heat source, and one in a dark closet. Discuss what happens to each group of seeds.

2. **Plants Contain Water**

   Cut off 1/4 inch from the bottom of a celery stalk. Fill a clear vase with water containing food coloring. Place the celery stalk in the vase. Encourage the children to observe color changes in the celery stalk. This activity can be repeated using a white carnation.

3. **Planting Seeds**

   Purchase bean and radish seeds. If space permits, plant outdoors. Otherwise, place soil in planters indoors. Plant the seeds with the children. Identify the plants by pasting the seed packages on the planters. This will help the children to recognize the plants as they emerge from the soil.

4. **The Science Table**

   Place a magnifying glass with different types of seeds and bulbs on the science table. During the week, add fresh flowers, plant leaves, and dried plants.

5. **Rooting an Organically Grown Sweet Potato**

   To root an organically grown sweet potato in water, push toothpicks halfway into the potato. Then place the potato in a glass of water with the toothpicks resting on the top rim. Make sure the end of the potato is immersed in water. Place the glass where it will receive adequate light. Maintain the water level so that the bottom of the potato is always immersed. Note that in a few weeks, roots will grow out of the sides and bottom of the potato, and leaves will grow out of the top. The plant can be left in the water or replanted in soil. This activity provides the children an opportunity to observe root growth.

6. **Worm Farm**

   Collect the following materials: a large clear jar with a wide mouth, soil, earthworms, gravel, and food for the worms (lettuce, cornmeal, and cereals). Place the gravel and soil in the jar. Add the worms. Add food on the top of the dirt and keep the soil moist, but not wet. Tape black construction paper around the outside of the jar. The paper can be temporarily removed to observe the worms and see their tunnels.

7. **Sunflower Seeds**

   Place a sunflower seed in a damp napkin and place in a Ziploc bag. Hang in a window. After a few days, you will see roots and eventually a sprout. Invite the children to look at the bags daily and observe any changes.

Sensory

1. **Place the following items in the sensory table:**

   - Soil
   - Seeds
   - Plastic plants
   - Beans
   - Measuring cups
   - Balance scales
   - Worms
   - Miniature garden tools
   - Cut grass or hay

2. Fill and Guess

After showing and discussing several kinds of fruits or vegetables with the children, place the fruits or vegetables in a bag. Individually let children reach in and touch one item. See if they can guess what it is before pulling it out of the bag. Older children may also be able to describe the item.

Social Studies

1. Salad and Soup Party

The children can plan and participate in a salad and soup party for their parents. The groceries will need to be purchased, cleaned, and prepared.

2. Plant Hunt

Go on a hunt to discover how many nonflowering plants, such as algae, fungi, lichens, mosses, and ferns, are found in the school yard. Make a display. How are these plants different from garden plants?

Books

The following books can be used to complement this theme:

Aston, Dianna Hutts. (2007). *A Seed Is Sleepy.* Illustrated by Sylvia Long. San Francisco: Chronicle Books.

Ayres, Katherine. (2007). *Up, Down, and Around.* Illustrated by Nadine Bernard Westcott. Cambridge, MA: Candlewick.

Bodach, Vijaya Khisty. (2007). *Seeds.* Mankato, MN: Capstone Press.

Brorstrom, Gay Bishop, and Kathy Geotzel. (2000). *A Class Trip to Miss Hallberg's Butterfly Garden.* Illustrated by Kathy Geotzel. Sebastopol, CA: Pipevine Press.

Brown, Peter. (2008). *The Curious Garden.* New York: Little, Brown Books for Young Readers.

Bunting, Eve. (2000). *Flower Garden.* Illustrated by Kathryn Hewitt. San Diego, CA: Harcourt Brace.

De Paola, Tomie. (2009). *Strega Nona's Garden.* New York: G.P. Putnam's Sons.

Ehlert, Lois. (2001). *Waiting for Wings.* San Diego, CA: Harcourt.

Ehlert, Lois. (2003). *Planting a Rainbow.* San Diego, CA: Harcourt.

Fine, Edith Hope. (2010). *Water, Weed, and Wait.* Illustrated by Colleen Madden. Berkeley, CA: Tricycle Press.

Flemming, Candace. (2002). *Muncha! Muncha! Muncha!* Illustrated by G. Brian Karas. New York: Atheneum Books for Young Readers.

Florian, Douglas. (1991). *Vegetable Garden.* New York: Harcourt Brace.

French, Vivian. (2010). *Yucky Worms.* Illustrated by Jessica Ahlberg. Somerville, MA: Candlewick Press.

Gordon, Elizabeth, and M. T. Ross. (2000). *Flower Children: The Little Cousins of the Field and Garden.* Illustrated by M. T. Ross. New York: Derrydale Books.

Henkes, Kevin. (2010). *My Garden.* New York: Greenwillow Books.

Krauss, Ruth. (1973). *The Carrot Seed.* Illustrated by Crockett Johnson. New York: HarperCollins.

Levenson, George. (2002). *Pumpkin Circle: The Story of a Garden.* Illustrated by Shmuel Thaler. Berkeley, CA: Ten Speed Press/ Tricycle.

Levenson, George. (2004). *Garden of Wheat and a Loaf to Eat.* Photography by Shmuel Thaler. Berkeley, CA: Ten Speed Press/ Tricycle.

Lionni, Leo. (2010). *Inch by Inch.* New York: Knof. Books for Young Readers.

Prelutsky, Jack. (2007). *In Aunt Giraffe's Green Garden.* Illustrated by Petra Mathers. New York: Greenwillow/HarperCollins.

Ray, Deborah Kogan. (2002). *Lily's Garden.* Brookfield, CT; Roaring Brook Press.

Richards, Jean, and Anca Hariton. (2002). *A Fruit Is a Suitcase for Seeds.* Minneapolis, MN: Millbrook Press.

Rockwell, Anne F. (1999). *One Bean.* New York: Walker and Co.

Schaefer, Lola M. (2003) *Pick, Pull, Snap.* Illustrated by Lindsay Barrett George. New York: Greenwillow Books.

Schatzer, Jeffery L., and Jeffrey Ebbeler. (2007). *The Runaway Garden.* Ann Arbor, MI: Mitten Press.

Shories, Pat. (1996). *Over Under in the Garden: An Alphabet Book.* New York: Farrar, Straus and Giroux.

Stewart, Sarah. (2007). *The Gardener.* New York: Square Fish.

Wellington, Monica. (2005). *Zinnia's Flower Garden.* New York: Dutton Children's Books.

Wojtowicz, Jen. (2005). *The Boy Who Grew Flowers.* Illustrated by Steve Adams. Cambridge, MA: Barefoot Books.

Technology and Multimedia

The following technology and multimedia products can be used to complement this theme:

Bread Comes to Life (A Garden of Wheat and a Load to Eat) [DVD]. (2003). A Project of Informed Democracy. Berkeley, CA: Ten Speed Press/Tricycle.

"The Garden Song" [CD]. (1985). In *10 Carrot Diamond.* Vancouver, BC: Hug Bug Records.

"In Grandma's Garden" [CD]. (2006). In *We've Got Harmony.* Long Branch, NJ: Kimbo Educational.

"In My Garden" [CD]. (1985). In *One Light, One Sun.* Cambridge, MA: Rounder/UMGD

"In the Garden" [CD]. (2010). In *What Are the Odds?* New York: Monkey Monkey Music.

"Oats and Beans and Barley" [CD]. (1980). In *Baby Beluga.* Cambridge, MA: Rounder/UMGD.

Planting a Rainbow [DVD]. (2005). New York: Weston Woods Studios/Scholastic.

Raffi. (1992). "Roots and Shoots Everywhere" [CD]. In *Let's Play.* Cambridge, MA: Rounder/UMGD.

Whose Garden Is It? [DVD]. (2006). Guilford, CT: Nutmeg Media, LLC.

Additional teaching resources to accompany this Theme can be found on the book's companion website. Go to www.cengagebrain.com to access the site for a variety of useful resources.

Theme 42
HALLOWEEN

Symbols
jack-o'-lantern
(pumpkin)
witch
ghost
skeleton
black cat

Colors
orange
black

Costumes and Masks
goblin
witch
ghost
television character
clown
animal
gypsy
cartoon character
funny people

Activities
trick-or-treating
bobbing for apples
parties
costume parades
making costumes
wearing makeup
safety

Theme Goals

Through participating in the experiences provided by this theme, the children may learn:

1. Halloween colors
2. Halloween costumes and masks
3. Halloween activities
4. Halloween symbols

Concepts for the Children to Learn

1. Orange and black are Halloween colors.
2. Costumes and masks are worn by some people on Halloween.
3. Some children make their costumes and wear makeup.
4. A costume is clothing put on for pretending.
5. A mask is a decorative covering we put over our face.
6. Sometimes people wear makeup instead of a mask.
7. A pumpkin can be carved to look like a face.
8. Ghosts, goblins, pumpkins, skeletons, black cats, and witches are symbols of Halloween.
9. People go trick-or-treating on Halloween.
10. A costume parade is a march with many children who are dressed in costumes.
11. Bobbing for apples is an activity at Halloween parties.
12. People often dress in costumes, such as goblins, witches, ghosts, or gypsies, on Halloween.
13. Funny people such as clowns are often seen on Halloween.
14. Costumes that are like cartoon, movie, television, and story book characters are often seen on Halloween.

Vocabulary

1. **costume**—clothing worn to pretend.
2. **ghost**—a make-believe being who wears all white.
3. **goblin**—a Halloween character.
4. **Halloween**—a day when children dress in costumes and go trick-or-treating.
5. **jack-o'-lantern**—a pumpkin cut to look like a face.
6. **mask**—face covering worn when pretending.
7. **pretending**—acting like something or someone else.
8. **trick-or-treating**—walking from house to house to ask for candy or treats.
9. **witch**—a make-believe being who wears black.

Bulletin Board

The purpose of this bulletin board is to have the children practice visual discrimination, problem-solving, and hand-eye coordination skills. To prepare the bulletin board, construct pumpkins out of orange-colored tagboard. The number prepared will be dependent on the developmental appropriateness for the group of children. An alternative would be to use white tagboard colored orange with paint or markers. Divide the pumpkins into pairs. Draw a different kind of face for each pair of pumpkins. Hang one pumpkin from each pair on the left side of the bulletin board as illustrated. Attach an orange string to each pumpkin. On the right side of the bulletin board, hang the matching pumpkins. (See illustration.) Attach a pushpin to each of these pumpkins. The child can match the faces on the pumpkins by winding the correct string around the correct pushpin.

Family Letter

InBox

Dear Families,

The month of October has a special holiday for children—Halloween! Therefore, our next theme will center on Halloween. Many learning experiences have been planned to promote an awareness of colors that are associated with Halloween, as well as symbols that represent Halloween such as costumes, pumpkins, black cats, bats, and witches. Perhaps not all children and families in our program celebrate this holiday, but we feel it is very important for children to learn about and respect others' beliefs. A general understanding of other cultures is also interesting and fun.

At School

Some of the Halloween activities planned include:

- Discussing Halloween safety procedures, especially while trick-or-treating
- Carving a jack-o'-lantern for the classroom
- Roasting pumpkin seeds and baking a pumpkin pie
- Trying on a variety of costumes in the dramatic play area
- Creating designs with pumpkin seeds and glue on paper

At Home

To get into the spirit of Halloween and to help your child develop language skills, practice the following Halloween rhyme:

"Five Little Pumpkins"

Five little pumpkins sitting on a gate.
The first one said, "Oh my, it's getting late."
The second one said, "There are witches in the air."
The third one said, "But we don't care."
The fourth one said, "Let's run. Let's run."
The fifth one said, "It's Halloween fun!"
"Wooooooooo," went the wind,
And out went the lights.
And the five little pumpkins rolled out of sight.

Have a safe and happy Halloween.

Arts and Crafts

1. **Spooky Easel**
   Provide orange and black paint at the paint easels.

2. **Pumpkin Seed Pictures**
   Dye pumpkin seeds many colors. Place the seeds with paste and paper on a table in the art area. The children then can create their own pictures.

3. **Crayon Wash**
   On the art table, place paper, light-colored crayons, tempera paint, and brushes. The children can draw on paper with light-colored crayons. After this, they can paint over the entire picture.

4. **Masks**
   Yarn, paper plates, felt-tip markers, and any other accessories needed to make interesting masks can be placed on a table in the art area. If desired, yarn can be used as hair on the mask.

5. **Pumpkin Play Dough**
   3 cups flour
   1 cup salt
   3 1/2 teaspoons cream of tarter
   4 tablespoons of pumpkin pie spice
   2 cups water

   Mix all of the ingredients together in a kettle. Cook over medium heat until all ingredients are mixed. Then knead until the mixture is smooth. Store in a plastic bag; otherwise, place in an airtight container.

Cooking

1. **Pumpkin Pie**
   1 unbaked pie shell
   2 cups (16–17 ounces) pumpkin
   1 can sweetened condensed milk
   1 egg
   1/2 teaspoon salt
   2 teaspoons pumpkin pie spice

   Blend all of the ingredients in a large mixing bowl. Pour the mixture into the pie shell. Bake the pie in an oven preheated to 375 degrees for 50 to 55 minutes or until a sharp knife blade inserted near the center of the pie is clean when removed. Cool and refrigerate the pie for 1 hour before serving. Top with whipped cream if desired.

2. **Pumpkin Patch Muffins**
   3 cups flour
   1 cup sugar
   4 teaspoons baking powder
   1 teaspoon salt
   1 teaspoon pumpkin pie spice
   1 cup milk
   1 cup canned pumpkin
   1/2 cup (1 stick) butter or margarine, melted
   2 eggs, beaten

   Sift the flour, sugar, baking powder, salt, and pumpkin pie spice into a large mixing bowl. Add the milk, pumpkin, melted butter, and eggs. Mix with a wooden spoon just until flour is moist. (Batter will be lumpy.) Place paper liners in the muffin tins and fill two-thirds full with batter. Bake in a preheated 400-degree oven for 20 minutes or until muffins are golden. Cool in muffin tins 10 minutes on a wire rack. Remove muffins from muffin tins, and finish cooling on wire racks. Pile into serving baskets and serve warm for a snack.

3. **Witches' Brew**
   5 cups cranberry juice
   5 cups apple cider
   1 or 2 cinnamon sticks
   1/4 teaspoon ground nutmeg

   Place ingredients in a large saucepan. Cover, heat, and simmer for 10 minutes. Serve warm.

4. **Roasted Pumpkin Seeds**
   Soak pumpkin seeds for 24 hours in saltwater (1/4 cup salt to 1 cup water). Spread on cloth-covered cookie sheet, and roast at 100 degrees for 2 hours. Turn oven off and leave seeds overnight.

5. Nonbake Pumpkin Pie

1 can prepared pumpkin pie filling
1 package vanilla instant pudding
1 cup milk

Mix and pour into a baked pie shell or graham cracker pie shell.

Dramatic Play

Costumes

Add Halloween costumes to the dramatic play area. (Some teachers purchase these at thrift stores or sales. From year to year, they are stored in a Halloween prop box.)

Field Trips and Resource People

1. Pumpkin Patch

Visit a pumpkin patch. During the tour, point out various-sized pumpkins. Discuss how the pumpkins grow, as well as their shapes, sizes, and so on.

2. Halloween Safety

A police officer can be invited to talk with the children about Halloween safety.

Fingerplays and Chants

Jack-o'-Lantern

I am a pumpkin, big and round.
  (show size with arms)
Once upon a time, I grew on the ground.
  (point to ground)
Now I have a mouth, two eyes, and a nose.
  (point to each)
What are they for, do you suppose?
  (point to forehead and "think")
Why—I'll be a jack-o'-lantern on Halloween night.

Five Little Jack-o'-Lanterns

Five little jack-o'-lanterns sitting on a gate.
The first one said, "My, it's getting late."
The second one said, "There are witches in the air."
The third one said, "But we don't care."
The fourth one said, "Let's run, let's run."
The fifth one said, "It's really Halloween fun."
Puff went the wind, out went the light.
And off ran the jack-o'-lanterns on Halloween night.

Five Little Witches

Five little witches standing by the door.
  (hold up five fingers)
One flew out and then there were four.
  (flying motion with hand)
Four little witches standing by a tree.
  (four fingers)
One went to pick a pumpkin and then there were three.
  (picking motion, then three fingers)
Three little witches stirring their brew.
  (stir)
One fell in and then there were two.
  (two fingers)
Two little witches went for a run.
  (run with fingers)
One got lost and then there was one.
  (one finger)
One little witch, yes, only one.
  (one finger)
She cast a spell and now there are none.
  (make motions as if to cast spell and then put hands in lap)

Halloween Fun

Goblins and witches in high-pointed hats,
  (hands above head to form hat)
Riding on broomsticks and chasing black cats.
  (ride broomstick)
Children in costumes might well give a fright.
  (look frightened)
Get things in order for Halloween night.
We like our treats
  (nod head)
And we'll play no mean pranks.
  (shake head)
We'll do you no harm and we'll only say, "Thanks!"

The Jack-o'-Lantern

Three little pumpkins growing on a vine.
(three fingers)
Sitting in the sunlight, looking just fine.
(arms up like sun)
Along came a ghost who picked just one
(one finger)
To take on home for some Halloween fun.
(smile)
He gave him two eyes to see where he goes.
(paint two eyes)
He gave him a mouth and a big handsome nose.
(point to mouth and nose)
Then he put a candle in.
(pretend to put in candle)
Now see how he glows.
(wiggle fingers from center of body out until arms are extended)

I've a Jack-o'-Lantern

I've a jack-o'-lantern
(make a ball with open fist, thumb at top)
With a great big grin.
(grin)
I've got a jack-o'-lantern
With a candle in.
(insert other index finger up through bottom of first)

Halloween Witches

One little, two little, three little witches,
(hold up one hand, nod fingers at each count)
Fly over the haystacks
(fly hand in up-and-down motion)
Fly over ditches
Slide down moonbeams without any hitches
(glide hand downward)
Heigh-ho! Halloween's here!

The Friendly Ghost

I'm a friendly ghost—almost!
(point to self)
And I chase you, too!
(point to child)
I'll just cover me with a sheet
(pretend to cover self, ending with hands covering face)

And then call "scat" to you.
(uncover face quickly and call out, "Scat!")

Witches' Cat

I am the witches' cat.
(make a fist with two fingers extended for cat)
Meoow. Meoow.
(stroke fist with other hand)
My fur is black as darkest night.
My eyes are glaring green and bright.
(circle eyes with thumb and forefingers)
I am the witches' cat.
(make a fist again with two fingers extended, and stroke fist with other hand)

My Pumpkin

See my pumpkin round and fat.
(make circle with hands, fingers spread wide, touching)
See my pumpkin yellow.
(make a smaller circle)
Watch him grin on Halloween.
(point to mouth, which is grinning wide)
He is a very funny fellow.

Group Time
(Games and Language)

1. **Thank-You Note**
Write a thank-you note to any resource person on a large sheet of paper. Encourage all of the children to participate by sharing what they liked or saw. After the note is finished, provide the children with orange and black crayons to decorate the note.

2. **Costume Parade**
On Halloween day, the children can dress up in costumes and march around the room and throughout the school to music. If available, a walk to a local nursing home may be enjoyed by the children as well as the nursing home residents.

Large Muscle

Ghost, Ghost, Witch

This game is played like "Duck, Duck, Goose." Form a circle and kneel. Choose one child to be "it" and to walk around the outside of the circle, chanting, "Ghost, ghost, ghost." When the child taps another child and says, "Witch," the tapped child chases the initiator around the circle, attempting to tag "it." If the child who is "it" returns to the empty child's spot before being tagged, he or she can sit in the circle. If not, the child continues walking around the circle, repeating the same procedure.

Math

1. **Counting Pumpkin Seeds**

   Cut circles from construction paper. The number needed will depend on the developmental level of the children. Write a numeral on each paper circle, and place each into a pie tin. The children may count enough pumpkin seeds into each tin to match the numeral on the circle.

2. **Weighing Pumpkin Seeds**

   In the math area, place a scale and pumpkin seeds. The children may elect to experiment by balancing the scale with the pumpkin seeds.

Music

1. **"Flying Witches"**

   (*Sing to the tune of "When the Saints Come Marching In"*)

   Oh, when the witches
   Come flying by.
   Oh, when the witches come flying by,

   It will be Halloween night,
   When the witches come flying by.

2. **"One Little, Two Little, Three Little Pumpkins"**

   (*Sing to the tune of "One Little, Two Little, Three Little Indians"*)

   One little, two little, three little pumpkins,
   Four little, five little, six little pumpkins,
   Seven little, eight little, nine little
       pumpkins,
   Ready for Halloween night!

3. **"Have You Made a Jack-o'-Lantern?"**

   (*Sing to the tune of "Muffin Man"*)

   Have you made a jack-o'-lantern,
   A jack-o'-lantern, a jack-o'-lantern?
   Have you made a jack-o'-lantern
   For Halloween night?

Science

1. **Carve Pumpkins**

   Purchase several pumpkins. Carve them and save the seeds for roasting. An alternative activity would be to use a black felt-tip marker to draw facial features on the pumpkin. Pumpkins can also have added accessories. For example, a large carrot can be used for a nose, parsley for hair, cut green peppers for ears, radishes for eyes, and a small green onion in a cut mouth for teeth.

2. **Roasting Pumpkin Seeds**

   Wash and dry pumpkin seeds. Then spread the seeds out on a cookie sheet to dry. Bake the seeds in a preheated oven at 350 degrees until brown. Salt if desired, cool, and eat at snack time.

3. **Plant Pumpkin Seeds**

   Purchase a packet of pumpkin seeds. Plant the pumpkin seeds in small paper cups. Set the paper cups with the pumpkin seeds in a sunny place. Water as needed. Observe daily to see if there is growth.

 **Sensory**

1. **Measuring Seeds**
   Pumpkin seeds and measuring cups can be added to the sensory table. The children will enjoy feeling and pouring seeds.

2. **Goop**
   Add dry cornstarch to the sensory table. Slowly add enough water to make it a "goopy" consistency. If desired, add coloring to make it black or orange.

 **Books**

The following books can be used to complement this theme:

Agran, Rick. (2003). *Pumpkin Shivaree.* Illustrated by Sara Anderson. Brooklyn, NY: Handprint Books.

Brenner, Tom. (2009). *And Then Comes Halloween.* Illustrated by Holly Meade. Somerville, MA: Candlewick Press.

Brown, Margaret Wise. (2003). *The Fierce Yellow Pumpkin.* New York: HarperCollins.

Carlson, Nancy L. (2002). *Harriet's Halloween Candy.* Minneapolis, MN: Carolrhoda Books.

Cooper, Helen. (1998). *Pumpkin Soup.* New York: Farrar, Straus and Giroux.

Donaldson, Julia. (2001). *Room on the Broom.* Illustrated by Alex Scheffler. New York: Dial Books for Young Readers.

Duval, Kathy. (2007). *The Three Bears Halloween.* Illustrated by Paul Meisel. New York: Holiday House.

Fleming, Denise. (2001). *Pumpkin Eve.* New York: Holt.

Gibbons, Gail. (1999). *The Pumpkin Book.* New York: Holiday House.

Gordon, Lynn, and Karen Johnson. (2000). *52 Tricks and Treats for Halloween.* Illustrated by Karen Johnson. New York: Chronicle Books.

Greene, Carol. (2004). *The Story of Halloween.* Illustrated by Linda Bronson. New York: HarperCollins.

Hall, Zoe. (1994). *It's Pumpkin Time!* Illustrated by Shari Halpern. New York: Scholastic.

Heiligman, Deborah. (2007). *Celebrate Halloween.* Illustrated by Jack Santino. Washington, DC: National Geographic Society.

Kessel, Joyce K. (2004). *Halloween.* Illustrated by Nancy Carlson. Minneapolis, MN: Carolrhoda Books.

Levenson, George. (2002). *Pumpkin Circle: The Story of a Garden.* Illustrated by Shmuel Thaler. Berkeley, CA: Ten Speed Press/ Tricycle.

Mayr, Diane. (2001). *Littlebat's Halloween Story.* Illustrated by Gideon Kendall. Morton Grove, IL: Albert Whitman and Company.

McCann, Jesse Leon. (1999). *Scooby-Doo and the Halloween Hotel Haunt: A Glow in the Dark Mystery.* New York: Scholastic.

Mcky, Katie. (2006*). Pumpkin Town! Or, Nothing Is Better and Worse Than Pumpkins.* Illustrated by Pablo Bernasconi. Boston: Houghton Mifflin.

Meddaugh, Susan. (2005). *The Witch's Walking Stick.* Boston: Houghton Mifflin.

Moler, Robert E. (2000). *If I Were a Halloween Monster: A Mirror-Mask Book with Pop-Up Surprises!* Boston: Little, Brown.

Murray, Marjorie Dennis. (2008). *Halloween Night.* Illustrated by Brandon Dorman. New York: Greenwillow Books.

Poydar, Nancy. (2001). *The Perfectly Horrible Halloween.* New York: Holiday House.

Prelutsky, Jack. (2002). *Halloween Countdown.* New York: HarperFestival.

Rau, Dana Meachen. (2001). *Halloween.* New York: Children's Press.

Robbins, Ken. (2007). *Pumpkins.* New York: Square Fish.

Rylant, Cynthia. (2003). *Moonlight: The Halloween Cat.* New York: HarperCollins Publishing.

Schulman, Janet. (2005). *10 Trick-or-Treaters: A Halloween Counting Book.* New York: Random House.

Spohn, Kate. (2002). *Turtle and Snake's Spooky Halloween.* New York: Viking.

Stoeke, Janet Morgan. (2009). *Minerva Louise on Halloween.* New York: Dutton Children's Books.

Stutson, Caroline. (2009). *By the Light of the Halloween Moon.* Illustrated by Kevin Hawkes. Tarrytown, NY: Marshall Cavendish Children.

Williams, Linda. (1998). *The Little Old Lady Who Was Not Afraid of Anything.* Illustrated by Megan Lloyd. New York: Harper and Row.

Technology and Multimedia

The following technology and multimedia products can be used to complement this theme:

"Halloween Song," "Halloween Is Here," and "Pumpkin Song" [CD]. (1998). In *Holiday Piggyback Songs.* Long Branch, NJ: Kimbo Educational.

Holiday Facts and Fun: Halloween [DVD]. (2004). Chicago: SVE & Churchill Media.

"It Must Be Halloween" [CD]. (1996). In *Halloween Howls.* Canoga Park, CA: Andrew Gold/QBRAIN Studios.

It's the Great Pumpkin, Charlie Brown [DVD]. (2008). Los Angeles: Warner Home Video.

"Monster Boogie" [CD]. (2010). In *The Best of the Laurie Berkner Band.* New York: Two Tomatoes.

"Monster Mash" [CD]. (2001). In *Dance Party Fun.* Long Branch, NJ: Kimbo Educational.

Palmer, Hap. (1997). "Have a Good Halloween Night." In *Holiday Songs and Rhythms* [CD]. Freeport, NY: Educational Activities.

Yo Gabba Gabba! Halloween! [DVD]. (2009). Los Angeles: Paramount Home Entertainment.

Additional teaching resources to accompany this Theme can be found on the book's companion website. Go to www.cengagebrain.com to access the site for a variety of useful resources.

Decorating a Pumpkin

While carving or decorating a pumpkin with the children, you can discuss:

- The physical properties of pumpkins—color, texture, size, and shape (both outside and inside)
- The food category to which pumpkins belong
- What other forms pumpkins can be made into after the shell is scooped out
- Where pumpkins grow (plant some of the seeds)
- What size and shape to make the features of the pumpkin, including eyes, nose, and mouth, and what kind of expression to make

Accessories:

1 bunch parsley (hair)
1 carrot (nose)
2 string beans (eyebrows)
2 radishes (eyes)
1 green pepper (ears)
1 stalk celery (teeth)
1 large pumpkin (head)

Prepare the pumpkin in the usual manner; that is, cut off the cap and scoop out the seeds inside. Save the seeds for roasting. If desired, individual vegetable pieces may be attached by carving or inserting toothpicks.

Theme 43
HANUKKAH
(Chanukah)

Foods
latkes
jelly doughnuts
chocolate coins (gelt)
Hanukkah cookies

Symbols
menorah
Star of David
dreidel

Celebration
lighting the menorah
gift giving
family togetherness
playing the dreidel game
singing

Theme Goals

Through participating in the experiences provided by this theme, the children may learn:

1. Foods eaten during Hanukkah
2. Symbols of Hanukkah
3. Hanukkah celebrations

Concepts for the Children to Learn

1. Hanukkah is a Jewish holiday celebrated for eight days.
2. Families celebrate together during Hanukkah.
3. Families and friends eat together, play dreidel, sing Hanukkah songs, and tell stories.
4. Hanukkah is a time for exchanging gifts and sharing with others.
5. The menorah and the dreidel are symbols of Hanukkah.
6. Some foods eaten during Hanukkah include latkes (potato pancakes), jelly doughnuts, chocolate coins, and Hanukkah cookies.

Vocabulary

1. **dreidel**—four-sided toy that spins like a top. Each side of the dreidel bears a letter of the Hebrew alphabet.
2. **Hanukkah**—eight-day Jewish festival of lights. A celebration of the Jewish people's fight long ago to keep the right to practice their religion. One candle on the menorah is lighted each day.
3. **latkes**—potato pancakes eaten during Hanukkah.
4. **menorah**—eight-branched candlestick. The middle or ninth candle is taller than the other eight and is called the "shammash."
5. **Star of David**—a six-pointed star that is a Jewish symbol.

Bulletin Board

The purpose of this bulletin board is to develop an awareness of the passage of time as well as the math concept of sets. This bulletin board starts out with the base of the menorah. Each day of Hanukkah, the children work together to construct a candle and a flame to add to the menorah. Candles and flames are most interesting when made using a wide variety of media: sequins, feathers, cut construction paper, yarn, and so on.

The festival of lights.

Family Letter

Dear Families,

For the next eight days, we will be celebrating Hanukkah. Hanukkah commemorates the victory of the Jews over the Syrians, and it is a celebration of religious freedom. Also known as the Festival of Lights, Hanukkah is observed for eight nights and days, starting on the 25th day of Kislev according to the Hebrew calendar, which may occur at any time from late November to late December. Legend states that, when the Jewish Temple was destroyed by the Syrians and rebuilt, there was only enough sacred oil to light the Temple lamp (an eternal flame) for one day. Miraculously, it burned for eight days and eight nights!

Hanukkah is celebrated by the lighting of a special candelabra called a menorah. On the menorah there is one holder for each of the eight nights and one for the shammash. "Shammash" means "helper" in Hebrew; this is the candle that is used to light the others. The candles are lit beginning on the right side and moving to the left.

Each night, after the lighting of the menorah, the children are given small gifts. Traditionally this gift was "gelt": money or chocolate money to be used while playing the dreidel game. Families get together for big dinners with friends and relatives. After dinner, everyone usually enjoys playing dreidel, singing Hanukkah songs, and telling stories.

Unlike most Jewish holidays, work and schooling continue during the eight-day celebration. Perhaps not all children and families in our program celebrate this holiday, but we feel it is very important for children to learn about and respect others' beliefs. A general understanding of other cultures is also interesting and fun. However, if you wish that your child not participate in this theme, please let us know.

At School
Some of the learning experiences the children will participate in include:
- Playing a game with a dreidel, which is similar to a toy top
- Preparing latkes (potato pancakes) for a snack
- Creating wax-resist drawings at the art table

Happy Hanukkah!

Arts and Crafts

1. **Menorahs**
   Provide the children with candles cut from different colored construction paper, along with flames cut out of red. Demonstrate to the children how to glue a candle onto the paper, and how to glue a flame on top of each candle.

2. **Play Dough Doughnuts**
   Give the children tan or yellow play dough, and a little bit of red play dough. Show them how you can make a jelly doughnut by putting a small ball of red play dough in the middle and putting tan or yellow play dough in a bigger ball all around it.

3. **Hanukkah Handprints**
   Provide the children with construction paper, brushes, and tempera paint in shallow pans. Paint each of the children's hands with a brush that has been dipped in tempera paint. The children then may place their hands on the construction paper, creating handprints.

4. **Dreidel**
   Collect and wash out half-pint milk containers. Tape the top down so that the carton forms a square. Provide construction paper squares for the children to paste to the sides of the milk carton. The children may decorate with crayons or felt-tip markers. Upon completion, punch an unsharpened pencil through the milk container so that the children may spin it like a top.

Cooking

1. **Latkes**
   6 medium-sized potatoes, washed, pared, and grated
   1 egg
   3 tablespoons flour
   1/2 teaspoon baking powder

   In a large bowl, mix the egg and the grated potatoes. Add the flour and baking powder.

Drop by spoonfuls into hot cooking oil in a frying pan. Brown on both sides. Drain on paper towels. Latkes may be served with a spoonful of applesauce or sour cream.

2. **Hanukkah Cookies**
   1 cup butter
   1 cup white sugar
   1 egg
   2 2/3 cups all-purpose flour
   1/4 teaspoon salt
   2 teaspoons vanilla extract

   In a large bowl, cream together the butter and sugar until light and fluffy. Beat in the egg, then the vanilla. Combine the flour and salt; stir into the butter mixture. Cover dough, and chill for at least one hour. Roll out and press onto wax paper. Have the children use Hanukkah-themed cookie cutters in the shapes of dreidels, the Star of David, and menorahs. Bake in a preheated 400-degree oven for 8–10 minutes. Cool. Once the cookies are cooked and cooled, children can ice the cookies and decorate with sprinkles. Blue and white would be traditional colors to use for Hanukkah, but are not essential.

Dramatic Play

1. **Family Celebration**
   Collect materials for a special family meal. These may include dresses, hats, coats, plates, cups, plastic food, napkins, and so on. The children can have a holiday meal.

2. **Gift Wrapping Center**
   Collect various-sized boxes, wrapping paper, tape, and ribbon. The children can wrap presents for Hanukkah.

Fingerplays and Chants

The Menorah Candle
I'm a menorah candle
  (stand, point at self)
Growing shorter you can see
  (bend down slowly)

Melting all my wax
   (go down more)
Until there's nothing left to see.
   (sit down)

Hanukkah Lights

One light, two lights, three lights, and four
   (hold up four fingers, one at a time)
Five lights, six lights, and three more,
   (hold up five fingers on other hand)
Twinkle, twinkle nine pretty lights,
   (move fingers)
In a golden menorah bright!
   (make cup with palm of hand)

My Dreidel

I have a little dreidel.
   (cup hands to form a square)
I made it out of clay.
   (move fingers in a molding motion)
And when it's dry and ready
   (flatten hands as if to hold in hand—
   palm up, pinkies together)
Then with it I will play.
   (pretend to spin dreidel on the floor)

 (Additional verses)
It has a lovely body.
With legs so short and thin.
And when it is tired
It drops and then I win!
My dreidel's always playful.
It loves to dance and spin.
A happy game of dreidel.
Come and play now, let's begin.

Group Time
(Games and Language)

1. Hot Potato

Ask the children to sit in a circle. Provide one child with a real potato, a plastic potato, or a potato constructed from tagboard. Play music. As the music is playing, the children pass the potato around the circle until the music stops. The one holding the potato is out of the circle. The game continues until one child is left or the children no longer wish to play.

2. Dreidel Game

Each player starts with 10 to 15 pennies, nuts, or raisins. Each player places an object in the center of the circle. The dreidel is spun by one of the players, while the following verse is chanted:

I have a little dreidel.
I made it out of clay.
And when it's dry and ready
Then with it I will play.

Whether the spinning player wins or loses depends on which side of the dreidel lands upward when it falls. Each side of the dreidel bears a letter of the Hebrew alphabet: נ (Nun), ג (Gimel), ה (Hei), and ש (Shin). The following may be used as a guide:

Nun (נ) means nothing: player receives
   nothing from the pot.
Gimmel (ג) means all: player receives
   everything from the pot.
Hei (ה) means half: player takes half
   of the pot.
Shin (ש) means put in: player adds two
   objects to the pot.

When one player has won all of the objects,
   the game is completed.

3. Gelt Hunt

Make a silver coin by cutting out a 4-inch round piece of cardboard and covering it with aluminum foil. Hide the coin (gelt) in the classroom, and play a hide-and-seek game. For younger children, hide the gelt in an obvious place.

   ("Gelt" is the Yiddish word for money. Traditionally, small amounts of gelt are given to children each night of Hanukkah.)

Large Muscle

1. Dreidel Dance

The children can dance the dreidel dance by standing in a circle and spinning as they sing this song to the tune of "Row, Row, Row Your Boat."

Dreidel, dreidel, dreidel,
A-spinning I will go.
Speed it up and slow it down,
And on the ground I'll go!

2. Frying Donuts: Dramatic Play

Children can act out frying donuts as they sing this song to the tune of "I Have a Little Turtle."

I have a little donut,
It is so nice and light,
And when it's all done cooking,
I'm going to take a bite!

Frying donuts usually pop up and out of the frying oil when they are finished cooking. The children can act out these motions. The oil used in frying the donuts is significant in the Hanukkah celebration. It signifies the oil burned in the Temple lamp.

 Math

1. **Sort the Candles**
   Provide children with various-colored candles. The children can match the colors. A variation would be to have candles of various sizes. The children could sequence the candles from largest to smallest.

2. **Hanukkah Puzzles**
   Mount pictures of a menorah and the Star of David on tagboard. Cut into pieces. Laminate. The number of pieces will depend on the children's developmental age.

3. **Candle Holder and Candle Match**
   Have a variety of candle holders set out with candles. The children will have to match the candles to the correct-sized candle holder.

 Music

"Hanukkah Oh Hanukah"
Hanukkah oh Hanukkah
come light the menorah,
we'll have a party,
we'll all dance the hora,
Gather round the table,
we'll give you a treat,
Dreidels to play with
and latkes to eat.

Resource People

Invite a rabbi or parent of the Jewish faith to come and talk about Hanukkah and how it is celebrated.

Science

1. **Potato Sprouts**
   Provide each child with a clear plastic cup. Fill the plastic cup half-full with water. Place a potato partway in the water supported by toothpicks to keep it from dropping into the jar. Put the end with tubers into the water. The other end should stick out of the water. Refill with fresh water as it evaporates, and watch the roots begin to grow and leaves start to sprout.

2. **Light**
   Light a flashlight. Discuss other sources of light. Examples can include the sun, a lamp, a candle, and traffic lights.

3. **Sunlight Power**
   Fill two glasses half-full of warm water. Stir some flour into one glass. In the other, dissolve a little yeast in the water, then add flour. Now set them both in a warm place for an hour and watch the results.

 Sensory

Sand Temples
Fill the sensory table with sand and moisten until the sand is wet enough to form shapes. The children may pack sand into cans to mold into desired shapes and build sand temples from the molded forms.

Social Studies

1. Menorah

Glue eight wooden or styrofoam spools of equal size to a piece of wood, leaving a space in the middle. Glue a larger spool in the middle, thus making four smaller spools on each side. Spray with gold or silver paint. The menorah can be lit during the eight days of Hanukkah during group time. Explain the meaning of the menorah to the group as well.

2. Hanukkah Celebration

Display pictures at the children's eye level of the Hanukkah celebration. Examples would include such pictures as lighting the menorah, a family meal, and playing with dreidels.

3. Human Menorah

The children can make a human menorah by positioning themselves to resemble a menorah. A menorah is a lamp with nine flames that is used to celebrate Hanukkah. Two children can lie head-to-toe on the floor to form the base. Have nine children stand behind the base to form the candles. The tallest child can stand in the middle and be the shammash. The shammash is the center candle that lights the other candles. The children can make pretend flames out of construction paper for the candles to hold over their heads as if they were lit.

 ## Books

The following books can be used to complement this theme:

Adler, David A. (1997). *Chanukah in Chelm.* Illustrated by Kevin O'Malley. New York: Lothrop, Lee & Shepard.

Baum, Maxie. (2006). *I Have a Little Dreidel.* Illustrated by Julie Paschkis. New York: Scholastic.

Bledsoe, Karen E. (2004). *Hanukkah Crafts.* Berkeley Heights, NJ: Enslow Publishers.

Chwast, Seymour. (2006). *The Miracle of Hanukkah.* Maplewood, NJ: Blue Apple Books.

Conway, Diana Cohen. (1994). *Northern Lights: A Hanukkah Story.* Rockville, MD: Kar-Ben Copies.

Da Costa, Deborah. (2007). *Hanukkah Moon.* Illustrated by Gosia Mosz. Minneapolis, MN: Kar-Ben Publishing.

Edwards, Michelle. (2004). *Papa's Latkes.* Cambridge, MA: Candlewick Press.

Glaser, Linda. (1997). *The Borrowed Hanukkah Latkes.* Illustrated by Nancy Cote. Park Ridge, IL: Albert Whitman & Company.

Glaser, Linda. (2004). *Mrs. Greenberg's Messy Hanukkah.* Illustrated by Nancy Cote. Park Ridge, IL: Albert Whitman & Company.

Goldin, Barbara Diamond. (2007). *The Best Hanukkah Ever.* Illustrated by Avi Katz. Tarrytown, NY: Marshall Cavendish.

Heiligman, Deborah. (2006). *Celebrate Hanukkah.* Washington, DC: National Geographic.

Holub, Joan. (2000). *Light the Candles: A Hanukkah Lift the Flap Book.* Illustrated by Lynne Avril Cravath. New York: Puffin.

Howland, Naomi. (2004). *Latkes, Latkes, Good to Eat: A Chanukah Story.* London: Sandpiper.

Kimmel, Eric A. (1992). *The Channukah Guest.* Illustrated by Giora Carmi. New York: Holiday House.

Kimmel, Eric A. (1996). *The Magic Dreidels: A Hanukkah Story.* Illustrated by Katya Krenina. New York: Holiday House.

Kroll, Steven. (2008). *The Hanukkah Mice.* Illustrated by Michelle Shapiro. Tarrytown, NY: Marshall Cavendish.

Martin, David. (2009). *Hanukkah Lights.* Illustrated By Melissa Sweet. Somerville, MA: Candlewick Press.

Newman, Leslea. (2002). *Runaway Dreidel!* New York: Henry Holt.

Oberman, Sheldon. (1997). *By the Hanukkah Light.* Illustrated by Neil Waldman. Honesdale, PA: Boyds Mills Press.

Penn, Malka. (1994). *The Miracle of the Potato Latkes: A Hanukkah Story.* Illustrated by Giora Carmi. New York: Holiday House.

Rosen, Michael J. (1992). *Elijah's Angel: A Story for Chanukah and Christmas*. Illustrated by Aminah B. L. Robinson. Orlando, FL: Harcourt Brace.

Roth, Susan. (2004). *Hanukkah Oh Hanukkah*. New York: Dial Books for Young Readers.

Rouss, Sylvia A. (1993). *Sammy Spider's First Hanukkah*. Illustrated by Katherine Janus Kahn. Minneapolis, MN: Kar-Ben Publishing.

Schnur, Steven. (1995). *The Tie Man's Miracle: A Chanukah Story*. Illustrated by Stephen Johnson. New York: William Morrow.

Schwartz, Linda, and Beverly Armstrong. (1998). *The Hanukkah Happenings*. Illustrated by Beverly Armstrong. Santa Barbara, CA: Learning Works.

Smith, Dian G. (2001). *Hanukkah Lights*. Illustrated by JoAnn Kitchel. San Francisco: Chronicle Books.

Sper, Emily. (2001). *Hanukkah*. New York: Scholastic.

Stillerman, Marci. (1998). *Nine Spoons: A Chanukah Story*. Brooklyn, NY: Hachai Publishers.

Wax, Wendy, ed. (1993). *Hanukkah, Oh Hanukkah! A Treasury of Stories, Songs, and Games to Share*. Illustrated by John Speirs. New York: Bantam Doubleday.

Technology and Multimedia

The following technology and multimedia products can be used to complement this theme:

Arthur's Perfect Christmas [DVD]. (2002). New York: Random House Home Video.

"Dreidel, Dreidel, Dreidel" [CD]. (2001). In *Seasonal Songs in Motion*. Long Branch, NJ: Kimbo Educational.

"The Dreidel Song." (1991). *Children of the World. Long Branch, NJ:* Kimbo Educational.

Elmo's World: Happy Holidays! [DVD]. (2002). Los Angeles: Sony Wonder.

"Hanukkah, Hanukkah," "Hanukkah Menorah," "Dreidel Song," and "The Latkes Are Frying in the Pan" [CD]. (1998). In *Holiday Piggyback Songs*. Long Branch, NJ: Kimbo Educational.

"Hanukkah, Oh Hanukkah," "Dreidel," and "How Many Candles?" [CD]. (2001). In *Sing 'N Sign Holiday Time (Gaia)*. Long Branch, NJ: Kimbo Educational.

"The Hanukkah Song" [CD]. (2002). In *Hanukkah and Chinese New Year*. Long Branch, NJ: Kimbo.

"Have Nagila" [CD]. (2002). In *Hanukkah and Chinese New Year*. Long Branch, NJ: Kimbo.

Lambchop's Chanukah and Passover Surprise [DVD]. (2002). New York: Sony Wonder.

"My Dreydel" [CD]. (1976). In *Singable Songs for the Very Young*. Cambridge, MA: Rounder/UMGD.

Palmer, Hap. (1997). "Hanukkah" [CD]. In *Holiday Songs and Rhythms*. Baldwin, NY: Educational Activities.

Rosenthal, Margie. (1997). *Just in Time for Chanukah!* [CD]. Portland, OR: Sheera Recordings.

Additional teaching resources to accompany this Theme can be found on the book's companion website. Go to www.cengagebrain.com to access the site for a variety of useful resources.

Theme 44
HATS

Parts
crown
brim

Materials
felt
plastic
canvas
wool
fur
yarn
leather
straw
fleece

Sizes
small
medium
large

Types
baseball hat
top hat
hard hat
bonnet
stocking cap
ski hat
cowboy hat
sombrero
helmet
hood
derby
graduation
birthday
yarmulke
headdress
veil
turban

Colors
red
blue
yellow
green
white
brown
purple
black
pink

Uses
ceremonial
occupational
protection
identification
decoration
religious
fraternal

Theme Goals

Through participating in the experiences provided by this theme, the children may learn:

1. Types of hats
2. Uses for hats
3. Materials used to make hats
4. Parts of a hat
5. Colors of hats
6. Sizes of hats

Concepts for the Children to Learn

1. Hats are coverings worn on our heads for protection, warmth, and identification.
2. Most hats have a crown and a brim.
3. Stocking and ski hats keep us warm.
4. Felt, plastic, wool, fur, straw, leather, cloth, plastic, fleece, and yarn are all materials used to make hats.
5. Hats come in many different sizes.
6. Hats come in different colors.
7. Hats can be red, blue, green, yellow, white, pink, brown, purple, or black.
8. Some hats have special names.
9. Some hats can keep us cool.
10. Hats can be worn for fun.
11. Some people wear hats when they are working.
12. Baseball hats can be worn for decoration and protection.
13. Motorcyclists, bicycle riders, and skiers should wear helmets for protection.
14. Construction workers and firefighters should wear hard hats for protection.
15. Police officers, train conductors, and airplane pilots wear hats for identification.
16. Brides often wear a headdress or veil at a wedding ceremony.
17. Cowboys wear cowboy hats for protection from the sun.
18. Bonnets can be worn for decoration.

Vocabulary

1. **brim**—the part of a hat that surrounds the crown.
2. **crown**—the top part of the hat.
3. **hat**—a covering for the head.

Bulletin Board

The purpose of this bulletin board is to have the children match the colored pieces to their corresponding shadow, thereby promoting the development of visual discrimination, hand-eye coordination, and problem-solving skills. To construct the bulletin board, draw different types of hats on white tagboard. Color the hats with watercolor markers, and cut them out. Trace the cut-out hats onto black construction paper to create shadows. Then cut out the shadows and attach to the bulletin board. A magnet piece or a pushpin can be fastened to the shadow. A magnet piece or a hole can be applied to the colored hats.

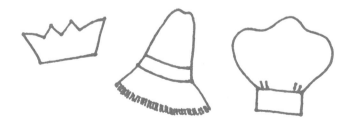

Family Letter

Dear Families,

Hats will be the focus of our next curriculum unit. Through this theme the children will become familiar with types, colors, and sizes of hats. They will also learn the materials used to construct hats, and the uses of hats, such as for protection, decoration, and identification.

At School

Some of the learning activities planned include:

- Playing in the hat store located in the dramatic play area

- Making paper plate hats at the art table

- Listening to and dramatizing the story *Caps for Sale* by Esphyr Slobodkina

Special Request!

On Friday, we will have a Hat Day. The children will show and wear hats that they have brought from home. If your child wishes to share a special hat, please label it and send it to school with your child in a paper bag. This will help us to keep track of which hat belongs to each child. Thank you for your help.

At Home

Ask your child to help you search the closets of your home for hats. To develop classification skills, discuss the colors and types of hats with your child. Are there more seasonal hats or sports hats? What are the hats made from? Why were those materials used?

Hats off to a fun unit!

Arts and Crafts

1. Easel Ideas

- Top hat–shaped paper
- Baseball cap–shaped paper
- Football helmet–shaped paper
- Graduation cap–shaped paper

2. Paper Plate Hats

Decorate paper plates with many different kinds of scraps, glitter, construction paper, and crêpe paper. Punch a hole, using a paper punch, on each side of the hat. Attach strings so that the hat can be tied on and fastened under the chin.

Cooking

The children may enjoy wearing baker's hats for the cooking experiences! Ask a bakery or fast-food restaurant to donate several paper hats for classroom use.

1. Cheese Crunchies

1/2 cup butter or margarine
1 cup all-purpose flour
1 cup shredded cheddar cheese
Pinch of salt
1 cup rice cereal bits

Cut the butter into six or eight slices, and mix together with the flour, cheese, and salt. Use fingers or a fork to mix. Knead in the cereal bits, and then roll the dough into small balls or snakes. Press them down flat, and place onto an ungreased cookie sheet. Bake at 325 degrees for approximately 10 minutes. Cool and serve for a snack.

2. Hamantaschen from Israel

Children in Israel eat hamantaschen on the holiday of Purim. A hamantasche is a pastry that represents the hat worn by the evil Haman, who plotted against the ancient Jews. Today, Israeli children dress in costumes, parade in the streets, and have parties on Purim.

7 tablespoons butter or margarine
1/3 cup sugar
2 eggs
2 1/2 cups flour
1/4 cup orange juice
1 teaspoon lemon juice
1 jar prune or plum jam

Cream the butter or margarine and sugar together in a large mixing bowl. Separate the eggs, and discard the whites. Add the yolks to the mixture and stir. Add the flour and juices to the mixture, and mix to form dough. On a floured board, roll the dough to about 1/8-inch thickness. Use a cookie cutter to cut into 4-inch circles. Spoon a tablespoon of jam into the center of each circle, and fold up three edges to create a triangle shape. Leave a small opening at the center. (Other fillings, such as poppy seeds or apricot jam, can be used.) Place the shaped dough on a cookie sheet, and bake for 20 minutes in a 350-degree preheated oven. Serve for a snack.

Dramatic Play

1. Sports Hats

Provide football helmets and jerseys, baseball hats, batters' helmets, and uniforms. Encourage the children to pretend they are football and baseball players.

2. Construction Site

Provide the children with toy tools, blocks, and construction hard hats.

3. Hat Store

Firefighter hats, bonnets, top hats, hard hats, bridesmaids' hats, baby hats, and so on can all be made available in the hat store. Encourage the children to buy and sell hats using a cash register and play money.

Field Trips

1. Hat Store

Visit a hat store or the hat department of a store. Examine the different kinds, sizes, and colors of hats.

2. Sports Store

Visit a sporting goods store. Locate the hat section. Observe the types of hats used for different sports.

Group Time
(Games and Language)

1. "My Favorite Hat Day"

Encourage the children to share their favorite hats with the class on a specific day. Talk about each hat, and ask where it was bought or found. Colors, sizes, and shapes can also be discussed.

2. Dramatization

Read the story *Caps for Sale* by Esphyr Slobodkina (see the "Books" section at the end of this chapter). After the children are familiar with the storyline, they may enjoy acting out the story.

Large Muscle

Hat Beanbag Toss

Lay several large hats on the floor. Encourage the children to stand about 2 feet from the hats and try to throw the beanbags into the hats.

Math

1. Hat Match

Construct pairs of hat puzzles out of tagboard. On each pair, draw a different pattern. Encourage the children to mix up the hats and sort them by design.

2. Hat Seriation

Collect a variety of hats. The children can arrange them from smallest to largest and from largest to smallest. Also, they can classify the hats by colors and uses.

Music

"My Hat"

(*traditional song*)

My hat it has three corners.
   (point to head, hold up three fingers)
Three corners has my hat.
   (hold up three fingers, point to head)
And had it not three corners
   (hold up three fingers)
It wouldn't be my hat.
   (shake head, point to head)

Variation: Make three-cornered paper hats to wear while acting out this song.

Science

What's It Made Of?

Hats representing a variety of styles and materials can be placed on the science table. Magnifying glasses can also be provided to allow the children to explore. They can look at, feel, and try on the hats.
Caution: Before letting the children try on the hats, make sure the children do not have head lice.

Social Studies

Many of these activities lend themselves to group time situations.

1. "Weather" or Not to Wear a Hat

Discuss the different kinds of hats that are worn in cold weather. Ask questions such as "What parts of our body does a hat keep warm?" "What kinds of hats do we wear when it is warm outside?" and "How does a hat help to keep us cool?"

2. **Sports Hats**

Make an arrangement of different sports hats. Place a mirror close by. The children can try on the hats.

3. **Community Helpers**

Many people in our community wear hats as part of their uniform. Collect several of these hats, such as those for a firefighter, police officer, mail carrier, baker, and so on, and place in a bag for a small-group activity. Identify one child at a time to pull a hat out of the bag. Once the hat is removed, the children can identify the worker. Older children may be able to describe the activities of the identified worker.

 **Books**

The following books can be used to complement this theme:

Adams, Pam. (2000). *Mrs. Honey's Hat: Giant Lap Book.* Auburn, ME: Child's Play.

Barroux, Stephanie. (2003). *Where's Mary's Hat?* New York: Viking.

Berenstain, Stan, and Jan Berenstain. (1999). *Old Hat, New Hat: The Berenstain Bears.* Illustrated by Jan Berenstain. New York: Random House.

Bogdanowicz, Basia. (1999). *Yellow Hat, Red Hat.* Brookfield, CT: Millbrook Press.

Brett, Jan. (1997). *The Hat.* New York: G. P. Putnam.

Carlson, Laurie. (1998). *Boss of the Plains: The Hat That Won the West.* Illustrated by Holly Meade. New York: Dorling Kindersley.

Carter, David A. (2005). *Who's under That Hat?* San Diego, CA: Red Wagon Books.

Dunrea, Olivier. (2004). *Peedie.* New York: Houghton Mifflin.

Fox, Mem. (2002). *The Magic Hat.* Illustrated by Tricia Tusa. San Diego, CA: Harcourt.

Kalman, Bobbie. (1998). *Bandanas, Chaps, and Ten-Gallon Hats.* New York: Crabtree.

Karon, Jan. (2002). *Miss Fannie's Hat.* New York: Puffin.

Katz, Cooper, and Sharon Muelenardt. (2007). *Whose Hat Is This?* Illustrated by Amy Bailey. Minneapolis, MN: Picture Window Book.

Katz, Karen. (2002). *Twelve Hats for Lena.* New York: Margaret K. McElderry Books.

Keats, Ezra Jack. (2003). *Jennie's Hat.* New York: Puffins

Kuskin, Karla. (2010). *A Boy Had a Mother Who Bought Him a Hat.* New York: HarperCollins.

Mayer, Mercer. (2004). *Good for Me and You.* New York: HarperFestival.

Rumford, James. (2007). *Don't Touch My Hat.* New York: A. A. Knopf Books for Young Readers

Slobodkina, Esphyr. (1947). *Caps for Sale.* New York: W. R. Scott.

Weeks, Sarah. (2005). *Who's under That Hat?* San Diego, CA: Harcourt.

 **Technology and Multimedia**

The following technology and multimedia products can be used to complement this theme:

"I Got a Hat" [CD]. (2001). In *Seasonal Songs in Motion.* Long Branch, NJ: Kimbo Educational.

 Additional teaching resources to accompany this Theme can be found on the book's companion website. Go to www.cengagebrain.com to access the site for a variety of useful resources.

Hats

A variety of hats can be collected for use in the dramatic play area. Some examples are:

Firefighter	Railroad engineer	Cowboy
Police officer	Motorcycle helmet	Stocking cap
Visor	Cloche	Mail carrier
Sunbonnet	Chef	Bicycle helmet
Sombrero	Sailor	Pillbox
Straw	Hard	Sports hats:
Mantilla	Ski cap	Football
Party (birthday)	Beret	Baseball
Nurse's cap	Top	Skiing

Theme 45
HEALTH

Occupations
doctors
dentists
nurses
excerise teachers
nutritionist

Exercise
running
aerobics
walking
bicycling
swimming
skiing

Exercise Clothing
shorts
sweatshirts
rubber-soled shoes
swimming suits
T-shirts

Foods
fruits
vegetables
meats
dairy products
beans
legumes
breads
cereal

Tools and Supplies
hairbrushes
toothbrushes
shampoo
soap
toothpaste
vitamins

Personal Habits
taking baths
brushing teeth
washing hair
taking naps
night sleep

Theme Goals

Through participating in the experiences provided by this theme, the children may learn:

1. Importance of exercise and good health
2. Healthy foods
3. Exercise clothing
4. Health tools and supplies
5. Personal habits related to health
6. Health occupations

Concepts for the Children to Learn

1. We need to take good care of our bodies to keep healthy.
2. Vitamins, shampoo, soap, and toothpaste are health aids.
3. Doctors, nurses, and dentists, nutritionists, exercise teachers provide health checkups.
4. Running, aerobics, and walking are all forms of exercise.
5. Bicycling, swimming, and skiing are other forms of exercise.
6. Fruits, vegetables, dairy products, beans, legumes, meat, breads, and cereals keep our bodies healthy.
7. Our bodies need rest, so we need to sleep and take naps.
8. Different types of clothing are worn during exercise.
9. Shorts, sweatshirts, T-shirts, and swimming suits are exercise clothing.
10. Rubber-soled shoes are exercise footwear.
11. Brushing teeth, washing hair, and bathing are ways to keep our bodies clean.
12. Hairbrushes and toothbrushes are health tools.
13. Taking naps, sleeping, and eating good foods are ways to have healthy bodies.

Vocabulary

1. **checkup**—a visit to a doctor to make sure you are healthy.
2. **cleanliness**—keeping our body parts free from dirt.
3. **diet**—the food we eat.
4. **exercise**—moving body parts.
5. **health**—feeling good.
6. **nutrition**—eating foods that are good for our body.

Bulletin Board

The purpose of this bulletin board is to have the children develop visual discrimination, hand-eye coordination, and problem-solving skills by matching the health aids to their corresponding shadow. Construct the health aid pieces from white tagboard. Include a toothbrush, toothpaste, comb, brush, and soap. Color the objects with colored felt-tip markers and laminate. Trace each of the health aids onto black construction paper to construct shadows as illustrated. Staple the shadow aids on the bulletin board by either affixing magnets or using pushpins. Punch a hole in each of the health aid pieces, allowing the children to hang them on the appropriate shadow.

Things that help us stay healthy.

Family Letter

InBox

Dear Families,

We will be starting a theme on health. We will be discussing foods that are good for us, important personal habits, and exercise. Through this theme, the children will develop an awareness of the importance of keeping their bodies healthy.

At School

Some of the learning experiences planned for the week include:

- Tracing our bodies at the art center
- Visiting Dr. Thomas, the dentist, at her office
- Having a visit by an aerobics instructor
- Creating healthy snacks
- Weighing and measuring ourselves

Field Trip

Arrangements have been made to visit Dr. Thomas's office on Thursday of this week. Dr. Thomas will give us a tour of the dental clinic and show us various pieces of dental equipment. We will walk to her office, leaving school at 10:00 a.m., and return just in time for lunch. Please have your child at school by 10:00 a.m. if he or she wishes to participate. Parents, please feel free to join us.

At Home

Help your child stay healthy by teaching and encouraging proper handwashing techniques. Preschool children need to be reminded to wash their hands after playing outside, before handling food and eating, after using the toilet, and after coughing, sneezing, rubbing the nose, or handling a handkerchief or tissue. They may also need supervision. Provide them liquid soap since germs can grow on bar soap. Then show them how to rub their hands together to create a soapy lather, washing both the fronts and backs of each hand. After this, the area between the fingers needs to be washed. Finally, the hands should be rinsed under warm, running water. The hands need to be kept below the wrists to prevent recontamination. While washing the hands, sing the song "Happy Birthday" twice to avoid rushing!

Arts and Crafts

1. **Paper Plate Meals**
   Magazines for the children to cut food pictures from the five food groups should be provided. The pictures can be pasted on a paper plate to represent a balanced meal. Plates from microwave dinners, if thoroughly cleaned, work well, too.

2. **Body Tracing**
   Instruct each child to lie on a large piece of paper. Trace the child's body, and let him or her take the tracing home and decorate it with his or her family. After this, it can be returned to school for display. This activity should help the children become aware of individual uniqueness and fosters parent-child interaction.

Cooking

Fruit Tree Salad
On a plate, place a lettuce leaf. On the lettuce, place a pineapple slice. Peel and slice a banana horizontally into 2-inch pieces, and place the pieces on the pineapple. Slice fresh strawberries or peaches. Spoon the fruit over the bananas.

Dramatic Play

1. **Health Club**
   Mats, fake weights (made from large tinker toys), headbands, and music to represent a health club can be placed in the dramatic play area.

2. **Doctor's Office (Hospital)**
   White clothing or scrubs, stethoscopes, strip thermometers, magazines, bandages, cots, sheets, and plastic syringes without needles can be placed in the dramatic play area to represent a hospital.

3. **Restaurant**
   Tables, tablecloths, menus, and tablets for taking orders can be placed in the dramatic play area. Paste pictures of food on the menus. A sign for the area could be "Eating for Health."

Field Trips and Resource People

1. **Take a field trip to the following places:**
   - Hospital
   - Health care facility
   - Doctor's office
   - Dentist's office
   - Health club
   - Drugstore

2. **Invite the following resource people to visit the classroom:**
   - Doctor
   - Nurse
   - Dentist
   - Dietician
   - Aerobics instructor

Fingerplays and Chants

Brushing Teeth
I jiggle the toothbrush again and again.
   (pretend to brush teeth)
I scrub all my teeth for a while.
I swish the water to rinse them and then
   (puff out cheeks to swish)
I look at myself and I smile.
   (smile at one another)

Group Time
(Games and Language)

Tasting Party

Prepare for a tasting party. Collect a wide variety of foods. For example, the children could experiment by dipping banana pieces in honey and then rolling them in wheat germ. To extend this activity, charts can be prepared listing the children's favorite foods.

Large Muscle

1. **Weight Awareness**

   The object of this activity is to become aware of weight and to feel the difference between heavy and light. To do this, the child should experiment with body force. Exercise in the following ways: lift arms slowly and gently, stomp on the floor, walk on tiptoes, kick out one leg as hard as possible, and very smoothly and lightly slide one foot along the floor. Music can be added to imitate aerobics.

2. **Mini-Olympics**

   Set up various areas for jumping jacks, jogging, relays, and a "beanbag launch." For the "launch," put a beanbag on the top edge of a child's foot and have the child launch it by kicking. Observe the distance each beanbag goes.

Math

1. **Food Group Sorting**

   Create a food group display. To do this, encourage the children to bring empty food containers. The food containers can be sorted into food groups. This could be a small-group activity or a choice during the self-selected play period.

2. **Height and Weight Chart**

   Weigh and measure each of the children at various times throughout the year. Record the data on a chart. This chart can be posted in the classroom.

Music

1. **"Brush Your Teeth"**

   by Raffi on *Get Up and Grow* (see "Technology and Multimedia" section at the end of this chapter)

2. **"My Body"**

   (Sing to the tune of "Where Is Thumbkin?")

   This is my body.
   This is my body.
   It's the only one I've got.
   It's the only one I've got.
   I'm going to take good care of it.
   I'm going to take good care of it.
   Yes I am. Yes I am.

3. **"Miss Polly Had a Dolly"**

   Miss Polly had a dolly
   Who was sick, sick, sick,
   So she called for the doctor
   To be quick, quick, quick.
   The doctor came
   With his bag and his hat,
   And he knocked at the door
   With a rat-a-tat-tat.
   He looked at the dolly
   And he shook his head,
   And he said, "Miss Polly,
   Put her straight to bed."
   Yes, I will, will, will!

Science

Soap Pieces

Add different kinds of soaps and a magnifying glass to the science area. Talk about what each one is used for.

Sensory

Add child safe shampoo or dish detergent to the sensory table.

Books

The following books can be used to complement this theme:

April, Elyse. (2007). *We Like to Move.* Illustrated by Diane Iverson. Prescott, AZ: Hohm Press.

Barron, Rex. (2004). *Showdown at the Food Pyramid.* New York: G.P. Putnam's Sons.

Carle, Eric. (1994). *The Very Hungry Caterpillar.* New York: Philomel/Penguin Young Readers.

Carlson, Nancy. (2006). *Get Up and Go!* New York: Puffin Books.

Cousins, Lucy. (2002). *Maisy Takes a Bath.* Cambridge MA: Candlewood Press.

Davis, Lambert. (2004). *Swimming with Dolphins.* New York: Blue Sky Press.

DeGezelle, Terri. (2006). *Taking Care of My Hair.* Mankato, MN: Capstone Press.

DeGezelle, Terri. (2006). *Taking Care of My Hands and Feet.* Mankato, MN: Capstone Press.

DeGezelle, Terri. (2006). *Taking Care of My Teeth.* Mankato, MN: Capstone Press.

Durant, Alan. (2006). *Burger Boy.* Illustrated by Mei Matsuoka. New York: Houghton Mifflin.

Edwards, Pamela Duncan. (2003). *Miss Polly Has a Dolly.* Illustrated by Elicia Castaldi. New York: Putnam's.

Ehrlich, Fred. (2005). *Does an Elephant Take a Bath?* Maplewood, NJ: Blue Apple Books.

Emberley, Rebecca. (2002*). My Food = Mi Comida.* Boston: Little, Brown.

Freymann, Saxton. (2006*). Fast Food.* New York: Arthur A. Levine Books.

Gordon, Sharon. (2003*). Exercise.* Chicago: Children's Press.

Hopman, Ellen Evert, and Steven Foster. (2000). *Walking the World in Wonder: A Children's Herbal.* Photography by Steven Foster. Rochester, VT: Healing Arts Press.

Lotu, Denize. (1996). *Running the Road to ABC.* Illustrated by Reynold Ruffins. New York: Simon & Schuster Books for Young Readers.

Miller, Edward. (2009). *The Tooth Book: A Guide to Healthy Teeth and Gums.* New York: Holiday House.

Owen, Ann. (2004). *Keeping You Healthy: A Book about Doctors.* Illustrated by Eric Thomas. Minneapolis, MN: Picture Window Books.

Redmond, E. S. (2009). *Felicity Visits the Zoo.* Somerville, MA: Candlewick Press.

Ricci, Christine. (2005). *Show Me Your Smile! A Visit to the Dentist.* Illustrated by Robert Roper. New York: Simon Spotlight/ Nick Jr.

Rockwell, Lizzy. (2009). *Good Enough to Eat.* New York: HarperCollins Publishers.

Savadier, Elivia. (2005). *No Haircut Today.* New Milford, CT: Roaring Brook Press.

Shuette, Sarah L. (2003). *Eating Pairs: Counting Fruits and Vegetables by Twos.* Mankato, MN: Capstone Press.

Schuette, Sarah L. (2003). *The Alphabet Soup: Fruits and Vegetables from A to Z.* Mankato, MN: Capstone Press.

Schuh, Mari C. (2006). *Being Active.* Mankato, MN: Capstone Press.

Schuh, Mari C. (2006). *Drinking Water.* Mankato, MN: Capstone Press.

Schuh, Mari C. (2006). *Healthy Snacks.* Mankato, MN: Capstone Press.

Schuh, Mari C. (2006). *The Milk Group.* Mankato, MN: Capstone Press.

Schuh, Mari C. (2007). *Mantenerse activo / Being Active.* Mankato, MN: Capstone Press.

Schuh, Mari C. (2007). *Meriendas saludables / Healthy Snacks.* Mankato, MN: Capstone Press.

Showers, Paul. (1997). *Sleep Is for Everyone.* Illustrated by Wendy Watson. New York: HarperCollins.

Teague, Mark. (1994). *Pigsty.* New York: Scholastic.

Thomas, Pat. (2001). *My Amazing Body.* Illustrated by Lesley Harker. Hauppauge, NY: Barron's Educational Series.

Thompson, Carol. (1997). *Piggy Washes Up.* New York: Candlewick Press.

Van Cleave, Janice. (1998). *Janice Van Cleave's Play and Find Out about the Human Body.* New York: Wiley.

Whitford, Rebecca, and Martina Selway. (2005). *Little Yoga: A Toddler's First Book of Yoga*. New York: Henry Holt.

Yolen, Jane. (2005). *How Do Dinosaurs Eat Their Food?* Illustrated by Mark Teague. New York: Blue Sky Press.

Technology and Multimedia

The following technology and multimedia products can be used to complement this theme:

"Brush Your Teeth" [CD]. (1976). In *Singable Songs for the Very Young*. Cambridge, MA: Rounder/UMGD.

Chef Combo's Fantastic Adventures in Tasting and Nutrition [kit]. (1996). Rosemont, IL: National Dairy Council.

Come See What the Doctor Sees [video]. (1994). Half Moon Bay, CA: Visual Mentor.

"Doctor, Doctor" [CD]. (1994). In *People in Our Neighborhood*. Long Branch, NJ: Kimbo Educational.

"Good Grooming" [CD]. (1995). In *Piggyback Songs*. Long Branch, NJ: Kimbo Educational.

Goofy over Dental Health [video]. (1991). Los Angeles: Disney Educational Productions.

"Hygiene" and "Respiration" [CD]. (1977). In *Science in a Nutshell*. Long Branch, NJ: Kimbo Educational.

K–6 Classroom Gallery [CD]. (1997). Lancaster, PA: Classroom Connect.

The Magic School Bus: Human Body [DVD]. (2005). Los Angeles: Warner Home Video.

"Physical Ed" and "Twelve Days of Gym Class" [CD]. (2000). In *Physical Ed*. Long Branch, NJ: Kimbo Educational.

Preschool Power! Jacket Flips and Other Tips [video]. (1991). Laguna Woods, CA: Concept Associates.

Raffi. (1987). "Bathtime" [CD]. In *Everything Grows*. Cambridge, MA: Rounder/UMGD.

Raffi. (1988). "Bathtime" [video]. In *Raffi in Concert with the Rise and Shine Band*. Hollywood, CA: Troubadour Records.

Raffi. (1994). "Brush Your Teeth," "I'm in the Tub," and "Let's Sing about Food" [CD]. In *Get Up and Grow*. Long Branch, NJ: Kimbo Educational.

Reading Rainbow. (2007). *Gregory, the Terrible Eater* [DVD]. Lincoln, NE: GNP Educational Media.

Rock 'n' Roll Fitness Fun [CD]. (1989). Long Branch, NJ: Kimbo Educational.

"Say No to Drugs" and "Please Don't Smoke" [CD]. (1989). In *Make the Right Choice*. Long Branch, NJ: Kimbo Educational.

Stewart, Georgiana. *Good Morning Exercises for Kids* [cassette]. (1987). Long Branch, NJ: Kimbo Educational.

"Sticky, Sticky" [CD]. (1994). In *Positively Singable Songs*. Long Branch, NJ: Kimbo Educational.

"Victor Vito" [CD]. (2010). In *The Best of the Laurie Berkner Band*. New York: Two Tomatoes.

"We Need Water" [CD]. (2000). In *Charlotte Diamond's World*. Vancouver, BC: Hug Bug Records.

The Wiggles. (2007). *Getting Strong* [DVD]. Los Angeles: Warner Home Video.

Additional teaching resources to accompany this Theme can be found on the book's companion website. Go to www.cengagebrain.com to access the site for a variety of useful resources.

Theme 46
HOMES

Rooms
living room
kitchen
bathroom
bedroom
den, dining room
closet, family room
office or study
garage, basement

Sizes
many

Workers
carpenters
architects
painters
plumbers
electricians
masons
cabinet makers
decorators

Parts
roof, garage
basement, toilets
stairs, ceiling
floors, walls
doors, windows
cupboards
sinks, bathtubs
showers

Types
apartments
houseboats
trailers, houses
condominiums
duplexes
cabins, tents
huts
townhouses

Materials
brick
straw
stone
wood
cement

Theme Goals

Through participating in the experiences provided by this theme, the children may learn about:

1. Home workers
2. Parts of a home
3. Rooms in a home
4. Types of homes
5. Materials for building a home
6. Sizes of homes

Concepts for the Children to Learn

1. A home is a place to live.
2. Apartments, condominiums, townhouses, duplexes, trailers, and houses are all kinds of homes.
3. Cabins, huts, tents, and houseboats are other types of homes.
4. Most homes have a kitchen, bedroom, bathroom, living room, and closets.
5. Some homes have a dining room, den, family room, garage, basement, and office or study.
6. Most homes have toilets, sinks, a bathtub, and a shower.
7. Homes come in many sizes.
8. Homes can be built from brick, stone, wood, and cement.
9. The ceiling, floor, roof, windows, doors, walls, and stairs are parts of a home.
10. Construction workers build houses.

Vocabulary

1. **apartment**—a building including many homes.
2. **architect**—a person who designs homes.
3. **bedroom**—a room for sleeping.
4. **construction worker**—a person who builds.
5. **duplex**—a house divided into two separate homes.
6. **house**—a place to live.
7. **kitchen**—a room for cooking.
8. **bathroom**—a room containing a sink and a toilet. Some bathrooms have a bathtub and shower.
9. **living room**—a room containing sofas and chairs where people can sit, talk, play, and relax.

Bulletin Board

The purpose of this bulletin board is to promote the development of classification skills. Begin by drawing an unfurnished model of a home on a large sheet of tagboard as illustrated. Include the basic rooms such as the kitchen, bedroom, and living room. Draw and cut furnishings to add to the home. Laminate home and furnishings. The children can place the furnishings in the proper room by using "fun tack" or magnetic strips on the furnishings.

Family Letter

InBox

Dear Families,

Homes will be the focus of our next curricular theme. Since everyone's home is unique, we will be discussing how homes differ. We will also be discussing home workers, materials for building a home, and the rooms in our homes.

At School

Some of our activities will include:

- Constructing homes out of cardboard boxes and paper in the art area
- Acting out the story of *The Three Little Pigs* in the dramatic play area
- Building at the workbench

A special activity will include making placemats, but we need your help. For our placemats, we will need a few pictures of your family, home, or both. These will be glued to construction paper and laminated during our project. They will not be returned in their original form. Thank you!

This week we will also be taking a neighborhood tour to observe the various types of homes in the area. We will be taking our walk at 10:00 a.m. on Thursday. Please feel free to join us!

At Home

To develop observation skills, take your child on a walk around your neighborhood to look at the houses in your area. Talk about the different colors and sizes of dwellings.

Enjoy the time you spend with your child!

Arts and Crafts

1. **Shape Homes**
    An assortment of construction paper shapes such as squares, triangles, rectangles, and circles should be placed on a table in the art area. Glue and large pieces of paper should also be provided.

2. **Tile Painting**
    Ask building companies to donate cracked, chipped, or discontinued tiles. The children can paint the tiles.

3. **Household Tracings**
    Several household items such as a spatula, wooden spoon, or cookie cutter can be placed on the art table. Also include paper, scissors, and crayons. These items can be traced. Some of the older children may color and cut their tracings.

Cooking

Homestyle Pizza
English muffins
Grated mozzarella cheese
Pizza sauce

Spread a tablespoon of sauce on each muffin half. Sprinkle the top with grated cheese. Bake in a preheated oven at 375 degrees until the cheese melts.

Dramatic Play

1. **Tent Living**
    A small tent can be set up indoors or outdoors depending upon weather and space. Accessories such as sleeping bags, flashlights, rope, cooking utensils, and backpacks should also be provided if available.

2. **Cardboard Houses**
    Collect large cardboard boxes. Place outdoors or in an open classroom area. The children may build their own homes.

If desired, tempera paint can be used for painting the homes. Wallpaper may also be provided.

3. **Cleaning House**
    Housecleaning tools such as a vacuum cleaner, a dusting cloth, sponges, mops, and brooms can be placed in the dramatic play area. During the self-selected play periods, the children may choose to participate in cleaning.

Field Trips and Resource People

1. **Neighborhood Walk**
    Walk around the neighborhood. Observe the construction workers' actions and tools.

2. **Construction Site**
    If available, visit a local construction site. Discuss the role of the construction worker.

3. **Resource People**
    The following resource people could be invited to the classroom:

    *   Builder
    *   Architect
    *   Plumber
    *   Painter
    *   Electrician

Fingerplays and Chants

My House
I'm going to build a little house
    (fingers make roof)
With windows big and bright
    (stand with arms in air)
Drifting out of sight.
In winter when the snowflakes fall
    (hands flutter down)
Or when I hear a storm
    (hand cupped to ear)
I'll go sit in my little house
    (sit down)
Where I'll be snug and warm.
    (cross arms over chest)

Where Should I Live?

Where should I live?
In a castle with towers and a moat?
    (make a point with arms over head)
Or on a river in a houseboat?
    (make wavelike motions)
A winter igloo made of ice may be just the
    thing
    (pretend to pack snow)
But what would happen when it turned to
    spring?
    (pretend to think)
I like tall apartments and houses made of
    stone,
    (stretch up tall)
But I'd also like to live in a blue mobile
    home.
    (shorten up)
A cave or cabin in the woods would give me
    lots of space
    (stretch out wide)
But I guess my home is the best place!
    (point to self)

Knocking

Look at _____ knocking on our door.
    (knock)
Look at _____ knocking on our door.
    (knock)
Come on in out of the cold
    (shiver)
Into our nice, warm home.
    (rub hands together to get warm)

My Chores

In my home, I wash the dishes
    (pretend to wash)
Vacuum the floor
    (push vacuum)
And dust the furniture.
    (dust)
Outside my home, I rake the leaves
    (rake)
Plant the flowers
    (plant)
And play hard all day.
    (wipe sweat from forehead)
When the day is over
    I eat my supper,
    (eat)
Read a story
    (read)
And go to sleep.
    (put head on hands)

Group Time
(Games and Language)

Construct a "My home is special because . . ." chart. Encourage the children to name a special thing about their homes. Display the chart at the children's eye level in the classroom for the week.

Large Muscle

Roofing Nails

Collect building materials such as soft pine scraps and styrofoam for the workbench. Provide safety goggles, a child-sized hammer, and roofing nails.
Caution: Adult supervision is always required with this activity.

Math

My House

Construct a "My House" book for each child. On the pages, write things like the following:

My house has _____ steps.
My house is the color _____.
My house has _____ windows.
There are _____ doors in my house.
My house has _____ keyholes.

Other ideas could include the number of beds, people, pets, and so on. Send this home with the child to complete with family.

Music

"This Is the Way We Build Our House"
(Sing to the tune of "Here We Go 'Round the Mulberry Bush")

This is the way we build our house,
Build our house, build our house.

This is the way we build our house,
So early in the morning.

(Other suggestions:)
This is the way we paint the house.
This is the way we wash the car.
This is the way we rake the leaves.

Science

Building Materials

Building materials and magnifying glasses should be placed in the science area. The children may observe and examine materials. Included may be wood, brick, canvas, tar paper, shingles, and so on.

Sensory

1. **Identifying Sounds**

   Record several sounds found in the home such as a vacuum cleaner, a television, water running, and a toilet flushing. Encourage children to name sounds. For older children, this could also be played as a lotto game. Make cards containing pictures of sounds, and vary pictures from card to card. When a sound is heard, cover the corresponding picture with a chip.

2. **Sand Castles**

   Add wet sand to the sensory table. Provide forms to create buildings, homes, and the like.
   Note: Examples may include empty cans, milk cartons, plastic containers, and so on.

Social Studies

Room Match

Collect several boxes. On one box, print "kitchen"; on another, print "bathroom"; on another, print "living room"; and on another, print "bedroom." Cut out objects related to each of these rooms from catalogs. The children may sort objects by placing them in the appropriate boxes. For example, dishes, silverware, and a coffeepot would be placed in the box labeled "kitchen."

Books

The following books can be used to complement this theme:

Adamson, Heather. (2008). *Homes in Many Cultures.* Mankato, MN: Capstone Press.

Baker, Jeannie. (2004). *Home.* New York: Greenwillow Books.

Brown, Margaret Wise. (2010). *The Fathers Are Coming Home.* Illustrated by Stephen Savage. New York: Margaret K. McElderry.

Burns, Marilyn. (2008). *Spaghetti and Meatballs for All!* New York: Scholastic.

Carle, Eric. (2005). *A House for Hermit Crab.* New York: Aladdin Paperbacks.

Chaconas, Dori. (2010). *Don't Slam The Door!* Illustrated by Wil Hullenbrand. Cambridge, MA: Candlewick Press.

Cowley, Joy, and Elizabeth Fuller. (2005). *Mrs. Wishy-Washy's Scrubbing Machine.* New York: Philomel Books.

Doering, Amanda. (2005). *Homes around the World ABC: An Alphabet Book.* Mankato, MN: Capstone Press.

Doss, Dayle Ann. (2009). *Full House.* Illustrated by Abby Carter. Cambridge, MA: Candlewick Press.

George, Lindsay Barrett. (2004). *Inside Mouse, Outside Mouse.* New York: Greenwillow Books.

Gregorie, Elizabeth. (2004). *Whose House Is This?* Minneapolis, MN: Picture Window Books.

Grimshaw, Caroline. (2000). *Our Homes.* London: Two-Can.

Johnston, Tony. (2000). *The Barn Owls.* Illustrated by Deborah Kogan Ray. Watertown, MA: Charlesbridge.

Kleven, Elisa. (2010). *Welcome Home, Mouse.* Berkeley, CA: Tricycle Press.

Lehman, Barbara. (2007). *Rainstorm.* Boston: Houghton Mifflin.

Lewiston, Wendy Cheyette. (2010) *There's a Mouse in the House!* New York: Cartwheel Books.

Masural, Claire. (2003). *Two Homes.* Illustrated by Kady MacDonald Denton. Somerville, MA: Candlewick Press.

Morris, Ann. (1992). *Houses and Homes.* Photography by Ken Heyman. New York: Lothrop, Lee & Shepard.

Raffi. (1999). *Down by the Bay.* Illustrated by Nadine Bernard Westcott. New York: Crown Books for Young Children.

Roemer, Heidi. (2009). *Whose Nest Is This?* Illustrated by Connie McLennan. Lanham, MD: North World.

Rylant, Cynthia. (2000). *The Old Woman Who Named Things.* Illustrated by Kathryn Brown. San Diego, CA: Voyager Books.

Rylant, Cynthia. (2002). *Let's Go Home.* Illustrated by Wendy Anderson Halperin. New York: Simon & Schuster Books for Young Readers.

Schuh, Mari C. (2006). *In My Home.* Mankato, MN: Capstone Press.

Smith, Alex T. (2009). *Once There Was a House That Was a Home.* Wilton, CT: Tiger Tales.

Squire, Ann O. (2002). *Animal Homes.* New York: Children's Press.

Taback, Simms. (2004). *This Is the House That Jack Built.* New York: Puffin.

Wood, Audrey. (2004). *The Napping House.* Illustrated by Don Wood. Orlando, FL: Harcourt.

Zweibel, Alan. (2005). *Our Tree Named Steve.* New York: G.P. Putnam's Sons.

Technology and Multimedia

The following technology and multimedia products can be used to complement this theme:

"All Around My Room" [CD]. (2008). In *Rocketship Run.* New York: Two Tomatoes.

"Down by the Bay" [CD]. (1976). In *Singable Songs for the Very Young.* Cambridge, MA: Rounder/UMGD.

Exploring Communities: Alike and Different [DVD]. (2007). Southington, CT: Mazzarella Media.

"Hungry Caterpillar" [CD]. (2001). In *Seasonal Songs in Motion.* Melbourne, FL: Learning Station.

Really Wild Animals: Totally Tropical Rain Forest [DVD]. (2005). Washington, DC: National Geographic.

Safety Smart at Home! [DVD]. (2008). Los Angeles: Disney Educational Productions.

"This Little House" [CD]. (1987). In *Raffi, Everything Grows.* Cambridge, MA: Rounder/UMGD.

Additional teaching resources to accompany this Theme can be found on the book's companion website. Go to www.cengagebrain.com to access the site for a variety of useful resources.

INSECTS AND SPIDERS

Insects

Types
ants, beetles
bees, butterflies
moths
grasshoppers
crickets
mosquitoes, flies

Body Parts
six legs, three parts
feelers, wings

Spiders

Types
daddy longlegs
tarantula
garden

Body Parts
eight legs
two parts

Origin
eggs

Uses
pest control
pollination
food

Homes
hives (bees)
hills (ants)
webs (spiders)
water, grass
ground, trees
plants

Movement
hop
crawl
fly
swim

Sounds
chirp
creak
buzz

Theme Goals

Through participating in the experiences provided by this theme, the children may learn:

1. Types and body parts of insects and spiders
2. Homes for insects and spiders
3. Movements of insects and spiders
4. Uses for insects and spiders
5. Sounds of insects and spiders
6. The origins of insects and spiders

Concepts for the Children to Learn

1. Ants, beetles, bees, butterflies, moths, grasshoppers, crickets, mosquitoes, and fleas are all insects.
2. Insects are different in many ways: size, shape, color, eyes, mouths, and number of wings.
3. Insects have six legs (three pairs) and, if winged, four wings.
4. Daddy longlegs, tarantula, and garden are types of spiders.
5. Spiders have two parts to their bodies, eight legs and no wings.
6. Insects and spiders come from eggs.
7. Insects can help us by making honey and pollinating flowers for fruit and vegetables.
8. Types of spiders include daddy longlegs, tarantulas, and garden-variety.
9. Some insects move by flying, others by walking.
10. Spiders spin a web to catch insects to eat.
11. Spiders and insects make sounds by chirping, creaking, or buzzing.
12. Bees live in hives, and ants live in hills.
13. Some insects and spiders may live in water, grass, the ground, trees, or plants.

Vocabulary

1. **antennae**—feelers on an insect that stick out from the head.
2. **caterpillar**—the wormlike larva of a butterfly or moth.
3. **cricket**—small leaping insect known for its chirping.
4. **insect**—small animal with six legs.
5. **moth**—night-flying insect with four wings, related to the butterfly.
6. **pollinate**—the way insects help flowers to grow.
7. **pupa**—intermediate stage of an insect; sometimes called a chrysalis.
8. **spider**—small animal with eight legs. Spiders have no wings. Spiders are not insects.
9. **spiderling**—a baby spider.
10. **wasp**—winged insect with a poisonous sting.

Bulletin Board

The purpose of this bulletin board is to develop visual discrimination as well as to promote problem-solving, matching, and hand-eye coordination skills. Construct several butterflies, each of a different shape, out of tagboard. Trace the butterfly figures onto black construction paper to create shadows. Cut out and laminate the butterfly figures and shadows. Staple shadow butterflies to bulletin board. Punch holes in colored butterflies for children to hang on the pushpin of the corresponding shadow butterfly.

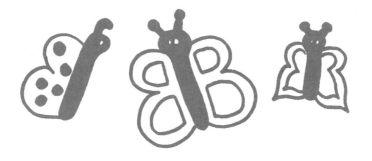

Family Letter

Dear Families,

We are continuing our study of animals. We are introducing a new category—insects and spiders. The children will become aware of the difference between insects and spiders and the ways that those creatures are helpful. Do you know the difference between insects and spiders? Most insects have three body parts and six legs. Spiders have two body parts and eight legs.

At School

Some of the learning experiences planned include:

- Singing and acting out the song "One Elephant Went out to Play." It's about an elephant that plays on a spiderweb!

- Listening to a flannel board version of the story *The Very Hungry Caterpillar* by Eric Carle

- Watching and observing an ant farm set up in the science area

- Creating spiders and insects out of a variety of materials in the art area

At Home

There are many ways to bring this unit into your home. Take a walk with your child and see how many spiders and insects you can find. Avoid touching unknown types of insects or spiders with your fingers. Instead, use a clear jar with a lid to observe the creature close up. Release the insect or spider after the observation.

We will be having a snack this week called ants on a log. Let your child make some for you! Spread cream cheese on pieces of celery. Top with raisins. Enjoy!

Enjoy your child!

Arts and Crafts

1. Make insects and spiders out of clay. Use toothpicks, straws, and chenille stem segments for the appendages.

2. Make insects and spiders with thumbprints. Children can draw crayon legs to make prints look like insects and spiders.

3. Egg carton caterpillars. Cut egg cartons in half, lengthwise. Each child paints a carton half. When dry, children can make a face on the end of the carton and insert chenille stems or straws for feelers.

4. Have children make spiders from black construction paper—one large black circle for a body and eight strips for legs. Children can paste on two yellow circles for eyes. Hang by a string around the room.

5. Make ladybug shapes out of red and orange construction paper. Have children sponge paint dots and legs on the bugs.

6. Sprinkle crayon shavings between two pieces of waxed paper, and iron. Put a butterfly template over the waxed paper, and glue it on. A pretty butterfly will be the final product!

7. Make tissue paper butterflies. Have children lightly paint white tissue paper or use colored tissue paper. Fasten a chenille stem around the middle. Add circles on the ends for antennae.

8. Make balloon bugs. Blow up several long balloons. Cover them with strips of paper dipped in wallpaper paste. Put on three to four layers of this sticky paper. Let dry for 2 to 3 days. Then paint your own giant bug!

Cooking

1. **Ants on a Log**
   Cut celery pieces into 3-inch strips. Fill the cavity of the celery stick with cream cheese. Garnish with raisins. (As with all recipes calling for celery, this might be more appropriate for older children.)

2. **Spider Snacks**
   Use chow mein noodles to place eight "spider legs" into a prune.

Dramatic Play

1. **Scientist**
   The children can dress up in white lab coats and observe spiders and insects with magnifying glasses.

2. **Spiderweb**
   Tie together a big piece of rope to resemble a spiderweb. Have children pretend they are spiders playing on their web.
   Caution: Closely supervise this activity.

3. **Spider Sac**
   Tape a 10-foot by 25-foot piece of plastic together on the sides. Blow it up with a fan to make a big bubble. Make a slit in the plastic for the entrance. The children can pretend to be baby spiders coming out of the spider sac when they are hatching.
   Caution: Closely supervise this activity.

4. The children can act out "Little Miss Muffet."

Field Trips and Resource People

1. Go on a walk to a nearby park to find bugs. Look under rocks, in cracks in sidewalks, in bushes, and so on.

2. Have someone who has a butterfly collection come in.

3. Visit a pet store. Ask them to show you what kind of insects they feed to the animals in the store. Do they sell any insects?

4. Invite a zoologist to come in and talk about insects and how important they are.

5. Invite an individual who raises bees to talk to the children. Ask him or her to bring in a honeycomb for the children to taste.

Fingerplays and Chants

Ants

Once I saw an anthill, with no ants about.
So I said "Little ants, won't you please come
    out?"
Then, as if they heard my call, one, two,
    three, four, five came out.
And that was all!

Bumblebee

Brightly colored bumblebee
Looking for some honey.
Flap your wings and fly away
While it still is sunny.

The Caterpillar

A caterpillar crawled to the top of a tree.
    (index finger of left hand moves up right
    arm)
"I think I'll take a nap," said he.
So under a leaf, he began to creep
    (wrap right hand over left fist)
To spin his chrysalis and he fell asleep.
All winter long he slept in his chrysalis bed,
    (keep right hand over left fist)
Till spring came along one day, and said,
"Wake up, wake up little sleepy head."
    (shake left fist with right hand).
"Wake up, it's time to get out of bed!"
So, he opened his eyes that sunshiny day
    (shake fingers and look into hand)
Lo—he was a butterfly and flew away!
    (move hand into flying motion)

Little Miss Muffet

Little Miss Muffet
Sat on a tuffet
Eating her curds and whey.
Along came a spider
And sat down beside her
And frightened Miss Muffet away!
Spiders can be prepared in the art area.

On a Spiderweb

On a spiderweb that once I saw.
Ten little spiders did creep and crawl.
    (show ten fingers)

They crawled and they crawled and they
    crawled around.
    (wiggle fingers)
Then one little spider fell down, down, down.
    (put one finger down)
Repeat, reducing the number of spiders by
    one each time.

Group Time
(Games and Language)

1. **Matching Insects**
    Divide children into two groups. For each
    group, hand out pictures of different spiders
    and insects that match pictures in the other
    group. Point to a child from one group and
    have that child act out his or her insect in
    some way (movement or noises). The child
    that has the same insect from the other
    group must go and meet the first child in
    the middle and act out the insect also.

2. Have many pictures of insects and spiders
    on display. Talk about a different insect or
    spider every day. Include where it lives, how
    it walks, what it might eat, and so on.

Large Muscle

1. Have children pretend to walk as different
    insects when in transition from one activity
    to another.

2. Explain to the children how bats eat
    insects. Play a version of "tag" where
    one child is the "bat" trying to catch the
    "insects." Make a bat headband out of black
    construction paper for the "bat" to wear.

Math

1. **Butterfly Match**
    Make several triangles of different colors.
    On one triangle, put the numbers 1 to 10;
    on the other, make dots to correspond to
    the numbers 1 to 10. Have the children
    match the dots to the numbers and clip the
    triangles together with a clothespin to form
    a butterfly.

2. **Ladybug Houses**
Paint several half-pint milk cartons red. Write the numerals 1 to 10 on each. Make 50 small ladybugs, dotting 5 sets of 1 to 10. Have children put ladybugs in their correct houses by matching dots to numerals.

3. **Numeral Caterpillar**
Make a caterpillar with 10 body segments and a head. Have the children put the numbers in order to complete the caterpillar's body.

4. Sing the song "The Ants Go Marching One by One," and have the children act out the song using their fingers as numbers.

5. Make an insect and spider lotto or concentration game with stickers for children to play.

Music

1. **"The Eensy Weensy Spider"**
(Traditional)

The eensy weensy spider crawled up the
water spout.
(walk fingers of one hand up other hand)
Down came the rain and washed the
spider out.
(lower hands to make rain, wash out
spider by placing hands together in
front and extending out to either side)
Out came the sun and dried up all the rain,
(form sun with arms in circle over head)
And the eensy weensy spider went
up the spout again.
(walk fingers up other arm)

2. **"The Elephant Song"**
(Chant)

One elephant went out to play
On a spider's web one day.
He had such enormous fun,
That he called for another elephant to come.

Elephant! Elephant! Come out to play!
Elephant! Elephant! Come out to play!

Two elephants …

3. **"The Insects and Spiders"**
(Sing to the tune of "The Wheels on the Bus")

The bugs in the air fly up and down,
up and down, up and down.
The bugs in the air fly up and down all
through the day.

The spiders on the bush spin a web.
The crickets in the field hop up and down.
The bees in their hive go buzz, buzz, buzz.

4. **"The Bees Are Buzzing All Around"**
(Sing to the tune of "The Ants Go Marching")

The bees are buzzing all around,
buzz, buzz, buzz, buzz.
The bees are buzzing all around,
buzz, buzz, buzz, buzz.
The bees are buzzing all around,
they're buzzing up and buzzing down.
Oh, the bees are buzzing all around.
Buzz, buzz, buzz.

5. **"Shoo Fly"**
Shoo fly, don't bother me,
(walk in a circle to the left)
Shoo fly, don't bother me,
(walk in a circle to the right)
Shoo fly, don't bother me,
(walk in a circle to the left)
For I belong to somebody.
(place hands on hips and shake head no)

Flies in the buttermilk,
(walk around shooing flies)
Shoo fly, shoo,
Flies in the buttermilk,
Shoo fly, shoo,
Flies in the buttermilk,
Shoo fly, shoo,
Please just go away.
(place hands on hips and shake head no)

Shoo fly, don't bother me,
(walk to the left in a circle)
Shoo fly, don't bother me.
(walk to the right in a circle)
Shoo fly, don't bother me,
(walk to the left in a circle)
Come back another day.
(wave goodbye)

Science

1. **Observe an Ant Farm**
   The children can watch the ants dig tunnels, build roads and rooms, eat and store food, and so on. (Ant farms are available in some commercial play catalogs.)

2. Go outside and observe anthills in the playground area.

3. Observe deceased flies and ants under a microscope.

4. Observe insects and spiders in a caged bug keeper or plastic jars with holes in the lids.

5. Listen to a cricket during quiet time.

6. Capture a caterpillar and watch it spin a chrysalis and turn into a butterfly.

Sensory

1. Add soil and plastic insects to the sensory table.

2. **Secret Smells**
   Discuss with children how bees use their sense of smell to find nectar. Prepare "secret smells" by placing cotton balls inside empty yogurt containers. Add a variety of fruit extracts to each canister. Use enough to soak the cotton ball. Ask the children to guess the flavor of the smell. Caution: Empty food containers need to be thoroughly washed in warm, soapy water before using them for classroom activities.

Social Studies

1. Take the children on an insect hunt near your school. When the children are finished, have everyone show the rest of the class what they found. Talk about where they found the insects (on a tree, under a log, etc.).

2. Have children make homes for all the insects they found. They can put dirt, grass, twigs, and small rocks in plastic jars and cans.

3. Discuss what it is like to be a member of a family. Ask the children if each member of their family has a certain job. Then focus on ant colonies as families. Ants live together much like people do, except that ants live in a larger community. Each ant has a certain task within the community. Some of the jobs are as follows:

   - Nurse: look after the young
   - Soldier: defend colony and attack enemies
   - Others: search for food, and enlarge and clean the nest (house)

Books

The following books can be used to complement this theme:

Allen, Judy, and Tudor Humphries. (2000). *Are You a Spider?* New York: Kingfisher.

Allen, Judy, and Tudor Humphries. (2001). *Are You a Bee?* Illustrated by Tudor Humphries. New York: Larousse Kingfisher Chambers.

Allen, Judy, and Tudor Humphries. (2003). *Are You a Butterfly?* New York: Kingfisher.

Allen, Judy, and Tudor Humphries. (2003). *Are You a Ladybug?* New York: Kingfisher.

Allen, Judy, and Tudor Humphries. (2004). *Are You a Dragonfly?* New York: Kingfisher.

Allen, Judy, and Tudor Humphries. (2004). *Are You a Grasshopper?* New York: Kingfisher.

Allen, Judy, and Tudor Humphries. (2004). *Are You an Ant?* New York: Kingfisher.

Aylesworth, Jim. (1992). *Old Black Fly.* Illustrated by Stephen Gammell. New York: H. Holt.

Brennan-Nelson, Denise. (1999). *Buzzy the Bumblebee.* Illustrated by Michael Glenn Monroe. Ann Arbor, MI: Sleeping Bear Press.

Carle, Eric. (1969). *The Very Hungry Caterpillar.* Harlow, NY: Longman.

Carle, Eric. (1984). *The Very Busy Spider.* New York: Philomel Books.

Carle, Eric. (1990). *The Very Quiet Cricket.* New York: Philomel Books.

Carle, Eric. (1995). *The Very Lonely Firefly.* New York: Philomel Books.

Carle, Eric. (1999). *The Very Clumsy Click Beetle*. New York: Philomel Books.

Cronin, Doreen. (2005). *Diary of a Spider*. Illustrated by Harry Bliss. New York: J. Cotter Books.

Cronin, Doreen. (2007). *Diary of a Fly*. Illustrated by Harry Bliss. New York: J. Cotter Books.

Dodd, Emma. (2010). *I Love Bugs!* New York: Holiday House.

Edwards, Pamela Duncan. (2004). *Clara Caterpillar*. Illustrated by Henry Cole. New York: HarperCollins.

Ehlert, Lois. (2001). *Waiting for Wings*. San Diego, CA: Harcourt.

Gibbons, Gail. (1993). *Spiders*. New York: Holiday House.

Gibbons, Gail. (1997). *The Honey Makers*. New York: William Morrow.

Gran, Julia. (2007). *Big Bug Surprise*. New York: Scholastic.

Hall, Margaret. (2005). *Ants*. Mankato, MN: Capstone Press.

Hall, Margaret. (2005). *Ladybugs*. Mankato, MN: Capstone Press.

Hall, Margaret. (2006). *Fireflies*. Mankato, MN: Capstone Press.

Hall, Margaret. (2007). *Hormigas / Ants*. Mankato, MN: Capstone Press.

Howard, Fran. (2005). *Bumble Bees*. Mankato, MN: Capstone Press.

Howard, Fran. (2005). *Butterflies*. Mankato, MN: Capstone Press.

O'Flatharta, Antoine. (2005) *Hurry and the Monarch*. New York: Knopf/Random House.

Sayre, April Pulley. (2005). *The Bumblebee Queen*. Illustrated by Patricia J. Wynne. Watertown, MA: Charlesbridge.

Sill, Cathryn. (2003). *About Insects: A Guide for Children*. Illustrated by John Sill. Atlanta, GA: Peachtree Publishing.

Singer, Marilyn. (2003). *Fireflies at Midnight*. Illustrated by Ken Robbins. New York: Atheneum Books for Young Readers.

Sturges, Philemon. (2005). *I Love Bugs!* Illustrated by Shari Halpern. New York: HarperCollins.

Tagliaferro, Linda. (2004). *Ants and Their Nests*. Mankato, MN: Capstone Press.

Ziefert, H. (1999). *Daddies Are for Catching Fireflies*. New York: Puffin.

Technology and Multimedia

The following technology and multimedia products can be used to complement this theme:

"Bumblebee" [CD]. 2010. In *The Best of Laurie Berkner*. New York: Two Tomatoes Records.

Butterfly and Moth [DVD]. (2007). New York: DK Publishing.

City of Bees [DVD]. (2005). Choices. Chicago, ILL: Moody Publishers. JH

Critter Quest [DVD]. (2006). New York: DK Publishing.

"Eensy Weensy Spider" [CD]. (2002). In *Raffi, Let's Play*. Cambridge, MA: Rounder/ UMGD.

"Eensy Weensy Spider," "Be My Little Baby Bumblebee/Bringing Home a Baby Bumblebee," and "Shoo! Fly, Don't Bother Me" [CD]. (2001). In *Four Baby Bumblebees*. Long Branch, NJ: Kimbo Educational.

"Firefly" [CD]. (2002). In *Night Time! Dan Zanes and Friends*. Brooklyn, NY: Festival Five Records.

Reading Rainbow. (2007). *Bugs* [DVD]. Lincoln, NE: GPN Educational Media.

"Spider on the Floor" [CD]. (1976). In *Singable Songs for the Very Young*. Cambridge, MA: Rounder/UMGD.

"Spiders" [CD]. (2008). In *Songs for the Whole Day*. Nashville, TN: Lamon Records.

 Additional teaching resources to accompany this Theme can be found on the book's companion website. Go to www.cengagebrain.com to access the site for a variety of useful resources.

KWANZAA

Foods
banana fritters
coconut biscuits
collard greens
and kale
cornbread
hoppin' John
(black-eyed peas
and rice)
fried chicken
sweet potato dishes

Colors
red
black
green

Symbols and Decorations
red, black, and
green candles
kinara
(candleholder)
mkeka (straw mat)
fruits and vegetable
basket
unity cup usually
filled with water
ears of dried corn
African baskets
cloth patterns

Preparation
making drums,
rattles, and rain
sticks, practicing
drumming and
dancing
buying or making
gifts for friends and
families
beading colored
necklaces
weaving mats
decorating homes

Principles
working together
helping others
making good choices
sharing

Celebration
candle lighting
storytelling
drumming
singing, dancing
reading poetry

Clothing
kaftans
keife
dashiki

Theme Goals

Through participating in the experiences provided by this theme, the children may learn:

1. Kwanzaa preparations
2. How people celebrate Kwanzaa
3. Kwanzaa principles
4. Special foods for Kwanzaa
5. Kwanzaa colors
6. Symbols of Kwanzaa

Concepts for the Children to Learn

1. Kwanzaa is an African-American holiday celebration that lasts for seven days.
2. The colors of Kwanzaa are red, green, and black.
3. Children and families prepare for Kwanzaa by decorating their houses, practicing drumming and dancing, and making gifts.
4. Special foods for Kwanzaa include fried chicken, black-eyed peas, greens, cornbread, banana fritters, coconut biscuits, and sweet potatoes.
5. Each night a new candle is lit on the kinara, a seven-candle candlestick.
6. The kinara is placed on a woven mat called the mkeka.
7. A unity cup is placed on the mkeka and a fruit and vegetable basket near it.
8. An ear of dried corn is placed in front of each child as they gather each night to celebrate Kwanzaa.
9. During Kwanzaa, we think about how to work together, help others, make good choices, and share.
10. People are singing, dancing, telling stories, reading poetry, and drumming during Kwanzaa.
11. People give and receive homemade gifts during Kwanzaa.
12. Kaftans, dashikis, and keifes are special clothing that may be worn during Kwanzaa.

Vocabulary

1. **dashiki**—a brightly-colored and loose-fitting shirt without buttons.
2. **harvest**—when you pick and collect ripe fruits and vegetables.
3. **jambo**—hello (in Swahili).
4. **kaftan**—a dress worn by women during a Kwanzaa celebration.
5. **keife**—a cap worn during Kwanzaa celebrations.
6. **kinara**—a candleholder for seven candles.
7. **Kwanzaa**—a special holiday to celebrate African-American history.
8. **mkeka**—a mat woven with black, green, and red.

Bulletin Board

The purpose of this bulletin board is to foster a positive self-concept as well as name recognition skills and visual-matching skills. Construct rectangle strips (approximately 2 × 8 inches) out of an assortment of red, black, and green construction paper so you have one for each child in your class. Print a child's name on each strip using black marker. Laminate all pieces. Staple 2- × 8-inch tagboard strips to the board to form a large rectangular shape so that you have a tagboard strip for each child and the strips are no more than 1/4 inch apart. Print each child's name on one of the tagboard strips. Punch a hole in the top of each colored piece with a paper punch. Attach a pushpin several inches above each tagboard strip. The children can hang their colored strips on the bulletin board as they arrive each day. When hung together, they will form the shape of an mkeka mat to welcome everyone to Kwanzaa. You can also point out how everyone is part of the whole, working together, sharing, and helping each other.

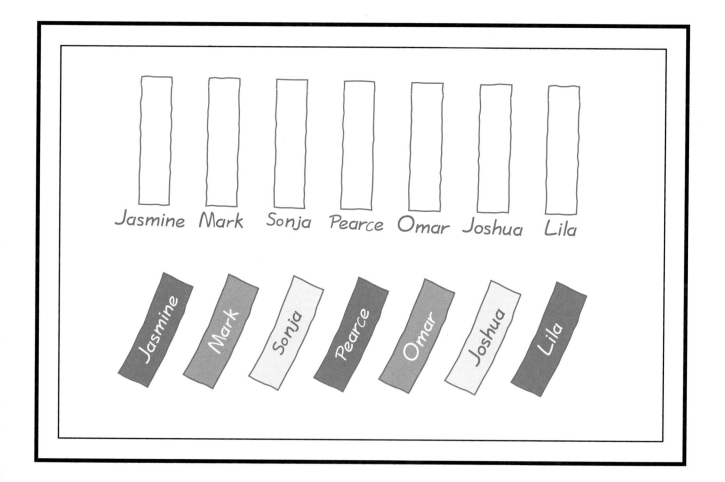

Family Letter

Dear Families,

It's the big season for holidays—Hanukkah, Christmas, and now Kwanzaa, which is our next theme. Kwanzaa is an African-American holiday celebrated during the week between December 26 and January 1 each year. Kwanzaa is a harvest holiday, not a religious holiday. It was established in 1966 to help African-Americans remember and celebrate their cultural heritage.

The word "Kwanzaa" comes from the Swahili language and means "first fruits." The celebration is organized around the number seven. Families and friends get together each night to light candles, eat together, play music, dance, and tell stories.

At School

Some of the Kwanzaa activities planned include:

- Making rain sticks and mkeka mats

- Gathering fruit for fruit baskets

- Cooking sweet potato pie and black-eyed peas

- Talking about how we work together, help each other, and make choices

Parent Involvement

If you have special knowledge or experience celebrating Kwanzaa, we would love to have you share it with our class. Please contact me so a time can be arranged for your visit.

You can learn more about Kwanzaa by doing a computer search!

Arts and Crafts

1. Rain Sticks

Encourage the children to decorate empty paper towel or wrapping paper tubes with African colored tissue paper (or paint)—red, green, and black. Cover one end of the tube with waxed paper and attach the paper tightly with a rubber band. Put a handful of small stones, sand, or pebbles into the open end. Seal the opening with waxed paper and a rubber band. Poke holes in the tube with a pushpin. Children can turn the tube slowly or shake it to listen to different sounds they can make. (Small dried pasta makes a rat-a-tat-tat sound; dried beans go tap tap tap; and rice makes a shushhhh sound.)

2. Kwanzaa Finger Painting

Place green and red fingerpaints on the art table with black paper or tagboard for the children to create designs.

3. Mkeka Mat Collages

Give the children black construction paper and square shapes cut out of red and green construction paper. Have them glue the square shapes onto their black paper to make a collage (similar to a woven Kwanzaa mat called the mkeka).

4. Unity Chains

Cut out strips of red, green, and black paper (each approximately 1–2 inches wide and 6–8 inches long). Teach the children how to make a chain by making links with the paper strips using tape. As each link of the paper chain is made, write the children's names on them to show how you are all united in friendship. (Unity is one of the principles of Kwanzaa.) Hang the long paper chain for decoration.

5. Kwanzaa Candle Pictures

On a piece of heavy paper, draw and reproduce a template of a simple seven-holed Kwanzaa candleholder. For candles, give your children three strips of red paper, three strips of green paper, and one strip of black paper. Help them glue the candles on the candleholder. (The black candle goes in the center, the red candles are on one side, and the green candles are on the other side.) Help them "light" the candles by dipping a finger into yellow finger paint and making a fingerprint flame at the top of each candle.

6. Beaded Necklaces

On the art table, lay out beads and cording that is cut in the lengths needed for a necklace. Make sure that the cording is stiff enough so the children easily thread the beads and create their own Kwanzaa necklaces.

Cooking

1. Fruit Kabobs

Since Kwanzaa means "fresh fruits," this is the perfect time for children to make fruit kabobs.
Banana chunks
Apple chunks
Orange segments
Pineapple chunks
Miniature marshmallows (optional)

Place each fruit on a plate. Give each child a plastic drinking straw, a beverage stirrer, or red or green toothpicks. Show them how to thread fruit onto the stick to make fruit kabobs for their snack.

2. Sweet Potato Pie

2 large eggs
1/2 cup sugar
Dash salt
1/2 tsp. cinnamon
1/4 tsp. allspice
1/8 tsp. nutmeg
1/4 tsp. lemon juice
1/2 tsp. vanilla
1/2 cup heavy cream
1 1/2 cups cooked, mashed sweet potatoes
1 unbaked pie shell

Preheat the oven to 350 degrees. Beat eggs well. Add sugar, salt, spices, lemon juice, and vanilla to the eggs. Mix thoroughly. Add cream and stir. Add mashed sweet potatoes and mix thoroughly. Turn into pie shell and bake for 1 hour or until firm. Let pie cool.

3. Mashed Sweet Potatoes

6–8 sweet potatoes
3–4 tablespoons butter
1/4 cup brown sugar

Preheat the oven to 400 degrees. Peel the sweet potatoes and poke them with a fork to make air holes. Bake them in a baking dish with a little water for 50–60 minutes, depending on the size. (Cutting the potatoes in half will allow them to bake more quickly.) The potatoes are done when soft. Mash the potatoes in a bowl with butter and brown sugar. Yum!

4. Coconut Biscuits

3 cups flour
1 tablespoon and 1 teaspoon baking powder
4 tablespoons of butter
3 tablespoons of sugar
1 1/3 teaspoon salt
1 1/3 cup milk
1/2 cup toasted coconut

Combine the first four ingredients—flour, baking powder, sugar, and salt. Add butter, and cut into the mixture until pea sized. Add milk and coconut. Stir. Drop onto a greased cookie sheet. Bake for 10 minutes at 450 degrees. Serve warm. Makes 20 biscuits.

Dramatic Play

1. Fruit and Vegetable Baskets

Set up a Kwanzaa fruit and vegetable basket center. Put out a few baskets (or platters), along with a variety of plastic fruits and vegetables. Invite the children to create fruit and vegetable baskets.

2. Decorate for Kwanzaa

Put on some African music and provide black, green, and red streamers. Invite the children to help hang and decorate with the streamers.

3. Costume Shop

Bring in black, red, and green clothes for Kwanzaa. If available, include African fabric strips for headbands, belts, and skirts.

4. Gift-Wrapping Center

Collect boxes, wrapping paper, construction paper, and ribbon (black, red, and green). The children can wrap presents for Kwanzaa.

Field Trips and Resource People

1. African-American Visitor

Invite someone who is African-American and celebrates Kwanzaa to come visit your school site. Have them talk with the children about how they and their family celebrate Kwanzaa. Encourage the visitor to bring any artifacts and pictures they may have.

Fingerplays and Chants

1. "One, Two, Three Little Candles"
(Sing to the tune of "Ten Little Indians")

One little, two little, three little candles
    (hold up fingers as you count on left hand)
four little, five little, six little candles
    (hold up fingers as you count on right hand)
seven little candles shine for Kwanzaa
    (hold up a seventh finger)
shining in the kinara
    (wiggle all seven fingers)

2. Seven Days of Kwanzaa
(Sing to the tune of "Three Blind Mice")

Seven days of Kwanzaa, seven days of Kwanzaa
    (hold up seven fingers)
Here they are, here they are
    (wiggle your seven fingers)
Each night we light a candle
    (hold up one finger on the left hand)
Each night we light a candle
    (hold up one finger on the right hand)

Black, red, green
(make a gentle fist and splay your
fingers three times)
Black, red, green
(make a gentle fist and splay your
fingers three times)

Group Time
(Games and Language)

1. **Hot Sweet Potato**
Play hot potato with a sweet potato (a
favorite food enjoyed during Kwanzaa).

2. **Black, Red, and Green
Color Games**
Since black, red, and green are the colors of
Kwanzaa, use the celebration to review the
colors with your children. Here are a few
things to try.

- Select items of red, green, or black
clothing to wear, and encourage your
children to do the same.
- Play an "I Spy" game with your
children looking for red, green, and
black objects.
- Go for a "red, green, and black walk" to
find things that are these colors.

Math

1. **Seven**
Make a mat with circles on it numbered 1
through 7. Draw one circle-shaped smiley
face in the number 1 circle, two smiley faces
in the number 2 circle, and so on. Put out
a bowl of pennies, dried pasta, or beans.
Children can count to seven by putting the
objects in the circles.

2. **Seven Giant Steps**
Using colored chalk, draw seven large
circles (in a line or a circle) on the yard
or walkway, and number them from one
to seven. The children can march, dance,
or hop while counting out the days of
Kwanzaa.

Music

1. **"Kwanzaa Light"**
(Sing to the tune of "Twinkle Twinkle")

Seven candles in a row,
Wait to join the bright bright glow.
We will light them one by one,
Until all seven join the fun.
Seven candles burning bright,
Fill the world with Kwanzaa light.

2. **"Kwanzaa's Here"**
(Sing to the tune of "Three Blind Mice")

Red, green, black
Red, green, black.
Kwanzaa's here,
Kwanzaa's here.

The colors are quite a sight,
We light a candle every night,
The holiday is filled with light,
Kwanzaa's here.

3. **Drums, Shakers, and Rain Sticks**
Provide drums, shakers, and rain sticks for
the children to create music.

Science

1. **Corn Display**
Place all types of corn, including corn on
the cob, popcorn, fresh cooked corn, canned
corn, or frozen corn, on the science table.
Provide a magnifying class for the children
to closely observe each type.

2. **Unity Cup Color Experiment**
Put water in a unity cup (a plastic wine
glass or goblet). Add yellow food coloring.
Ask the children what they think will
happen if you add blue food coloring. Show
them how it makes green. Repeat the
experiment with blue and red (to make
purple) or yellow and red (to make orange).

3. Sprout a Sweet Potato

Fill a jar halfway with cool water. Stick four toothpicks in a long, thin sweet potato, evenly spaced, about halfway between the top and bottom (roughly where 12, 3, 6, and 9 would be on a clock). Place the potato in the jar so the bottom inch or two is covered in water, but the potato bottom doesn't rest on the bottom of the jar. Keep the bottom of the potato covered with water and put in the sun. The eyes of the potato will begin to sprout, and purple vines will grow.

Sensory

The following items can be added to the sensory table:

- Small wax candles
- Red, green, and black colored streamers
- Colored water

Social Studies

1. Kwanzaa Symbols

Place a decorative mat on a table. Then place other Kwanzaa symbols such as corn, candleholders, children books, African baskets, and a red, black, and green flag on the decorative mat.

2. Sharing

Tell the children that Kwanzaa is a time to think about how we share. Give an example of how you share, and ask children about how they share—at home with siblings and at school with friends.

3. Helping Hands

Remind children that Kwanzaa is a time to think about how we help each other as a community. Draw outlines of two large hands on butcher paper. Have the kids dip their hands in fingerpaint and make handprints in the hand. Ask, "How do we help each other?" and write some examples around the hands.

Books

The following books can be used to complement this theme:

Ada, Alma Flor, and F. Isabel Campoy. (2007). *Celebrate Kwanzaa con Botitas y sus gatitos / Celebrate Kwanzaa with Boots and Her Kittens* (Spanish edition). Illustrated by Valeria DoCampo. Madrid, Spain: Alfaguara Infantil.

Anderson, Sheila. (2009). *Kwanzaa*. Cultural Holidays. Edina, MN: Magic Wagon.

Burden-Patmon, Denise. (1993). *Imani's Gift at Kwanzaa*. Illustrated by Floyd Cooper. Fullerton, CA: Aladdin Books.

Chocolate, Deborah. (1996). *A Very Special Kwanzaa*. New York: Scholastic Paperbacks.

Chocolate, Deborah. (1999). *My First Kwanzaa Book*. Illustrated by Cal Massey. New York: Scholastic Paperback.

Cooper, Melrose. (2007). *The Seven Days of Kwanzaa*. New York: Cartwheel Books.

Dickman, Nancy. (2011). *Kwanzaa*. Mankato, MN: Heinemann Publishers.

Doering, Amanda. (2006). *Kwanzaa: African American Celebration of Culture*. First Facts, Holidays and Culture. Illustrated by Robert Williams. Mankato, MN: Capstone.

Ford, Juwanda G. (2000). *Together for Kwanzaa*. Illustrated by Shelly Hehenberger. New York: Random House Books for Young Readers.

Ford, Juwanda G. (2003). *K Is for Kwanzaa*. Illustrated by Ken Wilson-Max. New York: Cartwheel Books.

Gayle, Sharon Shavers. (1996). *A Kwanzaa Miracle*. Illustrated by Frank Norfleet. New York: Troll Communications.

Goss, Linda, and Clay Goss. (2002). *It's Kwanzaa Time*. New York: Putnam Juvenile.

Grier, Ella. (2005). *Seven Days of Kwanzaa*. Illustrated by John Ward. New York: Sterling Publishers.

Holub, Joan. (2002). *Kwanzaa Kids*. A Lift-the-Flap Book. Illustrated by Ken Wilson-Max. New York: Puffin.

Katz, Karen. (2003). *My First Kwanzaa.* New York: Henry Holt.

Kotunbu, Dimitrea. (2009). *The Sound of Kwanzaa.* New York: Scholastic Press.

Otto, Carolyn. (2010). *Celebrate Kwanzaa: With Candles, Community, and the Fruits of the Harvest.* Holidays around the World. Washington, DC: National Geographic Children's Books.

Pinkney, Andrea Davis. (1998). *Seven Candles for Kwanzaa.* Illustrated by Brian Pinkney. New York: Puffin.

Porter, A. P. (1991). *Kwanzaa.* Carolrhoda On My Own Books. Illustrated by Janice Lee Porter. Minneapolis, MN: Carolrhoda Books

Ross, Kathy. (2006). *All New Crafts for Kwanzaa.* Illustrated by Sharon Lane Holm. Minneapolis, MN: First Avenue Editions.

Saint James, Synthia. (1994). *The Gifts of Kwanzaa.* Park Ridge, IL: Albert Whitman & Company.

Saint James, Synthia. (2001). *It's Kwanzaa Time.* A Lift-the-Flap Story. New York: Little Simon.

TK. (2004). *It's Beginning to Look a Lot like Kwanzaa.* JATS Holiday Classics. Illustrated by Rex Perry. New York: Hyperion Books.

Trueit, Trudi Strain. (2006). *Kwanzaa.* Rookie Read-About Holidays. Danbury, CT: Children's Press.

Washington, Donna. (1990). *The Story of Kwanzaa.* Illustrated by Stephen Taylor. New York: Harper Collins.

Washington, Donna. (2010). *Lil' Rabbit's Kwanzaa.* Illustrated by Shane W. Evans. New York: Katherine Tegen Books.

Williams, Nancy. (1995). *A Kwanzaa Celebration Pop-Up Book: Celebrating the Holiday with New Traditions and Feasts.* Illustrated by Robert Sabuda. New York: Little Simon.

Technology and Multimedia

The following technology and multimedia products can be used to complement this theme:

Kwanzaa Music [CD]. (1994). Boston: Rounder/Umgd.

Kwanzaa Party! A Celebration of Black Cultures in Song [CD]. (1996). Boston: Rounder/Umgd.

Smallwood, Frank. (2010). *Let's Celebrate Kwanzaa Sing-Along* [CD]. Newark, NJ: Peter Pan Records.

 Additional teaching resources to accompany this Theme can be found on the book's companion website. Go to www.cengagebrain.com to access the site for a variety of useful resources.

Theme 49
MAIL CARRIER

Symbols
hat
mailbag
mail truck
badge

Objects Delivered
letters
postcards
boxes
magazines
cards
books

Post Office Contents
post office boxes
stamp machines
address books
scales, mailboxes
envelopes
shelves
rubber stamps

Duties of Mail Carrier
delivers mail
picks up mail
sorts mail
stamps mail

Mailing Address
name
house number
street name
city name
state name
zip code, stamp

Types of Transportation
trucks
walking
bicycles
cars

Theme Goals

Through participating in the experiences provided by this theme, the children may learn:

1. Duties of a mail carrier
2. Symbols identifying a mail carrier
3. Contents found in a post office
4. Parts of a mailing address
5. Types of transportation
6. Objects delivered by mail carriers

Concepts for the Children to Learn

1. A man or woman who delivers mail is a mail carrier.
2. The mail carrier usually wears a badge and a hat for identification.
3. A mail carrier walks, rides a bicycle, or drives a car or truck to deliver mail.
4. Mail carriers deliver cards, letters, postcards, boxes, books, and magazines.
5. Mail carriers sort, stamp, pick up, and deliver mail.
6. Stamps are placed on objects for mailing.
7. Names, house numbers, street names, city names, state names, and zip codes are on mailing labels.
8. A post office has stamp machines, scales, address books, and mailboxes.
9. Envelopes and boxes can be purchased at the post office.
10. Scales are used to weigh mail.
11. Some mail carriers use mailbags to carry the mail.

Vocabulary

1. **address**—directions for the mail carrier.
2. **envelope**—a cover for a letter.
3. **letter**—a printed message that contains alphabet letters.
4. **mail**—letters, cards, postcards, and packages.
5. **mailbag**—a bag that holds letters and postcards.
6. **mail carrier**—a person who delivers mail.
7. **post office**—a place where mail is sorted.
8. **stamp**—a sticker put on mail.
9. **zip code**—the last numbers on a mailing address.

Bulletin Board

The purpose of this bulletin board is to reinforce the mathematical skill of matching a set to its written numeral. Construct mailboxes out of tagboard. Each mailbox should include a red flag and contain a numeral. The number will depend on developmental appropriateness. A set of dots, corresponding to the numeral on the flag, should be placed on the mailbox. Hang the mailboxes on the bulletin board. Next, construct letters by using small cards with sets of dots on them. The children can match the dots on the cards to the dots and numerals on the mailboxes. If desired, magnet pieces can be attached to both the mailboxes and the cards.

Family Letter

InBox

Dear Families,

During the past several weeks, we have been busy discussing the roles of a variety of community helpers. Next, we will focus the curriculum on the role of the mail carrier. The children will learn about letters, stamps, and addresses, and will be able to identify objects found in a post office. They will also become aware of what needs to be included on a letter or package before it is delivered. Moreover, they will learn the types of transportation used for delivering.

At School

Some of the many learning activities scheduled include:

- Listening to the story *Adventures of a Letter* by G. Warren Schloat
- Playing in a post office set up in the classroom
- Making mailboxes and postcards
- Weighing letters and packages
- Delivering mail to our friends in our room

At Home

Let your children help or watch you open the mail. Give your child the "junk mail" to play with. Show your child where your address is on your house and mailbox. You may also enjoy having your children dictate a letter to a grandparent, favorite aunt, or cousin. As you write the letter, show your child the printed alphabet letters to develop an awareness of alphabet letters. After you finish the letter, address an envelope. Let your child show the proper placement of the stamp. Then it's off to the post office!

Enjoy your child!

Arts and Crafts

1. **Postcards**

   Have children make postcards at school to send to family and friends. Provide index cards. Let the children design the postcards.

2. **Mailboxes**

   Make mailboxes out of old shoeboxes. Each child can decorate his or her own box. Names can be added by the child or teacher. Include a home address for older children.

3. **Mail Truck**

   Construct a mail truck out of a large cardboard box. Provide paint for the children to decorate it. When dried, place chairs and, if available, a steering wheel inside for the children to use.

4. **Stamps**

   Collect assorted stamps or stickers. Cancelled stamps can be reglued. The children can make a stamp collage.

Cooking

Zip Code Special

   1 1/2 cups nonfat dry milk
   2 cups fresh or frozen berries
   1 teaspoon vanilla
   1 cup water
   1 tray ice cubes

   Blend all ingredients in a blender. Serve and enjoy.

Dramatic Play

1. **Post Office**

   Develop the dramatic play area into a post office. Provide a mailbox, mail carrier hats, a mailbag, stamps, a cash register, rubber date stamps, and a letter scale. The children may enjoy acting out the role of a mail carrier or a post office worker.

2. **Letters**

   Provide a variety of writing materials. Include different colors of paper, writing tools, and envelopes. The children can dictate a letter to a friend or a family member. After all interested children have completed dictation, apply stamps and walk to the nearest mailbox or post office. (Contact a local printer, office supply store, or card shop and ask for discontinued samples or misprinted envelopes.)

Field Trips and Resource People

1. **Post Office**

   Plan a field trip to the local post office. Observe the mailboxes, stamp machines, address books, scales, and rubber stamps with the children. Mail a postcard back to the center. Count the number of days it takes to arrive.

2. **Mail Carrier**

   Invite the mail carrier who delivers mail or the local postmaster to your center or school to visit in the classroom. Ask the mail carrier to show his or her mailbag, hat, and so on to the children.

Fingerplays and Chants

Little Mail Carrier

   I am a little mail carrier
       (point to self)
   Who can do nothing better.
   I walk.
       (walk in place)
   I run.
       (run in place)
   I hop to your house.
       (hop in place)
   To deliver your letter.

Five Little Letters

Five little letters lying on a tray.
    (extend fingers of right hand)
Mommy came and took the first one away.
    (bend down thumb)
Daddy said, "This one's for me!"
I counted them twice, now there are three.
    (bend down pointer finger)
Brother Bill asked, "Did I get any mail?"
He found one and cried, "A letter from Gail."
    (bend down middle finger)
My sister Jane took the next to the last
And ran upstairs to open it fast.
    (bend down ring finger)
As I can't read, I am not able to see,
Whom the last one is for, but I hope it's for me!
    (wiggle last finger, clap hands)

The Mail Carrier

I come from the post office
    (walk from post office)
My mail sack on my back.
    (pretend to carry sack on back)
I go to all the houses
    (pretend to go up to a house)
Leaving letters from my pack.
    (pretend to drop letters into mailbox)
One, two, three, four
    (hold up fingers as you count)
What are these letters for?
    (pretend to hold letters as you count)
One for John. One for Lou.
    (pretend to hand out letters)
One for Tom and one for you!
    (pretend to hand out letters to others)

Letter to Grandma

Lick them, stamp them
    (make licking and stamping motions)
Put them in a box.
    (extend arms outward)
Hope that Grandma
Loves them a lot!
    (hug self)

Group Time
(Games, Language)

Thank You

Write a thank-you note to the postmaster or mail carrier after visiting.

Math

The number of items and numerals used in these activities needs to be adjusted to reflect children's level of development.

1. **Dominoes**
   Create dominoes out of envelopes. Have the children match the numbers and dots.

2. **How Many Stamps?**
   Write an individual numeral on an envelope. Make or collect many stamps. The children can place the correct number of stamps in the envelope with the corresponding numeral. A variation of this activity is to make mailboxes from shoeboxes. Again, write a numeral on each box. Make or collect many different envelopes. The children can put the correct number of letters in the corresponding mailboxes.

3. **Package Seriation**
   Prepare several packages and letters of different sizes. The children can place the letters and packages in order from largest to smallest or from smallest to largest.

Music

1. **"Mailing Letters"**
   (Sing to the tune of "The Mulberry Bush")

   This is the way we mail a letter,
   Mail a letter, mail a letter.
   This is the way we mail a letter,
   So early in the morning.

2. **"Let's Pretend"**
   (Sing to the tune of "Did You Ever See a Lassie?")

   Let's pretend that we are mail carriers,
   Are mail carriers, are mail carriers.
   Let's pretend that we are mail carriers,
   We'll have so much fun.
   We'll carry the letters and put them in
       boxes.
   Let's pretend that we are mail carriers,
   We'll have so much fun.

Science

1. **Dress the Mail Carrier**
   Place flannel board pieces representing seasonal clothing for a mail carrier. Let the children select the appropriate clothing for the weather. This may be an interesting activity to introduce daily during group time.

2. **Weighing Mail**
   A variety of letters, boxes, and stamps, and a scale, can be placed in the science area. The children can weigh letters and packages. This activity can be extended by placing materials in the boxes and weighing them, noting the difference.

3. **How Does the Mail Feel?**
   Place different types of envelopes and stationery on the sensory table for the children to explore. Include airmail paper, onionskin, bond paper, computer paper, and different kinds of stationery. Also, provide a magnifying glass.

Social Studies

Mailboxes
Plan a walk around the neighborhood. Observe the different types of mailboxes and addresses.

Books

The following books can be used to complement this theme:

Cuneo, Mary Louise, and Pamela Paparone. (2000). *Mail for Husher Town*. Illustrated by Pamela Paparone. New York: Greenwillow.

Flanagan, Alice K., and Christine Osinski. (1999). *Here Comes Mr. Eventoff with the Mail*. Our Neighborhood. Photography by Christine Osinski. New York: Children's Press.

Gibbons, Gail. (1987). *The Post Office Book: Mail and How It Moves*. New York: HarperCollins.

Keats, Ezra Jack. (1998). *A Letter to Amy* (reprint edition). New York: Viking.

Kottke, Jan. (2000). *A Day with a Mail Carrier*. Hard Work. New York: Children's Press.

Owen, Ann. (2003). *Delivering Your Mail: A Book about Mail Carriers*. Illustrated by Eric Thomas. Minneapolis, MN: Picture Window Books.

Schaefer, Lola M. (1999). *We Need Mail Carriers*. Mankato, MN: Pebble Books.

Scholat, G. Warren. (1949). *Adventures of a Letter*. New York: Schriber. JH

Scott, Ann Herbert. (1994). *Hi*. Illustrated by Glo Coalson. New York: Philomel Books.

Steffensmeier, Alexander. (2007). *Millie Waits for the Mail*. New York: Holzbrinck.

Teague, Mark. (2002). *Dear Mrs. La Rue: Letters from Obedience School*. New York: Scholastic.

Technology and Multimedia

The following technology and multimedia products can be used to complement this theme:

"The Community Helper Hop" [CD]. (1996). In *People in Our Neighborhood*. Long Branch, NJ: Kimbo Educational.

"Mail Carrier" [CD]. (2008). In *Songs for the Whole Day*. Nashville, TN: Lamon Records.

There Goes the Mail [video]. (1997). New York: KidVision.

 Additional teaching resources to accompany this Theme can be found on the book's companion website. Go to www.cengagebrain.com to access the site for a variety of useful resources.

Theme 50
MICE

Foods
insects
leaves
roots
seeds
leather
fruits
nuts
cheese
plants

Size
small

Homes
barns
attics
basements
fields
nests

Noises
squeaking
scratching
chattering

Types
house
American
harvest
grasshopper
deer

Needs
food
water
shelter

Enemies
people
dogs
hawks
foxes
snakes
owls
rats
other mice
cats

Body Parts
head
body
tail
ears
eyes
mouth
teeth
whiskers

Colors
white
black
brown

Theme Goals

Through participating in the experiences provided by this theme, the children may learn:

1. Body parts of mice
2. Size of mice
3. Needs of mice
4. Color of mice
5. Noises mice make
6. Foods mice eat
7. Homes mice make
8. Enemies of mice
9. Types of mice

Concepts for the Children to Learn

1. A mouse is a small animal with four legs.
2. Mice is the word to use when you refer to more than one mouse.
3. There are four main types of mice: house, American harvest, grasshopper, and deer.
4. The body of a mouse is 2 1/2 to 3 1/2 inches long. The tail is almost as long as the body.
5. The body of a mouse is covered with fur.
6. Mice may have white-, brown-, or black-colored fur.
7. Mice need water, food, and shelter to live.
8. Mice eat plants, insects, leaves, roots, seeds, leather, fruits, cheese, plants, and nuts.
9. Barns, attics, basements, fields, and nests are homes for mice.
10. Mice need food and shelter to live.
11. Mice have good hearing but poor sight.
12. Mice have strong, sharp front teeth that keep growing.
13. Mice have a head, a body, a tail, ears, eyes, a mouth, and whiskers.
14. A house mouse has a brown back and white belly.
15. People can sometimes hear mice squeaking, chattering, and scratching.
16. People, cats, dogs, hawks, foxes, snakes, owls, rats, and other mice can be enemies of mice.

Vocabulary

1. **mouse**—a small furry animal that has a head, ears, eyes, a mouth, whiskers, four legs, a body, and a tail.
2. **scratching**—a noise a mouse makes by rubbing its nails against a surface.
3. **squeaking**—a clear, sharp sound made by a mouse.
4. **chewing**—mice chew by crushing with their teeth.

Bulletin Board

The purpose of this bulletin board is to promote the identification of written numerals as well as match a set to a written numeral. Construct cheese and mice shapes out of construction paper or tagboard. Draw a set of dots on each piece of cheese. The number of dots used should correspond to the developmental level of the children. Print a corresponding numeral on each mouse. Staple the cheese pieces to the bulletin board along the side edges and the bottom, creating a pocket. The children should be encouraged to match the written numeral of each mouse to the corresponding set of dots on the cheese pieces and place the mice in the pockets.

Family Letter

Dear Families,

Squeak! Squeak! Squeak! We will be enjoying a new theme that will provide us with discoveries about small animals called mice. The children will be learning about the types, colors, care, needs, and enemies of mice. They will also learn about foods mice eat and the homes they make.

At School

Learning experiences planned for this unit include:

- Visiting the pet store to observe mice
- Pretending to be mice in the dramatic play area
- Listening to the stories titled *Mouse Paint* and *Mouse Count* by Ellen Stoll Walsh

At Home

Go to the library and check out some children's books about mice. Some titles to look for include:

- *If You Give a Mouse a Cookie* by Laura Numeroff
- *Mouse Poems* by John Foster

Enjoy the following fingerplay titled "Where Are the Baby Mice?" with your child.

> Where are the baby mice?
>   (hide fists behind back)
> Squeak, squeak, squeak.
> I cannot see them.
> Peek, peek, peek.
>   (show fists)
> Here they come out of their hole in the wall.
> One, two, three, four, five and that is all!
>   (show fingers one at a time)

Enjoy helping your child learn more about mice!

Arts and Crafts

1. Mouse Sponge Painting
Cut sponges into mice shapes. Place on the art table with paper and a shallow pan of thick tempera paint. The children can make designs by pressing the sponge into the paint and then on a piece of paper.

2. Seed Collage
Place a variety of seeds, glue, and paper on a table in the art area. The children can create designs with the materials.

Cooking

1. Macaroni and Cheese
Purchase prepackaged macaroni and cheese. Prepare following the directions provided on the container. Compare the flavor to that of the recipe that follows.

3–3 1/2 cups cooked macaroni
1/4 cup butter or margarine
1/4 cup chopped onion (optional)
1/2 teaspoon salt
1/2 teaspoon pepper
1/4 cup flour
1 1/2 cups milk
1/2 pound of Swiss or American cheese cut into small cubes

Combine butter, onion, salt, and pepper in a saucepan; cook over medium heat until onion is tender. Blend in the flour. Lower heat and stir constantly until the mixture is smooth and bubbly. Add milk and heat to boiling, stirring constantly. Stir and boil one minute. Remove from heat. Add cheese, and stir until melted.

Place macaroni in ungreased 1 1/2 quart casserole. Stir cheese sauce into the macaroni. Bake in an oven heated to 375 degrees for 30 minutes. Makes five servings.

2. Mouse Cookies
With the children, prepare a batch of drop cookie dough according to the recipe. Demonstrate how to drop three spoonfuls of dough onto a cookie sheet so that it will resemble a mouse head with two ears when baked. The mouse cookies can be frosted, or details can be added with raisins, chocolate chips, and string licorice.

Dramatic Play

1. Mouse House
The children can pretend to be mice! Construct mouse ears out of fabric or construction paper, and attach to headbands. Provide large cardboard boxes to represent houses for the mice.

2. Pet Store
Arrange the dramatic play area as a pet store. Provide props such as a cash register, play money, stuffed animals, animal cages, animal toys, and empty pet food boxes. Display posters of pets, including mice.

Field Trips

1. Pet Store
Visit a pet store to observe the colors of pet mice and animal accessories. Photographs can be taken during the trip and later displayed in the classroom.

2. Mouse Walk
Take a walk around your school and look for places mice might live.

Fingerplays and Chants

Where Are the Baby Mice?
Where are the baby mice?
   (hide fists behind back)
Squeak, squeak, squeak!
I cannot see them.
Peek, peek, peek.
   (show fist)

Here they come out of their hole in the wall.
One, two, three, four, five, and that is all!
(show fingers one at a time)

Five Little Baby Mice

Five little mice on the kitchen floor.
(hold up five fingers)
This little mouse peeked behind the door.
(point to thumb)
This little mouse nibbled at the cake.
(point to index finger)
This little mouse not a sound did he make.
(point to middle finger)
This little mouse took a bite of cheese.
(point to ring finger)
This little mouse heard the kitten sneeze.
(point to pinky)
"Ah-choo!" sneezed the kitten,
And "squeak" they cried.
As they found a hole and ran inside.
(move hand behind back)

Little Mouse

See the little mousie,
(place index and middle finger on thumb
to represent a mouse)
Creeping up the stair,
(creep mouse slowly up the forearm)
Looking for a warm rest.
There—Oh! There!
(spring mouse into an elbow corner)

Hickory Dickory Dock

Hickory, dickory, dock.
(bend arm at elbow; hold up and open
palm)
The mouse ran up the clock.
(run fingers up the arm)
The clock struck one,
(hold up index finger)
The mouse ran down,
(run fingers down arm)
Hickory, dickory, dock.

Mouse

Here is a mouse with ears so funny,
(place index and middle finger on thumb
to represent a mouse)
And here is a hole in the ground.
(make a hole with the other fist)
When a noise he hears, he pricks up his ears.
And runs to his hole in the ground.
(jump mouse into hole in other fist)

Group Time
(Games and Language)

1. **"Mouse, Mouse, Where's Your Cheese?"**
This game is played in a circle formation. Arrange the chairs and place one in the center of the circle. Place a block to represent the cheese under the chair. Select one child, the "mouse," to sit on the chair and close his or her eyes. Then point to another child. This child must try to remove the cheese without making a sound. After the child returns to his or her chair in the circle, instruct all of the children to place their hands behind their backs. Then, in unison, the children say, "Mouse, Mouse, where is your cheese?" The mouse then opens his or her eyes and tries to guess who is holding the cheese.

2. **Language Chart**
Across the top of a piece of tagboard, print the question "Where would you like to live if you were a mouse?" During group time, introduce the chart and record the children's responses. Display the chart in the classroom.

Music

1. **"Ten Little Mice"**
(*Sing to the tune of "Ten Little Indians"*)

One little, two little, three little mice.
Four little, five little, six little mice.
Seven little, eight little, nine little mice.
Ten little mice, all played nice.

2. **"Two Little Brown Mice"**
(*Sing to the tune of "Baa Baa Black Sheep"*)

Two little brown mice,
Scampering through the hall.
One named Sarah.
One named Paul.

Run away, Sarah.
Run away, Paul.
Come back, Sarah.
Come back, Paul.

Two little brown mice,
Scampering through the hall.
One named Sarah.
One named Paul.

3. "Find the Mouse"
(*Sing to the tune of "The Muffin Man"*)

Oh, can you find the little mouse,
The little mouse, the little mouse.
Can you find the little mouse,
He's somewhere in the house.

4. "One Little Mouse"
(*Sing to the tune of "Six Little Ducks"*)

One little brown and whiskery mouse
Lived in a hole in a cozy house.
When the cat came along to
Take a little peek,
The mouse ran away with a "Squeak,
    squeak, squeak."
"Squeak, squeak, squeak."
"Squeak, squeak, squeak."
"The mouse ran away with a "Squeak,
    squeak, squeak."

5. "Three Brown Mice"
(*Sing to the tune of "Three Blind Mice"*)

Three brown mice, three brown mice.
See how they run. See how they run.
They were chased through the house
    by the big black cat.
Lucky for them, she was lazy and fat.
Did you ever see such a sight as that?
Three brown mice, three brown mice.

Science

Mice
Purchase or borrow mice from a pet store to keep as classroom pets. Place the cage on the science table for the children to observe. Allow the children to assist in caring for the animals.

Sensory

Additions to the Sensory Table
- Grains with scoops, cups, and spoons
- Seeds with pails and shovels
- Clean cedar chips (animal bedding) with measuring cups, scoops, and pails

Books

The following books can be used to complement this theme:

Brett, Jan. (1994). *Town Mouse, Country Mouse.* New York: G. P. Putnam.

Cousins, Lucy. (1998). *Maisy on the Farm.* Cambridge, MA: Candlewick Press.

Cousins, Lucy. (2000). *Maisy Takes a Bath.* Cambridge, MA: Candlewick Press.

Cousins, Lucy. (2002). *Maisy Cleans Up.* Cambridge, MA: Candlewick Press.

Cousins, Lucy. (2010). *Maisy Goes to Preschool.* Cambridge, MA: Candlewick Press.

De Paola, Tomie. (1997). *Mice Squeak, We Speak* (poem by Arnold Shapiro). New York: Putnam.

Donofrio, Beverly. (2007). *Mary and the Mouse.* Illustrated by Barbara McClintock. New York: Schwartz & Wade Books.

Dunbar, Joyce. (2006). *Where's My Sock?* Illustrated by Sanja Rescek. New York: Chicken House.

Fleming, Denise. (1992). *Lunch.* New York: Henry Holt.

Foster, John. (1990). *Mouse Poems.* Oxford, England: Oxford University Press.

George, Lindsay Barrett. (2004). *Inside Mouse, Outside Mouse.* New York: Greenwillow Books.

Iwamura, Kazuo. (2010). *Hooray for Summer.* Fitzgerald, GA: North South.

King-Smith, Dick. (1999). *A Mouse Called Wolf.* New York: Yearling.

Kirk, Daniel. (2010). *Library Mouse: A World to Explore.* New York: Abrams Books for Young Readers.

Lewiston, Wendy Cheyette. (2010). *There's a Mouse in the House!* New York: Cartwheel Books.

Numeroff, Laura (2007). *If You Give A Mouse A Cookie.* Illustrated by Felicia Bond. New York: Harper Collins Publisher.

Pinkney, Jerry. (2009). *The Lion and the Mouse.* New York: Little Brown Books for Young Readers.

Ryan, Pam Munoz, and Joe Cepeda. (2001). *Mice and Beans.* Illustrated by Joe Cepeda. New York: Scholastic.

Rylant, Cynthia. (2008). *In November.* Orlando, FL: Voyager Books.

Scarry, Richard. (2001). *Is This the House of Mistress Mouse?* New York: Golden Books.

Shapiro, Arnold. (2000). *Mice Squeak, We Speak.* Illustrated by Tomie de Paola. New York: Penguin.

Smith, Jeff. (2009). *Little Mouse Gets Ready.* New York: RAW Junior.

Stoll, Ellen Walsh. (1991). *Mouse Count.* San Diego, CA: Harcourt Children's Books.

Stoll, Ellen Walsh. (1989). *Mouse Paint.* New York: Harcourt Brace and Company.

Stoll, Ellen Walsh. (2007). *Mouse Shapes.* San Diego, CA: Harcourt Children's Books.

Thompson, Lauren. (2004). *Mouse's First Summer.* Illustrated by Buket Erdogan New York: Simon and Schuster.

Urban, Linda. (2009*). Mouse Was Mad.* Illustrated by Henry Cole. Orlando, FL: Harcourt Children's Books.

Wallace, Nancy Elizabeth. (2006). *Look! Look! Look!* New York: Marshall Cavendish Children.

Wood, Don. (1990). *The Little Mouse, the Red Ripe Strawberry and the Big Hungry Bear.* New York: Child's Play.

Yee, Wong Herbert. (2009). *Mouse and Mole, Fine Feathered Friends.* Boston: Houghton Mifflin Books for Children.

Technology and Multimedia

The following technology and multimedia products can be used to complement this theme:

If You Give a Mouse a Cookie [CD]. (1995). New York: HarperCollins Interactive.

Mabela the Clever (an African Folktale of the Limba People of Sierra Leone) [DVD]. (2005). Guilford, CT: Nutmeg Media.

"Mouse in My Toolbox" [CD]. (2008). *Rocketship Run.* New York: Two Tomatoes.

Palmer, Hap. (1995). "The Mice Go Marching" [CD]. In *Rhythms on Parade.* Baldwin, NY: Educational Activities.

Play Time Maisy [DVD]. (2004). Burbank, CA: Universal Studios.

Reading Rainbow. (2007). *If You Give a Mouse a Cookie* [DVD]. Lincoln, NE: GPN Educational Media.

 Additional teaching resources to accompany this Theme can be found on the book's companion website. Go to www.cengagebrain.com to access the site for a variety of useful resources.

Theme 51
MUSIC

Body Sounds
stamping
clapping
whistling
marching
snapping
singing

Tempo
fast
slow

Equipment
compact disc player
computer
radio
iPod
MP3 player
DVD player

Language Concepts
numbers
colors
letters
shapes
animals
people

Sounds
high
low
loud
soft

Instruments
piano
autoharp
tambourine
drum
shakers
sandpaper blocks
bells
sticks
triangle
guitar

Kinds
rock and roll
classical
jazz
country

Theme Goals

Through participating in the experiences provided by this theme, the children may learn:

1. Kinds of music
2. Music tempos
3. Language concepts
4. Different sounds
5. Names of many musical instruments
6. Body sounds
7. Equipment used for playing and recording music

Concepts for the Children to Learn

1. Music is a language made up of sounds.
2. Music is a way of expressing ideas and feelings.
3. The piano, autoharp, tambourine, drum, shakers, sandpaper blocks, bells, sticks, triangle, and guitar are all musical instruments.
4. Each instrument has its own sound.
5. Music sounds can be high, low, loud, and soft.
6. Music can express different moods.
7. Music can be played in different rhythms.
8. Songs can tell stories.
9. Children's songs can be about numbers, colors, letters, shapes, animals, and people.
10. Our bodies can be used as musical instruments to produce songs.
11. We can clap our hands, stamp our feet and snap our fingers.
12. Our mouths can whistle and sing.
13. The piano, autoharp, and guitar are played with our fingers.
14. Sticks are used on the triangle, drum, xylophone, and bells to create music.
15. We shake bells, shakes, tambourines and rub sandpaper blocks.
16. We can record music on DVDs.
17. Rock and roll, classical, jazz, and country are kinds of music.
18. We can play music with a compact disc player, computer, radio, iPod, and MP3 player.

Vocabulary

1. **body sounds**—sounds made by moving one or more body parts.
2. **instrument**—a device that makes musical sounds.
3. **mallets**—special sticks used to play the xylophone and bells.
4. **music**—a way of expressing ideas and feelings through sound. The sounds made by instruments or by people singing are music.
5. **tempo**—the speed of music.

Bulletin Board

The purpose of this bulletin board is to promote the development of visual discrimination and visual memory skills. Create a musical bulletin board by drawing musical instruments on tagboard as illustrated. Color the instruments with markers, cut out, and laminate. Trace these pieces onto black construction paper. Cut out the pieces and attach to the bulletin board. A magnet strip should be attached to both the colored pieces and the black shadow pieces. The children can match the appropriately shaped instrument piece to its shadow on the bulletin board.

Family Letter

Dear Families,

We will be singing and playing instruments during our curriculum theme on music. Music is a universal language. It is a way of communicating and expressing oneself. Throughout the unit, the children will make interesting discoveries about the many sounds that we can make with our voices, body parts, and musical instruments.

At School

A few highlights of our scheduled musical learning activities include:

- Making musical instruments
- Painting at the easel while listening to music with headphones
- Trying on band uniforms (courtesy of Mead School) in the dramatic play area
- Forming a rhythm band outside in the play yard

Family Involvement

If you enjoy any special cultural or ethnic music or instruments, we invite you to share them with our class. Please contact me so a time for your visit can be arranged. The children, especially your own, will enjoy having you visit our class and learning more about music.

At Home

To stimulate creativity and language, create verses with your child for this song to the tune of "Old MacDonald Had a Farm":

> Mr. Roberts had a band,
> E-I-E-I-O.
> And in his band he had a drum
> E-I-E-I-O.
> With a boom, boom here, and a boom, boom, there,
> Here a boom, there a boom,
> Everywhere a boom, boom.
> Mr. Roberts had a band,
> E-I-E-I-O.
>
> And in his band he had a horn …
>
> Continue adding instruments that your child can think of.

Keep a song in your heart!

Arts and Crafts

1. Drums
Create drums out of empty coffee cans with plastic lids, plastic ice cream pails, or oatmeal boxes. The children can decorate as desired with paper, paint, felt-tip markers, or crayons.

2. Shakers
Collect a variety of empty yogurt cups and caps. Fill each yogurt cup with varying amounts of sand, peas, or rice, and securely tape or glue the covers shut. To compare sounds, empty cottage cheese containers can also be filled.

3. Cymbals
Make cymbals out of old tinfoil pans. Attach a string for the handles.

4. Tambourines
Two paper plates can be made into a tambourine. Begin by placing pop bottle caps or small stones between the plates. Staple the paper plates together. Shake to produce sound.

5. Rubber Band Instruments
Select several small cardboard boxes. Remove the covers. Then provide the children with rubber bands of different widths and lengths. Demonstrate how to wrap the rubber bands around the box. After the children make their rubber band instrument, show them how to pluck the different bands and tell them to listen. Discuss the different sounds, and encourage the children to pluck the rubber bands. Note the differences in sounds.

6. Musical Painting
On a table in the art area, place a tape recorder with headphones. The children can listen to music as they paint.

7. Kazoos
Kazoos can be made with empty paper towel rolls and waxed paper. The children can decorate the outside of the kazoos with colored felt-tip markers. After this, place a piece of waxed paper over one end of the roll and secure it with a rubber band. Poke two or three small holes into the waxed paper, allowing sound to be produced.

8. Rhythm Sticks
Two wooden dowels should be given to each interested child. The sticks can be decorated with paint or colored felt-tip markers.

Cooking

Popcorn
Make popcorn and have the children listen to the sounds of the oil and corn popping. *Caution:* Supervise this activity closely because the corn popper will become hot. This activity is most appropriate for older children—younger children may choke on popcorn.

Dramatic Play

1. Band
Collect materials for a band prop box, which may include band uniforms, a baton, a music stand, a CD player, and CDs with marching music. The children can experiment with instruments.

2. Dramatizing
Add a cassette recorder and a small microphone to the dramatic play area. The children may enjoy using it for singing and recording their voices.

3. Disc Jockey
In the music area, provide a CD player and CDs or an MP3 player for the children.

Field Trips and Resource People

1. Band Director
Visit a school band director. Observe the different instruments available to students. Listen to their sounds.

2. Who Can Play?

Invite parents, grandparents, brothers, sisters, relatives, friends, and so on to visit the classroom and demonstrate their talent.

3. Radio Station

Visit a local radio station.

4. Taping

Use a digital recorder to record the children singing and using rhythm instruments. Replay the video for the children. Save this for a future open house, parent meeting, or holiday celebration.

Fingerplays and Chants

I Want to Lead a Band

I want to lead a band
With a baton in my hand.
 (wave baton in air)
I want to make sweet music high and low.
Now first I'll beat the drum
 (drum-beating motion)
With a rhythmic tum-tum-tum,
And then I'll play the bells
A-ting-a-ling-a-ling,
 (bell-playing motion)
And next I'll blow the flute
With a cheery toot-a-toot.
 (flute-playing motion)
Then I'll make the violin sweetly sing.
 (violin-playing motion)
Now I'm leading a band
With a baton in my hand.
 (wave baton in air again)

If I Could Play

If I could play the piano
This is the way I would play.
 (move fingers like playing a piano)

If I had a guitar
I would strum the strings this way.
 (hold guitar and strum)

If I had a trumpet
I'd toot to make a tune.
 (play trumpet)

But if I had a drum
I'd go boom, boom, boom.
 (pretend to play a drum)

Musical Instruments

This is how a horn sounds
Toot! Toot! Toot!
 (play imaginary horn)
This is how guitars sound

Vrrroom, vrrroom, vrrroom
 (strum imaginary guitar)

This is how the piano sounds
Tinkle, grumble, brring.
 (run fingers over imaginary keyboard)

This is how the drum sounds
Rat-a-tat, grumble, brring.
 (strike drum, including cymbal)

Jack-in-the-Box

Jack-in-the-box all shut up tight
 (fingers wrapped around thumb)
Not a breath of air, not a ray of light.
 (other hand covers fist)
How tired he must be all down in a heap.
 (lift off)
I'll open the lid and up he will leap!
 (thumbs pop out)

Large Muscle

1. Body Movement Rhythms

Introduce a simple body movement. Then have the children repeat it until they develop a rhythm. Examples include the following:

- Stamp foot, clap hands, stamp foot, clap hands
- Clap, clap, stamp, stamp
- Clap, stamp, clap, stamp
- Clap, clap, snap fingers
- Clap, snap, stamp, clap, snap, stamp
- Clap, clap, stamp, clap, clap, stamp

2. Body Percussion

Instruct the children to stand in a circle. Repeat the following rhythmic speech:
We walk and we walk and we stop
 (rest)
We walk and we walk and we stop
 (rest)
We walk and we walk and we walk and we walk
We walk and we walk and we stop.
 (stop)

3. March

Play different rhythm beats on a piano or another instrument. Examples include hopping, skipping, gliding, walking, running, tiptoeing, galloping, and so on. The children can move to the rhythm.

4. Scarf Dancing

Give each child a scarf or streamer and play a variety of music. Encourage the children to move the scarf or streamer fast or slow according to the tempo of the music.

5. Musical Freeze

Arrange children in a circle. Pass around a beanbag as you play music. When the music stops, whoever is holding the beanbag "freezes" with it. When the music restarts, the child begins passing it again.

Math

1. Colors, Shapes, and Numbers

Sing the song "Colors, Shapes, and Numbers" that is mentioned in the "Shapes" unit, or make up a song about shapes. Hold up different colors, shapes, and numbers while you sing the song for the children to identify.

2. Number Rhyme

(*Say the following song to reinforce numbers*)

One, two, three, four
Come right in and shut the door.
Five, six, seven, eight
Come right in. It's getting late.
Nine, ten, eleven, twelve
Put your books upon the shelves.
Will you count along with me?
It's as easy as can be!

3. Ten in the Bed

(*Chant the following words to reinforce numbers*)

There were 10 in the bed and the little one said,
"Roll over, roll over."
So they all rolled over and one fell out.
There were nine in the bed and the little one said,

"Roll over, roll over."
So they all rolled over and one fell out.

(*Continue until there is only one left. The last line will be "… and the little one said, 'Good night!'"*)

4. Music Calendar

Design a calendar for the month of your music unit. The different days of the week can be made out of musical notes and different instruments.

5. Drum Beats

Arrange children in a circle and ask them to close their eyes. Have them listen for the number of times you beat the drum. (If it is too difficult for them to count in their heads, count out loud as you beat the drum.) Whoever names the correct number gets to beat the drum next.

Miscellaneous

Instrument of the Day

Focus on a different instrument each day. Talk about its construction, and demonstrate the instrument's sound.

Music

Music for this unit should consist of the children's favorite and well-known songs. The children will enjoy singing these songs, and you will be able to focus on the sound of the music. Here are some suggestions of traditional songs that most children enjoy:

1. **"Old MacDonald Had a Farm"**
2. **"Five Green Speckled Frogs"**
3. **"The Farmer in the Dell"**
4. **"Row, Row, Row Your Boat"**
5. **"Mary Had a Little Lamb"**
6. **"Hickory Dickory Dock"**

7. "If You're Happy and You Know It"
8. "ABC Song"
9. "The Little White Duck"
10. "Six Little Ducks"
11. "Do Your Ears Hang Low?"

Do your ears hang low?
Do they wobble to and fro?
Can you tie them in a knot?
Can you tie them in a bow?
Can you throw them over your
    shoulder?
Do your ears hang low?

12. "Old King Cole"
13. "Head, Shoulders, Knees, and Toes"
14. "I Am Special"

(*Sing to the tune of "Are You Sleeping?"*)

I am special, I am special.
    (child points to him or herself)
If you look, you will see.
    (place a mirror in front of the
    child's face)
Someone very special, someone very
    special.
That is me, that is me.
    (child points to him or herself)

15. **Here We Go 'round the Mulberry Bush**

Here we go 'round the mulberry bush.
The mulberry bush,
The mulberry bush.
Here we go 'round the mulberry bush,
So early in the morning.
These are the chores we'll do this week,
Do this week,
Do this week.
These are the chores we'll do this week,
So early in the morning.
This is the way we wash our clothes,
Wash our clothes,
Wash our clothes.
This is the way we wash our clothes,
So early Monday morning.
This is the way we iron our clothes,
Iron our clothes,
Iron our clothes.
This is the way we iron our clothes,
So early Tuesday morning.
This is the way we scrub the floor,
Scrub the floor,
Scrub the floor.

This is the way we scrub the floor,
So early Tuesday morning.
This is the way we mend our clothes.
Mend our clothes,
Mend our clothes.
This is the way we mend our clothes,
So early Thursday morning.
This is the way we sweep the floor.
Sweep the floor,
Sweep the floor.
This is the way we sweep the floor,
So early Friday morning.
This is the way we bake our bread,
Bake our bread,
Bake our bread.
This is the way we bake our bread,
So early Saturday morning.
This is the way we get dressed up,
Get dressed up,
Get dressed up.
This is the way we get dressed up,
So early Sunday morning.
Here we go 'round the mulberry bush,
The mulberry bush,
The mulberry bush.
Here we go 'round the mulberry bush,
So early in the morning.

Science

1. **Water Music**
Fill four identically sized crystal glasses each with a different amount of water. Supervise the children tracing their wet finger around the rim of each glass. Each glass will have a different tune. Older children may enjoy reordering the glasses from the highest to the lowest tone.

2. **Pop Bottle Music**
Fill six 12-ounce pop bottles, each with a different amount of water. For effect, in each bottle place a drop of food coloring, providing six different colors. Younger children can tap the bottles with a spoon as they listen for the sound. Older children may try blowing directly into the opening for sound production.

3. Throats

Show the children how to place their hands across their throat. Then have them whisper, talk, shout, and sing while feeling the differences in vibration.

4. Jumping Seeds

Set seeds or other small objects on top of a drum. Then beat the drum. What happens? Why? This activity can be extended by having the children jump to the drum beat.

5. Identifying Instruments

Prepare a CD of classroom musical instruments. Play the CD, encouraging the children to identify the correct instrument related to each sound.

6. Matching Sounds

Collect 12 containers, such as milk cartons or covered potato chip cans, that would be safe to use with the children. Fill two containers with rice, two cans with beans, two cans with pebbles, two cans with water, and the remaining cans with dry pasta. Coins, such as pennies, could be substituted. Color code each pair of containers on the bottom. Let the children shake the containers, listening to the sounds, in an attempt to find the matching pairs.

7. Musical Vibrations

Tie two pieces of string to a wire hanger near both ends. Hold the strings to your ears, and swing the hanger on the back of a chair or table. The vibration from the metal hanger will travel up the strings. Discuss with children the musical instruments that also make a vibration (triangles, drums, tone blocks, etc.).

Note: Supervise the children carefully when they are using hangers.

8. Paper Cup Telephones

For each telephone, you will need two large paper cups and a piece of string approximately 18 feet long. In the bottom of each cup, punch a hole. Then thread the ends of the string through the holes. Tie the string around a pipe cleaner or toothpick to keep it from pulling through the holes. Encourage the children to listen to each other from about 18 feet away.

Sensory

1. Rain Stick

Ask the children to close their eyes as you slowly turn a rain stick upside down. Ask the children to try to identify the sound they hear. Once they have guessed the correct sound, see if they can name the instrument. Allow time for children to experiment with the rain stick. (Rain sticks can easily be made with any cardboard roll and pebbles. Be sure to securely cap both ends before giving the rain stick to children.)

2. Bubble Wrap

Give each child a piece of bubble wrap. Let them experiment with making it pop. Sing "Pop Goes the Weasel," and ask the children to try to keep a beat or pop a bubble when the word "pop" is sung in the song.

Social Studies

1. Our Own Songs

Encourage the children to help you write a song about a common class experience. Substitute the words into a melody that everyone knows ("Twinkle, Twinkle, Little Star" or "The Mulberry Bush").

2. Pictures

Put up pictures of instruments and band players in the room to add interest and stimulate discussion.

3. Sound Tapes

Make a special CD of sounds heard in a home. Homes are full of different sounds. The following may be included:

- People knocking on doors
- Wind chimes
- Telephone ringing
- Teakettle whistling
- Clock ticking
- Toilet flushing
- Popcorn popping
- Vacuum cleaner

- Doorbell
- Running water
- Car horn
- Hands clapping
- Snapping fingers
- Alarm clock ticking
- Toast popping out of toaster
- Animal sounds
- Balls bouncing
- Bells ringing
- Baby crying
- Siren
- Door slamming

Play the CD and have the children listen carefully to identify the sounds.

 **Books**

The following books can be used to complement this theme:

Agell, Charlotte. (1994). *Dancing Feet.* San Diego, CA: Gulliver/Harcourt.

Aliki. (2003). *Ah, Music.* New York: HarperCollins.

Bradley, Kimberly. (2006). *Ballerina Nate.* New York: Dial.

Cox, Judy. (2003). *My Family Plays Music.* Illustrated by Elbrite Brown. New York: Holiday House.

Curtis, Gavin. (2001). *The Bat Boy and His Violin.* New York: Aladdin.

Edwards, Richard. (1994). *Moles Can Dance.* Cambridge, MA: Candlewick Press.

Ehrhardt, Karen. (2006). *This Jazz Man.* Illustrated by R. G. Roth. New York: Harcourt.

Feierabend, John M. (2003). *The Book of Children's Song Tales.* Illustrated by Tim Caton. Chicago: Gia Publications.

Feierabend, John M. (2003). *The Book of Echo Songs.* Illustrated by Tim Caton. Chicago: Gia Publications.

Feierabend, John M. (2003). *The Book of Finger Plays and Action Songs.* Illustrated by Tim Caton. Chicago: Gia Publications.

Feierabend, John M. (2004). *The Book of Movement Exploration.* Illustrated by Tim Caton. Chicago: Gia Publications.

Garriel, Barbara S. (2004). *I Know a Shy Fellow Who Swallowed a Cello.* Illustrated by John O'Brien. Honesdale, PA: Boyds Mills Press.

Johnson, Angela. (2004). *Violet's Music.* Illustrated by Laura Huliska-Beith. New York: Dial Books for Young Readers.

Krull, Kathleen. (2003). *M Is for Music.* Illustrated by Stacy Innerst. Orlando, FL: Harcourt.

Lach, William, and the Metropolitan Museum of Art. (2006). *Can You Hear It?* New York: Abrams Books for Young Readers.

McPhail. David. (1999). *Mole Music.* New York: Holt.

Miller, J. Philip, and Sheppard Greene. (2001). *We All Sing with the Same Voice.* Illustrated by Paul Meisel. New York: HarperCollins.

Morgan, Cindy, and Philomena O'Neil. (2009). *Dance Me Daddy.* Grand Rapids, MI: Zonderkidz.

Moss, Lloyd. (2000). *Zin! Zin! A Violin: A Violin.* Illustrated by Margorie Priceman. New York: Aladdin Paperbacks.

Parenteau, Shirley. (2007). *One Frog Sang.* Illustrated by Cynthia Jabar. Cambridge, MA: Candlewick Press.

Raschka, Chris. (1997). *Charlie Parker Played Be Bop.* New York: Scholastic.

Reynolds, Marilynn, Laura Fernandez, and Rick Jacobson. (2001). *The Magnificent Piano Recital.* Illustrated by Laura Fernandez and Rick Jacobson. Custer, WA: Orca Book Publishers.

Ryder, Joanne. (2007). *Dance by the Light of the Moon.* Illustrated by Guy Francis. New York: Hyperion Books for Young Children.

Shields, Carol Diggory, and Svjetlan Junakovic. (2000). *Animagicals: Music.* Illustrated by Svjetlan Junakovic. Brooklyn, NY: Handprint Books.

Wargin, Kathy-Jo. (2004). *M Is for Melody: A Music Alphabet.* Illustrated by Katherine Larson. Chelsea, MI: Sleeping Bear Press.

Weaver, Tess. (2002). *Opera Cat!* Illustrated by Andrea Wesson. New York: Clarion Books.

Weaver, Tess. (2009). *Encore, Opera Cat!* Illustrated by Andrea Wesson. New York: Clarion Books.

West, Jim, and Marshall Izen. (2004). *The Dog Who Sang at the Opera.* New York: H.N. Abrams.

Technology and Multimedia

The following technology and multimedia products can be used to complement this theme:

"Fast Slow" [CD]. (2010). In *The Best of the Laurie Berkner Band.* New York: Two Tomatoes.

Get Your Passport [DVD]. (2003). Washington, DC: National Geographic.

Grunsky, Jack. (2001). *Playground* [CD]. Toronto, Ontario, Canada: Jack Grunsky Productions.

I'd Like to Teach the World to Sing [DVD]. (2002). Ashville, NC: Video Master Video.

"I Really Love to Dance" [CD]. (2010). In *The Best of the Laurie Berkner Band.* New York: Two Tomatoes.

Jenkins, Ella. (1994). *This Is Rhythm* [CD]. Washington, DC: Smithsonian Folkways.

"Let's All Sing a Yodeling Song" [CD]. (2004). In *Celebration: A Tribute to Ella Jenkins.* Washington, DC: Smithsonian Folkways.

Music [DVD]. (2003). Suwanee, GA: Brainy Baby.

Reading Rainbow. (2006). *Music, Music, Everywhere* [DVD]. Lincoln, NE: Distributed by Educate Products.

"Shake It Loud" [CD]. (2010). In *What Are the Odds?* New York: Monkey Monkey Music.

"Song in My Tummy" [CD]. (2010). In *The Best of the Laurie Berkner Band.* New York: Two Tomatoes.

Songs about America [CD]. (2003). Long Branch, NJ: Kimbo Educational.

Stewart, Georgiana. (1992). *Multicultural Rhythm Stick Fun* [CD]. Long Branch, NJ: Kimbo Educational.

"Time to Sing" [CD]. (1985). In *One Light, One Sun.* Cambridge, MA: Rounder/UMGD.

"The Toy Symphony II" [CD]. (1998). In *Thye Mozart Effect.* Toronto: Children's Group.

"Twist! Stop! Hop!" "I Can Dance," "I Like Me," "Pelican Polka," and "My Chance to Dance" [CD]. (2002). In *Jump-Start Action.* Long Branch, NJ: Kimbo Educational.

"We Sing Out" [CD]. (2010). In *Pete Seeger, Tomorrow's Children.* Westchester, PA: Appleseed Records.

"You'll Sing a Song and I'll Sing a Song" [CD]. (2004). In *Celebration: A Tribute to Ella Jenkins.* Washington, DC: Smithsonian Folkways.

 Additional teaching resources to accompany this Theme can be found on the book's companion website. Go to www.cengagebrain.com to access the site for a variety of useful resources.

Multicultural Songs

Children's Folk Dances
By Georgiana Stewart

The following list includes excellent multicultural songs and folk dances for young children:

1. Polly Wolly Doodle
2. Walking Song
3. Go round and round the Village
4. Jump Jim Jo
5. Mi Jachol Lassim
6. Sma Grodorna
7. Unite Unite/Hobby Horse Parade
8. The French Musician
9. Where, Oh Where
10. Schottische
11. Troika
12. Everyone Likes Calypso
13. Ulili E
14. Cielito Lindo
15. Goodbye, Mrs. Durkin
16. Sur Le Pont D'Avignon
17. Die Hammerschiedsgesellen
18. Tarantella Doll
19. Carousel
20. Fado
21. Tant Hessie

Multicultural Rhythm Stick Fun
By Georgiana Stewart

1. Puerto Rico ("Ambos a Dos")
2. Caribbean ("Calypso")
3. Ireland ("Piper Piper")
4. Israel ("Zum Gali Gali")
5. Greece ("Children's Song")
6. Germany ("Hansel and Gretel Polka")
7. Span ("España Cani")
8. Australia ("Waltzing Matilda")
9. India ("Daysie")
10. Puerto Rico (instrumental)
11. Caribbean (instrumental)
12. Israel (instrumental)
13. West Africa ("Kourilengay")
14. Mexico ("La Cucaracha")
15. China ("Show Ha Mo")
16. Japan ("Haru Ga Kita")
17. Italy ("Tarantella")

18. Russia ("Trepak" from Tchaikovsky's ballet in the Nutcracker")
19. Brazil ("Tico Tico")
20. France ("Alouette")
21. Vietnam ("Chu Ech On")
22. Italy (instrumental)
23. Russia (instrumental)

Joining Hands with Other Lands
Kimbo Educational

1. Joining Hands with Other Lands
2. Mi Casa, My House
3. Sasha and Natasha
4. You Are Super the Way You Are
5. The Yodeling Song
6. How Do YOU Say Yes?
7. Many Ways to Say Hello
8. The Friendship Game
9. The Food Song
10. Let's Have a Party
11. The Caribbean Mango Song
12. Chinese New Year
13. Lady of the Light
14. Birthdays around the World
15. Uno, Uno, Dos, Dos
16. Native American Names

Folk Dance Fun
By Georgiana Stewart

Tracks 1–9 (Vocals and Music)
1. Hi to You
2. Mexican Hat Dance
3. Irish Jig
4. German Clapping Dance
5. Hawaiian Hukilau Dance ("Hukilau Song")
6. Italian Tarantella
7. American Virginia Reel ("Pop Goes the Weasel")
8. Greek Zorba Dance
9. So Long, Farewell (from *The Sound of Music*)

Tracks 10–18 (Music Only)
10. Hi To You
11. Mexican Hat Dance
12. Irish Jig
13. German Clapping Dance

(continued)

Multicultural Songs (Continued)

14. Hawaiian Hukilau Dance ("Hukilau Song")
15. Italian Tarantella
16. American Virginia Reel ("Pop Goes the Weasel")
17. Greek Zorba Dance
18. So Long, Farewell (from *The Sound of Music*)

Childern of the World
By Georgiana Stewart
1. Children of the World
2. Brazilian Carnival
3. A Visit to My Friend
4. Yolanda
5. The Wonders of the World
6. Haitian Alphabet Song
7. The Dreidel Song
8. Lullabies around the World
9. Polka Party
10. Funiculi, Funicula
11. Pata Pata

12. Wonderful Copenhagen
13. Love Makes the World Go Round
14. It's a Small World
15. I'd Like to Teach the World to Sing
16. Somewhere Out There

Songs about Native Americans
By Lois Skiera-Zucek
1. America Honors You
2. The Circle of Life
3. Indians Live Today
4. Sun and Rain
5. Food for My Family
6. The Tepee
7. Beautiful Music
8. Wake, Little Children
9. A Work of Art
10. Cradleboard Lullaby
11. An Indian Village
12. A Place Called Home
13. Many, Many Tribes

Theme 52
NUMBERS

Sources
clocks, rulers
telephones
calendars
games
computers

Recording Tools
calculator, pens
markers, pencils
computers
cash registers
phones
store scanners

Uses
communication
identification
time
age
address
telephone number

Theme Goals

Through participating in the experiences provided by this theme, the children may learn:

1. Uses of numbers
2. Sources of numbers
3. Number names
4. Tools for recording numbers

Concepts for the Children to Learn

1. A number is a word that tells how many.
2. Each number has a name.
3. Pencils and computers are tools used to make numbers.
4. Numbers can be found on clocks, rulers, telephones, calendars, computers, and games.
5. We can communicate our age with numbers.
6. Numbers are used to tell time.
7. Telephones, calculators, and cash registers have numerals.
8. Pens and markers can be used to make numbers.
9. House numbers are used to show where people live.
10. Numbers are on clocks to help us tell time.
11. Numbers are used to make telephone calls.

Vocabulary

1. **number**—a symbol used to represent an amount. A number tells how many.
2. **numeral**—a symbol that represents a number.

Bulletin Board

The objective of this bulletin board is to promote the concept of set. The children are to match the numeral to the set by winding the string around the other pushpin next to the items. Construct the numerals out of tagboard. Construct objects familiar to the children, and make one type of object correspond to each numeral. The number of objects and numerals should be developmentally appropriate for the group of children. Laminate. Staple the numbers down the left side of the bulletin board. Staple the sets of objects in random order down the right side of the bulletin board as illustrated. Affix a pushpin with an attached string of sufficient length next to each numeral. Affix a pushpin in front of each set row.

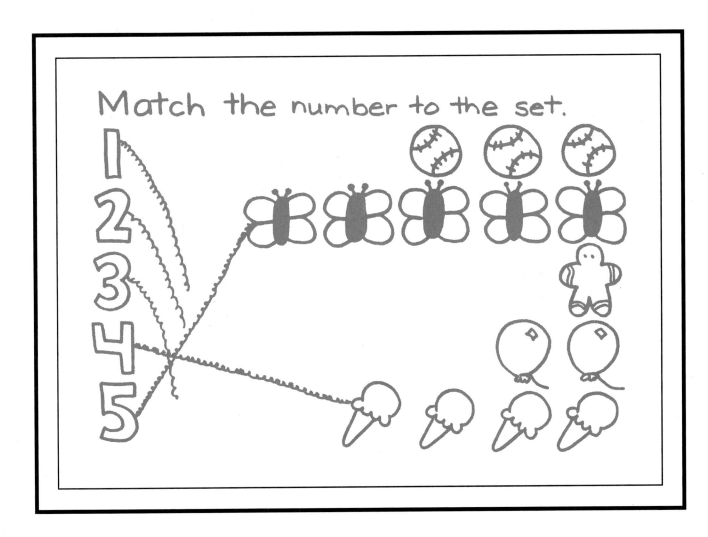

Dear Families,

Our next theme will focus on numbers. The curriculum will expose the children to the uses and sources of numbers. They will learn the names of numbers and use tools for recording numbers.

At School

Some of the play-related activities include:

- Measuring with scales and rulers at the science table
- Charting our weight and height
- Listening to the book titled *10 Little Rubber Ducks* by Eric Carle.
- Using number cookie cutters with play dough
- Bowling with numbered pins
- Learning to dial 911 on a toy telephone.

At Home

Cooking provides a concrete foundation for mathematical concepts. It involves amounts, fractions, and measures. While you are cooking, have your child help. Count how many spoonfuls it takes to fill a 1-cup measurer.

Your child can help you make this simple no-bake recipe for rice crispy treats.

Rice Crispy Treats

6 1/2 cups crispy rice cereal
1 package miniature marshmallows
3 tablespoons butter or margarine
1 teaspoon vanilla

Pour the crispy rice cereal in a large bowl. Melt the butter and marshmallows in the microwave. Stir vanilla into the butter and marshmallows. Pour this mixture over the rice cereal. Mix and pat into a 9-inch × 12-inch pan. Cool before cutting and serving.

Enjoy counting with your child!

Arts and Crafts

1. **Marker Sets**
   Using rubber bands, bind two watercolor markers together. Repeat this procedure, making several sets. Set the markers, including an unbound set, on the art table. The children can use the bound marker sets for creating designs on paper.

2. **Coupon Collage**
   Clipped coupons, paste, and paper can be placed on a table in the art area.

3. **Ruler Design**
   Collect a variety of rulers that are of different colors, sizes, and types. Using paper and a marking tool, the children can create designs.

4. **Numeral Cookie Cutter**
   Numeral cookie cutters should be provided with play dough.

Cooking

Rice Crispy Treats
6 1/2 cups crispy rice cereal
1 package miniature marshmallows
3 tablespoons butter or margarine
1 teaspoon vanilla

Pour the crispy rice cereal in a large bowl. Melt the butter and marshmallows in the microwave. Stir vanilla into the butter and marshmallows. Pour this mixture over the rice cereal. Mix and pat into a 9-inch × 12-inch pan. Cool before cutting and serving.

Dramatic Play

1. **Grocery Store**
   In the dramatic play area, arrange a grocery store. To do this, collect a variety of empty boxes, paper bags, sales receipts, and so on. Removable stickers can be used to indicate the grocery prices. A cash register and play money can also be added to **create** interest.

2. **Clock Shop**
   Collect a variety of clocks for the child**ren** to explore. Using discarded clocks, with **the** glass face removed, is an interesting **way** to let the children explore numerals **and** internal mechanisms.

3. **Telephoning**
   Prepare a classroom telephone book with all the children's names and telephone numbers. Place either toy **or** real telephones out on a table with the classroom telephone book. The children **can** practice dialing their own numbers as **well** as their classmates'.

Fingerplays and Chants

I Can Even Count Some More
One, two, three, four
I can even count some more.
Five, six, seven, eight
All my fingers stand up straight
Nine, ten are my thumb men.

Five Little Monkeys Swinging from a Tree
Five little monkeys swinging from the **tree**,
Teasing Mr. Alligator, "You can't catch **me**."
Along comes Mr. Alligator as sneaky **as**
   can be . . .
SNAP
Four little monkeys swinging from the **tree**.
Three little monkeys swinging from the **tree**.
Two little monkeys swinging from the **tree**.
One little monkey swinging from the **tree**.
No more monkeys swinging from the **tree**!

Five Little Birds
Five little birds without any home.
   (hold up five fingers)
Five little trees in a row.
   (raise hands high over head)
Come build your nests in our branches **tall**.
   (cup hands)
We'll rock them to and fro.

Ten Little Fingers

I have 10 little fingers and 10 little toes.
(children point to portions of body as
they repeat words)
Two little arms and one little nose.
One little mouth and two little ears.
Two little eyes for smiles and tears.
One little head and two little feet.
One little chin, that makes _____ complete.

Hands

Hands on shoulders, hands on knees
Hands behind you, if you please
Touch your shoulders, now your nose
Hands up high in the air
Down at your sides, now touch your head
Hands up high as before
Now clap your hands, one, two, three, four.

Group Time
(Games and Language)

1. **Squirrels in the Park**
   Choose five children to be squirrels. The
   children should sit in a row while one
   child pretends to go for a walk in the park
   carrying a bag of raisins or dried fruit.
   When the child who is walking approaches
   the squirrels, provide directions. These may
   include feeding the first squirrel, the fifth,
   the third, and so on.

2. **Block Form Board**
   On a large piece of cardboard, trace around
   one of each of the shapes of the blocks in the
   block area. Let children match blocks to the
   shape on the board.

3. **Match Them**
   Show the child several sets of identical
   picture cards, squares, objects, or flannel
   board pictures. Mix the items. Then have the
   children find matching pairs. One method of
   doing this is to hold up one item and have
   the children find the matching one.

4. **Follow the Teacher**
   At group time, provide directions containing
   a number. For example, say, "One jump,"
   "Two hops," "Three leaps," "Four tiptoe
   steps," and so on. The numbers used should

be developmentally appropriate for the
children.

Math

1. **Number Chain**
   Cut enough strips of paper to make a
   number chain for the days of the month.
   During group time each day, add a link
   to represent the passage of time. Another
   option is to use the chain as a countdown
   by removing a link per day until a special
   day. This is an interesting approach to an
   upcoming holiday.

2. **Flatware Set**
   Provide a flatware set. The children can sort
   the pieces according to sizes, shapes, or use.

3. **Constructing Numerals**
   Provide each interested child with a ball
   of play dough. Instruct children to form
   some numerals randomly. It is important
   for the teacher to monitor work and correct
   reversals. Then children can add the proper
   corresponding number of dots for the
   numeral just formed.
   An extension of this activity would be to
   make cards with numerals. The children
   roll their play dough into long ropes that
   can be placed over the lines of the numerals.

Music

1. **"Hickory Dickory Dock"**
   (Traditional)

   Hickory dickory dock.
   The mouse ran up the clock.
   The clock struck one,
   The mouse ran down.
   Hickory dickory dock.

2. **"Two Little Blackbirds"**
   (Traditional)

   Two little blackbirds sitting on a hill
   One named Jack,
   One named Jill.
   Fly away, Jack,

Fly away, Jill.
Come back, Jack,
Come back, Jill.
Two little blackbirds sitting on a hill
One named Jack,
One named Jill.

3. "One Elephant"
One elephant went out to play
Out on a spider's web one day.
He had such enormous fun,
He called for another elephant to come.

(Additional verses:)

Two elephants went out to play . . .
Three elephants went out to play . . .
Four elephants went out to play . . .
Five elephants went out to play . . .

Science

1. Height and Weight Chart
Design a height and weight chart for the classroom. The children can help by measuring each other. Record the numbers. Later in the year, measure the children and record their progress. Note the differences.

2. Using a Scale
Collect a variety of small objects and place on the science table with a balancing scale. The children can measure with the scale, noting the differences.

3. Temperature
Place an outdoor thermometer on the playground. Encourage the children to examine the thermometer. Record the temperature. Mark the temperature on the thermometer with masking tape. Bring the thermometer into the classroom. Check the thermometer again in half an hour. Show the children the change in temperature.

Sensory

Add colored water and a variety of measuring tools to the sensory table.

Books

The following books can be used to complement this theme:

Andreasen. Dan. (2007). *The Baker's Dozen.* New York. H. Holt.

Bajaj, Varsha. (2004). *How Many Kisses Do You Want Tonight?* Illustrated by Ivan Bates. New York: Little Brown.

Bates, Ivan. (2006). *Five Little Ducks.* Illustrated by Ivan Bates. New York: Scholastic.

Burns, Marilyn. (2008). *Spaghetti and Meatballs for All!* New York: Scholastic.

Carle, Eric. (2005). *10 Little Rubber Ducks.* New York: HarperCollins.

Cotton, Cynthia. (2002). *At the Edge of the Woods.* Illustrated by Reg Cartwright. New York: Henry Holt.

Davis, Rebecca Fjelland. (2007). *10, 9, 8 Polar Animals! A Counting Backward Book.* Mankato, MN: Capstone Press.

Doss, Dayle Ann. (2009). *Full House.* Illustrated by Abby Carter. Cambridge, MA: Candlewick Press.

Fjelland-Davis, Rebecca. (2007). *Counting Pets by Twos.* Mankato, MN: Capstone Press.

Fjelland-Davis, Rebecca. (2007). *Zoo Animals, 1, 2, 3.* Mankato, MN: Capstone Press.

Flemming, Candace. (2010). *Seven Hungry Babies.* Illustrated by Eugene Yelchin. New York: Atheneum Books for Young Readers.

Flemming, Denise. (1992). *Count!* New York: Holt.

Franco, Betsy. (2009). *Zero Is the Leaves on the Trees.* Berkeley, CA: Tricycle Press.

Jandl, Ernst, and Norman Junge. (2003). *Next Please.* New York: G.P. Putnam's Sons.

Jonas, Ann. (1995). *Splash!* New York: Greenwillow.

Knox, Barbara. (2003). *Baby Animals 1, 2, 3.* Mankato, MN: Capstone Press.

Knox, Barbara. (2003). *Under the Sea 1, 2, 3: Counting Ocean Life.* Mankato, MN: Capstone Press.

Marino, Gianna. (2010). *One Too Many: A Seek and Find Counting Book.* San Francisco: Chronicle Books.

Martin, Bill, Jr., and Michael Sampson. (2004). *Chick, Chicka, 1, 2, 3.* Illustrated by Lois Ehlert. New York: Simon & Schuster Books for Young Readers.

McGhee, Alison. (2002). *Countdown to Kindergarten.* Illustrated by Harry Bliss. San Diego, CA: Silver Whistle/Harcourt.

Miller, Virginia. (2002). *Ten Red Apples.* Cambridge, MA: Candlewick Press.

Moerbck, Kees. (2001). *Numbers.* Swindon, UK: Child's Play International.

Murphy, Stuart. (2003). *Double the Ducks.* Illustrated by Valeria Petrone. New York: HarperCollins.

Newman, Leslea. (2002). *Dogs, Dogs, Dogs!* New York: Simon & Schuster Books for Young Readers.

Pallotta, Jerry. (2003). *Apple Fractions.* Illustrated by Rob Bolster. New York: Cartwheel Books.

Parenteau, Shirley. (2007). *One Frog Sang.* Illustrated by Cynthia Jabar. Cambridge, MA: Candlewick Press.

Shuette, Sarah L. (2003). *Eating Pairs: Counting Fruits and Vegetables by Twos.* Mankato, MN: Capstone Press.

Smith, Danna. (2009). *Two at the Zoo.* New York: Clarion Books.

Stoll, Ellen Walsh. (1991). *Mouse Count.* San Diego, CA: Harcourt Children's Books.

Thong, Roseanne. (2004). *One Is a Drummer.* San Francisco: Chronicle Books.

Tufuri, Nancy. (2006) *Five Little Chicks.* New York: Simon & Schuster Books for Young Readers.

Wadsworth, Olive. (2002). *Over in the Meadow: A Counting Rhyme.* Illustrated by Anna Vojtech. New York: North-South Books.

Technology and Multimedia

The following technology and multimedia products can be used to complement this theme:

Chicka Chicka 1, 2, 3 [DVD]. (2006). Danbury, CT: Weston Woods.

Counting and Sorting [CD]. (1997). New York: DK Multimedia.

"Counting Together" [CD]. In *Children Love to Sing and Dance.* The Learning Station. Long Branch, NJ: Kimbo Educational.

"Five Days Old" [CD]. (2010). In *The Best of the Laurie Berkner Band.* New York: Two Tomatoes.

"Hey Ducky" [CD]. 2010. In *Rock and Roll Garden.* New York: Bari Koral Family Rock Band.

Learning about Numbers [DVD]. (2004). Los Angeles: Sony Wonder.

"Numba Rhumba." (1998). In *Sing, Dance 'N Sing (Gaia).* Long Branch, NJ: Kimbo Educational.

"One Two Buckle My Shoe" [CD]. (2000). In *Early Childhood Classics: Old Favorites with a New Twist.* Sherman Oaks, CA: Hap-Pal Music.

"One, Two, Buckle My Shoe," "Five Green and Speckled Frogs," "Four Leaf Clover," and "Five Little Monkeys" [CD]. (1999). In *Five Little Monkeys.* Long Branch, NJ: Kimbo Educational.

"One, Two, Buckle My Shoe" and "Five Little Monkeys" [CD]. (1997). In *Tony Chestnut.* The Learning Station. Long Branch, NJ: Kimbo Educational.

"One, Two, Buckle My Shoe" and "Three Little Kittens" [CD]. (1986). In *Singable Nursery Rhymes.* Long Branch, NJ: Kimbo Educational.

"123" [CD]. (2001). In *Whaddaya Think of That, Laurie Berkner.* New York: Two Tomatoes.

Reader Rabbit's Preschool [CD]. (1997). Cambridge, MA: Learning Company.

"Rocketship Run" [CD]. (2010). In *The Best of the Laurie Berkner Band.* New York: Two Tomatoes.

Tell Me Why [DVD]. (2007). Venice, CA: TMW Media Group.

"There Are Seven Days in the Week" and "My Five Senses" [CD]. (2004). In *Circle*

Time Activities. Long Branch, NJ: Kimbo Educational.

"This Old Man," "Five Little Monkeys," and "Six Little Ducks" [CD]. (1997). In *Six Little Ducks.* Long Branch, NJ: Kimbo Educational.

 Additional teaching resources to accompany this Theme can be found on the book's companion website. Go to www.cengagebrain.com to access the site for a variety of useful resources.

Manipulatives for Math Activities

Buttons
Beads
Bobbins
Craft pompons
Spools
Shells
Seeds (corn, soybeans)

Toothpicks
Pennies
Checkers
Crayons
Plastic caps from markers, milk containers, or plastic bottles

Golf tees
Stickers
Fishing bobbers
Keys
Small toy cars
Plastic bread ties
Marbles
Cotton balls
Bottle caps

Poker chips
Paper clips
Clothespins
Erasers

Theme 53
NURSERY RHYMES

Uses
enjoyment
learning words
learning numbers
bedtime rituals

Forms
written
spoken
sung

Characters
animals
people

Favorites

Little Bo Peep

Mary Had a Little Lamb

Old Mother Hubbard

Hey, Diddle Diddle

Little Miss Muffet

Humpty Dumpty

Jack and Jill

Mary Mary Quite Contrary

Jack Be Nimble

Rub-a-Dub-Dub

The Muffin Man

Little Jack Horner

Old MacDonald Had a Farm

Two Little Blackbirds

Hickory Dickory Dock

Three Kittens' Mittens

Theme Goals

Through participating in the experiences provided by this theme, the children may learn:

1. Favorite nursery rhymes
2. Uses of nursery rhymes
3. Forms of nursery rhymes
4. Characters portrayed in nursery rhymes

Concepts for the Children to Learn

1. Nursery rhymes are short, simple poems or rhymes.
2. Nursery rhymes are fun to listen to and say.
3. Nursery rhymes help us learn new words.
4. Nursery rhymes can be said at bedtime.
5. Nursery rhymes can be written, spoken, or sung.
6. Nursery rhymes can contain real or pretend words.
7. Nursery rhymes can be about animals, people, or objects.
8. Some nursery rhymes help us learn numbers and counting.
9. Some nursery rhymes teach us about different people.
10. There are many favorite nursery rhymes, such as Little Bo Beep, Mary Had a Little Lamb, Old Mother Hubbard, and many more that will be explored in this Theme.

Vocabulary

nursery rhyme—a short, simple poem or rhyme.

Bulletin Board

The purpose of this bulletin board is to promote visual discrimination and name recognition skills, and call attention to the importance of the printed word. If desired, this can be used as an attendance bulletin board. Each child should be provided a bulletin board piece with his or her name printed on it. To assist children who cannot recognize their name, a digital photograph can also be added to the name tag. When the children arrive each morning at school, they should be encouraged to hang their name on the bulletin board. To create a "Find Your Mitten" bulletin board, cut a mitten out of tagboard for each child in the class. Use a paper punch to cut a hole in the top of each mitten. Three kittens can be constructed and attached to the bulletin board to represent the three little kittens who lost their mittens. Hang pushpins on the bulletin board for the children to hang their mittens.

Family Letter

InBox

Dear Families,

Nursery rhymes will be the focus of our next theme. These rhymes can serve as a bridge between the home and school. I'm sure many of you have shared favorite nursery rhymes with your child at home. Nursery rhymes are an easy introduction to poetry, as well as to the concept of rhyming words.

At School

We have a fun-filled curriculum planned for our unit on nursery rhymes. A few highlights include:

- Acting out various rhymes with puppets that represent different characters from familiar nursery rhymes

- Unraveling the riddle of the "Humpty Dumpty" nursery rhyme. (Why couldn't Humpty be put back together? Because Humpty was an egg!)

- Creating "Little Miss Muffet" spiders in the art area

- Taking turns being nimble and quick as we jump over a "candlestick" to dramatize the rhyme of "Jack Be Nimble"

At Home

To foster concepts of the unit at home, try the following:

- Let your child help you crack eggs open to make scrambled eggs. Children like to feel that they have accomplished a grown-up task when they crack the eggs.

- Sing or recite some of the many rhymes your child already knows, such as "Jack and Jill" and "Mary Had a Little Lamb." These also develop an enjoyment of music and singing.

Share a nursery rhyme with your child today!

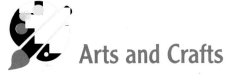

Arts and Crafts

1. Spiders
Add black tempera paint to a play dough mixture. In addition to the play dough, provide black chenille stems or yarn. Using these materials, spiders or other objects can be created.

2. Spider Webs
Cut circles of black paper to fit in the bottom of a pie tin. Mix thin silver or white tempera paint. Place a marble and two teaspoons of paint on the paper. Gently tilt the pie tin, allowing the marble to roll through the paint, creating a spider web design.

3. Twinkle, Twinkle Little Stars
The children can decorate stars with glitter and sequins. The stars can be hung from the ceiling. During group time, sing "Twinkle, Twinkle, Little Star."

Cooking

1. Bran Muffins
(Use with the "Muffin Man" rhyme)

3 cups whole-wheat bran cereal
1 cup boiling water
1/2 cup shortening or oil
2 eggs
2 1/2 cups unbleached flour
1 1/2 cups sugar
2 1/2 teaspoons baking soda
2 cups buttermilk

Preheat the oven to 400 degrees. Line the muffin tins with paper baking cups. In a large bowl, combine the cereal and boiling water. Stir in the shortening and eggs. Add the remaining ingredients. Blend well. Spoon the batter into cups about 3/4 full. Bake at 400 degrees for 18 to 22 minutes or until golden brown. Eat at snack and sing the "Muffin Man" song.

2. Cottage Cheese
2 quarts pasteurized skim milk (to make 1 to 3/4 pounds of cottage cheese)
Salt
Liquid rennet or a junket tablet

Heat the water to 80 degrees Fahrenheit in the bottom part of a double boiler. Use a thermometer to determine the water temperature—*do not guess.*

Pour the skim milk into the top of the double boiler. Dilute 1 or 2 drops of liquid rennet in a tablespoon of cold water, and stir it into the milk. If rennet is not available, add 1/8 of a junket tablet to a tablespoon of water and add it to the milk. Allow the milk to remain at 80 degrees until it curdles, about 12 to 18 hours. During this period, no special attention is necessary. If desired, the milk may be placed in a warm oven overnight. Place the curd in a cheese cloth over a container to drain the whey. Occasionally, pour out the whey that collects in the container so that the draining will continue. In 15 to 20 minutes, the curd will become mushy and will drain more slowly. When it is almost firm and the whey has nearly ceased to flow, the cheese is ready for salting and eating. Salt the cheese to taste. The cottage cheese can be spread on crackers for a snack.
Note: This activity is time-consuming. It may be more appropriate for older children.

3. Miss Muffet's Curds and Whey
2 cups whole milk
1 teaspoon vinegar

Heat the milk to lukewarm and add vinegar. Stir as curds separate from the whey. Curds are the milk solids, and whey is the liquid that is poured off. You can let your children taste the whey, but they probably will not be thrilled by it. Strain the curds from the whey, and then dump the curds onto a paper towel and gently press the curds with more towels to get out the liquid. Sprinkle with salt and refrigerate. Eat as cottage cheese. You can also serve the curds at room temperature. Stir them until they are smooth. Add different flavorings (such as cinnamon, orange flavoring, vanilla, etc.). Use as a spread on crackers. Serves 12 (two crackers each).

Dramatic Play

1. **Baker**
Baking props such as hats, aprons, cookie cutters, baking pans, rolling pins, mixers, spoons, and bowls can be placed in the dramatic play area.

2. **Puppets**
A puppet theater can be placed in the dramatic play area for the duration of the unit. To add variety, each day a different set of puppets can be added for the children.

Field Trips and Resource People

1. **Candle Making**
Invite a resource person to demonstrate candle making, or take a field trip to a craft center so that the children can view candles being made.

2. **Greenhouse**
Visit a florist or greenhouse to observe flowers and plants.

Fingerplays and Chants

Listening Time
(Follow the actions for each phrase)

Sometimes my hands are at my side
Then they hide behind my back.
Sometimes I wiggle my fingers,
Shake them fast, shake them slow.
Sometimes my hands go clap, clap, clap.
Then I rest them in my lap,
Because it's listening time, you see.

Humpty Dumpty
Humpty Dumpty sat on a wall,
Humpty Dumpty had a great fall.
All of the king's horses and all of the king's
    men,
 Couldn't put Humpty Dumpty together again.

Little Boy Blue
Little Boy Blue, come blow your horn.
The sheep's in the meadow, the cow's in the
    corn.
Where is the little boy that looks after the
    sheep?
 He is under the hay stack, fast asleep.
Will you wake him? No, not I.
For if I do, he'll be sure to cry.

Little Jack Horner
Little Jack Horner
Sat in a corner
Eating a Christmas pie.
    (pretend you're eating)
He put in his thumb,
    (thumb down)
And pulled out a plum
    (thumb up)
And said, "What a good boy am I!"
    (say out loud)

Pat-a-Cake
Pat-a-cake, pat-a-cake, baker's man.
Bake me a cake as fast as you can!
    (clap hands together lightly)
Roll it
    (roll hands)
And pat it
    (touch hands together lightly)
And mark it with a "B"
    (write "B" in the air)
And put it in the oven for baby and me.
    (point to baby and to yourself)

Wee Willie Winkie
Wee Willie Winkie runs through the town
    (pretend to run)
Upstairs, downstairs in his nightgown,
    (point up, point down, then point to
    clothes)
Rapping at the window, crying through the
    lock
    (knock in the air, peek through a hole)
"Are the children all in bed, for now it's
    eight o'clock!"
    (shake finger)

Old King Cole

Old King Cole was a merry old soul
    (lift elbows up and down)
And a merry old soul was he.
    (nod head)
He called for his pipe.
    (clap two times)
He called for his bowl.
    (clap two times)
And he called for his fiddlers three.
    (clap two times then pretend to play
    violin)

Hickory Dickory Dock

Hickory dickory dock
    (swing arms back and forth together,
    bent down low)
The mouse ran up the clock.
    (run fingers up your arm)
The clock struck one
    (clap, and then hold up one finger)
The mouse ran down.
    (run fingers down your arm)
Hickory dickory dock.
    (swing arms back and forth together,
    bent down low)

Group Time
(Games and Language)

Old Mother Hubbard's Doggie Bone Game

Save a bone or construct one from tagboard. Ask one child to volunteer to be the doggie. Seat the children in a circle with the doggie in the center and the bone in front of him or her. The doggie closes his or her eyes. A child from the circle quietly comes and steals the bone. When the child is reseated with the bone out of sight, the children will call,

"Doggie, doggie, where's your bone?
Someone took it from your home!"

The doggie gets three chances to guess who has the bone. If he or she guesses correctly, the child who took the bone becomes the doggie.

Large Muscle

1. **Jack Be Nimble's Candlestick**
   Make a candlestick out of an old paper towel holder and tissue paper for the flame. Repeat the rhyme by substituting each child's name.

   Jack be nimble. Jack be quick.
   Jack jump over the candlestick.

2. **Hey, Diddle Diddle Jump**
   Make cow headbands for the children to wear. Create a large moon and tape it to the floor. Encourage children to jump over the moon while saying the rhyme.

   Hey, Diddle Diddle,
   the cat and the fiddle.
   The cow jumped over the moon.
   The little dog laughed to see such a sport,
   And the dish ran away with the spoon.

3. **Wall Building**
   Encourage the children to create a large wall out of blocks for Humpty Dumpty. Act out the rhyme.

4. **London Bridge**
   Play London Bridge game while chanting
       the rhyme:

   London Bridge is falling down,
   falling down, falling down.
   London Bridge is falling down,
   my fair lady.

   Build it up with needles and pins,
   Needles and pins, needles and pins.
   Build it up with needles and pins,
   My fair lady.

   Pins and needles rust and bend,
   Rust and bend, rust and bendf.
   Pins and needles rust and bend,
   My fair lady.

   Build it up with silver and gold,
   Gold and silver I've not got,
   Here is a prisoner I have got.

 **Math**

1. **Puzzles**

   Draw or cut out several pictures of different nursery rhymes ("Jack and Jill," "Jack Be Nimble," etc.) and mount on tagboard. Laminate and cut each picture into five to seven pieces. The children can match nursery rhyme puzzle pieces.

2. **Rote Counting**

   Say or sing the following nursery rhyme to help the children with rote counting.

   1, 2 buckle my shoe
   3, 4 shut the door
   5, 6 pick up sticks
   7, 8 lay them straight
   9, 10 a big fat hen.

3. **Matching**

   Draw from 1 to 10 simple figures from a nursery rhyme (mittens, candlesticks, pails, etc.) on the left side of a sheet of tagboard and the corresponding numeral on the right side. Laminate the pieces and cut each in half, creating different-shaped puzzle pieces. The children can match the number of figures to the corresponding numeral.

4. **Mitten Match**

   Collect several matching pairs of mittens. Mix them up, and have children match the pairs.

5. **Muffin Man Math Game**

   Place several empty muffin tins on the table. Place one large die on the table. Each child takes turns rolling the die and placing the corresponding number of chips into the muffin tin. The game is over when one player has filled his or her muffin tin.

6. **Humpty Dumpty Egg Match**

   On the bottom of a devil egg dish, paint different colors that correspond to painted Easter Eggs. Encourage the children to match the colored Easter Eggs with the color of the painted slots on the dish.

7. **Little Bo Peep Sheep**

   Make sheep cutouts. Place a numeral on each sheep and have children glue the corresponding number of cotton balls on the sheep.

8. **Twinkle, Twinkle Star Count**

   Write numerals 1 through 10 on cutout stars. Have children arrange the stars in the correct order. Dots may also be placed beneath the numeral if more appropriate.

 Music

1. **"Hickory Dickory Dock"**
   (Traditional)

   Hickory dickory dock
   The mouse ran up the clock.
   The clock struck one, the mouse ran down,
   Hickory dickory dock.

2. **"Peter, Peter, Pumpkin Eater"**
   (Traditional)

   Peter Peter pumpkin eater,
   Had a wife and couldn't keep her!
   He put her in a pumpkin shell,
   And there he kept her very well!

3. **"The Muffin Man"**
   (Traditional)

   Oh, do you know the muffin man,
   The muffin man, the muffin man?
   Oh, do you know the muffin man
   Who lives on Drury Lane?

   Yes, I know the muffin man . . .

4. **"Twinkle, Twinkle Little Star"**
   (Traditional)

   Twinkle, twinkle, little star,
   How I wonder what you are!
   Up above the world so high,
   Like a diamond in the sky.
   Twinkle, twinkle, little star,
   How I wonder how you are!

5. "Two Little Blackbirds"

(Traditional)

Two little blackbirds sitting on a hill
One named Jack. One named Jill.
Fly away, Jack. Fly away, Jill.
Come back, Jack. Come back, Jill.
Two little blackbirds sitting on a hill.
One named Jack. One named Jill.

6. "Jack and Jill"

(Traditional)

Jack and Jill went up a hill
To fetch a pail of water.
Jack fell down and broke his crown
And Jill fell tumbling after.

7. "A Peanut Sat on a Railroad Track"

A peanut sat on a railroad track,
His heart was all a-flutter,
Round the bend came number ten.
Toot! Toot! Peanut butter!
SQUISH!

8. "Jack Be Nimble"

Jack be nimble,
Jack be quick;
Jack jump over
the candlestick.

(Additional verses:)

Jack be nimble,
Jack be late;
Jack jump over
the dinner plate.

Jack be nimble,
Jack be soon;
Jack jump over
the silver spoon.

Jack be nimble,
Jack be up;
Jack jump over
the sippy cup.

9. "Little Bo-Peep"

Little Bo-Peep has lost her sheep,
And can't tell where to find them;
Leave them alone, and they'll come home,
Wagging their tails behind them.

Little Bo-Peep fell fast asleep,
And dreamt she heard them bleating;
But when she awoke, she found it a joke,
For they were still a-fleeting.

Then up she took her little crook,
Determined for to find them;
She found them indeed, but it made her
   heart bleed,
For they left all their tails behind them.

10. "Little Miss Muffet"

Little Miss Muffet sat on her tuffet,
Eating her curds and whey.
Along came a spider,
And sat down beside her,
And frightened Miss Muffet away.

11. "London Bridge Is Falling Down"

London Bridge is falling down,
Falling down, falling down.
London Bridge is falling down,
My fair lady.

Build it up with needles and pins,
Needles and pins, needles and pins.
Build it up with needles and pins,
My fair lady.

Pins and needles rust and bend,
Rust and bend, rust and bend.
Pins and needles rust and bend,
My fair lady.

Build it up with silver and gold . . .
Gold and silver I've not got . . .
Here's a prisoner I have got . . .
Take the key and lock him (her) up . . .

12. "Looby Loo"

(Chorus:)

Here we go Looby-Loo
Here we go Looby-Light
Here we go Looby-Loo
All on a Saturday night.

You put your right hand in,
You put your right hand out,
You give your hand a shake, shake, shake,
And turn yourself about.

(Repeat chorus)
(Other verses:)

You put your left hand in . . .
You put your right foot in . . .
You put your left foot in . . .
You put your whole self in . . .

13. "Miss Polly Had a Dolly"

Miss Polly had a dolly
Who was sick, sick, sick,
So she called for the doctor
To be quick, quick, quick.

The doctor came
With his bag and his hat,
And he knocked at the door
With a rat-a-tat-tat.

He looked at the dolly
And he shook his head,
And he said, "Miss Polly,
Put her straight to bed."

14. "Mary Had a Little Lamb"

Mary had a little lamb,
Little lamb, little lamb,
Mary had a little lamb,
Its fleece was white as snow.

And everywhere that Mary went,
Mary went, Mary went,
And everywhere that Mary went
The lamb was sure to go.

It followed her to school one day,
School one day, school one day,
It followed her to school one day,
Which was against the rules.

It made the children laugh and play,
Laugh and play, laugh and play,
It made the children laugh and play,
To see a lamb at school.

"Why does the lamb love Mary so?
Love Mary so? Love Mary so?"
"Why does the lamb love Mary so?"
The eager children cry.

"Why, Mary loves the lamb, you know.
Loves the lamb. Loves the lamb."
"Why, Mary loves the lamb, you know."
The teacher did reply.

15. "Old King Cole"

Old King Cole was a merry old soul,
And a merry old soul was he.
He called for his pipe,
And he called for his bowl,
And he called for his fiddlers three.
Ev'ry fiddler had a fiddle,
And a very fine fiddle had he.
Tweedle dee, tweedle dee,
Tweedle dee, tweedle dee,

Tweedle dee, tweedle dee,
Went the fiddlers three,
Oh, there's none so rare
As can compare,
With King Cole and his fiddlers three.

16. "Open, Shut Them"

Open, shut them.
    (hold hands up and open and close
    fingers)
Open, shut them.
Give a little clap.
    (clap)
Open, shut them.
    (hold hands up and open and close
    fingers)
Open, shut them.
Put them in our lap.
    (place hand in lap)
Walk them, walk them,
    (walk fingers up chest to chin)
Walk them, walk them.
Way up to your chin.
Walk them, walk them,
    (walk fingers around face, but not into
    mouth)
Walk them, walk them,
But don't let them walk in.

17. "Pat-a-Cake"

Pat-a-cake, pat-a-cake, baker's man.
    (clap hands together)
Bake me a cake as fast as you can.
Roll it,
    (roll hands over each other)
And pat it,
    (pat hands together)
And mark it with B,
    (draw B in the air)
And put it in the oven for baby and me.
    (point to a child or tickle child's tummy)

18. "Pop! Goes the Weasel"

All around the cobbler's bench
The monkey chased the weasel.
The monkey thought 'twas all in fun . . .
Pop! Goes the weasel.

Johnny has the whooping cough,
Mary has the measles.
That's the way the money goes . . .
Pop! Goes the weasel.

A penny for a spool of thread
A penny for a needle.
That's the way the money goes . . .
Pop! Goes the weasel.

All around the mulberry bush,
The monkey chased the weasel.
The monkey thought 'twas all in fun . . .
Pop! Goes the weasel.

19. "Rock-a-Bye Baby"

Rock-a-bye, baby,
In the tree top,
When the wind blows,
The cradle will rock.
When the bough breaks,
The cradle will fall,
And down will come baby,
Cradle and all.

20. "Row, Row, Row Your Boat"

Row, row, row your boat
Gently down the stream.
Merrily, merrily, merrily, merrily,
Life is but a dream.

21. "Teddy Bear, Teddy Bear"

Teddy bear, teddy bear,
Turn around.
Teddy bear, teddy bear,
Touch the ground.
Teddy bear, teddy bear,
Touch your shoes.
Teddy bear, teddy bear,
Say how-di-do.
Teddy bear, teddy bear,
Go up the stairs.
Teddy bear, teddy bear,
Say your prayers.
Turn out the light.
Say good night.

22. "There Was an Old Woman"

There was an old woman,
Who lived in a shoe.
She had so many children,
She didn't know what to do.
She gave them some broth,
With butter and bread,
Then kissed them all sweetly,
And sent them to bed.

23. "This Old Man"

This old man, he played one.
   (hold up one finger)
He played knick-knack on my thumb.
   (pretend to knock on thumb)

(Chorus:)

With a knick-knack paddy whack give a dog
   a bone.
   (knock on head, clap twice, pretend to
      throw a bone over your shoulder)
This old man came rolling home.
   (roll hand over hand)

(Second verse:)

This old man, he played two.
   (hold up two fingers)
He played knick-knack on my shoe.
   (knock on shoe)

(Repeat chorus)

This old man, he played three.
   (hold up three fingers)
He played knick-knack on my knee.
   (knock on knee)

(Chorus)

This old man, he played four.
   (hold up four fingers)
He played knick-knack on the door.
   (pretend to knock on the door)

(Chorus)

This old man, he played five.
   (hold up five fingers)
He played knick-knack on a hive.
   (pretend to knock on a hive)

(Chorus)
(Continue hand motions with additional verses:)

six . . . sticks
seven . . . heaven
eight . . . gate
nine . . . line
ten . . . over again!

24. "Are You Sleeping?"

Are you sleeping?
Are you sleeping?
Brother John, Brother John?
Morning bells are ringing,
Morning bells are ringing.
Ding! Dong! Ding!
Ding! Dong! Ding!

25. "Where Is Thumbkin?"

Where is Thumbkin?
    (hands behind back)
Where is Thumbkin?
Here I am. Here I am.
    (bring out right thumb, then left)
How are you today, sir?
    (bend right thumb)
Very well, I thank you.
    (bend left thumb)
Run away. Run away.
    (put right thumb behind back, then left
    thumb behind back)

(Other verses:)

Where is Pointer?
Where is Middle One?
Where is Ring Finger?
Where is Pinky?
Where are all of them?

26. "Hey, Diddle Diddle"

Hey, diddle diddle,
The cat and the fiddle,
The cow jumped over the moon.
The little dog laughed to
See such a sport,
And the dish ran away with the spoon.

Science

1. Mary's Garden

A styrofoam cup with the child's name printed on it and a scoop of soil should be provided. Let everyone choose a flower seed. Be sure to save the seed packages. The children can plant their seed, water it, and care for it. When the plant begins to grow, try to identify the names of the plants by comparing them to pictures on the seed packages.

2. Hickory Dickory Dock Clock

Draw and cut out a large Hickory Dickory Dock clock from cardboard. Move the hands of the clock and see if the children can identify the numeral.

3. Wool

Pieces of wool fabric mounted on cardboard can be matched with samples.

4. Pumpkin Tasters

Plan a Peter, Peter, Pumpkin Eater pumpkin-tasting party.

5. Jack and Jill's Pail

See what objects will sink or float in Jack and Jill's pail.

Sensory

Water and Pails

Add water, pails, and scoopers to the sensory table.

Social Studies

1. Table Setting

On a sheet of tagboard, trace the outline of a plate, cup, knife, fork, spoon, and napkin. Laminate. The children can match the silverware and dishes to the outline on the placemat in preparation for a snack or meals. This activity can be extended by having the children turn over the placemat and arrange the place setting without the aid of an outline.

2. Shoe House

Create a large boot or shoe out of tagboard. Print digital photographs of each child. Invite the children to take turns gluing their picture onto the shoe. (*Note:* If photographs are not available, have each child draw his or her picture on the shoe.)

Books

The following books can be used to complement this theme:

Adams, Pam, and Child's Play. (2000). *There Was an Old Woman Who Swallowed a Fly.* Illustrated by Pam Adams. Auburn, ME: Child's Play International.

Child, Lauren. (2007) *Charlie and Lola's Numbers.* Cambridge, MA: Candlewick Press.

Chorao, Kay. (2009). *Rhymes 'round the World.* New York: Penguin Group.

Conway, David. (2009). *The Great Nursery Rhyme Disaster.* Illustrated by Melanie Williamson. Wilton, CT: Tiger Tales.

Cravath, Lynne Woodcock, and Steven Carpenter. (2000). *My First Action Rhymes.* Illustrated by Lynne Woodcock Cravath and Steven Carpenter. New York: HarperFestival.

Dillon, Leo, and Diane Dillon. (2007). *Mother Goose Numbers on the Loose.* Orlando, FL: Harcourt.

Dunn, Opal. (2006). *Un, Deux, Trois: First French Rhymes.* London: Frances Lincoln.

Engelbreit, Mary. (2005). *Mary Engelbreit's Mother Goose: One Hundred Best-Loved Verses.* New York: HarperCollins.

Fisher Wright, Blanche. (2000). *My First Real Mother Goose Bedtime Book.* New York: Scholastic.

Galdone, Paul, (2007). *Three Little Kittens.* New York: Clarion Books.

Gill, Shelley. (2002). *The Alaska Mother Goose: North Country Nursery Rhymes.* Seattle, WA: Sasquatch Books.

Gustafson, Scott. (2007). *Favorite Nursery Rhymes from Mother Goose.* Shelton, CT: Greenwich Workshop Press.

Herman, R.A. (2006). *Jack and Jill.* Brooklyn, NY: Handprint Books.

Hines, Anna Grossnickle. (2008). *1, 2, Buckle My Shoe.* Orlando, FL: Harcourt.

Hoberman, Mary Ann. (2005). *You Read to Me, I'll Read to You: Very Short Mother Goose Tales to Read Together.* Illustrated by Michael Emberley. New York: Little, Brown.

Janovitz, Marilyn. (2002). *Three Little Kittens.* New York: North-South Books.

Joyce, William, and Kerry Milliron, eds. (2001). *William Joyce's Mother Goose.* New York: Random House.

Keats, Ezra Jack. (1999). *Over in the Meadow.* New York: Viking.

Kubler, Annie. (2001). *Here We Go round the Mulberry Bush.* Auburn, ME: Child's Play.

Lansky, Bruce. (2004). *Mary Had a Little Jam and Other Silly Rhymes.* Minnetonka, MN: Meadowbrook.

Miranda, Anne. (1997). *To Market, to Market.* Illustrated by Janet Stevens. Orlando, FL: Harcourt Brace.

Opie, Iona Archibald, ed. (1996). *My Very First Mother Goose.* Illustrated by Rosemary Wells. Cambridge, MA: Candlewick Press.

Opie, Iona Archibald. (1997). *Humpty Dumpty and Other Rhymes.* Cambridge, MA: Candlewick Press.

Opie, Iona Archibald. (1997). *Pussycat Pussycat and Other Rhymes.* Cambridge, MA: Candlewick Press.

Opie, Iona Archibald. (1997). *Wee Willie Winkie and Other Rhymes.* Cambridge, MA: Candlewick Press.

Pearson, Tracey Campbell. (2005). *Little Miss Muffet.* New York: Farrar, Straus and Giroux.

Ross, Tony. (2009). *Three Little Kittens and Other Favorite Nursery Rhymes.* New York: Henry Holt.

Scarry, Richard. (1999). *Richard Scarry's Best Mother Goose Ever.* New York: Golden Books.

Weber, Paige. (2006). *Classic Nursery Rhymes.* New York: Gramercy Books.

Wright, Danielle, Mique Moriuchi, and Michael Rosen. (2010). *My Village: Rhymes from around the World.* London: Frances Lincoln.

Technology and Multimedia

The following technology and multimedia products can be used to complement this theme:

"Baa Baa Black Sheep" [CD]. (1976). In *Singable Songs for the Very Young.* Cambridge, MA: Rounder/UMGD.

"I'm a Little Tea Pot" [CD]. (2000). In *Early Childhood Classics: Old Favorites with a New Twist.* Sherman Oaks, CA: Hap-Pal Music.

"Itsy Bitsy Spider" [CD]. (2000). In *Early Childhood Classics: Old Favorites with a New Twist.* Sherman Oaks, CA: Hap-Pal Music.

Palmer, Hap. (1991). *Hap Palmer Sings Classic Nursery Rhymes* [cassette]. Freeport, NY: Educational Activities.

"Pop Goes the Weasel" and "Hickory Dickory Dock" [CD]. (2001). In *Four Baby Bumblebees.* Long Branch, NJ: Kimbo Educational.

Richard Scarry's Best Sing-Along Mother Goose Video Ever [DVD]. (2002). Los Angeles: Sony Wonder, Random House Home Video.

"Rock-N-Roll Pat-a-Cake" [CD]. (2008). In *Songs for the Whole Day.* Nashville, TN: Lamon Records.

"Simon Says" [CD]. (2001). *Dance Party Fun.* Long Branch, NJ: Kimbo Educational.

Singable Nursery Rhymes [CD]. (1986). Long Branch, NJ: Kimbo Educational.

Singleton-Prather, Anita. [DVD] (2006). *Tales from the Land of Gullah for Kids* [DVD]. (2006). Charleston, SC: Matrix Media.

"Twinkle Twinkle Little Star" [CD]. (2000). In *Early Childhood Classics: Old Favorites with a New Twist.* Sherman Oaks, CA: Hap-Pal Music.

 Additional teaching resources to accompany this Theme can be found on the book's companion website. Go to www.cengagebrain.com to access the site for a variety of useful resources.

Theme 54
OCCUPATIONS

Transportation
taxi driver
bus driver
car salesperson
pilot
ambulance driver
truck driver
gas station
attendant
astronaut

Production
farmer
cook
chef
baker
miner
factory worker
artist

Community Helpers
police officer
firefighter
mail carrier
judge

Health
doctor
nurse
dentist
hygienist
paramedic
child care

Sports
announcer
umpire
coach
athlete
hockey players
baseball players
golfers
tennis players
soccer players

Other
homemaker
seasonal
part-time
self-employed
shift
cottage

Service Workers
teacher
librarian
food server
banker, cashier
custodian
secretary
auto mechanic
butcher, clerk
sanitation engineer

Communications
computer operator
television reporter
newspaper reporter
actor

Construction
carpenter
plumber
cabinetmaker
architect
electrician

Theme Goals

Through participating in the experiences provided by this theme, the children may learn:

1. Occupations of community helpers
2. Sports figure occupations
3. Health occupations
4. Transportation occupations
5. Communications occupations
6. Construction occupations
7. Production occupations
8. Service occupations
9. Community helpers
10. Other types of occupations

Concepts for the Children to Learn

1. An occupation is a job a person does to earn money to live.
2. There are many different kinds of occupations.
3. Truck drivers, gas station attendants, and astronauts are in transportation occupations.
4. Taxi drivers, bus drivers, pilots, and ambulance drivers are in transportation occupations.
5. Doctors, nurses, hygienists, paramedics, child care workers, and dentists are in health occupations.
6. A community helper is someone who helps us.
7. Police officers, firefighters, mail carriers, and judges are community helpers.
8. Teachers, librarians, and custodians work to help us.
9. Farmers, cooks, chefs, and factory workers make or create things for us.
10. There are many sporting occupations.
11. Hockey players, golfers, tennis players, and soccer players are in sports occupations.
12. Announcers, umpires, and coaches are also in sports occupations.
13. Football and baseball players are in sports occupations.
14. Television and newspaper reporters are in communications occupations.
15. Builders, carpenters, plumbers, cabinetmakers, and electricians are in construction occupations. They build things such as houses, schools, and other buildings.
16. Architects design buildings.

Vocabulary

1. **job**—type of work that someone has to do.
2. **occupation**—the job a person performs to earn money.
3. **service**—helping people.

Bulletin Board

The purpose of this bulletin board is to learn about gender. Both men and women can be doctors, farmers, construction workers, teachers, judges, and so on. In addition, visual discrimination, hand-eye coordination, and problem-solving skills are promoted. To prepare the bulletin board, construct a boy and girl out of tagboard. Design several occupational outfits that may be worn by either sex. Color and laminate the pieces. Magnet pieces or pushpins and holes should be provided to affix clothing on the children.

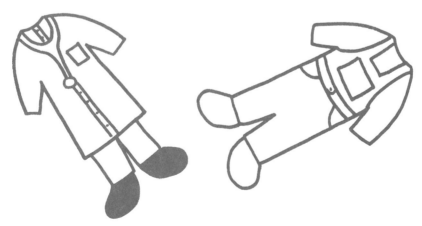

Family Letter

InBox

Dear Families,

Hello! We will explore a new unit on occupations. Through experiences provided by this theme, the children will become aware of a great number of occupations and the way these workers help us today. Transportation, health care, sports, community helpers, communication, production, construction, and service workers will all be included.

At School

Some learning experiences include:

- Listening to books and recordings about people in our neighborhoods

- Making occupation hats

- Visiting a police station on Wednesday at 2:00 p.m. Join us if you can!

- Observing an ambulance and talking with a paramedic

- Designing a job chart for our classroom

At Home

Page through magazines with your child. Discuss equipment and materials that are used in various occupations. Questions such as the following can be asked to stimulate thinking skills: Who might use a computer to perform a job? What occupations involve the use of a cash register? Your child might be interested in visiting your place of employment!

Enjoy your child!

Arts and Crafts

1. Mail Truck

Cut out mail truck parts including one rectangle, one square, and two circles. The children can paste the pieces together and decorate. This activity is most appropriate for older children.

2. Occupation Vests

Cut a circle out of the bottom of a large paper grocery bag. Then, from the circle, cut a slit down the center of the bag and turn bag inside out. Cut out armholes. Provide felt-tip colored markers for the children to decorate the vests. They may elect to be a pilot, police officer, mail carrier, baker, flight attendant, doctor, firefighter, and so on.

3. Mail Pouch

Cut the top half off a large grocery bag. Use the cutaway piece to make a shoulder strap. Staple it to the bag. The children can decorate the bag with crayons or markers.

Dramatic Play

1. Hat Shop

Police officer hats, firefighter hats, construction worker hats, businessperson hats, and other occupation-related hats should be placed in the dramatic play area.

2. Classroom Cafe

Cover the table in the dramatic play area with a tablecloth. Provide menus, a tablet for the waitress to write on, a space for a cook, and the like. A cash register and play money may also be added to encourage play.

3. Hairstylist

Collect empty shampoo bottles, combs, barrettes, ribbons, hair spray containers, and magazines. Cut the cord off a discarded hair dryer and curling iron, and place these in the dramatic play area.

4. Our Library

Books on a shelf, a desk for the librarian, and a stamper and ink pad to check out books should be placed in the dramatic play area. A small table for children to sit and read their books would also add interest.

5. Workbench

A hammer, nails, saws, vises, a carpenter's apron, and so forth should be added to the workbench. Eye goggles for the children's safety should also be included. *Caution:* Constant supervision is needed for this activity.

6. An Airplane

Create an airplane out of a large cardboard refrigerator box. If desired, the children can paint the airplane.

7. Post Office

A mailbox, letters, envelopes, stamps, and mail carrier bags can be set up in the dramatic play or art area.

8. Fast-Food Restaurant

Collect bags, containers, and hats to set up a fast-food restaurant.

9. A Construction Site

Hard hats, nails, a hammer, large blocks, and scrap wood can be provided for outdoor play. Cardboard boxes and masking tape should also be made available.

10. Prop Boxes

The following prop boxes can be made by collecting the materials listed.

Police Officer

- Badge
- Hat
- Uniform
- Whistle
- Walkie-talkie

Mail Carrier

- Letter bag
- Letter
- Uniform
- Mailbox
- Wrapped
- Cardboard boxes
- Paper
- Stamps
- Rubber stamp
- Ink pad
- Envelopes
- Pencil

Firefighter

- Boots
- Helmet
- Hose
- Uniform
- Gloves
- Raincoat
- Suspenders
- Goggles

Doctor

- Stethoscope
- Medicine bottles
- Adhesive tape
- Cotton balls
- Red Cross armband
- Chart holder

Field Trips and Resource People

1. Take field trips to the following:

- Bank
- Library
- Grocery store
- Police station
- Doctor or dentist office
- Beauty salon or barber
- Television or radio station
- Courthouse
- Airport
- Farm
- Restaurant

2. Invite the following resource people to school:

- Police officer with squad car
- Firefighter with truck
- Ambulance driver with ambulance
- Truck driver with truck
- Taxi driver with cab
- Librarian with books

Fingerplays and Chants

Farm Chores

Five little farmers woke up with the sun.
   (hold up hand, palm forward)
It was early morning and the chores must be done.
The first little farmer went out to milk the cow.
   (hold up hand, point to thumb)

The second little farmer thought he'd better plow.
   (hold up hand, point to index finger)
The third little farmer cultivated weeds.
   (point to middle finger)
The fourth little farmer planted more seeds.
   (point to fourth finger)
The fifth little farmer drove his tractor round.
   (point to last finger)
Five little farmers, the best that can be found.
   (hold up hand)

Traffic Policeman

The traffic policeman holds up his hand.
   (hold up hand, palm forward)
He blows the whistle,
   (pretend to blow whistle)
He gives the command.
   (hold up hand again)
When the cars are stopped
   (hold up hand again)
He waves at me.
Then I may cross the street, you see.
   (wave hand as if indicating for someone to go)

The Carpenter

This is the way he saws the wood
   (right hand saws left palm)
Sawing, sawing, sawing.
This is the way he nails a nail
   (pound right fist on left palm)
Nailing, nailing, nailing.
This is the way he paints the house
   (right hand paints left palm)
Painting, painting, painting.

Group Time
(Games and Language)

1. Brushes as Tools

Collect all types of brushes, and place in a bag. The children can reach into the bag and feel one. Before removing it, the child describes the kind of brush. When using with younger children, limit the number of brushes. Also, before placing the brushes in the bag, show the children each brush and discuss its use.

2. Machines as Helpers Chart

Machines and tools help people work and play. Ask the children to think of all of the machines they or their parents use around the house. As they name a machine, list it on a chart and discuss how it is used.

3. Mail It

Play a variation of "Duck, Duck, Goose." The children can sit in a circle. One child holds an envelope and walks around the circle saying, "Letter," and taps each child on the head. When he or she gets to the one he or she wants to be chased by, have the child drop the letter and say, "Mail it!" Then both children run around the circle until they return to the letter. The chaser gets to "mail" the letter by walking around and repeating the game.

 Large Muscle

Cut large cardboard boxes to make squad cars. Take the boxes and spray paint them either blue or white. Emblems can be constructed for the sides.

 Music

1. "Do You Know the Muffin Man?"

Oh, do you know the muffin man,
The muffin man, the muffin man?
Oh, do you know the muffin man
Who lives on Drury Lane?
Oh, yes, I know the muffin man,
The muffin man, the muffin man.
Oh, yes, I know the muffin man
Who lives on Drury Lane.

2. "What Is My Job?"

(Sing to the tune of "Are You Sleeping?")
What is my job? What is my job?
Can you guess? Can you guess?

I keep your body healthy, I keep your body healthy.
Who am I? Who am I?

(Variations in song:)

I keep your pets healthy. (Veterinarian)
I deliver letters. (Mail carrier)
I keep your teeth healthy. (Dentist)
I keep your building clean. (Custodian)
I put out the fires. (Firefighter)

 Sensory

The following materials can be added to the sensory table:

- Sponge hair rollers with water
- Wood shavings with scoops and scales
- Sand with toy cars, trucks, and airplanes
- Pipes with water

 Social Studies

1. Occupation Pictures

Pin occupation pictures on classroom bulletin boards and walls.

2. A Job Chart

Make a chart containing classroom jobs. Include tasks such as feeding the class pet, watering plants, sweeping the floor, wiping tables, and so on.

 Books

The following books can be used to complement this theme:

Carter, Don. (2002). *Get to Work Trucks!* Brookfield, CT: Roaring Brook Press.

Chapman, Jane. (2003). *Let's Build.* Cambridge, MA: Candlewick Press.

Cordsen, Carol Foskett. (2005). *The Milkman.* Illustrated by Douglas B. Jones. New York: Dutton Children's Books.

Cousins, Lucy. (2005). *Maisy Goes to the Library.* Cambridge, MA: Candlewick Press.

Crews, Donald. (1995). *Sail Away.* New York: Scholastic.

Davis, Kate, and Kate Endle. (2000). *What Do You Want to Be?* Illustrated by Kate Endle. Norwalk, CT: Innovative Kids.

Downs, Mike, and David Gordon. (2005). *The Noisy Airplane Ride.* Berkeley CA: Tricycle Press.

Hill, Susanna Leonard. (2009). *Airplane Flight.* Illustrated by Ana Martin Larranaga. New York: Little Simon.

Hoena, B. A. (2004). *A Visit to the Doctor's Office.* Mankato, MN: Capstone Press.

Jackson, Thomas Campbell. (1994). *Hammers, Nails, Planks, and Paint.* Illustrated by Randy Chewing. New York: Scholastic.

Lenski, Lois, and Heidi Kilgras, eds. (2001). *Policeman Small.* New York: Random House.

Lewis, Kevin. (2001). *Big Machines! Big Buildings!* Illustrated by Reg Cartwright. New York: Scholastic.

Lindeen, Carol K. (2005). *Fire Trucks.* Mankato, MN: Capstone Press.

Lindeen, Carol K. (2005). *Police Cars.* Mankato, MN: Capstone Press.

Macken, JoAnn Early. (2008). *Construction Tools.* Mankato, MN: Capstone Press.

Macken, JoAnn Early. (2009). *Building a House.* Mankato, MN: Capstone Press.

Markes, Julie. (2005). *Shhhhhh! Everybody's Sleeping.* Illustrated by David Parkins. New York: HarperCollins.

McMullan, Kate, and Jim McMullan. (2002). *I Stink!* New York: Joanne Cotler Books.

Metzger, Steve. (2008). *The Wheels on the Truck.* Illustrated by Tammie Lyon. New York: Scholastic.

Murphy, Patricia J. (2005). *A Visit to the Dentist's Office.* Mankato, MN: Capstone Press.

Neitzel, Shirley. (1999). *I'm Taking a Trip on My Train.* Illustrated by Nancy Winslow Parker. New York: Greenwillow Books.

Rey, Margaret, and H. A. Rey. (2003). *Curious George Visits the Library.* Illustrated in the style of H. A. Rey by Martha Weston. Boston: Houghton Mifflin.

Rockwell, Anne. (1997). *I Fly.* Illustrated by Annette Cable. New York: Crown.

Samuels, Barbara. (2010). *The Trucker.* New York: Farrar, Straus and Giroux.

Schaefer, Lola M. (2001). *Zoo. Who Works Here?* Chicago: Heinemann Library.

Schubert, Leda. (2010). *Feeding the Sheep.* Illustrated by Andrea U'Ren. New York: Farrar, Straus and Giroux.

Schuh, Mari C. (2008). *At the Dentist.* Mankato, MN: Capstone Press.

Schuh, Mari. (2009). *Fire Stations in Action.* Mankato, MN: Capstone Press.

Smith, Marie, and Roland Smith (2005). *Z Is for Zookeeper.* Illustrated by Henry Cole. Ann Arbor, MI: Sleeping Bear Press.

Stewart, Sarah. (2007). *The Gardener.* New York: Square Fish.

Thomas, Mark. (2001). *A Day with a Plumber.* New York: Children's Press.

Troupe, Thomas Kingsley. (2010). *If I Were a Ballerina.* Mankato, MN: Capstone Press.

Winne, Joanne. (2001). *A Day with a Mechanic.* New York: Children's Press.

Technology and Multimedia

The following technology and multimedia products can be used to complement this theme:

"The Airplane Song" [CD]. (2001). In *Whaddaya Think of That, Laurie Berkner.* New York: Two Tomatoes.

Exploring Communities and Its Workers [DVD]. (2007). Southington, CT: Mazzarella Media.

Reading Rainbow. (2007). In *Fox on the Job* [DVD]. Lincoln, NE: Distributed by GPN Educational Media.

"Riding in an Airplane" [CD]. (1985). In *One Light, One Sun.* Cambridge, MA: Rounder/UMGD.

Spend a Day with Firefighters [DVD]. (2003). Century City, CA: First Look Home Entertainment.

What I Want to Be! [DVD]. (2002). Beverly Hills, CA: Image Entertainment.

 Additional teaching resources to accompany this Theme can be found on the book's companion website. Go to www.cengagebrain.com to access the site for a variety of useful resources.

Excursions

Special excursions and events in an early childhood program give opportunities for widening the young child's horizons by providing exciting direct experiences. The following places or people are some suggestions:

Train station	Offices	Hospital	Print shop
Dentist office	Animal hospital	Meat market	Artist's studio
Post office	Fire station	Library	Bowling alley
Grocery store	Tree farm	Apple orchard	Department store
Zoo	Car wash	Farm	windows
Dairy	Children's houses	Airport	Potter's studio
Family garden	Garage mechanic	Riding stable	Teacher's house
Poultry house	Television studio	Barber shop	Street repair site
Construction site	Drugstore	College dormitory	
Beauty shop	Bakery	Shoe repair shop	

Theme 55
PETS

Body Covering
fur
feathers
scales
shell

Movement
swimming
walking
flying
hopping
running
crawling

Care
food
water
loving care
exercise
grooming
shelter

Sounds
barking
meowing
squeaking
chirping
hissing

People
breeders
trainers
groomers
owners
veterinarians

Kinds

house
dogs, cats
hamsters, gerbils
turtles, guinea pigs
fish, birds
rabbits, snakes
lizards, spiders
mice, ferrets
chinchillas

farm
pig, horse
ponies
sheep, goat
cow

Theme Goals

Through participating in the experiences provided by this theme, the children may learn:

1. People who work with pets
2. Pet care
3. Kinds of pets
4. Body coverings of pets
5. Sounds of pets
6. Movements of pets

Concepts for the Children to Learn

1. A favorite animal kept for pleasure is called a pet.
2. Dogs, cats, fish, hamsters, gerbils, turtles, guinea pigs, and birds can all be house pets.
3. Rabbits, snakes, lizards, spiders, mice, ferrets, and chinchillas can also be house pets.
4. Pigs, ponies, horses, sheep, goats, and cows can be pets on a farm.
5. Pets need food, water, shelter, exercise, and loving care.
6. Some pets need to be groomed.
7. Barking, meowing, squeaking, hissing, and chirping are pet sounds.
8. To move, pets may swim, walk, fly, hop, run, or crawl.
9. The care of a pet depends on the type of animal.
10. Body coverings on pets differ.
11. Body coverings can be fur, feathers, scales, or a shell.
12. A veterinarian is an animal doctor.
13. Breeders and trainers also work with pets.
14. Groomers wash, brush, and care for animals.

Vocabulary

1. **collar**—a band worn around an animal's neck.
2. **feathers**—skin covering of birds.
3. **fur**—hairy coating covering the skin of some animals.
4. **leash**—a cord that attaches to a collar.
5. **pet**—a favorite animal that is kept for pleasure. Cats and dogs are pets.
6. **scales**—skin covering of fish and reptiles.
7. **veterinarian**—an animal doctor.
8. **whiskers**—stiff hair growing around the animal's nose, mouth, and eyes.

Bulletin Board

The purpose of this bulletin board is to encourage the development of mathematical, visual discrimination, hand-eye coordination, and problem-solving skills. To prepare the bulletin board, construct fishbowls out of white tagboard or construction paper. Write a numeral beginning with 1 on each fishbowl and the corresponding number of dots. Hang the fishbowls on the bulletin board. Next, construct pieces as illustrated that will fit on top of the fishbowl to represent water in the bowl. Draw fish to match the numerals in each bowl. The pieces can be attached to each other to hang on the bulletin board by using magnet pieces, or pushpins and a paper punch. The children should count the fish in each water piece and match it to the corresponding numbered fishbowl.

Family Letter

Dear Families,

Children are naturally curious about animals. To build on their interests, we are starting a curriculum unit on pets, and I'm sure that we'll be busy! The children will discover the kinds of animals most people keep as pets. They will also learn sounds, care, body coverings, and movements of pets. Also, the children will learn the occupations of people who work with pets.

At School

The following are some of the learning experiences in which your child will participate during our pet unit:

- Making a special treat for Greta, our classroom gerbil

- Creating a large doghouse out of an appliance box for the dramatic play area

- Interacting with a variety of pets. Dani and Donny will bring their rabbit on Tuesday, and Cindy will bring her bird on Wednesday. If you are willing to bring your family pet to school to show the children, we welcome you. Contact me, and we can arrange a time that would be convenient for you (and your pet).

- Listening to the story *Clifford, the Big Red Dog* by Norman Birdwell

At Home

Is your family considering adding a pet to your household? If so, there are many variables to take into consideration because not all households are meant to include pets. Allergies, fears, and lifestyles are three things that need to be considered. Also, you need to consider your child's readiness for a pet.

To develop fine motor skills, provide magazines and newspapers for your child to cut or tear out pictures of animals. These can be used to create an animal alphabet book or a collage to hang in your child's bedroom.

Enjoy your child!

Arts and Crafts

1. Pet Sponge Painting
Cut sponges into a variety of pet shapes. Place on the art table with paper and a shallow pan of tempera paint.

2. Doghouse
Provide an old, large cardboard box for the children to make a doghouse with adult supervision. They can cut holes in it, paint it, and decorate it. When dry, the doghouse can be moved into the dramatic play area or to the outdoor play yard.

3. Cookie Cutters and Play Dough
Pet-shaped cookie cutters and play dough can be placed on the art table.

Cooking

Animal Cookies

1 1/2 cups powdered sugar
1 cup butter or margarine
1 egg
1 teaspoon vanilla extract
2 1/2 cups flour
1 teaspoon baking soda
1 teaspoon cream of tartar

Mix powdered sugar, margarine, egg, and vanilla extract. Mix in flour, baking soda, and cream of tartar. Cover and refrigerate for 2 hours. Preheat oven to 375 degrees. Divide dough into halves. Roll out 1/2-inch thick on a lightly floured, cloth-covered board. Cut the dough into animal shapes with cookie cutters, or let the children cut it. Place on a lightly greased cookie sheet. Bake 7 to 10 minutes. Serve for snack.

Dramatic Play

1. Pet Store
The children can all bring in their stuffed animals to set up a pet store. A counter, a cash register, and several empty pet food containers should be provided to stimulate play.

2. Veterinarian Prop Box
Collect materials for a veterinarian prop box. Include a stethoscope, empty pill bottles, fabric cut as bandages, splints, and stuffed animals.

Field Trips and Resource People

1. Pet Show
Plan a pet show. Each child who wants to show a pet should sign up for a time and day. If children can all bring in a pet on the same day, have a big pet show. Award prizes for longest tail, longest ears, biggest, smallest, best groomed, loudest barker, most obedient, and so on. Children who do not have a pet or cannot arrange to bring it to school can bring a stuffed toy.

2. Veterinarian
Invite a veterinarian to talk to the children about how a veterinarian helps pets and animals. Pet care can also be addressed.

3. Pet Store
Visit a pet store to observe types of pets, their toys, and other accessories. Pictures can be taken on the trip and later placed on the bulletin board of the classroom.

4. Pet Groomer
Visit a pet groomer. Observe how pets are bathed and groomed.

Fingerplays and Chants

My Puppy

I like to pet my puppy.
   (pet puppy)
He has such nice soft fur.
   (pet puppy)
And if I don't pull his tail
   (pull tail)
He won't say "Grr!"
   (make face)

If I Were

If I were a dog
I'd have four legs to run and play.
   (down on all four hands and feet)
If I were a fish
I'd have fins to swim all day.
   (hands at side fluttering like fins)
If I were a bird
I could spread my wings out wide.
And fly all over the countryside.
   (arms out from sides fluttering like
    wings)
But I'm just me.
I have two legs, don't you see?
And I'm just as happy as can be.

The Bunny

Once there was a bunny
   (fist with two fingers tall)
And a green, green cabbage head.
   (fist of other hand)
"I think I'll have some breakfast," this little
    bunny said.
So he nibbled and he cocked his ears to say,
"I think it's time that I be on my way."

Sammy

Sammy is a super snake.
   (wave finger on opposite palm)
He sleeps on the shore of a silver lake.
   (curl finger to indicate sleep)
He squirms and squiggles to snatch a snack
   (wave finger and pounce)
And snoozes and snores till his hunger is
    back.
   (curl finger on palm)

Not Say a Single Word

We'll hop, hop, hop like a bunny
   (make hopping motion with hand)
And run, run, run like a dog.
   (make running motion with fingers)
We'll walk, walk, walk like an elephant
   (make walking motion with arms)
And jump, jump, jump like a frog.
   (make jumping motions with arms)
We'll swim, swim, swim like a goldfish
   (make swimming motion with hand)
And fly, fly, fly like a bird.
   (make flying motion with arms)
We'll sit right down and fold our hands
   (fold hands in lap)
And not say a single word!

Music

1. "Rags"

I have a dog and his name is Rags.
   (point to self)
He eats so much that his tummy sags.
   (hold tummy)
His ears flip-flop and his tail wig-wags.
   (flip hands by ears and wag hands at
    back)
And when he walks he zigs and zags.
   (put hands together and zig-zag them)

Flip-flop
Wiggle-waggle
Zig-zag (Repeat the same actions)
Flip-flop
Wiggle-waggle
Zig-zag

2. "Six Little Pets"
(Sing to the tune of "Six Little Ducks")

Six little gerbils I once knew,
Fat ones, skinny ones, fair ones, too.
But the one little gerbil was so much fun.
He would play until the day was done.

Six little dogs that I once knew,
Fat ones, skinny ones, fair ones, too.
But the one little dog with the brown curly
    fur,
She led the others with a grr, grr, grr.

Six little fish that I once knew,
Fat ones, skinny ones, fair ones, too.
But the one little fish who was the leader of
    the crowd,
He led the others around and around.

Six little birds that I once knew,
Fat ones, skinny ones, fair ones, too.
But the one little bird with the pretty little
    beak,
She led the others with a tweet, tweet, tweet.

Six little cats that I once knew,
Fat ones, skinny ones, fair ones, too.
But the one little cat who was as fluffy as a
    ball,
He was the prettiest one of all.

3. "Have You Ever Seen a Rabbit?"

(Sing to the tune of "Have You Ever Seen a Lassie?")

Have you ever seen a rabbit, a rabbit, a rabbit?
Have you ever seen a rabbit go hopping around?
Go hopping, go hopping, go hopping, go hopping
Have you ever seen a rabbit go hopping around?

 ## Science

1. Pet Foods

Cut out pictures of pets and pet foods, and place on the science table. Include different foods such as meat, fish, carrots, lettuce, nuts, and acorns. The children can match the food to a picture of the animal that would eat each type of food.

2. Bird Feathers

Bird feathers with a magnifying glass can be placed on the science table for the children to examine.

 ## Sensory

1. Minnows

Fill the sensory table with cold water. Place minnows purchased from a bait store into the water. The children will attempt to catch the minnows. Teachers should stress the importance of being gentle with the fish and follow through with limits set for the activity. After participating in this activity, the children should wash their hands.

2. Texture Rubbings

Cut out sandpaper "footprints" representing a variety of animals (cat, dog, birds, etc.). Tape the prints on the table, and have children place a piece of paper over the print. Rub the side of a crayon over the sandpaper to form a print. Have the children guess what kind of pet made each print.

 ## Social Studies

1. Animal Sounds

Tape several animal sounds and play them back for the children to identify.

2. Feeding Chart

Design and prepare a feeding chart for the classroom pets.

3. Weekend Visitor

Let children take turns bringing class pets home on weekends. Prepare a card for each animal's cage outlining feeding and behavioral expectations.

 ## Books

The following books can be used to complement this theme:

Blackaby, Susan. (2006). *A Cat for You.* Illustrated by Charlene Delage. Minneapolis, MN: Picture Window Books.

Blackaby, Susan. (2006). *A Dog for You.* Illustrated by Charlene Delage. Minneapolis, MN: Picture Window Books.

Blackaby, Susan. (2006). *Fish for You.* Illustrated by Charlene Delage. Minneapolis, MN: Picture Window Books.

Bluemle, Elizabeth. (2008). *Dogs on the Bed.* Illustrated by Anne Wilsdorf. Cambridge, MA: Candlewick Press.

Boelts, Maribeth. (2007). *Before You Were Mine.* Illustrated by David Walker. New York: G.P. Putnam's Sons.

Calmenson, Stephanie. (2007). *May I Pet Your Dog?* Illustrated by Jan Ormerod. New York: Clarion Books

Dahl, Michael. (2005). *Pets ABC: An Alphabet Book.* Mankato, MN: Capstone Press.

Dodd, Emma. (2003). *Dog's Colorful Day.* New York: Puffin Books.

Doyle, Malachy. (2008). *Horse.* Illustrated by Angelo Rinaldi. New York: M.K. McElderry Books.

Fjelland-Davis, Rebecca. (2007). *Counting Pets by Twos*. Mankato, MN: Capstone Press.

Florian, Douglas. (2003). *Bow Wow Meow Meow*. San Diego, CA: Harcourt.

Graham, Bob. (2007). *"The Trouble with Dogs," Said Dad*. Cambridge, MA: Candlewick Press.

Gravett, Emily. (2010). *Dogs*. New York: Simon & Schuster Books for Young Readers.

Grover, Jan Zita. (2008). *A Home for Dakota*. Minneapolis, MN: Gryphon House.

Jenkins, Steve. (2007). *Dogs and Cats*. Boston: Houghton Mifflin.

Kasza, Keiko. (2005). *The Dog Who Cried Wolf*. New York: G.P. Putnam's Sons.

Kimble, Warren. (2006). *The Cat's Meow*. New York: Walker & Co.

L'Engle, Madeleine, and Christine Davenier. (2001). *The Other Dog*. Illustrated by Christine Davenier. New York: Seastar.

MacLeod, Elizabeth. (2008). *Why Do Cats Have Whiskers?* New York: Kids Can Press.

McDonald, Megan, and Nancy Poydar. (2000). *Beezy and Funnybone*. Illustrated by Nancy Poydar. New York: Orchard Books.

Meyers, Susan. (2007). *Kittens, Kittens, Kittens!* New York: Abrams Books for Young Readers.

Nelson, Robin. (2003). *Pet Fish*. Minneapolis MN: Lerner.

Peters, Stephanie True. (2009). *Rumble Tum*. Illustrated by Robert Papp. New York: Dutton Children's Books.

Schaefer, Lola M. (2008). *Family Pets*. Mankato, MN: Capstone Press.

Scillian, Deven. (2007). *Memoirs of a Goldfish*. Illustrated by Tim Bowers. Ann Arbor, MI: Sleeping Bear Press.

Simon, Seymour. (2009). *Cats*. New York: Smithsonian/Collins.

Sovak, Jan. (2001). *Learning about Farm Animals*. New York: Dover.

Stainton, Sue. (2007). *I Love Cats*. Illustrated by Anne Mortimer. New York: Katherine Tegen Books.

Wahman, Wendy. (2009). *Don't Lick the Dog: Making Friends with Dogs*. New York: Henry Holt.

Technology and Multimedia

The following technology and multimedia products can be used to complement this theme:

Dogs Nature Special Presentation [DVD]. (2003). Questar: Chicago, Ill.

DogTown: New Beginnings [DVD]. (2008). Washington, DC: National Geographic.

Elmo's World: Pets [DVD]. (2006). Los Angeles: Sony Music Entertainment.

"Little Black Dog" [CD]. (1996). In *Diamonds and Daydreams*. Vancouver, BC: Hug Bug Records.

"My Little Kitty" [CD] (1998). In *Birds, Beasts, Bugs and Fishes Little and Big*. Washington, DC: Smithsonian Folkways.

Paws, Claws, Feathers and Fins [DVD]. (2005). Goldhil Video: Los Angeles, CA.

"Snuggle with Your Puppy" [CD]. (2000). In *Charlotte Diamond's World*. Vancouver, BC: Hug Bug Records.

Additional teaching resources to accompany this Theme can be found on the book's companion website. Go to www.cengagebrain.com to access the site for a variety of useful resources.

Theme 56
PLANTS

Origin
seed
another plant

Parts
roots
seeds
stems
leaves
buds
flowers
fruit

Types of Plants
medicinal
flowers
shrubs
trees, grasses
bushes
poisonous

Growth Sites
rainforest
garden
greenhouse or nursery
house, field
forest or wood
pond or lake

Plants We Can Eat
carrot, radish
celery
asparagus
rhubarb
lettuce, cabbage
spinach

Plants That Grow Food We Can Eat
beanstalk
cornstalk
apple tree
berry bush
grapevine

Growth Needs
sunshine
water
soil

Theme Goals

Through participating in the experiences provided by this theme, the children may learn:

1. Types of plants
2. Growth needs of plants
3. The parts of a plant
4. Plant growth sites
5. Edible plants
6. Origin of plants

Concepts for the Children to Learn

1. Plants are living things, usually green, that grow in the soil.
2. There are many kinds of plants.
3. Flowers, shrubs, trees, grasses, and bushes are all plants.
4. Some plants grow from seeds.
5. Some plants grow from another plant.
6. Plants need water, sunlight, and soil to grow.
7. People and animals eat some types of plants.
8. The parts of a plant are the stem, roots, buds, leaves, flowers, fruit, and seeds.
9. Carrots, radishes, beanstalks, celery, asparagus, and rhubarb are plants.
10. Lettuce, cabbage, spinach, cornstalks, apple trees, berry bushes, and grapevines are all plants.
11. There are different sizes, colors, and shapes of seeds.
12. Plants grow in homes, gardens, greenhouses, nurseries, fields, forests, and the woods.
13. Plants can also grow in a pond or lake.

Vocabulary

1. **flower**—a colored plant part that contains seeds.
2. **fruit**—an edible part of a plant. Fruits usually contain seeds. Oranges, apples, and strawberries are fruits.
3. **garden**—ground for growing vegetable and flower plants.
4. **leaf**—part of a plant or tree that grows on the stem. Most leaves are green.
5. **plant**—living thing, usually green, that grows in the soil. Bushes, flowers, grass, and trees are all plants.
6. **root**—part of the plant that grows below the ground. Plants use roots to get their food and water.
7. **seed**—part of a plant that can grow into a new plant. By planting a pumpkin seed, you get a new pumpkin plant.
8. **sprout**—first sign of growth on a plant.
9. **stem**—part of the plant that supports the leaves and grows upward. Leaves, flowers, and fruit have stems.
10. **vegetable**—a plant grown for food. Beans, carrots, and corn are vegetables.

Bulletin Board

The purpose of this bulletin board is to promote visual discrimination, hand-eye coordination, problem-solving, and numeral recognition skills. To prepare the bulletin board, construct flowerpots out of construction paper. Color each pot and draw dots on it as illustrated. Hang the pots on the bulletin board. Next, construct the same number of flowers with stems as pots. In the center of each flower, write a numeral. The children can place each flower in the flowerpot with the corresponding number of dots.

Family Letter

InBox

Dear Families,

Plants will be the focus of our next theme. Through the unit, the children will become aware of the origin and parts of a plant. They will also discover where plants can be grown and what plants can be eaten. They will be exposed to the parts of plants, plant growth sites, as well as foods that are edible plants.

At School

Some of the learning experiences related to plants will include:

- Listening to the story *The Plant Sitter* by Gene Zion

- Sprouting alfalfa seeds to add to a salad

- Walking around our play yard to collect plants

- Playing hopscotch in the shape of a flower

At Home

There are many ways to foster the concepts of this unit at home. If you have plants, let your child help water them. If you are planning to start a garden, section off a small portion for your child to grow plants.

At mealtimes, identify various parts of plants that are eaten. For example, we eat the leaves of lettuce, the stems of celery, the root of a carrot, and so on.

Plant some flower seeds with your child! Or, perhaps you could root a vegetable. To do this, place a potato or carrot in a jar, root end down so that one-third is covered by water. A potato can be held upright by inserting toothpicks or small nails at three points so that the vegetable can be rested on the rim of the jar. Encourage your child to water the vegetable as needed. Label the plant. Roots should grow out from the bottom of the vegetable. Likewise, shoots will grow from the top.

Enjoy your child!

Arts and Crafts

1. **Grass Hair**
   Save half-pint milk cartons. The children can decorate the outside of the carton like a face. Place soil in the cartons, and add grass seeds. After approximately 7 days, the grass will start to grow, and it will look like hair. If the grass becomes too long, have the child give it a haircut.

2. **Flower Collage**
   Collect flowers and weeds. Press the flowers and weeds between paper and books. Old telephone directories can be used. Dry them for 7 to 10 days. The children can use the pressed foliage to create their own collages on paper plates or construction paper.

3. **Nature Tree**
   Cut a branch off a tree, and place it in a pail of plaster of Paris. The children can decorate the tree with a ribbon and different forms of plant life that they have collected or made. Included may be flowers, plants, fruits, vegetables, and seeds.

4. **Leaf Rubbings**
   Place a thin piece of paper over a leaf. Rub gently with the long side of a crayon.

5. **Easel Ideas**
   Cut easel paper into different shapes, such as the following:
   - Leaves
   - Flowers
   - Flowerpots
   - Fruits and vegetables

6. **Egg Carton Flowers**
   Use egg cartons and chenille stems to make flowers. To make the flower stand up, place a chenille stem into the egg carton as well as a Styrofoam block.

7. **Hand and Foot Flowers**
   Create a flower by using the child's hands and feet. Trace and cut two left and right hands and one set of left and right feet. Put one set of hands together to form the top of the flower and the other set (facing down) to form the bottom side. Add a circle to the middle. Cut a stem from green paper, and add the green feet as leaves. This makes a cute Mother's Day idea. Mount on white paper.

Cooking

1. **Vegetable-Tasting Party**
   Prepare raw vegetables for a tasting party. Discuss the color, texture, and flavor of each vegetable.

2. **Sprouts**
   Provide each interested child with a small jar. Fill the bottom with alfalfa seeds. Fill the jar with warm water, and cover with cheesecloth and a rubber band. Each day, rinse and fill the jar with fresh warm water. In three or four days, the seeds will sprout. The sprouts may be used on sandwiches or salads at lunchtime.

3. **Latkes (Potato Pancakes)**
   2 potatoes, peeled and grated
   1 egg, slightly beaten
   1/4 cup flour
   1 teaspoon salt
   Cooking oil

   Mix the ingredients in a bowl. Drop the mixture by tablespoons into hot oil in an electric skillet. Brown on both sides. Drain on paper towels.
   Caution: This activity must be carefully supervised.

Dramatic Play

1. **Greenhouse**
   Provide materials for a greenhouse. Include a window space, pots, soil, water, watering cans, seeds, plants, posters, work aprons, garden gloves, a terrarium, and seed packages to mount on sticks.

2. **Jack and the Beanstalk**
   Act out the story "Jack and the Beanstalk." The children can dramatize a beanstalk growing.

3. Vegetable and Fruit Stand

Display plastic fruits and vegetables. Set up a shopping area with carts, cash registers, and play money. Provide a balance scale for children to weigh the produce.

4. Garden Planting

Plant a small garden outdoors. Provide seeds, watering cans, garden tools, gloves, and garden hats.

 Field Trips

1. Greenhouse

Visit a greenhouse or a tree nursery to observe the different plants and trees and inquire about their care.

2. Farm

Plan a visit to a farm. While there, observe the various forms of plant life.

3. Florist

Visit a florist. Observe the different colors, types, and sizes of flowering plants.

 Fingerplays and Chants

My Garden

This is my garden.
    (extend one hand forward, palm up)
I'll rake it with care
    (make raking motion on palm with other hand)
And then some flower seeds
    (make planting motion with thumb and index fingers)
I'll plant in there.
The sun will shine
    (make circle above head)
And the rain will fall
    (let fingers flutter down to lap)
And my garden will blossom
    (cup hands together, extend upward slowly until fingers stand straight)
And grow straight and tall.

Plants

Plants need care to help them grow.
    (make fist with hand)
Just like boys and girls you know.
Good soil, water, sunshine bright.
Then watch them pop overnight.
    (extend fingers from fist)

 Group Time
(Games and Language)

Feltboard Fun

Construct felt pieces representing the stages of a flower's growth. Include a bulb, a seed, cuttings, roots, a stem, leaves, and a flower. During group time, review the name and purpose of each part with the children. The children can take turns coming up to the flannel board and adding the pieces. After group time, the felt pieces should be left out so that children can reconstruct the growth during self-selected activity periods.

 Large Muscle

1. Leaf Jumping

Cut out eight large leaves from tagboard. Arrange the leaves in a pattern on the floor. Encourage the children to jump from one leaf to another. This game could also be played outdoors by drawing the leaves on the sidewalk with chalk.

2. Flower Hopscotch

Design a hopscotch in the form of a flower. Chalk can be used on a sidewalk outdoors, or masking tape can be used indoors to make the form.

3. Vegetable, Vegetable, Plant

Play "Vegetable, Vegetable, Plant" as a variation of "Duck, Duck, Goose."

4. Raking and Hoeing

Provide the children with plastic child-sized hoes and rakes to tend to the play yard.

 Math

1. **Charting Growth**
   The children can observe the growth of a small plant by keeping a chart of its growth. Record the dates of the observation and the height. For convenience, place the chart near the plant table.

2. **Flowerpot Match Game**
   Construct flowerpots. The number constructed will depend on the developmental appropriateness for the children. Write a numeral on each, beginning with the numeral 1. Make the same number of flowers, with the petals varying from one to the total number of flowerpots constructed. The children match the flowerpot to the flower with the same number of petals.

3. **Counting and Classifying Seeds**
   Place a variety of seeds on a table. Encourage the children to count and classify them into groups. To assist in counting and classifying, an egg carton with each section given a number from 1 to 12 may be helpful. Encourage the children to observe the numeral and place a corresponding number of seeds in each section.

4. **Plant Growth Seriation**
   Construct pictures of plants through stages of growth. Begin with a seed, followed by the seed sprouting. The third picture should be the stem erupting from the soil surface. Next, a stem with leaves can be constructed. Finally, flowers can be added to the last picture. This could also be made into a bulletin board.

5. **Seed Match**
   Collect a variety of seeds such as corn, pumpkin, orange, apple, lima bean, watermelon, pea, and peach. Cut several rectangles out of white tagboard. On the top half of each rectangle, glue one of the seed types you have collected. Encourage the children to sort the seeds, matching them to those seeds glued on the individual cards.

 Music

1. **"The Seed Cycle"**
   (Sing to the tune of "The Farmer in the Dell")
   (Children can dramatize the parts for each verse)

   The farmer sows his seeds.
   The farmer sows his seeds.
   Hi-ho the dairy-o
   The farmer sows his seeds.

   (Other verses:)

   The wind begins to blow . . .
   The rain begins to fall . . .
   The sun begins to shine . . .
   The seeds begin to grow . . .
   The plants grow big and tall . . .
   The farmer cuts his corn . . .
   He puts it in his barns . . .
   And now the harvest is in . . .

2. **"This Is the Way We Rake the Garden"**
   (Sing to the tune of "Here We Go Round the Mulberry Bush")

   This is the way we rake the garden,
   Rake the garden, rake the garden.
   This is the way we rake the garden,
   So early in the morning.

   (Other verses:)

   This is the way we plant the seeds . . .
   This is the way the rain comes down . . .
   This is the way we hoe the weeds . . .
   This is the way the garden grows . . .
   This is the way we pick the vegetables . . .
   This is the way we eat the vegetables . . .

3. **"The Farmer in the Dell"**
   (Traditional)

   The farmer in the dell,
   The farmer in the dell,
   Hi-ho the dairy-o
   The farmer in the dell.
   The farmer takes a wife (husband).
   The farmer takes a wife (husband).
   Hi-ho the dairy-o
   The farmer in the dell.

(Other verses:)

The wife (husband) takes the child
The child takes the nurse
The nurse takes the dog
The dog takes the cat
The cat takes the rat
The rat takes the cheese.

(The final verse:)

The cheese stands alone.
The cheese stands alone.
Hi-ho the dairy-o
The cheese stands alone.

Science

1. **Watch Seeds Grow**
   A pan and paper toweling is needed for this activity. Moisten the paper towel and place on the pan. On top of the moist toweling, place various seeds—corn, peas, squash seeds, beans, and so on. Add 1/2-inch water to the pan. Watch the seeds sprout and grow. (Make sure to check the water level in the pan so that the seeds do not dry out.)

2. **Colored Celery**
   In clear containers, place several celery stalks with leaves. In each container, add 3 inches of water and drop a different color of food coloring. The leaves of the celery should turn colors in a few hours. Try splitting a celery stalk in half, but do not split the stalk all the way up to the top. Put one-half of the stalk in red water, and the other half in blue water. Watch what happens to the leaves.

3. **Sunlight Experiment**
   Place seeds in two jars with a half-inch of soil. Place one jar in a dark place such as a closet or cupboard, and avoid watering it. Keep the other jar in a sunny area, and water it frequently. Which one grew? Why?

4. **Growing Bean Plants**
   Each child can grow a bean plant.

5. **Tasting Plants**
   Various fruits and vegetables grown from plants should be provided for the children to taste and smell.

6. **Feely Box**
   In the feely box, place different parts of a plant such as the root, stems, leaves, flowers, fruit, and buds. The children can feel and verbally identify the part of the plant before looking at it.

7. **Root a Vegetable**
   Place a potato or carrot in a jar, root end down so that one-third is covered by water. A potato can be held upright by inserting toothpicks or nails at three points. This can be rested on the rim of the jar. The children can water as needed. Roots should grow out from the bottom and shoots from the top. Plant the root in soil for an attractive plant.

8. **Beans**
   Soak dry navy beans in a jar of water overnight. The next day, compare soaked beans with dry beans. Note the difference in texture and color. Open some beans that were soaked. A tiny plant should be inside the bean. These can be placed under a microscope for closer observation.

9. **Budding Branches**
   Place a branch that has buds ready to bloom in a jar of water on the science table. Let the children observe the buds bloom. Notice that after all the stored food of the plant is used, the plant will die.

Social Studies

1. **Plant Walk**
   Walk around the neighborhood, and try to identify as many plants as you can.

2. **Play Yard Plants**
   Make a map of the play yard. The children can collect a part of each plant located in the playground. The plant samples can be mounted on the map.

3. **Planting Trees**
   Plant a tree on your playground. Discuss the care needed for trees.

4. Family Tree

Make a family tree by mounting a bunch of branches in a pail of dirt. Each child can bring in a family picture to be placed on a leaf shape and hung on the tree branches.

 **Books**

The following books can be used to complement this theme:

Aston, Diana Hutts. (2007). *A Seed Is Sleepy*. Illustrated by Sylvia Long. San Francisco: Chronicle Books.

Batten, Mary, and Paul Mirocha. (2000). *Hungry Plants*. Illustrated by Paul Mirocha. New York: Golden Book Family Entertainment.

Bodach, Vijaya Khisty. (2007). *Flowers*. Mankato, MN: Capstone Press.

Bodach, Vijaya Khisty. (2007). *Fruits*. Mankato, MN: Capstone Press.

Bodach, Vijaya Khisty. (2007). *Leaves*. Mankato, MN: Capstone Press.

Bodach, Vijaya Khisty. (2007). *Roots*. Mankato, MN: Capstone Press.

Bodach, Vijaya Khisty. (2007). *Seeds*. Mankato, MN: Capstone Press.

Bodach, Vijaya Khisty. (2007). *Stems*. Mankato, MN: Capstone Press.

Cole, Henry. (1997). *Jack's Garden*. New York: Greenwillow Books.

Hall, Zoe. (1996). *The Apple Pie Tree*. New York: Scholastic.

Krauss, Ruth. (2005). *The Carrot Seed* (60th anniversary edition). Illustrated by Crockett Johnson. New York: HarperCollins.

Levenson, George. (2002). *Pumpkin Circle: The Story of a Garden*. Illustrated by Shmuel Thaler. Berkeley, CA: Ten Speed Press/ Tricycle.

Macken, JoAnn Early. (2008). *Flip, Float, Fly: Seeds on the Move*. Illustrated by Pam Paparone. New York: Holiday House.

Miranda, Anne. (2001). *To Market, to Market*. Illustrated by Janet Stevens. San Diego, CA: Harcourt Brace.

Mitton, Tony, and Ant Parker. (2009). *Rainforest Romp*. New York: Kingfisher Books.

Muldrow, Diane. (2010). *We Planted a Tree*. Illustrated by Bob Staake. New York: Random House Children's Books.

Pallotta, Jerry. (2010). *Who Will Plant a Tree?* Illustrated by Tom Leonard. Ann Arbor, MI: Sleeping Bear Press.

Ray, Deborah Kogan. (2002). *Lily's Garden*. Brookfield, CT: Roaring Brook Press.

Richards, Jean, and Anca Hariton. (2002). *A Fruit Is a Suitcase for Seeds*. Minneapolis, MN: Millbrook Press.

Rustad, Martha E. H. (2008). *Leaves in Fall*. Mankato, MN: Capstone Press.

Schaefer, Lola M. (2003) *Pick, Pull, Snap*. Illustrated by Lindsay Barrett George. New York: Greenwillow Books.

Stewart, Sarah. (2007). *The Gardener*. New York: Square Fish.

Wade, Mary Dodson. (2009). *Flowers Bloom!* Berkeley Heights, NJ: Enslow Elementary.

Wellington, Monica. (2005). *Zinnia's Flower Garden*. New York: Puffin Books.

Zion, Gene (1959). *The Plant Sitter*. New York, Harper Collins.

 Technology and Multimedia

The following technology and multimedia products can be used to complement this theme:

Max & Ruby: Max and the Beanstalk [DVD]. (2008). New York: KaBoom! Entertainment.

Reading Rainbow. (2007). *Legend of the Indian Paintbrush* [DVD]. Lincoln, NE: GPN Educational Media.

Rock 'N Learn. (2009). *Life Science* [DVD]. Conroe, TX: Rock 'N Learn.

 Additional teaching resources to accompany this Theme can be found on the book's companion website. Go to www.cengagebrain.com to access the site for a variety of useful resources.

Theme 57
PUPPETS

Purposes
express feelings
entertainment
communication

Stages
tables
bookcases
cardboard boxes
blankets
sheets

Kinds
finger
hand
stick
cloth
rod
shadow
marionette
dummy

Movement
string
wire
rods
hands
fingers

Types
animals
people
pretend creatures

Materials
paper
paper bags
novelty sticks
cloth, socks
wooden spoons
string, felt
coat hangers
pot holders
mittens, gloves
paper plates
flyswatters

Theme Goals

Through participating in the experiences provided by this theme, the children may learn:

1. The purpose of using puppets
2. Kinds of puppets
3. Types of puppets
4. Materials used to make puppets
5. Ways of moving puppets
6. Types of puppet stages

Concepts for the Children to Learn

1. A puppet is a toy that looks like a person, animal, or pretend creature.
2. Puppets can be moved by the hand, the finger, or a string.
3. There are finger, hand, stick, and cloth puppets.
4. Our hands and fingers can be decorated and used as puppets.
5. Rod, shadow, marionette, and dummy are types of puppets.
6. Puppets can be fun; they can be used for communication and entertainment.
7. We can use puppets to express feelings.
8. People talk for puppets.
9. Puppets can be made from paper bags, socks, felt, wooden spoons, novelty sticks, cloth, or even wood.
10. Puppets can also be made from coat hangers, pot holders, mittens, gloves, paper plates, and flyswatters.
11. Some puppets can be moved with strings, wires, or rods.
12. Large cardboard boxes, tables, bookcases, blankets, and sheets can be used for puppet stages.

Vocabulary

1. **entertainment**—things we enjoy seeing and listening to.
2. **imaginary**—something that is not real.
3. **marionette**—a puppet that has its head, body, arms, and legs attached with strings.
4. **puppet**—a toy that looks like an animal, person, or pretend creature.
5. **puppet show**—a show using puppets to tell a story.
6. **puppeteer**—a person who makes a puppet move and talk.
7. **puppet stage**—a place for puppets to act.

Bulletin Board

The purpose of this bulletin board is to expose the children to a variety of puppets. The children's expressive language skills will be stimulated by interacting with the puppets. Design the bulletin board by constructing about five or six simple puppets for the children to take off the bulletin board to play with. Include a flyswatter puppet, paper bag puppet, hand puppet, sock puppet, and wooden spoon puppet. Hooks or pushpins can be used to attach the puppets to the bulletin board.

Family Letter

Dear Families,

Our new curriculum theme will focus on puppets. They are magical and motivating to young children. Sometimes a child will respond or talk to a puppet in a situation when he or she might not talk to an adult or another child. Through learning experiences involving puppets, the children will become aware of the different types, kinds, and movements of puppets. They will also learn materials that can be used to make puppets. Through using puppets in their play, they will learn to express themselves creatively and imaginatively.

At School

Some of the activities related to puppets include:

- Creating our own puppets with a variety of materials
- Using the puppet stage throughout the week, putting on puppet shows for one and all
- Exploring various types of puppets, including finger, hand, stick, shadow, and marionette puppets

At Home

The children enjoy retelling familiar stories and making up original stories for puppet characters. To stimulate this type of play, you and your child can make simple puppets at home with objects found around the house.

Paper Bag Puppets: Using small paper lunch bags, children can use crayons or markers to create a puppet. The fold in the bag can be used as the mouth. After the child's hand is in the bag, the puppet can talk. Yarn scraps can easily be glued on for hair, and construction paper scraps can add a decorative touch.

Enjoy your child!

Arts and Crafts

1. **Making Puppets**
Puppets can be made from almost any material. Some suggestions are listed here.

- Cotton covered with cloth attached to a tongue depressor
- Paper sacks stuffed with newspaper
- A cork for a head with a hole in it for a finger
- Socks
- Cardboard colored with crayon attached to a tongue depressor
- Wooden spoon
- Flyswatter
- Oatmeal box attached to a dowel
- Pantyhose stretched over a hanger bent into an oval shape
- Empty toilet paper and paper towel rolls

2. **Puppet Stages**
Puppet stages can be made from the following materials:

- Box, with tempera paint and markers for decorating
- Large paper bag
- Half-gallon milk carton
- Towel draped over an arm
- Towel draped over the back of a chair
- Blanket covering a card table

Cooking

1. **Puppet Faces**
Make open-faced sandwiches using jelly or cream cheese spread onto a slice of bread or a bun. Carrot curls can be used to represent hair. Raisins and green or purple grape halves can be used for the eyes, nose, and mouth.

2. **Dog Puppet Salad**
Place a pear half onto a plate. Two apple slices can be added to resemble a dog's ears hanging down. Raisins or grape halves can be used to represent the eyes and nose of a dog.

Dramatic Play

1. **Puppet Show**
A puppet stage should be available throughout the entire unit in the dramatic play area. Change or add the puppets on a regular basis using as many different kinds of puppets as possible.

2. **Puppet Shop**
A variety of materials should be provided for the children to construct puppets. Include items such as buttons, bows, felt, paper bags, cloth pieces, socks, tongue depressors, and so on.

Field Trips and Resource People

1. **Puppet Show**
Place puppets by the puppet stage to encourage the children to put on puppet shows.

2. **Puppeteer**
Invite a puppeteer to visit the classroom and show the children the many uses of puppets.

Fingerplays and Chants

Speckled Frogs
(This fingerplay can be told using puppets made from felt or tagboard)

Five green-speckled frogs
Sitting on a speckled log
Eating the most delicious bugs,
Yum, yum!
    (rub tummy)
One jumped into the pool
Where it was nice and cool
Now there are four green-speckled frogs.
Repeat until there are no green-speckled frogs.

Chickadees
(This fingerplay can be told using puppets made from felt or tagboard)

Five little chickadees sitting in a door
(hold up hand)
One flew away and then there were four.
(put down one finger at a time)
Four little chickadees sitting in a tree
One flew away and then there were three.
Three little chickadees looking at you
One flew away and then there were two.
Two little chickadees sitting in the sun
One flew away and then there was one.
One little chickadee sitting all alone
He flew away and then there were none.

Two Little Puppets

Two little puppets,
(hold up both hands)
One on each hand.
(wave hands)
Isn't she pretty?
(look at right hand, wave fingers)
Isn't he grand?
(look at left hand, wave fingers)
Her name is Bella.
(wave right hand fingers)
His name is Beau.
(wave left hand fingers)
Hear her say, "Good morning."
(bend right hand)
Hear him say, "Hello!"
(bend left hand)

Group Time
(Games and Language)

Puppet Show
Using your favorite classroom stories, put on a puppet show. The children can volunteer to be the various characters. Pretape the story so that the children can listen to it while they practice. This might be a good activity to invite parents to attend.

Large Muscle

1. Creative Movement
Demonstrate how to manipulate a marionette. Then have the children pretend that they are marionettes and that they have strings

attached to their arms and legs. Say, "Someone is pulling up the string that is attached to your arm; what would happen to your arm?" Allow the children to make that movement. Continue with other movements.

2. Large Puppets
Large puppets such as stick or rod puppets can provide the children with a lot of large-muscle movement.

3. Pin the Nose on the Puppet
This game is a variation of the traditional "Pin the Tail on the Donkey." (This game would be more appropriate for five-, six-, seven-, and eight-year-old children.)

Math

1. Examine a Puppet
With the children, examine a puppet and count all of its various parts. Count its eyes, its legs, its arms, the stripes on its shirt, and so on. Discuss how it was constructed.

2. Puppet Dot-to-Dot
Draw a large puppet on a sheet of tagboard. Laminate or cover the tagboard sheet with clear adhesive paper. A grease pencil or felt-tip watercolor marker should be provided for the children for drawing. Also, felt scraps should be available to remove grease markings. Otherwise, a damp cloth or paper towel should be available.

Music

"Eensy Weensy Spider"
(Traditional)

The eensy weensy spider crawled up the
water spout.
(walk fingers of one hand up other hand)
Down came the rain and washed the
spider out.

(lower hands to make rain, wash out
spider by placing hands together in
front and extending out to either side)
Out came the sun and dried up all the rain,
(form sun with arms in circle over head)
And the eensy weensy spider went up the
spout again.
(walk fingers up other arm)

Science

1. **Classify Puppets**
   During group time, let the children classify
   the various puppets into special categories
   such as animals, people, insects, imaginary
   things, and so on.

2. **Button Box**
   A large box of buttons should be provided.
   The children can sort the buttons according
   to color, size, or shape into a muffin tin or
   egg carton.

Sensory

Sensory Table
During this unit, add to the sensory table
all of the various materials that puppets are
made of.

- String
- Buttons
- Felt
- Toilet paper rolls
- Cardboard
- Paper
- Sticks
- Wood shavings

Social Studies

Occupation Puppets
Introduce various types of occupation
puppets such as police officer, mail carrier,
fire fighter, doctor, nurse, etc. Ask the
children to describe each.

Books

The following books can be used to complement
this theme:

Almoznino, Albert. (2002). *The Art of Hand
Shadows.* Mineola, NY: Dover Publications.

Baric, Maija. (2007). *Puppet Theatre.* Illustrated
by Kristiina Louhi. Stroud, UK: Hawthorn
Press.

Bulloch, Ivan. (1997). *I Want to Be a Puppeteer.*
Illustrated by Diane James. Chicago: World
Book.

Fowler, Richard. (2006). *Lights Out! Shadow
Pop-Up and Play.* Hauppauge, NY: Barron's
Educational Series.

Little Red Riding Hood. (1997). Finger Puppet
Theater. Illustrated by Peter Stevenson.
St. Paul, MN: Cartwheel Books.

Piumini, Roberto. (2010). *Pinocchio.* Mankato,
MN: Capstone Press.

Wood, David, and Richard Fowler. (2000). *The
Toy Cupboard.* London: Pavilion Books.

Technology and Multimedia

The following technology and multimedia
products can be used to complement this
theme:

*Jim Henson's The Song of the Cloud Forest
and Other Earth Stories* [DVD]. (2010). Los
Angeles: Lionsgate.

Pinocchio [DVD]. (2009). Los Angeles: Walt
Disney Studios Home Entertainment.

Rainy Day Art [DVD]. (2003). St. Louis, MO:
Jumby Bay Studios.

Additional teaching resources to accompany this
Theme can be found on the book's companion
website. Go to www.cengagebrain.com to
access the site for a variety of useful resources.

Theme 58
PURPLE

Flowers
violet
iris
lilac

Foods
grapes
eggplant
cabbage

Shades
lavender (pale purple)
violet (bluish purple)

Color Mixing
red + blue = purple
purple + white = lavender

Theme Goals

Through participating in the experiences provided by this theme, the children may learn:

1. Color mixing to make the color purple
2. Shades of purple
3. Purple flowers
4. Foods that are purple

Concepts for the Children to Learn

1. Purple is the name of a color.
2. Mixing the color red with the color blue makes purple.
3. Many objects are purple in color.
4. Violets, irises, and lilacs are flowers that are purple in color.
5. Grapes, eggplant, and cabbage are foods that are purple in color.
6. There are light and dark shades of purple.
7. Lavender is a pale purple color.
8. Violet is a bluish purple color.

Vocabulary

1. **purple**—a color created by mixing red and blue.
2. **shade**—lightness or darkness of color.
3. **tint**—a variety of a color produced by mixing it with white.

Bulletin Board

The purpose of this bulletin board is to promote name recognition skills and call attention to the printed word. Interaction promotes the development of visual discrimination, problem-solving, and hand-eye coordination skills. This bulletin board can also be used to check attendance. Trace and cut a crayon for each child in the class from purple tagboard. Then print each child's name on a crayon. Laminate and cut out the crayon pieces. Use a paper punch to cut a hole in the top of each crayon. Hang pushpins on the bulletin board for the children to hang their crayons.

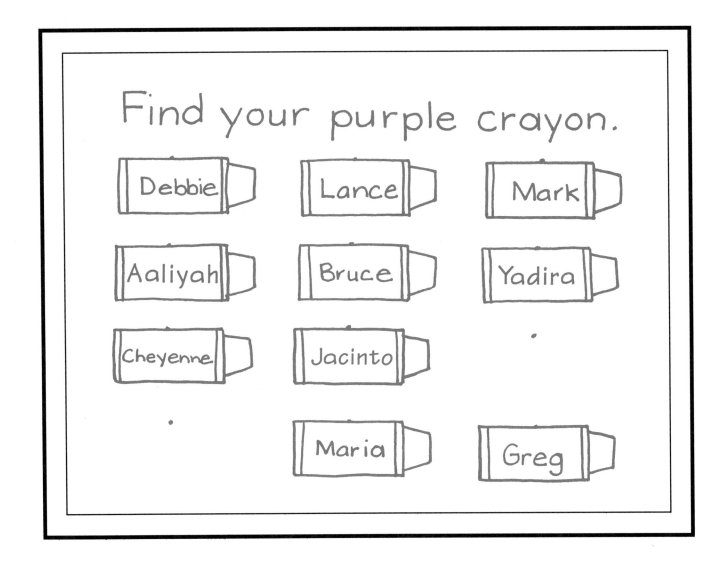

Family Letter

InBox

Dear Families,

What color is made when blue is mixed with red? The popular color PURPLE! Our next theme will focus on exploring the royal color purple. The children will learn from what colors purple is made and learn to identify items that are purple.

At School

A few of this week's learning experiences include:

- Creating designs and drawings in the art area with purple crayons, paints, markers, yarn, tissue paper, pompons, and glitter

- Listening to the story *Harold and the Purple Crayon* by Crockett Johnson. Afterward, we will each make a page to create a classroom purple crayon book. Look for it in the book area by the end of the week!

- Looking at various items that are purple. Could you help your child find an object that is purple and bring it to school on Wednesday? Thank you for your help!

At Home

The theme of purple can be explored at home as well. Feel free to try the following purple activities:

- Preparing purple foods with your child for meals or snacks such as grapes, purple cabbage, gelatin, grape juice, or jelly

- Making grape popsicles by freezing grape juice or grape-flavored fruit drink

- Creating a purple collage by cutting out purple pictures and letters from magazines. Glue pictures on a purple sheet of construction paper.

Have a good week!

Arts and Crafts

1. Marble Painting

For each child, place a 9-inch × 12-inch piece of white construction paper in a dishpan. Squeeze a few teaspoons of purple liquid tempera paint onto the paper. Place two or three marbles on the paper. Designs are created by holding the pan and tilting it back and forth, allowing the marbles to slide through the paint.

2. Grape Prints

Wrap a piece of masking tape around three toilet paper tubes to create a stamp to make designs of grapes. The children can then dip the end of the stamp into a shallow tray of purple paint, and then press it down on white construction paper to print bunches of grapes. After the paint is dry, crayons or markers can be used to add stems or leaves.

3. Purple Glitter Dough

Make purple play dough using your favorite recipe (or combine 1 cup flour, 1/2 cup salt, 1 cup water, 1 tablespoon vegetable oil, 2 teaspoons cream of tartar, and red and blue food coloring). Cook for 3 minutes, stirring frequently until the mixture thickens and pulls away from the pan. Cool play dough. Give each child a lump of play dough, and sprinkle a small amount of purple glitter on the tabletop. The children can work the glitter into the dough.
Caution: Supervision is required with glitter activities.

4. Wacky Watercolors

Combine 1 1/2 tablespoons corn syrup and 3 tablespoons cornstarch. Add 3 tablespoons baking soda and 3 tablespoons vinegar. Mix and watch it foam! Add food coloring of choice (red and blue to make purple). Pour mixture into shallow paint cups, and allow to dry for two days. Use watercolors to create designs on paper.

5. Purple Play Dough Grapes

Make a batch of red play dough and a batch of blue play dough using your favorite play dough recipe. Give each child a small lump of the two play dough colors. The children can squeeze the lumps together to create purple. Then, small balls of play dough can be rolled to represent grapes. Allow to dry if desired.

Cooking

1. Purple Pops

1 3-ounce package grape-flavored gelatin
1 cup boiling water
1 6-ounce can frozen grape juice concentrate
3 cups water
15 3-ounce paper cups
15 wooden sticks

In a medium bowl, dissolve gelatin in boiling water. Add frozen juice concentrate and stir until melted. Add water and stir. Pour about 1/3 cup of juice mixture into each paper cup. Cover each cup with foil. Insert a stick through the foil into the juice mixture. Freeze overnight or until firm. To serve, peel paper cups off pops.

2. Purple Popcorn

10 cups popped popcorn (remove all
    unpopped kernels)
1 cup butter or margarine
3/4 cup sugar
1 3-ounce package grape-flavored gelatin
3 tablespoons water
1 tablespoon light corn syrup

Place the popcorn in a greased 17- × 12- × 2-inch baking dish. Keep popcorn warm in a 300-degree oven while making syrup mixture. In a heavy 2-quart saucepan, combine butter, sugar, gelatin, water, and corn syrup. Cook mixture over medium heat until it boils, stirring constantly. Clip a candy thermometer to the side of the pan. Continue cooking over medium heat, stirring constantly, until the thermometer reaches 255 degrees (hard-ball stage).

Pour syrup mixture over popcorn, and stir gently to coat popcorn. Bake in a 300-degree oven for 5 minutes. Stir once and bake 5 minutes longer. Place popcorn mixture onto a large piece of foil. Cool completely. Break popcorn mixture into clusters. Store in an airtight container. Serves 14–16 children.

3. Purple Pudding

Spoon vanilla pudding into small paper cups. Add a few drops of red and blue food coloring to each cup. Children can stir their pudding with spoons to observe what happens.

4. Purple Cow

Pour 1 quart of milk into a blender. Add one 6-ounce can of frozen grape juice concentrate. Blend until ingredients are well mixed. Pour into cups and serve. Serves six.

5. Purple Coleslaw

6 cups shredded purple cabbage
1 cup sliced purple grapes
1 cup mayonnaise
3 tablespoons lemon juice
2 tablespoons sugar
1 teaspoon salt

Combine mayonnaise, lemon juice, sugar, and salt. Stir in cabbage and grapes. Cover and chill until ready to eat.

Dramatic Play

Flower Shop

Collect artificial flowers, focusing on the color purple if possible, to create a flower shop in the dramatic play area. Additional props for the area could include vases, flower pots, small garden tools, sheets of tissue paper, pictures and posters of flowers, and a cash register. Books on flowers and mail-order catalogs of bulbs and flowers can also be displayed.

Field Trips and Resource People

1. Art or Paint Store

Visit an art supply or paint store. Observe the many shades of purple paints and papers.

2. Flower and Garden Shop

Make arrangements to tour a greenhouse or flower shop. Take note of the varieties of purple-colored flowers and plant leaves.

Fingerplays and Chants

Purple Lollipop

Here is a purple, sweet lollipop.
  (make fist pretending to hold a stick
  of lollipop)
I bought it today at a candy shop.
One lick, mmm, it tastes so good.
  (pretend to lick)
Two licks, oh, I knew it would.
Three licks, yes, I like the taste.
Four licks, now I will not waste.
Five licks, keep on and on.
Six licks, oh! It's nearly gone!
Seven licks, it's getting small.
Eight licks and still not all.
Nine licks, my tongue goes fast.
Ten licks and that's the last!

One Grape and One Grape

One grape and one grape, that makes two.
  (hold up two fingers)
But you have three friends, now what do
  you do?
  (shrug shoulders and hold hands up)
Go to the store and buy a few more.
Then you'll have a whole bunch.
  (hold out arms to create circle shapes)
They're great with your lunch!

Group Time
(Games and Language)

1. "I Spy" Game

Have the children glance around the room. Begin game by saying, "I spy with my little eye something *purple*." Have the children try to guess what the object is. When a player guesses correctly, he or she is the next "spy."

2. Purple Color Bag or Box

Use purple fabric to make a drawstring bag for "Purple Day," or cover a box and lid with purple wrapping paper. Fill the bag or box with small purple items. At circle time, each child in turn can describe an item from the bag or box for others to identify. Repeat the activity throughout the week.

3. **Purple Shapes "Hokey Pokey"**
Cut a set of geometric shapes from purple construction paper for each child to use for this game. Game is played in circle formation.

"Purple Hokey Pokey"
(Sing to the tune of "Hokey Pokey")

Put your purple (shape name) in,
Put your purple (shape name) out,
Put your purple (shape name) in,
And shake it all about.

Do the hokey pokey,
And turn yourself around.
That's what it's all about.

 Large Muscle

Purple Shape March
Using purple construction paper, cut large geometric shapes and tape them to the floor. Play music as the children walk, march, hop, and so forth across the shapes.

 Math

1. **Purple Chain**
Provide 8-inch × 1 1/2-inch strips of purple, lilac, and white construction paper. If necessary, demonstrate to children how to create a paper chain using tape or glue to fasten strips. Encourage children to create a pattern with the colored strips. Display chains in the classroom.

2. **Shades of Purple Sort**
Collect purple paint color strips from a hardware, paint, or building supply store. Have children assist in cutting the color strips apart. The paint chips can be used for sorting activities (light purple, dark purple, etc.) or for counting activities.

 Music

1. **"A Lilac, a Lilac"**
(Sing to the tune of "A Tisket, a Tasket")

A lilac, a lilac, a pretty purple lilac.
There's a lilac bush on the way to school.
And on the way I picked some,
I picked some, I picked some.
And on the way I picked some.
There's a lilac bush on the way to school.
And on the way I picked some.

2. **"Purple Things"**
(Sing to the tune of "Mary Had a Little Lamb")

Many things are colored purple,
Colored purple, colored purple.
Many things are colored purple,
Can you think of some?

3. **"Here's a Grape"**
(Sing to the tune of "Hot Cross Buns")

Here's a grape,
A purple grape.
What a yummy little fruit,
A purple grape.

 Science

1. **Purple Bubble Prints**
In a small plastic bowl or cup, mix 1 tablespoon purple liquid tempera paint with 2 tablespoons liquid dishwashing detergent, and gently stir in a small amount of water. One child at a time can put a straw in the paint mixture and blow until bubbles rise above the rim of the bowl or cup. Remove the straw, and lay a piece of white paper on top of the bubbles. As the bubbles pop, they will leave prints on the paper.

Note: Supervise this activity closely.

2. **Purple Carnation**
Insert a white carnation into a clear glass or vase of water. To the water, add drops of red and blue food coloring to create a dark

purple. In a few days, the children should be able to observe the petals of the flower turning purple.

3. **Purple Glasses**

Help the children view the world through purple-tinted eyeglasses. For each child, cut frame shapes out of tagboard. Assist the children in gluing purple cellophane squares over the eye holes. Attach chenille stems to the sides of the frames, and bend them to fit over the children's ears.

4. **Making Raisins**

Purchase 1 or 2 pounds of purple grapes. Wash them thoroughly. Spread grapes in a single layer on baking sheets. Dry by placing in a sunny windowsill for several days or by baking in a slow oven. To bake, turn the oven to 165 degrees and let fruit dry for eight hours. Turn off the oven, and leave the fruit in it overnight.

Sensory

1. **Purple Water**

Add red and blue food coloring to 3 inches of water in the sensory table. Add water toys (look for purple ones!) as tools to explore the properties of water.

2. **Purple Shaving Cream**

Spray the contents of one or two cans of shaving cream in a sensory table. Color the shaving cream purple by mixing in drops of red and blue food coloring.

3. **Purple Goop**

In a sensory table or dishpan, combine 2 cups cornstarch, 2 cups water, and red and blue food coloring.

Social Studies

Occupation: Painter

Invite a local house painter to come to the classroom and talk about his or her job. If possible, perhaps painting tools and supplies could be shown and demonstrated.

Books

The following books can be used to complement this theme:

Adams, Jean Ekman. (2000). *Clarence Goes Out West and Meets a Purple Horse.* Flagstaff, AZ: Rising Moon.

Burrowes, Adjoa J. (2000). *Grandma's Purple Flowers.* New York: Lee & Low Books.

German, Donna Rathmell. (2006). *Octavia and Her Purple Ink Cloud.* Illustrated by Connie McLennan. Mt. Pleasant, SC: Sylvan Dell Publishing.

Jenkins, Steve. (2007). *Living Color.* Boston: Houghton Mifflin.

Johnson, Crockett. (1965). *Harold and the Purple Crayon.* New York: Harper and Brothers.

Kessler, Leonard P. (2000). *Mr. Pine's Purple House.* Keller, TX: Purple House Press.

Low, Alice. (2004). *Blueberry Mouse.* Illustrated by David Friend. New York: Mondo.

Martin, Bill, Jr. (1992). *Brown Bear, Brown Bear, What Do You See?* Illustrated by Eric Carle. New York: H. Holt.

Schuette, Sarah L. (2003). *Purple: Seeing Purple All around Us.* Mankato, MN: Capstone Press.

Shannon, George. (2005). *White Is for Blueberry.* Illustrated by Laura Dronzek. New York: Greenwillow Press.

Williams, Rozanne Lanczak, and Mary Grandpre. (2000). *The Purple Snerd.* Illustrated by Mary Grandpre. San Diego, CA: Harcourt Brace.

Technology and Multimedia

The following technology and multimedia products can be used to complement this theme:

"Color Parade" [CD]. (1993). In *Can A Cherry Pie Wave Goodbye?* Sherman Oaks, CA: Hap-Pal Music.

"Colors" [CD]. 2010. In *Rock and Roll Garden.* New York: Bari Koral Family Rock Band.

"De Colores" [CD]. (1996). In *One Light, One Song.* Cambridge, MA: Rounder/UMGD.

"De Colores" [CD]. (2010). In *Pete Seeger, Tomorrow's Children.* Westchester, PA: Appleseed Records.

Discovering Colors [DVD]. (2006).Long Beach, CA: Visual Entertainment.

Planting a Rainbow [DVD]. (2005). Norwalk, CT: Weston Woods Studios/Scholastic.

Reading Rainbow. (2007). *Legend of the Indian Paintbrush* [DVD]. Lincoln, NE: GPN Educational Media.

 Additional teaching resources to accompany this Theme can be found on the book's companion website. Go to www.cengagebrain.com to access the site for a variety of useful resources.

RAIN

Effects
rainbow
puddles
mud
floods

Origins
clouds

Watering
plants
crops
grass

Filling
creeks
ponds
lakes
rivers
ocean

Uses

Drinking and Bathing
people
animals

Clothing
rain hat
raincoat
rain shoes
umbrella

Forms
drizzle
shower
snow, dew, hail

Measurements
gauge

Theme Goals

Through participating in the experiences provided by this theme, the children may learn:

1. Uses of rain
2. Effects of rain
3. Clothing worn for protection from the rain
4. Forms of rain
5. Origin of rain
6. The tool used for the measurement of rain

Concepts for the Children to Learn

1. Rain are the drops of water that fall from the clouds in the sky.
2. Rain can fall in the form of drizzle, dew, hail, snow, or a shower.
3. Rain can be used for watering lawns, plants, crops, and grass.
4. Rain fills ponds, creeks, lakes, rivers, and oceans.
5. A rainbow sometimes appears when it rains while the sun is shining.
6. A rainbow is colorful.
7. An umbrella is used in the rain to keep us dry.
8. Raincoats, hats, and rubber shoes are clothing worn in the rain to keep us dry.
9. Puddles of water can form during a rainfall.
10. The amount of rain can be measured by a tool called a water gauge.
11. Farmers need rain to water the crops.
12. Rain waters people's outdoor plants and grass.
13. People and animals can use rainwater for drinking and bathing.
14. Mud is formed when soil is mixed with water.

Vocabulary

1. **gauge**—a tool for measuring rain.
2. **puddle**—a shallow pool of water often made by rain.
3. **rain**—drops of water that fall from the clouds in the sky.
4. **rainbow**—a colorful band of many colors that stretches across the sky. It is formed when the sun is reflected in raindrops, spray, or mist.
5. **snow**—frozen drops of water. When it is cold during winter, snow comes from the clouds.
6. **umbrella**—a tool held in the hand to protect against rain, sun, or snow.

Bulletin Board

The purpose of this bulletin board is to develop an awareness of sets, as well as to identify written numerals. Interaction with the board will also promote visual discrimination, problem-solving, and hand-eye coordination skills. Construct clouds out of gray tagboard. Write a numeral on each cloud. Cut out and laminate. Next, trace and cut cloud shadows from construction paper. Attach the shadows to the bulletin board. A set of raindrops, from 1 to 10, should be attached underneath each cloud shadow. Magnet pieces or pushpins and holes in the cloud piece can be used for the children to match each cloud to a corresponding shadow, using the raindrops as a clue.

Family Letter

Dear Families,

"Rain, rain, go away/Come again some other day" is a familiar nursery rhyme. It is one that we may often hear as our theme on rain begins. Through the experiences provided, the children will become aware of the origins, effects, uses, and forms of rain as well as how rainbows are created. They will become aware of the clothing worn in the rain.

At School

The following activities are just a few that have been planned for the rain unit:

- A visit by TV 8's weatherman: Tom Hector will come at 2:00 p.m. on Tuesday to show us a video made for preschoolers that depicts various weather conditions.

- Finding out about evaporation by setting out a shallow pan of water and marking the water level each day

- Creating a rainbow on a sunny day outdoors with a garden hose

At Home

To develop language skills, practice this rain poem with your child:

> Rain on the green grass
> And rain on trees.
> Rain on the rooftops,
> But not on me!!

Use an empty can or jar to make a rain gauge. Place the container outdoors to measure rainfall. Several gauges could be placed in various places in your yard.

Enjoy your child!

Arts and Crafts

1. **Eyedropper Painting**
   Use eyedroppers filled with colored water as applicators.

2. **Waxed Paper Rainbows**
   Cut waxed paper in the shape of large rainbows. Then prepare red, yellow, green, and blue crayon shavings. After this, the children can sprinkle the crayon shavings on one sheet of waxed paper. Place another sheet of waxed paper on the top of the sheet with sprinkled crayon. Finally, the teacher should place a towel over the top of the waxed paper sheets. A warm iron should be applied to melt the two pieces together. Cool and attach a string. Hang from the window.
   Caution: This activity needs constant adult supervision.

3. **Rainbow Yarn Collage**
   Using rainbow-shaped paper and rainbow-colored yarn, the children can make rainbow yarn collages.

4. **Thunder Painting**
   Tape-record a rain or thunderstorm. Leave this tape, with a tape recorder and earphones, at the easel. Gray, black, and white paint can be provided. Let the children listen to the rainstorm and paint to it. Ask the children how the music makes them feel.

5. **Rainbow Mobiles**
   Precut rainbow arcs. On these, the children can paste Styrofoam packing pieces. After this, they can paint the pieces. Display the mobiles in the room.

6. **Crêpe Paper Water**
   Cut strips of colored crêpe paper. Provide small bowls of water. Encourage the children to dip the crêpe paper into the bowls of water. Observe the change in color.

Cooking

Rainbow Fruits
Serve a different colored snack each day to correspond with the colors of the rainbow.

- Strawberries
- Oranges
- Lemon finger gelatin
  (see a gelatin box for recipe)
- Blueberries added to yogurt
- Grape juice
- Grapes or blackberries
- Lettuce salad

Dramatic Play

1. **Rainy Day Clothing**
   Umbrellas, raincoats, hats, rain shoes, and a tape containing rain sounds should be added to the dramatic play area.
   Caution: Be careful when selecting umbrellas for this activity. Some open quickly and can be dangerous.

2. **Weather Station**
   A map, a pointer, adult clothing, and a pretend microphone should be placed in the dramatic play area. The children can play weather person. Pictures depicting different weather conditions can be included.

Field Trips and Resource People

1. **Reflection**
   Take a walk after it rains. Enjoy the puddles, overflowing gutters, and swirls of water caught by sewers. Look in the puddles. Does anyone see a reflection? Look up in the sky. Do you see any clouds, the sun, or a rainbow? What colors are in a rainbow?

2. **The Weather Person**
   Take a field trip to a television station and see what equipment a weather person uses.

Fingerplays and Chants

Little Raindrop

This is the sun, high up in the sky.
    (hold hands in circle above head)
A dark cloud suddenly comes sailing by.
    (slide hands to side)
These are the raindrops,
    (make raining motion with fingers)
Pitter patter down,
Watering the flowers,
    (pouring motion)
Growing on the ground.
    (hands pat the ground)

Rainy Day Fun

Slip on your raincoat.
    (pretend to put coat on)
Pull up your galoshes.
    (pretend to pull up galoshes)
Wade in puddles,
Make splishes and sploshes.
    (make stomping motions)

Thunderstorm

Boom, bang, boom, bang!
    (clap hands)
Rumpety, lumpety, bump!
    (stomp feet)
Zoom, zam, zoom, zam!
    (swish hands together)
Rustles and bustles
    (pat thighs)
And swishes and zings!
    (pat thighs)
What wonderful noises
A thunderstorm brings.

Rain

From big black clouds
    (hold up arms)
The raindrop fell.
    (pull finger down in air)
Drip, drip, drip one day,
    (hit one finger on palm of hand)

Until the bright sunlight changed them
Into a rainbow gay!
    (make a rainbow with hands)
Note: First four fingerplays (above) from Wilmes, Dick, and Liz Wilmes. *Everyday Circle Times.* (1983). Mt. Rainier, MD: Distributed by Gryphon House.

Group Time
(Games and Language)

Jump in Puddles

This game is played like "Musical Chairs." The puddles are made from circles on the floor with one child in each and one fewer circle than children so one child is not in a circle. On the signal "Jump in the puddles," the children have to switch puddles. The child who was out has a chance to get in a puddle. The child who does not get into a puddle waits until the next round. This can be played indoors or outdoors. Hula hoops could also be used in small groups of four children using three hoops. (This activity is most appropriate for older children.)

Large Muscle

Worm Wiggle

The purpose of this game is to imitate worm motions. Show the children how to lie on their stomachs, holding their arms in at their sides. The children should try to move forward without using their hands or elbows like a worm would wiggle.

Math

Rainbow Match

Fabrics of all the colors of the rainbow can be cut into pieces. The children can sort these and group them into different colors, textures, and sizes.

Music

1. "Rainy"
(Sing to the tune of "B-I-N-G-O")
(Repeat each verse, eliminating a letter and substituting it with a clap until the last chorus is all claps to the same beat.)
There was a day when we got wet
and rainy was the weather
R-A-I-N-Y, R-A-I-N-Y, R-A-I-N-Y
and rainy was the weather.

2. "Rain, Rain, Go Away"
Rain, rain, go away.
Come again another day.
Clouds, clouds, go away.
Little children want to play.
Thunder, thunder, go away.
Little children want to play.
Rain, rain, come back soon.
Little flowers want to bloom.

Science

1. Tasting Water
Collect tap water, soda water, mineral water, and distilled water. Pour the different types of water into paper cups, and let children taste them. Discuss the differences.

2. Evaporation
The children can pour water into a clear, plastic jar. Mark a line at the water level. Place the jar on a window ledge and check it every day. The disappearance is called evaporation.

3. Catching Water
If it rains one day during your unit, place a bucket outside to catch the rain. Return the bucket to your science table. Place a bucket of tap water next to the rainwater, and compare.

4. Color Mixing
Using water and food coloring or tempera, mix the primary colors. Discuss the colors of the rainbow.

5. Ice Cubes Observation
Fill three ice cube trays with water. Place one in the sun, one in the refrigerator, and the third in a freezer. Encourage the children to observe. Then ask what happened and why.

Sensory

Additions to the Sensory Table

- Water with scoops, cups, and spoons
- Sand and water (Make puddles in the sand.)
- Rainbow-colored sand, rice, and pasta
- Rainwater
- Measuring cups
- Colanders
- Thermometers
- Water wheels
- Fishing bobs
- Hoses
- Nesting cups
- Scrub brushes
- Toy boats
- Dish detergent

Books

The following books can be used to complement this theme:

Arnosky, Jim. (1997). *Rabbits and Raindrops.* New York: Putnam.

Base, Graeme. (2001). *The Water Hole.* New York: Harry N. Abrams.

Conway, David. (2009). *Lila and the Secret of the Rain.* London: Frances Lincoln.

Cotton, Cynthia. (2008). *Rain Play.* New York: Henry Holt.

Gibbons, Gail. (2009) *Hurricanes!* New York: Holiday House.

Goin, Miriam. (2009). *Storms!* Washington, DC: National Geographic.

Hallowell, Edward M. (2004). *A Walk in the Rain with a Brain.* Illustrated by Bill Mayer. New York: ReganBooks.

Herman, Charolette. (2010). *First Rain.* Chicago: Albert Whitman & Co.

Iwamura, Kazuo. (2010). *Hooray for Summer.* Fitzgerald, GA: North South.

Kurtz, Jane. (2002). *Rain Romp.* New York: Greenwillow Books.

Lehman, Barbara. (2007). *Rainstorm.* New York: Houghton Mifflin.

Macken, JoAnn Early. (2010). *Waiting Out the Rain.* Illustrated by Susan Gaber. Somerville, MA: Candlewick Press.

Munsch, Robert N. (1982). *Mud Puddle.* Illustrated by Sami Suomalainen. Toronto: Annick Press.

Ray, Mary Lyn. (2000). *Red Rubber Boot Day.* Illustrated by Lauren Stringer. Orlando, FL: Harcourt.

Ray, Mary Lyn. (2001). *Mud.* Illustrated by Lauren Stringer. New York: Harcourt.

Rustad, Martha E. H. (2006). *Today Is Rainy.* Mankato, MN: Capstone Press.

Schaefer, Lola M., and Jane Wattenberg. (2001). *This Is the Rain.* Illustrated by Jane Wattenberg. New York: Greenwillow.

Shannon, David. (2000). *The Rain Came Down.* New York: Blue Sky Press.

Stojic, Manya. (2009). *Rain.* New York: Dragonfly Books.

Tekavec, Heather. (2002). *Storm Is Coming.* Illustrated by Margaret Spengler. New York: Dial Books for Young Readers.

Wong, Herbert Yee. (2007). *Who Likes Rain?* New York: H. Holt.

Technology and Multimedia

The following technology and multimedia products can be used to complement this theme:

"After It Rains" [CD]. (2010). In *Laurie Berkner: Under a Shady Tree.* New York: Two Tomatoes.

Bringing the Rain to Kapiti Plain [DVD]. (2007). Lincoln, NE: Distributed by GPN.

"Brush Your Teeth" [CD]. (1976). In *Singable Songs for the Very Young.* Cambridge, MA: Rounder/UMGD.

Jim Henson's The Song of the Cloud Forest and Other Earth Stories [DVD]. (2010). Los Angeles: Lionsgate.

"Raining like Magic" [CD]. (2002). In *Raffi, Let's Play.* Cambridge, MA: Rounder/UMGD.

"Rain Song" [CD]. (1995). In *Piggyback Songs.* Long Branch, NJ: Kimbo Educational.

Rainy Day Stories [DVD]. (2005). Norwalk, CT: Weston Woods Studios.

Sid the Science Kid: Weather Kid Sid [DVD]. (2009). Dallas, TX: Distributed by NCircle Entertainment.

"Singing in the Rain" [CD]. (1997). In *Rock 'n' Roll Songs That Teach.* The Learning Station. Long Branch, NJ: Kimbo Educational.

"Singin' in the Rain" [CD]. (2000). In *Charlotte Diamond's World.* Vancouver, BC: Hug Bug Records.

"Thunderstorm" [CD]. (2008). In *Rocketship Run.* New York: Two Tomatoes.

Totally Tropical Rain Forest [DVD]. (2004). Washington, DC: National Geographic.

The Umbrella [DVD]. (2008). Holmes, New York: Spoken Arts.

Water and Weather: Ecosystems and Environment [DVD]. (2007) Venice, CA: TMW Media Group.

 Additional teaching resources to accompany this Theme can be found on the book's companion website. Go to www.cengagebrain.com to access the site for a variety of useful resources.

RAMADAN

Foods
rice porridge
fruit with coconut
cinnamon and dates
hummus and vegetables
curry and tandoori dishes
lentil soup

Preparation
decorate the house with
candles and lights
get ready for the new
moon

Celebration
wear new or finest clothes
and shoes
eat dinner with family and
friends after dark
receive gifts and gold coins
from relatives
celebrate Eid-al-Fitr, give
treats to children

greet others with
a hug and "Eid mubarak,"
which means "holiday
blessings"
collect food and money
for people in need
give thanks
special prayers

Theme Goals

Through participating in the experiences provided by this theme, the children may learn:

1. Special foods eaten during Ramadan
2. Preparation for Ramadan
3. Ways to celebrate Ramadan

Concepts for the Children to Learn

1. Ramadan is a month-long Muslim holiday.
2. Ramadan begins with the cycle of the new moon.
3. Children look forward to wearing new clothes and shoes.
4. People decorate their homes with candles and lights.
5. Adults fast (they don't eat or drink) between breakfast and dinner during the month of Ramadan.
6. Special prayers are said during the month of Ramadan.
7. People who observe Ramadan think about those who are less fortunate, and give money and food to the poor.
8. Ramadan celebrations include having special dinners with family and friends.
9. Some foods eaten during Ramadan include rice porridge; lentil soup; hummus and vegetables; curry and tandoori; and fruits with cinnamon, coconut and dates.
10. Ramadan ends with a three-day Eid festival.
11. People say "Eid mubarak," which means "holiday blessings."
12. Children eat treats and receive gifts or gold coins from relatives.

Vocabulary

1. **appreciate**—feel grateful for something or someone.
2. **Eid**—three-day celebration at the end of Ramadan (full name is Eid-al-fitr).
3. **lunar**—related to the moon or its movement.
4. **lunar calendar**—marking time according to changes in the moon.
5. **Muslim**—a person who follows the religion of Islam.
6. **new moon**—when the moon is directly between the earth and sun and you can't really see it.
7. **Ramadan**—means "parched thirst" and is a 30-day Muslim holiday observed in the ninth month of the Islamic lunar calendar.
8. **tandoori dishes**—meals cooked in a clay container.

Bulletin Board

The purpose of this bulletin board is to aid in visual and number-matching skills. Construct and cut a large black circle out of construction paper. Using white chalk, draw a line down the middle to create two halves. On each half, draw three crescent-shaped "slices" for a total of six crescents all together. Number the slices 1–6, laminate the circle, and hang it on the bulletin board. Repeat the process on a white piece of paper, and once the crescents are numbered, go ahead and actually cut the six numbered slices apart. Punch a hole in the top of each numbered piece with a paper punch. Attach a pushpin several inches above each numbered slice. The children can match the numbered crescents to the ones on the full moon in the middle of the bulletin board.

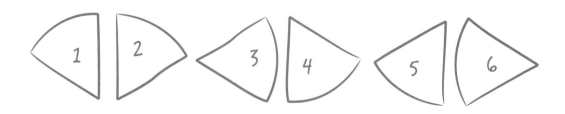

Family Letter

InBox

Dear Families,

Our next theme is Ramadan, the ninth month in the Islamic lunar calendar when Muslims over 12 all over the world fast daily from dawn to sunset to work toward self-purification and betterment.

Naturally, you may be asking, "Why introduce Ramadan to such young children?" Your children may not fully understand the history or meaning of Ramadan, but learning about this Muslim holiday can be part of their ongoing development and knowledge of the world. Through all of our multicultural holiday themes, children gain a valuable window into how others live, celebrate, tell stories, and spend time together.

At School
Some planned activities include:

- Doing art and science explorations related to the moon (lunar cycles)
- Making a charity jar to collect for those less fortunate
- Preparing and eating rice pudding and fruit salad with dates
- Counting and marching all the way to 30

Parent Involvement
If you have special knowledge or experience observing Ramadan, we would love to have you share it with our class. Please contact me so a time can be arranged for your visit.

Kul'am wa entra bi-khair! (May every year find you in good health!)

Arts and Crafts

1. **New Crescent Moon**
   Using a white crayon, draw a thin crescent moon on white paper. (The holiday begins at the new moon, but this is a phase we can't actually see.) Press hard with the crayon as you draw the shape of the moon. Give the children some black tempera paint mixed with a little water. Show them how to paint over your drawing to reveal a new crescent moon in the black night sky.

2. **Foil Moons**
   Precut thin crescent moon shapes with aluminum foil. Have the children glue the crescent moon shapes onto pieces of black construction paper. You can also give them a few silver star stickers to add to their pictures.

3. **Crescent Moon Play Dough Shapes**
   Roll out play dough circles, and show children how to create crescent moon shapes. (Slice each circle in half, then slice each half into three pieces to create crescent shapes.) Or use a crescent moon–shaped cookie cutter, along with a letter "R" cookie cutter for Ramadan.

   You can also have children make circular coins out of gold- or silver-colored play dough. Children often receive coins as gifts at the end of Ramadan.

4. **New Clothes Group Collage**
   Look through magazines, store catalogs, and appropriate advertisements for pictures of children (and adults) wearing new clothes. Cut or have the children cut these pictures out. Invite them to glue the pictures onto a large piece of construction paper to make a group collage of clothes that might be fun to wear for an Eid-al-Fitr celebration. You can also have the children make individual collages of new clothes.

5. **Festival Coin Bank**
   Rinse and dry small milk cartons (one for each child), and staple the tops closed.

On each milk carton, cut coin slots in one of the slanted sides. Have children cover the carton with tempera paint mixed with a small amount of dishwashing liquid (to help the paint adhere). After the paint dries, help children collect and count pennies as they drop them in the slots. You can give each child 5–10 pennies, invite them to bring them from home, or use plastic coins.

Cooking

1. **Hummus, Pita, and Vegetables**
   Help children dip pita bread triangles and raw vegetables (carrot sticks, celery sticks, green beans, and snap peas) into store-bought hummus.

2. **Fruit Salad with Chopped Dates and Flaked Coconut**
   Cut up some fresh fruit and serve it to children with chopped dates and flaked coconut as toppings.

3. **Rice Pudding with Dates**
   2 cups cooked white rice
   2 cups 2% milk
   3 tablespoons white sugar
   15 dates, pitted and chopped

   Place the rice in a food processor or blender, and process until coarse but not pureed. Transfer to a saucepan. Stir in the milk, sugar, and dates. Cook over a low heat, stirring occasionally until the dates are tender, about 20 minutes.

4. **Spiced Pears and Pomegranate**
   3 pears, peeled, cored, and cut into wedges
   1 pomegranate, skin and rind removed
   1 tablespoon fresh lemon juice
   2 tablespoons light brown sugar
   1/2 teaspoon ground cinnamon
   4 sprigs fresh mint leaves for garnish (optional)

   Place the sliced pears and pomegranate seeds into a bowl. Toss with lemon juice to coat. Combine the brown sugar and cinnamon in a small cup or bowl, then mix into the fruit. Cover and refrigerate for at least 1 hour before serving to blend the flavors. Garnish with a sprig of mint.

Dramatic Play

1. Have a Feast for Eid
Set up a feast center by putting out plates, cups, cutlery, and a tablecloth, along with a variety of plastic fruits and vegetables. Invite the children to create and enjoy a make-believe feast.

2. Decorate for Ramadan
Have children clean up your center and decorate with streamers, strings of lights, crescent moons, and other decorations for the Eid celebration at the end of Ramadan. Cover tagboard stars in tin foil, and help children string them across the room.

3. New Clothes
Bring in dress-up clothes and shoes. Invite the children to get dressed up for Ramadan.

Field Trips and Resource People

1. Invite a Visitor
Invite someone who celebrates Ramadan to come visit your site. Have them talk with the children about how they and their family observe and celebrate the holiday. Encourage the visitor to bring any artifacts and pictures they may have.

2. Helping Others
Remind the children that during Eid (the last three days of Ramadan), families remember the needy by sharing food. Help the children put together a basket or bags of nonperishable food items such as soups, pasta, tuna fish, beans, and cereal. Then take the items to a local food bank or family shelter. You might want to check ahead of time to find out what kinds of foods are needed.

Fingerplays and Chants

1. Ten Little Stars
(Sing to the tune of "Ten Little Indians")

One little, two little, three little stars,
  (hold up and add one finger at a time as you count)
Four little, five little, six little stars.
  (hold up and add one finger at a time as you count)
Seven little, eight little, nine little stars,
  (hold up and add one finger at a time as you count)
Ten stars in the sky.
  (wiggle all ten fingers above your head)

Group Time
(Games and Language)

1. Who Stole the Pear? (Or Any Plastic Food Item)
Play this game by having children sit in a circle with a plastic food item in the middle. Ask player number 1 to leave the area for one minute. Identify one child who will "steal the pear" and hide it in his or her lap or under a leg. Invite player number 1 back to stand in the middle, look around, and guess who stole the pear. When he or she guesses correctly, the two players switch places. (Or, if player number 1 does not guess after three guesses, player number 1 reveals him or herself and the players switch places.) Player number 2 goes out of the room, a new player is chosen to "steal the pear," and the game repeats.

2. Costume Fun
Halfway through Ramadan, Muslim kids often celebrate Girgian (which means "mixture of things") by dressing up in costumes and go door-to-door collecting candy and money from friends and neighbors. Get out the dress-up clothes and have the children play a game of dress-up and door-to-door by pretending to give each other candy. You can also have them give each other pretend gold coins.

Math

1. **Full Moon**
Cut out circles. Cut each circle in half, then cut each half into three pieces to create six crescent-shaped moons. Number the pieces on the back to help children remember which piece comes next. Have children put the moon together by putting the pieces in order to put the circle back together. Explain to the children that each piece represents a stage of the moon, and it would take two weeks or 14 days for the moon to develop into a full moon.

2. **Count to Eid**
At the beginning of Ramadan, mark the first day of Ramadan with a colorful number 1 on a big calendar, and then mark the beginning of the Eid-al-Fitr, or Eid, festival, which everyone looks forward to. (Eid-al-Fitr begins on day 27 and lasts for three days.) Each day, invite children to gather round while one child puts a sticker on the calendar to mark the current day. Then you can count or sing aloud together to see how many days are left until Eid.

    Tip: To find out when Ramadan begins, you might want to search the Internet for "Ramadan calendar 2012" or whatever year it happens to be.

Music

1. **"Ramadan Is Coming Soon"**
(Sing to the tune of "Mary Had a Little Lamb")

Ramadan is coming soon,
Coming soon, coming soon,
Ramadan is coming soon,
Time to fast all day.
When we see the thin new moon,
Thin new moon, thin new moon,
When we see the thin new moon,
We'll celebrate and play.

Science

1. **Moon Chart**
Invite parents and children to look at the moon each night and take time during the day to ask children what they saw. Draw what they describe every day or two on a moon chart. Explain how the Islamic calendar is based on phases of the moon. You can also do this by having different moon phases (crescent, half, and full) on a felt or Velcro board and help them pick the one that looks most like the current moon phase.

Social Studies

1. **Ramadan Greetings**
Teach the children some Arabic greetings for the Ramadan holiday.

    - "Eid Saeed!" means "Happy Eid!" and is said during the three-day festival at the end of Ramadan.
    - "Kul'am wa entra bi-khair!" means "May every year find you in good health!"

2. **Charity Jar**
Ramadan is the time of year to remember the poor and needy. Charity is a big part of the celebration. Bring in a large jar, and help the children decorate it with stickers, ribbons, and glitter glue. Have them collect coins in the jar by bringing some to school. (You will want to send home a note to parents explaining what the coins are being collected for.) At the end of the month, help the children count the change and decide which charity that helps feed or cloth those in need to give it to.

3. **Ramadan Calendar Chain**
Cut six-inch lengths of construction paper. Each child will need 30 lengths, one for each day until the end of Ramadan. The children can use paste, transparent tape, or a stapler to connect the links of the chain.

 **Books**

The following books can be used to complement this theme:

Addasi, Maha. (2008). *The White Nights of Ramadan.* Illustrated by Ned Gannon. Honesdale, PA: Boyds Mills Press.

Dickmann, Heidi. (2010). *Ramadan and Id-ul-fitr.* Acorn: Holidays and Festivals. Portsmouth, NH: Heinemann Press.

Dickmann, Nancy. (2011). *Ramandan and id-ul-Fitr.* Chicago: Heinemann Publishers.

Dougherty, Terri. (2006). *Ramadan: Islamic Holy Month.* First Facts: Holidays and Culture. Mankato, MN: Capstone Press.

Gilani-Williams, Fawzia. (2010). *Nabid's New Pants: An Eid Tale.* Illustrated by Proiti Roy. Tarrytown, NY: Marshall Cavendish Children's Books.

Hall, M. C. (2010). *Ramadan.* Little World Holidays and Celebrations. Vero Beach, Florida: Rourke Publishing.

Hamed, Melissa. (2007). *The Last Night of Ramadan.* Illustrated by Mohamed El Wakil. Great Barrington, MA: Bell Pond Books.

Hamid Ghazi, Suhaib. (1996). *Ramadan.* Illustrated by Omar Rayya. New York: Holiday House.

Heiligman, Deborah. (2009). *Holidays around the World: Celebrate Ramadan and Eid-al-Fitr.* Washington, DC: National Geographic Children's Books.

Jalali, Reza. (2010). *Moon Watchers: Shirin's Ramadan Miracle.* Illustrated by Anne Sibley O'Brien. Gardiner, ME: Tilbury House Publishers.

Katz, Karen. (2007). *My First Ramadan.* Illustrated by Laura Jacobsen. New York: Henry Holt.

Kerven, Rosalind. (2011). *Ramadan and Id-Ul-Fitr.* Festivals and Faiths. London: Evans Brothers.

Marx, David F. (2002). *Ramadan.* Rookie Read-About Holidays. Danbury, CT: Children's Press.

Mobin-Uddin, Asma. (2007). *The Best Eid Ever.* Illustrated by Laura Jacobsen. Honesdale, PA: Boyds Mills Press.

Mobin-Uddin, Asma, and Laura Jacobsen. (2009). *A Party in Ramadan.* Honesdale, PA: Boyds Mills Press.

Na'ima, Robert B. (2009). *Ramadan Moon.* Illustrated by Shirin Adl. London: Frances Lincoln Children's Books.

Pirotta, Saviour. (2007). *Id-Ul-fitr.* We Love Holidays. New York: PowerKids Press.

Whitman, Sylvia. (2008). *Under the Ramadan Moon.* Illustrated by Sue Williams. Park Ridge, IL: Albert Whitman & Company.

Worsham, Adria F. (2008). *Max Celebrates Ramadan.* Read-It! Readers. Illustrated by Mernie Gallagher-Cole. Mankato, MN: Picture Window Books.

Zucker, Jonny. (2004). *Fasting and Dates: A Ramadan and Eid-ul-Fitr Story.* Festival Time! Illustrated by Jan Barger. Hauppauge, NY: Barron's Educational Series.

Zucker, Jonny. (2004). *Sweet Dates to Eat: A Ramadan and Eid Story.* Festival Time! Illustrated by Jan Barger. London: Frances Lincoln Publishers.

 Additional teaching resources to accompany this Theme can be found on the book's companion website. Go to www.cengagebrain.com to access the site for a variety of useful resources.

Theme 61
RED

Food	Flowers	Color Mixing	Signs
apples	roses	red + yellow =	stop (danger)
strawberries	tulips	orange	traffic light
raspberries	carnations	red + blue =	fire trucks (some)
cherries		purple	fire hydrants
tomatoes		red + white = pink	(some)
beets			
radishes			

Theme Goals

Through participating in the experiences provided by this theme, the children may learn:

1. Red can be mixed with other colors to make different colors
2. Some foods are red
3. Some flowers are colored red
4. Red signs

Concepts for the Children to Learn

1. Red is a primary color.
2. Some foods, such as apples, tomatoes, beets, radishes, raspberries, cherries, and strawberries, are a red color.
3. Some flowers are colored red.
4. Red can be mixed with other colors to create a new color.
5. Red and yellow mixed together make orange.
6. Red and blue mixed together make purple.
7. Red and white mixed together make pink.
8. Some fire trucks and fire hydrants are red.
9. Red signs warn us of danger.
10. A stop sign is colored red.
11. Some flowers are red.
12. Roses, tulips, and carnations can be a red color.

Vocabulary

1. **primary colors**—red, yellow, and blue are primary colors.
2. **red**—a primary color. Strawberries are red.

Bulletin Board

The purpose of this bulletin board is to reinforce the mathematical skills of matching sets of objects to a written numeral. Green produce baskets or other small baskets can be hung on the bulletin board for a strawberry-counting bulletin board. Attach baskets to the bulletin boards using staples or pushpins. Collect small plastic strawberries, or make strawberries out of tagboard. On each basket, mark a numeral. The children can place the appropriate number of strawberries into each basket.

Family Letter

Dear Families,

Colors are everywhere, and they make our world beautiful. That's why we'll focus on a specific color during our next curriculum theme: the color red! It's a popular color with young children, and many objects in our world are red. The experiences provided will also help the children become aware of colors that are formed when mixed with red.

At School

A few of the curriculum experiences include:

- Mixing the color red with yellow (to make orange) and blue (to make purple)

- Setting up an art store in the dramatic play area where the children can act out the buying and selling of art supplies

- Exploring red-colored crayons, markers, pencils, chalk, paint, and paper

- Filling the sensory table with red goop

- Listening to stories related to the color red

At Home

To reinforce the concepts in this unit, try the following activities at home with your child:

- To develop observation skills, look around your house with your child for red items. How many red objects can you find in each room?

- Prepare meals using red foods such as apples, strawberries, tomatoes, and jam.

- Prepare red ice cubes to cool your drinks. To do this, just add a few drops of red food coloring to the water before freezing it.

Enjoy making colorful discoveries with your child.

Arts and Crafts

1. Red Paint
Red and white paint can be provided at the easels. By mixing these colors, children can discover shades of red.

2. Red Crayon Rubbings
Red crayons, red paper, or both can be used to do this activity. Place an object such as a penny, button, or leaf under paper. Use the flat edge of a crayon to color over the item. An image of the object will appear on the paper.

3. Paint Blots
Fold a piece of paper in half. Open up and place a spoonful of red paint on the inside of the paper. Refold paper, and press flat. Reopen and observe the design. Add two colors such as blue and yellow, and repeat the process to show color mixing.

4. Paint over Design
Paint over a crayon picture with watery red paint. Observe how the paint will not cover the crayon marks.

5. Glitter Pictures
The children make a design using glue on a piece of paper. Shake red glitter onto the glue. Shake the excess glitter into a pan. *Caution:* Carefully supervise this activity.

6. Red Fingerpaint
Red fingerpaint and foil should be placed on an art table. Yellow and blue paint can be added to explore color mixing.

7. Shaving Cream Fingerpainting
Spray a small amount of fingerpaint in front of each child who wishes to participate in the activity. Then provide each child with a small amount of colored tempera paint or food coloring. Encourage the child to blend the shaving cream and food coloring. Then they can use this medium for fingerpainting.

Cooking

Raspberry Slush

4 10-ounce packages frozen raspberries
1 6-ounce can frozen lemonade concentrate, thawed
2 quarts ginger ale, chilled

Thaw and cook raspberries for 10 minutes. Use a wooden spoon to rub the cooked raspberries through a strainer. Cool. Add lemonade concentrate. Just before serving, stir in ginger ale. Makes 24 servings, about 1/2 cup each.

Dramatic Play

1. Art Store
Set up an art supply store. Include paints, crayons, markers, paper, chalk, brushes, money, and a cash register.

2. Fire Station
Firefighter hats can be added to the dramatic play area.

3. Colored Hats
After reading *Caps for Sale* by Esphyr Slobodkina, set out colored hats for children to use to retell the story.

Field Trips and Resource People

1. Art Store
Visit an art store. Observe all the red items for sale.

2. Take a Walk
Take a walk around the neighborhood, and look for red objects.

3. Floral Shop
Visit a floral shop, and specifically observe red flowers.

4. Fire Station

Visit a fire station. Note the color of the engine, hats, sirens, and other red items.

5. Resource People

Invite the following resource people to the classroom:

- Artist
- Gardener
- Firefighter

Fingerplays and Chants

Tulips

Five little tulips—red and bright
    (hold up hand)
Let us water them every day.
    (make sprinkle motion with other hand)
Watch them open in the bright sunlight.
    (cup hand, then open)
Watch them close when it is night.
    (close hand again).

My Apple

Look at my apple, it's red and round.
    (make ball shape with hands)
It fell from a tree down to the ground.
    (make downward motion)
Come let me share my apple, please do!
    (beckoning motion)
My mother can cut it right in two—
    (make slicing motion)
One half for me and one half for you.
    (hold out two hands, sharing halves)

Five Red Apples

Five red apples in a grocery store.
    (hold up five fingers)
Bobby bought one, and then there were four.
    (bend down one finger)
Four red apples on an apple tree.
Susie ate one, and then there were three.
    (bend down one finger)
Three red apples. What did Alice do?
Why, she ate one, and then there were two.
    (bend down one finger)
Two red apples ripening in the sun.

Timmy ate one, and then there was one.
    (bend down one finger)
One red apple and now we are done.
I ate the last one, and now there are none.
    (bend down last finger)

The Red Balloon

I had a big red balloon.
So I blew, and blew, and blew.
    (pretend to blow up an imaginary big balloon)
Till it became all large and fat
    (show the large balloon)
And grew, and grew, and grew.
I tossed it up into the air
    (make a tossing motion)
And never let it drop.
    (catch the large balloon)
But once it bounced on the ground.
    (make a bouncing motion)
And suddenly went POP!
    (jump back)

Group Time
(Games and Language)

1. Colored Jars

Collect five large clear jars. Fill three with red water, one with yellow water, and one with blue water. Show children the three red jars. Discuss the color red. Discuss that it can make other colors too. Show them the yellow jar. Add yellow to red. What happens? Add blue water to the other red jar. What happens? Discuss color mixing.

2. Play "Red Light, Green Light"

Pick one child to be your traffic light. Place the "traffic light" about 30 feet away from the other children facing away from children who have formed a long line. With his or her back to the other children, the traffic light says, "Green light." Children try to creep toward the traffic light. Traffic light may then say, "Red light," and turn toward the children. Children must freeze. If the traffic light sees a child move, he or she needs to go back to the starting line. The game continues with "Green light." The first child to reach the traffic light becomes the new light.

Large Muscle

1. **Ribbon Dance**
   Attach strips of red crêpe paper to short wooden dowels or unsharpened pencils to make ribbons. The children can use the ribbons to move to their favorite songs.

2. **Red Bird, Red Bird**
   The children should form a circle by holding hands. Choose a child to be a bird, and start the game. Children chant,

   Red bird, red bird through my window
   Red bird, red bird through my window
   Red bird, red bird through my window
   Oh!

   The bird goes in and out, under the children's arms. The bird stops on the word "Oh!" and bows to the child facing him or her. This child becomes the new bird. The color of the bird can be determined by the color of the clothing of each child picked to be the bird.

Math

1. **Color Cards**
   Construct color cards that start with white and gradually become cherry red. The children can sequence the cards from white to red or from red to white. Discontinued sample color cards could be obtained from a paint store.

2. **Bead Stringing**
   Yarn and a variety of colored beads should be available to the children. After initial exploration, the children can make patterns with beads, such as red-yellow-red-yellow-red.

3. **Colored Bags**
   Place three bags labeled red, yellow, and blue and a variety of blocks on a table. The children can sort the blocks by placing them in the matching colored bag.

4. **Color Sort**
   Obtain paint color sample cards and cut apart. Tape each color onto a container.

Provide objects for the children to sort into each container.

Science

Mixing Colors
Place two or three ice cube trays and cups filled with red-, yellow-, and blue-colored water on the science table. Using an eyedropper, the children can experiment mixing colors in the ice cube trays. Smocks should be provided to prevent stained clothing.

Sensory

1. **Red Water**
   Fill the sensory table with water and red food coloring. The children can add coloring and observe the changes.

2. **Red Shaving Cream**
   Shaving cream with red food coloring added can be placed in the sensory table. During self-selected play, the children can explore the shaving cream.

3. **Red Goop**
   Mix together red food coloring, 1 cup cornstarch, and 1 cup water in the sensory table.

4. **Red Funny Putty**
   Mix together red food coloring, 1 cup liquid starch, and 2 cups white glue. This mixture usually needs to be stirred continuously for an extended period of time before it jells.

Social Studies

1. **Discussion about Colors**
   During group time, discuss colors and how they make us feel. Hold up a color card and ask a child how it makes him or her feel.

2. Color Chart

Construct a "My Favorite Color Is ..." chart. Encourage each child to name his or her favorite color. After each child's name, print his or her favorite color with a colored marker. Display the chart in the classroom.

3. Colored Balloons

Each child should be provided with a balloon. The balloons should be the colors of the rainbow: red, orange, yellow, green, blue, and purple. Arrange the children in the formation of a rainbow. Children with red balloons should stand together, and so on. Take a picture of the class. Place the picture on the bulletin board. *Caution:* This activity needs to be carefully supervised.

 Books

The following books can be used to complement this theme:

Bailey, Carolyn Sherwin, Jacqueline Rogers, and Monique Z. Stephens, eds. (2001). *The Little Rabbit Who Wanted Red Wings.* Illustrated by Jacqueline Rogers. Los Angeles: Price Stern Sloan.

Bunting, Eve. (2008). *My Red Balloon.* Honesdale, PA: Boyds Mills Press.

Carle, Eric. (2001). *Hello, Red Fox.* New York: Aladdin Paperbacks.

Dewdney, Anna. (2005). *Llama Llama Red Pajama.* New York: Viking Juvenile.

Dunrea, Olivier. (2004). *Peedie.* New York: Houghton Mifflin.

Elffers, Joost, and Saxton Freymann. (2005). *Food for Thought.* New York: Arthur A. Levine Books.

Glass, Eleri. (2008). *The Red Shoes.* Illustrated by Ashley Spires. Vancouver, BC: Simply Read Books.

Horacek, Petr. (2001). *Strawberries Are Red.* Cambridge, MA: Candlewick Press.

Jay, Alison. (2010). *Red, Green, Blue.* New York: Dutton Juvenile.

Johnson, Steven. (2009). *My Little Red Fire Truck.* New York: Simon & Schuster Books for Young Readers.

Lindeen, Carol K. (2005). *Fire Trucks.* Mankato, MN: Capstone Press.

Lowell, Susan. (2002). *Little Red Cowboy Hat.* Illustrated by Randy Cecil. New York: Henry Holt.

Martin, Bill, Jr. (1992). *Brown Bear, Brown Bear, What Do You See?* Illustrated by Eric Carle. New York: H. Holt.

Miller, Virginia. (2002). *Ten Red Apples.* Cambridge, MA: Candlewick Press.

Murphy, Stuart. (2000). *Beep Beep, Vroom Vroom!* Illustrated by Chris L. Demarest. New York: HarperCollins.

Ray, Mary Lyn. (2000). *Red Rubber Boot Day.* Illustrated by Lauren Stringer. Orlando, FL: Harcourt.

Schuette, Sarah L. (2008). *Red: Seeing Red All Around Us.* Mankato, MN: Capstone Press.

Seeger, Laura Vaccaro. (2004). *Lemons Are Not Red.* Brookfield, CT: Roaring Brook Press.

Sidman, Joyce. (2009). *Red Sings from Treetops: A Year in Colors.* Illustrated by Pamela Zagarenski. Boston: Houghton Mifflin Harcourt.

Slobodkina, Esphyr. (1985). *Caps for Sale.* New York: Harper & Row.

Thomas, Jane. (2001). *The Big Red Sled.* Illustrated by Priscilla Burris. New York: Scholastic.

Thong, Roseanne. (2008). *Red Is a Dragon.* Illustrated by Grace Lin. San Francisco: Chronicle Books.

Walsh, Ellen Stoll. (1989). *Mouse Paint.* Orlando, FL: Harcourt Brace.

Wood, Don. (1990). *The Little Mouse, the Red Ripe Strawberry and the Big Hungry Bear.* New York: Child's Play.

Yoo, Taeeun. (2007). *The Little Red Fish.* New York: Dial Books for Young Readers.

Ziefert, Harriet. (2009). *One Red Apple.* Illustrated by Karla Gudeon. Maplewood, NJ: Blue Apple Books.

Technology and Multimedia

The following technology and multimedia products can be used to complement this theme:

"Color Parade" [CD]. (1993). In *Can a Cherry Pie Wave Goodbye?* Sherman Oaks, CA: Hap-Pal Music.

"Colors" [CD]. (2010). In *Rock and Roll Garden.* New York: Bari Koral Family Rock Band.

"De Colores" [CD]. (2010). In *Pete Seeger, Tomorrow's Children.* Westchester, PA: Appleseed Records.

Discovering Colors [DVD]. (2006). Los Angles, CA: Distributed by Visual Entertainment.

"Mary Wore Her Red Dress" [CD]. (1987). In *Raffi, Everything Grows.* Cambridge, MA: Rounder/UMGD.

Planting a Rainbow [DVD]. (2005). New York: Weston Woods Studios/Scholastic.

"Put a Little Color on You" [CD]. (1993). In *Can a Cherry Pie Wave Goodbye?* Sherman Oaks, CA: Hap-Pal Music.

Reading Rainbow. (2007). *Legend of the Indian Paintbrush* [DVD]. Lincoln, NE: GPN Educational Media.

Additional teaching resources to accompany this Theme can be found on the book's companion website. Go to www.cengagebrain.com to access the site for a variety of useful resources.

SAFETY

Indoors
walking
scissors care
fire drills
metal detectors
rules

Field Trips
rules

Vehicles
traffic signs
seat belts
rules
airbags

Outdoors
rules
animals
street
bicycles
helmets

People
police officers
firefighters
doctors
nurses
ambulance drivers
strangers

Theme Goals

Through participating in the experiences provided by this theme, the children may learn:

1. Indoor safety precautions
2. Outdoor safety
3. People who keep us safe
4. Field trip safety
5. Vehicle safety

Concepts for the Children to Learn

1. Safety means freedom from danger or harm.
2. We walk indoors.
3. Play yard rules help keep us safe.
4. Rules are the way we are to act.
5. We have special rules for field trips.
6. Fire drills prepare us for emergencies.
7. Scissors need to be handled carefully.
8. Wearing a seat belt is practicing car safety.
9. Wearing a helmet when riding a bicycle is practicing safety.
10. Traffic signs help prevent accidents.
11. Police officers, firefighters, doctors, nurses, and ambulance drivers help keep us safe.
12. Talk only to people you know; do not talk to strangers.
13. Pet only friendly animals you know.

Vocabulary

1. **fire drill**—practicing leaving the building in case of a fire.
2. **rule**—the way we are to act. A rule tells what we should do and not do.
3. **safety**—freedom from danger or harm.
4. **seat belt**—strap that holds a person in a vehicle.
5. **sign**—a lettered board that tells you what to do and not do.

Bulletin Board

The purpose of this bulletin board is to help the children recognize safety signs. To prepare this bulletin board, construct six safety signs out of tagboard, each a different shape. Color appropriately and laminate. Trace the outline of these signs onto black construction paper to create shadow signs as illustrated. Staple the shadow signs to the bulletin board. Punch holes in the safety signs using a hole punch. The children can match the shape of the safety signs to the shadow signs by hanging them on the appropriate pushpins.

Family Letter

InBox

Dear Families,

Safety will be the focus of our next theme. We will be learning about safety at school, at home, and outdoors. Through this curriculum, the children will also become more aware of traffic signs and their importance.

At School

A few of the activities planned for this unit include:

- Taking a safety walk to practice crossing streets

- Counting the number of traffic signs that are in our school neighborhood

- Visiting the fire station on Tuesday morning. We will be leaving at 9:30 a.m. and should return to school by 11:00 a.m.

At Home

One of the songs we will learn follows. It will help your child become aware of the purpose and colors of a traffic light. You may enjoy singing the song at home with your child. The song is sung to the tune of "Twinkle, Twinkle, Little Star." The words are as follows:

> Twinkle, twinkle, traffic light,
> Standing on the corner bright.
> When it's green it's time to go.
> When it's red it's stop, you know.
> Twinkle, twinkle, traffic light,
> Standing on the corner bright.

During your daily routines, share safety tips with your child.

 ## Arts and Crafts

1. **Firefighter Hats**
   Cut firefighter hats out of large sheets of red construction paper for the children to wear.

2. **Easel Painting**
   On the easel, place cutout shapes of fire hats or boots.

3. **Traffic Lights**
   Construct stop-and-go lights out of shoeboxes. Tape the lid to the bottom of the box. Cover with black construction paper and have children place green, yellow, and red circles in the correct order on the box. The red circle should be placed on the top, yellow in the middle, and green on the bottom.

4. **Officer Hats and Badges**
   Police officer hats and badges can be constructed out of paper and colored with crayons or felt-tip watercolor markers.

 ## Cooking

1. **Banana Rounds**
   4 medium bananas
   1/2 tablespoon honey
   1/8 teaspoon nutmeg
   1/8 teaspoon cinnamon
   1/4 cup wheat germ

   The children can peel the bananas and then slice them with a plastic knife. Measure the spices, wheat germ, and honey. Finally, mix them with the bananas. Chill. Serves 8.

2. **Stop Signs**
   Eight-sided crackers
   Cream cheese
   Jelly

   Spread a thin layer of cream cheese or jelly on each cracker.

3. **Yield Signs**
   Triangle crackers
   Yellow cheese

   Cut yellow cheese into triangles. Put the cheese on the crackers.

 ## Dramatic Play

1. **Fire Engine**
   A large cardboard box can be decorated by the children as a fire engine with yellow or red tempera paint. When the fire engine is dry, place it in the dramatic play area with short hoses and firefighter hats. This prop could also be placed outdoors, weather permitting.

2. **Prop Boxes**
   Develop prop boxes such as the following:

Firefighter	Police Officer
Bell	Hat
Jacket or uniform	Badges
Boots	Handcuffs
Whistle	Stop sign (for holding)
Hose	
Oxygen mask	
Hat	

3. **Firefighter Jackets**
   Construct firefighter jackets out of large paper bags. Begin by cutting three holes. One hole is used for the child's head at the top of the bag. Then cut two large holes for arms. These props may encourage the children to dramatize the roles of the firefighters.

4. **Seat Belts**
   Collect child-sized car seats. Place them around like chairs, and let the children adjust them for themselves or their dolls.

 ## Field Trips and Resource People

1. **Firefighter**
   Invite a firefighter to the classroom. Ask him or her to bring firefighter clothing and equipment and to discuss each item.

2. **Police Car**
   Invite a police officer to visit the classroom. Ask him or her to bring a police car to show the children.

Fingerplays and Chants

Silly Teddy Bear

Silly little teddy bear
Stood up in a rocking chair.
(make rocking movement)
Now he has to stay in bed
(lay head on hands)
With a bandage round his head.
(circular movement of hand around head)

Crossing Streets

At the curb before I cross
I stop my running feet
(point to feet)
And look both ways to left and right
(look left and right)
Before I cross the street.
Lest autos running quietly
Might come as a surprise.
I don't just listen with my ears
(point to ears)
But look with both my eyes.
(point to eyes)

Red Light

Red light, red light, what do you say?
I say, "Stop and stop right away!"
(hold palms of both hands up)
Yellow light, yellow light, what do you say?
I say, "Wait till the light turns green."
(hold one palm of hand up)
Green light, green light, what do you say?
I say "Go, but look each way."
(circle arm in forward motion and turn head to the right and left)
Thank you, thank you, red, yellow, green
Now I know what the traffic light means.

Five Police Officers

Five strong police officers standing by a store.
(hold up the one hand)
One became a traffic cop, then there were four.
(hold up four fingers)
Four strong police officers watching over me.

One took a lost boy home, then there were three.
(hold up three fingers)
Three strong police officers all dressed in blue.
One stopped a speeding car and then there were two.
(hold up two fingers)
Two strong police officers, how fast they can run.
One caught a bad man and then there was one.
(hold up one finger)
One strong police officer saw some smoke one day.
He called a firefighter who put it out right away.

The Crossing Guard

The crossing guard keeps us safe
As he works from day to day.
He holds the stop sign high in the air.
(hold palm of hand up)
For the traffic to obey.
And when the cars have completely stopped
And it's as safe as can be,
He signals us to walk across
(make a beckoning motion)
The street very carefully.

Group Time
(Games and Language)

Toy Safety

Collect a variety of unsafe toys that may have sharp edges, such as a broken wagon and the like. During group time, discuss the dangers of each toy. As soon as group activity is finished, remove the toys from the classroom.

Large Muscle

1. **Safety Walk**

   Take a safety walk. Practice observing traffic lights when crossing the street. Point out special hazards to the children.

2. Stop, Drop, and Roll

Practice "Stop, Drop, and Roll" with the children. This will be valuable to them if they are ever involved in a fire and their clothes happen to catch on fire. Usually a firefighter will teach them this technique while they are visiting the fire station.

3. Traffic Light

Cut a green circle and red circle from construction paper. Choose one child to be the officer. Give other children toy vehicles to "drive" on the floor. The other children should line up away from the officer. When the officer shows the green light, the children "drive" toward him or her. When the officer shows the red light, the children should stop.

 Math

1. Sequencing Hats

Draw pictures of three police hats. Make each picture identical except design three different sizes. The children can sequence the objects from largest to smallest or from smallest to largest. Discuss the sizes and ask which is largest, smallest, and in the middle.

2. Safety Items

Walk around the school and observe the number of safety items. Included may be exit signs, fire drill posters, fire extinguishers, sprinkler systems, fire alarm, drill bells, and so on.

 Music

1. "Twinkle, Twinkle, Traffic Light"

(Sing to the tune of "Twinkle, Twinkle, Little Star")

Twinkle, twinkle, traffic light,
Standing on the corner bright.
When it's green it's time to go.
When it's red it's stop, you know.
Twinkle, twinkle, traffic light,
Standing on the corner bright.

2. "Do You Know the Police Officer?"

(Sing to the tune of "The Muffin Man")
(This song can be extended. For example, the song can be continued by substituting "who helps me when I'm lost" or "who helps one cross the street.")

Oh, do you know the police officer,
The police officer, the police officer?
Oh, do you know the police officer
Who helps me cross the street?

 Science

1. Sorting for Safety

Collect and thoroughly wash empty household product containers. Include safe and dangerous items such as cleaning supplies, orange juice containers, and so on. Place all the items in one large box. The children can separate the containers into "safe" and "dangerous" categories. Younger children may be able to separate the containers into edible and inedible categories.

2. All about Me

On a table, place identification items. Prepare a separate card for each child. Record the following information on the cards:

- Height
- Weight
- Color hair
- Color eyes
- Fingerprint
- Signature (if child can or a teacher can help)

 Sensory

1. Pumps and Hoses

Water pumps, hoses, and water can be placed in the sensory table.

2. Trucks

Small toy fire trucks and police cars can be placed in the sensory table with sand.

Social Studies

1. **Safety Pictures and Signs**
   Post safety pictures and signs around the room.

2. **Stop-and-Go Light**
   Draw a large stop-and-go light on a piece of tagboard. Color with felt-tip markers. Print the following across from the corresponding colors:

   Green means go we all know.
   Yellow means wait even if you're late.
   Red means stop!

3. **Safety Signs**
   Take a walk and watch for safety signs. Discuss the colors and letters on each sign.

 Books

The following books can be used to complement this theme:

Berenstain, Stan, and Jan Berenstain. (1999). *My Trusty Car Seat: Buckling Up for Safety.* New York: Random House.

Calmenson, Stephanie. (2007). *May I Pet Your Dog?* Illustrated by Jan Ormerod. New York: Clarion Books.

Cuyler, Margery. (2001). *Stop Drop and Roll.* Illustrated by Arthur Howard. New York: Simon & Schuster Children's Publishing.

Irma, Joyce. (2000). *Never Talk to Strangers.* New York, NY: Golden Books.

King, Kimberly. (2008). *I Said No!* Illustrated by Sue Rama. Weaverville, CA: Boulden Publishing.

Llewellyn, Claire. (2006). *Watch Out! Around Town.* Illustrated by Mike Gorden. Hauppauge, NY: Barron's Educational Series.

Llewellyn, Claire. (2006). *Watch Out! At Home.* Illustrated by Mike Gorden. Hauppauge, NY: Barron's Educational Series.

Llewellyn, Claire. (2006). *Watch Out! Near Water.* Illustrated by Mike Gorden. Hauppauge, NY: Barron's Educational Series.

Llewellyn, Claire. (2006). *Watch Out! On the Road.* Illustrated by Mike Gorden. Hauppauge, NY: Barron's Educational Series.

Mattern, Joanne. (2007). *Staying Safe at School.* Milwaukee, WI: Weekly Reader Early Learning Library.

Mattern, Joanne. (2007). *Staying Safe in the Car.* Milwaukee, WI: Weekly Reader Early Learning Library.

Mattern, Joanne. (2007). *Staying Safe on My Bike.* Milwaukee, WI: Weekly Reader Early Learning Library.

Mattern, Joanne. (2007). *Staying Safe on the School Bus.* Milwaukee, WI: Weekly Reader Early Learning Library.

Pendziwo, Jean E. (2005). *No Dragons for Tea: Fire Safety for Kids.* Illustrated by Martine Gourbault. Toronto: Kids Can Press.

Pendziwo, Jean E. (2005). *Once Upon a Dragon: Stanger Safety for Kids.* Illustrated by Martine Gourbault. Toronto: Kids Can Press.

Pendziwo, Jean E. (2006). *A Treasure at Sea for Dragon and Me: Water Safety for Kids.* Illustrated by Martine Gourbault. Toronto: Kids Can Press.

Saltz, Gail. (2008). *Amazing You! Getting Smart About Your Private Parts.* Illustrated by Lynne Avril Cravath. New York: Puffin Books.

Schuh, Mari. (2009). *Fire Safety in Action.* Mankato, MN: Capstone Press.

Thomas, Pat, and Leslie Harker. (2003). *I Can Be Safe: A First Look at Safety.* Hauppauge, NY: Barron's Educational Series.

Thomas, Pat, and Leslie Harker. (2003). *Is It Right to Fight? A First Look at Anger.* Hauppauge, NY: Barron's Educational Series.

Technology and Multimedia

The following technology and multimedia products can be used to complement this theme:

Disney's Wild About Safety. (2009). *Safety Smart About Fire!* [DVD]. Los Angeles: Distributed by Disney Educational Productions.

Fire Songs and Safety Tips [DVD]. (2008). Barrington, IL: Marshall Publishing and Promotions.

Safety Smart at Home! [DVD]. (2009). Los Angeles: Disney Educational Productions.

"Stop Look and Listen" [CD]. 2010. In *Time for the Bubblepops.* Nottingham, UK: Bubblepop Music.

The Wiggles Go Bananas! [DVD]. (2009). Los Angeles: Warner Home Video.

 Additional teaching resources to accompany this Theme can be found on the book's companion website. Go to www.cengagebrain.com to access the site for a variety of useful resources.

Theme 63
SCISSORS

Care
cleaning
storing
handling
sharpening

Construction
plastic
metal

Types
left-handed
paper
pinking
cloth
cuticle
shears
haircutting

electric
toenail
kitchen
children's

Materials to Cut
paper
cardboard
fabric
hair
fingernails
toenails
yarn or thread
pastry

Parts
handle
blade

Purpose
cutting tool
trimming tool

Users
barber
hairstylist
tailor or dressmaker
sheep shearer
cook or chef
animal groomer
adult
child

Theme Goals

Through participating in the experiences provided by this theme, the children may learn:

1. Parts of scissors
2. Users of scissors
3. Materials that can be cut with scissors
4. Care of scissors
5. Scissor construction
6. Purposes of scissors
7. Types of scissors

Concepts for the Children to Learn

1. Scissors are tools for cutting and trimming.
2. Two blades and ring-shaped handles are the parts of scissors.
3. Scissors help us do our work.
4. Scissors can be made from plastic or metal.
5. Scissors cut paper, fingernails, hair, and other materials.
6. Paper, pinking, cloth, cuticle, and shears are names for scissors.
7. Toenail, kitchen, and children's are also names for scissors.
8. Some people need scissors to do their job.
9. Barbers, hairstylists, tailors, dressmakers, cooks, chefs, and animal groomers use scissors.
10. Adults and children use scissors.
11. Hand motions make scissors cut.
12. Scissors need to be handled carefully.
13. Scissors need care; they need to be cleaned and sharpened.
14. Scissors can cut many materials.
15. Paper, cardboard, fabric, and hair can be cut with scissors.
16. Fingernails, toenails, yarn, thread, and pastry can be cut with scissors.

Vocabulary

1. **blade**—cutting edge of scissors.
2. **pinking shears**—sewing scissors.
3. **scissors**—a tool for cutting or trimming.
4. **shears**—large scissors.

Bulletin Board

The purpose of this bulletin board is to have the children match the colored scissors to the corresponding colored skein of yarn. To prepare the bulletin board, construct six scissors out of tagboard. With felt-tip markers, color each scissor a different color and laminate. Fasten the scissors to the top of the bulletin board. Next, construct six skeins of yarn out of tagboard. Color each skein a different color to correspond with the scissors. Attach the skeins to the bottom part of the bulletin board. Fasten a string to each of the scissors and a pushpin to each of the skeins of yarn.

Family Letter

Dear Families,

Snip, snip, snip! This sound will be heard frequently in the classroom as we start a curriculum theme focusing on scissors. Through the experiences provided, the children will be introduced to various kinds and uses of scissors. They will also learn the proper care and safety precautions to consider when handling and using scissors.

At School

Some activities related to scissors will include:

- Discussing safety and the proper uses of scissors

- Experimenting cutting with different kinds of scissors

- Cutting a variety of materials such as yarn, fabric, paper, wallpaper, and aluminum foil

- Visiting Tom's Barber Shop on Wednesday morning. We will leave at 10:00 a.m. and expect to watch a haircut demonstration. Also, we will observe the tools and equipment used by a barber.

- Listening to the story "Michael's New Hair Cut"

At Home

Children need many experiences working with scissors before they are able to master cutting skills. Each child will learn this skill at his or her own rate. To assist your child, save scraps of paper and junk mail. Allow your child to practice cutting the paper using child-sized scissors. Once the cutting skills have been mastered, your child may enjoy cutting coupons out of newspaper sections or magazines.

Have fun with your child!

Arts and Crafts

1. Scissor Snip

Strips of paper with scissors can be provided for snipping.

2. Cutting

For experimentation, a wide variety of materials and types of scissors can be added to the art area for the children.

Cooking

Pretzels

1 1/2 cups warm water
1 envelope yeast
4 cups flour
1 teaspoon salt
1 tablespoon sugar
Coarse salt
Egg

Mix the warm water, yeast, and sugar together. Set this mixture aside for 5 minutes. Pour salt and flour into a bowl. Add the yeast mixture to make dough. Roll the dough into a long snake form. Cut the dough into smaller sections using scissors. The children can then form individual shapes with dough. Brush egg on the shapes with a pastry brush, and sprinkle with salt. Preheat the oven and bake the pretzels at 425 degrees for 12 minutes.

Dramatic Play

1. Beauty Shop

Set up a beauty shop in the dramatic play area. Include items such as curling irons, hair dryers, combs, and wigs. Also include a chair, a plastic covering, and a "Beauty Shop" sign. A cash register and money can be added to encourage play. *Caution:* For safety purposes, cut the cords off the hair dryer and curling irons.

2. Tailor and Dressmaking Shop

Materials that are easy to cut should be provided. Likewise, a variety of scissors should be placed next to the material. Older children may want to make doll clothes.

3. Bake Shop

Play dough, scissors, and other cooking tools can be placed on a table. If desired, make paper baker hats and a sign.

4. Dog Groomer

A dog-grooming area can be set up in the dramatic play corner with stuffed animals, brushes, and combs. If available, cut off the cord of an electric dog shaver and provide it for the children.

Field Trips and Resource People

1. Hairstylist

Visit a hairstylist. While there, observe a person's hair being cut. Notice the different scissors that are used and how they are used.

2. Pet Groomer

Invite a pet groomer to class. If possible, arrange for a dog to be groomed.

Fingerplays and Chants

Open, Shut Them

Open, shut them, open, shut them.
   (use index and middle finger to make
   scissors motion)
Give a little snip, snip, snip.
   (three quick snips with fingers)
Open, shut them, open, shut them.
   (repeat scissors motion)
Make another clip.
   (make another scissors motion)

Group Time
(Games and Language)

Scissors Safety

Discuss safety while using scissors. The children can help make a list titled "How We Use Our Scissors Safely." Display chart in room.

Math

Shape Sort

Cut out different-colored shapes. Place the shapes on a table for the children to sort by color, shape, and size.

Science

1. **Scissor Show**

   Place a variety of scissors on an overhead projector. Encourage the children to describe each by naming it and explaining its use.

2. **Shadow Profiles**

   Tape a piece of paper on a wall or bulletin board. Stand a child in front of the paper. Shine a light source to create a shadow of the head. Trace the outline of each child's shadow. Provide scissors for the children to use to cut out their own shadows.

3. **Weighing Scissors**

   On the science table, place a variety of scissors and a scale. The children should be encouraged to note the differences in weight.

Sensory

Play Dough

Scissors can be placed next to the play dough in the sensory area.

Books

The following books can be used to complement this theme:

Battle-Lavert, Gwendolyn. (2004). *The Barber's Cutting Edge.* San Francisco: Children's Book Press.

Frandsen, Karen. (1986). *Michael's New Hair Cut.* Chicago, ILL: Children's Press.

Glatzer, Jenna. (2005). *Hattie, Get A Haircut!* Illustrated by Monica Kendall. Warwick, NY: Moo Press

Klinting, Lars. (1996). *Bruno the Tailor.* New York: Holt.

Moore, Eva. (1997). *The Day of the Bad Haircut.* Illustrated by Meredith Johnson. St. Paul, MN: Cartwheel Books.

Ruediger, Beth. (1997). *The Barber of Bingo.* Illustrated by John McPherson. Kansas City, MO: Andrews McMeel.

Tarpley, Natasha. (2002). *Bippity Bop Barbershop.* Illustrated by E. B. Lewis. Boston: Little, Brown.

Strickland, Michael R., and Keaf Holliday. (1998). *Haircuts at Sleepy Sam's.* Illustrated by Keaf Holliday. Honesdale, PA: Boyds Mills.

Woram, Catherine. (2010). *Paper Scissors Glue.* New York: Ryland Peters & Small.

Ziefert, Harriet. (2006). *There Was a Little Girl, She Had a Little Curl.* Illustrated by Elliot Kreloff. Maplewood, NJ: Blue Apple Books.

Technology and Multimedia

The following technology and multimedia products can be used to complement this theme:

Reading Rainbow. (2007). *Uncle Jed's Barbershop* [DVD]. Lincoln, NE: Distributed by GPN Educational Media.

Additional teaching resources to accompany this Theme can be found on the book's companion website. Go to www.cengagebrain.com to access the site for a variety of useful resources.

Pastes

Paste is a staple in early childhood classrooms and children can participate in making it. It can be colored, if desired, for special occasion. For example, green food coloring can be added for St. Patrick's Day or red for Valentine's day. When not being used, paste should always be stored in a covered, airtight container.

Bookmaker's Paste

1 teaspoon flour
2 teaspoons cornstarch
1/4 teaspoon powdered alum
3 ounces water

Mix dry ingredients. Add water slowly, stirring out all lumps. Cook over slow fire (preferably in a double boiler), stirring constantly. Remove when paste begins to thicken. It will thicken more as it cools. Keep in covered unbreakable container. Thin with water if necessary.

Cooked Flour Paste

1 cup boiling water
1 tablespoon powdered alum
1 pint cold water

1 pint flour
1 teaspoon oil of cloves
Oil of wintergreen (optional)

To 1 cup boiling water, add powdered alum. Fold flour into cold water until smooth; pour mixture gradually into boiling alum water. Cook until it has a bluish cast, stirring all the time. Remove from fire, add oil of cloves, and stir well. Keep in airtight jars. Thin when necessary by adding water. A drop or two of oil of wintergreen may be added to give the paste a pleasing aroma.

Colored Salt Paste

Mix 2 parts salt to 1 part flour. Add powdered paint and enough water to make a smooth heavy paste. Keep in an airtight container.

Crêpe Paper Paste

Cut or tear 2 tablespoons crêpe paper of a single color. The finer the paper is cut, the smoother the paste will be. Add 1/2 tablespoon flour, 1/2 tablespoon salt, and enough water to make a paste. Stir and squash the mixture until it is as smooth as possible. Store in an airtight container.

Theme 64
SHAPES

Names
circle
triangle
rectangle
square
oval
lines
round
four sides
three sides

Types
open
closed
tall
short
big or large
small or little

Theme Goals

Through participating in the experiences provided by this theme, the children may learn:

1. The names of basic shapes
2. Lines used in shapes
3. Objects have shapes

Concepts for the Children to Learn

1. The shape is the way something looks.
2. There are many shapes of different sizes and colors in our world.
3. Some shapes have names.
4. Circles, triangles, rectangles, squares, and ovals are all shapes.
5. A circle is round.
6. Triangles have three sides.
7. A rectangle is a shape with four sides.
8. An oval is shaped like an egg.
9. A square has four sides all the same size.
10. All objects contain one or more shapes.
11. We can draw lines to make shapes.

Vocabulary

1. **circle**—a shape that is round.
2. **line**—a mark made with a marking tool such as a pencil, crayon, or felt-tip marker to make a shape.
3. **oval**—a shape that looks like an egg.
4. **rectangle**—a shape with four sides. Two sides are longer. A wagon is a rectangle.
5. **shape**—the way something looks. A shape is the outside form of an object.
6. **square**—a shape with four sides of equal length.
7. **triangle**—a shape with three sides.

Bulletin Board

The purpose of this bulletin board is to develop visual discrimination, hand-eye coordination, and problem-solving skills by making a shape train. To prepare the bulletin board, use the model shown to construct a train using basic shapes. Color the shapes, cut them out, and laminate. Trace laminated shapes onto black construction paper to construct shadow shapes. Cut out the shadow shapes. Staple the shadow shapes onto the board in a train pattern. The children can affix the colored shape pieces to the shadows by using magnets.

All aboard the shape train.

Family Letter

Dear Families,

Hello again! Shapes are the focus of our new curriculum theme. Our world consists of shapes. The children will become aware of this on an introductory walk around the block. They also will become familiar with the names of shapes and will classify objects according to their shapes. Consequently, the children will be more aware of all the shapes in our world. In addition, the children who are developmentally ready will practice drawing some of the basic shapes.

At School

Some of the fun-filled learning activities scheduled for this unit include:

- Playing a game called "Shape Basket Upset"
- Listening to the story *Shapes and Things* by Tana Hoban
- Feeling and identifying objects by shape in a feely box
- Making and baking cookies of various shapes

At Home

You can reinforce the activities included in this curriculum unit at home by observing shaped objects in your house. Each day at school, we will have a special shape theme. Your child can bring in an object from home to fit the shape of the day. I will send home the shape the night before so you and your child will have time to look for an object.

Enjoy your child!

Arts and Crafts

1. Sponge Painting
Cut sponges into the four basic shapes. The children can hold the sponges with a clothespin. The sponge can be dipped in paint and printed on the paper. Make several designs and shapes.

2. Shape Mobiles
Trace shapes of various sizes on colored construction paper. If appropriate, encourage the children to cut the shapes from the paper and punch a hole at the top of each shape. Next, put a piece of string through the hole and tie onto a hanger. The mobiles can be hung in the classroom for decoration.

3. Easel Ideas
Feature a different shape of easel paper each day at the easel.

4. Shape Collage
Provide different-colored paper shapes and glue for the children to create collages from shapes.

5. My Shape Book
Stickers, catalogs, and magazines should be placed on the art table. Also, prepare booklets cut into the basic shapes. Encourage the children to find, cut, and glue the objects in each shape book.

6. Shape Stamps
Collect jar lids and pieces of thick cardboard. Cut the cardboard into shapes, and glue them to jar lids. The children can dip them in paint and stamp them onto paper.

7. Shape Stencil Painting
Cut the basic shapes out of cardboard using a safety razor blade. Provide paints and paper with the stencils.

8. Gadget Painting
Collect items that have a basic shape such as cookie cutters, plastic berry boxes, fly swatters, or plastic lids to use as painting tools. Provide paper, paint, and the gadgets.

Encourage the children to form designs or pictures by combining and overlapping their designs.

Cooking

1. Shaped Bread
The children can cut bread with different-shaped cookie cutters. Spread soft cheese, cream cheese, or other toppings on the bread.

2. Fruit Cutouts
1/2 cup sugar
4 envelopes unflavored gelatin
2 1/2 cups pineapple juice, apple juice, orange juice, grape juice, or fruit drink

In a mixing bowl, stir the sugar and gelatin with a rubber scraper until well mixed. Pour fruit juice into a 1-quart saucepan. Put the pan on the burner. Turn the burner to high heat. Cook until the juice boils. Turn burner off. Pour the boiling fruit juice over the sugar mixture. Stir with a rubber scraper until all the gelatin is dissolved. Pour into a 13-inch × 9-inch × 2-inch pan. Place in the refrigerator and chill until firm. Cookie cutters can be used to make shapes. Enjoy! *Caution:* This activity requires close supervision.

3. Shape Snacks
Spread cheese onto variously shaped crackers and serve.

Serve cheese cut into circles, triangles, squares, and rectangles.

Serve vegetable circles—cucumbers, carrots, and zucchini.

Cut fruit snacks into circles—bananas, grapefruit wedges, apple slices, and grapes—and serve.

4. Nachos
4 flour tortillas
3/4 cup grated cheese
1/3 cup chopped green pepper (optional)

With clean kitchen scissors, cut each tortilla into 4 or 6 triangle wedges. Place on a cookie sheet, and sprinkle the tortilla wedges with the cheese. Garnish with green pepper if desired. Bake in a 350-degree oven for 4 to 6 minutes or until the cheese melts. Makes 16 to 20 nachos.

5. Swedish Pancakes

3 eggs
1 cup milk
1 1/2 cups flour
1 tablespoon sugar
1/2 teaspoon salt
4 tablespoons butter
1 cup heavy cream
2 tablespoons confectioners' sugar or a
    12-ounce jar of fruit jelly

Using a fork or whisk, beat the eggs lightly in a large mixing bowl. Add half the milk. Fold in the flour, sugar, and salt. Melt the butter and add it, the cream, and the remaining milk to the mixture. Stir well. Lightly grease a frying pan or griddle, and place it over medium-high heat on a hot plate or stove. Carefully pour small amounts of the mixture onto the frying pan or griddle. Cook until the pancakes are golden around the edges and bubbly on top. Turn the pancakes over with a spatula and cook until the other sides are golden around the edges. Remove to a covered plate. Repeat until all the mixture is used. Sprinkle pancakes lightly with confectioners' sugar, or spread jelly over them. Makes 3 dozen pancakes.

Dramatic Play

1. Baker
Provide play dough, cake pans, and cookie cutters.

2. Puppets
A puppet prop box should be placed in the dramatic play area. A puppet stage should be added if available. Otherwise, a puppet stage can be made from cardboard.

Field Trips

Shape Walk
Walk around the school neighborhood. During the walk, observe the shapes of the traffic signs and houses. After returning to the school, record the shapes observed on a chart.

Fingerplays and Chants

Right Circle, Left Square
Close my eyes, shut them tight.
    (close eyes)
Make a circle with my one hand.
    (make circle with one hand)
Keep them shut; make it fair.
    (keep eyes shut)
With my other hand, make a square.
    (make square with other hand)

Lines
One straight finger makes a line.
    (hold up one index finger)
Two straight lines make one "t" sign.
    (cross index fingers)
Three lines make a triangle there
    (form triangle with index fingers
    touching and thumbs touching)
And one more line will make a square.
    (form square with hands)

Draw a Square
Draw a square, draw a square
Shaped like a tile floor.
Draw a square, draw a square
All with corners four.

A Circle
Around in a circle we will go.
    (walk in a circle as a group)
Little tiny baby steps make us go very slow.
    (walk in a circle with little steps)
And then we'll take some great giant steps,
    (walk in a circle with big steps)

as big as they can be.
Then in a circle we'll stand quietly.
  (stand in a circle)

Draw a Triangle
Draw a triangle, draw a triangle
With corners three.
Draw a triangle, draw a triangle
Draw it just for me.

Draw a Circle
Draw a circle, draw a circle
Made very round.
Draw a circle, draw a circle
No corners can be found.

What Am I Making?
This is a circle.
  (draw circle in the air)
This is a square.
  (draw square in the air)
Who can tell me
What I'm making there?
  (draw another shape in the air)

 **Group Time**
(Games and Language)

1. **Shape Hunt**
   Throughout the classroom, hide colorful shapes. Each of the children can find a shape.

2. **Twister**
   On a large old bedsheet, secure many shapes of different colors, or draw the shapes on with magic markers. Make a spinner with these different shapes or colors on it. Have children place parts of their bodies on the different shapes.

3. **Shape Day**
   Each day, highlight a different shape. Collect related items that resemble the shape of the day, and display throughout the classroom. During group time, have each child find an object in the classroom

that is the same shape as the shape of the day.

 **Large Muscle**

1. **Walk and Balance**
   Using masking tape, outline the four basic shapes on the floor. The children can walk and balance on the shapes. Older children may walk forward, backward, and sideways.

2. **Hopscotch**
   Draw a hopscotch board with chalk on the sidewalk outdoors. Masking tape can be used to form the grid on the floor indoors.

3. **Spinning Hula Hoops**
   Provide hula hoops for each child. First, practice using positional words. Encourage the children to stand inside the hoop, in front of the hoop, behind the hoop, and beside the hoop. Then demonstrate how to spin the hoops around your waist and encourage the children to try.

 Math

1. **Wallpaper Shape Match**
   From scraps of old wallpaper, cut out two sets of basic shapes. Mix all of the pieces. The children can match the sets by pattern and shape.

2. **Shape Completion**
   On several pieces of white tagboard, draw a shape. Leave one side, or part of a circle, unfinished or dotted. Laminate the tagboard. The children can complete the shape by drawing with watercolor markers or grease pencils. Erase with a damp cloth.

Music

"Twinkle, Twinkle, Little Star"
Twinkle, twinkle, little star,
How I wonder what you are.
Up above the world so high,
Like a diamond in the sky.
Twinkle, twinkle, little star.
How I wonder what you are.
When the blazing sun is set,
And the grass with dew is wet,
Then you show your little light,
Twinkle, twinkle, all the night.

Science

1. **Feely Box**
   Cut many shapes out of different materials such as felt, cardboard, wallpaper, carpet, and so on. Place the shapes into a feely box. The children can be encouraged to reach in and identify the shape by feeling it before removing it from the box.

2. **Evaporation**
   Pour equal amounts of water into a large round and a small square cake pan. Mark the water level with a grease pencil. Allow the water to stand for a week. Observe the amount of evaporation.

3. **Classifying Objects**
   Collect four small boxes. Mark a different shape on each box. Include a circle, triangle, square, and rectangle. Cut shapes out of magazines. The children can sort the objects by placing them in the corresponding boxes.

4. **What Shape Is It?**
   Place objects with distinct shapes, such as marbles, dice, a pyramid, a deck of cards, a book, a ball, a button, and so on, in the feely box. Encourage the children to reach in and identify the shape of the object they are feeling before they pull it out.

Sensory

Add the following items to the sensory table:
1. Marbles and water
2. Different-shaped sponges and water
3. Colored water
4. Scented water
5. Soapy water

Books

The following books can be used to complement this theme:

Aboff, Marcie. (2009). *If You Were a Polygon.* Illustrated by Francesca Carabelli. Minneapolis, MN: Picture Window Books.

Aboff, Marcie. (2009). *If You Were a Triangle.* Illustrated by Sarah Dillard. Minneapolis, MN: Picture Window Books.

Aigner-Clark, Julie, and Nadeem Zaidi. (2001). *See and Spy Shapes.* Baby Einstein Books. Illustrated by Nadeem Zaidi. New York: Hyperion Press.

Blackstone, Stella. (2006). *Bear in a Square.* Illustrated by Debbie Harter. Cambridge, MA: Barefoot Books.

Blaisdell, Molly. (2009). *If You Were a Triangle.* Illustrated by Francesca Carabelli. Minneapolis, MN: Picture Window Books.

Burns, Marilyn. (2008). *The Greedy Triangle.* New York: Scholastic.

Carter, David A. (2007). *600 Black Dots.* New York: Little Simon.

Carter, David A. (2007). *Whoo? Whoo?* New York: Little Simon.

Carter, David A. (2008). *Yellow Square.* New York: Little Simon.

Casmar, Tom. (2005). *Henry and Pawl and the Round Yellow Ball.* New York: Dial Books for Young Readers.

Ehlert, Lois. (1989). *Color Zoo.* New York: Lippincott.

Ehlert, Lois. (1990). *Color Farm.* New York: Lippincott.

Ehlert, Lois. (2010). *Lots of Spots*. New York, Beach Lane Books.

Elffers, Joost, and Saxton Freymann. (2005). *Food for Thought*. New York: Arthur A. Levine Books.

Greene, Rhonda Gowler. (2001). *When a Line Bends … a Shape Begins*. Illustrated by James Kaczman. New York: Houghton Mifflin.

Hoban, Tana. (1986). *Shapes and Things*. New York: Greenwillow Books.

Hoban, Tana. (1998). *So Many Circles, So Many Squares*. New York: Greenwillow Books.

Metropolitan Museum of Art. (2005). *Museum Shapes*. New York: Little, Brown.

Scarry, Richard. (2008). *Richard Scarry's Shapes and Opposites*. New York: Sterling Publishing Company.

Schuette, Sarah L. (2003). *Circles: Seeing Circles All around Us*. Mankato, MN: Capstone Press.

Schuette, Sarah L. (2003). *Ovals: Seeing Ovals All around Us*. Mankato, MN: Capstone Press.

Schuette, Sarah L. (2003). *Rectangles: Seeing Rectangles All around Us*. Mankato, MN: Capstone Press.

Schuette, Sarah L. (2003). *Squares: Seeing Squares All around Us*. Mankato, MN: Capstone Press.

Schuette, Sarah L. (2003). *Stars: Seeing Stars All around Us*. Mankato, MN: Capstone Press.

Schuette, Sarah L. (2003). *Triangles: Seeing Triangles All around Us*. Mankato, MN: Capstone Press.

Shaw, Charles Green. (1947). *It Looked Like Spilt Milk*. New York: Harper.

Stoll, Ellen Walsh. (2007). *Mouse Shapes*. San Diego, CA: Harcourt Children's Books.

Thong, Roseanne, and Grace Lin. (2000). *Round Is a Mooncake: A Book of Shapes*. Illustrated by Grace Lin. San Francisco: Chronicle Books.

Touch and Feel Shapes. (2000). New York: Dorling Kindersley.

Technology and Multimedia

The following technology and multimedia products can be used to complement this theme:

"Circle" [CD]. (2010). In *What Are the Odds?* New York: Monkey Monkey Music.

"Circles (All My Life's a Circle)" [CD]. (2000). In *Charlotte Diamond's World*. Vancouver, BC: Hug Bug Records.

"Circle Songs" [CD]. (2000). In *Early Childhood Classics: Old Favorites with a New Twist*. Sherman Oaks, CA: Hap-Pal Music.

"Everything Has a Shape" [CD] (2001). In *Sally the Swinging Snake*. Sherman Oaks, CA: Hap-Pal Music.

Guess That Shape and Color [DVD]. (2006). Los Angeles: Sony Wonder.

"I Am a Bubble" [CD]. (2000). In *Charlotte Diamond's World*. Vancouver, BC: Hug Bug Records.

Meet the Shapes [DVD]. (2005). Danville, CA: Preschool Prep.

Shapes [DVD]. (2009). Beverly Hills, CA: Echo Bridge Home Entertainment.

Additional teaching resources to accompany this Theme can be found on the book's companion website. Go to www.cengagebrain.com to access the site for a variety of useful resources.

To Teach Math Concepts

Before a child can learn the more abstract concepts of arithmetic, he or she must be visually, physically, and kinesthetically aware of basic quantitative concepts. Form discrimination of shapes must be included such as circle, square, triangle and rectangle. The following vocabulary should also be introduced:

big	top	all	more
little	bottom	none	less
small	long	some	through
smaller	short	first	around
large	tall	last	fast
larger	high	middle	slow
heavy	low	near	up
light	thick	far	down
in	thin	above	most
out	front	below	least
over	back	many	patterns
under	behind	few	

Theme 65
SPORTS

Participants
spectators
players
coaches
umpires
scorekeepers
announcers

Clothing
uniforms
swimsuits
shorts, jerseys
sweatshirts
sweatpants
hats
ski clothing
jacket
gloves
pants
goggles

Types
baseball, basketball
football, soccer
rugby, swimming
tennis, volleyball
skiing, biking
hiking, bowling
skating
track and running
fishing
golf
hockey

Equipment
balls, bats
shoulder pads
rackets, bikes
skis, boots
poles, gloves
special shoes
helmets
golf clubs
skates

Places Indoors and Outdoors
yards, fields
swimming pools
tennis courts
roads, gyms
golf courses
bowling alleys
ski slopes
lakes

Theme Goals

Through participating in the experiences provided by this theme, the children may learn:

1. Places used for sports participation
2. Types of sports people play
3. Equipment used for sports
4. Kinds of clothing worn for sports participation
5. The many people who participate in sports

Concepts for the Children to Learn

1. Sports are activities played for fun and exercise.
2. Exercise means to move our body to improve health.
3. Swimming pools, playing fields, tennis courts, roads, gyms, golf courses, backyards, bowling alleys, lakes, and ski slopes are all places that are used for sports.
4. Spectators, players, and coaches are all sports participants.
5. Umpires, scorekeepers, and announcers work at sporting activities.
6. Baseball, biking, hiking, hockey, football, and golf are all types of sports.
7. Soccer, rugby, swimming, and volleyball are sports.
8. Skiing, skating, bowling, fishing, running, and hockey are also sports.
9. Balls, bikes, and golf clubs are sports equipment.
10. Uniforms are special clothes worn when playing some sports. Uniforms can identify the sport being played.
11. Football and basketball players wear uniforms and helmets.
12. Some sports are played indoors, and others are played outdoors.
13. Skating, track and running, and fishing are also sports.
14. Different sports require different equipment.
15. Baseball players have bats, baseballs, and gloves for equipment.
16. Skiers have skis, boots, gloves, poles, hats, ski suits, and sometimes goggles.
17. Golfers have golf clubs, gloves, golf balls, and special shoes.
18. Swimsuits, shorts, jerseys, sweatshirts, and sweatpants are clothing worn in some sports.

Vocabulary

1. **ball**—equipment used for sports. Most balls are round.
2. **sport**—an activity played for fun that gives exercise.
3. **exercise**—moving your body. Exercise improves our health.
4. **team**—a group of people who play together.
5. **uniform**—special clothing worn for some sports.

Bulletin Board

The purpose of this bulletin board is to encourage visual discrimination skills. The children are to hang each ball with a numeral on the glove that has the corresponding number of dots. To prepare the bulletin board, construct baseball mitts out of brown tagboard. Cut out the mitts, and attach dots starting with one on each of the gloves. The number of gloves prepared (and the corresponding number of dots) will depend on the developmental maturity of the children. Hang the gloves on the bulletin board. Next construct white baseballs. Write a numeral, starting with 1, on each of the balls.

 **Family Letter**

InBox

Dear Families,

Sports are the focus of our next theme. Through the experiences provided, the children will become familiar with types of sports equipment and clothing, and people who participate in sports. They will also recognize sports as a form of exercise.

At School

Activities planned to foster sports concepts include:

- Exploring balls used in different sports and classifying them into groups by size, color, and ability to bounce and roll

- Trying on a variety of clothing used in different sports, including a swim cap; goggles; shoulder, leg, and knee pads; helmets; gloves; and uniforms

- Skating in the room by wrapping squares of waxed paper around our feet and attaching them with rubber bands around our ankles. Our feet will then easily glide over the carpet!

At Home

You can incorporate sports concepts at home by:

- Looking through sports magazines with your child and pointing out the equipment that is used or the clothing that is worn. This will develop your child's observation skills.

- Observing a sporting event with your child, such as basketball, baseball, or football. Likewise, let your child watch you participate in a sport!

- Participating in a sport together. Your child will enjoy spending special time with you!

Enjoy your child!

Arts and Crafts

1. **Easel Ideas**
   Cut easel paper in various sports shapes.

   - Baseball glove
   - Baseball diamond
   - Tennis racket
   - Bike
   - Tennis shoe
   - Football
   - Baseball cap
   - Football helmet
   - Different sizes of balls

2. **Team Pennants**
   Prepare triangular pennants using a variety of colors of construction paper or fun foam. Allow the children to use sequins, pompons, and so on to decorate the pennants.

3. **Ball Collages**
   Balls used in various sports come in all different sizes. Using construction paper or wallpaper, cut the paper in various round shapes, as well as football shapes. Encourage the children to paste them on a large piece of construction paper and decorate.

4. **Golf Ball Painting**
   Place a piece of paper in a shallow tray or pie tin. Spoon 2 or 3 teaspoons of thin paint onto the paper. Next, put a golf ball or ping-pong ball in the tray and tilt the pan in several directions, allowing the ball to make designs in the paint.

Cooking

Cheese Balls

8 ounces cream cheese, softened
1 stick of butter, softened
2 cups grated cheddar cheese
1/2 package of onion soup mix

Blend all of the ingredients together. Shape the mixture into small balls.

Dramatic Play

1. **Baseball**
   Baseball caps, plastic balls, uniforms, catcher's masks, and gloves can be placed in the dramatic play area.

2. **Football**
   Balls, shoulder pads, uniforms, and helmets can be provided for the children to use outdoors.

3. **Tennis**
   Tennis rackets, balls, visors, sunglasses, and shorts for the children can be placed outdoors. A variation would be to use balloons for balls and hangers with pantyhose pulled around them for rackets.

4. **Skiing**
   Ski boots and skis can be provided for the children to try on.

5. **Skating**
   Waxed paper squares for children to wrap around their feet and ankles can be provided. The children can attach the waxed paper with rubber bands around their ankles. Encourage the children to slide across the carpeting.

Field Trips

Suggested trips include:
1. A football field
2. A baseball field
3. Tennis court
4. Health (fitness) club
5. Stadium
6. A swimming pool
7. The sports facilities of a local high school or college

Fingerplays and Chants

Here Is a Ball

Here's a ball
    (make a circle with your thumb and
    pointer finger)
And here's a ball
    (make a bigger circle with two thumbs
    and pointers)
And a great big ball I see.
    (make a large circle with arms)
Now let's count the balls we've made,
One, two, three.
    (repeat)

Football Players

Five big football players standing in the
    locker room door.
One had a sore knee
And then there were four.

Four big football players down on their
    knees.
One made a touchdown
And then there were three.

Three big football players looking up at you.
One made a tackle
And then there were two.

Two big football players running in the sun.
One was offsides
And then there was one.

One big football player standing all alone.
He decided to go home
And then there were none.

Group Time
(Games and Language)

"What's Missing?"

Provide a large group of children with a
tray of sports equipment such as a ball,
a baseball glove, a golf ball, sunglasses,
goggles, and so on. Let the children examine
the tray of items. Then have the children
close their eyes and place their heads in
their laps. Remove one item from the tray
and see if the children can guess what
is missing. This activity will be more
successful if the numbers are related to the
age of the child. For example, with two-year-
old children, use only two items. Three-year-
olds may be successful with an additional
item. If not, remove one.

Large Muscle

1. **Going Fishing**
   Use a large wooden rocking boat or a large
   box that two to three children can sit in.
   Make fish out of construction paper or
   tagboard, and attach paper clips to the
   top. Tie a magnet to a string and pole. The
   magnet will attract the fish.

2. **Kickball**
   Many sports involve kicking a ball. Discuss
   these sports with the children. Then provide
   the children with a variety of balls to kick.
   Let the children discover which balls go the
   farthest and which are the easiest to kick.

3. **Sports Charades**
   Dramatize various sports, including
   swimming, golfing, tennis, and bike riding.

4. **Golfing**
   Using a child-sized putter and regular golf
   balls, the children hit golf balls. ***Note:*** This
   is an outdoor activity that requires a lot of
   teacher supervision.

5. **Beach Volleyball**
   Use a large beach ball and a rope or net in
   a central spot outdoors. Let the children
   volley the beach ball to one another.

Math

1. **Ball Sort**
   Sort various balls by size, texture, and color.

2. Hat Sorting

Sort hats such as a baseball cap, a football helmet, a biking helmet, a visor, and others by color, size, texture, and shape.

3. Soccer Ball Pattern

Cut large balls from white construction paper. Cut out small octagons from black construction paper. Encourage the children to glue the black octagons on the white ball to create a pattern. Help the children identify a black-white-black-white pattern to create a soccer ball.

 Science

1. Feely Box

Place a softball, baseball, golf ball, and tennis ball in a feely box. The children can reach into the box, feel, and try to guess the type of ball.

2. Ball Bounces

Observe the way different balls move. Check to see if footballs, basketballs, and soccer balls can be bounced. Observe to see if some go higher than others. Also repeat using smaller balls such as tennis balls, baseballs, and golf balls.

3. Wheels

Observe the wheels on a bicycle. If possible, bring a bike to the classroom and demonstrate how peddling makes the wheels move.

4. Examining Balls

Observe the composition of different balls. Ask the children to identify each. Then place the balls in water. Observe to see which ones float and which ones sink.

5. Types of Grass

Place real grass and artificial turf on the science table. The children can feel both types of grass and describe differences in texture.

6. Stethoscopes

Place stethoscopes on the science shelf. Show children how to listen to their heart rate. Have children run in place for 30 seconds and again listen to their heartbeats. What did they notice?

Note: Be certain the stethoscope earplugs are cleaned after each use.

 Sensory

1. Swimming

Add water to the sensory table with dolls or small people figures.

2. Weighing Balls

Fill the sensory table with small balls, such as golf balls, foam balls, Wiffle balls, or tennis balls. Add a balance scale so that the children can weigh the balls.

3. Measuring Mud and Sand

Add a mud and sand mixture to the sensory table with scoops and spoons.

4. Feeling Turf

Line the bottom of the sensory table with artificial turf.

 Books

The following books can be used to complement this theme:

Adamson, Heather. (2006). *Let's Play Soccer.* Mankato, MN: Capstone Press.

Bouchard, David. (2004). *That's Hockey.* Illustrated by Dean Griffiths. Custer, WA: Orca Book Publishers.

Christopher, Matt, and Daniel Vasconcellos. (2000). *Hat Trick.* Illustrated by Daniel Vasconcellos. Boston: Little, Brown.

Davis, Lambert. (2004). *Swimming with Dolphins.* New York: Blue Sky Press.

DeGezelle, Terri. (2006). *Let's Play Baseball!* Mankato, MN: Capstone Press.

Diehl, Davis. (2007). *Sports A to Z.* New York: Lark Books.

Falk, Laine. (2008). *Let's Talk Baseball.* New York: Children's Press.

Falk, Laine. (2008). *Let's Talk Soccer.* New York: Children's Press.

Falk, Laine. (2008). *Let's Talk Tae Kwon Do.* New York: Children's Press.

Jones, Melanie Davis. (2003). *I Can Ski.* Illustrated by Terry Boles. New York: Children's Press.

Lature, Denize. (2000). *Running the Road to ABC.* Illustrated by Reynold Ruffins. New York: Simon & Schuster Children's Publishing.

Lewis, Maggie, and Michael Chesworth. (1999). *Morgy Makes His Move.* Illustrated by Michael Chesworth. Boston: Houghton Mifflin.

Lindeen, Carol K. (2006). *Let's Ice Skate!* Mankato, MN: Capstone Press.

Lindeen, Carol K. (2006). *Let's Play Basketball!* Mankato, MN: Capstone Press.

Lindeen, Carol K. (2006). *Let's Swim!* Mankato, MN: Capstone Press.

London, Jonathan. (1994). *Let's Go Froggy!* Illustrated by Frank Remkiewicz. New York: Viking.

London, Jonathan. (1995). *Froggy Learns to Swim.* Illustrated by Frank Remkiewicz. New York: Viking.

Mader, Jan. (2007). *Let's Play Football!* Mankato, MN: Capstone Press.

Martin, Bill, and Michael Sampson. (1997). *Swish.* Illustrated by Michael Chesworth. New York: Holt.

McG, Shane. (2007). *Tennis Anyone?* Minneapolis, MN: Carolrhoda Books.

McKissack, Patricia C. (1996). *A Million Fish … More or Less.* Illustrated by Dena Schutzer. New York: Random House.

Miller, Amanda. (2008). *Let's Talk Basketball.* New York: Children's Press.

Miller, Amanda. (2008). *Let's Talk Swimming.* New York: Children's Press.

Napier, Matt. (2002). *Z Is for Zamboni.* Illustrated by Melanie Rose. Chicago: Sleeping Bear Press.

Norworth, Jack, and Alec Gillman. (1999). *Take Me out to the Ballgame.* Illustrated by Alec Gillman. New York: Scholastic Trade.

Parish, Peggy. (1996). *Play Ball, Amelia Bedelia.* Illustrated by Wallace Tripp. New York: HarperCollins.

Prelutsky, Jack. (2007). *Good Sports.* Illustrated by Chris Raschka. New York: Knopf.

Prosek, James. (2004). *A Good Day's Fishing.* New York: Simon & Schuster Children's Publishing.

Pulver, Robin. (1997). *Alicia's Tutu.* Illustrated by Mark Graham. New York: Dial Books.

Rex, Michael. (2005). *Dunk Skunk.* New York: G.P. Putnam's Sons.

Rice, Eve. (1996). *Swim!* Illustrated by Marisabina Russo. New York: Greenwillow.

Sampson, Michael. (1996). *The Football That Won …* Illustrated by Ted Rand. New York: Holt.

Wells, Eva. (2006). *Wishing I Was Fishing.* Illustrated by Chandra Dale. Edina, MN: Beaver's Pond Press.

Technology and Multimedia

The following technology and multimedia products can be used to complement this theme:

The Magic School Bus: Super Sports Fun [DVD]. (2004). Los Angeles: Warner Home Video.

Olivia Takes Ballet [DVD]. (2010). Los Angeles: Paramount Home Entertainment.

"Perseverance" [CD]. (2005). In *Red Grammer Be Bop Your Best.* Brewerton, NY: Red Note Records.

Reading Rainbow. (2007). *Sports Pages* [DVD]. Lincoln, NE: GPN Educational Media.

"Take Me Out to the Ballgame" [CD]. (1996). In *One Light, One Song.* Cambridge, MA: Rounder/UMGD.

"Take Me Out to the Ballgame" [CD]. (1997). In *Six Little Ducks.* Long Branch, NJ: Kimbo Educational.

Wow! Wow! Wubbzy! Go for Gold! [DVD]. (2010). Beverly Hills, CA: Anchor Bay Entertainment.

Additional teaching resources to accompany this Theme can be found on the book's companion website. Go to www.cengagebrain.com to access the site for a variety of useful resources.

Theme 66
SPRING

Plants
flowers
dandelions
grass
tree buds

Activities
flying kites
gardening
fishing
baseball
picnics
golf
tennis
camping
walking
bicycling

Colors
green
white
yellow
pastels

Weather
rain
wind
warm
thunderstorms

Animals
chicks
lambs
birds
calves
robins

Holidays
St. Patrick's Day
Mother's Day
Arbor Day
May Day
Memorial Day
Passover
Easter

Insects
caterpillars
butterflies
spiders
ants

Theme Goals

Through participating in the experiences provided by this theme, the children may learn:

1. Spring colors
2. Spring weather
3. Plants that grow in the spring
4. Insects seen during the spring
5. Springtime holidays
6. Spring animals
7. Spring activities

Concepts for the Children to Learn

1. Spring is a season that comes after winter and before summer.
2. It rains in the spring, and there can be thunderstorms and wind.
3. Spring is usually warmer than winter.
4. Light colors are seen during the spring.
5. Green, white, yellow, and pastels are spring colors.
6. Caterpillars, butterflies, spiders, and ants are insects seen in the spring.
7. Some holidays are celebrated in the spring: Mother's Day, Passover, Easter, St. Patrick's Day, May Day, Arbor Day, and Memorial Day.
8. Chicks, lambs, calves, and robins are springtime animals.
9. Some people go on picnics, to baseball games, fishing, and golfing in the spring.
10. Picnics, camping, walking, bicycling, and flying kites are spring activities.
11. Many gardens are planted in the spring.
12. Flowers, dandelions, and grass are spring plants.
13. Gardens are often planted in the spring.

Vocabulary

1. **garden**—a place where flowers, fruits, and vegetables are grown.
2. **rain**—water that comes from the clouds.
3. **spring**—one of the four seasons. Spring is the season that comes after winter and before summer.

Bulletin Board

The purpose of this bulletin board is to promote the development of mathematical skills. Have the children place the proper number of ribbons on each kite tail. To do this, they need to count the number of dots on the kite. Construct kites, and print the numerals beginning with 1 and the corresponding number of dots on each. Construct ribbons for the tails of the kites as illustrated. Color the kites and tails, and laminate. Staple the kites to the bulletin board. Affix magnetic strips to each kite as the string. Affix a magnetic piece in the middle of each ribbon.

InBox

Dear Families,

The temperature is slowly rising, and the grass on the playground is getting greener. In other words, spring is here! And spring is the theme we will explore at school. Throughout the week, the children will become more aware of the many changes that take place during this season, as well as common spring activities. They will be exposed to spring holidays, weather, colors, plants, animals, insects, and activities. We will also talk about spring activities.

At School

Some of the learning experiences for this curriculum unit include:

- Finding a suitable place on the playground to plant flowers
- Taking a walk around the neighborhood to observe signs of spring
- Planting grass seed in eggshells at the science table
- Creating pictures and designs with pastel watercolor markers in the art area

At Home

To foster concepts of spring at home, save seeds from fruits such as oranges and apples. Assist your child in planting the seeds. Your child can also sort the seeds by color, size, or type to develop classification skills. The seeds could also be used for counting. Happy seed collecting!

Enjoy your child as you explore concepts related to spring.

Arts and Crafts

1. Butterfly Wings
Fold a sheet of light-colored paper in half. Show the children how to paint on only one side of the paper. The paper can be folded again and pressed. The result will be a symmetrical painting. Antennae can be added by using crayons and markers to make butterflies.

2. Pussy Willow Fingerprints
Trace around a tongue depressor with a colored marker. Then, using ink pads or fingerpaint, the children can press a finger on the ink pad and transfer the fingerprint to the paper. This will produce pussy willow buds.

3. Caterpillars
Cut egg cartons in half lengthwise. Place the long rows on the art table with short pieces of chenille stems, markers, and crayons. From these materials, the children can make caterpillars.

4. Kites
Provide diamond-shaped construction paper, string, a hole punch, crêpe paper, glue, glitter, and markers. For older children, provide the paper with a diamond already traced. This provides them an opportunity to practice finger motor skills by cutting out the shapes. Using the triangle shapes, the children can create kites and use them outdoors.

Cooking

1. Lemonade
1 lemon
2 to 3 tablespoons sugar
1 1/4 cups water
2 ice cubes

Squeeze lemon juice out of lemon. Add the sugar and water. Stir to dissolve the sugar.

This makes one serving. Adjust the recipe to accommodate your class size.

2. Watermelon Popsicles
Remove the seeds and rind from a watermelon. Puree the melon in a blender or food processor. Pour into small paper cups. Freeze partially, then insert popsicle sticks and freeze completely. These fruit popsicles can be served at snack time.

Dramatic Play

1. Fishing
Using short dowels, prepare fishing poles with a string taped to one end. Attach a magnet piece to the loose end of the string. Construct fish from tagboard, and attach a paper clip to each fish. The magnet will attract the paper clip, allowing the children to catch the fish. Add a tackle box, canteen, hats, and life jackets for interest.

2. Garden
A small plastic hoe, rake, and garden shovel can be placed outdoors to encourage gardening. A watering can, flower pots, seed packages, and sun hats will also stimulate interest.

3. Flower Shop
Collect plastic flowers, vases, wrapping paper, seed packages, and catalogs, and place in the dramatic play area. A cash register and play money can be added.

4. Spring Cleaning
Small mops, brooms, feather dusters, and empty pails can be placed in the dramatic play area. A spray bottle filled with blue water, which can be used to wash designated windows, can also be provided.

Field Trips

1. Nature Walk
Walk around your neighborhood, looking for signs of spring. Robins and other birds are

often early signs of spring and can usually
be observed in most areas of the country.

2. **Farm**

Arrange a field trip to a farm. It is an
interesting place to visit during the spring.
Ask the farmer to show you the farm
equipment, buildings, crops, and animals.

Fingerplays and Chants

See, See, See

See, see, see
>(shade eyes with hands)

Three birds are in a tree.
>(hold up three fingers)

One can chirp
>(point to thumb)

And one can sing.
>(point to index finger)

One is just a tiny thing.
>(point to middle finger, then rock baby bird in arms)

See, see, see
Three birds are in a tree
>(hold up three fingers)

Look, look, look
>(shade eyes)

Three ducks are in a brook.
>(hold up three fingers)

One is white, and one is brown.
One is swimming upside down.
>(point to a finger each time)

Look, look, look
Three ducks are in a brook.
>(hold up three fingers)

This Little Calf

(Extend fingers, and push each down in succession)

This little calf eats grass.
This little calf eats hay.
This little calf drinks water.
This little calf runs away.
This little calf does nothing
But just lies down all day.
>(rest last finger in palm of hand)

Raindrops

Rain is falling down.
Rain is falling down.
>(raise arm, flutter fingers to ground, tapping the floor)

Pitter-patter
Pitter-patter
Rain is falling down.

Creepy Crawly Caterpillar

A creepy crawly caterpillar that I see
>(shade eyes)

Makes a chrysalis in the big oak tree.
>(make body into a ball)

He stays there and I know why
>(slowly stand up)

Because soon he will be a butterfly.
>(flap arms)

My Garden

This is my garden.
>(extend one hand forward, palm up)

I'll rake it with care
>(make raking motion on palm with three other fingers)

And then some flower seeds
I'll plant there.
>(planting motion)

The sun will shine
>(make circle with hands)

And the rain will fall.
>(let fingers flutter down to lap)

And my garden will blossom
And grow straight and tall.
>(cup hands together, extend upward slowly)

Caterpillar

The caterpillar crawled from a plant, you see.
>(left hand crawls up and down right arm)

"I think I'll take a nap," said he.
So over the ground he began to creep
>(right hand crawls over left arm)

To spin a chrysalis, and he fell asleep.
>(cover right fist with left hand)

All winter he slept in his bed
Till spring came along and he said,
"Wake up, it's time to get out of bed!"
>(shake fist and pointer finger)

So he opened his eyes that sunny spring
    day.
    (spread fingers and look into hand)
"Look I'm a butterfly!" … and he flew away.
    (interlock thumbs and fly hands away)

Group Time
(Games and Language)

1. What's Inside?
Inside a large box, place many spring items. Include a kite, an umbrella, a hat, a fishing pole, and the like. Select an item without showing the children. Describe the object and give clues about how the item can be used. The children should try to identify the item.

2. Insect Movement
During transition time, ask the children to move like the following insects: worm, grasshopper, caterpillar, butterfly, bumblebee, and others.

Large Muscle

1. Windmills
The children can stand up, swing their arms from side to side, and pretend to be windmills. A fan can be added to the classroom for added interest. Sing the song "Let's Be Windmills," which is listed in the "Music" section.

2. Puddles
Construct puddles out of tagboard, and cover with aluminum foil. Place the puddles on the floor. The children can jump from puddle to puddle. A variation would be to do this activity outside, using chalk to mark puddles on the ground.

3. Caterpillar Crawl
During a transition time, the children can imitate caterpillar movements.

Math

1. Seed Counting
On an index card, mark a numeral. The number of cards prepared will depend on the developmental appropriateness for the children. The children are to glue the appropriate number of seeds onto the card.

2. Insect Seriation
Construct flannel board pieces representing a ladybug, an ant, a caterpillar, a butterfly, and so on. The children can arrange them on the flannel board from smallest to largest.

Music

1. "Catch One if You Can"
(Sing to the tune of "Skip to My Lou")

Butterflies are flying. Won't you try and
    catch one?
Butterflies are flying. Won't you try and
    catch one?
Butterflies are flying. Won't you try and
    catch one?
Catch one if you can.

Raindrops are falling. Won't you try and
    catch one?
Raindrops are falling. Won't you try and
    catch one?
Raindrops are falling. Won't you try and
    catch one?
Catch one if you can.

2. "Signs of Spring"
(Sing to the tune of "Muffin Man")

Do you see a sign of spring,
A sign of spring, a sign of spring?
Do you see a sign of spring?
Tell us what you see.

3. "Let's Be Windmills"
(Sing to the tune of "If I Were a Lassie")

Oh I wish I were a windmill, a windmill, a
    windmill.

Oh I wish I were a windmill. I know what
I'd do.
I'd swing this way and that way, and this
way and that way.
Oh I wish I were a windmill, when the wind
blew.

Science

1. **Alfalfa Sprouts**
Each child who wishes to participate should
be provided with a small paper cup, soil,
and a few alfalfa seeds. The seeds and soil
can be placed in the cup and watered. Place
the cups in the sun, and watch the sprouts
grow. The sprouts can be eaten for snack. A
variation is to plant the sprouts in eggshells
as an Easter activity.

2. **Weather Chart**
A weather chart can be constructed that
depicts weather conditions such as sunny,
rainy, warm, cold, windy, and so on. Attach at
least two arrows to the center of the chart so
that the children can point the arrow at the
appropriate weather conditions.

3. **Thermometers**
On the science table, place a variety
of outdoor thermometers. Also, post a
thermometer outside a window, at a low
position, so the children can read it.

4. **Sprouting Carrots**
Cut the large end off a fresh carrot, and
place it in a small cup of water. In a few
days, a green top will begin to sprout.

5. **Nesting Materials**
Place string, cotton, yarn, and other small
items outside on the ground. Birds will collect
these items to use in their nest building.

6. **Grass Growing**
Grass seeds can be sprinkled on a wet
sponge. Within a few days, the seeds will
begin to sprout.

7. **Ant Farm**
An ant farm can by made by using a large
jar with a cover. Fill the jar 2/3 full with
sand and soil, and add ants. Punch a few air
holes in the cover of the jar, and secure the
cover to the top of the jar. The children can
watch the ants build tunnels.

Sensory

The following items can be added to
the sensory table:

- String, hay, sticks, and yarn to make
  birds' nests
- Tadpoles and water
- Dirt with worms
- Seeds
- Water and boats
- Ice cubes to watch them melt

Social Studies

1. **Animal Babies**
Collect pictures of animals and their young.
Place the adult animal pictures in one
basket and the pictures of the baby animals
in another basket. The children can match
adult animals to their offspring.

2. **Dressing for Spring**
Flannel board figures with clothing items
should be provided. The children can dress
the figures for different kinds of spring
weather.

3. **Spring Clothing**
Collect several pieces of spring clothing
such as a jacket, a hat, galoshes, and short-
sleeved shirts. Add these to the dramatic
play area.

Books

The following books can be used to complement
this theme:

Alarcon, Francisco X. (2005). *Laughing
Tomatoes: And Other Spring Poems.*
Illustrated by Maya Christina Gonzalez.
San Francisco: Children's Book Press.

Albee, Sarah, and Carol Niklaus. (2001). *Spring Fever.* Illustrated by Carol Niklaus. New York: Random House.

Bernard, Robin. (2001). *Tree for All Seasons.* Washington, DC: National Geographic Children's Books.

Bodach, Vijaya Khisty. (2007). *Flowers.* Mankato, MN: Capstone Press.

Esbaum, Jill. (2010). *Everything Spring.* Washington, DC: National Geographic.

Fleming, Denise. (1993). *In the Small, Small, Pond.* New York: H. Holt.

Glaser, Linda. (2002) *It's Spring.* Illustrated by Susan Swan. Minneapolis, MN: Millbrook Press.

Hopkins, Lee Bennett. (2010) *Sharing the Seasons: A Book of Poems.* Illustrated by David Diaz. New York: Margaret K. McElderry Books.

Howard, Fran. (2005). *Butterflies.* Mankato, MN: Capstone Press.

Iwamura, Kazuo. (2009). *Hooray for Spring.* Fitzgerald, GA: North South.

Jackson, Ellen B. (2003). *The Spring Equinox.* Illustrated by Jan Davey Ellis. Brookfield, CT: Millbrook Press.

Lindeen, Carol K. (2004). *Life in a Pond.* Mankato, MN: Capstone Press.

Na, Il Sung. (2011). *Snow Rabbit, Spring Rabbit.* New York: Alfred A. Knopf.

Ouellet, Debbie. (2009). *How Robin Saved Spring.* Illustrated by Nicoletta Ceccoli. New York: Henry Holt.

Raczka, Bob. (2007). *Spring Things.* Illustrated by Judy Stead. Morton Grove, IL: Albert Whitman and Company.

Ray, Mary Lyn. (1996). *Mud.* Illustrated by Lauren Stringer. Orlando, FL: Harcourt Brace.

Roca, Nuria. (2004). *Spring.* Four Season Series. Hauppauge, NY: Barron's Educational Series.

Rockwell, Anne F. (1996). *My Spring Robin.* Madison, WI: Demco Media.

Rustad, Martha E. H. (2006). *Today Is Rainy.* Mankato, MN: Capstone Press.

Schuette, Sarah L. (2007). *Let's Look at Spring.* Mankato, MN: Capstone Press.

Thayer, Tanya. (2001). *Spring.* Minneapolis, MN: First Avenue Editions.

Thompson, Lauren. (2005). *Mouse's First Spring.* Illustrated by Buket Erdogan. New York: Simon and Schuster Books for Young Readers.

Walters, Catherine. (1998). *When Will It Be Spring?* New York: Dutton.

Wong, Herbert Yee. (2007). *Who Likes Rain?* New York: H. Holt.

Yolleck, Joan. (2010). *Paris in the Spring with Picasso.* New York: Schwartz & Wade.

Technology and Multimedia

The following technology and multimedia products can be used to complement this theme:

"My Umbrella" [CD]. (2008). In *Songs for the Whole Day.* Nashville, TN: Lamon Records.

Peep and the Big Wide World [DVD]. (2005). Boston: WGBH Boston Video.

Sesame Street: Elmo's Rainbow and Other Springtime Stories [DVD]. (2010). New York: Sesame Street Workshop.

"Singin' in the Rain" [CD]. (2000). In *Charlotte Diamond's World.* Vancouver, BC: Hug Bug Records.

Spring Science [DVD]. (2005). New York: Scholastic.

"Thunderstorm" [CD]. (2008). In *Rocketship Run.* New York: Two Tomatoes.

 Additional teaching resources to accompany this Theme can be found on the book's companion website. Go to www.cengagebrain.com to access the site for a variety of useful resources.

Science Activities

Try these 25 other interesting science activities:

1. Observe **food forms** such as potatoes in the raw, shredded, or sliced form. Fruits can be juiced, sliced, or sectioned.

2. **Prepare tomatoes** in several ways, such as sliced, juiced, stewed, baked, and pureed.

3. **Show corn** in all forms, including on the cob, popcorn, freshly cooked, and canned.

4. **Sort** picture cards into piles of living and nonliving things.

5. **Record voices.** Encourage the children to recognize each others' voices.

6. **Record familiar sounds** from their environment. Include a ticking clock, telephone ringing, doorbell, toilet flushing, horn beeping, and so on.

7. Take the children on a **sensory walk.** Fill dishpan-sized containers with different items. Foam, sand, leaves, pebbles, mud, cold and warm water, and grains can be used. Have the children remove their shoes and socks to walk through the items.

8. **Enjoy a nature walk.** Provide each child with a grocery bag and instructions to collect leaves, rocks, soil, and so on.

9. Provide the children with **bubbles.** To make the solution, mix 2 quarts water, 3/4 cup liquid soap, and 1/4 cup glycerin (available from a local druggist). Dip plastic berry baskets and plastic six-pack holders into the solution. Wave to produce bubbles.

10. Show the children how to feel their **heartbeat** after a vigorous activity.

11. Observe **popcorn** popping.

12. Record **body weights and heights**.

13. Prepare **hair and eye color charts.** This information can be made into bar graphs.

14. If climate permits, **freeze water outdoors.** Return it to the class, and observe the effects of heat.

15. **Introduce water absorption** by providing containers with water. Allow the children to experiment with coffee filters, paper towels, newspaper, sponges, dishcloths, waxed paper, aluminum foil, and plastic wrap.

16. Explore **magnets.** Provide magnets of assorted sizes, shapes, and strengths. With the magnets, place paper clips, nuts, bolts, aluminum foil, copper pennies, metal spoons, jar lids, feathers, and so on.

17. Plan a **seed party.** Provide the children with dried beans, sunflower seeds, flower seeds, and coconuts. Observe the different sizes, shapes, textures, and flavors.

18. Make a **desk garden.** Cut carrots, turnips, and a pineapple 1 1/2 inches from the stem. Place the stem in a shallow pan of water.

19. Create a **worm farm.** Place gravel and soil in a clear, large-mouth jar. Add worms, and keep soil moist. Place lettuce, corn, or cereal on top of the soil. Tape black construction paper around the outside of the jar. Remove the paper temporarily and see the tunnels the worms have built.

20. Place a **celery stalk** with leaves in a clear container of water. Add blue or red food coloring. Observe the plant's absorption of the colored water. A similar experiment can be introduced with a white carnation.

21. Make a **rainbow** with a garden hose on a sunny day. Spray water across the sun rays. The rays of the sun contain all of the colors, but the water, acting as a prism, separates the colors.

22. Make **shadows.** In a darkened room, use a flashlight. Place a hand or object in front of the light source, making a shadow.

23. Produce **static electricity** by rubbing wool fabric over inflated balloons.
    Note: Supervise the use of balloons.

24. Install a **bird feeder** outside the classroom window.

25. During large group, play the **What's Missing? game.** Provide children with a variety of small familiar items. Tell them to cover their eyes or put their heads down. Remove one item. Then tell the children to uncover. Ask them what is missing. As children gain skill, remove a second and a third item.

Theme 67
SUMMER

Weather
warm
sunny
rainy
humid

Activities
vacationing
swimming
biking
boating
water sports
baseball
camping
golfing
picnics

Holidays
Bastille Day
Memorial Day
Labor Day
Fourth of July
Father's Day
Grandparents' Day

Clothing
shorts
swimsuits
sunglasses
sundresses
lightweight fabrics

Theme Goals

Through participating in the experiences provided by this theme, the children may learn:

1. Summer holidays
2. Types of weather
3. Summer clothing needs
4. Summer activities

Concepts for the Children to Learn

1. Summer is one of the four seasons.
2. Summer comes after spring and before fall.
3. Summer is usually the warmest season.
4. Summer months are usually warm and sunny.
5. It can rain and become humid in the summer.
6. Lightweight clothing is worn in the summer.
7. Shorts, swimsuits, and sundresses are summer clothing.
8. Shade trees protect us from the sun during the summer.
9. Memorial Day, Father's Day, Grandparents' Day, the Fourth of July, Bastille Day, and Labor Day are all summer holidays.
10. There are many summer activities.
11. Swimming, biking, boating, water sports, and camping are all summer activities.
12. Baseball, golfing, and picnicking are also summer activities.
13. Many people take vacations during the summer.

Vocabulary

1. **beach**—a sandy place used for sunbathing and playing.
2. **hot**—a warmer temperature experienced during summer months.
3. **shade**—out of direct sunlight. Sitting under a large tree provides shade.
4. **shorts**—short pants worn in warm weather. Shorts are between the upper thigh and the knee.
5. **summer**—one of the four seasons. Summer comes after spring and before fall.
6. **swimming**—a water sport involving moving through the water with legs and arms. It can be for fun or exercise.

Bulletin Board

The purpose of this bulletin board is to promote the identification of written numerals as well as matching sets of objects to a written numeral. Pairs of pails are constructed out of various scraps of tagboard. Using a black marker, print a different numeral on each pail. The number of pairs made and numerals used should depend on the developmental level of the children. Cut seashells out of tagboard, and decorate as desired. Laminate all pieces. Attach pails to the bulletin board by stapling them along the side and bottom edges, leaving the tops of the pails open. The children should place the corresponding sets of shells in each pail.

Family Letter

InBox

Dear Families,

Summer is the favorite season of most children. As summer approaches, we will start a unit on the season. Through this unit, the children will become more aware of summer weather, activities, holidays, and clothing.

At School

Learning experiences planned to highlight summer concepts include:

- Exploring the outside and inside of a watermelon, and then eating it!
- Trying on shorts, sunglasses, and sandals in the dramatic play area
- Preparing fruit juice popsicles
- Eating a picnic lunch on Wednesday. We will walk to Wilson Park at 11:45 a.m. Please feel free to pack a lunch and meet us there!

At Home

To reinforce summer concepts at home, try the following:

- Plan a family picnic and allow your child to help plan what food and items will be needed.
- Take part in or observe any summer activity such as boating, fishing, camping, or taking a bike ride.

Have a good summer!

Arts and Crafts

1. **Outdoor Painting**
   An easel can be placed outside. The children can choose to use the easel during outdoor playtime. If the sun is shining, encourage the children to observe how quickly the paint dries.

2. **Chalk Drawings**
   Large pieces of chalk should be provided for the children to draw on the sidewalks outdoors. Small plastic berry baskets make handy chalk containers.

3. **Foot Painting**
   This may be used as an outdoor activity. The children can dip their feet in a thick tempera paint mixture and make prints by stepping on large sheets of paper. Sponges and pans of soapy water should be available for cleanup.

4. **Shake Painting**
   Tape a large piece of butcher paper on a fence or wall outdoors. Let the children dip their brushes in paint and stand 2 feet from the paper. Then show them how to shake the brush, allowing the paint to fly onto the paper.

5. **Sailboats**
   Color Styrofoam meat trays with markers. Stick a chenille stem in the center of the tray, and secure it by bending the end underneath the carton. Prepare a sail, and glue to the chenille stem.

Cooking

1. **Popsicles**
   Pineapple juice
   Grape juice
   Cranapple juice
   Craft sticks
   Small paper cups

   If frozen juice is used, mix according to the directions on the can. Fill the paper cups 3/4 full of juice. Place the cups in the freezer.

When the juice begins to freeze, insert a craft stick in the middle of each cup. When frozen, peel away the cup and serve.

2. **Watermelon Popsicles**
   Remove the seeds and rind from a watermelon. Puree the melon in a blender. Follow the recipe for popsicles.

3. **Zippy Drink**
   2 ripe bananas
   2 cups orange juice
   2 cups orange sherbet
   Ice cubes
   Orange slices

   Peel the bananas, place in a bowl, and mash with a fork. Add orange juice and sherbet, and beat with a rotary beater or whisk until smooth. Pour into pitcher. Add ice cubes and orange slices.

4. **Indian Yogurt Dessert**
   8 ounces plain yogurt
   1 can sweetened condensed milk
   1 can evaporated milk
   4 cardamom seeds, crushed, or 1 teaspoon
       ground cardamom
   1/4 teaspoon nutmeg
   Pinch cinnamon
   1/2 cup raisins

   Blend the first six ingredients, and pour into a baking dish. Bake at 275 degrees for 1 hour. After the first 1/2 hour, add raisins by sprinkling over the top. Continue to bake for another 30 minutes. This recipe serves six children and will need to be adjusted to group size if served for a snack.

5. **Sand Dollar Cookies**
   1 cup butter
   1 cup oil
   1 cup sugar
   2 eggs
   1 teaspoon vanilla
   4 1/4 cups flour
   1 teaspoon salt
   1 teaspoon baking soda
   1 teaspoon cream of tartar
   Dried fruit bits or sunflower seeds

   Place the butter and sugar in a large bowl and mix until light and fluffy. Add the eggs and beat. Combine the salt and flour and gradually add to the cream mixture. Mix well. Cover with plastic food wrap and refrigerate for an hour and a half or until easy to handle. Provide each child with a spoonful of dough. Demonstrate how to roll the dough into a ball and press into cookies. Place 5 sunflower seeds or pieces of dried fruit in the middle of the cookie to resemble a sand dollar. Bake 8–10 minutes in a 350-degree oven.

Dramatic Play

1. Juice Stand
Set up a lemonade or orange juice stand. Use real oranges and lemons. Let the children squeeze the fruit and make the drinks. The juice or lemonade can be served at snack time.

2. Ice Cream Stand
Trace and cut ice cream cones from brown construction paper. Cotton balls or small yarn pompons can be used to represent ice cream. The addition of ice cream buckets and ice cream scoopers can make this activity more inviting during self-selected play periods.

3. Indoor or Outdoor Picnic
A blanket, a picnic basket, plastic foods, a small cooler, paper plates, plastic silverware, napkins, and so on can be placed in the classroom to stimulate play.

4. The Beach
In the dramatic play area, place beach blankets, lawn chairs, buckets, sunglasses, beach balls, magazines, and books. If the activity is used outdoors, a sun umbrella can be added to stimulate interest in play.

5. Camping Fun
A small freestanding tent can be set up indoors, if room permits, or outdoors. Sleeping bags can also be provided. Blocks or logs could represent a campfire.

6. Traveling by Air
Place a telephone, tickets, travel brochures, and suitcases in the dramatic play area.

Field Trips and Resource People

1. Picnic at the Park
A picnic lunch can be prepared and eaten at a park or in the play yard.

2. Resource People
The following resource people may be invited to the classroom:

- A lifeguard can talk about water safety.
- A camp counselor can talk to the children about camping and sing some camp songs with the children.

Fingerplays and Chants

Here Is the Beehive
Here is the beehive. Where are the bees?
   (make a fist)
They're hiding away so nobody sees.
Soon they're coming creeping out of their
   hive,
1, 2, 3, 4, 5. Buzz-z-z-z-z.
   (draw fingers out of fist on each count)

Green Leaf
Here's a green leaf
   (show hand)
And here's a green leaf.
   (show other hand)
That, you see, makes two.

Here's a bud
   (cup hands together)
That makes a flower.
Watch it bloom for you!
   (open cupped hands gradually)

A Roly-Poly Caterpillar
Roly-poly caterpillar
Into a corner crept.
Spun around himself a blanket
   (spin around)
Then for a long time slept.
   (place head on folded hands)

Roly-poly caterpillar
Wakened by and by.
    (stretch)
Found himself with beautiful wings
Changed into a butterfly.
    (flutter arms like wings)

Group Time
(Games and Language)

1. Exploring a Watermelon
Serve watermelon for snack. Talk about the color of the outside, which is called the rind. Next, cut the watermelon into pieces. Give each child a piece to examine carefully. "What color is the inside? Are there seeds? Do we eat the seeds? What can we do with them?" The children can remove all the seeds from their piece of watermelon. They also may eat the watermelon. Collect all the seeds. After circle time, wash the seeds. When dry, they can be used for a collage.

2. Puppet Show
Weather permitting, bring puppets and a puppet stage outdoors and have an outdoor puppet show.

Large Muscle

1. Barefoot Walk
Check the playground to ensure that it is free of debris. Sprinkle part of the grass and sandbox with water. Go on a barefoot walk.

2. Balls
In the outdoor play yard, place a variety of large balls.

3. Catching Balloons
Balloons can be used indoors and outdoors. Close supervision is required.
Caution: If a balloon breaks, all its pieces must be immediately discarded.

4. Parachute Play
Use a real parachute or a sheet to represent one. The children should hold onto the edges. Say a number, and then have the children count and wave the parachute in the air that number of times.

5. Balloon Racket Ball
Bend coat hangers into diamond shapes. Bend the handles closed, and tape them for safety. Pull nylon stockings over the diamond shapes to form swatters. The children can use the swatters to keep the balloons up in the air by hitting them.
Caution: If a balloon breaks, all its pieces must be discarded immediately.

Math

1. Sand Numbers and Shapes
During outdoor play, informally make shapes and numbers in the sand, and let children identify the shape or number.

2. Kites
Make a kite out of construction paper. Write a numeral on the kite. Children can glue the appropriate number of ties onto the string.

Music

1. "Summer Clothing"
(Sing to the tune of "The Farmer in the Dell")
(In additional verses, include sandals, tennis shoes, flowers, a sundress, blue jeans, belt, barrettes, and so on. This song can be used during transition times to point out children's summer clothing.)

Oh, if you are wearing shorts,
If you are wearing shorts,
You may walk right to the door,
If you are wearing shorts.

2. "Summer Activities"
(Sing to the tune of "Skip to My Lou")
(In additional verses, include jump, hop, skip, run, walk, and so on. Use this song as a transition song to introduce summer activities.)

Swim, swim, swim in a circle.
Swim, swim, swim in a circle.
Swim, swim, swim in a circle.
Swim in a circle now.

3. "Oh, the Sun Is Shining Brightly"

(Sing to the tune of "She'll Be Coming around the Mountain")

Oh, the sun is shining brightly in the sky!
Oh, the sun is shining brightly in the sky!
Oh, the sun is far away,
but shines down all through the day.
Oh, the sun is shining brightly in the sky!

Science

1. Science Table

Add the following items to the science table:

- All kinds of sunglasses with different-colored shades
- Grass seeds planted in small cups of dirt for the children to water daily
- Dirt and grass with magnifying glasses
- Sand with scales and magnifying glasses
- Pinwheels (children blow on them to make them move)
- Bubbles to blow outdoors

2. Water and Air Make Bubbles

Bubble solution:

3/4 cup liquid soap
1/4 cup glycerin (obtain at a drugstore)
2 quarts water

Mix ingredients of solution, place in a shallow pan, and let the children place the bubble makers in the solution. Bubble makers can be successfully made from the following:

- A plastic six-pack drink holder
- Straws
- Bent wire with no sharp edges
- Funnels

3. Flying Kites

On a windy day, make and fly kites.

4. Making Rainbows

If you have a hose available, the children can spray the hose into the sun. The rays of the sun contain all the colors mixed together. The water acts as a prism and separates the water into colors, creating a rainbow.

Sensory

1. Sensory Table

The following items can be added to the sensory table:

- Sand with toys
- Colored sand
- Sand and water
- Water with toy boats
- Shells
- Small rocks and pebbles
- Grass and hay

2. Kool-Aid Smell

Purchase several different kinds of Kool-Aid or powdered drink mix. Pour each packet into a container. Give children a spray bottle to spray water over the powdered Kool-Aid. Ask them to smell each kind and try to identify the flavor.

Social Studies

1. Making Floats

To celebrate the Fourth of July, decorate tricycles, wagons, and scooters with crêpe paper, streamers, balloons, and so on. Parade around the school or neighborhood.

2. Summer at School

Take pictures or slides of community summer activities. Construction workers, parades, children playing, sports activities, people swimming, library hours, picnics, band concerts, and people driving are examples. Show the slides and discuss them during group time.

3. Summer Fun Book

Magazines should be provided for the children to find pictures of summer activities. The pictures can be pasted on a sheet of paper. Bind the pages by stapling them together to make a book.

 **Books**

The following books can be used to complement this theme:

Asch, Frank. (2008). *The Sun Is My Favorite Star*. Orlando, FL: Harcourt Books.

Cousins, Lucy. (2001). *Maisy at the Beach*. Cambridge, MA: Candlewick Press.

Fleming, Denise. (1991). *In the Tall, Tall Grass*. New York: H. Holt.

Franco, Betsy. (2007). *Summer Beat*. Illustrated by Charlotte Middleton. New York: Margaret McElderry Books.

George, Lindsay Barrett. (1996). *Around the Pond: Who's Been Here?* New York: Greenwillow.

Glaser, Linda. (2003). *It's Summer*. Illustrated by Susan Swan. Minneapolis, MN: Millbrook Press.

Hopkins, Lee Bennett. (2010). *Sharing the Seasons: A Book of Poems*. Illustrated by David Diaz. New York: Margaret K. McElderry Books.

Iwamura, Kazuo. (2010). *Hooray for Summer*. Fitzgerald, GA: North South.

Jackson, Ellen B. (2003). *The Summer Solstice*. Illustrated by Jan Davey Ellis. Brookfield, CT: Millbrook Press.

Lindeen, Carol K. (2006). *Let's Swim!* Mankato, MN: Capstone Press.

London, Jonathan. (2001). *Sun Dance Water Dance*. New York: Viking.

Low, Alice, and Roy McKie. (2001). *Summer*. Illustrated by Roy McKie. New York: Beginner Books.

McClure, Nikki. (2010). *Mama, Is It Summer Yet?* New York: Abrams Books for Young Readers.

Munoz Ryan, Pam. (2001). *Hello Ocean*. Illustrated by Mark Astrella and translated by Yanitzia Canetti. Watertown, MA: Charlesbridge Publishing.

Pfeffer, Wendy. (2010). *The Longest Day: Celebrating the Summer Solstice*. Illustrated by Linda Bleck. New York: Dutton Juvenile.

Raczka, Bob. (2009). *Summer Wonders*. Illustrated by Judy Stead. Morton Grove, IL: Albert Whitman.

Roca, Nuria. (2004). *Summer*. Hauppauge, NY: Barron's Educational Series.

Roosa, Karen. (2001). *Beach Day*. Illustrated by Maggie Smith. New York: Clarion Books.

Schuette, Sarah L. (2007). *Let's Look at Summer*. Mankato, MN: Capstone Press.

Seeger, Laura Vaccaro. (2010). *What If?* New York: Roaring Brook Press.

Thompson, Lauren. (2004). *Mouse's First Summer*. Illustrated by Buket Erdogan. New York: Simon and Schuster Books for Young Readers.

Williams, Karen Lynn. (2010). *A Beach Tail*. Illustrated by Floyd Cooper. Honesdale, PA: Boyds Mills Press.

Wing, Natasha. (2002). *The Night before Summer Vacation*. Illustrated by Julie Durrell. New York: Grosset & Dunlap.

 **Technology and Multimedia**

The following technology and multimedia products can be used to complement this theme:

Arthur's Great Summer [DVD]. (2002). New York: Random House Home Video.

"A Day at the Beach" [CD]. (2007). In *Bari Koral Rock Band*. New York: Bari Koral Rock Band.

Elmo's World: Summer Vacation [DVD]. (2008). Studio City, CA: JH Genius Entertainment.

"Just Like the Sun" [CD]. (1987). In *Raffi, Everything Grows*. Cambridge, MA: Rounder/UMGD.

"Just Like the Sun" [CD]. (2010). In *Laurie Berkner: Under a Shady Tree*. New York: Two Tomatoes.

"Mr. Sun" [CD]. (1976). In *Singable Songs for the Very Young*. Cambridge, MA: Rounder/UMGD.

"Seasons" [CD]. (2004). In *Circle Time Activities*. Long Branch, NJ: Kimbo Educational.

"Summertime, Summertime" [CD]. (2000). In *Bean Bag Rock and Roll*. Long Branch, NJ: Kimbo Educational.

"Sunscreen" [CD]. (2001). In *Seasonal Songs in Motion*. Long Branch, NJ: Kimbo Educational.

 Additional teaching resources to accompany this Theme can be found on the book's companion website. Go to www.cengagebrain.com to access the site for a variety of useful resources.

THANKSGIVING

Symbols
Native Americans
harvest
turkey
cornucopia
fruits
vegetables
Pilgrims

Traditions
family celebrations
giving thanks

Foods
turkey
dressing
potatoes and gravy
corn
squash
cornbread
cranberries
pumpkin pie

Giving Thanks
our health
our friends
our families

Theme Goals

Through participating in the experiences provided by this theme, the children may learn:

1. The purpose of Thanksgiving
2. Thanksgiving traditions
3. Thanksgiving foods
4. Thanksgiving symbols

Concepts for the Children to Learn

1. Thanksgiving is a holiday.
2. Holidays are special days to celebrate something that has happened.
3. Thanksgiving is a time for giving thanks.
4. Families and friends celebrate together on Thanksgiving.
5. People give thanks for their family, friends, and health on Thanksgiving.
6. Turkey, dressing, potatoes, gravy, corn, squash, cranberries, and pumpkin pie are eaten on Thanksgiving by many families.
7. A turkey, cornucopia, Pilgrims, and Native Americans are Thanksgiving symbols.

Vocabulary

1. **holiday**—a special day to celebrate something.
2. **cornucopia**—a horn-shaped container with fruits, vegetables, and flowers.
3. **Native Americans**—natives who lived in America when the Pilgrims first arrived.
4. **Pilgrims**—early settlers who sailed to America.
5. **thankful**—expressing thanks.
6. **Thanksgiving**—a holiday in November to give thanks.
7. **turkey**—a large white or brown bird with a long neck. Turkey is the meat cooked and served at Thanksgiving.

Bulletin Board

The purpose of this bulletin board is to have the children hang the color-coded card with the printed word onto the corresponding colored feather. Construct a large turkey out of tagboard. Color each feather a different color. Hang the turkey on the bulletin board. Next, hang a pushpin in each feather. On small index cards, make a circle of each color and write the color name above it as illustrated. Use a hole punch to make a hole in each card

Family Letter

InBox

Dear Families,

During the month of November each year, we celebrate Thanksgiving. To coincide with this holiday at school, we will focus our curriculum on a Thanksgiving theme. Through the activities provided, the children will develop an understanding of Thanksgiving symbols and foods. They will also become more aware of the many people and things for which we are thankful.

At School

Planned learning experiences related to Thanksgiving include:

- Popping corn
- Creating hand turkeys
- Visiting a turkey farm
- Exploring various types of corn with scales and magnifying glasses

At Home

There are many ways for you to incorporate Thanksgiving concepts at home. Talk with your child about the special ways your family celebrates Thanksgiving. Involve your child in the preparation of a traditional Thanksgiving dish. Also, emphasize things and people for which you are thankful.

Reminder

There will be no school on Thursday, November   , and Friday, November   . For those of you who are traveling during the Thanksgiving weekend, drive safely!

Happy Thanksgiving from the staff!

Arts and Crafts

1. **Thanksgiving Collage**
Place magazines on the art table so the children can cut out things for which they are thankful. After the pictures are cut, they can be pasted on paper to form a collage.

2. **Cornmeal Play Dough**
Make cornmeal play dough. Mix 2 1/2 cups flour with 1 cup cornmeal. Add 1 tablespoon oil and 1 cup water. Additional water can be added to make the desired texture. The dough should have a grainy texture. Cookie cutters and rolling pins can extend this activity.

3. **Popcorn Collage**
Place popped popcorn and dried tempera paint into small sealable bags. Have children shake the bags to color the popcorn. Have them create designs and pictures by gluing the popcorn onto the paper. You can also use unpopped colored popcorn. *Caution:* Make sure the children do not eat any of the popcorn after it has been mixed with paint.

4. **Hand Turkey**
Paper, crayons, or pencils are needed. Begin by instructing the children to place a hand on a piece of paper. Next, tell them to spread their fingers. If possible, have the children trace their own fingers. Otherwise, you need to trace them. The hand can be decorated to create a turkey. Eyes, a beak, and a wattle can be added to the outline of the thumb. The fingers can be colored to represent the turkey's feathers. Legs can be added below the outline of the palm.

5. **Pumpkin Pie Play Dough**
This smells great, so remind small children that it is not for eating.
6 1/2 cups flour
2 cups salt
9 teaspoons cream of tarter
3/4 cup vegetable oil
1 (1 1/2 ounce) container pumpkin pie spice
Orange food coloring (4 drops yellow and 2 drops red)
4 1/2 cups water

Combine all of the ingredients. Over medium heat, cook and stir until all lumps disappear. Knead the dough on a floured surface, and add additional flour if necessary, until it is smooth. Store in an airtight container.

Cooking

1. **Fu Fu from West Africa**
3 or 4 yams
Water
1/2 teaspoon salt
3 tablespoons honey or sugar (optional)

Wash and peel yams, and cut into 1/2-inch slices. Place slices in a large saucepan, and add water to cover them. Bring to a boil over a hot plate or stove. Reduce heat, cover saucepan, and simmer for 20 to 25 minutes until yams are soft enough to mash. Remove saucepan from stove, and drain off liquid into a small bowl. Let yams cool for 15 minutes. Place yam slices in a medium-sized mixing bowl, mash with a fork, add salt, and mash again until smooth. Roll mixture into small, walnut-sized balls. If the mixture is too dry, moisten it with a tablespoon of the reserved yam liquid. For sweeter Fu Fu, roll yam balls in a dish of honey or sugar. Makes 24 balls.

2. **Muffins**
1 egg
3/4 cup milk
1/2 cup vegetable oil
2 cups all-purpose flour
1/3 cup sugar
3 tablespoons baking powder
1 teaspoon salt

Heat oven to 400 degrees. Grease bottoms only of 12 medium muffin cups. Beat egg. Stir in milk and oil. Stir in remaining ingredients all at once, just until flour is moistened. Batter will be lumpy. Fill muffin cups about 3/4 full. Bake until golden brown, about 20 minutes.

For pumpkin muffins: stir in 1/2 cup canned pumpkin and 1/2 cup raisins with the milk, and 2 teaspoons pumpkin pie spice with the flour.

For cranberry-orange muffins: stir in 1 cup cranberry halves and 1 tablespoon grated orange peel with milk.

3. **Cranberry Freeze**
    1 16-ounce can (2 cups) whole cranberry
        sauce
    1 8-ounce can (1 cup) crushed pineapple,
        drained
    1 cup sour cream or yogurt

    In a medium bowl, combine all the ingredients and mix well. Pour the mixture into an 8-inch square pan or an ice cube tray. Freeze 2 hours or until firm. To serve, cut into squares or pop out of the ice cube tray.

Dramatic Play

Shopping
    Set up a grocery store in the dramatic play area. To stimulate play, provide a cash register, shopping bags, and empty food containers such as boxes, packages, and plastic bottles.

Field Trips and Resource People

Turkey Farm
    Visit a turkey farm. The children can observe the behavior of the turkeys as well as the food they eat.

Fingerplays and Chants

Thanksgiving Dinner
    Every day we eat our dinner.
    Our table is very small.
        (palms of hands close together)

There's room for father, mother, sister,
    brother, and me—that's all.
    (point to each finger)
But when it's Thanksgiving Day and the
    company comes,
You'd scarcely believe your eyes.
    (rub eyes)
For that very same reason, the table
    stretches until it is just this size!
    (stretch arms wide)

Gobble, Gobble
    The turkey is a funny bird,
    His head goes wobble wobble.
        (place hands together and go back and
        forth)
    And all he knows is just one word,
    Gobble, gobble, gobble.

The Big Turkey
    The big turkey on the farm is so very proud.
        (form fist)
    He spreads his tail like a fan
        (spread fingers of other hand behind fist)
    And struts through the animal crowd.
        (move two fingers of fist as walking)
    If you talk to him as he wobbles along
    He'll answer back with a gobbling song:
    "Gobble, gobble, gobble."
        (open and close hand)

Little Turkey
    I saw a little turkey
        (use hands to show the little)
    Standing by a tree.
    It gobbled and wobbled.
        (use hands to show gobbling and wobbling)
    Then it ran away from me.

    Oh, turkey, turkey, turkey.
    Please come back out and play!
        (use hands to motion come)
    I promise I will not eat you.
    On Thanksgiving Day.

Group Time
(Games and Language)

1. **Turkey Chase**
    Have the children sit in a circle formation. The game requires two balls of different

colors. Vary the size, depending on the age of the children. Generally, the younger the child, the larger the ball size. Begin by explaining that the first ball passed is the "turkey." The second ball is the "turkey farmer." The first ball should be passed from child to child around the circle. Shortly after, pass the second ball in the same direction. The game ends when the turkey farmer, the second ball, catches up to the turkey, the first ball. This game is played like "Hot Potato."

2. **Feast**

Place several kinds of food on a plate in the middle of the circle. Tell the children to cover their eyes. Choose one child to take something from the plate to eat. The child hides one item, and the others open their eyes and try to guess which food item the child has eaten! The number of items included in this activity should be determined by the children's developmental age. It may be advisable to begin with only two food items.

3. **Turkey Keeper**

To play this game, you need a turkey cut from cardboard or a small plastic replica. Instruct one child to cover his or her eyes. Quietly hide the turkey in the classroom. Next, instruct the child to open his or her eyes and look for the turkey. When the child begins walking in the direction of the turkey, the rest of the children provide a clue by saying quietly, "Gobble gobble." As the child approaches the turkey, the children's voices serve as a clue by becoming louder. Once the turkey is located, another child becomes the turkey keeper.

4. **Drop the Wishbone**

Tell the children to sit in a circle formation. Choose one child to walk around the outside of the circle and drop a wishbone behind another child. (If a real wishbone is unavailable, a wishbone can be cut from cardboard.) The child who had the wishbone dropped behind him or her must pick it up and chase the first child. If the first child is tagged before he or she runs around the circle and sits in the second child's place, he or she is "it" again. If not, the second child is "it." This is a variation of "Drop the Handkerchief."

5. **Turkey Waddle**

Provide the children with verbal and visual clues to waddle like turkeys. The following terms may be used:

- Big turkey
- Little turkey
- Fast turkey
- Slow turkey
- Tired turkey
- Happy turkey
- Proud turkey
- Sad turkey
- Hungry turkey
- Full turkey

 **Large Muscle**

Popping Corn

Pretend to be popping corn. Begin by demonstrating how to curl down on the floor, explaining that everyone is a kernel of corn. Then plug in the popcorn popper and listen to the sounds. Upon hearing popping sounds, jump up and down to the sounds.

 Math

1. **Turkey Shapes**

Give children several geometric shapes to create their own turkeys with circles, squares, and triangles. Have children identify the shapes and colors as they create their turkeys.

2. **Colored Popcorn**

Provide the children with colored popcorn seeds. Place corresponding colored circles in the bottom of muffin tins or egg cartons. Encourage the children to sort the seeds by color.

 Music

1. **"Popcorn Song"**
(Sing to the tune of "I'm a Little Teapot")

I'm a little popcorn in a pot.
Heat me up and watch me pop.
When I get all fat and white, then I'm done.
Popping corn is lots of fun.

2. "If You're Thankful"

(Sing to the tune of "If You're Happy")
(Additional verses could include "stamp your feet," "tap your head," "turn around," "shout hooray," and so on)

If you're thankful and you know it, clap
    your hands.
If you're thankful and you know it, clap
    your hands.
If you're thankful and you know it, then
    your face will surely show it,
If you're thankful and you know it, clap
    your hands.

Science

1. Corn
Display several types of corn on the science table. Include field corn, popcorn, and popped popcorn.

2. Wishbone
Bring in a wishbone from a turkey and place it in a bottle. Pour some vinegar in the bottle to cover the wishbone. Leave the wishbone in the bottle for 24 hours. Remove it and feel it. It will feel and bend like rubber.

Sensory

The following items can be placed in the sensory area for the children to discover:

- Unpopped or popped popcorn
- Pinecones
- Cornmeal and measuring cups

Books

The following books can be used to complement this theme:

Arnosky, Jim. (1998). *All about Turkeys*. New York: Scholastic.

Atwell, Debby. (2006). *The Thanksgiving Door*. New York: Houghton Mifflin.

Bateman, Teresa. (2004). *A Plump and Perky Turkey*. Illustrated by Jeff Shelly. New York: Scholastic.

Boelts, Maribeth. (2004). *The Firefighter's Thanksgiving*. Illustrated by Terry Widener. New York: Putnam's Sons.

Cowley, Joy. (1996). *Gracias, the Thanksgiving Turkey*. Illustrated by Joe Cepeda. New York: Scholastic.

Crane, Carol. (2007). *P Is for Pilgram: A Thanksgiving Alphabet*. Chelsea, MI: Sleeping Bear Press.

Frienman, Laurie B., and Teresa Murfin. *Thanksgiving Rules*. Minneapolis, MN: Carolrhoda Books.

Gibbons, Gail. (2005). *Thanksgiving Is …* New York: Holiday House.

Gibbons, Gail. (2009). *Corn*. New York: Holiday House.

Glaser, Linda. (2001). *It's Fall*. Illustrated by Susan Swan. Minneapolis, MN: Millbrook Press.

Jackson, Alison, et al. (1997). *I Know an Old Lady Who Swallowed a Pie*. Illustrated by Byron Schachner. New York: Dutton.

Johnston, Tony. (2004). *10 Fat Turkeys*. Illustrated by Rich Deas. New York: Cartwheel.

Jules, Jacqueline. (2009). *Duck for Turkey Day*. Illustrated by Kathryn Mitter. Morton Grove, IL: Albert Whitman.

Kamma, Anne. (2001). *If You Were at the First Thanksgiving*. Illustrated by Bert Dodson. New York: Scholastic.

Markes, Julie. (2008). *Thanks for Thanksgiving*. New York: HarperCollins.

Melmed, Laura Krauss. (2003). *The First Thanksgiving Day: A Counting Story*. New York: HarperCollins.

Pilkey, Dav. (2004). *Twas the Night before Thanksgiving*. New York: Scholastic.

Roberts, Bethany. (2005). *Thanksgiving Mice!* Illustrated by Doug Cushman. New York: Clarion Books.

Silvano, Wendi. (2009) *Turkey Trouble*. Tarrytown, NY: Marshall Cavendish.

Spinelli, Eileen. (2007). *The Perfect Thanksgiving*. Illustrated by JoAnn Adinolfi. New York: Square Fish.

Stewart, Pat. (2001). *Learning about Thanksgiving*. New York: Dover.

Sutherland, Margaret. (2000). *Thanksgiving Is for Giving Thanks*. Illustrated by Sonja Lamut. New York: Grosset & Dunlap.

Wing, Natasha, and Tammie Lyon. (2001). *The Night before Thanksgiving*. Illustrated by Tammie Lyon. New York: Grosset & Dunlap.

Ziefert, Harriet. (2004). *This Is Thanksgiving*. Illustrated by Deborah Zemke. Maplewood, NJ: Blue Apple Books.

Technology and Multimedia

The following technology and multimedia products can be used to complement this theme:

Holiday Facts and Fun: Thanksgiving [DVD]. (2004). Chicago, ILL:SVE & Churchill Media.

"I'm Gonna Eat" [CD]. (2001). In *Whaddaya Think of That, Laurie Berkner.* New York: Two Tomatoes.

Squanto and the First Thanksgiving [DVD]. (2005). Norwalk, CT: Rabbit Ears Entertainment, Clearvue & SVE.

Stories for Thanksgiving [DVD]. (2003). Norwalk, CT: Weston Woods.

"Thanks Alot" [CD]. (1980). In *Baby Beluga*. Cambridge, MA: Rounder/UMGD.

 Additional teaching resources to accompany this Theme can be found on the book's companion website. Go to www.cengagebrain.com to access the site for a variety of useful resources.

TREES

Fruit
apple
banana
pear
tangerine
lemon
grapefruit
apricot

Kinds
hardwoods
softwoods
evergreens
deciduous

Parts
buds
leaves
branches
bark
sap
trunk
roots

Purpose
shade
wood
wood products
clean air
create oxygen for
breathing
food
animal homes

Care
soil
water
sunlight

Animal Homes
owls
squirrels
birds
chipmunks

Theme Goals

Through participating in the experiences provided by this theme, the children may learn:

1. Parts of a tree
2. Kinds of trees
3. Care of trees
4. The purpose of trees
5. Types of fruit trees
6. Animal homes in trees

Concepts for the Children to Learn

1. A tree is a large plant.
2. There are many kinds of trees, including hardwoods and softwoods.
3. A tree has many parts: buds, leaves, branches, bark, trunk, and roots.
4. The leaves of some trees are like needles.
5. The trunk is the stem of the tree and is covered with bark.
6. The roots of a tree are underground.
7. Roots help the tree stand; they also get water and nutrients from the soil.
8. Sap is a liquid that supplies food to the tree.
9. Trees need soil, water, and sunlight to grow.
10. Trees provide us with wood.
11. Many items are made from wood, such as houses, chairs, tables, some toys, doors, fences, paper, and paper products.
12. Some trees provide us with food.
13. Some fruits grow on trees.
14. Apples, bananas, pears, lemons, tangerines, apricots, and grapefruits grow on trees.
15. Trees provide homes for many animals.
16. Owls, squirrels, birds, and chipmunks live in trees.
17. Trees provide us with shade to keep us cool and protect us from the sun.
18. Trees help provide oxygen for us to breathe.

Vocabulary

1. **bark**—the tough, outer covering of a tree.
2. **root**—the underground part of a plant.
3. **sap**—the fluid part of a tree.
4. **tree**—a large plant.
5. **trunk**—the main stem and largest part of a tree.

Bulletin Board

The purpose of this bulletin board is to provide numeral identification as well as matching sets of objects to numerals. To prepare the bulletin board, construct tree trunks out of brown tagboard. Print a numeral on each trunk. Next, construct treetops out of green tagboard. Draw leaves on each treetop. Trace and cut out treetop shadows from black construction paper. Using the illustration as a guide, attach the shadows and tree trunks to the bulletin board. Adhesive magnet pieces or map tacks can be used by the children to match each tree trunk to the corresponding treetop.

Family Letter

InBox

Dear Families,

Did you ever stop to think about what our world would be like without trees? Trees serve many purposes; consequently, we will explore a theme on trees beginning this week. Through the experiences provided in this curriculum unit, the children will become aware of the parts, kinds, care, and importance of trees.

At School

We will use wood to build houses, schools, chairs, tables, and several other objects. We will make paper. We will talk about foods that grow on trees. The foods served at snack time will be foods that grow on trees. Some of the week's activities will include:

- Creating leaf and bark rubbings in the art area
- Going on a "tree walk" and recording the number and kinds of trees we see
- Cooking with foods we get from trees
- Creating our own books in the writing center
- Planting citrus fruit seeds and an avocado seed
- Listening to stories related to trees

At Home

Walk around your home and find all the things that are made from wood. Which room contains the most wood items?

Polish your furniture with your child. Show him or her how to care for fine wood products.

Try preparing the following recipe with your child:

Enjoy your child!

There are many kinds of trees, with many kinds of leaves.

Arts and Crafts

1. Tree Rubbing

Use crayons or chalk to create rubbings of various tree parts. Place leaves under a single sheet of newsprint. Rub the crayon over the top of the paper until the imprint of the leaf appears. Try making additional rubbings using bark and maple seeds.

2. Twig Painting

Twigs from trees can be used as painting tools. Provide the children with trays of tempera paint of a thick consistency and construction paper to create designs. The children may also enjoy experimenting with the twig as a writing tool.

3. Pine Needle Brushes

Cut branches from a pine needle tree. Place the branches at the easel so that the children can use them as brushes to apply paint.

4. Decorating Pinecones

Collect pinecones of different sizes. Place them on the art table with trays of thick, colored tempera paints, glitter, glue, yarn, sequins, and strips of paper for the children to decorate the pinecones.

5. Sawdust Play Dough

Combine 2 cups of sawdust, 3 cups of flour, and 1 cup of salt. Add water as needed to make a pliable dough. (Sawdust can be obtained, usually at no cost, from a local lumber company.)

6. Textured Paint

Add sawdust to prepared paints for use at the art table or easel.

7. Make a Tree

Collect paper towel and toilet paper rolls. The children can paint or cover them with construction paper to resemble tree trunks. Branches and leaves can be fabricated from chenille stems and construction paper. The branches and leaves can then be attached to the trunk.

Cooking

1. Guacamole Dip

1 medium avocado
2 tablespoons chopped onion
1/4 teaspoon chili powder
1/4 teaspoon garlic salt
2 tablespoons mayonnaise or salad dressing

Peel and cut the avocado into pieces and process at medium speed in a blender. Add remaining ingredients and blend. Serve the dip with tortilla or corn chips.

2. Orange Raisin Cookies

1 cup sugar
3/4 cup softened butter or margarine
1/4 cup milk
1 teaspoon vanilla
1 egg
2 cups flour
1/2 cup raisins
2 tablespoons grated orange peel
1 teaspoon baking powder
3/4 teaspoon salt

Combine sugar, butter, milk, vanilla, and egg in a large mixing bowl. Add remaining ingredients and blend well. Drop by rounded teaspoonfuls onto ungreased cookie sheets. Bake for 9–12 minutes or until lightly browned in a 370-degree oven. Remove cookies from sheet and cool.

3. **Prepare recipes that include the following items that come from trees:**

Apples	Limes
Apricots	Maple syrup
Avocados	Nectarines
Cherries	Nutmeg
Cinnamon	Olives
Cloves	Oranges
Dates	Peaches
Figs	Pears
Grapefruit	Prunes
Lemons	

Caution: Beware of the potential of children choking on fruit seeds. Remove seeds such as avocado, cherry, apricot, peach, and olive pits when using in recipes for young children. Also, check for children's allergies before food experiences.

4. **Broccoli Trees**
Use broccoli florets to resemble trees and eat as a healthy snack.

Dramatic Play

1. **Construction Site**
Design a construction site in the dramatic play area. Provide props such as hard hats, blueprints, floor plans, rulers, tape measures, lumber scraps, wooden blocks, and cardboard boxes.

2. **Birds**
Trace and cut bird masks and wings from tagboard for the children to wear. Display pictures of trees and birds. Play a tape of bird songs. A variation would be to decorate a climber with green crêpe paper to resemble a tree.

Field Trips and Resource People

Nature Walk

Take the children on a nature walk. Bring magnifying glasses to observe interesting specimens and bags to collect specimens. Observe leaves, tree stumps, tree bark, twigs, and flowers.

The following sources can be contacted for more information:

- Area forest industries such as paper mills and logging companies
- Department of Natural Resources
- University or county extension offices
- National, state, and local parks
- Nature centers
- University departments of biology, botany, construction, forestry, and horticulture

Fingerplays and Chants

The Apple Tree
Way up high in the apple tree
    (raise arms over head)
Two little apples smiled at me.
    (make fists or circles with hands)
I shook that tree as hard as I could
    (move hands as if shaking something)
Down came the apples
    (falling motion with fists)
Mmmmmmmmmm—were they good!
    (rub tummy)

Orange Tree
This is the orange tree with leaves so green
    (raise arms over head, making a circle)
Here are the oranges that hang in between.
    (make fists)
When the wind blows the oranges will fall.
Here is the basket to gather them all.
    (make circle with arms in front of body)

I Am a Tall Tree

I am a tall tree.
I reach toward the sky
    (reach upward with both hands)
Where the bright stars twinkle
And white clouds float by.
    (sway arms above head)
My branches toss high
As the wild winds blow.
    (wave arms rapidly)
Now they bend forward
Loaded with snow.
    (arms out front swaying)
I like it best
When I rock birds to sleep in their nest.
    (place hands at the side of head and
    close eyes)

The Wind

Who has seen the wind?
Neither I nor you;
But when the leaves hang trembling,
    (hold hands downward and wiggle
    fingers)
The wind is passing through.

Who has seen the wind?
Neither you nor I;
But when the trees bow down their heads,
    (move head downward)
The wind is passing by.

Group Time
(Games and Language)

1. **Tree Chart**
On a large piece of tagboard, print the title "Things Made from Trees." During group time, present the chart and record the children's responses. Display the completed chart and refer to it throughout the theme.

2. **Movement Activity: "Happy Leaves"**
Cut leaves out of various colors of construction paper. During group time, give each child one leaf. When the children hear the color of their leaf in the following rhyme, they may stand up and move like leaves:

Little red leaves are glad today,
For the wind is blowing them off and away,
They are flying here, they are flying there.
Oh, little red leaves, you are everywhere.
Repeat the rhyme and insert additional
    color words.

Large Muscle

1. **Wooden Climber**
If available, set up a wooden climber on the playground or in the classroom so the children can practice their climbing skills.

2. **Wooden Balance Beam**
If available, set up a wooden balance beam in an open area of the classroom. Suggest ways for the children to cross the beam: walking heel to toe, walking sideways, crawling, and walking holding an object. Older children may be able to walk backward.

Math

1. **Tree Walk**
Record the number of trees observed on a walk. If appropriate, the trees might also be classified as "broadleaf" or "evergreen" or by the type of tree, such as maple, oak, pine, and so on.

2. **Sorting and Counting Activities**
The following items can be collected and used for various sorting and counting activities:

- Acorns
- Small pinecones
- Apple seeds
- Citrus fruit seeds

3. **Items Made from Trees**
Collect items from the classroom for children to sort and then classify those made from trees as "wooden items" and

others as "nonwooden items." Label and provide boxes or similar containers for the children to place the items. If appropriate, the children can count the number of items in each category and record the results.

Music

1. **"Little Leaves"**
(Sing to the tune of "Ten Little Indians")

One little, two little, three little leaves.
Four little, five little, six little leaves.
Seven little, eight little, nine little leaves.
Ten little leaves fall down.

2. **"Foods That Grow on Trees"**
(Sing to the tune of "The Farmer in the Dell")

Foods that grow on trees.
Foods that grow on trees.
Let's sing a song about
Foods that grow on trees.

Apples grow on trees.
Apples grow on trees.
Pick them, red and sweet.
Apples grow on trees.

Bananas grow on trees.
Bananas grow on trees.
Pick them, yellow and long.
Bananas grow on trees.

Oranges grow on trees.
Oranges grow on trees.
Pick them, sweet and juicy.
Oranges grow on trees.

Walnuts grow on trees.
Walnuts grow on trees.
Pick them, brown and crunchy.
Walnuts grow on trees.

Science

1. **Weighing Items from Trees**
Provide a balance scale and acorns, pinecones, or seed pods at the science table.

2. **Planting Seeds**
Collect and plant seeds from fruits that grow on trees such as apples and citrus fruits. Make and record predictions about when the plants will sprout.

3. **Grow an Avocado Tree**
Remove a seed from an avocado. Peel the brown outer covering of the seed. Poke three toothpicks into the avocado seed at equal distances from one another. Place the seed in a glass of lukewarm water with the largest end submerged. Replace the water once a week. Sprouts will appear in about three weeks. When the stem and roots are several inches long, transplant the avocado into a pot that is about 1 inch wider than the avocado.

4. **Leaf Book**
Collect leaves from various trees. Mount each leaf on a piece of construction paper or tagboard. Then print the name of the tree the leaf represents. Gather the pages and bind with loose-leaf rings. Place the book in the science area for the children to review.

5. **Shade versus Sun**
Place an outdoor thermometer in direct sunlight and another beneath the shade of a tree. Compare results. A chart could also be made for this activity, and results could be compared for several days.

6. **Pinecone Bird Feeders**
Collect pinecones. Attach a piece of yarn or string to the stem. Use a plastic knife to spread shortening, lard, or soft butter over the pinecone and then roll in birdseed. Hang the feeder outside.

7. **Make Paper**
Cut a piece of screen 7 inches × 11 inches and frame with wood. Tear construction paper or tissues into 1-inch pieces. Place the shredded paper pieces in a blender. Add enough water to cover and blend the paper into pulp. Pour the pulp into a 9-inch × 13-inch tray. Use the framed screen to pan the pulp, moving it to get an even layer of pulp. Lift the screen out of the pan in a straight, upward direction. Place the screen on a stack of newspapers. Roll with a rolling pin to squeeze out water. Lift off the

newspaper, and gently peel the homemade paper from the screen; allow it to dry on paper towels or newspaper.

Sensory

1. Wood Shavings
Obtain wood shavings from a local lumber company. Place them in the sensory table along with scoops and pails.

2. Pinecones
Collect pinecones of various sizes, and place them in the sensory table. Small boxes, pails, and scoops can be added.

3. Acorns
Collect acorns and allow them to dry thoroughly before placing in the sensory table. Add accessories to encourage participation such as pails, small paper bags, scoops, and spoons.

Social Studies

Family Tree
Cut a tree trunk out of brown tagboard. Cut a treetop out of green tagboard. Attach the trunk and treetop to a bulletin board, and display on a wall. Ask the children to bring family photographs that can be displayed on the tree.

Books

The following books can be used to complement this theme:

Aston, Dianna Hutts. (2007). *A Seed Is Sleepy.* Illustrated by Sylvia Long. San Francisco: Chronicle Books.

Berger, Carin. (2008). *The Little Yellow Leaf.* New York: Greenwillow Books.

Bosca, Francesca. (2001). *The Apple King.* Illustrated by Giuliano Ferri. New York: North-South Books.

Chin, Jason. (2009). *Redwoods.* New York: Roaring Brook Press.

Ehlert, Lois. (1991). *Red Leaf, Yellow Leaf.* Orlando, FL: Harcourt Brace.

Formento, Alison. (2010). *This Tree Counts!* Illustrated by Sarah Snow. Chicago: Albert Whitman.

Hall, Zoe. (1996). *The Apple Tree.* Illustrated by Shari Halpern. New York: Scholastic.

Iwamura, Kazuo. (2009). *Hooray for Fall.* Fitzgerald, GA: North South.

Iwamura, Kazuo. (2009). *Hooray for Spring.* Fitzgerald, GA: North South.

Iwamura, Kazuo. (2010). *Hooray for Summer.* Fitzgerald, GA: North South.

Martin, Bill, Jr., and Michael Archambault. (1989). *Chicka, Chicka Boom Boom.* Illustrated by Lois Ehlert. New York: Simon & Schuster Books for Young Readers.

Muldrow, Diane. (2010). *We Planted a Tree.* Illustrated by Bob Staake. New York: Random House Children's Books.

Pallotta, Jerry. (2010). *Who Will Plant a Tree?* Illustrated by Tom Leonard. Ann Arbor, MI: Sleeping Bear Press.

Parr, Todd. (2010). *The EARTH Book.* New York: Hachette Book Group.

Pfeffer, Wendy. (2007). *A Log's Life.* Illustrated by Robin Brickman. New York: Simon & Schuster Books for Young Children.

Ray, Jane. (2008). *The Apple-Pip Princess.* Cambridge, MA: Candlewick Press.

Salas, Laura Purdie. (2009). *From Seed to Maple Tree.* Illustrated by Jeff Yesh. Minneapolis, MN: Picture Window Books.

Sis, Peter. (2003). *The Tree of Life: A Book Depicting the Life of Charles Darwin, Naturalist, Geologist and Thinker.* New York: Farrar, Straus and Giroux.

Slade, Suzanne. (2009). *From Seed to Pine Tree.* Illustrated by Jeff Yesh. Minneapolis, MN: Picture Window Books.

Tagliaferro, Linda. (2007). *The Life Cycle of an Apple Tree.* Mankato, MN: Capstone Press.

Tagliaferro, Linda. (2007). *The Life Cycle of an Oak Tree.* Mankato, MN: Capstone Press.

Tagliaferro, Linda. (2007). *The Life Cycle of a Pine Tree.* Mankato, MN: Capstone Press.

Ward, Helen, and Wayne Anderson. (2001). *The Tin Forest*. New York: Dutton.

Zweibel, Alan. (2005). *Our Tree Named Steve*. New York: G.P. Putnam's Sons.

Technology and Multimedia

The following technology and multimedia products can be used to complement this theme:

The Legend of Johnny Appleseed and Pecos Bill [DVD]. (2004). Los Angeles: Disney Educational Productions.

Reading Rainbow. (2007). *Once There Was a Tree* [DVD]. Lincoln, NE: GPN Educational Media.

Really Wild Animals: Totally Tropical Rain Forest [DVD]. (2005). Washington, DC: National Geographic.

The Song of the Cloud Forest [DVD]. (2010). Los Angeles: Lionsgate.

The Umbrella [DVD]. (2008). Holmes NY: Spoken Arts.

"Under a Shady Tree" [CD]. 2010. In *The Best of Laurie Berkner*. New York: Two Tomatoes Records.

"Willow Tree in the Wind" [CD]. (2010). In *What Are the Odds?* New York: Monkey Monkey Music.

Additional teaching resources to accompany this Theme can be found on the book's companion website. Go to www.cengagebrain.com to access the site for a variety of useful resources.

VALENTINE'S DAY

Purpose
share feelings
show love

Colors
red
pink
white

Activities
parties
card giving
flowers
gifts

Symbols
hearts
Cupid
cards
candy
arrows
flowers

Theme Goals

Through participating in the experiences provided by this theme, the children may learn:

1. Valentine's Day colors
2. Valentine's Day activities
3. Symbols of Valentine's Day
4. Purpose of Valentine's Day

Concepts for the Children to Learn

1. On Valentine's Day, we share our love with others.
2. Red, pink, and white are Valentine's Day colors.
3. Hearts, Cupids, candy, arrows, and flowers are symbols of Valentine's Day.
4. People send cards on Valentine's Day.
5. Valentine cards share our feelings and show our love.
6. Some people attend or give parties on Valentine's Day.
7. Flowers and gifts are given to special people on Valentine's Day.

Vocabulary

1. **card**—a decorative paper with a written message. Valentine cards show love.
2. **Cupid**—a symbol of Valentine's Day, usually a baby boy with a bow and arrows.
3. **heart**—the shape of a heart is a symbol of love.
4. **Valentine**—a card designed for someone special.
5. **Valentine's Day**—a special day when we share our love with others. Cards, flowers, and presents may be given to people we love on Valentine's Day.

Bulletin Board

The purpose of this bulletin board is to promote numeral recognition, visual discrimination, hand-eye coordination, and problem-solving skills by having the children place the correct number of hearts into the corresponding numbered box. Using decorated boxes as illustrated, a Valentine's Day bulletin board can be created. The bottom of each box should be cut, so it can be taped shut while putting hearts in and easily opened to release the hearts. Mark each box with a numeral and a corresponding number of hearts, as illustrated. The number of numerals will depend on developmental appropriateness. Attach the boxes to the bulletin board using pushpins or staples. Next, construct many small hearts.

Family Letter

Dear Families,

Valentine's Day is a special day, and it will be the focus of our next theme. It is a day when we share our positive feelings about special people. This day also provides an opportunity to talk about the importance of sharing, giving, loving, and friendship. The children will also learn the purpose, symbols, colors, and activities related to Valentine's Day.

Perhaps not all children and families celebrate this holiday, but we feel it is very important for children to learn about and respect others' beliefs. A general understanding of other cultures is also interesting and fun. However, if you wish that your child not participate in this theme, please let us know.

At School

Some of the activities related to Valentine's Day will include:

- Having a post office in the dramatic play area to mail valentines to friends
- Constructing valentine mobiles to decorate our room
- Constructing a "What a Friend Is …" chart to hang in our room
- Sending and receiving valentines
- Watching the video *Valentine's Day*
- Inviting special people at school, including the custodian and secretary, to a party
- Listening to valentine stories and poems

At Home

Try to set aside time to have a heart-to-heart chat with your child. To develop self-esteem, talk to your child about feelings and why you are proud of him or her. Also, help your child make a valentine for a grandparent, aunt, uncle, or other person. A special note could be dictated by your child and written by you.

Have a Happy Valentine's Day!

Arts and Crafts

1. Easel Painting
Mix red, white, and pink paint, and place at the easel.

2. Chalk Drawings
White chalk and red and pink construction paper can be used to make chalk drawings.

3. Classroom Valentine
Cut out one large paper heart. Encourage all children to decorate and sign it. The valentine can be hung in the classroom or be given to a classroom friend. The classroom friend may be the cook, custodian, center director, or principal.

4. Heart Prints
On the art table, place white paper and various heart-shaped cookie cutters. Mix pink and red tempera paint, and pour into shallow pans. The children can print hearts on white construction paper using the cookie cutters as a tool and then paint them.

5. Heart Materials
The children can cut hearts out of construction paper and decorate them with lace scraps, yarn, and glitter to make original Valentine's Day cards. Precut hearts should be available for children who have not mastered the skill. For other children who have cutting skills, a heart shape can be traced on paper for them to cut.

 ## Cooking

1. Valentine Cookies
2/3 cup shortening
1 egg
3/4 cup sugar
1 teaspoon vanilla
1 1/2 cups flour
1 1/2 teaspoons baking powder
4 teaspoons milk
1/4 teaspoon salt

Mix all of the ingredients together. If time permits, refrigerate the dough. Roll out

Individual bags can be made to hold valentines.

dough. Use heart-shaped cookie cutters. Bake at 375 degrees for 12 minutes. Frost. The children can make two cookies, one for themselves and one to give to a friend.

2. Heart-Shaped Sandwiches
1 loaf bread
Heart-shaped cookie cutters
Strawberry jam or jelly

Give each child one or two pieces of bread (depending on the size of the cutter). Cut out two heart shapes from bread. Spread on jam or jelly to make a sandwich. Eat at snack time.

3. Valentine Mints
2 8-ounce packages cream cheese at room temperature
2 teaspoons peppermint extract
10 drops red food coloring
8–9 cups powdered sugar

Combine the first three ingredients in a mixing bowl. Gradually add the powdered sugar, mixing at a low speed until well blended. Next, place the dough on a pastry cloth; keep kneading and adding additional powdered sugar until the dough is very stiff. Roll out the dough. Use a heart-shaped cookie cutter to make the candy hearts. Chill overnight to harden.

Dramatic Play

1. Mailboxes
Construct an individual mailbox for each child using shoeboxes, empty milk cartons, paper bags, or partitioned boxes. Print each child's name on the box, or encourage the child to do so. The children can sort mail, letters, and small packages into the boxes.

2. Florist
Plastic flowers, vases, Styrofoam pieces, tissue paper, ribbons, candy boxes, a cash register, and play money can be used to make a flower shop.

3. Card Shop
Stencils, paper, markers, scraps, stickers, and so forth can be provided to make a card-making shop.

4. Make a Valentine
Across the top of a large piece of cardboard, print "Make a Valentine." Then print the following slogans on large strips of paper:

I want you for my valentine.
Happy Valentine's Day.
Be my valentine,
Be mine.

Paste the strips on the piece of tagboard. Post the chart and provide crayons, felt-tip markers, and paper for the children to make valentines by copying the phrases.

Field Trips

1. Visit a Post Office
Visit the local post office. Valentine's Day cards made in the classroom can be mailed.

2. Visit a Floral Shop
Visit a flower store. Observe the different valentine arrangements. Call attention to the beautiful color of the flowers, arrangements, and containers.

Fingerplays and Chants

Five Little Valentines
Five little valentines were having a race.
The first little valentine was frilly with lace.
    (hold up one finger)
The second little valentine had a funny face.
    (hold up two fingers)
The third little valentine said, "I love you."
    (hold up three fingers)
The fourth little valentine said, "I do too."
    (hold up four fingers)
The fifth little valentine was sly as a fox.
He ran the fastest to the valentine box.
    (make five fingers run behind back)

Group Time
(Games and Language)

Valentine March
Place large fabric or paper hearts with numerals on them on the floor. Include one valentine per child. Play a marching song, and encourage children to march from heart to heart. When the music stops, so do the children. Each child then tells the numeral on which he or she is standing. To make the activity developmentally appropriate for young children, use symbols. Examples might include a ball, car, truck, glass, cup, door, and so on.

Large Muscle

1. Hug Tag
One child is "it" and tries to tag another child. Once tagged, the child is "frozen" until another child gently hugs him or her to "unfreeze" him or her.

2. Balloon Ball

Blow up two or three red, pink, or white balloons. The children can hit the balloons to each other. The object is to try to keep the balloon off the floor or ground. This activity needs to be carefully supervised. **Caution:** If a balloon breaks, all its pieces must be discarded immediately.

Math

1. Broken Hearts

Cut heart shapes out of red and pink tagboard. Print a numeral on one side and a number set of heart stickers or drawings on the other side. Cut the hearts in half as a puzzle. The children can match the puzzle pieces.

2. Heart Seriation

Cut various-sized hearts from pink, red, and white construction paper. The children can sequence the heart shapes from small to big or vice versa.

3. Sorting Hearts

Cut out red, white, and pink hearts of varying sizes (small, medium, and large). Provide containers for the children to sort the hearts according to their size or color.

Music

1. "My Valentine"

(Sing to the tune of "The Muffin Man")

Oh, do you know my valentine,
My valentine, my valentine?
Oh, do you know my valentine?
His name is _____.

(Chosen valentine then picks another child)

2. "Ten Little Valentines"

(Sing to the tune of "Ten Little Indians")

One little, two little, three little valentines.
Four little, five little, six little valentines.
Seven little, eight little, nine little
    valentines.
Ten little valentines here!

3. "Two Little Cupids"

(Sing to the tune of "Two Little Blackbirds")
(For each _____, insert a child's name)

Two little cupids sitting on a heart.
    (hold hands behind back)
One named _____. One named _____.
    (bring out one pointer for each name)
Fly away, _____. Fly away, _____.
    (place one pointer behind back for each
    name)
Come back, _____. Come back, _____.
    (bring out pointers one at a time again)
Two little cupids sitting on a heart.
    (hold up two fingers)
One named _____. One named _____.
    (wiggle each pointer separately)

4. "Will You Be My Valentine?"

(Children will try to guess who you are thinking of. The child who guesses correctly gets to choose the next person for others to guess.)

Will you be my V-A-L-E-N-T-I-N-E?
If you will, you know how very happy I will be.

Science

1. Valentine's Day Flowers

In the science area, place various flowers and magnifying glasses. The children can observe and explore the various parts of the flowers.

2. Valentine's Day Colors

Mixing red and white tempera paint, the children can make various shades of red or pink.

Sensory

Soap

Mix dish soap, water, and red food coloring in the sensory table. Provide eggbeaters for the children to make bubbles.

Social Studies

1. **Sorting Feelings**
    Cut pictures of happy and sad people out of magazines. On the outside of two boxes, draw a smiling face on one and a sad face on the other. The children can sort the pictures into the corresponding boxes.

2. **Sign Language**
    Show the children how to say, "I love you," in sign language. They can practice with each other. When the parents arrive, the children can share with them.
    I   (point to self)
    love   (cross arms over chest)
    you   (point outward)

Books

The following books can be used to complement this theme:

Bond, Felicia. (2006). *The Day It Rained Hearts.* New York: HarperCollins.

Capucilli, Alyssa Satin, and Pat Schories. (2001). *Biscuit's Valentine's Day.* Illustrated by Pat Schories. New York: HarperFestival.

Crites, Susan E. (2007). *I Love You More Than Rainbows.* Nashville, TN: Thomas Nelson.

Davies, Simon, Serena Feneziani, and A. J. Wood. (2000). *Pucker Up, Buttercup!* Illustrated by Serena Feneziani. Brookfield, CT: Millbrook Press.

Douglas, Lloyd G. (2003). *Let's Get Ready for Valentine's Day.* New York: Children's Press.

Erlbach, Arlene. (2004). *Valentine's Day Crafts.* Berkeley Heights, NJ: Enslow Publishers.

Friedman, Laurie B. (2006). *Love, Ruby Valentine.* Minneapolis, MN: Carolrhoda Books.

Gibbons, Gail. (2006). *Valentine's Day Is.* New York: Holiday House.

Inches, Alison, and Alison Winfield. (2001). *Be My Valentine (Raggedy Ann and Andy).*

Illustrated by Alison Winfield. New York: Little Simon.

Katz, Karen. (2001). *Counting Kisses.* New York: Margaret McElderry.

Kroll, Steven. (2006). *The Biggest Valentine Ever.* Illustrated by Jeni Bassett. New York: Cartwheel Books.

Mayer, Mercer. (2005). *Little Critter: Happy Valentine's Day Little Critter!* New York: HarperFestival.

O'Connor, Jane. (2009). *Fancy Nancy: Heart to Heart.* Illustrated by Robin Preiss Glasser. New York: HarperCollins Children's Books.

Parish, Herman. (2009). *Amelia Bedelia's First Valentine.* Illustrated by Lynne Avril. New York: HarperCollins Children's Books.

Parr, Todd. (2009). *The I Love You Book.* New York: Little Brown.

Roberts, Bethany. (2001). *Valentine Mice.* Illustrated by Doug Cushman. New York: Houghton Mifflin.

Samuels, Barbara. (2008). *Happy Valentine's Day, Dolores.* New York: Square Fish.

Scotton, Rob. (2008). *Love, Splat.* New York: HarperCollins.

Sutherland, Margaret. (2007). *Valentines Are for Saying I Love You.* Illustrated by Amy Wummer. New York: Grosset & Dunlap.

Van Lieshout, Maria. (2007). *Boom! A Little Book about Finding Love.* New York: Feiwel & Friends.

Wing, Natasha. (2000). *The Night before Valentine's Day.* Illustrated by Heidi Petach. New York: Grosset & Dunlap.

Technology and Multimedia

The following technology and multimedia products can be used to complement this theme:

"Blow a Kiss" [CD]. (2002). In *Laurie Berkner: Under a Shady Tree.* New York: Two Tomatoes.

"Caring and Compassion" [CD]. (2005). In *Red Grammer Be Bop Your Best.* Brewerton, NY: Red Note Records.

Franklin. (2009). *Franklin's Valentines* [DVD]. North Hollywood, CA: KaBOOM! Entertainment, distributed by Phase 4 Films.

"Open Your Heart" [CD]. (2010). In *The Best of Laurie Berkner.* New York: Two Tomatoes Records.

We Love Our Friends [DVD]. (2010). Los Angeles: Paramount Home Entertainment.

 Additional teaching resources to accompany this Theme can be found on the book's companion website. Go to www.cengagebrain.com to access the site for a variety of useful resources.

Materials to Collect for the Art Center

Aluminum foil	Fabrics	Paper doilies	Sweaters
Ball bearings	Felt	Paper napkins	Tacks
Barrel hoops	Felt hats	Paper tissue	Tape
Beads	Flannel	Paper towels	Thread
Belts	Floor covering	Paper tubes	Tiles
Bottles	Glass	Paper wrapping	Tin cans
Bracelets	Gourds	Phonograph	Tin foil
Braiding	Hat boxes	records	Tongue
Brass	Hooks	Photographs	depressors
Buckles	Inner tubes	Picture frames	Towels
Burlap	Jars	Pinecones	Tubes
Buttons	Jugs	Pins	Twine
Candles	Lacing	Plastic board	Wallpaper
Canvas	Lampshades	Plastic paint	Wax
Cartons	Leather remnants	Pocket books	Window shades
Cellophane	Linoleum	Reeds	Wire
Chains	Marbles	Ribbon	Wire eyelets
Chalk	Masonite	Rings	Wire hairpins
Chamois	Metal foil	Rope	Wire hooks
Chenille stems	Mirrors	Rubber bands	Wire mesh
Clay	Muslin	Rug yarn	Wire paper clips
Cloth	Nails	Safety pins	Wire screen
Colored pictures	Necklaces	Sand	Wire staples
Confetti	Neckties	Sandpaper	Wooden beads
Containers	Newspaper	Seashells	Wooden blocks
Copper foil	Oilcloth	Seeds	Wooden
Cord	Ornaments	Sheepskin	clothespins
Cornhusks	Pans	Shoelaces	Wooden sticks
Cornstalks	Paper (cardboard)	Shoe polish	Wool
Costume jewelry	Paper	Snaps	Yarn
Crayon pieces	(corrugated)	Soap	Zippers
Crystals	Paper bags	Sponges	
Emery cloth	Paper boxes	Spools	
Eyelets	Paper dishes	Stockings	

Theme 71
WATER

Places
ponds
lakes
rivers
oceans

Purposes
drinking
cleaning
energy
recreation

Forms
liquid
solid
vapor

Uses
soak
dilute
spray
sprinkle
flood
moisten

Sports
swimming
fishing
skiing
boating

Reaction
mix
absorb

Conserving
brushing teeth
washing hands
bathing
flushing toilets

Theme Goals

Through participating in the experiences provided by this theme, the children may learn:

1. Uses of water
2. Forms of water
3. Water sports
4. Purposes of water
5. Reactions of water
6. Places water is found
7. Conservation of water

Concepts for the Children to Learn

1. Water is a clear, colorless liquid with no taste or smell.
2. Water can be found in ponds, lakes, rivers, and oceans.
3. All living things need water.
4. Water takes three forms: liquid, vapor, and solid.
5. Ice is a solid form of water and steam is a vapor form of water.
6. Some things mix with water and other things absorb water.
7. Some things float when placed on water.
8. Some animals and plants live in bodies of water.
9. Animals, people, and plants need water.
10. Water can be used to soak, dilute, spray, sprinkle, flood, and moisten.
11. Swimming, fishing, skiing, and boating are water sports.
12. Care must be taken not to waste water while brushing our teeth, washing our hands, bathing, and flushing the toilet.

Vocabulary

1. **cloud**—water droplets formed high in the sky. Clouds can be gray or white.
2. **float**—to move on top of a liquid.
3. **freeze**—to become hard and cold.
4. **ice**—water that has frozen.
5. **lake**—a large body of water surrounded by land.
6. **liquid**—a substance that can be poured. Milk and water are liquids.
7. **melt**—to change from a solid to a liquid. Ice cream and popsicles melt.
8. **ocean**—a large body of saltwater. Sometimes the word "sea" is used for ocean.
9. **rain**—drops of water that fall from clouds.
10. **sink**—to drop or go down to the bottom of a liquid.
11. **snow**—drops of water that freeze and fall from the sky.
12. **swimming**—moving yourself through water with arm and leg movements.
13. **water**—a clear, colorless, odorless, tasteless liquid.

Bulletin Board

The purpose of this bulletin board is to develop visual discrimination, problem-solving, and matching skills. Construct and color four or five pictures of swimming- and water-related items from tagboard. Laminate. Trace these pictures on black construction paper to make shadows. Staple the shadows on the bulletin board. Encourage the children to hang the colored picture over the correct shadow.

Family Letter

Dear Families,

Did you know all living things have something in common? They all need water to survive. Water will be the theme that we explore with our next curriculum unit. The children will become familiar with the purpose, forms, uses, and reactions of water, as well as sports that require water.

At School

Some of the learning experiences planned to include water concepts are:

- Placing celery stalks in colored water to observe plants' use of water

- Experimenting with objects that sink or float when placed in water

- Washing doll clothes in the sensory table

- Observing ice with magnifying glasses and watching it change from a solid to a liquid

- Looking at books about water

At Home

There are many ways that you can reinforce water concepts at home. Try any of the following with your child:

- Allow your child to assist in washing dishes after a meal. This will give your child a sense of responsibility and will develop self-esteem.

- Provide water and large paintbrushes for your child to paint sidewalks and fences outdoors.

- Bubbles made with an eggbeater in a container of soapy water are fun for children of all ages!

Enjoy your child!

Arts and Crafts

1. Liquid Painting
Paper, straws, thin tempera, and spoons can be placed on the art table. Spoon a small amount of paint onto paper. Using a straw, blow paint on the paper to make a design.

2. Bubble Prints
Collect the following materials: 1/2 cup water, 1/2 cup liquid soap, food coloring, straws, and light-colored construction paper. Mix together the water, soap, and food coloring in a container. Place a straw in the solution and blow until the bubbles reach about 1 inch to 2 inches over the top of the container. Remove the straw and place a piece of paper over the jar. The bubbles will pop as they touch the paper, leaving a print.

3. Wet Chalk Drawings
Chalk, paper, and water in a shallow pan are needed for this activity. The children can dip chalk into water and then draw on paper. Encourage children to note the difference between wet and dry chalk.

Cooking

1. Fruit Ice
Mix a 1/2 can partially thawed juice concentrate with 2 cups of crushed ice in the blender. Liquefy until the contents become snowy. Serve immediately.

2. Filipino Floating Cake
2 cups sweet rice flour
1 cup water
1/2 to 3/4 cup sugar
1/2 cup toasted sesame seeds, hulled
1 cup grated coconut

Mix rice flour and water. Form into 10 to 20 small balls. Flatten each ball into a round or elongated shape, and drop into 8 to 10 cups boiling water. As each cake floats to the surface, remove from water with a slotted spoon. Roll in grated coconut, and coat with sugar and sesame seeds. Adult supervision is required. Makes four servings.

Dramatic Play

1. Firefighter
Place hoses, hats, coats, and boots in the dramatic play area.

2. Doll Baths
Fill the dramatic play sink with water. Children can wash dishes or give dolls baths.

3. The Beach
Provide towels, sunglasses, umbrellas, pails, shovels, and beach toys for the children to use indoors or outdoors.

4. Canoeing
Bring a canoe into the classroom or onto the play yard. Provide paddles and life vests for the children to wear.

Fingerplays and Chants

Five Little Ducks
Five little ducks
   (hold up five fingers)
Swimming in the lake.
   (make swimming motions)
The first duck said,
   (hold up one finger)
"Watch the waves I make."
   (make waves motions)
The second duck said,
   (hold up two fingers)
"Swimming is such fun."
   (smile)
The third duck said,
   (hold up three fingers)
"I'd rather sit in the sun."
   (turn face to sun)
The fourth duck said,
   (hold up four fingers)
"Let's swim away."
   (swimming motions)
The fifth duck said,
   (hold up five fingers)
"Oh, let's stay."

Then along came a motorboat.
With a Pop! Pop! Pop!
(clap three times)
And five little ducks
Swam away from the spot.
(put five fingers behind back)

Swimming

I can dive.
(make diving motion with hands)
I can swim.
(swimming motion)
I can float.
(hands outstretched with head back)
I can fetch.
But dog paddle
(paddle like dog)
Is the stroke I do best.

Five Little Fishes

Five little fishes swimming in a pond.
(wiggle five fingers)
The first one said, "I'm tired," as he yawned.
(yawn)
The second one said, "Well, let's take a nap."
(put hands together on side of face)
The third one said, "Put on your sleeping cap."
(pretend to pull on hat)
The fourth one said, "Wake up! Don't sleep."
(shake finger)
The fifth one said, "Let's swim where
it's deep."
(point down and say with a low voice)
So, the five little fishes swam away.
(wiggle fingers and put behind back)
But they came back the very next day.
(wiggle fingers out front again)

The Rain

I sit before the window now
(sit down)
And look out at the rain.
(shade eyes and look around)
It means no play outside today,
(shake head)
So inside I remain.
(rest chin on fist; look sad)

I watch the water dribble down
(look up and down)
As it turns the brown grass green.
And after a while I start to smile
At Nature's washing machine.
(smile and lean back)

Group Time
(Games and Language)

Water Fun

Discuss the various recreational uses of water. Included may be swimming, boating, ice fishing, ice skating, fishing, and canoeing. Also discuss water safety issues, such as wearing a life vest. Encourage the children to name their favorite water activities. Prepare a chart using each child's name and favorite water activity, along with a small picture of that activity. Display in the room.

Large Muscle

Catch Me

Children form a circle with one child in the middle. While walking in a circle, they chant,

(Insert child's name:)
_____ over the water.
_____ over the sea.
_____ caught a tuna fish.
But he can't catch me!

On "me," all the children stoop quickly. If the child in the middle touches another child before he or she stoops, that child is it and now goes into the middle. This game is for older children.

Math

1. **Measuring**
   Assorted measuring cups in a variety of sizes can be added to the sensory table or sandbox.

2. **Clipping Raindrops**
   Cut raindrops in a variety of sizes from construction paper. Tie a small string to the bottom of two chair legs, and have the children use clothespins to clip the raindrops in order from smallest to largest. *Note:* The children will need to sit on the floor for this activity.

3. Drops of Water

Using an eyedropper, count the number of drops of water you can put into a marker cap before it overflows. Be sure to cover the table with a towel. Invite the children to guess how many drops it will hold before it overflows.

4. Sliding Drops

Cover a piece of cardboard with aluminum foil and prop up one end. Color water and begin to drop water on the top of the board with an eyedropper. Count how many drops it takes before the water begins to "slide" down the ramp.

5. Counting Raindrops

Place large, blue beads into a bucket. Provide a sand shovel for the children to scoop out the "raindrops" and count how many they have. Type or write a rain poem (like "Rain, Rain, Go Away"), and glue it to the bucket so the children can say it as they scoop out the raindrops.

Music

1. "Raindrops"

(Sing to the tune of "London Bridge")

Raindrops falling from the sky,
From the sky, from the sky.
Raindrops falling from the sky
On my umbrella.

2. "Raindrops Falling"

(Sing to the tune of "Twinkle, Twinkle")

I see raindrops falling down.
Falling down upon the ground.
See them falling in the air.
See them falling everywhere.
I see raindrops falling down.
Falling down upon the ground.

Science

1. Painting Sidewalks

On a sunny day, allow children to paint sidewalks with water. To do this, provide various paintbrushes and buckets of water. Call attention to the water evaporation.

2. Measuring Rainfall

During spring, place a bucket outside with a plastic ruler set vertically by securing it to the bottom. Check the height of the water after each rainfall. With older children, make a chart to record rainfall.

3. Testing Volume

Containers that hold the same amounts of liquid are needed. Try to include containers that are tall, skinny, short, and flat. Ask the children, "Do they hold the same amount?" Encourage them to experiment by pouring liquids from one container to another.

4. Freezing Water

Freeze a container of water. Periodically observe the changes. In colder climates, the water can be frozen outdoors. The addition of food coloring may add interest.

5. Musical Scale

Make unique musical tone jars by pouring various levels of water into glass bottles or jars. Color each bottle of water differently. Provide the children with spoons, encouraging them to experiment with sounds by tapping each bottle. *Caution:* Supervise this activity carefully.

6. Plants Use Water

Place celery stalks in colored water. Observe how water is absorbed in their veins.

7. Chase the Pepper

Collect the following materials: water, pepper, a shallow pan, a piece of soap, and sugar. Fill the pan with water, and shake the pepper on the water. Take a piece of wet soap and dip it into the water. What happens? (The pepper moves away from the soapy water to the clear water.) The surface of water pulls, and on soapy water the pull is weak. On clear water, it is strong and pulls the pepper. Now take some sugar and shake it into the soapy water. What happens? Sugar gives the surface a stronger pull.

8. Warm Water and Cold Water

Collect the following materials: a small aquarium, a small bottle, food coloring, and water. First, fill the aquarium with very warm water. Fill the small bottle with colored cold water. Put your thumb on the mouth of the bottle. Hold the bottle sideways and lower it into the warm water. Take away your thumb. What happens? (The cold water sinks to the bottom of the tank. The cold water is heavier than the warm water.) Now fill the tank with cold water and fill the small bottle with colored warm water. What do you predict will happen when you repeat the procedure?

9. Wave Machine
Collect the following materials: mineral oil, water, food coloring, and a transparent jar. Fill the jar 1/2 to 2/3 full with water. Add a few drops of food coloring. Add mineral oil to completely fill the jar. Secure the lid on the jar. Tilt the jar slowly from side to side to make waves. Notice that the oil and water have separate layers and do not stay mixed after the jar is shaken.

10. Water and Vinegar Fun
Collect the following materials: two small plastic jars with lids, water, and white vinegar. Pour water into one jar and an equal amount of vinegar into the other jar. Replace the caps. Let the children explore the jars of liquids and discuss the similarities, and then let the children smell each jar.

11. Color Mixing
Mix water and food coloring to make a variety of colors. Place a different color of water in a separate place on a muffin tin. Give children an eyedropper and an empty muffin tin to experiment with mixing the colors of water to make a new color.

Sensory

1. Colored Ice
Fill the sensory table with colored ice cubes for the children to explore.

2. Sink and Float
Fill the sensory table with water. Provide the children with a variety of items that will sink and float. Let them experiment.

A chart may be prepared listing items that sink and float.

3. Boating
Fill the water table. Let the children add blue food coloring. Provide a variety of boats for them to play with.

4. Moving Water
Provide the children with a variety of materials that move water. Include the following:

- Sponges
- Basters
- Eye droppers
- Squeeze bottles
- Empty and cleaned yogurt containers
- Funnels
- Pitchers
- Plastic tubing
- Measuring cups

5. Making Rain
Punch or cut out holes (vary the size and number) in the bottoms of containers (nondairy whipped topping, yogurt, etc.). Place in the sensory table with water, and encourage children to scoop water into them and compare the amount of "rain" coming from each container.

Books

The following books can be used to complement this theme:

Arnosky, Jim. (2010). *Slow Down for Manatees.* New York. G. P. Putnam's Sons.

Base, Graeme. (2001). *The Water Hole.* New York: Harry N. Abrams.

Cousins, Lucy. (2001). *Maisy at the Beach.* Cambridge, MA: Candlewick Press.

Cowley, Joy, and Fuller, Elizabeth. (2005). *Mrs. Wishy-Washy's Splishy-Sploshy.* New York: Philomel.

Davis, Lambert. (2004). *Swimming with Dolphins.* New York: Blue Sky Press.

Falwell, Cathryn. (2001). *Turtle Splash! Countdown at the Pond.* New York: Greenwillow Books.

Fleming, Denise. (1993). *In the Small, Small Pond.* New York: Holt.

Franco, Betsy. (2009). *Pond Circle.* New York: Margaret K. McElderry Books.

Jarnow, Jill, ed., and Elizabeth Hathon. (2000). *Splish! Splash!* All Aboard Books. Illustrated by Elizabeth Hathon. New York: Grosset & Dunlap.

Kerley, Barbara. (2002). *A Cool Drink of Water.* Washington, DC: National Geographic.

Knox, Barbara. (2003). *Under the Sea: Counting Ocean Life.* Mankato, MN: Capstone Press.

Lindeen, Carol K. (2004). *Life in an Ocean.* Mankato, MN: Capstone Press.

Lindeen, Carol K. (2004). *Life in a Pond.* Mankato, MN: Capstone Press.

Lindeen, Carol K. (2004). *Life in a Stream.* Mankato, MN: Capstone Press.

London, Jonathan. (2001). *Sun Dance Water Dance.* New York: Viking.

Munoz Ryan, Pam. (2001). *Hello Ocean.* Illustrated by Mark Astrella and translated by Yanitzia Canetti. Watertown, MA: Charlesbridge Publishing.

Schafer, Lola, M. (2006). *An Island Grows.* Illustrated by Cathie Felstead. New York: Greenwillow Books.

Schuh, Mari C. (2006). *Drinking Water.* Mankato, MN: Capstone Press.

Seeger, Laura Vaccaro. (2010). *What If?* New York: Roaring Brook Press.

Sidman, Joyce. (2005). *Song of the Water.* Illustrated by Beckie Prange. Boston: Houghton Mifflin.

Williams, Karen Lynn. (2010). *A Beach Tail.* Illustrated by Floyd Cooper. Honesdale, PA: Boyds Mills Press.

Winter, Jeanette. (2006). *Mama.* New York: Harcourt Books.

Wong, Herbert Yee. (2007). *Who Likes Rain?* New York: H. Holt.

Technology and Multimedia

The following technology and multimedia products can be used to complement this theme:

"Baby Beluga" [CD]. (1980). In *Baby Beluga.* Cambridge, MA: Rounder/UMGD.

"Down by the River" [CD]. (2010). In *Pete Seeger, Tomorrow's Children.* Westchester, PA: Appleseed Records.

"Hey Ducky" [CD]. 2010. In *Rock and Roll Garden.* New York: Bari Koral Family Rock Band.

Jim Henson's The Song of the Cloud Forest and Other Earth Stories [DVD]. (2010). Los Angeles: Lionsgate.

"My Blue Sailboat" [CD]. (2008). In *Rocketship Run.* New York: Two Tomatoes.

Really Wild Animals: Deep Sea Dive [DVD]. (2005). Washington, DC: National Geographic.

"River" [CD]. (2010). In *Pete Seeger, Tomorrow's Children.* Westchester, PA: Appleseed Records.

"There'll Come a Day" [CD]. (2010). In *Pete Seeger, Tomorrow's Children.* Westchester, PA: Appleseed Records.

"Walk along the River" [CD]. (2006). *We Are the Laurie Berkner Band.* New York: Razor & Tie.

Water and Weather: Ecosystems and Environment [DVD]. (2007). Conshohocken, PA: TMW Media Group.

"Water Dance" [CD]. (1980). In *Baby Beluga.* Cambridge, MA: Rounder/UMGD.

"We Need Water" [CD]. (2000). In *Charlotte Diamond's World.* Vancouver, BC: Hug Bug Records.

"When the Tide Goes Out" [CD]. (2000). In *Charlotte Diamond's World.* Vancouver, BC: Hug Bug Records.

Who Lives in the Sea? [DVD]. (2007). Seattle, Washington: All Images and Media.

Additional teaching resources to accompany this Theme can be found on the book's companion website. Go to www.cengagebrain.com to access the site for a variety of useful resources.

Water Play and Sensory Experiences

Sensory experiences are especially appealing to young children. They delight in feeling, listening, smelling, tasting, and seeing. They also love to manipulate objects by pulling, placing, pouring, tipping, shoving, as well as dipping. As they interact, they learn new concepts and solutions to old problems. When accompanied by other children, these experiences lead to cooperative, social interactions. As a result, the child's egocentricity is reduced, allowing him or her to become less self-centered.

Containers

Begin planning sensory experiences by choosing an appropriate container. Remember that it should be large enough so that several children may participate at any given time. If you select a dishpan, due to its size, you may want to use several. Other containers that may be used include a commercially made sensory or water table, baby bathtub, wash tub, pail, wading pool, sink, or bathtub.

Things to Add to Water

A variety of substances can be added to water to make it more inviting. Food coloring is one example. Start by individually choosing and adding one primary color. Later soaps can be added. These may be in liquid or flake form. Baking soda, cornstarch, and salt will affect the feel of the water. Baby and vegetable oil may leave a residue on the child's hand. Extracts add another dimension. Lemon or pine oil and peppermint, anise, and orange extracts all provide variety for the child. On the other hand, ice cubes allow the child to experience an extreme touch.

Tools and Utensils

A wide variety of household tools can be used in the water play table. Measuring cups, small pitchers, small pots and pans, and clean yogurt containers can all be used for pouring. Scoops, spoons, turkey basters, small squeeze bottles, and funnels can be used for transferring the liquid from one container to another. Pipes, rubber hoses, sponges, wire whisks, and eggbeaters all can be used for observing water in motion. Plastic toys, corks, spools, strainers, boots, and so forth also encourage exploration.

Other Sensory Experiences

There are wide varieties of other materials that can be used in the sensory table. Natural materials such as sand, gravel, rocks, grain, mud, wood chips, clay, corn, and birdseed can be used. Children also enjoy having minnows and worms in the table. They delight in visually tracking the minnow and worm movement. As they attempt to pick them up, eye-hand coordination skills are practiced. Styrofoam pieces and shavings are attractive materials that can lend variety.

A strange mixture called goop is a fun material to play with. To prepare goop, empty 1 box of cornstarch into a dishpan or similar container. Sprinkle a few drops of food coloring on the cornstarch. Measure 1/c cup water and dd small amounts at a time and mix with a spoon or with fingers. (This is a unique sensory experience which the children will enjoy!) The mixture feels hard when you touch it on the surface, yet melts in your hands when you pick some up! (This will keep for up to 1 week if kept covered when not in use. You will probably need to add water the next time you use it.)

Silly putty is just as easy to prepare as goop. This mixture is prepared by combining 1 part liquid starch, 2 parts white glue, and dry tempera paint for color. Begin by measuring the liquid starch first, as it will prevent the glue from sticking to the measuring cup. Mix with a spoon, adding single tablespoons of liquid starch to get the right consistency. Next, knead with hands. Store in an airtight container (such as a zipper-sealed bag) in the refrigerator. You will be thrilled to find that it will keep for several weeks.

Enjoy yourself with the children, but always change the sensory experiences on a daily basis. In doing so, you stimulate the child's curiosity as well as provide a meaningful curriculum.

For health purposes, children should be encouraged to wash their hands after sensory play.

Theme 72
WHEELS

Purpose
movement
transportation

Materials
rubber
plastic
wood
metal

Sizes
small
medium
large

Uses
bicycles, motorcycles
tricycles, scooters, cars, trucks, buses
planes, unicycles, wagons
wheelbarrows, carts, chairs
trailers, roller skates, in-line skates
pulleys, gears, trains
wheelchairs, pizza cutters

Theme Goals

Through participating in the experiences provided by this theme, the children may learn:

1. Sizes of wheels
2. Purposes of wheels
3. Materials used to make wheels
4. Uses of wheels

Concepts for the Children to Learn

1. Wheels are round.
2. Wheels come in different sizes.
3. Wheels can help us do our work.
4. Wheels help move people and things.
5. Cars, trains, trucks, buses, planes, motorcycles, tricycles, and bicycles have wheels.
6. Wagons, wheelbarrows, carts, and trailers have wheels.
7. Some chairs have wheels.
8. Wheelchairs have wheels.
9. In-line skates and roller skates have wheels.
10. Pulleys and gears have wheels.
11. Wheels can be different sizes.
12. A unicycle is a one-wheeled cycle.
13. A pizza cutter is a wheel.
14. Wheels can be made of rubber, plastic, metal, or wood.

Vocabulary

1. **bicycle**—a two-wheeled vehicle.
2. **pulley**—a wheel that can be connected to a rope to move things.
3. **unicycle**—a vehicle with one wheel.
4. **wheel**—a form in the shape of a circle. Wheels help things move and work.
5. **wheelbarrow**—a vehicle that is pushed and used for moving small loads.
6. **wheelchair**—a chair on wheels used to move people.

Bulletin Board

The purpose of this bulletin board is to promote the development of mathematical concepts. To prepare the bulletin board, draw pictures of a unicycle, bicycle, and tricycle on tagboard. Color, cut out, and post on the bulletin board. Next, construct the numerals 1, 2, and 3 out of tagboard. Hang the numerals on the top of the bulletin board. A corresponding set of dots can be placed below the numeral to assist children in counting. A string can be attached to each numeral by using a stapler. Have the children wind the string around a pushpin connected to the vehicle with the corresponding number of wheels.

Family Letter

InBox

Dear Families,

Wheels! Wheelchairs, wheelbarrows, tricycle wheels, bicycle wheels, and car wheels! Children see wheels almost every day of their lives. We are studying wheels. Through participating in the activities planned for this unit, the children will discover the purpose, uses, and sizes of wheels. They will also learn what materials are used to make wheels.

At School

We have many learning experiences planned for this unit, including:

- Examining tire rubber at the science table
- Painting with toy cars at the art table
- Singing a song called "The Wheels on the Bus"

At Home

There are many ways that you can incorporate this unit in your home. Try any of these activities with your child:

- Walk around the neighborhood with your child. To develop observation skills, look for different wheels.
- Count the wheels on the different types of transportation. Semi-trucks have several, whereas a unicycle has only one.

Enjoy your child!

Arts and Crafts

1. Car Painting
Provide small plastic cars, tempera paint, and paper. Place the tempera paint in a shallow pan. Car tracks can be created by dipping the car wheels in the tempera paint and rolling them across paper.

2. Wheel Collage
Provide magazines for the children to cut out pictures of wheels. The pictures can be pasted or glued onto sheets of paper.

3. Tracing Wheels
Provide sewing tracing wheels, pizza cutters, pastry wheels, carbon paper, and construction paper. The children can place the carbon paper on the construction paper and run one of the wheels over the carbon paper, making a design on the construction paper.

Cooking

1. Cheese Wheels
Using a cookie cutter, cut cheese slices into circle shapes to represent wheels. Top the pieces with raisins, or serve with crackers.

2. Pizza Rounds
Provide each child with half of an English muffin. Demonstrate how to spread pizza sauce on a muffin. Next, lay a few skinny strips of cheese across the top, making the cheese look like wheel spokes. Now let the children prepare their own. Bake in an oven at 350 degrees for 5 to 7 minutes or until the cheese melts. Cool slightly before serving.

Dramatic Play

1. Car Mechanic
Outdoors, place various wheels, tires, tools, overalls, and broken tricycles. The children can experiment using tools.

2. Floats
Paper, tape, crêpe paper, and balloons can be provided to decorate the wheels on tricycles, wagons, and scooters.

Field Trips and Resource People

1. Cycle Shop
Visit a cycle shop. Observe the different sizes of wheels that are in the shop. Talk about the different materials that wheels can be made of.

2. Machine Shop
Visit a machine parts shop. Look at the different gears, pulleys, and wheels. Discuss their sizes, shapes, and possible uses.

3. Resource People
- Cycle specialist
- Mechanic
- Machinist
- Person who uses a wheelchair

Fingerplays and Chants

My Bicycle
One wheel, two wheels on the ground.
 (revolve hand in forward circle to form each wheel)
My feet make the pedals go round and round.
 (move feet in pedaling motion)
Handlebars help me steer so straight
 (pretend to steer bicycle)
Down the sidewalk, through the gate.

Wheels
Wheels big.
 (form big circles with fingers)
Wheels small.
 (form little circles with fingers)
Count them one by one

Turning as they're pedaled
(make pedaling motion with hands)
In the springtime sun.
1-2-3-4-5.
(count fingers)

Group Time
(Games and Language)

Who Took the Wheel?
(Variation of "Who Took the Cookie from the Cookie Jar?")
(After the first verse, the chant continues as the chosen child picks another child. Continue repeating the chant using the children's names.)

Who took the wheel off the car today?
_____ took the wheel off the car today.
(fill _____ with a child's name)
(Chosen child says:) "Who me?"
(Class responds:) "Yes, you!"
(Chosen child says:) "Couldn't be!"
(Class responds:) "Well then, who?"

Large Muscle

1. **Wheelbarrow**
   Place child-safe wheelbarrows in the play yard. Provide materials of varying weights for the children to move.

2. **Wagons**
   Place child-safe wagons in the playground. Provide objects for the children to move.

Math

1. **Wheel Sequence**
   Cut out various-sized circles from tagboard to represent wheels. The children can sequence the wheels from largest to smallest.

2. **How Many Wheels?**
   Pictures of a unicycle, bicycle, tricycle, cars, scooters, and trucks of all sizes can be cut from magazines and catalogs. Mount the pictures on tagboard. Laminate. Sort the pictures according to the number of wheels.

Music

"The Wheels on the Bus"
The wheels on the bus go round and round,
Round and round, round and round.
The wheels on the bus go round and round
All through the town.

(Other verses:)

The wipers on the bus go swish, swish, swish.
The doors on the bus go open and shut.
The horn on the bus goes beep, beep, beep.
The driver on the bus says, "Move on back."
The people on the bus go up and down.

Science

1. **Tire Rubber**
   Cut off several pieces of rubber from old bicycle tires. Provide magnifying glasses. Encourage the children to observe similarities and differences.

2. **Pulley**
   Set up a pulley. Provide the children with blocks so they may lift a heavy load with the help of a wheel. Supervision may be necessary for this activity.

3. **Gears**
   Collect gears and place on the science table. The children can experiment, observing how the gears move. When appropriate, discuss their similar and different characteristics.

4. **Wheels and Axles**
   Set out a few wheels and axles. Discuss how they work as a lever to help lift heavy loads. Encourage the children to think about where they might find wheels and axles.

Sensory

Sensory Table

Add the following items to the sensory table:

- Sand with wheel molds
- Rubber from tires
- Gravel and small toy cars and trucks

Social Studies

Wheelchair

Borrow a wheelchair (child sized if possible) from a local hospital or pharmacy. During group time, discuss how wheelchairs help some people to move. Children can experience moving and pushing a wheelchair.

Books

The following books can be used to complement this theme:

Barton, Byron. (1997). *Machines at Work.* New York: HarperFestival.

Carter, Don. (2002). *Trucks!* Get to Work. Brookfield, CT: Roaring Brook Press.

Cousins, Lucy. (2010). *Maisy's Book of Things That Go.* Somerville, MA: Candlewick Press.

Dahl, Michael. (2002). *Tires, Spokes, and Sprockets: A Book about Wheels and Axles.* Minneapolis, MN: Picture Window Books.

Day, Nancy Raines. (2003). *Double Those Wheels.* New York: Dutton Children's Books

Graham, Ian. (2008). *Monster Trucks.* Laguna Hills, CA: QEB Publishing.

Johnson, Stephen T. (2006). *My Little Yellow Taxi.* San Diego, CA: Red Wagon Books/ Harcourt.

Kubler, Annie. (2001). *The Wheels on the Bus.* Bridgemead, UK: Child's Play.

Lillegard, Dee. (2006). *Go! Poetry in Motion.* Illustrated by Valeri Gorbachev. New York: Knopf.

Lyon, George Ella, and Craig Frazier. (2007). *Trucks Roll!* New York: Atheneum/Richard Jackson Books.

Marzollo, Jean, and Walter Wick. (1998). *I Spy Little Wheels.* I Spy. Photography by Walter Wick. New York: Scholastic.

Michalak, Jamie. (2009). *Joe and Sparky Get New Wheels.* Somerville, MA: Candlewick Press.

Murphy, Stuart. (2000). *Beep Beep, Vroom Vroom!* Illustrated by Chris L. Demarest. New York: HarperCollins.

Pienkowski, Jan. (1997). *Trucks and Other Working Wheels.* New York: Dutton Children's Books.

Prince Jones, April. (2006). *What Do Wheels Do All Day?* Illustrated by Giles Laroche. Boston: Houghton Mifflin.

Raffi. (1998). *Wheels on the Bus.* New York: Crown Books.

Rockwell, Anne. (2006). *Big Wheels.* New York: Walker & Co.

Samuels, Barbara. (2010). *The Trucker.* New York: Farrar, Straus and Giroux.

Shannon, David. (2002). *Duck on a Bike.* New York: Scholastic.

Shirley, Debra. (2008). *Best Friend on Wheels.* Morton Grove, IL: A. Whitman and Co.

Todd, Mark. (2003). *Monster Trucks.* Boston: Houghton Mifflin.

Walton, Rick. (2002). *Cars at Play.* New York: G.P. Putnam's Sons.

Willems, Mo. (2005). *The Pigeon Loves Things That Go!* New York: Scholastic.

Zane, Alex. (2005). *Wheels on the Race Car.* New York: Orchard Books.

Technology and Multimedia

The following technology and multimedia product can be used to complement this theme:

The Best of Mighty Machines [DVD]. (2007). Coral Springs, FL: NCircle Entertainment.

"Drive My Car" [CD]. (2002). In *Laurie Berkner: Under a Shady Tree.* New York: Two Tomatoes.

"Let's Go Riding in the Car" [CD]. (2008) In *Pete Seeger's Children's Concert At Town Hall.*

Mighty Machines: Chomp! Crunch! Tear! [DVD]. (2010). Coral Springs, FL: NCircle Entertainment.

Mighty Machines: MakingTracks [DVD]. (2007). NCircle Entertainment.

"Wheels" [CD]. (2010). In *What Are the Odds?* New York: Monkey Monkey Music.

"The Wheels on the Bus" [CD]. (2000). In *Early Childhood Classics: Old Favorites with a New Twist.* Sherman Oaks, CA: Hap-Pal Music.

 Additional teaching resources to accompany this Theme can be found on the book's companion website. Go to www.cengagebrain.com to access the site for a variety of useful resources.

Theme 73
WINTER

Weather Characteristics
colder
may be icy
may be snowy
may be sleety
may be shivery

Outdoor Clothing
hats, jackets
coats
mittens and gloves
boots, scarves
earmuffs, snowpants
snowsuits

Animals That Hibernate
chipmunks
bears
snakes
turtles
frogs and toads

Cold Weather Sports
ice skating, sledding
snowmobiling
ice fishing, hockey
skiing, tobogganing

Impact
trees shed leaves
lakes and ponds may freeze

Months
December
January, February

Holidays
Christmas
Hanukkah
Kwanzaa
New Year's Day
Valentine's Day

Theme Goals

Through participating in the experiences provided by this theme, the children may learn:

1. Winter holidays
2. Characteristics of winter weather
3. Winter sports
4. Winter outdoor clothing
5. Hibernating animals

Concepts for the Children to Learn

1. Winter is one of the four seasons.
2. Winter is usually the coldest season.
3. Winter comes after fall and before spring.
4. Ice, snow, and sleet are found during the winter in some places.
5. People wear warmer clothes in the winter.
6. Hats, jackets, coats, mittens, gloves, boots, scarves, snowpants, earmuffs, and snowsuits are worn during the winter.
7. Some animals hibernate in the winter.
8. Chipmunks, bears, snakes, turtles, frogs, and toads hibernate for the winter.
9. Trees may lose their leaves in the winter.
10. Lakes, ponds, and water may freeze in the winter.
11. Sledding, skiing, tobogganing, snowmobiling, ice fishing, hockey, and ice skating are winter sports in colder areas.
12. To remove snow, people shovel and plow.
13. December, January, and February are winter months.
14. Christmas, Kwanzaa, New Year's Day, Hanukkah, and Valentine's Day are winter holidays.

Vocabulary

1. **boots**—clothing worn on feet to keep them dry and warm.
2. **cold**—not warm. Winter weather is often cold.
3. **frost**—very small ice pieces.
4. **hibernate**—to sleep during the winter.
5. **ice**—frozen water.
6. **icicle**—a hanging piece of frozen ice.
7. **shiver**—to shake from cold or fear.
8. **ski**—a runner that moves over snow and ice.
9. **sled**—transportation for moving over snow and ice.
10. **sleet**—mixture of rain and snow.
11. **snow**—frozen particles of water that fall to the ground.
12. **snowperson**—snow shaped in the form of a person.
13. **temperature**—indicates how hot or cold something is.
14. **winter**—one of four seasons. Winter comes after fall and before spring.

Bulletin Board

The purpose of this bulletin board is to provide the children with an opportunity to develop their visual discrimination skills by matching patterns. Construct several pairs of mittens out of tagboard, each with a different pattern, as illustrated. Laminate the pieces. On the bulletin board, string one of each pair of the mittens through a rope or clothesline (one or two rows). Tie enough clothespins in place by putting the line through the wire spring of the clothespins so children can attach the matching mittens. (Tie a clothespin beside each mitten.) Children can match the mittens by hanging the second next to the first with a clothespin. This is mainly a small motor exercise for older children, unless you make the mittens with patterns or colors that are similar. More detailed patterns will increase the difficulty of the task.

Family Letter

InBox

Dear Families,

We are beginning a curriculum theme on winter. The children will learn about the coldest season by taking a look at winter clothing, weather characteristics that occur during this season, and winter sports. Throughout the unit, the children will develop an awareness of winter activities. The children will also learn to identify the winter holidays and the animals that hibernate during the winter.

At School

Some of our learning experiences related to winter include:

- Creating cottonball snowpeople

- Sorting mittens by size, shape, and color

- Enjoying stories about winter

- Setting up an ice-skating rink in the dramatic play area

- Experiencing snow and ice in the sensory table

At Home (Teachers: delete this paragraph if snow is unavailable)

To experience winter at home, try this activity—snow in the bathtub! Bring in some snow from outside, and place it in your bathtub. Also place some measuring cups, spoons, and scoops in the bathtub and let your child use mittens to play in the snow. In addition, a spray bottle filled with colored water (made with food coloring) will allow your child to make colorful sculptures. This is sure to keep your children busy and will develop an awareness of the senses.

Happy Winter from all of us!

 **Arts and Crafts**

1. Whipped Soap Painting
Mix 1 cup Ivory Snow flakes with 1/2 cup warm water in bowl. The children can beat with a hand eggbeater until the mixture is fluffy. Apply the mixture to dark construction paper with various tools (toothbrushes, rollers, tongue depressors, brushes, etc.). To create variety, food coloring can be added to the paint mixture.

2. Cotton Ball Snowperson
Cut a snowperson figure from dark construction paper. Provide the children with cotton balls and glue. They can decorate the snowperson by gluing on cotton balls.

3. Snowflakes
Cut different-sized squares out of white construction paper. Fold the squares in half, and then in half again. Demonstrate and encourage the children to cut and open their own designs. The snowflakes can be hung in the entry or classroom for decoration.

4. Ice Cube Art
Place a craft stick in each ice compartment of a tray and fill with water. Freeze. Sprinkle dry tempera paint on paper. To make their own design, the children can move an ice cube on the paper.

5. Frosted Pictures
Mix 1 part Epsom salts with 1 part boiling water. Let the mixture cool. Encourage the children to make a crayon design on paper. The mixture can be brushed over the picture. Observe how the crystals form as the mixture dries.

6. Winter Shape Printing
Cut sponges into various winter shapes such as boots, snowmen, mittens, snowflakes, fir trees, and stars. The children can use the sponges as a tool to print on different pieces of colored construction paper.

7. Easel Ideas
Feature white paint at the easel for snow pictures on colored paper. Or, cut easel paper into winter shapes: snowmen, hats, mittens, scarves, snowflakes, and so on.

8. Snow Drawings
White chalk and dark construction paper can be placed in the art area.

9. Snow Painting
Using old spray bottles filled with colored water, let the children make pictures in the snow outside. *Note:* This activity is limited to areas where snow is available.

 **Cooking**

1. Banana Snowpeople
2 cups raisins
2 bananas
Shredded coconut

Chop the bananas and raisins in a blender. Place them in a mixing bowl. Refrigerate until the mixture is cool enough to be handled. Roll the mixture into balls and into shredded coconut. Stack three balls, and fasten with toothpicks. *Caution:* Close supervision is needed when using toothpicks with young children.

2. Hot Chocolate
Add warm water or milk to instant hot chocolate, and mix. Heat as needed.

3. Snow Cones
Crush ice, and spoon into small paper cups. Pour a fruit juice over the ice. Serve.

 **Dramatic Play**

1. Ice-Skating Palace
Make a masking tape border on a carpeted floor. Give each child two pieces of waxed paper. Show children how to fasten waxed paper to their ankles with rubber bands. Play instrumental music and encourage the children to skate around on the carpeted floor.

2. Dress Up

If available, put outdoor winter clothing such as coats, boots, hats, mittens, scarves, and earmuffs in the dramatic play area of the classroom with a large mirror. The children may enjoy trying on a variety of clothing items.

Field Trips and Resource People

1. Visit an ice-skating rink. Observe the ice and watch how it is cleaned.
2. Visit a sledding hill. Bring sleds and go sledding.
3. Invite a snowplow operator to school to talk to the children. After a snowfall, the children can observe the plowing.
4. Take the children to a grocery store and view the freezer area. Also, observe a refrigerated delivery truck.

Fingerplays and Chants

Five Little Snowpeople

Five little snowpeople standing in the door.
This one melted and then there were four.
  (hold up all five fingers, put down thumb)
Four little snowpeople underneath a tree.
This one melted and then there were three.
  (put down pointer finger)
Three little snowpeople with hats and
  mittens too.
This one melted and then there were two.
  (put down middle finger)
Two little snowpeople outside in the sun.
This one melted and then there was one.
  (put down ring finger)
One little snowperson trying hard to run.
He melted too, and then there were none.
  (put down pinky)

Variations:

- Make five little snowpeople finger puppets, and remove them one by one.
- Make five stick puppets for children to hold and sit down one by one at appropriate times during fingerplay.

Making a Snowperson

Roll it, roll it, get a pile of snow.
  (make rolling motions with hands)
Rolling, rolling, rolling, rolling, rolling here
  we go.
Pat it, pat it, face it to the south.
  (patting motion)
Now my little snowperson's done, eyes and
  nose and mouth.
  (point to eyes, nose, and mouth)

Zippers

Three little zippers on my snowsuit,
  (hold up three fingers)
Fasten up as snug as snug can be
It's a very easy thing as you can see
Just zip, zip, zip!
  (do three zipping motions)
I work the zippers on my snowsuit.
Zippers really do save time for me
I can fasten them myself with one, two,
  three.
Just zip, zip, zip!
  (do three zipping motions)

The Snowperson and the Bunny

A chubby little snowperson
  (make a fist)
Had a carrot nose.
  (poke thumb out)
Along came a bunny
And what do you suppose?
  (other hand, make rabbit ears)
That hungry little bunny
Looking for his lunch
  (bunny hops around)
Ate that snowperson's carrot nose.
  (bunny nibbles at thumb)
Crunch, crunch, crunch.

Build a Snowperson

First you make a snowball,
  (rolling motion)
Big and fat and round.
  (extend arms in large circle)
Then you roll the snowball,
  (rolling motion)
All along the ground.
Then you build the snowperson
One-two-three!
  (place three pretend balls on top of each
  other)

Then you have a snowperson,
Don't you see?
    (point to eyes)
Then the sun shines all around and
Melts the snowperson to the ground.
    (drop to the ground in a melting motion)

Group Time
(Games and Language)

1. Who Has the Mitten?
Ask the children to sit in a circle. One child should sit in the middle. Make a very small mitten out of felt or construction paper. Tell the children to pass the mitten around the circle. All the children should imitate the passing actions, even if they do not have the mitten in hand. When the verse starts, the child in the middle tries to guess who has the mitten. Chant the following verse while passing a mitten.

I pass the mitten from me to you to you,
I pass the mitten and that is what I do.

2. Hat Chart
Prepare a hat chart by listing all the types and colors of hats worn by the children in the classroom.

Large Muscle

1. Freeze
Play music, and have the children walk around in a circle. When the music stops, the children freeze by standing still in a stooped position. Vary the activity by substituting other actions such as hopping, skipping, galloping, sliding, and the like.

2. Snowperson
During outdoor play, make a snowperson. Decorate with radish eyes, a carrot nose, a scarf, and a hat, and have the snowperson hold a stick. Other novel accessories can be substituted by using the children's ideas.

3. Snowpeople
After a snowfall, have the children lie down in the snow and move their arms and legs to make shapes.

4. Snowball Target
Because children love throwing snowballs, set up a target outside for children to throw snowballs.

5. Shovel
Provide child-sized shovels for the children to help shovel a walk.

6. Balance
Make various tracks in the snow, such as a straight line, zig-zag line, circle, square, triangle, and rectangle.

2+3= Math

1. Shape Sequence
Cut three different-sized white circles from construction paper for each child to make a snowperson. Which is the largest? Smallest? How many do you have? What shape? Have children sequence the circles from largest to smallest and from smallest to largest.

2. Winter Dominoes
Trace and cut 30 squares out of white tagboard. Section each square into four spaces diagonally. In each of the four spaces, draw different winter objects or stick on winter stickers. The children can match the pictures by playing dominoes.

3. Dot to Dot
Make a dot-to-dot snowperson. The children connect the dots in numerical order. You can also make dot-to-dot patterns of other winter objects such as hats, snowflakes, mittens, and so on. This activity requires numeral recognition and order, so it is restricted to the school-aged child.

4. Puzzles
Mount winter pictures or posters on tagboard sheets. Cut into pieces. The number of pieces cut will depend on the children's developmental age. Place in the small manipulative area of the classroom for use during self-selected activity periods.

Music

1. "Snowperson"
(Sing to the tune of "Twinkle, Twinkle, Little Star")

Snowperson, snowperson, where did you go?
I built you yesterday out of snow.
I built you high and I built you fat.
I put on eyes and a nose and a hat.
Now you're gone all melted away
But it's sunny outside so I'll go and play.

2. "Winter Clothes"
(Sing to the tune of "Did You Ever See a Lassie?")
(In additional verses, replace "coats" with hats, boots, mittens, etc.)

Children put your coats on, your coats on,
    your coats on.
Children put your coats on, one, two, and
    three.

3. "Mitten Song"
Thumbs in the thumb place, fingers all
    together.
This is the song we sing in mitten weather.

Science

1. Weather Doll
Make a felt weather doll. Encourage the children to dress and undress the doll according to the weather.

2. Make Frost
Changes in temperature cause dew. When dew freezes, it is called frost. Materials needed are a tin can with no lid, rock salt, and crushed ice. Measure and pour 2 cups of crushed ice and 1/2 cup rock salt in a can. Stir rapidly. Let the mixture sit for 30 minutes. After 30 minutes, the outside of the can will have dew on it. Wait longer, and the dew will change to frost. To hasten the process, place in a freezer.

3. Make Bird Feeders
Roll pinecones in a mixture of cornmeal with shortening, lard, or softened butter, and then roll in bird seed. Attach a string to the pinecones, and hang them outside. Encourage the children to check the bird feeders frequently.

A bird feeder can also be prepared from suet. To do this, wrap suet in netting. Gather up the edges, and tie together with a long string. Another method is to place suet in a net citrus fruit bag.

4. Snow
Bring a large container of snow into the classroom. After it is melted, add colored water and place the container outdoors. When frozen, bring a colored block of ice back into the classroom and watch it melt.

5. Examine Snowflakes
Examine snowflakes with a magnifying glass. Each is unique. For classrooms located in warmer climates, make a snow-like substance by crushing ice.

6. Catching Snowflakes
Cover a piece of cardboard with dark felt. Place the cardboard piece in the freezer. Place the board outside, and let snowflakes land on the board. Snowflakes will last longer for examination.

7. Coloring Snow
Provide children with spray bottles containing colored water, preferably red, yellow, and blue. Allow them to spray the snow and mix colors.

8. Thermometers
Experiment with a thermometer. Begin introducing the concept by observing and discussing what happens when the thermometer is placed in a bowl of warm water and a bowl of cold water. Demonstrate to the children, and encourage them to experiment under supervision during the self-selected activity period.

9. Signs and Sounds of Winter
On a winter walk in colder climates, have the children watch and listen for signs and sounds of winter. The signs of winter are

(1) weather: cold, ice, daylight is shorter, and darkness is earlier; (2) plants: all but evergreen trees are bare; and (3) people: we wear warmer clothes, we play inside more, we shovel snow, and we play in the snow. Some of the sounds of winter arc boots crunching, rain splashing, wind howling, and so on. **Note:** Adapt this activity to the signs of winter in your climate.

Sensory

The following items can be placed in the sensory table:

- Snow and ice (plain or colored with drops of food coloring)
- Cottonballs with measuring and balancing scale
- Pinecones
- Ice cubes (colored or plain)
- Snow and magnifying glasses

Social Studies

1. **Travel**
   Discuss ways people travel in winter, such as by sled, toboggan, snowmobile, snowshoes, skis, and the like.

2. **Winter Happenings**
   Display pictures of different winter happenings—for example, sports, clothing, snow, and so forth—around the room at the children's eye level.

3. **Winter Book**
   Encourage the children to make a book about winter. Do one page a day. The following titles could be used:
   - *What I Wear in Winter*
   - *What I Like to Do Outside in Winter*
   - *What I Like to Do Inside in Winter*
   - *My Favorite Food during Winter*
   - *My Favorite Thing about Winter*

   Note: This activity may be more appropriate for the school-aged child.

4. **Winter Clothing Match**
   Draw large paper figures of a boy and of a girl. Design and cut winter clothing to fit each figure. The children can dress the figures for outdoor play.

Books

The following books can be used to complement this theme:

Allue, Joseph M., M. E. Sole, N. C. Canals, and M. P. Pons. (2001). *100 Games for Winter.* Illustrated by Joseph M. Allue, M. E. Sole, and M. P. Pons. Hauppage, NY: Barron Juveniles.

Barclay, Jane. (2000). *How Cold Was It?* Montreal: Lobster Press.

Brett, Jan. (2007). *The Three Snow Bears.* New York: Putnam Juvenile.

Brett, Jan. (2009). *The Mitten* (20th anniversary edition). New York: Putnam Juvenile.

Brunelle, Nicholas. (2005). *Snowman.* New York: Viking.

Gay, Marie-Louise. (2000). *Stella, Queen of Snow.* Toronto: Douglas & McIntyre.

Glaser, Linda. (2002). *It's Winter!* Minneapolis, MN: Millbrook Press.

Hest, Amy. (2003). *You Can Do It Sam.* Illustrated by Anita Jeram. Cambridge, MA: Candlewick Press.

Hopkins, Lee Bennett. (2010). *Sharing the Seasons: A Book of Poems.* Illustrated by David Diaz. New York: Margaret K. McElderry Books.

Iwamura, Kazuo. (2008). *Hooray for Snow.* Fitzgerald, GA: North South.

Kohara, Kazuno. (2009). *Here Comes Jack Frost.* New York: Roaring Brook Press.

Laminack, Lester L. (2007). *Snow Day!* Illustrated by Adam Gustavson. Atlanta, GA: Peachtree.

Lenski, Lois. (2000). *I Like Winter.* New York: Random House.

Lindeen, Carol K. (2006). *Let's Ice Skate!* Mankato, MN: Capstone Press.

London, Jonathan. (1992). *Froggy Gets Dressed.* Illustrated by Frank Remkiewicz. New York: Viking.

Maass, Robert. (1993). *When Winter Comes.* New York: H. Holt.

Quattlebaum, Mary. (2005). *Winter Friends.* Illustrated by Hiroe Nakata. New York: Doubleday Books for Young Readers.

Rustad, Martha E. H. (2009). *Animals in Winter.* Mankato, MN: Capstone Press.

Rustad, Martha E. H. (2009). *Christmas.* Mankato, MN: Capstone Press.

Rustad, Martha E. H. (2009). *People in Winter.* Mankato, MN: Capstone Press.

Rustad, Martha E. H. (2009). *Snowflakes.* Mankato, MN: Capstone Press.

Rylant, Cynthia. (2007). *Snow.* Illustrated by Lauren Stringer. Orlando, FL: Harcourt.

Schoenherr, Ian. (2007). *Pip and Squeak.* New York: Greenwillow Books.

Schuette, Sarah L. (2007). *Let's Look at Winter.* Mankato, MN: Capstone Press.

Stoick, Jean, and Carl R. Sams II. (2000). *Stranger in the Woods.* Auburn Hills, MI: EDCO Publishing.

Tafuri, Nancy. (2001). *Where Did Bunny Go?* New York: Scholastic Press.

Thomas, Jane. (2001). *The Big Red Sled.* Illustrated by Priscilla Burris. New York: Scholastic.

Van Laan, Nancy, and Susan Gaber. (2000). *When Winter Comes.* New York: Atheneum / Anne Schwartz Books.

Technology and Multimedia

The following technology and multimedia products can be used to complement this theme:

Bear Snores On [DVD]. (2005). New York: Scholastic.

Caillou: Caillou's Winter Wonders [DVD]. (2008). Los Angeles: Paramount Home Entertainment.

Curious George Plays in the Snow [DVD]. (2007). Burbank, CA: Universal Studios Home Entertainment.

"I'm a Little Snowflake" [CD]. (2001). In *Whaddaya Think of That, Laurie Berkner.* New York: Two Tomatoes.

Kipper [DVD]. (2003). London, England: Hit Entertainment.

The Snowy Day and Other Caldecott Classics [DVD]. (2003). New York: Scholastic.

"Winter Lullaby" [CD]. (2008). In *The Laurie Berkner Band, Rocketship Run.* New York: Razor & Tie.

 Additional teaching resources to accompany this Theme can be found on the book's companion website. Go to www.cengagebrain.com to access the site for a variety of useful resources.

Theme 74
WORMS

Earthworm Enemies	Purpose	Places	Foods	Sizes
birds	fishing bait	soil or	dirt	small
lizards	tunnels in soil	underground	rotting leaves	medium
frogs		oceans	plants	large
toads		ponds		
turtles				
moles				
shrews				

Theme Goals

Through participating in the experiences provided by this theme, the children may learn:

1. Places worms live
2. Sizes of worms
3. Earthworm enemies
4. Foods worms eat
5. Purpose of earthworms

Concepts for the Children to Learn

1. Worms are thin animals that have long, soft bodies.
2. Worms can be different sizes and lengths.
3. Earthworms live underground.
4. An earthworm moves by stretching itself thin and then pulling its body together.
5. Earthworms make tunnels in the soil.
6. Earthworms help keep soil healthy for plant growth.
7. Earthworms breathe through their skin.
8. Many insects at the caterpillar stage of growth are worms, such as apple worms, inchworms, and tomato worms.
9. Earthworms are food for many animals, including birds, lizards, frogs, toads, turtles, moles, and shrews.
10. Earthworms are sometimes used as fishing bait.
11. Earthworms eat dirt, rotting leaves, and plants.

Vocabulary

1. **burrow**—a tunnel in the earth made by a worm.
2. **soil**—top layer of the earth in which plants grow.
3. **worm**—an animal that has a soft, slender body and no backbone or legs.

Bulletin Board

The purpose of this bulletin board is to identify written numerals, as well as match sets of objects to a written numeral. Construct bucket shapes out of tag board. Print a different numeral on each bucket. (Numerals used should depend on the developmental level of the children.) Cut worms out of tag board and decorate as desired. Laminate all pieces. Attach the buckets to the bulletin board by stapling them along the side and bottom edges, leaving the tops of the buckets open. The children are to place the corresponding number of worms in each bucket.

Family Letter

InBox

Dear Families,

Did you know that there are thousands of kinds of worms? Worms are fascinating. They are any of several kinds of animals that have a soft, slender body, with no backbone or legs. The smallest worms cannot be seen without a microscope, and the largest can be many feet long. At school this week, we will focus on the common earthworm, which is a member of the segmented worm group. Through the experiences provided by this theme, the children will learn the places worms live and the foods they eat.

At School

Some of this week's learning experiences include:

- Creating a worm farm to place on the science table and observe worms

- Sorting gummi worm candies by colors

- Making pretzels in the shape of worms!

- Playing with plastic worms and sand in the sensory table

At Home

After a rainfall, look for worms and worm holes with your child to reinforce concepts of this unit at home. Also, we will learn the following song. You may want to try it with your child.

"I'm a Little Worm"
(Sing to the tune of "I'm a Little Teapot")

I'm a little worm in the soft, cool ground.
I like to wiggle and squirm around.
When a bird comes near,
I scoot away.
Back into the ground is where I'll stay!

Have a good week!

Arts and Crafts

1. Worm Painting

Plastic fishing worms on string, paint, and paper are needed for this activity. Children dip a worm or string into paint and apply to the paper, moving it around the paper.

2. Package Worm Collages

Save Styrofoam package "worms" and place on the art table with paper, markers, and glue. The children can use materials to create designs of their choice.

Cooking

1. Mud Cake

  1 1/2 cups flour
  1 cup sugar
  1/4 cup unsweetened cocoa powder
  1 teaspoon baking soda
  1/2 teaspoon salt
  1/3 cup vegetable oil
  1 tablespoon vinegar
  1 teaspoon vanilla
  1 cup water
  Gummi worm candies (for decoration)

Place dry ingredients in an 8-inch × 8-inch × 2-inch baking pan. Mix well. Using a fork, make a hole shape in the middle of the flour mixture. Pour liquid ingredients into the hole. Stir together all ingredients with a fork. Bake for 40 to 45 minutes in a 350-degree oven. Cool in pan. Decorate cake by gently pushing worm candies into each piece.

2. Worm Pretzels

Use frozen bread dough to make worm-shaped pretzels. Follow directions on the package for thawing and baking.

3. Worm and Dirt Cupcakes

  1 package fudge brownie mix
  1/2 cup shredded sweetened coconut
  1/2 cup semisweet chocolate chips
  2 teaspoons coconut extract

Preheat oven to the directions provided on the mix. Follow the directions for preparation of the mix. Stir in the extract, shredded coconut, and chocolate chips.

  Divide the batter into a regular-size cupcake tin and bake according to the directions on the brownie mix. Recipe should make 12 cupcakes. Depending on the size of the class, you may want to use more than one mix.

4. Dirty Worm Snack

Prepare desired amount of chocolate pudding. Place in cups and add gummy worms.

Dramatic Play

Bait Shop

In the dramatic play area, place tackle boxes, plastic worms (in small containers), fishing lures (with the hooks removed), bobbers, nets, fishing poles, cash register, and play money. The children can pretend to be customers and bait shop workers.

Field Trips

1. Bait Store

Plan a trip to an area bait store. Ask to see the variety of worms that are sold. Also, look closely at worm bedding.

2. Go Fishin'

If appropriate and with plenty of adult supervision, arrange a fishing trip to a pond, lake, or fish farm. Bring along a picnic lunch and enjoy the day!

Fingerplays and Chants

A Robin

  When a robin cocks his head
   (tilt head to side)
  Sideways in a flower bed,
  He can hear the tiny sound
  Of a worm beneath the ground.
   (make crawling motion with fingers)

Little Worm

The little tiny wiggly worm
    (move index finger)
Went crawling through the ground.
Down came the rain
    (wiggle all fingers downward)
It was muddy all around.

Rain filled the tunnels
    (make slow fist)
And out came the little worm.
    (push index finger of one hand through
    fist of other)
So the puddles on the ground
Were the only place to squirm.
    (move index finger)

Group Time
(Games and Language)

1. Hide the Worm

Ask several children to close or cover their eyes. Then hide a plastic worm in an observable place in the room. Children uncover their eyes and try to find the worm. The first child to find the worm hides it again, and the game continues until all have had a chance to look for the worm.

2. Drop the Worm (A Variation of Drop the Handkerchief)

To play this game, children stand in a circle formation. One child is chosen to hold a plastic worm and walk around the outside of the circle, dropping the worm behind another child. The child who has the worm dropped behind him or her must pick it up and chase the child who dropped it. The first child tries to return to the vacated space by running before he or she is tagged.

Large Muscle

Wiggle Worms

Encourage children to move like worms by wiggling on the floor. A "freeze" game could be played. Children wiggle while music plays and stop or "freeze" when the music stops.

Math

1. Gummi Worm Candy Sort

As a group, sort a package of gummi worm candies by color. Count the number of each color. Count all gummi worms. If appropriate, record information on a graph.

2. Set of Worms

Using plastic fishing worms and number cards, encourage children to count sets of worms to match written numbers.

3. How Many Worms?

Create "inchworms" by drawing a worm (or pasting a clip art worm) in a strip of paper one inch long. Make one full sheet and photocopy for desired amount. Cut apart and give some to each child. Give children a variety of objects to "measure" by placing inchworms end to end. *Variation:* You could also make inchworm measuring cubes by taping inchworms to cubes that are approximately one inch long.

Music

1. "I'm a Little Worm"
(Sing to the tune of "I'm a Little Teapot")

I'm a little worm in the soft, cool ground.
I like to wiggle and squirm around.
When a bird comes near,
I scoot away.
Back into the ground is where I'll stay!

2. "Did You Ever See a Wiggly Worm?"
(Sing to the tune of "Did You Ever See a Lassie?")

Did you ever see a wiggly worm,
A wiggly worm, a wiggly worm?
Did you ever see a wiggly worm,
Move on the ground?

It stretches and scrunches,
And stretches and scrunches.
Did you ever see a wiggly worm,
Move on the ground?

3. "Here's a Little Worm"
(Sing to the tune of "Where Is Thumbkin?")

Here's a little worm, here's a little worm,
Crawling around, in the ground.
Making little tunnels, making little tunnels,
Crawling around, in the ground.

4. "Just a Little Worm"
(Sing to the tune of "Mary Had a Little Lamb")

I am just a little worm,
Little worm, little worm.
I am just a little worm,
In the nice cool ground.

Wiggling is what I do,
What I do, what I do.
Wiggling is what I do,
When I want to move around.

5. "Wiggle, Wiggle, Little Worm"
(Sing to the tune of "Twinkle, Twinkle")

Wiggle, wiggle, little worm.
Wiggle, wiggle, jiggle, squirm.
If a robin you should see,
hide as quick as quick can be.
Wiggle, wiggle, little worm.
Wiggle, wiggle, jiggle, squirm.

Science

1. Worm Farm
Fill a large, clear jar with earthworm bedding or soil. Add a few worms to the jar. Poke holes in the cover and attach to the jar. Because worms prefer dark areas, cover the glass with black construction paper pieces. Remove periodically to observe the worms and their trails. Sprinkle cornmeal in the jar a few times a week.

2. Worm Hunt
After a rainfall, join the children in a worm hunt! Collect worms in buckets or similar containers. Use magnifying glasses to get a closer look at the worms. Return the worms to the soil (or a garden) on completion of the hunt.

Sensory

1. Plastic Worms
Place plastic fishing worms in the sensory table with sand, potting soil, or water. Add small nets, scoops, and bowls to add interest.

2. Package "Worms"
Collect Styrofoam packing "worms" and place in the sensory table with scoops and buckets.

Books

The following books can be used to complement this theme:

Bailey, Jill. (2001). *Worm.* Oxford: Heinemann Library.

Bosca, Francesca. (2001). *The Apple King.* Illustrated by Giuliano Ferri. New York: North-South Books.

Brendler, Carol. (2009). *Winnie Finn, Worm Farmer.* Illustrated by Ard Hoyt. New York: Farrar, Straus and Giroux.

Caple, Kathy. (2001). *Wow, It's Worm.* London: Walker.

Cronin, Doreen. (2003). *Diary of a Worm.* Illustrated by Harry Bliss. New York: J. Cotter Books.

French, Vivian. (2010). *Yucky Worms.* Illustrated by Jessica Ahlberg. Somerville, MA: Candlewick Press.

Himmelman, John. (2000). *An Earthworm's Life.* New York: Children's Press.

Kalman, Bobbie. (2004). *The Lifecycle of an Earthworm.* New York: Crabtree Press.

Koontx, Robin. (2007). *Composting: Nature's Recyclers.* Illustrated by Matthew Harrad. Minneapolis, MN: Picture Window Books.

Loewen, Nancy. (2006). *Garden Wigglers: Earthworms in Your Backyard.* Illustrated by Rick Peterson. Minneapolis, MN: Picture Window Books.

Pfeffer, Wendy. (2004). *Wiggling Worms at Work.* Illustrated by Steve Jensen. New York: HarperCollins.

Pinczes, Elinor J., and Randall Enos. (2000). *Inchworm and a Half.* Boston: Houghton Mifflin.

Raschka, Christopher. (2000). *Wormy Worm.* New York: Hyperion Books for Children.

Rosinsky, Natalie M. (2003). *Dirt: The Scoop on Soil.* Minneapolis, MN: Picture Window Books.

Rustad, Martha. (2009). *Mealworms.* Watch It Grow. Mankato, MN: Capstone Press.

Silverstein, Alvin, and Virginia Silverstein. (2000). *Life in a Bucket of Soil.* Illustrated by Elsie Wrigley. Mineola, NY: Dover.

Williams, Rozanne. (2008). *Watch Out for Worms!* Huntington Beach, CA: Creative Teaching Press.

Technology and Multimedia

The following technology and multimedia products can be used to complement this theme:

Diary of a Worm [DVD]. (2006). Norwalk, CT: Weston Woods.

Slither & Slime and Other Yucky Things [DVD]. (2004). Port Washington, NY: Koch Vision.

 Additional teaching resources to accompany this Theme can be found on the book's companion website. Go to www.cengagebrain.com to access the site for a variety of useful resources.

Theme 75
YELLOW

Animals
chicks
canaries
cats

Color Mixing
yellow + blue = green
yellow + red = orange

Traffic Signs
traffic light
yield signs

Flowers
daisy
dandelion
rose
daffodil

Objects
sun
paint
cars
toys
bikes
clothes

Foods
pineapple
banana
lemon
corn
grapefruit
cheese
egg yolk

Theme Goals

Through participating in the experiences provided by this theme, the children may learn:

1. Yellow-colored flowers
2. Yellow traffic signs
3. Yellow animals
4. Many objects that are colored yellow
5. Yellow objects
6. Colors formed by adding yellow

Concepts for the Children to Learn

1. Yellow is a primary color.
2. Yellow mixed with blue makes green.
3. Yellow mixed with red makes orange.
4. Some objects are colored yellow.
5. The sun is yellow.
6. Bikes, clothing, cars, toys, and paint can be a yellow color.
7. The middle color on a traffic light is yellow.
8. Yield traffic signs are colored yellow.
9. Some flowers can be a yellow color.
10. Daisies, dandelions, and daffodils are yellow flowers.
11. Some roses are a yellow color.
12. Canaries, chicks, and some cats are a yellow color.
13. Toys, paints, cars, bikes, and clothing can be yellow.
14. Some foods are a yellow color.
15. Pineapples, bananas, and corn are yellow foods.
16. Lemons, corn, and egg yolks are yellow.
17. Some grapefruit and cheeses are yellow.

Vocabulary

1. **primary colors**—red, blue, and yellow.
2. **yellow**—a primary color.

Bulletin Board

The purpose of this bulletin board is to have the children match the shapes, providing practice in visual discrimination and hand-eye coordination skills. To prepare the bulletin board, collect yellow tagboard, a black felt-tip marker, scissors, yellow string, and pushpins. Using yellow tagboard, draw sets of different-shaped balloons as illustrated. Outline with a black felt-tip marker, and cut out. Take one balloon from each set, and attach to the top of the bulletin board as illustrated. Staple a yellow string to hang from each balloon. Next, attach the remaining balloons on the bottom of the bulletin board. A pushpin can be fastened next to each balloon, and the children can match the balloons by shape.

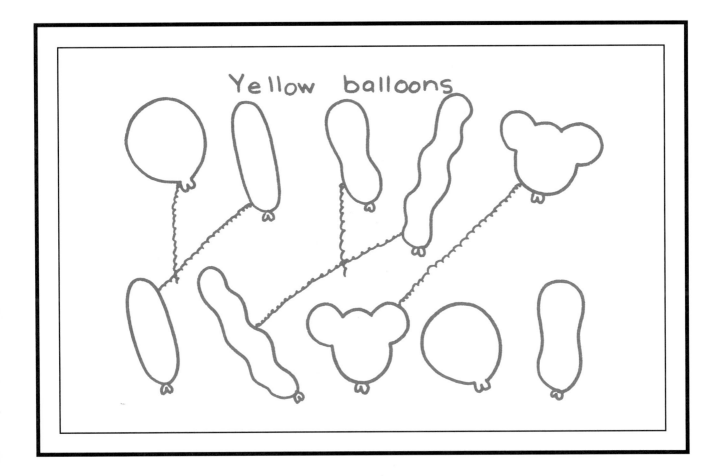

Family Letter

InBox

Dear Families,

Colors are such a big part of our world. Consequently, our new theme focuses on the color yellow. Throughout this week, the children will become aware of the color in their environment. It should be a bright time discovering the color yellow! They will learn to identify the signs, flowers, animals, foods, and objects that are colored yellow.

At School

Some learning experiences planned for the unit include:

- Making scrambled eggs
- Visiting a paint store
- Learning the fingerplay "Six Yellow Chickadees"
- Making yellow soap crayons
- Playing with corn kernels in the sensory table

At Home

At school, we will make yellow play dough. The children enjoy helping prepare the play dough and, of course, playing with it! It would be great fun for them to make it at home, and they will be exposed to the mathematical concepts of amounts, fractions, and measurements. Here is the recipe:

2 cups flour
1 cup salt
1 cup water
2 tablespoons cooking oil
Food coloring

Let your child assist in gathering and measuring the ingredients. Next, mix all the ingredients together. To encourage play, provide some tools for your child to use: rolling pins, cookie cutters, spatulas, or potato mashers. Have fun!

Enjoy your child!

Arts and Crafts

1. Yellow Paint
Provide yellow fingerpaint and yellow tempera paint in the art area.

2. Corncob Painting
Cover the bottom of a shallow pan with thick yellow tempera paint. Using a corncob as an applicator, apply paint to paper.

3. Popsicle Stick Prints
Cover the bottom of a shallow pan with thick yellow tempera paint. Apply the paint to paper using a popsicle stick or craft stick as an applicator.

4. Yellow Play Dough
Combine 2 cups flour, 1 cup salt, 1 cup water, and 2 tablespoons cooking oil. Add yellow food coloring. Mix well. If prepared dough becomes sticky, add more flour.

5. Baker's Clay
Combine 4 cups flour, 1 cup salt, and 1 1/2 cups water. Mix the ingredients. The children can shape forms. Place the forms on a cookie sheet, and bake at 350 degrees for about 1 hour. The next day, the children can paint the objects yellow.

6. Yellow Collage
Provide different yellow items such as crêpe paper, colored paper, magazine pictures, and yellow glitter for the children to construct a collage.

Cooking

1. Banana Bobs
Cut bananas into chunks and dip into honey. Next, roll the bananas in wheat germ and use large toothpicks for serving.
Caution: Close supervision is needed when using toothpicks with young children.

2. Caribbean Banana Salad
3 green (unripe) bananas, peeled
2 cups water
1 teaspoon salt
2 medium carrots, shredded
1 small cucumber, sliced
1 medium tomato, chopped
1 avocado, cubed
1 stalk celery, sliced
Vinaigrette dressing

Heat bananas, water, and salt to boiling; reduce heat. Cover and simmer until bananas are tender, about 5 minutes. Drain and cool. Cut bananas crosswise into 1/2-inch slices. Toss bananas and remaining ingredients with vinaigrette dressing.

Note: From *Betty Crocker's International Cookbook,* 1980, New York: Random House. Reprinted with permission.

3. Corn Bread
1 cup flour
1 cup yellow cornmeal
2 tablespoons sugar
4 teaspoons baking powder
1 teaspoon salt
1 cup milk
1/4 cup cooking oil or melted shortening
1 egg, slightly beaten

Preheat oven to 425 degrees. Grease (do not oil) an 8- or 9-inch square pan. In a medium mixing bowl, combine the dry ingredients. Stir in the remaining ingredients, beating by hand until just smooth. Pour the batter into the prepared pan. Bake for 20 to 25 minutes or until a toothpick inserted in the center comes out clean.

Dramatic Play

Paint Store
Set up a paint store by including paint caps, paintbrushes, pans, rollers, drop cloths, paint clothes, a cash register, and play money.

Field Trips

1. Paint Store

Visit a paint store and observe the different shades of yellow. Collect samples of paint for use in the art area. If possible, also observe the manager mixing yellow paint.

2. Yellow in Our World

Take a walk and look for yellow objects. Prepare a language experience chart when you return to the classroom.

3. Greenhouse

Visit a greenhouse and observe the different kinds of yellow flowers.

Fingerplays and Chants

Six Yellow Chickadees

(Suit the actions to the words)

Six yellow chickadees sitting by a hive.
One flew away and then there were five.
Five yellow chickadees sitting by the door.
One flew away and then there were four.
Four yellow chickadees sitting in a tree.
One flew away and then there were three.
Three yellow chickadees sitting by my shoe.
One flew away and then there were two.
Two yellow chickadees sitting by my thumb.
One flew away and then there was one.
One yellow chickadee flying around the sun.
She flew away and then there were none.

Ten Fluffy Chickens

Five eggs and five eggs
    (hold up two hands)
That makes ten.
Sitting on top is the mother hen.
    (fold one hand over the other)
Crackle, crackle, crackle
    (clap hands three times)
What do I see?
Ten fluffy chickens
    (hold up ten fingers)
As yellow as can be!

Group Time
(Games and Language)

Guessing Game: What's Missing?

Use any yellow familiar objects or toys that can be easily handled. The number will depend upon developmental appropriateness. For two-year-olds, choose only two objects. On the other hand, several objects can be used for five-year-olds. Spread them out on the floor, and ask children to name each item. Then ask the group to close their eyes. Remove one item. When the group opens their eyes, ask them to tell you which item is missing.

Math

1. Sorting Shapes

Cut circles, triangles, and rectangles out of yellow tagboard. Place on the math table. The children can sort the yellow shapes into groups. For younger children, the objects can be cut from different colors. Then the objects can be sorted by color.

2. Block Patterning

Place a bucket of yellow and white cubes on the table. Encourage the children to make yellow-white-yellow-white patterns with the blocks. This activity can be extended by making pattern cards for the children to copy the pattern with the blocks.

Science

1. Paper Towel Dip

Fold a paper towel in half several times. Dip the towel into red water, and then into yellow water. Open the towel carefully, and allow it to dry. Orange designs will appear on the paper towel.

2. Carnation Coloring

Put a white carnation into a glass of water that has been dyed yellow with food coloring. Soon the carnation will show yellow streaks. During the summer, other white garden flowers can be substituted.

3. Yellow Soap Crayons

Measure 1 cup of mild powdered laundry soap. Add 1 tablespoon of food coloring. Add water by the teaspoonful until the soap is in liquid form. Stir well. Pour the soap into ice cube trays. Set in a sunny, dry place until hard. Soap crayons are great for writing in the sink, tub, or sensory table.

4. Yellow Paint Mixing

Place 2 tablespoons of yellow tempera paint on one side of a zipper closure plastic storage bag. Then place 2 tablespoons of red tempera paint on the other side. Ensure that the zipper closure is secure before giving it to the children. Then encourage the children to gently mix the colors. Ask, "What happened?" Then repeat using yellow and blue and green and yellow tempera paints.

Sensory

1. Shaving Cream Fun

Spray the contents of one can of shaving cream in the sensory table. Color the shaving cream by adding yellow food coloring.

2. Corn Kernels

Place corn kernels in the sensory table.

3. Yellow Goop

In the sensory table, mix 1 cup cornstarch, 1 cup water, and yellow food coloring. Mix together well.

4. Water Toys

Add yellow food coloring to 3 inches of water in the sensory table. Provide water toys as accessories to encourage play during self-selected play activities.

Social Studies

Tasting Party

Cut a banana, a pineapple, a lemon, and a piece of yellow cheese into small pieces. Let the children sample each during snack time.

The concepts of color, texture, and taste can all be discussed.

Books

The following books can be used to complement this theme:

Adler, David A. (2008). *Bones and the Big Yellow Mystery.* Illustrated by Barbara Johansen Newman. New York: Puffin Books.

Barry, Frances. (2008). *Big Yellow Sunflower.* Cambridge, MA: Candlewick Press.

Berger, Carin. (2008). *The Little Yellow Leaf.* New York: Greenwillow Books.

Bogdanowicz, Basia. (1999). *Yellow Hat, Red Hat.* Brookfield, CT: Millbrook Press.

Brown, Margaret Wise. (2003). *The Fierce Yellow Pumpkin.* New York: HarperCollins.

Carle, Eric. (1998). *Let's Paint a Rainbow.* New York: Scholastic.

Carter, David A. (2008). *Yellow Square.* New York: Little Simon.

Casmar, Tom. (2005). *Henry and Pawl and the Round Yellow Ball.* New York: Dial Books for Young Readers.

Catalanotto, Peter. (2005). *Kitten Red, Yellow, Blue.* New York: Atheneum Books for Young Readers.

Dematons, Charlotte. (2003). *The Yellow Balloon.* Asheville, NC: Front Street / Lemniscaat.

Dunbar, Joyce. (2006). *Where's My Sock?* Illustrated by Sanja Rescek. New York: Chicken House.

Elffers, Joost, and Saxton Freymann. (2005). *Food for Thought.* New York: Arthur A. Levine Books.

Gardner, Charlie. (2004). *Yellow Submarine / The Beatles.* Cambridge, MA: Candlewick Press.

Jenkins, Steve. (2007). *Living Color.* Boston: Houghton Mifflin.

Johnson, Stephen. (2006). *My Little Yellow Taxi.* San Diego, CA: Red Wagon Books / Harcourt.

Larios, Julie Hofstrand. (2006). *Yellow Elephant: A Bright Bestiary.* Paintings by Julie Paschkis. Orlando, FL: Harcourt.

Lionni, Leo. (1994). *Little Blue and Little Yellow.* New York: William Morrow.

Martin, Bill, Jr. (1992). *Brown Bear, Brown Bear, What Do You See?* Illustrated by Eric Carle. New York: H. Holt.

Munsch, Robert. (1992). *Purple, Green, and Yellow.* Illustrated by Helene Desputeaux. Willowdale, ON: Annick Press.

Murphy, Stuart. (2000). *Beep Beep, Vroom Vroom!* Illustrated by Chris L. Demarest. New York: HarperCollins.

Porter, Pamela Paige. (2008). *Yellow Moon Apple Moon.* Toronto: Groundwood Books / House of Anansi Press.

Schuette, Sarah L. (2003). *Yellow: Seeing Yellow All Around Us.* Mankato, MN: Capstone Press.

Stewart, Melissa. (2009). *Why Are Animals Yellow?* Berkeley Heights, NJ: Enslow Elementary Publishers.

Tufuri, Nancy. (2006) *Five Little Chicks.* New York: Simon & Schuster Books for Young Readers.

Walsh, Ellen Stoll. (1989). *Mouse Paint.* Orlando, FL: Harcourt Brace.

Technology and Multimedia

The following technology and multimedia products can be used to complement this theme:

"Color Parade" [CD]. (1993). In *Can a Cherry Pie Wave Goodbye?* Sherman Oaks, CA: Hap-Pal Music.

"De Colores" [CD]. (2010). In *Pete Seeger, Tomorrow's Children.* Westchester, PA: Appleseed Records.

Discovering Colors [DVD]. (2006). Long Beach, CA: Distributed by Visual Entertainment.

Planting a Rainbow [DVD]. (2005). New York: Weston Woods Studios/Scholastic.

"Put a Little Color on You" (1993). [CD]. In *Can A Cherry Pie Wave Goodbye?* Sherman Oaks, CA: Hap-Pal Music.

Reading Rainbow. (2007). *Legend of the Indian Paintbrush* [DVD]. Lincoln, NE: GPN Educational Media.

"Yellow Submarine" [CD]. (2002). In *Raffi, Let's Play.* Cambridge, MA: Rounder/UMGD.

 Additional teaching resources to accompany this Theme can be found on the book's companion website. Go to www.cengagebrain.com to access the site for a variety of useful resources.

Theme 76
ZOO ANIMALS

Homes
cages
fences
water
trees

Kinds
elephants, giraffes
tigers, parrots
monkeys, snakes
lions, bears
zebras, camels

Needs
food
water
shelter
air

Caretakers
zookeeper
veterinarian

Theme Goals

Through participating in the experiences provided by this theme, the children may learn:

1. Kinds of zoo animals
2. Needs of zoo animals
3. Types of animal homes
4. The caretakers of zoo animals

Concepts for the Children to Learn

1. A zoo is a place where animals are kept.
2. People enjoy going to the zoo to look at animals.
3. Zoo animals are housed in cages, fences, water, or trees.
4. Elephants, giraffes, monkeys, snakes, lions, zebras, camels, parrots, tigers, and bears are zoo animals.
5. A zookeeper gives food and water to the animals.
6. Zoo animals need food, water, shelter, and air.
7. Veterinarians are doctors who care for animals.

Vocabulary

1. **cage**—a home for animals.
2. **veterinarian**—a doctor who cares for animals.
3. **zoo**—a place where animals are kept. People go to the zoo to look at animals.
4. **zookeeper**—a person who feeds the zoo animals.

Bulletin Board

The purpose of this bulletin board is to encourage the children to place the correct number of balls above each seal corresponding to the numeral written on the drum. To prepare the bulletin board, construct seals sitting on a drum as illustrated. Place a numeral on each drum with the corresponding number of dots. Construct colored balls from tagboard. Laminate and cut out the pieces. Staple the seal figures and drums to the bulletin board. Place a magnetic strip above each seal. Also adhere a magnetic strip to the back of each ball.

Family Letter

Dear Families,

This week's curriculum unit will focus on a favorite topic of children: zoo animals.

This is an appropriate theme to introduce to the children because they are fascinated by the zoo and the animals that live there. Through our study of zoo animals, the children will become familiar with the names, needs, and homes of many zoo animals. They will also be introduced to new occupations: the zookeeper and the veterinarian.

At School

Some of the experiences planned for the zoo animal unit include

- Looking at peek-a-boo pictures of zoo animals

- Using zoo animal–shaped cookie cutters with play dough at the art table

- Pretending to be caged zoo animals using boxes as cages in the dramatic play area

Field Trip

Our class is taking a field trip to the Dunn County Reserve Park on Friday. There we can see some unusual animals. Please let me know by Wednesday if you are interested in accompanying the group. We will leave the center at 9:30 a.m. and return by 11:30 a.m.

At Home

To develop observation skills, you can show your child pictures of zoo animals from books or magazines. Plan a family trip to a zoo. Many opportunities for learning present themselves at the zoo. Children can actually see different kinds of animals and many times, such as at petting zoos, are able to touch and feed them. What a great way to develop an appreciation and respect for animal life!

Enjoy your child!

Arts and Crafts

1. Paper Plate Lions
Collect paper plates, sandwich bags, and yellow cotton. Color the cotton balls by pouring powdered tempera paint into the sandwich bag and shaking. The children can trim the cut side of the paper plate with the yellow cotton to represent a mane. Facial features can also be added.
Note: This activity is for older children.

2. Cookie Cutters
Play dough and zoo animal–shaped cookie cutters can be placed on a table in the art area.

Cooking

Animals on Grass
Take a graham cracker and spread green-tinted cream cheese on the top. Stand an animal cracker on the top of the graham cracker.

Dramatic Play

1. The Zoo
Collect large appliance boxes. Cut slits to resemble cages. Old fur coats or blankets can be added. The children may use the fur pieces while pretending to be animals in the zoo.

2. Pet Store
Cages and many small stuffed animals can be added to the dramatic play area.

3. Block Play
Set out many blocks and rubber, plastic, or wooden models of zoo animals.

Field Trips

1. Zoo
Visit a local zoo if available. Observe the animals that are of particular interest to the children such as the elephants, giraffes, bears, and monkeys.

2. Reserve Park
If your community has a reserve park, or an area where wild animals are secured in a natural environment, take the children to visit. Plan a picnic snack to take along.

Fingerplays and Chants

Lion
I knew a little lion who went roar, roar, roar.
(make sounds)
Who walked around on all fours.
(walk on both hands and feet)
He had a tail we could see behind the bars
(point to tail)
And when we visit we should stand back far.
(move backward)

Alligator
The alligator likes to swim.
(two hands flat on top of the other)
Sometimes his mouth opens wide.
(hands open and shut)
But when he sees me on the shore,
Down under the water he'll hide.

The Monkey
The monkey claps, claps, claps his hands.
(clap hands)
The monkey claps, claps, claps his hands.
(clap hands)
Monkey see, monkey do.
The monkey does the same as you.
(use pointer finger)
(change actions)

Zoo Animals

This is the way the elephant goes.
>(clasp hands together, extend arms,
>move back and forth)

With a curly trunk instead of a nose.
The buffalo, all shaggy and fat.
Has two sharp horns in place of a hat.
>(point to forehead)

The hippo with his mouth so wide—
Let's see what's inside.
>(hands together and open wide and close
>them)

The wiggly snake upon the ground
Crawls along without a sound.
>(weave hands back and forth)

But monkey see and monkey do is the
>funniest animal in the zoo.
>(place thumbs in ears and wiggle fingers)

The Zoo

The zoo holds many animals inside
>(make a circle with your hands and peer
>inside)

So unlatch the doors and open them wide.
>(open your hands wide)

Elephants, tigers, zebras, and bears
>(hold up one finger for each animal)

Are some of the animals you'll find there.

Bear Hunt

This is a rhythmic chant that may be
easily varied. Start by chanting each line,
encouraging the children to repeat the
line. Say, "Let's go on a bear hunt," while
slapping your knees alternately. Then
have the children repeat while slapping
their knees alternately. Continue with the
following:

>I see a wheat field.
>Can't go over it.
>Can't go under it.
>Let's go through it.
>>(arms straight ahead like you're parting
>>wheat)
>
>I see a bridge.
>Can't go over it.
>Can't go under it.
>Let's swim.
>>(arms in swimming motions)
>
>I see a tree.
>Can't go over it.
>Can't go under it.

>Let's go up it.
>>(climb and look)
>
>I see a swamp.
>Can't go over it.
>Can't go under it.
>Let's go through it.
>>(pull hands up and down slowly to
>>imitate pushing branches away.)
>
>I see two eyes. I see two ears.
>I see a nose. A see a mouth.
>It's a BEAR!!!
>>(Do all in reverse very fast)

Group Time
(Games and Language)

What Am I?
Give the children verbal clues to describe an
animal. Have the children guess which zoo
animal you are describing. An example is "I
am very large, gray colored, and have a long
nose that looks like a hose. What zoo animal
am I?"

Large Muscle

1. **Walk Like the Animals**
   "Walk Like the Animals" is played like
   "Simon Says." Say, "The zookeeper says to
   walk like a giraffe." The children can walk
   as they believe that particular zoo animal
   would walk. Repeat using different animals
   such as monkeys, elephants, lions, tigers,
   bears, and so on. This activity can also be
   used for transition.

2. **Zookeeper, May I?**
   Designate one child to be the zookeeper.
   This child should stand about 6 feet in front
   of the remaining children. The zookeeper
   provides directions for the other children.
   To illustrate, they may say, "Take three
   elephant steps," "Take one kangaroo hop,"
   "Take two alligator glides," and the like.
   Once the children reach the zookeeper, the
   zookeeper chooses a child to be his or her
   successor.

Math

1. **Animal Sort**
   Collect pictures of elephants, lions, giraffes, monkeys, and other zoo animals from magazines, calendars, or coloring books. Encourage the children to sort the pictures into labeled baskets. For example, one basket may be for large animals and another for small animals.

2. **Which Is Bigger?**
   Collect many toy models of zoo animals in various sizes. Encourage the children to order from smallest to biggest, from biggest to smallest, and so on.

3. **Animal Sets**
   Cut and mount pictures of zoo animals. The children can classify the pictures by sorting. Examples might include birds, four-legged animals, furry animals, and so on.

4. **Zoo Sort Hula Hoops**
   Collect pictures of zoo animals that live on land or live on water. Place two hula hoops on the floor, and place a picture of land inside one hoop and a picture of water inside the other hoop. Have children sort animals into the appropriate hoop.

5. **Giraffe Math**
   Make a giraffe cutout. Place a numeral on the giraffe, and have the children place a corresponding number of black stickers on the giraffe.

6. **Zebra Stripes**
   Make a zebra cutout and strips of black paper. Encourage children to glue the black strips of paper on the zebra to make a black-white-black-white pattern.

Music

1. **"Zoo Animals"**
   (Sing to the tune of "Muffin Man")
   (Adapt this song and use other zoo animals such as the monkey, elephant, giraffe, lion, turtle, bear, snake, etc.)

   Do you know the kangaroo
   The kangaroo, the kangaroo?
   Oh, do you know the kangaroo
   That lives in the zoo?

2. **"One Elephant"**
   (Makes a nice flannel board story, or choose one child to be an "elephant." Add another "elephant" with each verse.)

   One elephant went out to play
   On a spiderweb one day.
   He had such enormous fun
   That he called for another elephant to come.

3. **"Animals at the Zoo"**
   (Sing to the tune of "Frère Jacques")

   See the animals, see the animals
   At the zoo, at the zoo.
   Elephants and tigers, lions and seals
   Monkeys too, monkeys too.

4. **"The Bear Went over the Mountain"**
   (Sing to the tune of "For He's a Jolly Good Fellow")

   The bear went over the mountain,
   The bear went over the mountain,
   The bear went over the mountain
   To see what he could see.
   To see what he could see,
   To see what he could see.
   The bear went over the mountain
   To see what he could see.

5. **"Five Little Monkeys (Jumping on the Bed)"**
   (Repeat this verse, subtracting a monkey each time. Sing the rhyme while using fingers or acting it out.)

   Five little monkeys jumping on the bed.
   One fell off and bumped her head.
   Mamma called the doctor, and the doctor said,
   "No more monkeys jumping on the bed!"

Science

1. **Animal Skins**

   Place a piece of snakeskin, a patch of animal hide, and animal fur out on the science table. The children can see and feel the differences. These skins can usually be borrowed from the Department of Natural Resources.

2. **Habitat**

   On the science table, place a bowl of water, a tray of dirt, and a pile of hay or grass. Also, include many small toy zoo animals. The children can place the animals in their correct habitat.

Sensory

Additions to the Sensory Table

- Zoo animal models
- Sand
- Seeds and measuring scoops
- Corn and scales
- Hay
- Water

Social Studies

Helpful Zoo Animals

During large group, discuss how some animals can be useful. Show the children pictures of various helping animals, and discuss their uses. Examples include:

- Camel (transportation in some countries)
- Elephant (often used to pull things)
- Dogs (Seeing Eye dogs and sled dogs)
- Goats (used for milk)

Books

The following books can be used to complement this theme:

Aliki. (1997). *My Visit to the Zoo.* New York: HarperCollins.

Doudna, Kelly. (2009). *It's a Baby Giraffe!* Edina, MN: ABDO Publishing.

Doudna, Kelly. (2009). *It's a Baby Zebra!* Edina, MN: ABDO Publishing.

Fjelland-Davis, Rebecca. (2007). *Zoo Animals 123.* Mankato, MN: Capstone Press.

Guiberson, Brenda Z. (2010). *Moon Bear.* Illustrated by Ed Young. New York: Holt.

Hall, Michael. (2010). *My Heart Is Like a Zoo.* New York: Greenwillow Books.

Halls, Kelly Milner, and William Sumner. (2009). *Saving the Baghdad Zoo.* New York: Greenwillow Books.

Hatkoff, Isabella, Craig Hatkoff, and Dr. Paula Kahumbu. (2006). *Owen and Mzee: The True Story of a Remarkable Friendship.* Photography by Peter Greste. New York: Scholastic.

Hillenbrand, Will. (1999). *Down by the Station.* San Diego, CA: Harcourt Brace.

Hoena, B. A. (2004). *A Visit to the Zoo.* Mankato, MN: Capstone Press.

Hort, Lenny. (2000). *The Seals on the Bus.* Illustrated by G. Brian Karas. New York: Henry Holt.

Ipcizade, Catherine. (2008). *Giraffes.* Mankato, MN: Capstone Press.

Ipcizade, Catherine. (2008). *Lions.* Mankato, MN: Capstone Press.

Ipcizade, Catherine. (2008). *Zebras.* Mankato, MN: Capstone Press.

Jay, Alison. (2008). *Welcome to the Zoo.* New York: Dial Books for Young Readers.

Jenkins, Steve, and Robin Page. (2010). *How to Clean a Hippopotamus.* Boston: Houghton Mifflin Harcourt.

Larios, Julie Hofstrand. (2006). *Yellow Elephant: A Bright Bestiary.* Paintings by Julie Paschkis. Orlando, FL: Harcourt.

Lillegard, Dee. (2009). *Sitting in My Box.* Illustrated by Jon Agee. New York: Marshall Cavendish.

Lima, Carolyn W., and Rebecca L. Thomas. (2010). *A to Zoo.* Santa Barbara, CA: Libraries Unlimited.

Lluch, Alex. (2005). *Zoo Clues Animal Alphabet.* Illustrated by David Defenbaugh. San Diego, CA: Wedding Solutions.

Martin, Bill. (1991). *Polar Bear, Polar Bear, What Do You Hear?* Illustrated by Eric Carle. New York: H. Holt.

Marzollo, Jean. (2010). *Pierre Penguin.* Illustrated by Laura Regan. Ann Arbor, MI: Sleeping Bear Press.

McClatchy, Lisa. (2009). *Eloise Visits the Zoo.* Illustrated by Tammie Lyon. New York: Aladdin.

Meltzer-Kleinhenz, Sydnie. (2008). *Elephants.* Mankato, MN: Capstone Press.

Munari, Bruno. (2005). *Bruno Munari's Zoo.* San Francisco: Chronicle Books.

Rathmann, Peggy. (1994). *Good Night, Gorilla.* New York: G. P. Putnam.

Ryder, Joanne. (2001). Little Panda: The World Welcomes Hua Mei at the San Diego Zoo. New York: Simon & Schuster.

Rylant, Cynthia. (2007). *Alligator Boy.* Illustrated by Diane Goode. Orlando, FL: Harcourt.

Sierra, Judy, and Barney Saltzberg. (2000). *There's a Zoo in Room 22.* Illustrated by Barney Saltzberg. San Diego, CA: Harcourt Brace.

Smith, Danna. (2009). *Two at the Zoo.* New York: Clarion Books.

Weeks, Sarah. (2004). *If I Were a Lion.* Illustrated by Heather M. Solomon. New York: Aladdin Paperbacks.

Wolff, Ashley. (2004). *Me Baby, You Baby.* New York: Dutton Children's Books.

Technology and Multimedia

The following technology and multimedia products can be used to complement this theme:

Choo Choo to the Zoo [CD]. (2006). Long Branch, NJ: Kimbo Records.

A Day with the Animals [DVD]. (2002). Image Entertainment. Chatsworth, CA.

"The Elephant" [CD]. (2000). In *Early Childhood Classics: Old Favorites with A New Twist.* Sherman Oaks, CA: Hap-Pal Music.

"Going to the Zoo" [CD]. (1976). In *Singable Songs for the Very Young.* Cambridge, MA: Rounder/UMGD.

Good Night, Gorilla [DVD]. (2002). Norwalk, CT: La Crosse, WI: Weston Woods Studios.

The Impossible Elephant [DVD]. (2008). Echo Bridge Home Entertainment. La Crosse, WI.

"Joshua Giraffe" [CD]. (1980). In *Baby Beluga.* Cambridge, MA: Rounder/UMGD.

Mama Mirabelle's Home Movies: It's Movie Time [DVD]. (2008). Washington, DC: National Geographic.

Really Wild Animals [DVD]. (2005). Washington, DC: National Geographic.

 Additional teaching resources to accompany this Theme can be found on the book's companion website. Go to www.cengagebrain.com to access the site for a variety of useful resources.

Appendix A

Overview of the NAEYC Early Childhood Program Standards

1. Relationships

Program Standard: The program promotes positive relationships among all children and adults to encourage each child's sense of individual worth and belonging as part of a community and to foster each child's ability to contribute as a responsible community member.

Rationale: Positive relationships are essential for the development of personal responsibility, capacity for self-regulation, for constructive interactions with others, and for fostering academic functioning and mastery. Warm, sensitive, and responsive interactions help children develop a secure, positive sense of self and encourage them to respect and cooperate with others. Positive relationships also help children gain the benefits of instructional experiences and resources. Children who see themselves as highly valued are more likely to feel secure, thrive physically, get along with others, learn well, and feel part of a community.

2. Curriculum

Program Standard: The program implements a curriculum that is consistent with its goals for children and promotes learning and development in each of the following areas: social, emotional, physical, language, and cognitive.

Rationale: A curriculum that draws on research assists teachers in identifying important concepts and skills as well as effective methods for fostering children's learning and development. When informed by teachers' knowledge of individual children, a well-articulated curriculum guides teachers so they can provide children with experiences that foster growth across a broad range of developmental and content areas. A curriculum also helps ensure that the teacher is intentional in planning a daily schedule that (a) maximizes children's learning through effective use of time, materials used for play, self-initiated learning, and creative expression as well as (b) offers opportunities for children to learn individually and in groups according to their developmental needs and interests.

3. Teaching

Program Standard: The program uses developmentally, culturally, and linguistically appropriate and effective teaching approaches that enhance each child's learning and development in the context of the program's curriculum goals.

Rationale: Teaching staff who purposefully use multiple instructional approaches optimize children's opportunities for learning. These approaches include strategies that range from structured to unstructured and from adult directed to child directed. Children bring to learning environments different backgrounds, interests, experiences, learning styles, needs, and capacities. Teachers' consideration of these differences when selecting and implementing instructional approaches helps all children succeed. Instructional approaches also differ in their effectiveness for teaching different elements of curriculum and learning. For a program to address the complexity inherent in any teaching-learning situation, it must use a variety of effective instructional approaches. In classrooms and groups that include teacher assistants or teacher aides and specialized teaching and support staff, the expectation is that these teaching staff work as a team. Whether one teacher works alone or whether a team works together, the instructional approach creates a teaching environment that supports children's positive learning and development across all areas.

4. Assessment of Child Progress

Program Standard: The program is informed by ongoing systematic, formal, and informal assessment approaches to provide information on children's learning and development. These assessments occur within the context of reciprocal communications with families and with sensitivity to the cultural contexts in which children develop. Assessment results are used to benefit children by informing sound decisions about children, teaching, and program improvement.

Rationale: Teachers' knowledge of each child helps them to plan appropriately challenging curricula and to tailor instruction that responds to each child's strengths and needs. Further, systematic assessment is essential for identifying children who may benefit from more intensive instruction or intervention or who may need additional developmental evaluation. This information ensures that the program meets its goals for children's learning and developmental progress and also informs program improvement efforts.

5. Health

Program Standard: The program promotes the nutrition and health of children and protects children and staff from illness and injury.

Rationale: To benefit from education and maintain quality of life, children need to be as healthy as possible. Health is a state of complete physical, oral, mental, and social well-being and not merely the absence of disease or infirmity (World Health Organization 1948). Children depend on adults (who also are as healthy as possible) to make healthy choices for them and to teach them to make healthy choices for themselves. Although some degree of risk taking is desirable for learning, a quality program prevents hazardous practices and environments that are likely to result in adverse consequences for children, staff, families, or communities.

6. Teachers

Program Standard: The program employs and supports a teaching staff that has the educational qualifications, knowledge, and professional commitment necessary to promote children's learning and development and to support families' diverse needs and interests.

Rationale: Children benefit most when their teachers have high levels of formal education and specialized early childhood professional preparation. Teachers who have specific preparation, knowledge, and skills in child development and early childhood education are more likely to engage in warm, positive interactions with children, offer richer language experiences, and create more high-quality learning environments. Opportunities for teaching staff to receive supportive supervision and to participate in ongoing professional development ensure that their knowledge and skills reflect the profession's ever-changing knowledge base.

7. Families

Program Standard: The program establishes and maintains collaborative relationships with each child's family to foster children's development in all settings. These relationships are sensitive to family composition, language, and culture.

Rationale: Young children's learning and development are integrally connected to their families. Consequently, to support and promote children's optimal learning and development, programs need to recognize the primacy of children's families, establish relationships with families based on mutual trust and respect, support and involve families in their children's educational growth, and invite families to fully participate in the program.

8. Community Relationships

Program Standard: The program establishes relationships with and uses the resources of the children's communities to support the achievement of program goals.

Rationale: As part of the fabric of children's communities, an effective program establishes and maintains reciprocal relationships with agencies and institutions that can support it in achieving its goals for the curriculum, health promotion, children's transitions, inclusion, and diversity. By helping to connect families with needed resources, the program furthers children's healthy development and learning.

9. Physical Environment

Program Standard: The program has a safe and healthful environment that provides appropriate and well-maintained indoor and outdoor physical environments. The environment includes facilities, equipment, and materials to facilitate child and staff learning and development.

Rationale: The program's design and maintenance of its physical environment support high-quality program activities and services as well as allow for optimal use and operation. Well organized, equipped, and maintained environments support program quality by fostering the learning, comfort, health, and safety of those who use the program. Program quality is enhanced by also creating a welcoming and accessible setting for children, families, and staff.

10. Leadership and Management

Program Standard: The program effectively implements policies, procedures, and systems that support stable staff and strong personnel, fiscal, and program management so all children, families, and staff have high quality experiences.

Rationale: Excellent programming requires effective governance structures, competent and knowledgeable leadership, as well as comprehensive and well functioning administrative policies, procedures, and systems. Effective leadership and management create the environment for high-quality care and education by:

- Ensuring compliance with relevant regulations and guidelines;
- Promoting fiscal soundness, program accountability, effective communication, helpful consultative services, positive community relations, and comfortable and supportive workplaces;
- Maintaining stable staff; and
- Instituting ongoing program planning and career development opportunities for staff as well as continuous program improvement.

Appendix B

Multicultural Materials for the Early Childhood Classroom

Teaching children about diversity is an important role of an early childhood professional. Supporting diversity needs to be an ongoing and continuous process. Early childhood teachers must help young children feel good about themselves, their families, and their communities. Young children need to develop respect and tolerance toward all who are different. As a result, multiculturalism must permeate the environment. It is important that preschool and kindergarten children are exposed to differences, including experiences and things that are different than those in their immediate surroundings. To do this, they need to interact and play with a variety of diverse materials.

Teachers must carefully plan and examine all classroom materials so that they can positively and realistically introduce children to a variety of cultural backgrounds. The center materials, room décor, and books you select for the classroom can influence children's judgments, social attitudes, and behaviors. Each center needs to include cultural artifacts. The music center should include different musical instruments. The dramatic play center should include dress-up clothes representing different cultural groups. The block center should include people and families of other cultures. Likewise, wooden or plastic animals from other parts of the world can be introduced in this area.

Bulletin boards containing people need to include a variety of different cultures and should be included in the center. Travel brochures and pictures from travel magazines can be posted. Inexpensive art prints can also add to the class environment.

The contents of this Appendix will help you choose books, music, and dramatic play props that can be added to the environment to reflect a variety of cultures.

Multicultural Musical Instruments

Using musical instruments is an excellent opportunity to expose children to a variety of cultures. Following is a list of instruments you might want to add to your music shelf for the children to experiment with:

- Agogo bells
- Chilean rainstick
- Ankle bells
- Steel drum
- Maracitos
- Samba whistles
- Casaba
- Vibra slap
- Tambourine
- Castanets
- Claves
- Maracas
- Bongos
- Guiro tone block
- Conga drum
- Tom tom drum

Multicultural Dramatic Play Center

- Dolls from all racial groups
- Multicultural puppets and props
- Clothing from different countries
- Chopsticks
- Plastic multicultural foods
- Empty cans or boxes of foods printed with a foreign language
- Empty spice cans of cinnamon, cardamom, and curry

719

Multicultural Books

There are many wonderful multicultural folktales, fairy tales, and fables from all over the world that can be introduced in our programs. These books can delight children and dispel misconceptions. Regardless of the theme, multicultural books should always be available on bookshelves in the classroom. Children need to learn that all people everywhere have the same needs.

Aardema, Verna. (1995). *How the Ostrich Got Its Long Neck: A Tale from the Akamba of Kenya.* Illus. by Marcia Brown. New York: Scholastic.

Ada, Alma Flor (selected by). (2003). *Pio Peep!* Illus. by Vivi Escriva. New York: HarperCollins.

Ada, Alma Flor. (2010). *Let Me Help!* Illus. by Angela Dominguez. New York: HarperCollins.

Adamson, Heather. (2008). *Homes in Many Cultures.* Mankato, MN: Capstone Press.

Adoff, Arnold. (2004). *Black Is Brown Is Tan.* New York: Amistad/HarperCollins.

Agassi, Martine. (2002). *Hands Are Not for Hitting.* Illus. by Marieka Heinlen. Minneapolis, MN: Free Spirit Pub.

Ajmera, Maya, and John D. Ivanko. (2002). *Animal Friends: A Global Celebration of Children and Animals.* Watertown, MA: Charlesbridge.

Ajmera, Maya, and John D. Ivanko. (2004). *Be My Neighbor.* With words of wisdom from Fred Rogers. Washington, DC: Shakti for Children; Watertown, MA: Charlesbridge.

Ajmera, Maya, and John D. Ivanko. (2004). *To Be a Kid.* Watertown, MA: Charlesbridge; Washington, DC: Shakti for Children.

Ajmera, Maya. (2004). *To Be An Artist.* Watertown, MA: Charlesbridge.

Argueta, Jorge. (2005). *Moony Luna (Luna, Lunita Lunera).* Illus. by Elizabeth Gomez. San Francisco: Children's Book Press.

Bae, Hyun-Joo. (2007). *New Clothes for New Year's Day.* La Jolla, CA: Kane/Miller.

Bang, Molly. (1985). *Ten, Nine, Eight.* New York: Puffin Books.

Bannerman, Helen. (1996). *The Story of Little Babaji.* Illus. by Fred Marcellino. New York: HarperCollins Publishers.

Barnwell, Ysaye M. (1998). *No Mirrors in My Nana's House.* Painting by Synthia Saint James. San Diego: Harcourt Brace.

Bloom, Suzanne. (2001). *The Bus for Us.* Honesdale, PA: Boyds Mills Press.

Brett, Jan. (2005). *Honey . . . Honey . . . Lion! A Story from Africa.* New York: G.P. Putnam's Sons.

Brown, Margaret Wise. (1996). *El gran granero rojo (The Big Red Barn).* Illus. by Felicia Bond. New York: Harper Arco Iris.

Brown, Margaret Wise. (1998). *Buenas noches, Luna / Good Night Moon.* Illus. by T. Mlawer. New York: Harper Festival.

Brown, Monica. (2010). *Chavela and the Magic Bubble.* Illus. by Magaly Morales Boston: Clarion Books.

Carle, Eric. (1994). *La oruga muy hambrienta (The Very Hungry Caterpillar).* New York: Philomel Books.

Carryl, Charles E. (2004). *The Camel's Lament.* Illus. by Charles Santore. New York: Random House.

Chamberlin, Mary and Rich. (2005). *Mama Panya's Pancakes: Village Tale From Kenya.* Illus. by Julia Cairns. Bath, ME: Barefoot Books.

Cheng, Andrea. (2000). *Grandfather Counts.* Illus. by Ange Zhang. New York: Lee and Low Books.

Cheng, Andrea. (2003). *Goldfish and Chrysanthemums.* Illus. by Michelle Cheng. New York: Lee & Low Books

Chorao, Kay. (2009). *Rhymes 'round the World.* New York: Penguin Group

Christelow, Eileen. (2005). *Cinco monitos brincando en la cama (Five little monkeys jumping on the bed).* New York: Clarion Books.

Crews, Donald. (1985). *Freight Train.* New York: Puffin Books.

Cumpiano, Ina. (2005). *Quinito's Neighborhood / El Vecindario de Quinito.* Illus. Jose Ramirez. San Francisco: Children's Book Press.

Cumpiano, Ina. (2008). *Quinto, Day and Night / Quinito, dia y noche.* Illus. by José Ramirez. San Francisco: Children's Book Press.

Demarest, Chris L. (2000). *Firefighters A to Z.* New York: Margaret K. McElderry Books.

Demi. (1990). *The Empty Pot.* New York: H. Holt.

Demi. (2000). *Liang and the Magic Paintbrush / Liang Hab Tug Cwg Mem Pleev Kws muaj Yeeg Siv.* Saint Paul:

Minnesota Humanities Commission, Motheread/Fatheread.

Doering, Amanda. (2005). *Homes around the World ABC: An Alphabet Book*. Mankato, MN: Capstone Press.

Douglas, Lloyd. (2003). *Let's Get ready for Martin Luther King Jr. Day*. New York: Children's Press/Scholastic.

Dunn, Opal. (2006). *Un, Deux, Trois: First French Rhymes*. London: Frances Lincoln.

Dwight, Laura. (2005). *Brothers and Sisters*. New York: Star Bright Books.

Edwards, Michelle. (2004). *Papa's Latkes*. Cambridge, MA: Candlewick Press.

Ehlert, Lois. (1996). *A sembrar sopa de verdures (Growing Vegetable Soup)*. San Diego, CA: Libros Viajeros.

Ehrhardt, Karen. (2006). *This Jazz Man*. Illus. by R.G. Roth. New York: Harcourt.

Elya, Susan Middleton. (2005). *Cowboy José*. Illus. by Tim Raglin. New York: G. P. Putnam's Sons.

Elya, Susan. (2006). *F Is for Fiesta*. New York: Putnam.

Emberley, Rebecca. (2002). *My animals = Mis animales*. Boston: Little, Brown.

Emberley, Rebecca. (2005). *My city = Mi ciudad*. New York: Little, Brown.

Emberley, Rebecca. (2002). *My clothes / Mi ropa*. Boston: Little, Brown.

Emberley, Rebecca. (2000). *My colors = Mis colores*. Boston: Little, Brown.

Emberley, Rebecca. (2002). *My food = Mi comida*. Boston: Little, Brown.

Emberley, Rebecca. (2005). *My garden = Mi jardin*. New York: Little, Brown.

Emberley, Rebecca. (2005). *My room = Mi cuarto*. New York: Little, Brown.

Emberley, Rebecca. (2005). *My school = Mi escuela*. New York: Little, Brown.

Fine, Edith Hope, and Judith Pinkerton Josephson. (2007). *Armando and the Blue Tarp School*. Illus. by Hernan Sosa. New York: Lee & Low Books.

Flack, Marjorie, and Kurt Wiese. (2000). *The Story about Ping*. New York: Grosset & Dunlap.

Fleming, Denise. (2000). *The Everything Book*. New York: Henry Holt.

Fleming, Denise. (2005). *The First Day of Winter*. New York: Henry Holt.

Fleming, Denise. (1993). *In the Small, Small Pond*. New York: Henry Holt.

Fleming, Denise. (1991). *In the Tall, Tall Grass*. New York: Henry Holt.

Forman, Ruth (2007). *Young Cornrows Callin Out the Moon*. Illus. by Cbabi Bayoc. San Francisco: Children's Book Press.

Freeman, Don. (1968). *Corduroy*. New York, Viking Press.

Frost, Helen. (1999). *Going to the Dentist*. Mankato, MN: Pebble Books.

Gershator, David, and Phillis Gershator. (1995). *Bread Is for Eating*. Illus. by Emma Shaw-Smith. New York: Holt.

Gill, Shelley. (2002). *The Alaska Mother Goose: North Country Nursery Rhymes*. Seattle WA: Sasquatch Books.

Global Fund for Children. (2007). *Global Babies*. Watertown, MA : Charlesbridge.

Gomi, Taro. (2006). *My Friends = Mis Amigos*. San Francisco: Chronicle Books.

Gonzalez, Maya C. (2007). *My Colors, My World / Mis colores, mi mundo*. San Francisco: Children's Book Press.

Gonzalez, Maya C. (2009). *I Know the River Loves Me*. San Francisco: Children's Book Press

Gonzalez, Maya C. (2011). *My Colors, My World / Mis colores, mi mundo* (Board Book. San Francisco: Children's Book Press.

Gordon, Sharon. (2007). *What's izznside a Hospital? / Que Hay Dentro De Un Hospital?* Tarrytown, NY: Marshall Cavendish Benchmark.

Greenberg, Polly. (1968). *Oh Lord, I Wish I Was a Buzzard*. Illus. by Aliki. New York: Macmillan.

Greenfield, Eloise. (2003). *Honey, I Love*. Illus. by Jan Spivey Gilchrist. New York: HarperCollins.

Gresco, M.S. (2000). *A Ticket to Israel*. Minneapolis, MN: Carolrhoda Books.

Guy, Ginger Foglesong. (1996). *Fiesta!* Pictures by Rene King Moreno. New York: Greenwillow Books.

Guy, Ginger Foglesong. (2005). *Siesta*. Pictures by Rene King Moreno. New York: Greenwillow Books.

Hall, Margaret. (2007). *Hormigas / Ants*. Mankato, MN: Capstone Press.

Hamanaka, S. (1999). *All the Colors of the Earth*. New York: Harper Trophy.

Heelan, Jamee Riggio. (2000). *Rolling Along: The Story of Taylor and His Wheelchair*. Illus. by Nicola Simmonds. Atlanta, GA: Peachtree.

Hester, Denia Lewis. (2005). *Grandma Lena's Big Ol' Turnip*. Illus. by Jackie Urbanovic. Morton Grove, IL: Albert Whitman.

Hindley, Judy. (1999). *Eyes, Nose, Fingers, and Toes: A First Book All about You*. Illus. by Brita Granstrom. Cambridge, MA: Candlewick Press.

Holiday, Billie, and Arthur Herzog Jr. (2004). *God Bless the Child*. Illus. by Jerry Pinkney. New York: HarperCollins/ Amistad.

Holub, Joan. (2003). *Apples and Honey*. Illus. by Cary Pillo-Lassen. New York: Puffin Books.

Hooks, Bell. (2001). *Happy to be Nappy*. Illus. by Chris Raschka. New York: Jump at the Sun.

Howell, Theresa. (2003). *A Is for Airplane. A es para Avion*. Illus. by David Brooks. Flagstaff, AZ: Rising Moon.

Hubbell, Will. (2002). *Apples Here!* Illus. by Will Hubbell. Morton Grove, IL: Albert Whitman.

Isadora, Rachel. (2002). *Peekaboo Morning*. New York: G.P. Putnam's Sons.

Jadoul, Emile. (2004). *Todo El Mundo Va!* Zaragoza, Spain: Edelvives.

Jarkins, Sheila. (2008). *Marco Flamingo / Marco Flemenco*. McHenry, IL: Raven Tree.

Jocelyn, Marthe and Tom Slaughter. (2005). *ABC 3 3*. Plattsburgh, NY: Tundra Books.

Jonas, A. (1984). *The Quilt*. New York: Puffin.

Jones, Bill T., and Susan Kuklin. (1998). *Dance*. Photographed by Susan Kuklin. New York: Hyperion Books for Children.

Joosse, Barbara M. (2000). *Mama, Do You Love Me?* Illus. by Barbara Lavallee. San Francisco: Chronicle Books.

Katz, K. (2002). *The Colors of Us*. New York: Henry Holt.

Keats, Ezra Jack. (1967). *The Snowy Day*. London: Bodley Head.

Keeler, Patricia. (2006). *Drumbeat in Our Feet*. New York: Lee & Low Books.

Khan, Rukhsana. (2005). *Silly Chicken*. Pictures by Yunmee Kyong. New York: Viking.

Kroll, Virginia. (2005). *Forgiving a Friend*. Illus. by Paige Billin-Frye. Morton Grove, IL: Albert Whitman.

Lee, Huy Voun. (2005). *In the Leaves*. New York: Holt.

Lewis, E.B. (2005). *This Little Light of Mine*. New York: Simon & Schuster Books for Young Readers.

Lin, Grace. (2004). *Fortune Cookie Fortunes*. New York: Alfred A. Knopf.

Lindman, Maj. (1995). *Snipp, Snapp, Snurr and the Buttered Bread*. Morton Grove, IL: Albert Whitman.

Lindsay, Jeanne Warren. (1991). *Do I Have a Daddy? A Story about a Single Parent Child*. Illus. by Cheryl Boeller. Buena Park, CA: Morning Glory Press.

Lionni, Leo. (2006). *A Color of His Own*. New York: Alfred A. Knopf.

Lo, Ginnie. (2005). *Mahjong All Day Long*. Illus. by Beth Lo. New York: Walker & Co.

Lunge-Larsen, Lise, and Margi Preus. (1999). *The Legend of the Lady Slipper: An Ojibwe Tale*. Illus. by Andrea Arroyo. Boston: Houghton Mifflin.

Manders, John. (2003). *Señor Don Gato: A Traditional Song*. Illus. by John Manders. Cambridge, MA: Candlewick Press.

Manning, Jane K. (2001). *My First Baby Games*. New York: HarperFestival.

Markes, Julie. (2005). *Shhhhh! Everybody's Sleeping*. Illus. by David Parkins. New York: HarperCollins.

Martin, Bill. (1998). *Oso pardo, oso pardo, que ves ahi? (Brown Bear, Brown Bear, What Do You See?)* Illus. by Eric Carle. New York: Holt.

Martin, Bill, and John Archambault. (1998). *Here Are My Hands*. Illus. by Ted Rand. New York: H. Holt.

Medearis, Angela Shelf. (2004). *Snug in Mama's Arms*. Illus. by John Sandford. Columbus, Ohio: Gingham Dog Press.

Miller, J. Philip, and Sheppard M. Greene. (2001). *We All Sing with the Same Voice*. Illus. by Paul Meisel. New York: HarperCollins.

Morales, Yuyi. (2003). *Just a Minute: A Trickster Tale and Counting Book*. San Francisco: Chronicle Books.

Morris, Ann. (1993). *Bread Bread Bread*. Photographs by Ken Heyman. New York: Mulberry Books.

Morris, Ann. (2000). *Families*. New York: HaperCollins.

Morris, Ann. (1993). *Hats Hats Hats*. Photographs by Ken Heyman. New York: Mulberry Books.

Morris, Ann. (1992). *Houses and Homes*. Photographs by Ken Heyman. New York: Lothrop, Lee & Shepard Books.

Morris, Ann. (1995). *Weddings*. New York: Lothrop, Lee & Shepard Books.

Mosel, Arlene. (1989). *Tikki Tikki Tembo*. Illus. by Blair Lent. New York: Henry Holt.

Munoz, Isabel. (2005). *Es Mio / It's Mine*. Illus. by Gustavo Mazali. New York: Scholastic.

Nelson, Kadir. (2005). *He's Got the Whole World in His Hands*. New York: Dial Books for Young Readers.

Newman, Leslea. (2002). *Runaway Dreidel!* New York: Henry Holt.

Nishizuka, Koko. (2009). *The Beckoning Cat: Based on a Japanese Folktale*. Illus. by Rosanne Litzinger. New York: Holiday House

Orozco, José-Luis (selected, arranged, and translated). (1994). *De Colores and Other Latin-America Folk Songs for Children*. Illus. by Elisa Kleven. New York: Dutton Children's Books.

Orozco, José-Luis (selected, arranged, and translated). (1997). *Diez Deditos / Ten Little Fingers and Other Play Rhymes*. Illus. by Elisa Kleven. New York: Dutton Children's Books.

Orozco, José-Luis, and David Diaz. (2005). *Rin, Rin, Rin, Do, Re, Mi*. New York: Orchard Books.

Owen, Ann. (2004). *Keeping You Healthy: A Book about Doctors*. Illus. by Eric Thomas. Minneapolis, MN: Picture Window Books.

Oxenbury, Helen. (1987). *All Fall Down*. New York: Aladdin Books.

Oxenbury, Helen. (1987). *Clap Hands*. New York: Aladdin Books.

Oxenbury, Helen. (1987). *Tickle, Tickle*. New York: Aladdin Books.

Park, Linda Sue. (2005). *Bee-Bim Bop!* Illus. by Ho Baek Lee. New York: Clarion Books.

Parr, Todd. (1998). *Somewhere Today: A Book of Peace*. Photographs by Eric Futran. Morton Grove, IL: Albert Whitman.

Pedersen, Janet. (2005). *Pino and the Signora's Pasta*. Cambridge, MA: Candlewick Press.

Picayo, Mario. (2008). *A Very Smart Cat / Una Gata Muy Inteligente*. Illus. by Yolanda V. Fundora. New York: Editorial Campanita Books.

Pilobous. (2005). *The Human Alphabet*. Photographs by John Kane. Brookfield, CT: Roaring Brook Press.

Pinkney, Andrea Davis, and Brian Pinkney. (1997). *I Smell Honey*. San Diego, CA: Harcourt Brace.

Pinkney, Andrea Davis, and Brian Pinkney. (1997). *Pretty Brown Face*. San Diego, CA: Harcourt Brace.

Pinkney, Sandra L. (2000). *Shades of Black: A Celebration of Our Children*. Photographs by Myles Pinkney. New York: Scholastic.

Raschka, Christopher. (1992). *Charlie Parker Played Be Bop*. New York: Orchard Books.

Reiser, Lynn. (1998). *Tortillas and Lullabies*. Pictures by Corazones Valientes. Coordinated and translated by Rebecca Hart. New York: Greenwillow Books.

Rosa-Mendoza, Gladys. (2000). *My family and I = Mi familia y yo*. Illus. by Jackie Snider edited by Carolina Cifuentes. Wheaton, IL: Me+mi Pub.

Rosenthal, Betsy R. (2006). *It's Not Worth Making a Tzimmes Over!* Illus. by Ruth Rivers. Morton Grove, IL: Albert Whitman.

Roth, Susan. (2004). *Hanukkah Oh Hanukkah*. New York: Dial Books for Young Readers.

Rylant, Cynthia. (2005). *The Stars Will Still Shine*. Illus. by Tiphanie Beeke. New York: HarperCollins.

Rylant, Cynthia. (1982). *When I Was Young in the Mountains*. Illus. by Diane Goode. New York: Dutton.

Saenz, Benjamin Alire. (2009). *The Dog Who Loved Tortillas / La Perrita Que Le Encantaban Las Tortillas*. Illus. by Geronimo Garcia. El Paso, TX: Cinco Puntos Press.

Sakai, Kimiko. (1990). *Sachiko Means Happiness*. Illus. by Tomie Arai. San Francisco: Children's Book Press.

Sanger, Amy Wilson. (2001). *First Book of Sushi*. Berkeley, CA: Tricycle Press.

Sanger, Amy Wilson. (2002). *Hola! Jalapeno*. Berkeley, CA: Tricycle Press.

Sanger, Amy Wilson. (2002). *Let's Nosh!* Berkeley, CA: Tricycle Press.

Sanger, Amy Wilson. (2004). *A Little Bit of Soul Food*. Berkeley, CA: Tricycle Press.

Sanger, Amy Wilson. (2005). *Mangia! Mangia!* Berkeley, CA: Tricycle Press.

Sanger, Amy Wilson. (2003). *Yum Yum Dim Sum*. Berkeley, CA: Tricycle Press.

Sata, Wakiko. (2004). *Grandma Baba's Birthday Party*. Boston: Tuttle.

Schiller, P., R. Lara-Alecio and B.J. Irby. (2004). *Bilingual Book of Rhymes, Songs, Stories, and Fingerplays*. Beltsville, MD: Gryphon House.

Schuh, Mari C. (2007). *Mantenerse active / Being Active*. Mankato, MN: Capstone Press.

Schuh, Mari C. (2007). *Meriendas saludables / Healthy Snacks*. Mankato, MN: Capstone Press.

Scott, Ann Herbert. (1992). *On Mother's Lap*. Illus. by Glo Coalson. New York: Clarion Books.

Seeger, Pete. (2005). *ABIYOYO*. Illus. by Michael Hays. New York: Aladdin Paperbacks.

Senisi, Ellen B. (2002). *All Kinds of Friends, Even Green!* Photographed by Ellen B. Senisi. Bethesda, MD: Woodbine House.

Shaham, S. (2004). *Spicy Hot Colors: Colores Picantes*. Little Rock, AR: August House.

Simon, Norma. (2003). *All Families Are Special*. Illus. by Teresa Flavin. Morton Grove, IL: Albert Whitman.

So, Meilo. (2004). *Gobble, Gobble, Slip, Slop*. New York: Alfred A. Knopf.

Sockabasin, Allen. (2005). *Thanks to the Animals*. Illus. by Rebekah Raye. Gardiner, ME: Tilbury House.

Spinelli, Eileen. (2005). *City Angel*. Illus. by Kyrsten Brooker. New York: Dial Books for Young Readers.

Spinellie, Eileen. (2000). *Night Shift Daddy*. Illus. by Melissa Iwai. New York: Hyperion Books for Children.

Sturges, Philemon. (2004). *I Love School!* Illus. by Shari Halpern. New York: HarperCollins.

Taback, Simms. (1999). *Joseph Had a Little Overcoat*. New York: Viking.

Tarpley, Natasha Anastasia. (1998). *I Love My Hair!* Illus. by E.B. Lewis. New York: Little, Brown.

Truong, Tran. (2003). *Going Home, Coming Home*. Illus. by Ann Phong. San Francisco: Children's Book Press.

Verdick, Elizabeth. (2004). *Feet Are Not for Kicking*. Illus. by Marieka Heinlen. Minneapolis, MN: Free Spirit Pub.

Verdick, Elizabeth. (2005). *Tails Are Not for Pulling*. Illus. by Marieka Heinlen. Minneapolis, MN: Free Spirit Pub.

Verdick, Elizabeth. (2003). *Teeth Are Not for Biting*. Illus. by Marieka Heinlen. Minneapolis, MN: Free Spirit Pub.

Verdick, Elizabeth. (2004). *Words Are Not for Hurting*. Illus. by Marieka Heinlen. Minneapolis, MN: Free Spirit Pub.

Weinstein, Ellen. (2008). *Everywhere the Cow Says "Moo!"* Illus. by Kenneth Anderson. Honesdale, PA: Boyds Mills Press.

Williams, Sue. (2006). *Sali de paseo (I Went Walking)*. Illus. by Julie Vivas. Orlando: Harcourt.

Williams, Vera B. (1982). *A Chair for My Mother*. New York: Greenwillow Books.

Williams, Vera B. (1990). *More More More, Said the Baby*. New York: Greenwillow Books.

Willis, Jeanne, and Tony Ross. (2004). *Shhh!* New York: Hyperion Books for Children.

Winter, Jeanette. (2004). *The Librarian of Basra*. Orlando: Harcourt, Inc.

Winthrop, Elizabeth. (2005). *Squashed in the Middle*. Illus. by Pat Cummings. New York: Henry Holt.

Wolff, Ashley. (2003). *The Baby Chicks Are Singing = Los Pollitos Dicen*. Boston: Little, Brown.

Wolff, Ashley. (2003). *Oh, the Colors = De colores*. Boston: Little, Brown.

Woodson, Jacqueline. (2001). *The Other Side*. Illus. by Earl B. Lewis. New York: Putnam's.

Woodson, Jacqueline. (2002). *Our Gracie Aunt*. Illus. by Jon J. Muth. New York: Hyperion Books for Children/Jump at the Sun.

Woodson, Jacqueline. (2002). *Visiting Day*. Illus. by James Ransome. New York: Scholastic Press.

Wright, Danielle, Mique Moriuchi, and Michael Rosen. (2010). *My Villiage: Rhymes from around the World*. London: Frances Lincoln.

Yashima, Taro. (1958). *Umbrella*. New York: Viking Press.

Yolleck, Joan. (2010). *Paris in the Spring with Picasso*. New York: Schwartz & Wade.

Young, Ed. (1995). *Night Visitors*. New York: Philomel Books.

Young, Ed. (2004). *I, Doko: The Tale of a Basket*. New York: Philomel Books.

Multicultural Dramatic Play Ideas

Multicultural props should be included in the dramatic play area. These props can be authentic or teacher made. Following is a list of ideas for props that can be used in the dramatic play area.

Grocery Store: Use containers and boxes that include a variety of products that appeal to many cultures and both genders. Create ethnically diverse foods from clip art or play dough to display in the store. Some ideas for multicultural materials to include in this area could be:

- Taco or rice boxes
- Variety of spice containers
- Variety of plastic fruits and vegetables
- Play money (from other countries)

Restaurants: A variety of restaurants that reflect ethnically diverse foods can be set up in the dramatic play area. Include the cooking utensils, special dishes, and menus for the type of restaurant you choose (Mexican, Indian, Chinese, Korean, Italian, etc.). If the materials are not available from a restaurant in your area, make them using clip art. Some ideas for multicultural materials to include in this area could be:

- Karahi or wok
- Chopsticks
- Floor mats (instead of chairs)
- Take-out containers
- Rice pot
- Wooden spoons
- Escobeta (Mexican cooking brush)
- Flan pan
- Bean masher

Department Store: Include a variety of clothing, hats, scarves, jewelry, or home décor that represents many cultures. Some ideas for multicultural materials to include in this area could be:

- Kimonos
- Turbans
- Stone/shell necklaces
- African beads
- Headband/headdress
- Various shades of nylons and tights
- Ceramics/pottery
- Woven baskets

Multicultural Music

Kimbo Educational. (1993). *Joining Hands with Other Lands.* Long Branch, NJ: Kimbo Educational.

Skiera-Zucek, Lois. (1994). *Songs about Native Americans.* Long Branch, NJ: Kimbo Educational.

Stewart, Georgiana Liccione. (1991). *Children of the World Multicultural Rhythmic Activities.* Long Branch, NJ: Kimbo Educational.

Stewart, Georgiana Liccione. (1998) *Children's Folk Dances.* Long Branch, NJ: Kimbo Educational.

Stewart, Georgiana Liccione. (1992). *Multicultural Rhythm Stick Fun.* Long Branch, NJ: Kimbo Educational.

Appendix C

International Holidays and Celebrations

When planning the curriculum, it is important to note international holidays and celebrations. The exact date of the holiday may vary from year to year. Consequently, it is important to check with parents or use a computer search engine. International holidays for Buddhist, Chinese, Christian, Eastern Orthodox, Hindu, Jewish, and Muslim faiths are as follows.

African-American

Kwanzaa: a celebration lasting from December 26 to January 1 that celebrates "good harvest, life, and prosperity."

Martin Luther King, Jr. Day: a holiday celebrating Martin Luther King, Jr. and his contributions to the civil rights movement.

Juneteenth: celebrates the day on which slaves were set free.

Black History Month: a month-long celebration in February stemming from the pride associated with African heritage.

Buddhist

Nirvana Day (Mahayana Sect): observes the passing of Sakyamuni into Nirvana. He obtained enlightenment and became a Buddha.

Magna Puja (Theravada Sect): one of the holiest Buddhist holidays; it marks the occasion when 1250 of Buddha's disciples gathered spontaneously to hear him speak.

Buddha Day (Mahayana Sect): this service commemorates the birth of Gautama in Lumbini Garden. Amida, the Buddha of Infinite Wisdom and Compassion, manifested himself among men in the person Gautama.

Versakha Piya (Theravada Sect): the most sacred of the Buddhist days. It celebrates the birth, death, and enlightenment of Buddha.

Maharram: marks the beginning of Buddhist Lent; it is the anniversary of Buddha's sermon to the first five disciples.

Vassana (Theravada Sect): the beginning of the three-month period when monks stay in their temple to study and meditate.

Bon (Mahayana Sect): an occasion for rejoicing in the enlightenment offered by the Buddha; often referred to as a "Gathering of Joy." Buddha had saved the life of the mother Moggallana. The day is in remembrance of all those who have passed away.

Pavarana (Theravada Sect): celebrates Buddha's return to earth after spending one Lent season preaching in heaven.

Bodhi Day (Mahayana Sect): celebrates the enlightenment of Buddha.

Chinese

Chinese New Year: the most important traditional Chinese holiday; it celebrates the beginning of the Chinese Lunar New Year. In China, it is known as the Spring Festival.

Qingming Festival: a day set aside to offer sacrifices to their ancestors.

Dragon Boat Festival: a festival characterized by boat racing and eating zongziong, which is a pyramid-shaped dumpling.

Mid-Autumn Day: family members gather to admire the bright moon.

National Day: celebrated every year on October 1 with portraits of revered leaders displayed, fireworks, and concerts.

Christian

Ash Wednesday: the first day of Lent.

Palm Sunday: the Sunday before Easter; commemorates the triumphant entry of Jesus into Jerusalem.

Holy Thursday: also known as Maundy Thursday; it is the Thursday of Holy Week.

Good Friday: commemorates the crucifixion of Jesus.

Easter: celebrates the resurrection of Jesus.

Christmas Day: commemorates the birth of Jesus.

Eastern Orthodox

Christmas: commemorates the birth of Jesus.

First Day of Lent: begins a period of fasting and penitence in preparation for Easter.

Easter Sunday: celebrates the resurrection of Jesus.

Ascension Day: the fortieth day after Easter; commemorates the ascension of Jesus to heaven.

Pentecost: commemorates the descent of the Holy Spirit upon the Apostles, 50 days after Easter Sunday. Marks the beginning of the Christian Church.

Hindu

Diwali: celebrated to show respect to Hindu gods and goddesses.

Pongal Sankrandi: a three-day harvest festival.

Vasanta Pachami: celebrated in honor of Saraswati, the charming and sophisticated goddess of scholars.

Shivarari: a solemn festival devoted to the worship of Shiva, the most powerful of deities of the Hindu pantheon.

Holi: celebrates the advent of spring.

Ganguar: celebrated in honor of Parvati, the consort of Lord Shiva.

Ram Navami: birthday of the God Rama.

Hanuman Jayanti: birthday of Monkey God Humumanji.

Meenakshi Kalyanam: the annual commemoration of the marriage of Meenakshi to Lord Shiva.

Teej: celebrates the arrival of the monsoon; Parvati is the presiding deity.

Jewish

Yom Kippur: the most holy day of the Jewish year, it is marked by fasting and prayer as Jews seek forgiveness from God and man.

Sukkot: commemorates the 40-year wandering of Israelites in the desert on the way to the Promised Land; expresses thanksgiving for the fall harvest.

Simchat Torah: celebrates the conclusion of the public reading of the Pentateuch and its beginning anew, thus affirming that the study of God's word is an unending process. Concludes the Sukkot Festival.

Hanukkah: the eight-day festival that celebrates the rededication of the Temple to the service of God. Commemorates the ancient Maccabean victory over Antiochus, who sought to suppress freedom of worship.

Purim: marks the salvation of the Jews of ancient Persia, through the intervention of Queen Esther, from Haman's plot to exterminate them.

Passover: an eight-day festival marking ancient Israel's deliverance from Egyptian bondage.

Yom Hashoah: day of remembrance for victims of the Nazi Holocaust during World War II.

Shavuot: celebrates the covenant established at Sinai between God and Israel and the revelation of the Ten Commandments.

Rosh Hashanah: the Jewish New Year and the first of the High Holy Days; it marks the beginning of a ten-day period of penitence and spiritual renewal.

Muslim

Isra and Miraj: commemorates the anniversary of the night journey of the Prophet and his ascension to heaven.

Ramadan: the beginning of the month of fasting from sunrise to sunset.

Id al-Fitr: end of the month of fasting from sunrise to sunset; the first day of pilgrimage to Mecca.

Hajj: the first day of pilgrimage to Mecca.

Day of Amfat: gathering of the pilgrims.

Id al-adha: commemorates the Feast of the Sacrifice.

Muharram: the Muslim New Year; marks the beginning of the Hejira Year 1412.

Id al-Mawlid: commemorates the nativity and death of Prophet Muhammad and his flight from Mecca to Medina.